THE OXFORD HANDBOO

ORGANIZATIO
DECISION MAKING

THE OXFORD HANDBOOK OF

ORGANIZATIONAL DECISION MAKING

Edited by

GERARD P. HODGKINSON

and

WILLIAM H. STARBUCK

OXFORD

UNIVERSITY PRESS

OXFORD

UNIVERSITY PRESS

Great Clarendon Street, Oxford OX2 6DP
United Kingdom

Oxford University Press is a department of the University of Oxford.
It furthers the University's objective of excellence in research, scholarship,
and education by publishing worldwide. Oxford is a registered trade mark of
Oxford University Press in the UK and in certain other countries

First published 2008
First published in paperback 2012
Reprinted 2013

British Library Cataloguing in Publication Data
Data available

Library of Congress Cataloging in Publication Data
Data available

ISBN 978-0-19-964458-2

To James G. March and the Memory of Herbert A. Simon

Contents

PART I   THE CONTEXT AND CONTENT OF DECISION MAKING

PART II   DECISION MAKING DURING CRISES AND HAZARDOUS SITUATIONS

PART III   DECISION MAKING PROCESSES

PART IV   CONSEQUENCES PRODUCED BY DECISIONS

PART V   TOWARD MORE EFFECTIVE DECISION MAKING

LIST OF FIGURES

LIST OF TABLES

Notes on Contributors

Editors

Gerard P. Hodgkinson is Professor of Strategic Management and Behavioural Science at Warwick Business School, University of Warwick, UK. The author of over 60 scholarly articles and chapters in edited volumes, on topics ranging from socio-cognitive processes in competitive strategy to intuition and the nature and role of mental models in organizational decision making, and applied psychometrics, his work has appeared in a number of distinguished outlets including the *Annual Review of Psychology, Organizational Research Methods, Personnel Psychology,* and *Strategic Management Journal.* He has also (co-)authored three books. Registered with the UK Health Professions Council (HPC) as an Occupational Psychologist, in 2001 he was elected a fellow of both the British Psychological Society and the British Academy of Management. In recent years, his work on managerial and organizational cognition has been taken forward through the award of a senior fellowship of the UK ESRC/EPSRC Advanced Institute of Management (AIM) Research (2004–07). He was the Editor-in-Chief of the *British Journal of Management* (1999–2006) and currently co-edits the *International Review of Industrial and Organizational Psychology* and serves on several editorial boards including the *Academy of Management Review, Journal of Organizational Behavior,* and *Journal of Management.*

William H. Starbuck is Professor in Residence at the Lundquist College of Business of the University of Oregon and Professor Emeritus at New York University. He has held faculty positions in economics, sociology, and management at Purdue University, the Johns Hopkins University, Cornell University, the University of Wisconsin–Milwaukee, and New York University, as well as visiting positions in universities and business schools in England, France, New Zealand, Norway, and Sweden. He was also a senior research fellow at the International Institute of Management in Berlin. He has been Editor of *Administrative Science Quarterly*; he has chaired the screening committee for senior Fulbright awards in business management; he has directed the doctoral program in business administration at New York University, and he was the President of the Academy of Management. He has published over 150 articles on accounting, bargaining, business strategy, computer programming, computer simulation, forecasting, decision making, human–computer interaction, learning, organizational design, organizational growth and development, perception, scientific methods, and social revolutions. He has also authored two books and edited 16 books, including the *Handbook of Organizational Design*, which was chosen the best book on management published during the year ending May 1982.

CONTRIBUTING AUTHORS

Eric Abrahamson is a tenured full professor of management at Columbia Business School. He holds degrees from New York University (PhD and MPh Beta Gamma Sigma). He is internationally recognized for his research on innovation diffusion generally, fashions in business techniques, and fashions in artifacts with both technological and aesthetic qualities. His work has won two of the most prestigious awards in management, the Award for the Best Article published in the *Academy of Management Journal* and two Best Paper Awards of the Academy of Management Organization and Management Theory Division (1990, 1997). He was a consulting editor for the *Academy of Management Review* and Program Chair of the Organizational and Management Theory Division of the Academy of Management. He is or has been on the editorial boards of, and published in, numerous academic journals. He authored the award winning book, *Change Without Pain*, and his most recent book, *A Perfect Mess* (2007), explores his current interest in what happens to systems when they deviate from perfect organization.

Julia Balogun is the Professor Sir Roland Smith Chair in Strategic Management at Lancaster University Management School and an AIM Ghoshal Fellow. Her research centers on strategy development, strategic change, and renewal. She has a particular interest in how large corporations and MNEs transform themselves to both retain and regain competitive advantage in the face of declining performance. She adopts a sociological perspective, focussing on how strategists accomplish their work through political, cultural, cognitive, and discursive processes and practices, consistent with the strategy-as-practice field. Julia also has a concern for how strategic activity is initiated and championed at multiple levels within organizations, exploring the strategizing work of both senior executives and middle managers. She has published in a wide range of journals including the *Academy of Management Journal, Organization Studies, Journal of Management Studies,* and *Human Relations,* and her book, *Exploring Strategic Change,* is in its third edition. She also serves on a number of editorial boards including the *Academy of Management Journal, Organization Science, Organizational Studies,* and *Long Range Planning.*

Michael L. Barnett (PhD, New York University) is Professor of Strategy at the Saïd Business School and Fellow in Management at St. Anne's College, University of Oxford. Mike's research focuses on how firms interface with their stakeholders. In particular, he studies how firms individually and collectively manage their relationships with stakeholders, and how their efforts at stakeholder management, through acts of corporate social responsibility and via communal institutions such as industry trade associations, influence their reputations and financial performance.

Philippe Baumard is a tenured Professor of Strategic Management at Ecole Polytechnique, Innovation & Regulation Chair. His research addresses the collective use of tacit knowledge by executives in times of crisis. He has authored nine books, including *The Strategic Vacuum* (CNRS, 2012), and directed the national strategy report of the French High Council for Strategic Education and Research as President of its Scientific Council (http://www.csfrs.fr/en.html). He held Visiting Professorships at Stanford University's School of Engineering (2008–2010), UC Berkeley's Haas School of Business (2004–2007), New York University, Lund University, and University of Technology Sydney. Philippe's research currently focuses on the use of artificial intelligence for the reproduction of human reasoning and decision-making, a domain in which he holds European and US patents.

Nicole Bourque (PhD in social anthropology, University of Cambridge) is a senior lecturer in social anthropology in the Department of Sociology, Anthropology and Applied Social Science at the University of Glasgow, Scotland. She is also a research associate of AIM Research. Her main research interests are ritual and religious change. She has carried out fieldwork looking at the economics of festivals, ritual symbolism, syncretism, and religious conversion in the Andean regions of Ecuador and Bolivia. She has also carried out research on conversion to Islam and the processes of identity reformation in Scotland. More recently, she has turned her attention to the use of anthropological ritual theory in the analysis of corporate strategy events.

Laure Cabantous is Associate Professor at ESCP Europe, in Paris. Previously, she worked as an assistant professor at Nottingham University Business School (2007–2011). She received her Masters in economics from Ecole Normale Supérieure (ENS) de Cachan and University Paris I-Panthéon Sorbonne and, earned a PhD in economics from the Toulouse School of Economics (University of Toulouse – Sciences Sociales) in 2006. Her research in behavioral decision-making investigates the effect of ambiguity on choices (in particular in the field of insurance). Other areas of research include organizational decision-making processes and practice, calculability, and the performativity of theories. Her research has been published in *Organization Science, Organization Studies,* the *Journal of Risk and Uncertainty, Theory and Decision,* and *La Revue Economique.*

Prithviraj Chattopadhyay is Professor of Management at the Hong Kong University of Science and Technology. He received his PhD in management from the University of Texas at Austin. His research interests include relational demography, managerial cognition and emotions, and employment externalization. His research has been published in journals such as *Academy of Management Review*, *Academy of Management Journal*, *Administrative Science Quarterly*, *Journal of Applied Psychology*, and *Strategic Management Journal*.

Kevin Daniels is Professor of Organizational Behaviour at the University of East Anglia. He has a PhD in applied psychology and is a Fellow of the British Psychological Society. From 1998–2006 he was an associate editor of the *Journal of Occupational and Organizational Psychology*, and from 2007–2011, he was an associate editor of *Human Relations*. He is currently on the editorial boards of *Human Relations*, *Journal of Management*, and *Journal of Occupational and Organizational Psychology*. Broadly, his research interests concern relationships between affect and cognition in organizational contexts, with a recent focus on affect, problem solving, and job design in safety critical and innovative work contexts.

Jerker Denrell is Professor of Strategy and Decision Making at the Saïd Business School, University of Oxford. He received his PhD from Stockholm School of Economics. His research focuses on why firms and individuals may learn the wrong lessons from their experience and the opportunities created by such flawed learning. In several papers, he has illustrated how ordinary learning processes can lead to biases in beliefs and behavior when individuals develop beliefs based on samples of their own and others experiences. His papers on these and other topics on organizational learning, risk taking, and strategy have been published in *Psychological Review*, *Management Science*, *Organization Science*, and *Strategic Management Journal*.

Vinit M. Desai is an assistant professor of strategy and organization theory at the University of Colorado at Denver and Health Sciences Center. His research interests include organizational learning, strategic decision making, crisis management, and the causes and consequences of organizational failures. His work spans various industries including space exploration, healthcare, telecommunications, naval aviation, and natural gas exploration. He has worked in the private and public sectors, and has a PhD in business administration from the University of California at Berkeley.

Giovanni Dosi is Professor of Economics at the Scuola Superiore Sant'Anna in Pisa, Italy, where he also coordinates the Laboratory of Economics and Management (LEM). His major research areas include economics of innovation and technological change, industrial organization and industrial dynamics, theory of the firm and corporate governance, economic growth and development. Professor Dosi is Co-Director of the task forces "Industrial Policy" and "Intellectual Property Rights" within the *Initiative for Policy Dialogue*, founded and chaired by Joseph Stiglitz, at Columbia University (New York); editor for Continental Europe of *Industrial and Corporate Change*; and Visiting Professor at the University of Manchester, UK. He is author and editor of several works in the areas of economics of innovation, industrial economics, evolutionary theory, and organizational studies. A selection of his works has been published in *Innovation, Organization and Economic Dynamics: Selected Essays* (Edward Elgar, 2000).

Roger L. M. Dunbar is Professor of Management at the Stern School of Business, New York University. He is interested in sensemaking processes in organizations and in particular, how framing processes and language use determine meaning. With Bill Starbuck, he edited a special issue of *Organization Science* (March–April 2006) that focused on organization design. He is a senior editor of *Organization Studies*. He was born in Dunedin, New Zealand, and studied at the University of Otago, moving to Cornell University to do a doctorate and to Dallas, Texas, for a first academic appointment at Southern Methodist University. He then spent almost five years in Berlin, Germany, at the International Institute of Management, a part of the Science Center of Berlin before moving to New York University. He has held visiting appointments at Victoria University and Auckland University in New Zealand as well as at the Free University in Berlin.

Stephen M. Fiore holds a joint appointment with the University of Central Florida's Cognitive Sciences Program in the Department of Philosophy and UCF's Institute for Simulation and Training and Team Performance Laboratory. He earned his PhD (2000) in cognitive psychology from the University of Pittsburgh, Learning Research and Development Center. He maintains a multidisciplinary research interest that incorporates aspects of the cognitive, organizational, and computational sciences in the investigation of learning and performance in individuals and teams. He is Co-editor of a recent volume on *Distributed Learning* as well as a volume on *Team Cognition* and he has published in the area of learning, memory, and problem solving at the individual and the group level. He has helped to secure and manage over US$6 million in research funding from organizations such as the National Science Foundation, the European Science Foundation, the Office of Naval Research, and the Air Force Office of Scientific Research.

Mark A. Fuller is the Dean and the Thomas O'Brien Endowed Chair of the Isenberg School of Management at the University of Massachusetts, Amherst. Professor Fuller received his PhD in Management Information Systems from the University of Arizona. His research focuses on virtual teamwork, technology supported learning, and trust and efficacy in technology-mediated environments, and has appeared in outlets such as *Information Systems Research, Management Information Systems Quarterly, Journal of Management Information Systems, Decision Sciences, Journal of the Association for Information Systems, Journal of Organizational Behavior, IEEE Transactions of Engineering Management,* and *Decision Support Systems*. Professor Fuller has won multiple teaching awards, has published a textbook on *Information Systems Project Management*, and has taught graduate and undergraduate courses on a variety of topics, including global information systems and strategy, information systems project management, and collaborative technology.

Michael Shayne Gary is a senior lecturer of strategy and entrepreneurship at the Australian Graduate School of Management (AGSM). He is also Associate Director of the Accelerated Learning Laboratory at AGSM. His research focuses on the impact of managerial policies and decision making on performance in complex decision environments. At the firm level, he examines managerial policies adopted to pursue organizational strategies—such as corporate growth and diversification—and the impact on firm performance of implementing different policies. In another line of related research at the micro level, he investigates mental models, dynamic decision making, and learning, through behavioral experiments using management flight simulators. His research has been published in the *Strategic Management Journal* and other leading journals. He received his PhD at the London Business School.

Elizabeth George is Professor of Management at the Hong Kong University of Science and Technology. Her research interests include employment externalization, institutional theory, and workforce diversity. Her work has appeared in journals such as the *Journal of Applied Psychology, Academy of Management Review, Academy of Management Journal, Organization Science,* and *Administrative Science Quarterly.* She received her PhD from the University of Texas at Austin.

Jean-Pascal Gond is Visiting Professor at HEC Montreal. Previously, he worked as an Assistant Professor in corporate social responsibility at Nottingham University Business School, UK. He graduated from Ecole Normale Supérieure (ENS) de Cachan and received his Masters in economic sociology from the University of Toulouse, France. He received his PhD in Management from the University of Toulouse in 2006. J.-P. Gond's research focuses on the topic of corporate social responsibility (CSR) and the concept of performativity. His work has appeared in journals such as *Organization Science, Organization Studies, Journal of Management Studies, Economy and Society, Human Relations,* the *Journal of Business Ethics, Business and Society,* and *Finance Controle Stratégie.*

Paul Goodwin is Professor of Management Science at the University of Bath. He has an MSc in Management Science and Operational Research from the University of Warwick and a PhD in Management Science from the University of Lancaster. His research interests are concerned with the role of management judgment in forecasting and decision making. Paul is an Editor of the *International Journal of Forecasting* and a member of the editorial board of the *Journal of Behavioral Decision Making.* He also writes a column in *Foresight,* the international journal of applied forecasting, that is aimed at practitioners. He was, until recently, a Director of the International Institute of Forecasters and he has advised a large number of companies and public sector organizations on forecasting and decision making. A book he co-authored with George Wright, *Decision Analysis for Management Judgment* (Wiley), is recommended reading on a number of US and UK government web sites.

Terri L. Griffith is a professor of management in the Leavey School of Business at Santa Clara University. Her MSc and PhD are from Carnegie Mellon, her BA is from UC Berkeley. Her research and consulting interests include the mixing of new technologies and organizational practices to improve work and innovation. This research includes fieldwork in two Fortune 100 tech companies, funded by the National Science Foundation. Her research is published in journals such as: *Organization Science, Information Systems Research, MIS Quarterly, Organizational Behavior and Human Decision Processes,* and the *Academy of Management Review.* She recently published *The Plugged-In Manager* to bring these ideas to a broader audience.

Mark P. Healey is Lecturer in Strategic Management at Manchester Business School, University of Manchester, UK. After receiving his PhD in Management Sciences from UMIST, he was Senior Research Fellow in Organizational Psychology and Lecturer in Organizational Behaviour and Strategic Management, both at Leeds University Business School. His research focuses on cognition in organizations and its influence on individual, group, and organizational responsiveness. He is particularly interested in managerial and organizational cognition, including cognitive adaptation—how decision makers update their knowledge and thinking in response to changing conditions. Dr Healey's work has been published in leading scholarly journals including *Organization Studies* and *Strategic Management Journal.* He serves as an editorial board member for international journals in both management studies and organizational behavior.

Gerry Johnson is Emeritus Professor of Strategic Management at Lancaster University Management School and Senior Fellow of AIM Research. He received a BA in anthropology from University College London and his PhD from Aston University. His research interests are in the field of strategic management practice, in particular with regard to strategy development and change in organizations. He has published in the *Academy of Management Review, Academy of Management Journal, Journal of Management Studies, Strategic Management Journal, Organization Studies, British Journal of Management,* and *Human Relations.* He serves on the editorial boards of the *Academy of Management Journal, Strategic Management Journal,* and the *Journal of Management Studies.* He is also co-author of Europe's best selling strategic management text, *Exploring Corporate Strategy* (Prentice Hall).

Michael Johnson-Cramer is Associate Professor of Global Strategy and Ethics at Bucknell University. His research focuses on the sources of change and conflict in organizational and stakeholder relationships. His research has been published in such publications as the *Journal of Management Studies,* the *Journal of Business Ethics,* and the *California Management Review.* He completed his doctoral work at Boston University School of Management.

Alfred Kieser is Full Professor of Management and Vice President of Research at Zeppelin University at Friedrichshafen, Germany. He studied business administration and sociology at the University of Cologne and the Carnegie-Mellon University, Pittsburgh. In 1968, he received his doctoral degree in business administration from the University of Cologne, Germany. From 1974 to 1977, he was Full Professor of Personnel Administration and Organizational Behavior at the Free University of Berlin, and from 1977 to 2010, he was Full Professor of Organizational Behavior at Mannheim University. His research interests include the history of organization, organizational evolution, cross-cultural comparisons of organizations, management fashions, consulting, organizational learning, and systems for management education in different cultures. He has published in *Administrative Science Quarterly, Journal of Management Inquiry, Organization Science, Organization Studies, Organization*, and in German journals. He has published two textbooks on organizational theory (in German), one is now in its sixth, the other in its fifth edition. He has received honorary doctoral degrees from the University of Munich and from Corvimus University, Budapest, and is a member of the Heidelberg Academy of Sciences.

Ann Langley is Professor of Management at HEC Montréal and Canada Research Chair in strategic management in pluralistic settings. Her research focuses on strategic change, decision making, leadership, innovation, and the use of management tools in complex organizations with an emphasis on processual research approaches. She has published over 50 articles and two books. She is adjunct professor at the Norwegian School of Economics and Business Administration and the Department of Health Administration at University of Montréal.

Eleanor T. Lewis is an organizational sociologist currently working at the Center for Health Care Evaluation in the US Department of Veterans Affairs (VA). At the VA, she is leading studies on medication safety and substance use disorders, and conducting program evaluation of VA mental health programs. She received a PhD in Organization Science and Sociology from Carnegie Mellon University where her dissertation received the Herbert A. Simon dissertation award. She has studied how hospitals learn from medication errors, the role of communication networks in safety, and how healthcare systems can improve prescribing practices for prescription pain medication.

Dan Lovallo is Professor of Business Strategy at the University of Sydney Business School. His research focuses on the psychology of strategic decision making and has been published in the *American Economic Review, Management Science*, and the *Harvard Business Review*. He has previously held positions at Wharton, the Australian Graduate School of Management, and McKinsey & Co.

Rebecca Lyons is a doctoral candidate in the industrial and organizational psychology program at the University of Central Florida. She also works as a graduate research associate at the Institute for Simulation and Training where her research interests include individual and team training, simulation, performance measurement, and individual and team decision making and adaptability.

Much of this work has related to teams working in complex environments, such as healthcare and military populations. Rebecca is currently lead graduate student on projects funded by ARL-STTC and the National Institutes of Health. She has co-authored ten peer-reviewed articles, and six book chapters.

Peter M. Madsen is an assistant professor in the Marriott School of Management at Brigham Young University. His doctoral degree is from the University of California at Berkeley's Walter A. Haas School of Business. Peter's research interests focus on organizational reliability, corporate social performance, and the effects of social, environmental, and safety regulation on organizations. His current research deals with how organizational safety and environmental performance interrelate with institutional and technological change. Specifically, he studies the relationship between corporate social responsibility and the socio-political legitimacy of organizations, organizational forms, and technological systems. He is examining these issues in the aerospace, healthcare, insurance and automobile assembly industries.

John Maule is Emeritus Professor of Human Decision Making and a member of the Centre for Decision Research at Leeds University Business School. He is also a former President of the European Association for Decision Making. He carries out research on how people make judgements and take decisions and how we can use this knowledge to improve the effectiveness of these activities. Particular research interests include: the effects of emotion and time pressure on decision making; and the perception and communication of risk and how this varies across experts, the public, and other stakeholders. He has a strong commitment to applying academic theory and research on risk and decision making to work contexts, including the development of training courses to identify and overcome the factors that inhibit security awareness, acted as a consultant on risk and risk communication for Government Agencies, and run courses on this topic for private and public sector organizations.

John M. Mezias is an associate professor at the University of Miami's School of Business Administration. He received his PhD from New York University's Stern School of Business in 1998. His research examines managerial cognition, international human resource management, strategic leadership, and legal consequences of strategic actions. He has published in a variety of scholarly journals including the *Harvard Business Review, Strategic Management Journal, Journal of International Business Studies, Organization Science, British Journal of Management, Journal of Management, Long Range Planning, Journal of International Management, Journal of Organizational Behavior,* and the *Industrial-Organizational Psychologist.* He serves on the editorial boards of the *Strategic Management Journal* and *Journal of International Business Studies,* and was a guest editor of the *Journal of International Management.*

Nigel Nicholson is Professor of Organizational Behaviour and a former research dean at the London Business School. His research and writing have been extensive and wide ranging, including over 15 books and monographs, and over 200 articles in leading academic and practitioner journals. He has been pioneering the application of evolutionary psychology to business, and his current research is on leadership and family business. In addition he is known for his work on careers and transitions, absence from work, employee relations, behavioral risk in finance, leadership and personality. His last book was *Traders: Risks, Decisions and Management in Financial Markets* (Oxford University Press, 2005), and he has a book in press under the title *Family Wars*. He directs two major leadership programs at London Business School: *High Performance People Skills,* and one of the world's most innovative programs: *Proteus.*

Gregory B. Northcraft is the Harry J. Gray Professor of Executive Leadership and Associate Dean of Faculty and Research in the College of Business at the University of Illinois. He is a former editor of the *Academy of Management Journal,* and a former senior editor of *Organization Science.* His major research interests include collaboration in teams, conflict management, managerial decision making, and employee motivation and job design, particularly in high-tech manufacturing settings.

David Oliver is Associate Professor of Management at HEC Montréal, where he teaches strategy and management skills. His current research is focused on the areas of organizational identity and the practice of strategy. David was previously a research fellow at the Swiss-based Imagination Lab Foundation (www.imagilab. org), where he experimented with the use of building materials such as LEGO® to help managers develop shared organizational identity representations and engage in innovative strategizing. Prior to joining the Lab, he spent several years in the research department of the IMD business school (www.imd.ch) in Lausanne, Switzerland, where he conducted research on self-managed teams and complex adaptive systems theory. David's recent work has appeared in the *British Journal of Management, Organization Studies and Human Relations.* He holds a PhD in management from HEC, Lausanne, and an MBA from York University in Toronto, Canada.

Annie Pye (PhD) is Professor of Leadership Studies and Director of Research at the University of Exeter's Centre for Leadership Studies. Her enduring research interest is in 'making sense' of how small groups of people 'run' complex organizations, integrating concepts of leadership, governance, strategy, and board/director process research, from a sensemaking perspective. Funded by a series of three ESRC grants, she has researched Chief Executives, Chairmen, and board members in large FTSE companies such as Prudential, Marks & Spencer, and Lloyds Banking Group, over a twenty five year period. Current research includes: an ESF-funded study of senior leadership roles in bringing about change to achieve low carbon procurement; and continuing long-term research with Dr Louise Knight (University of Aston) into network leadership and learning. Annie publishes in a range of journals including *Organization Science, Journal of Management Studies, Human Relations, British Journal of Management, Management Learning* and *Corporate Governance: An International Review.*

Karlene H. Roberts is a professor at the Walter A. Haas School of Business, at the University of California at Berkeley. Karlene Roberts earned her Bachelor's degree in psychology from Stanford University and her PhD in industrial psychology from the University of California at Berkeley. She also received the docteur honoris causa from the Universite Paul Cezanne, Aix Marseilles III. She has done research on job attitudes, cross-national management, and organizational communication. She has also contributed to the research methodology literature. Since 1984 she has been investigating the design and management of organizations and systems of organizations in which error can result in catastrophic consequences. She has studied both organizations that failed and those that succeed in this category. Some of the industries Roberts has worked in are the military, commercial marine transportation, health care, railroads, petroleum production, commercial aviation, banking, and community emergency services.

Jacques Rojot is Professor Emeritus at the University of Paris II. He has served as a consultant and scientific advisor to the OECD, the EU, the World Bank and the European Foundation in Dublin as well as to several corporations, French ministries, and public bodies. He is the author and co-author of 12 books and more than 120 papers in French and journals of various other countries, is the French foreign correspondent to the US National Academy of Arbitrators, has been a visiting professor in several universities internationally, sits on the editorial boards of several academic journals and the management board of professional societies, nationally and internationally, is a board member of the French Foundation for the Teaching of Management, and is the President of the French Society of University Professors of Management. He is a knight in the national order of the Legion of Honour.

Michael A. Rosen, PhD, is an assistant professor at the Armstrong Institute for Patient Safety and Quality and the Department of Anesthesiology and Critical Care Medicine at the Johns Hopkins University School of Medicine. His research and applied work focus on understanding teamwork, decision making, and problem solving in healthcare delivery systems, as well as strategies to improve these types of performance including simulation, systems design, and performance measurement and feedback. He has published over 50 peer-reviewed articles and chapters in these areas. Prior to his appointment at Johns Hopkins, he was a consultant to the Department of Defense Patient Safety Program. He completed his PhD in Human Factors Psychology at the University of Central Florida and the Institute for Simulation and Training in 2010.

Isabelle Royer is a professor of management and research methods at IAE Lyon, France, the business school of the University of Lyon 3. She holds a PhD in business administration from the University of Paris-Dauphine and spent 18 months as a postdoc at the Wharton School of the University of Pennsylvania. Her research centers on decision making and innovation, with a particular interest in escalation of commitment. She has published in *Harvard Business Review* and French academic journals.

Eugene Sadler-Smith is Professor of Management Development and Organizational Behaviour and an Associate of AIM Research at the School of Management, the University of Surrey. His current research and teaching interests centre on the role of intuitive judgment in management decision making and management development. His research has been published in journals such as *Academy of Management Executive*, *Academy of Management Learning and Education*, *Journal of Organizational Behavior*, *Organization Studies*, and the *British Journal of Psychology*, He is the author of three books, including *Inside Intuition* (Routledge).

Eduardo Salas is Trustee Chair and Professor of Psychology at the University of Central Florida. He also holds an appointment as Program Director for the Human Systems Integration Research Department at the Institute for Simulation & Training. Eduardo Salas has co-authored over 300 journal articles and book chapters and has co-edited 16 books. He is on or has been on the editorial boards of *Journal of Applied Psychology*, *Personnel Psychology*, *Military Psychology*, *Interamerican Journal of Psychology*, *Applied Psychology: An International Journal*, *International Journal of Aviation Psychology*, *Group Dynamics*, *Journal of Organizational Behavior*, and is a past editor of *Human Factors* journal. He is a fellow of the American Psychological Association (SIOP and Divisions 19 & 21), and the Human Factors and Ergonomics Society. He received his PhD degree (1984) in industrial and organizational psychology from Old Dominion University.

Kristyn A. Scott is Assistant Professor of Organizational Behaviour and Human Resources Management at the Ted Rogers School of Business at Ryerson University. She received her PhD in industrial organizational psychology from the University of Waterloo. Her primary research interests are in the area of leadership and information processing, with a specific focus on subordinate perceptions of male and female leaders. Kristyn's research has appeared in *Organizational Behavior and Human Decision Processes* and *Human Resources Management Journal*.

Zur Shapira is the William Berkley Professor of Entrepreneurship and Management at the Stern School of Business, New York University. He received his PhD in psychology and management from the University of Rochester. He has taught at the University of Rochester, Hebrew University, Carnegie-Mellon University, University of California at Berkeley, and the University of Chicago before joining New York University in 1988. He has been a research fellow at the International Institute of Management in Berlin, a visiting scholar at the Russell Sage Foundation, a resident scholar at the Rockefeller Foundation, and a visiting scholar at the Center for the Study of Rationality in Jerusalem. He is a fellow of the American Psychological Society. Zur Shapira is known professionally for his work on risk taking and organizational decision making. Among his publications are the books: *Risk Taking: A Managerial Perspective* (1995); *Organizational Decision Making* (1997*)*; *Technological Learning: Oversights and Foresights* (1997); and *Organizational Cognition* (2000).

Carolyne Smart is Professor Emerita of Business Strategy at the Beedie School of Business, Simon Fraser University in Vancouver, B.C. Canada. Carolyne's research centers on crisis management in public and private organizations. Her most recent work examines the management of major public health crises and the significant policy and governmental issues involved. She also has a long-term interest in female entrepreneurship and the factors that lead to successful female owned enterprises. A long time professor with SFU Business, Carolyne has held a number of executive positions within the faculty, most recently as Dean Pro Tem. She also established and ran the former Resource Centre for Women Entrepreneurs.

Gerald F. Smith is a professor in the Department of Management, College of Business Administration, at the University of Northern Iowa. He received a PhD in decision sciences from the Wharton School at the University of Pennsylvania (1985). Gerald Smith's research has focused on managerial problem solving, the thinking managers do when faced with complex organizational problems. Much of his early research, published in journals like *Management Science* and *Organizational Behavior and Human Decision Processes*, used conceptual analysis to reach a clearer understanding of notions like problem definition and problem structure. A later stream of research, concerned with problem solving aimed at improving the quality of organizational products and processes, culminated in the publication of *Quality Problem Solving* (1998). Professor Smith's more recent publications have appeared in educational journals and address controversies regarding the nature of thinking skills and the challenges of teaching students how to think effectively.

Emma Soane is Lecturer in the Department of Management at the London School of Economics and Political Science and Programme Director, MSc Management. She teaches applied psychology at post-graduate level. Her research interests include personality, decision making, risk management, and the implications of individual differences for organizations. Emma holds several EPSRC grants and has collaborative projects with colleagues at other universities nationally and internationally. Emma co-authored the book, *Traders: Managing Risks and Decisions in Financial Markets* (Oxford University Press), and has published a number of academic and practitioner journal articles. She is a referee for several journals, and the ESRC and has spoken at many international conferences and works as a consultant to organizations. Prior to her current post, Emma was a research fellow at London Business School. She worked on two ESRC projects examining the decision making and performance of traders in financial markets. Emma holds a PhD in psychology from University of Sheffield and is a chartered occupational psychologist and chartered scientist.

Paul R. Sparrow is Director of the Centre for Performance-led HR and Professor of International Human Resource Management at Lancaster University Management School. He has worked as a research fellow at Aston University, senior research fellow at Warwick University, consultant/principal consultant at PA Consulting Group, reader/professor at Sheffield University, and while at Manchester Business School he took up the Ford Chair from 2002–04 and was Director, Executive Education 2002–05. He has consulted with major multinationals, public sector organizations, and intergovernmental agencies, and is an Expert Advisory Panel member to the UK Government's Sector Skills Development Agency. His research interests include cross-cultural and international HRM, HR strategy, cognition at work, and changes in the employment relationship. He has published over 100 journal articles and book chapters, and several books.

Matt Statler is the Richman Family Director of Business Ethics and Social Impact Programming and Clinical Assistant Professor of Management and Organizations at NYU Stern School of Business. Previously, Matt served NYU's Center for Catastrophe Preparedness and Response as the Director of Research, and as Associate Director of the International Center for Enterprise Preparedness. He worked as Director of Research and as a Research Fellow at the Imagination Lab Foundation in Lausanne, Switzerland, following several years as a management consultant in New York City. His research has appeared in the *Journal of Business Ethics* and *Long Range Planning*, and he is the co-editor of the recent *Encyclopedia of Disaster Relief* (2010, with K. Bradley Penuel) and *Learning from the Global Financial Crisis: Creatively, Reliably, Sustainably* (2011, with Paul Shrivastava).

Kathleen M. Sutcliffe is the Gilbert and Ruth Whitaker Professor of Business Administration and Professor of management and organizations at the Stephen M. Ross School of Business at the University of Michigan. Her research interests include topics such as organizational resilience and reliability, how organizations and their members sense emerging problems and cope with uncertainty, cognitive and experiential diversity in top management teams, and team and organizational learning. Her most recent work examines how elements of an organizational system influence errors in health care settings. Her work has been published in a wide variety of journals, including the *Academy of Management Review*, the *Academy of Management Journal*, *Strategic Management Journal*, and *Organization Science*.

Michal Tamuz, PhD, is an organizational sociologist with research interests in decision making, organizational learning, improving patient safety, and risk management. Michal Tamuz received a PhD in sociology from Stanford University. She is an associate professor in the Department of Health Policy and Management in the School of Public Health at SUNY Downstate Medical Center in Brooklyn, New York. In her research, she explores how organizations learn from small samples and under conditions of ambiguity. Her research focuses on near accident reporting in hospitals and in an array of high hazard industries, from aviation to chemical manufacturing plants and blood banks. Her current research, funded in part by the Agency for Healthcare Research and Quality, examines how hospitals learn from medical errors.

Teri Jane Ursacki-Bryant received her PhD from the University of British Columbia and joined the Faculty of Management (now the Haskayne School of Business) at the University of Calgary in 1990. Her research has focused on managerial and public policy issues in Asia, particularly Japan, China, and Korea. Most recently her work has dealt with crisis management in an international context. Her research has appeared in journals such as *Strategic Management Journal, Journal of Banking and Finance, Pacific Affairs*, and the *Asia-Pacific Journal of Management* as well as in numerous book chapters. She is a past president of the Japan Studies Association of Canada.

Ilan Vertinsky is the Vinod Sood Professor of International Business Studies, Operations Logistics, Strategy and Business Economics in the Sauder School of Business. He is also the director of the Centre for International Business Studies and a member of the Institute of Asian Research at the University of British Columbia. He has published more than 250 journal articles, book chapters, and monographs. His current research projects include a study of organizational sense making in crises, a study of competitive behaviors in knowledge intensive industries, and a study of the effects of cultural diversity on performances of syndicates of international venture capitalists.

Bénédicte Vidaillet is Associate Professor of Management and Organizational Behavior at the Institute for Business Administration (Institut d' Administration des Entreprises), University of Lille 1 (France). She graduated from ESSEC Business School, France, and received her PhD from Paris Dauphine University, France. Her research focuses on the processes of managerial decision making, sensemaking in organizations, and emotion at work. She has co-edited a multidisciplinary book about decision making with economists, psychologists, and researchers in organization theory (2005). Among her other publications are the books *Le sens de l'action. Karl Weick: sociopsychologie de l'organisation* (2003) and *Les ravages de l'envie au travail* (2006) as well as several book chapters and articles published in *Human Relations, International Studies in Management and Organizations, Management Learning*, and *Organization Studies*.

Jane Webster received her PhD from New York University and is the E. Marie Shantz Professor of MIS in the School of Business at Queen's University in Canada. She has served as a senior editor for *MIS Quarterly*, guest associate editor of *Information Systems Research*, and the VP of publications for the *Association for Information Systems*. She has published in a variety of journals including the *Academy of Management Journal, Communication Research, Journal of Organizational Behavior, MIS Quarterly*, and *Organization Science*. Her current research concerns information systems and technologies for environmental sustainability. She also investigates the impacts of technologies in the support of distributed work, organizational communication, employee recruitment and selection, employee monitoring, training and learning, and human-computer interaction.

Karl E. Weick is the Rensis Likert Distinguished University Professor of Organizational Behavior and Psychology at the University of Michigan. He joined the Stephen M. Ross School of Business at the University of Michigan in 1988 after previous faculty positions at the University of Texas, Cornell University, the University of Minnesota, and Purdue University. He received his PhD from Ohio State University in social and organizational psychology. He is a former editor of the journal, *Administrative Science Quarterly* (1977–85). Weick's books include *The Social Psychology of Organizing* and *Sensemaking in Organizations* (Sage, 1995). Karl Weick's research interests include collective sensemaking under pressure, handoffs and transitions in dynamic events, organizing for resilient performance, and continuous change.

Benjamin Wellstein is Managing Director of the Institute for Business to Business I4B2B (Vallendar, Germany), a spin-off from the WHU – Otto Beisheim School of Management. In 2008 he received his PhD from Mannheim University researching on knowledge management. He studied business administration at Mannheim University, Friedrich Schiller University, Jena, and at the European Business Management School in Swansea, UK. He worked as strategy consultant for leading internationally operating top-management firms in Europe and the United States. He has published scientific work in international journals and book series and received an award from the Academy of Management for outstanding practice-based research. His current research interests concentrate on sales management and systemic approaches in the consulting of organizations.

George Wright is Professor of Operational Research and Management Science at Warwick Business School, University of Warwick, UK. George is the Founding Editor of *Journal of Behavioral Decision Making* and an associate editor of two forecasting journals: *International Journal of Forecasting* and *Journal of Forecasting*. He is also an associate editor of *Decision Support Systems*. His publications have appeared in a range of US-based management journals—including *Organizational Behavior and Human Decision Processes, Management Science,* and the *Strategic Management Journal.* George's books include, *Decision Analysis for Management Judgement* (3rd edn., Wiley, 2004, co-authored with Paul Goodwin); *Strategic Decision Making: A Best Practice Blueprint* (Wiley, 2001); and *The Sixth Sense: Accelerating Organizational Learning with Scenarios* (Wiley, 2002, co-authored).

Frank Yu received his PhD in Management of Organizations from Haas School of Business of UC Berkeley, and is currently an Assistant Professor of Management at City University of Hong Kong. His research interests include High Reliability Organizations and reliability-enhancing practices; risk and uncertainty management; discretion and accountability; and social constructionism and research methods. He is especially interested in how organizations can achieve reliable performances from appropriate discretion, flexibility, justification, and accountability. Furthermore, he pays particular attention to the socially constructed nature of organizational reality. Serving as the Academy of Management (AOM) All Academy Practice Theme Committee PDW chair from 2007 to 2012, he is committed to applying scholarship and producing rigorous and relevant knowledge.

David Zweig received his PhD in industrial/organizational psychology at the University of Waterloo and is currently an associate professor of organizational behaviour at the University of Toronto in Canada. He has published in a variety of journals including the *Journal of Organizational Behavior, Personnel Psychology, Human Resources Management Journal,* and the *Journal of Vocational Behavior.* His research interests include the impact of employee monitoring technologies, goal orientation and learning outcomes, structured interviews, and knowledge hiding in organizations.

ACKNOWLEDGEMENTS

The Oxford Handbook of Organizational Decision Making originated from a series of conversations between Gerard and Peter Herriot, during the course of co-authoring a sequence of publications concerning the growing divide between academic researchers and practitioners in the field of industrial, work, and organizational psychology. Prior to his retirement, Peter suggested that the topic of organizational decision making would present a great opportunity to demonstrate the applicability of their evolving ideas regarding the problems of attempting to produce knowledge that is both academically rigorous but also socially useful and how they might be resolved. Subsequently, Gerard met Bill while serving on the Academy of Management's Executive Committee of the Managerial and Organizational Cognition Division (2002–05). Over this period, we discovered that we share a passionate interest in both organizational decision making and the nature and production of social scientific knowledge, a passion that led us to embark upon the production of this volume. The award of a senior fellowship under the auspices of the UK ESRC/EPSRC Advanced Institute of Management (AIM) Research (grant number RES-331-25-0028), provided Gerard with the financial resources to devote the necessary time and space to complete his share of the task, while Bill similarly benefited from the support of the Stern School of Business, New York University— his former employer.

We are extremely grateful to David Musson, the Business and Management Editor, and to Matthew Derbyshire and Emma Lambert, the Assistant Commissioning Editors (Business and Management) at Oxford University Press, for their unstinting support of the project, from its inception to the final stages of the production and marketing of the finished product. We are equally grateful to Liam Irwin, Gerard's PA, whose organizational ability, together with his meticulousness and painstaking attention to detail, ensured that the project as a whole ran smoothly throughout and that the final manuscript met the exacting standards of the Oxford production team. Finally, but by no means least, we would like to thank the contributors for their commitment to ensuring that *The Oxford Handbook of Organizational Decision Making* is of the quality of scholarship worthy of its title.

Gerard P. Hodgkinson and William H. Starbuck

ORGANIZATIONAL DECISION MAKING: MAPPING TERRAINS ON DIFFERENT PLANETS

GERARD P. HODGKINSON*
WILLIAM H. STARBUCK

THE *Oxford Handbook of Organizational Decision Making* comprises 30 chapters authored by leading social and behavioral scientists and scientist-practitioners whose work addresses cutting edge issues in decision research in applied contexts. Targeted at professional decision researchers, management and organizational scientists, and reflective practitioners, the *Handbook* provides an authoritative overview of the main theoretical, methodological, and substantive developments in the analysis of decision making in organizations. The volume also offers insights for improving organizational decision making.

* The financial support of the UK ESRC/EPSRC Advanced Institute of Management (AIM) Research in the preparation of this chapter, under grant number RES-331–25-0028 (Hodgkinson), is gratefully acknowledged.

The *Handbook*'s design expresses an underlying belief that research can often meet the twin imperatives of scholarly rigor and social usefulness. This philosophy is gaining momentum among behavioral and social scientists (Pettigrew 1997; Anderson et al. 2001; Dunbar and Starbuck 2006; Starbuck 2006; Van de Ven and Johnson 2006; Van de Ven 2007), although debate continues (Grey 2001; McKelvey 2006). The need for a volume that accords with this philosophy is all too evident from the various high profile decision fiascos that continue to dog public service and business organizations. From the Enron debacle to the multiagency mishandling of the 9/11 crisis and the recent floods of New Orleans, organizations have repeatedly failed to heed the lessons of similar cases. They adopt decision processes that perpetuate errors of judgment and miscommunication, leading them into inappropriate courses of action and escalating commitments to failing strategies (Staw 1981, 1997). Readers will recognize this tendency in the construction of many public works, where costs often spiral out of control.

The widely publicized space shuttle disasters of NASA illustrate the high costs of mismatches between decision-making practices and their technological and organizational contexts. These events also illustrate the complexity of organizational and environmental influences on decision making and the difficulty of attributing specific consequences to specific decisions. NASA's official goals imply that the agency should pioneer new technologies, which inevitably entail risk, and NASA's technologies tend to be very complex ones in which many components can fail, so the risks are high (Starbuck and Stephenson 2005). History suggests that each launch has roughly a 2 percent probability of killing an astronaut (Whoriskey 2003), yet much of NASA's technology is many years out of date. NASA's political and mass communications environments have consistently emphasized the importance of meeting planned schedules for achieving various targets such as launch dates, which has pressured NASA to de-emphasize technological progress and safety. NASA's political environment has demonstrated little enthusiasm for the agency's official goals and has loaded it with numerous additional "performance targets" that have tangential or no relationships to its official goals. In 2004, NASA claimed to be trying to achieve 211 distinct performance targets.

NASA's internal structure is also complex and mutually inconsistent. One result of the diverse performance targets is that NASA contains many subunits that are partially in conflict with each other. Furthermore, NASA's largest subunits have autonomous political support of their own, and the two largest centers have occasionally refused to comply with instructions from NASA's official headquarters. The centers use distinct rules for everyday activities such as travel to conferences and expense re-imbursement. NASA's leaders have tried to manage the organization by specifying rules and procedures, in effect turning the agency into a mechanistic bureaucracy. Not only is mechanistic organization inconsistent with the agency's goal of technological development, but it contradicts the realities of subunits that conflict and does not recognize central authority.

NASA personnel include managers, engineers, and scientists who pursue different goals, espouse different values, and speak somewhat different languages (Vaughan 1996; Starbuck and Milliken 1988). These distinct cultures nurture intra-organizational conflict and impede and distort communication. One of several persistent differences between these cultures has been that engineers have emphasized safety over cost or adherence to planned schedules, whereas managers have sought to keep costs within budgets and activities on schedule. One of NASA's senior leaders, Hans Mark, has said, "When I was working as Deputy Administrator, I don't think there was a single launch where there was some group of subsystem engineers that didn't get up and say 'Don't fly.' You always have arguments" (Bell and Esch 1987: 48).

Much of NASA's activity involves performing incremental experiments. Although these experiments may have laboratory precursors, the crucial experiments occur during space flights. Investigations of the 1986 Challenger disaster revealed that managers and engineers had drawn very different inferences from several years of flight experience (Starbuck and Milliken 1988). Some engineers at both NASA and Morton Thiokol had inferred that the Shuttle was becoming increasingly likely to have a catastrophic failure. They met in early 1986 to discuss the reasons for escalating evidence of burn damage to O-rings in the solid rocket boosters (SRBs). Meanwhile, managers at NASA and Thiokol had been observing that the Shuttle had continued to fly successfully despite escalating evidence of burn damage to O-rings, and they had inferred that the Shuttle was much more tolerant of problems than their engineering colleagues had said. As a result, the managers in charge of the SRBs had gradually lowered their standards for "acceptable" risk.

These differences led to several explicit disagreements between managers and engineers during the year before the fatal launch of Challenger. In the summer of 1985, engineers proposed that NASA ground the Shuttles for three years to wait for new SRBs. In August 1985, NASA held a meeting to discuss this proposal, which led to a decision to continue flying the Shuttles until new boosters became available. This meeting omitted some key personnel, including the astronauts and the top manager of the Shuttle program, and participants did not see some of the displays that engineers had produced about the O-ring problems. Disagreements between engineers and managers arose at Thiokol during the fall of 1985, when a team of engineers was trying to study and produce a report about the O-ring problems; these engineers complained that managers were giving them inadequate cooperation and financial resources. Disagreements between engineers and managers arose again on the afternoon before the fatal launch. Engineering managers from Marshall Space Flight Center met privately at a motel before their teleconference with engineers and managers from Thiokol. The Director of the Marshall Center had declared that his organization would never be responsible for a delayed launch, and it appears that the Director of the Marshall Center may have instructed his personnel to make sure that that this launch would occur as scheduled no matter what the people from Thiokol said. Thus, the teleconference placed pressure on the Thiokol managers to do what the NASA managers wanted to happen, and the Thiokol managers proceeded to construct a rationale for doing what their customer had demanded (Esser and Lindoerfer 1989). When Thiokol's Vice President for engineering expressed agreement with his engineers and reluctance to endorse the launch, the Chief Executive of Thiokol's operations told him, "Take off your engineering hat and put on your management hat" (Presidential Commission 1986: 108).

The Challenger disaster also illustrates the hazards of retrospective analyses of decisions. Just a few days before the disaster, engineers from NASA and Thiokol discussed 11 somewhat contradictory hypotheses about the causes of burn damage to the SRBs' O-rings. The commission that investigated the disaster came up with two more hypotheses. Thus, at the time of the accident, there was no consensus about what might be wrong, and before the disaster there was no consensus that the burn damage had very serious implications. Yet, only a few months after the disaster, the press and academic analyses had developed a consensus about the causes of the disaster, and they had agreed that specific managers made the crucial errors. Such conversion of complexity, uncertainty, and ambiguity into simplicity, certainty, and clarity is typical of retrospective analyses (Fischhoff 1980). However, this distortion means that retrospective analyses generate deceptive guidance for future decisions, because the people who are making the future decisions will not possess certainty and clarity and they will not see simple situations. In order for analyses of past events to generate useful guidance for future decisions, analysts have to surmount their tendencies to know more than they could have known, and they must formulate prescriptions that help decision makers to operate effectively amid complexity, uncertainty, and ambiguity.

NASA and Thiokol reacted to the Challenger disaster by dismissing almost everyone who had participated in those events and by making numerous changes to rules and procedures. These changes created an impression within NASA that the agency was unlikely to repeat the errors associated with the Challenger disaster. Yet, 17 years later, the Space Shuttle Columbia suffered a catastrophic failure, and the decision processes preceding this second disaster had many similarities to those preceding the earlier one (Starbuck and Farjoun 2005). Again, years of successful launches had led NASA personnel to underestimate the risks posed by signs of damage... in this case damage to foam insulation on the large fuel tank. Pieces of foam had been coming off the fuel tank for 22 years. Engineers again showed more concern for safety than did managers, who again showed more concern for adherence to schedules. Again, managers paid little heed to protests and proposals from engineers. Of course, NASA's shuttles were still using much the same technology as in 1986, and NASA's political and public relations environments were still emphasizing low costs and conformity to plans and schedules.

We, the editors of this *Handbook*, draw two sets of inferences from stories such as the NASA one. Firstly, decision makers in practical situations can benefit from academic research. At a minimum, decision makers can gain insights by observing academic debates about how to interpret events. Decision makers may also find useful some of the prescriptions that academics have extracted from their observations. Secondly, academic researchers can benefit from considering the practical implications of their studies. Such reflections help researchers to identify contingencies that differentiate situations and to frame analyses in relation to variables that have practical meanings. Academic researchers may also be able to contribute to better decisions that produce a better world. Thus, this *Handbook* aims to meet "double hurdles," providing both an up to the minute overview of theoretical and substantive advances and ongoing debates, and doing so in ways that will enable decision makers to benefit from these scientific endeavors (Pettigrew 1997).

The Past, Present, and Future of Organizational Decision Research

This introductory chapter outlines major historical developments that have shaped organizational decision research and highlights themes that surface in the chapters that follow. Several of the themes have been visible for many years; these raise questions about decision makers' rationality, their heuristics and simplifications, their political behaviors, and their interpretations of experience. Other themes, however, are nascent ones that promise to become more visible in the future; these deal with decision makers' expertise, intuitions, and emotions. The chapter concludes with an overview of the structure and contents of the *Handbook* as a whole.

Persistent Themes

Rational Decision Makers

People did not perceive organizations as making decisions until the late 1930s and 1940s. Before that time, talk and writing about organizations focused on their administrative hierarchies but people took for granted the activities that these hierarchies performed. Obviously, the hierarchies were making decisions but neither managers nor academics saw these decisions as worthy of discussion or study. In the late 1940s, Simon (1947) wrote the book, *Administrative Behavior,* in which he discussed decisions. He argued that observers could best understand administrative behaviors in terms of decision processes, that decision premises are the key factors in decision processes, and that decision premises and organizational structures influence each other. Simon also introduced a term that has had widespread influence: "bounded rationality." People have bounded rationality, he said, because, "The capacity of the human mind for formulating and solving complex problems is very small compared with the size of the problems whose solution is required for objectively rational behavior in the real word" (Simon 1957: 198). Simon's formulations not only made decision making a focal point for understanding organizational behavior, they also placed organization theory amid the behavioral sciences, especially psychology.

Although Simon had pointed to mutual influence between decision premises and organizational structures, *Administrative Behavior* said little about organizations as systems. A decade later, March and Simon (1958) described organizations as complex interactive systems, and discussed how organizational activities modify the bounded rationality of individual decision makers, and vice versa. Still later, Cyert and March (1963) described how actual decision makers in department stores make routine decisions about prices and quantities to order. They showed that human decision makers adhere to very detailed rules of thumb. However, Cyert and March studied and described microscopic decisions that occurred repeatedly and routinely, not major strategic decisions that occur rarely.

Debates about decision makers' rationality have routinely displayed miscomprehension of the opposing viewpoints (Salgado et al. 2002). Both the proponents of rational theories and the critics of these theories agree that individual decision makers do not exhibit in their everyday behaviors the kind of rationality that microeconomic theories purport to assume. As observed by March (1997), rational theories commonly assume that every decision maker:

1. knows all the alternatives for action;
2. knows all the consequences of every alternative action, at least well enough to be able to state a probability distribution;
3. has a consistent preference ordering for alternative courses of action; and
4. uses decision rules that can select a single action to take.

Critics of rational theories have remarked that the everyday realities of organizational life do not allow decision makers to have complete data or well defined objectives and decision makers do not use entirely logical information processes. Decision makers have neither full information nor the competence and capacities to process the myriad of information that is available, nor do they have perfect knowledge of the issues at hand. Empirical studies going back to the 1930s have shown that business decision makers have little confidence in their knowledge of marginal costs, and that their firms set prices not by optimizing but by applying traditional mark-up rules (Hall and Hitch 1939; Harrod 1939; Lester 1946). Furthermore, those who have studied it have described actual decision making as iterative and complex, punctuated by digressions, and warped by biases and misperceptions (Mintzberg et al. 1976). Witte (1972) analyzed the documents generated by 233 decision processes, and found only four of these processes flowed in one direction from problem definition to solution selection.

March (1971) remarked that rational theories ignore the obvious fact that goals change over time, and they said people first specify preferences and then they choose actions, whereas people often discover their preferences through taking actions and experiencing the consequences. Thus, people need a technology of foolishness to supplement the technology of rationality. Sensible foolishness (or playfulness) enables people to experiment and discover but it requires a loosening of the requirement to behave consistently. March (1991) weighed the advantages and disadvantages of allocating resources to exploiting the knowledge an organization already has versus exploring the organization's environment in search of new knowledge. As an example, he cited choices between refining an existing technology versus inventing a new technology. Returns from such choices depend, he said, on their variability, timing, and external effects as well as on their expected values, and exploration generally entails consequences that are more variable, have longer time horizons, and exert weaker effects on other organizations.

Proponents of rational theories, who have been mainly economists, have said that these theories are not intended to describe either decision processes or choices in the short-run. Economic theories of rational decision making are not about one person's behavior or one firm's behavior in the immediate future, but about industry level phenomena over the very long run. Economic theories of rational decision making focus narrowly on prices and quantities. Machlup (1946), for example, pointed out that empirical studies did not allow for the fact that the theory of the firm deals with expectations about the future rather than actual experiences, and that studies had assumed that business decision makers understand concepts such as marginal cost and elasticity of demand. Alchian (1950) argued that economists do not have to look at actual decision processes in order to predict the behaviors that survive in the long-run. No matter what decision rules firms might use, they can survive only by earning positive profits: firms that lose money go out of business. In addition, firms that behave more optimally have higher probabilities of survival, he said. Friedman (1953) maintained that economic theory does not have to describe firms' actual behaviors as long as it helps economists to analyze firms' behaviors. That is, the appropriate frame of reference for analysis is that of the analysts, not that of the decision makers.

Throughout the 1950s, Carnegie hosted a never ending debate between Modigliani, who said that people are rational, and Simon, who said rationality has bounds. What Simon, Modigliani, and those who watched them did not see clearly was that they were debating two different topics. Simon was talking about the behavior one can observe when one watches one decision maker at a time or at least obtains data from individual decision makers. Modigliani, on the other hand, was talking about the behavior one can observe when one watches hundreds or thousands of decision makers who are responding to similar stimuli (e.g., financial markets). In a way, this debate continues today with similar non-recognition of the fundamental differences due to aggregation. Economists' notions about rational expectations obviously make no sense when applied to individuals, who cannot know the future, yet these ideas have some predictive value when applied to large aggregates. Students of individual decisions are still criticizing economists for their blind disregard for the many factors that can influence choices and actions microscopically.

"Behavioral" Decision Makers

One subgroup of researchers that has applied economic rationality to individual people has been the behavioral decision theorists. However, behavioral decision theorists soon discovered that actual behavior deviates from what statistical models recommend as being "optimal." For instance, Edwards (1954, 1961), who is usually regarded as the founder of behavioral decision theory, sought to describe human choice as maximizing "subjective expected utility." However, even as early as 1961, Edwards was ready to say that maximizing subjective expected utility "does not fit the facts" (1961: 474). Hence, behavioral decision theorists have devoted themselves to finding ways in which human choice deviates from the maximization of subjective expected utility.

Researchers have identified a variety of rules of thumb, "heuristics," that enable people to cut through the detailed information bombarding them (Kahneman et al. 1982; Payne et al. 1993; Gilovich et al. 2002). The "availability" heuristic says that the more easily people can recall past examples of events and outcomes, the more people will expect them to occur in the future. For example, recent media coverage of business failures would tend to increase the percentage of retail managers who predict that a major competitor will fail in the next year. The "representativeness" heuristic says an observer's estimate of the likelihood that an event will occur depends on that observer's generalizations about similar events, and an observer's estimate of the likelihood that a given person or object belongs to a particular category depends on that observer's generalizations about similar persons or objects. For example, if an employee's physical appearance closely resembles a manager's stereotypical image of a potential "high-flyer" (e.g., smartly dressed and quick to offer forthright opinions in meetings), the manager will tend to classify the employee accordingly. Although use of heuristics reduces the information-processing requirements of decision makers, their use may also yield poor judgments and choices.

Researchers have amassed much evidence about the relevance of behavioral decision theory (BDT) concepts for decisions and the design of interventions (Bazerman 1984; Schwenk 1984 1988; Bateman and Zeithaml 1989a, b; Das and

Teng 1999; Hodgkinson et al. 1999; Highhouse 2001; Neale et al. 2006). Nonetheless, growing numbers of researchers have questioned BDT's adequacy on philosophical, theoretical, and methodological grounds. So far, BDT has made no significant contributions that take meaningful account of social interactions or organizational complexity.

Decision Makers With Simple Mental Models

Another enduring contribution of Simon is the computer metaphor of the human mind that has dominated the cognitive sciences over the past 50 years (Newell and Simon 1956; Newell et al. 1958). One legacy of this metaphor is the notion that decision makers develop simplified internal representations of problems that help them cope with their information-processing limitations (Porac and Thomas 1989). The development of methods to probe more deeply organizational decision makers' mental representations has gathered pace over the past two decades, following the publication of Huff's (1990) influential volume and Walsh's (1995) landmark review. Unfortunately, from the late 1980s to the early 1990s, management and organizational scientists borrowed a plethora of terms from the basic cognitive sciences including "mental models" (Johnson Laird 1983); "schemata" (Bartlett 1932); "scripts" (Schank and Abelson 1977); and "cognitive maps" (Tolman 1932). Inconsistent usage of terms and concepts has likely impeded scientific progress. More recently, however, a number of conceptual and methodological refinements have advanced understanding of actors' mental representations; some of these contributions have focused on the sharing of mental models among members of single organizations (e.g., Daniels et al. 1994; Hodgkinson and Johnson 1994) and across industries (e.g., Porac et al. 1989; Porac et al. 1995). Furthermore, research about mental models has inspired the design of interventions to enhance decision processes. These design interventions seek to stimulate more effortful information processing and, where appropriate, requisite cognitive change (Eden and Ackermann 1998; Hodgkinson et al. 1999; van der Heijden et al. 2002).

Adaptive Decision Makers

Gigerenzer and colleagues (Gigerenzer 1991; Gigerenzer and Goldstein 1996) have criticized BDT as an incomplete portrayal of human cognitive abilities in that it pays insufficient attention to humans' adaptive capacities. Furthermore, Gigerenzer has maintained that many of the experimental studies central to the development and validation of BDT involve probabilistic reasoning and other forms of abstract judgment that are far removed from the real-world environments to which humans have adapted (cf., Kahneman and Tversky 1996).

Predicated upon a fundamentally different conception of Simon's bounded rationality, ecological rationality, Gigerenzer and his colleagues have identified an alternative category of heuristics, fast and frugal heuristics, that they allege adaptively match the informational structure and demands of decision makers' environments. According to Gigerenzer and Todd (1999), people behave in an ecologically rational manner when they use heuristics that suit their environments. They maintain that Simon's notion of satisficing and fast and frugal heuristics suit the real-life environments of decision makers and are thus ecologically valid. Gigerenzer and Todd claim that fast and frugal heuristics not only make minimal computational demands on decision makers, but they cause less error and bias than the heuristics identified by conventional BDT researchers. However, researchers attempting to identify and analyze fast and frugal heuristics in relation to organizationally relevant decisions have done so mainly in laboratory settings, or they have employed simulated data to compare the performance of fast and frugal heuristics with BDT counterparts (Hogarth and Karelaia 2005; Newell et al. 2003; Bryant 2007). The few studies of fast and frugal heuristics in natural settings (e.g., Astebro and Elhedhli 2006), have yielded mixed findings regarding the extent to which organizational decision makers actually rely on fast and frugal heuristics and with what consequences. There is a clear need, therefore, for further investigations in both controlled and organizational field settings, before researchers should draw definitive conclusions about the applicability of this notion to real-world organizations.

Politically Aware Decision Makers

Miller and Wilson (2006: 471) observed,

In Simon's definition of the term, "bounded rationality" is largely the result of human and organizational constraints. Arguably, this view underplays the role of power and political behavior in setting those constraints. Many writers have pointed out that decision-making may be seen more accurately as a game of power in which competing interest groups vie with each other for the control of scarce resources.

Pettigrew's (1973, 1985) longitudinal analyses of decision processes in a British retail organization and the pharmaceutical and industrial chemicals giant, ICI, illustrate the potential contributions of a political perspective (see also Pfeffer and Salancik 1974, 1978; Pfeffer 1981; Wilson 1982). This body of work emphasizes the influence of multiple and contending stakeholders and of coalitions that assemble loosely on an issue-by-issue basis, each pursuing a distinct rationality (Cyert and March 1963).

Cohen et al. (1972) pointed out that decision making often creates occasions in which heterogeneous problems, miscellaneous potential solutions, and diverse actors come together erratically. The authors described these occasions as resembling "garbage cans" into which people dump their preferences, technological alternatives, potential solutions, and participants, many of which have weak relations to the problems that gave rise to the occasions. Cohen et al. (1972: 1) observed,

... organizations can be described for some purposes as collections of choices looking for problems, issues and feelings looking for decision situations in which they might be aired, solutions looking for issues to which they might be an answer, and decision makers looking for work.

As formulated, garbage-can decision making is much more likely to occur during decision making by organizations than during decision making by individuals. Cohen et al. said that garbage-can decision making is particularly prevalent and conspicuous in public, educational, and illegitimate organizations, although it may occur in any organization. Other researchers have observed garbage-can decision making in business firms. The conditions that elicit garbage-can decision making are ambiguity of goals, lack of clarity in technology, and transient participants. The decision processes of individuals may also look like garbage cans when they have ambiguous goals and unclear technological alternatives and their thinking mixes disparate issues and cherished solutions.

Brunsson (2007) has contributed many case studies of rationality in political contexts such as local governments. Brunsson (1982, 1985) observed that the various activities that comprise "rational" decision making tend to lower the likelihood that decisions will lead to actions. When participants in a decision process become aware that a chosen action is only one of several alternatives, or when participants see that a chosen action may yield different consequences that are not entirely predictable, they may feel less commitment to that action. Actions become more likely when the people who carry them out do not see alternatives and expect only good results. Thus, irrational decisions are more likely to produce actions. At least in political contexts, said Brunsson (1989), decision making is a process of talking that participants engage in as a means of building rationales for action, creating visions of future states, and mobilizing resources. Because organizations have diverse goals and stakeholders that cannot all be satisfied simultaneously, organizational leaders have to espouse different visions at different times and support mutually inconsistent actions. Such hypocrisy helps organizations to make controversial decisions and to take forceful actions. Decision processes also create responsibility in that people hold to account those whom they perceive to have advocated actions or made decisions. The ways in which decision processes unfold create external perceptions of about the legitimacy of the decisions, the ensuing actions, and the deciding organization.

Decision Makers Who Process Information, Interpret, and Enact

Weick's (1969, 1979) much cited book, *The Social Psychology of Organizing*, challenged the idea that environments are stable, objective entities. He said people "enact" their environments when they make sense of their perceptions and experiences and act on these interpretations, and he portrayed organizations as operating in environments of human interpretation. *The Social Psychology of Organizing* was the first comprehensive analysis of organizations as information-processing systems. March and Simon (1958) had devoted two chapters of *Organizations* to information processing, but they focused on a few propositions and did not attempt a comprehensive theory. Cyert and March (1963) had also offered general propositions, but they had concentrated on routinized decision making. Weick's book treated information processing as the essence of organized activity. Indeed, Weick argued that organizations are not static systems and that organizing is a never ending process so that organizations continuously evolve. This evolution occurs primarily in ideas, perceptions, data, beliefs, and communications, and people are endlessly choosing whether or not to follow standardized routines (recipes). Thus, organizations become interpretation systems (Daft and Weick 1984).

Weick's theorizing has reflected especially the ideas of Schutz (1932), who pointed out how interpretation was involved in selecting an experience out of one's stream of experience and how the meaning of action to an actor depends upon the actor's long-run goals. Schutz argued that understanding conscious choice requires the knowledge of the perspective of the actor at the time of choice; an action that appears irrational after the fact might have appeared perfectly rational when the actor chose it. He also observed that actors learn through experience recipes and rules that guide their behavior.

For Weick (1995), sensemaking involves more than interpretation and wrestling with cognitive dissonances. Sensemaking encompasses: (a) changes in perceptions to render them mutually consistent (consonant); (b) changes in goals and expectations to render them consistent with perceptions; (c) changes in perceptions to render them consistent with actions that have already occurred; and (d) active efforts to manipulate environments to render them consistent with one's perceptions and desires. Even when performed by individuals, sensemaking is intrinsically social because it relies on words to define concepts and categories. Weick has studied sensemaking in various crises and hazardous situations, such as aircraft landings, forest fires, NASA space shuttles, and nuclear power plants. One persistent theme in his writings is the importance of maintaining the coherence of sensemaking; he has argued that situations go out of control when sensemaking breaks down. Another enduring theme is the sharing of perceptions and expectations that enables teams of workers to act coherently during crises. Weick has referred to the latter as "collective mind," and he has argued that people (individually or collectively) must develop effective "mindfulness"—meaning useful categories and appropriate attention to different kinds of stimuli. An influential article by Weick and Roberts (1993) described the activities of flight operations crews on the decks of aircraft carriers, demonstrating that such crews cooperate effectively in turbulent situations without overt communication because they have rehearsed their activities until each person understands what the others are doing without anyone having to speak.

Theorists disagree about whether computational perspectives, such as BDT, and interpretive perspectives, exemplified by the work of Weick and his colleagues, describe complementary processes that coexist in a dynamic interplay or constitute irreconcilable accounts. Several commentators have advocated unification (Lant and Shapira 2001a, b; Hodgkinson and Sparrow 2002; Lant 2002; Hodgkinson and Healey 2008). Finkelstein and Hambrick (1996), for example, offered a model of strategic decision making in which selective attention and limited search processes by the organization's dominant coalition precede interpretation and choice. However, interpretive perspectives imply that much BDT research has been off-target. Rather, as Miller and Wilson (2006) observed, interpretive perspectives call for frameworks and metaphors commensurate with sensemaking (Weick 1995), ones capable of supporting decision makers who confront ambiguity and indeterminacy.

Nascent Themes

Expert Decision Makers in Naturalistic Environments

Like Gigerenzer and his colleagues, researchers who study naturalistic decision making (NDM) reject the notion of equivalency between barren laboratories and the much richer, more complex settings in which organizational decision makers conduct their everyday affairs. These researchers have been seeking alternative concepts, theories, and methods that reflect specific decision contexts.

NDM originated in studies of domain experts making complex, high stakes, and ill-structured decisions under time pressure, often in dangerous situations (Lipshitz et al. 2001). Klein's (1993) recognition primed decision making model epitomizes the NDM approach. It emphasizes the crucial role of pattern recognition in obviating the need for extensive deliberation about multiple alternatives. NDM applications in organizational contexts have been gathering momentum (Lipshitz et al. 2006), and this work demonstrates that expert decision makers in naturalistic settings are surprisingly adept at making rapid fire and largely error free decisions.

Intuitive Decision Makers

A further challenge to rational theories comes from research on the nature and role of intuition in organizational decision making. Intuition had received scant scholarly attention until recently, but advances in cognitive neuroscience (Lieberman 2007) and managerial and organizational cognition (Sinclair and Ashkanasy 2005; Dane and Pratt 2007) have rejuvenated the construct. Intuition now lies at the heart of a number of dual-process theories of cognition (Chaiken and Trope 1999; Gilovich et al. 2002; Evans 2007, 2008) and has potential relevance across a range of domains of application, from education to management to health (Hodgkinson et al. 2008). Dual-process theories assert that two modes of processing are necessary for many tasks: both automatic processing that is beyond conscious control and conscious, analytic processing. The former, automatic mode enables people to cut through vast quantities of information rapidly, while the latter, conscious mode entails detailed analysis. Substantial neuropsychological and psychometric evidence supports dual-process conceptions, but researchers are currently debating the adequacy of these formulations (Hayes and Allinson 1994; Hayes et al. 2003; Hodgkinson and Sadler-Smith 2003a, b; Sinclair and Ashkanasy 2005; Dane and Pratt 2007; Sadler-Smith and Shefy 2007).

Emotional Decision Makers

Yet another challenge to rational theories comes from research on emotion and affect in organizations. Reflecting Mumby and Putnam's (1992) notion that people in organizations are constrained by "bounded emotionality," Ashkanasy and Ashton-James (2005: 221) have speculated, "Perhaps the reason scholars have been so reluctant to address the role of emotions in organizations is because of the inherent complexity and ambiguity surrounding emotion." Again, advances in cognitive neuroscience (Phelps 2006) have been building useful bases for investigations that could elevate the relevance of emotion (cf., Fisher and Ashkanasy 2000; Brief and Weiss 2002). For example, such research may help to explain how emotional traits and states influence the extent to which decision makers rely on conscious or automatic processing (Daniels et al. 2004). Such research could also clarify how anticipated (fear, dread) and felt (anxiety, stress) emotions constrain behavior relating to difficult decisions. However, the time has come for conceptual advances that go beyond linear, single-step analyses of affective influences on cognition or, conversely, of the cognitive determinants of affect (cf., Brief and Weiss 2002).

Researchers need to consider recursive processes by which affectively informed appraisals produce discrete emotions, in turn shaping subsequent cognitions, both within discrete episodes and over time (Hodgkinson and Healey 2008).

With few exceptions, these nascent themes have been focusing on microscopic behaviors. They have said virtually nothing about macroscopic behaviors. However, developments in strategic management could be signaling a new orientation. Drawing on anthropology, economics, management, psychology, and sociology, researchers are attempting to enrich understanding of the dynamic interplay between the micro processes and practices of strategic actors and the macro sociological and economic contexts of those actors and their practices (Wilson and Jarzabkowski 2004; Hodgkinson and Wright 2006; Hodgkinson et al. 2006; Whittington 2006; Jarzabkowski et al. 2007). Suitably developed, this new line of inquiry has the potential to advance the study of organizational decision making beyond an impasse that has limited scholarly and practical progress over much of the past 50 years.

OVERVIEW OF THE *HANDBOOK*

The *Handbook* comprises five sections that focus variously on the context and content of decision making, decision making during crises and hazardous situations, decision making processes, the consequences of decisions, and efforts to make decisions more effectively. Although the table of contents divides the chapters into sections with such titles, the sections are not distinct. The chapters under context and content also discuss decision processes, consequences, and ways to make decisions more effectively. Similarly, the chapters under decision processes also discuss context, content, and consequences and they offer suggestions for improving decision making, while the chapters under consequences of decision making also discuss context, content, and decision processes.

Within sections, chapters with more similar topics are closer together. However, there are many ways to describe each chapter and consequently many ways to classify and sequence them. For example, some chapters talk mainly about decision making by individual people, others about group decisions, and others about the behaviors of organizations or other large collectivities. A number of the chapters discuss rationality—its meaning, existence, nature, implications, and usefulness. These chapters surface repeatedly the underlying tensions discussed above concerning the relative merits of the computational and interpretive approaches to the analysis of decision making. The four chapters about consequences of decision making all talk about non-obvious or deceptive consequences.

Part I: The Context and Content of Decision Making

Boom and Bust Behavior: On the Persistence of Strategic Decision Biases, by Michael Shayne Gary, Giovanni Dosi, and Dan Lovallo (Chapter 2), points to several cognitive and behavioral factors that drive boom and bust dynamics that are widespread and persistent. Firms react to economic booms by trying to expand their capacities, but these expansions rely on too-simple mental models and imperfect forecasts, and firms implement their decisions slowly so they tend to overexpand or overcontract. Furthermore, firms do not learn to avoid the errors they made in previous cycles. In concluding, the authors argue that firms could improve their decision making by using schemata of logistic demand growth when they manage product lifecycles and by paying attention to historical time data about capacity building.

In Information Overload Revisited (Chapter 3), Kathleen Sutcliffe and Karl Weick question some of the effects observers have attributed to "information overload." It has been widely accepted that distractions, large amounts of noisy information, excessive task demands, and time pressure lead people to overlook relevant information. The authors propose that overload depends on people's abilities to interpret information and situations, and hence on their prior learning. As well, overload is a transitory condition that fluctuates over time. One effect of overload is that it changes how people infer what they need to interpret, which tells them what they need to decide. That is, interpretation dominates deciding.

Decision Making with Inaccurate, Unreliable Data, by John Mezias and William Starbuck (Chapter 4), looks at consequences of inaccurate, unreliable data. Such data may arise from social construction, from subjective extrapolations of sparse objective data, from noisy collection and transmission processes, or from forecasting errors. The authors propose that when decision makers recognize that they have unreliable data, they seek more data, collapse probability distributions into certainties, revert to ideology, act incrementally, and play to their audiences. Noisy, unreliable data present the challenges of how to design organizations that act effectively despite such data and how better to educate and inform decision makers.

Terri Griffith, Gregory Northcraft, and Mark Fuller ask, "Borgs in the Org?" Organizational Decision Making and Technology (Chapter 5). The authors point out that decision-aiding technologies can facilitate searches for information, uses of information, and interactions among group members. Decision-aiding technologies can also undermine decision making, and empirical studies have shown that technologies have mixed effects. In particular, such technologies reflect the human limitations of their designers. Searches for information and uses of it depend on how designers characterize and classify information, so technologies can at best make rationality less bounded. Technologies to support group processes have revealed some unexpected effects. Thus, decision-aiding technologies are works in progress.

In Making the Decision to Monitor in the Workplace: Cybernetic Models and the Illusion of Control (Chapter 6), David Zweig, Jane Webster, and Kristyn Scott evaluate the trend toward electronic surveillance and monitoring in the workplace. The authors argue that cybernetic models of control that underpin the decisions of many organizations to adopt surveillance practices yield illusory consequences that can generate a repetitive spiral of increased control at the expense of employees' trust and respect. The authors advise leaders to entrust employees with responsibility for decision making and to intervene only when essential. Building on cognitively oriented leadership theory, the authors assert that such behavior by leaders should yield better consequences than the use of electronic monitoring.

Jacques Rojot's chapter, Culture and Decision Making (Chapter 7), describes ways that cultural assumptions influence decision makers. For instance, differences in the traditions of France and Germany appear to influence wages, hierarchical control, and the content of work assignments. However, because prevalent ideas about cultures are vague and inconsistent, they make unreliable foundations for discussions of decision making. Rojot argues that people can understand cultures' effects more usefully as limitations on rationality. For example, national traditions, occupational customs, and organizational systems limit the options that decision makers perceive. This approach to cultural effects has the advantage of drawing upon theories that have grounding in research.

Part II: Decision Making During Crises and Hazardous Situations

Facing the Threat of Disaster: Decision Making When the Stakes are High, by Michal Tamuz and Eleanor Lewis (Chapter 8), considers effects of extreme potential consequences such as accidents or disasters. High stakes decisions occur in diverse settings such as natural disasters, industrial accidents, military planning, and medical treatment. This chapter examines decision making under the threat of disaster, in the midst of disaster, and during post-disaster investigations. It also points out that organizations have developed decision-making practices to avert or mitigate disasters. Organizations collect and analyze data about small failures and near misses, mobilize support from other organizations in their environment, and draw on local expertise to generate and test hypotheses about how to recognize and remove hazards.

In The Fit Between Crisis Types and Management Attributes as a Determinant of Crisis Consequences (Chapter 9), Teri Jane Ursacki-Bryant, Carolyne Smart, and Ilan Vertinsky discuss the consequences of "fit" between decision processes and different types of crises. They propose that various properties of a crisis require good performance on corresponding dimensions, and they identify organizational properties that support good performance on each of these dimensions. Weakness of the appropriate organizational properties causes organizations to respond pathologically.

Karlene Roberts, Kuo Frank Yu, Vinit Desai, and Peter Madsen's chapter, Employing Adaptive Structuring as a Cognitive Decision Aid in High Reliability Organizations (Chapter 10), reviews research about high reliability organizations. These organizations seek to meet stringent requirements for safety and performance in hazardous environments that spawn crises. The authors present three contrasting case studies that illustrate structural and cognitive mechanisms that support rapid and effective decision making in crises. The authors infer that those organizations that achieve high reliability use structural properties to augment the capabilities of individual decision makers.

In Expertise and Naturalistic Decision Making in Organizations: Mechanisms of Effective Decision Making (Chapter 11), Michael Rosen, Eduardo Salas, Rebecca Lyons, and Stephen Fiore review the growing body of research about how expert decision makers handle "naturalistic" decision situations. This work has investigated decision makers in real world settings that entail complexity, high stakes, and time pressure, such as military battle fields and emergency control rooms. The authors identify mechanisms that enable expert decision makers to make rapid and largely error-free decisions in such situations.

Part III: Decision-Making Processes

In Cognitively Skilled Organizational Decision Making: Making Sense of Deciding (Chapter 12), Julia Balogun, Annie Pye, and Gerard Hodgkinson offer a sociological perspective on decision-making skills. They suggest that decision makers with different agendas and personal interests use their differing power resources to influence and shape meaning, leading to particular definitions of the situations at particular moments in time. This chapter highlights the importance of understanding conversational and social practices through which people negotiate and renegotiate their worlds. It points out that people not only make sense of their situations but also influence the sensemaking or those around them. Thus, one power of skillful decision makers arises from molding perceptions and interpretations.

In Linking Rationality, Politics, and Routines in Organizational Decision Making (Chapter 13), Isabelle Royer and Ann Langley explore the roles of decision routines in altering the relative influence of socio-political and procedurally rational elements of organizational decision making. They suggest that generalization from a single period or a global characterization of decision making as entirely rational or political is likely erroneous. The complex influence of routines on decision making implies a need for longitudinal and multilevel research. Moreover, people naturally favor decision-making patterns in which procedural rationality and socio-political processes are more symbiotic than contingent.

Jerker Denrell's chapter, Superstitious Behavior as a Byproduct of Intelligent Adaptation (Chapter 14), offers a perspective as to why organizations often fail to learn from their past decisions. Denrell argues that the requirement of obtaining excellent results prevents managers from experimenting with actions that they expect to produce inferior results. Limited experimentation leads to superstitious routines; in other words, to behavior performed repeatedly despite the absence of clear evidence about causal connections between actions and consequences. Denrell's analysis suggests why managers should limit experimentation and why superstitious routines constitute intelligent responses. He says organizational learning only eliminates practices having direct and severely negative consequences. When practices do not have such negative consequences, organizations avoid experimenting with alternatives, with the result that some behavior is superstitious.

Zur Shapira's chapter, On the Implications of Behavioral Decision Theory for Managerial Decision Making: Contributions and Challenges (Chapter 15), reviews the origins and major developments in BDT and considers its implications for managerial decisions in organizations. According to Shapira, research on BDT and organizational decision making have few similarities and many differences, notwithstanding the fact that the two traditions share common roots and have pursued similar research agendas for over 50 years. One reason, as observed above, is that BDT has relied on lab experiments with simple decision problems involving statistical reasoning, and researchers who study organizational decision making have doubts about the realism and relevance of such experiments; studies of organizational decision making, in contrast, have emphasized longitudinal analyses of sensemaking and social construction.

Eugene Sadler-Smith and Paul Sparrow examine implications of Intuition in Organizational Decision Making (Chapter 16). Recent theorizing portrays intuition as an expression of tacit knowledge in which cognitive and affective processes interact below the level of conscious awareness. BDT researchers have portrayed intuitive judgments based upon heuristics as being both useful and error prone. Drawing on the insights of this body of work, this chapter argues intuition and rational analysis are different facets of information processing that may operate in parallel and interact contingently, depending on the person's expertise, the task, and the social setting.

Kevin Daniels' chapter, Affect and Information Processing (Chapter 17), considers the influence of cognitions on emotions and moods, and vice versa. Daniels describes affect as having independent negative and positive dimensions; negative affect varies from relaxation to anger, whereas positive affect varies from boredom to enthusiasm. Affect reflects social contagion and situational influences, and individual people exhibit affective traits. Research studies lead Daniels to infer that affect is both a major determinant and consequence of cognition and individual level decision making, and a factor in effectiveness and well-being.

In Individual Differences and Decision Making (Chapter 18), Emma Soane and Nigel Nicholson survey the range of individual differences that affect decision making. In line with the aforementioned dual-process conceptions of decision making, the authors argue that many decisions reflect automatic processing whereas others involve conscious, effortful information processing, and that individual difference variables influence the thresholds between these two modes as well as behaviors within each mode. In particular, people exhibit systematic and consistent preferences and traits. The authors develop a person–situation framework that portrays decisions as both causes and effects of individual differences.

Group Composition and Decision Making, by Elizabeth George and Prithviraj Chattopadhyay (Chapter 19), discusses the effects of group diversity on decision making. Diversity has been increasing due to globalization, the creation of cross-functional teams, and the employment and promotion of more women, people of differing ethnicities, older workers, and workers with more education. This chapter considers the influence of diversity on access to information, information-processing biases, and commitment to group decisions. The authors surmise that diversity can be beneficial but its benefits are uncertain and subject to complex influences.

Part IV: Consequences Produced by Decisions

Making Sense of Real Options Reasoning: An Engine of Choice that Backfires? by Michael Barnett and Roger Dunbar (Chapter 20), discusses a proposed strategy for managing risk and uncertainty by generating future opportunities. Real-options reasoning allocates a proportion of the organization's current resources to support the exploration of potential future actions, thus gaining information while postponing major commitments. However, this strategy can inadvertently create future obligations that foreclose future choices, and attempts to avert escalation of commitment can render real-option positions incapable of generating a wedge capable of holding open future decision-making opportunities in the face of rivalry. Barnett and Dunbar's analysis offers a number of insights into the question of when and how decisions makers might find real-options reasoning more or less appropriate.

In The Social Construction of Rationality in Organizational Decision Making (Chapter 21), Laure Cabantous, Jean-Pascal Gond, and Michael Johnson-Cramer focus on the divergent perspectives of economists and organization theorists. As observed earlier, whereas economists have prescribed a normative model for rational decision making, organization theorists have rejected the hypotheses of this normative model, disputed the model's explanatory power, and rejected the idea that humans can behave as prescribed. The authors argue that managers attempt to follow the dictates of the normative model by using its concepts and compatible analytic tools and that the tools compensate for decision makers' biases and limitations. The results include "rituals" of rationality and markets for rationality—as exemplified by demand for courses, tools, and advice from consultants.

In a chapter entitled When "Decision Outcomes" are not the Outcomes of Decisions (Chapter 22), Bénédicte Vidaillet points out that "so-called decision outcomes" are often not the consequences of decisions because consequences also depend upon actions. Vidaillet remarks that both rational and political concepts of decision making incorporate similar assumptions—that different decision making processes lead to different decisions, that different decisions lead to different actions, and that different actions lead to different consequences. Prescriptions usually focus on decision processes as if consequences follow automatically from decisions, and analyses usually attribute consequences to decisions. According to Vidaillet, actions influence consequences at least as decisions, and are driven by their own dynamics. Moreover, consequences result from interactions of multiple issues that mobilize the organization's attention rather than from specific and identifiable decisions.

What Lies Behind Organizational Façades and How Organizational Façades Lie: An Untold Story of Organizational Decision Making (Chapter 23) proposes that decision processes are not what they seem to be. Eric Abrahamson and Philippe Baumard argue that three types of façades pervade organizational decisions—rational, progressive, and reputation. Rational facades give the impression that decisions are creating technically efficient means toward important financial ends. Progressive façades convey the impression that decisions mirror the norms of progress, in line with management fashions and fads. Reputation facades enhance organizations' legitimacy by painting positive images of activities and accomplishments. The chapter shows that façades play positive roles in decision making that go beyond the obfuscation of organizational deficiencies.

Part V: Toward More Effective Decision Making

In designing this *Handbook,* as noted above, we, the editors, sought not only a comprehensive survey of scholarly developments but also state of the art guidance for practical applications. Trying to identify useful implications encourages authors and researchers to define operational variables and to consider contingencies. Evidently, the authors of the *Handbook* chapters accepted these premises, for nearly all the chapters offer prescriptions or point to some practical implications. However, the seven chapters in Part V evaluate explicitly practices that purport to enhance decision making.

Gerald Smith discusses his insights and experiences while Teaching Decision Making (Chapter 24). He argues that logical calculation is appropriate for some situations and intuitive "gut feel" appropriate for other situations, and mistakes occur when decision makers adopt the wrong mode. Smith develops a broader account of decision-making rationality, one that seeks to do justice to the human capacity for reflective thought. Rejecting dual-process conceptions as bases for developing decision-making skills and capabilities, he construes reflective thought as forming a middle ground between intuition and logical calculation, and he says it is potentially decision makers' most valuable resource. One implication of this analysis is that curricula should put less emphasis on the rational model and should incorporate concepts, heuristics, and methods pertaining to functional parts of decision processes such as problem definition or diagnosis.

In Facilitating Serious Play (Chapter 25), Matt Statler and David Oliver give an account of their work at the Imagination Lab (I-Lab), a charitable foundation that conducts research on "play," "imagination," and "emergence" in organizing and strategizing. In conjunction with academic and business collaborators, research staff in I-Lab have developed an approach to facilitation in the context of strategy making, organizational development, team dynamics, and leadership initiatives. The authors reflect critically on the practices that have emerged through these collaborations and extract lessons about the effectiveness of different practices.

Alfred Kieser and Benjamin Wellstein ask, Do Activities of Consultants and Management Scientists Affect Decision Making by Managers? (Chapter 26). The authors analyze the proposition that the activities of consultants and management scientists can enhance the processes or consequences of decision making through collaborative working, and their analysis leaves them highly skeptical. They challenge the notion that organizations can bridge the widely documented communication gap between academics and managers through joint activities or by hiring consultants. According to their analysis, managers, academics, and consultants inhabit separate self-referential systems, each characterized by its own goals, values, norms, and interests. They say the idea of applied science contains fundamental flaws because neither consultants' knowledge nor academic knowledge integrates well with managerial knowledge and managerial problems.

John Maule provides a state of the art overview of research on Risk Communication in Organizations (Chapter 27). The central message emanating from Maule's review is that the effective communication of risk requires far more than merely passing on formal risk assessments. Risk managers have given inadequate attention to recipients' acceptance of assumptions underlying risk assessments, to their interpretations of such assessments, and to whether recipients act in accordance with these assessments. Skillful risk communicators need to take account of a broad range of individual and social processes that attenuate or amplify perceptions of risk; they also need to consider whether their communications ought to inform or persuade.

In Structuring the Decision Process: An Evaluation of Methods (Chapter 28), George Wright and Paul Goodwin describe and assess various formal methods that purport to enhance decision making. They identify a number of "best practices" at both individual and group levels and conclude that formal methods can be helpful but users need to match them to specific decision situations.

In Strategy Workshops and "Away-Days" as Ritual (Chapter 29), Nicole Bourque and Gerry Johnson consider the effectiveness of strategy workshops, the practice of taking time out from day to day routines to plan the longer-term direction of organizations. Drawing on anthropological theories about ritual, the authors argue that many of these events have designs that assure failure. The very act of removal from everyday work contexts generates outputs (chiefly, ideas and feelings) that are less likely to transfer readily from the ritualized contexts in which many of these workshops and away-days occur to normal workplaces. The authors offer suggestions for how designers of these events could engineer them to improve the chances of attaining the required transfer.

Finally, in Troubling Futures: Scenarios and Scenario Planning for Organizational Decision Making (Chapter 30), Mark Healey and Gerard Hodgkinson review research about the effects of scenario thinking on judgment and choice, pointing to both benefits and potential liabilities. One widespread claim in popular management literature is that analyzing multiple scenarios leads people to perceive wider ranges of possible futures, but this chapter shows that unskillful use of scenarios can anchor and confine thinking because people who construct scenarios build assumptions into them. Scenarios may also decrease or increase decision makers' confidence, thus creating excessive optimism, excessive pessimism, or rigid adherence to chosen courses of action. The authors propose that scenario users can mitigate these undesirable effects by providing decision makers with continuous feedback on the accuracy of predictions and by encouraging reflective thought about ideas that arise from discussing scenarios.

In sum, the study of organizational decision making is a vibrant, multidisciplinary endeavor. Intentionally varied in style and purpose, and drawing upon fields as diverse as anthropology, business and management studies, economics, psychology, and sociology, the above chapters reveal the richness and variety of theoretical and methodological approaches that characterize this eclectic domain. With contributions from leading researchers from around the globe, *The Oxford Handbook of Organizational Decision Making* provides a comprehensive overview of developments at the forefront of the field.

References

ALCHIAN, A. A. (1950). 'Uncertainty, Evolution, and Economic Theory.' *Journal of Political Economy*, 58: 211–21.

ANDERSON, N., HERRIOT, P., and HODGKINSON, G. P. (2001). 'The Practitioner–Researcher Divide in Industrial, Work and Organizational (IWO) Psychology: Where are We Now and Where do We Go From Here?' *Journal of Occupational and Organizational Psychology*, 74: 391–411.

ASHKANASY, N. M. and ASHTON-JAMES, C. E. (2005). 'Emotion in Organizations: A Neglected Topic in I/O Psychology, But With a Bright Future', in G. P. Hodgkinson and J. K. Ford (eds.), *International Review of Industrial and Organizational Psychology— Volume 20*. Chichester, UK: Wiley, 221–68.

ASTEBRO, T. and ELHEDHLI, S. (2006). 'The Effectiveness of Simple Decision Heuristics: Forecasting Commercial Success for Early-Stage Ventures'. *Management Science*, 52: 395–409.

BARTLETT, F. C. (1932). *Remembering: A Study in Experimental and Social Psychology*. Cambridge: Cambridge University Press.

BATEMAN, T. S. and ZEITHAML, C. P. (1989a). 'The Psychological Context of Strategic Decisions: A Model and Convergent Experimental Findings.' *Strategic Management Journal*, 10: 59–74.

—— —— (1989b). 'The Psychological Context of Strategic Decisions: A Test of Relevance to Practitioners.' *Strategic Management Journal*, 10: 587–92.

BAZERMAN, M. H. (1984). 'The Relevance of Kahneman and Tversky's Concept of Framing to Organizational Behavior.' *Journal of Management*, 10: 333–43.

BELL, T. E. and ESCH, K. (1987). 'The Fatal Flaw in Flight 51-L.' *IEEE Spectrum*, 24/2: 36–51.

BRIEF, A. P. and WEISS, H. M. (2002). 'Organizational Behavior: Affect in the Workplace.' *Annual Review of Psychology*, 53: 279–307.

BRUNSSON, N. (1982). 'The Irrationality of Action and Action Rationality: Decisions, Ideologies and Organizational Actions.' *Journal of Management Studies*, 19: 29–44.

—— (1985). *The Irrational Organization: Irrationality as a Basis for Organizational Action and Change*. Chichester, UK: Wiley.

—— (1989). *The Organization of Hypocrisy: Talk, Decisions, and Action in Organizations*. Chichester, UK: Wiley.

—— (2007). *The Consequences of Decision-Making*. Oxford: Oxford University Press.

BRYANT, D. J. (2007). 'Classifying Simulated Air Threats with Fast and Frugal Heuristics.' *Journal of Behavioral Decision Making*, 20: 37–64.

CHAIKEN, S. and TROPE, Y. (eds.) (1999). *Dual-Process Theories in Social Psychology*. New York: Guilford Press.

COHEN, M. D., MARCH, J. G. and Olson, J. P. (1972). 'The Garbage Can Model of Organizational Choice.' *Administrative Science Quarterly*, 17: 1–25.

CYERT, R. M. and MARCH, J. G. (1963). *A Behavioral Theory of the Firm*. Englewood Cliffs, NJ: Prentice-Hall.

DAFT, R. L. and WEICK, K. E. (1984). 'Toward a Model of Organizations as Interpretation Systems.' *Academy of Management Review*, 9: 284–95.

DANE, E. and PRATT, M. G. (2007). 'Exploring Intuition and its Role in Managerial Decision Making.' *Academy of Management Review*, 32: 33–54.

DANIELS, K., JOHNSON, G., and de CHERNATONY, L. (1994). 'Differences in Managerial Cognitions of Competition.' *British Journal of Management*, 5/Special Issue: S21–S29.

—— HARRIS, C. and BRINER, R. B. (2004). 'Linking Work Conditions to Unpleasant Affect: Cognition, Categorization and Goals.' *Journal of Occupational and Organizational Psychology*, 77: 343–63.

DAS, T. K. and TENG, B.-S. (1999). 'Cognitive Biases and Strategic Decision Processes.' *Journal of Management Studies*, 36: 757–78.

DUNBAR, R. L. M. and STARBUCK, W. H. (2006). 'Learning to Design Organizations and Learning from Designing Them.' *Organization Science*, 17/2: 171–78.

EDEN, C. and ACKERMANN, F. (1998). *Making Strategy: The Journey of Strategic Management.* London: Sage.

EDWARDS, W. (1954). 'The Theory of Decision Making.' *Psychological Bulletin*, 51: 380–417.

—— (1961). 'Behavioral Decision Theory.' *Annual Review of Psychology*, 12: 473–98.

ESSER J. K. and LINDOERFER J. S. (1989). 'Groupthink and the Space Shuttle Challenger Accident: Towards a Quantitative Case Analysis.' *Journal of Behavioral Decision Making*, 2: 167–77.

EVANS, J. St. B.T. (2007). *Hypothetical Thinking: Dual Processes in Reasoning and Judgement.* Hove, UK: Psychology Press.

—— (2008). 'Dual-Processing Accounts of Reasoning, Judgment, and Social Cognition.' *Annual Review of Psychology*, 59: 255–278.

FINKELSTEIN, S. and HAMBRICK, D. C. (1996). *Strategic Leadership: Top Executives and their Effects on Organizations.* St. Paul, MN: West.

FISCHHOFF, B. (1980). 'For Those Condemned to Study the Past: Reflections on Historical Judgment', in R. A. Shweder and D. W. Fiste (eds.), *New Directions for Methodology of Behavioral Science.* San Francisco, CA: Jossey-Bass, 79–93.

FISHER, C. D. and ASHKANASY, N. M. (2000). 'The Emerging Role of Emotions in Work Life: An Introduction.' *Journal of Organizational Behavior*, 21: 123–9.

FRIEDMAN, M. (1953). *Essays in Positive Economics.* Chicago, IL: University of Chicago Press.

GIGERENZER, G. (1991). 'How to Make Cognitive Illusions Disappear: Beyond Heuristics and Biases,' in W. Stroebe and M. Hewstone (eds.), *European Review of Social Psychology—Volume* 2. Chichester: Wiley, 83–115.

—— GOLDSTEIN, D. G. (1996). 'Reasoning the Fast and Frugal Way: Models of Bounded Rationality.' *Psychological Review*, 103: 650–69.

—— TODD, P. M. (1999). 'Fast and Frugal Heuristics: The Adaptive Toolbox,' in G. GIGERENZER, P. M. TODD, and the ABC Research Group (eds.), *Simple Heuristics That Make Us Smart.* New York: Oxford University Press, 3–34.

GILOVICH, T., GRIFFITH, D., and KAHNEMAN, D. (eds.) (2002). *Heuristics and Biases: The Psychology of Intuitive Judgment.* Cambridge, UK: Cambridge University Press.

GREY, C. (2001). 'Re-imagining Relevance: A Response to Starkey and Madan.' *British Journal of Management*, 12/Special Issue: S27–S32.

HALL, R. L. and C. J. HITCH (1939). 'Price Theory and Business Behavior.' *Oxford Economic Papers*, 2: 12–45.

HARROD, R. F. (1939). 'Price and Cost in Entrepreneurs' Policy.' *Oxford Economic Papers*, 2: 1–11.

HAYES, J. and ALLINSON, C. W. (1994). 'Cognitive Style and its Relevance for Managerial Practice.' *British Journal of Management*, 5: 53–71.

HAYES, J. and ALLINSON, C. W., HUDSON, R. S., and KEASEY, K. (2003). 'Further Reflections on the Nature of Intuition-Analysis and the Construct Validity of the Cognitive Style Index.' *Journal of Occupational and Organizational Psychology, 76:* 269–78.

HIGHHOUSE, S. (2001). 'Judgment and Decision-Making Research: Relevance to Industrial and Organizational Psychology,' in N. Anderson, D. S. Ones, H. K. Sinangil, and C. Viswesvaran (eds.), *Handbook of Industrial, Work and Organizational Psychology: Volume 2—Organizational Psychology.* London: Sage, 314–31.

HODGKINSON, G. P. and HEALEY, M. P. (2008). 'Cognition in Organizations'. *Annual Review of Psychology, 59:* 387–417.

—— JOHNSON, G. (1994). 'Exploring the Mental Models of Competitive Strategists: The Case for a Processual Approach.' *Journal of Management Studies, 31:* 525–51.

—— SADLER-SMITH, E. (2003a). 'Complex or Unitary? A Critique and Empirical Reassessment of the Allinson-Hayes Cognitive Style Index.' *Journal of Occupational and Organizational Psychology, 76:* 243–68.

—— —— (2003b). 'Reflections on Reflections . . . On the Nature of Intuition, Analysis and the Construct Validity of the Cognitive Style Index.' *Journal of Occupational and Organizational Psychology, 76:* 279–81.

—— SPARROW, P. R. (2002). *The Competent Organization: A Psychological Analysis of the Strategic Management Process.* Buckingham, UK: Open University Press.

—— WRIGHT, G. (2006). 'Neither Completing the Practice Turn, nor Enriching the Process Tradition: Secondary Misinterpretations of a Case Analysis Reconsidered.' *Organization Studies, 27:* 1895–901.

HODGKINSON, G. P., BOWN, N. J., MAULE, A. J., GLAISTER, K. W., and PEARMAN, A. D. (1999). 'Breaking the Frame: An Analysis of Strategic Cognition and Decision Making Under Uncertainty.' *Strategic Management Journal, 20:* 977–85.

—— LANGAN-FOX, J., and SADLER-SMITH, E. (2008). 'Intuition: A Fundamental Bridging Construct in the Behavioural Sciences.' *British Journal of Psychology, 99:* 1–27.

—— WHITTINGTON, R., JOHNSON, G., and SCHWARZ, M. (2006). 'The Role of Strategy Workshops in Strategy Development Processes: Formality, Communication, Coordination and Inclusion.' *Long Range Planning, 39:* 479–96.

HOGARTH, R. M. and KARELAIA, N. (2005). 'Simple Models for Multiattribute Choice with Many Alternatives: When it Does and Does Not Pay to Face Trade-offs with Binary Attributes.' *Management Science, 51:* 1860–72.

HUFF, A. S. (ed.) (1990). *Mapping Strategic Thought.* Chichester, UK: Wiley.

JARZABKOWSKI, P., BALOGUN, J., and SEIDL, D. (2007). 'Strategizing: The Challenges of a Practice Perspective.' *Human Relations, 60:* 5–27.

JOHNSON-LAIRD, P. N. (1983). *Mental Models.* Cambridge, UK: Cambridge University Press.

KAHNEMAN, D. and TVERSKY, A. (1996). 'On the Reality of Cognitive Illusions.' *Psychological Review, 103:* 582–91.

—— SLOVIC, P., and TVERSKY, A. (eds.) (1982). *Judgment under Uncertainty: Heuristics and Biases.* Cambridge: Cambridge University Press.

KLEIN, G. A. (1993). 'A Recognition-Primed Decision (RPD) Model of Rapid Decision Making,' in G. Klein, J. Orasanu, R. Calderwood, and C. Zsambok (eds.), *Decision Making in Action: Models and Methods.* Norwood, CT: Ablex, 138–47.

LANT, T. K. (2002). 'Organizational Cognition and Interpretation', in J. A. C. Baum (ed.), *The Blackwell Companion to Organizations.* Oxford: Blackwell, 344–62.

—— SHAPIRA, Z. (2001a). 'Introduction: Foundations of Research on Cognition in Organizations', in T. K. Lant and Z. Shapira (eds.), *Organizational Cognition: Computation and Interpretation.* Mahwah, NJ: Erlbaum, 1–12.

—— —— (2001b). 'New Research Directions on Organizational Cognition,' in T. K. Lant and Z. Shapira (eds.), *Organizational Cognition: Computation and Interpretation.* Mahwah, NJ: Erlbaum, 367–76.

LESTER, R. A. (1946). 'Shortcomings of Marginal Analysis for Wage-Employment Problems.' *American Economic Review,* 36: 62–82.

LIEBERMAN, M. D. (2007). 'Social Cognitive Neuroscience: A Review of Core Processes.' *Annual Review of Psychology,* 58: 259–89.

LIPSHITZ, R., KLEIN, G., ORASANU, J., and SALAS, E. (2001). 'Focus Article: Taking Stock of Naturalistic Decision Making.' *Journal of Behavioral Decision Making,* 14: 331–52.

—— —— Carroll, J. S. (eds.) (2006). 'Special Issue on "Naturalistic Decision Making and Organizational Decision Making: Exploring the Intersections".' *Organization Studies,* 27/Special Issue: 917–1057.

MACHLUP, F. (1946). 'Marginal Analysis and Empirical Research.' *American Economic Review,* 36: 519–54.

MARCH, J. G. (1971). 'The Technology of Foolishness.' *Civiløkonomen* (Copenhagen), 18/4: 4–12.

—— (1991). 'Exploration and Exploitation in Organizational Learning.' *Organization Science,* 2: 71–87.

—— (1997). 'Understanding How Decisions Happen in Organizations,' in Z. Shapira (ed.), *Organizational Decision Making.* Cambridge, UK: Cambridge University Press, 9–32.

—— SIMON, H. A. (1958). *Organizations.* New York: Wiley.

MCKELVEY, B. (2006). 'Van de Ven and Johnson's "Engaged Scholarship": Nice Try, But...' *Academy of Management Review,* 31: 822–29.

MILLER, S. J. and WILSON, D. C. (2006). 'Perspectives on Organizational Decision Making,' in S. R. Clegg, C. Hardy, T. B. Lawrence, and W. R. Nord (eds.), *The Sage Handbook of Organization Studies* (2nd edn.) London: Sage, 469–84.

MINTZBERG, H., RAISINGHANI, D., and THÉORÊT, A. (1976). 'The Structure of "Unstructured" Decision Processes.' *Administrative Science Quarterly,* 21: 246–75.

MUMBY, D. K. and PUTNAM, L. L. (1992). 'The Politics of Emotion: A Feminist Reading of Bounded Rationality.' *Academy of Management Review,* 17: 465–86.

NEALE, M. A., TENBRUNSEL, A. E., GALVIN, T., and BAZERMAN, M. H. (2006). 'A Decision Perspective on Organizations: Social Cognition, Behavioural Decision Theory and the Psychological Links to Micro- and Macro-Organizational Behaviour,' in S. R. Clegg, C. Hardy, T. B. Lawrence, and W. R. Nord (eds.), *The Sage Handbook of Organization Studies* (2nd edn.) London: Sage, 485–519.

NEWELL, A., SHAW, J. C., and SIMON, H. A. (1958). 'Chess-Playing Programs and the Problem of Complexity.' *IBM Journal of Research and Development,* 2/4: 320–35.

NEWELL, A. and SIMON, H. A. (1956). 'The Logic Theory Machine, A Complex Information Processing System.' *IEEE Transactions on Information Theory,* IT-2/3: S-61–79.

NEWELL B. R., WESTON, N. J., and SHANKS, D. R. (2003). 'Empirical Tests of a Fast-and-Frugal Heuristic: Not Everyone "Takes-the-Best".' *Organizational Behavior and Human Decision Processes,* 91: 82–96.

PAYNE, J. W., BETTMAN, J. R. and JOHNSON, E. J. (1993). *The Adaptive Decision Maker.* Cambridge: Cambridge University Press.

PETTIGREW, A. M. (1973). *The Politics of Organizational Decision Making*. London: Tavistock.

—— (1985). *The Awakening Giant: Continuity and Change in ICI*. Oxford: Blackwell.

—— (1997). 'The Double Hurdles for Management Research,' in T. Clarke (ed.), *Advancement in Organizational Behaviour: Essays in Honour of Derek S. Pugh*. London: Dartmouth Press, 277–96.

PFEFFER, J. (1981). *Power in Organizations*. Cambridge, MA: Ballinger.

—— SALANCIK, G. R. (1974). 'Organizational Decision Making as a Political Process: The Case of a University Budget'. *Administrative Science Quarterly*, 19: 135–51.

—— —— (1978). *The External Control of Organizations: A Resource Dependence Perspective*. New York: Harper and Row.

PHELPS, E. A. (2006). 'Emotion and Cognition: Insights from Studies of the Human Amygdala.' *Annual Review of Psychology*, 57: 27–53.

PORAC, J. F. and THOMAS, H. (1989). 'Managerial Thinking in Business Environments.' *Journal of Management Studies*, 26/4: 323–4.

—— —— BADEN-FULLER, C. (1989). 'Competitive Groups as Cognitive Communities: The Case of Scottish Knitwear Manufacturers.' *Journal of Management Studies*, 26: 397–416.

—— —— WILSON, F., PATON, D., and KANFER, A. (1995). 'Rivalry and the Industry Model of Scottish Knitwear Producers.' *Administrative Science Quarterly*, 40: 203–27.

PRESIDENTIAL COMMISSION (1986). *Report of the Presidential Commission on the Space Shuttle Challenger Accident*. Washington, DC: US Government Printing Office.

SADLER-SMITH, E. and SHEFY, E. (2007). 'Developing Intuitive Awareness in Management Education.' *Academy of Management Learning and Education*, 6: 186–205.

SALGADO, S. R., STARBUCK, W. H., and MEZIAS, J. M. (2002). 'The Accuracy of Managers' Perceptions: A Dimension Missing from Theories about Firms,' in M. Augier and J. G. March (eds.), *The Economics of Choice, Change, and Organizations: Essays in Memory of Richard M. Cyert*. Cheltenham: Edward Elgar, 168–85.

SCHANK R. C. and ABELSON, R. (1977). *Scripts, Plans, Goals, and Understanding: An Inquiry into Human Knowledge Structures*. Hillsdale, NJ: Lawrence Erlbaum Associates.

SCHUTZ, A. (1932). *Der sinnhafte Aufbau der sozialen Welt: Eine Einleitung in die verstehenden Soziologie*. Vienna: Springer. (English translation: *The Phenomenology of the Social World*, translated by G.Walsh and F. Lehnert, Evanston, IL: Northwestern University Press, 1967.)

SCHWENK, C. R. (1984). 'Cognitive Simplification Processes in Strategic Decision Making.' *Strategic Management Journal*, 5: 111–28.

—— (1988). 'The Cognitive Perspective on Strategic Decision Making.' *Journal of Management Studies*, 25: 41–55.

SIMON, H. A. (1947). *Administrative Behavior: A Study of Decision-Making Processes in Administrative Organizations*. New York: Macmillan.

—— (1957). *Administrative Behavior: A Study of Decision-Making Processes in Administrative Organizations* (2nd edn.). New York: Macmillan.

SINCLAIR, M. and ASHKANASY, N. M. (2005). 'Intuition: Myth or a Decision-Making Tool?' *Management Learning*, 36: 353–70.

STARBUCK, W. H. (2006). *The Production of Knowledge: The Challenge of Social Science Research*. Oxford: Oxford University Press.

—— FARJOUN, M. (eds.) (2005). *Organization at the Limit: Lessons from the Columbia Disaster.* Maldon, MA: Blackwell.

—— MILLIKEN F. J. (1988). 'Challenger: Changing the Odds Until Something Breaks.' *Journal of Management Studies,* 25: 319–40.

—— STEPHENSON, J. (2005). 'Making NASA More Effective', in W. H. Starbuck and M. Farjoun (eds.), *Organization at the Limit: Management Lessons from the Columbia Disaster.* Oxford: Blackwell Publishers.

STAW, B. M. (1981). 'The Escalation of Commitment to a Course of Action.' *Academy of Management Review,* 6: 577–87.

—— (1997). 'The Escalation of Commitment: An Update and Appraisal,' in Z. Shapira (ed.), *Organizational Decision Making.* Cambridge: Cambridge University Press, 191–215.

TOLMAN, E. C. (1932). *Purposive Behavior in Animals and Men.* New York: Century.

VAN DE VEN, A. H. (2007). *Engaged Scholarship: A Guide for Organizational and Social Research.* Oxford: Oxford University Press.

—— JOHNSON, P. (2006). 'Knowledge for Science and Practice.' *Academy of Management Review,* 31: 802–21.

VAN DER HEIJDEN, K., BRADFIELD, R., BURT, G., CAIRNS, G., and WRIGHT, G. (2002). *The Sixth Sense: Accelerating Organizational Learning with Scenarios.* New York: John Wiley.

VAUGHAN, D. (1996). *The Challenger Launch Decision: Risky Technology, Culture, and Deviance at NASA.* Chicago, IL: University of Chicago Press.

WALSH, J. P. (1995). 'Managerial and Organizational Cognition: Notes from a Trip Down Memory Lane.' *Organization Science,* 6: 280–321.

WEICK, K. E. (1969). *The Social Psychology of Organizing.* Reading, MA: Addison-Wesley.

—— (1979). *The Social Psychology of Organizing* (2nd edn.). Reading, MA: Addison-Wesley.

—— ROBERTS, K. H. (1993). 'Collective Mind in Organizations: Heedful Interrelating on Flight Decks.' *Administrative Science Quarterly,* 38: 357–81.

—— (1995). *Sensemaking in Organizations.* Thousand Oaks, CA: Sage.

WHITTINGTON, R. (2006). 'Completing the Practice Turn in Strategy Research.' *Organization Studies,* 27: 613–34.

WHORISKEY, P. (2003). 'Shuttle Failures Raise a Big Question: With a 1-in-57 Disaster Rate, is Space Exploration Worth the Risk?' *Washington Post,* February 10.

WILSON, D. C. (1982). 'Electricity and Resistance: A Case Study of Innovation and Politics.' *Organization Studies,* 3: 119–40.

—— JARZABKOWSKI, P. (2004). 'Thinking and Acting Strategically: New Challenges for Interrogating Strategy.' *European Management Review,* 1: 14–20.

WITTE, E. (1972). 'Field Research on Complex Decision Making Processes—The Phase Theorem.' *International Studies of Management and Organization,* 2: 156–82.

PART I

THE CONTEXT AND CONTENT OF DECISION MAKING

BOOM AND BUST BEHAVIOR: ON THE PERSISTENCE OF STRATEGIC DECISION BIASES

MICHAEL SHAYNE GARY

GIOVANNI DOSI

DAN LOVALLO

INTRODUCTION

BOOM and bust or overshoot and collapse dynamics are common among firms in a large range of different industries. Durable consumer electronics (e.g., televisions, VCR's, calculators, etc.), telecommunications, medical equipment, chemicals, real estate, pulp and paper, agricultural commodities, natural resources, toys and games, tennis equipment, bicycles, semiconductors, and running shoes, are examples of industries where boom and bust dynamics have occured (Paich and Sterman 1993; Sterman 2000; Sterman et al. 2007). Such dynamics occur in both traditional cyclical industries (Meadows 1970) and industries with pronounced product and/or category lifecycles (Klepper 1996).

The common managerial behavior underpinning boom and bust dynamics (B&B) across all of these industries is aggressive capacity expansion in the boom period when demand typically outstrips supply. Aggressive capacity expansion strategies in the boom phase ultimately result in excess capacity turning the boom into bust (Sterman 1989a, b, 2000; Bakken et al. 1992; Paich and Sterman 1993; Moxnes 1998). The fundamental problem is that in many cases capacity adjustments cannot be made quickly enough to match demand. Time delays associated with expanding or reducing capacity require firms to forecast demand and make strategic decisions to initiate capacity changes far in advance. This combination of boundedly rational decision making and capacity adjustment delays gives rise to boom and bust dynamics (Sterman et al. 2007). The combination is so difficult to manage that agents, including firms, rarely learn from boom and bust experiences. In some cases, the bust phase is so severe that the firms involved go bankrupt and disappear altogether. In other cases, the firms involved survive the bust only to fall into the same trap a few years later.

This chapter examines the underlying cognitive and behavioral factors responsible for strategic decisions driving B&B dynamics, discusses the reasons firms do not learn to avoid boom and bust, and identifies tentative strategies for mitigating B&B behavior. At the same time, we shall conjecturally conclude, there might be a positive collective side to B&B behavior fostering accumulation of knowledge and physical infrastructure, especially regarding new technological paradigms.

The next section discusses a number of real world cases of boom and bust dynamics. The examples illustrate quite common dynamic behaviors and highlight the crucial role of capacity investment decisions in B&B outcomes. Subsequent sections review the findings from prior experimental research on B&B dynamics and discuss some key decision biases and heuristics that play important roles in B&B decision making. The final section outlines some tentative strategies for moderating B&B decision making. In the conclusion, we highlight some of the collectively positive aspects of booms and busts.

Examples of Boom and Bust Dynamics

There are numerous examples of companies that have experienced B&B dynamics. Examples include Atari in home video games (Coughlan 2001, 2004), JDS Uniphase in telecommunications (Sterman et al. 2007), Worlds of Wonder in toys ("Toy Maker Finds a Buyer" 1989), Tensor Corporation in lighting (Salter 1969), and Swatch in fashion watches (Pinson 1987). This section discusses two brief case examples of organizational B&B dynamics—EMI in CT scanners and

Lucent Technologies in telecommunications equipment. Both businesses experienced booming growth phases of tremendous success and then, within a very short period of time, suffered equally dramatic collapses and financial bust. These examples just scratch the surface of the wealth of cases documenting boom and bust.

EMI CT Scanners

EMI Laboratories invented Computed Tomography (CT) imaging in 1972 and installed the first seven CT scanners in hospitals in 1973. Figure 2.1 provides time series data for the number of CT scanners sold in the United States from 1973–80 (Figure 2.1a) along with the estimated remaining potential customers in the US market (Figure 2.1b) (Bartlett 1983a, b; EMI 1973–80). By 1976, 17 companies were selling CT scanners, including a number of well established medical equipment and devices firms such as GE and Siemens, and had installed over 475 CT scanners. At this stage, existing players invested rapidly to expand their production capacity to improve the 9–12 month delivery delays (Bartlett 1983c). New entrants were also rapidly increasing the amount of capacity in the industry during this period. Unit sales across the industry were very strong in 1977, with approximately 40 scanners installed per month. However, during 1978 the unit sales rate fell by nearly half and

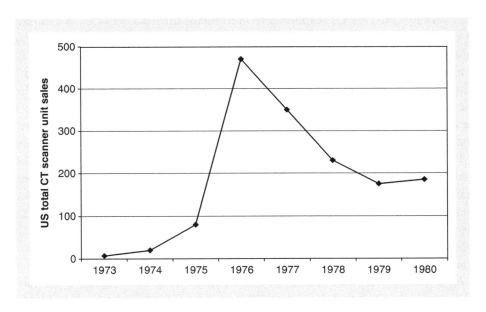

Fig. 2.1a US total CT scanner unit sales, 1973–80.
Source: Bartlett, 1983c.

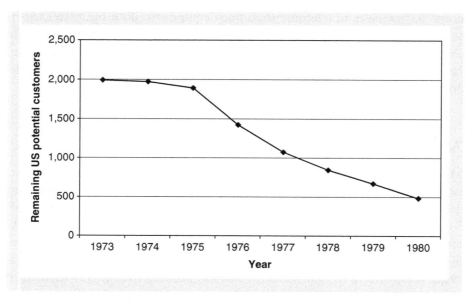

Fig. 2.1b Remaining US potential customers, 1973–80.
Source: Bartlett, 1983c.

then continued to fall further in 1979 and 1980. The precipitous decline in scanner sales in 1977 and 1978 caused many firms to exit the industry during this bust phase.

As the first and dominant manufacturer of CT scanners for the first three years after they invented the CT scanner, EMI epitomized the B&B behavior of a number of companies in the CT market during the period 1973–80. Following a US$29.1 million profit in 1977, the medical electronics division of EMI, including the CT scanner business, incurred major losses in both fiscal years 1978 (−US$28.7 million) and in 1979 (−US$27.8 million). In December 1979, Thorn Electrical Industries acquired EMI, and several months later sold the CT scanner business to General Electric. In the eight years after inventing the CT scanner, EMI went through a spectacular boom period in which they could not keep up with demand, followed by an even steeper bust leading to large financial losses. A post hoc analysis of overall market potential compared with cumulative sales in 1976 reveals that the saturation point of the product lifecycle was being approached very rapidly even as capacity expansion was just starting to ramp up (Bartlett 1983c). Figure 2.1b provides estimates of remaining "potential" US customers from 1973 to 1980. The subsequent period of excess capacity in the industry plummeted many firms into financial turmoil.

As is true in most B&B scenarios, EMI or other industry members could have, relatively easily, predicted the potential demand for CT scanners from the available knowledge of the number of hospitals and the required scanning capacity for CT diagnostics. Furthermore, almost all successful durable products follow a similar pattern of slow initial acceptance followed by rapid sales growth until the market becomes saturated. Demand stagnates and then falls to the level of replacement sales during the mature and decline phases of the lifecycle. Senior managers could have used the well established product lifecycle curve plus knowledge of delays in adjusting production capacity in the industry when planning their strategies and capacity investment decisions to avoid the deep trough and losses of the bust.

Lucent Technologies

AT&T spun off Lucent Technologies in an initial public offering in 1996 and the new company morphed overnight into a hot technology stock. Deregulation of the telecommunications industry that same year fueled rapid growth in demand for telecommunications equipment by enabling new companies to sell phone services. These upstarts needed the networking equipment Lucent sold, and investors willingly furnished the cash required (Greenwald et al. 2001). The technology boom was in full swing. By the end of 2000, Lucent was the largest telecommunications equipment maker in the United States and had the leading share of the world's US$250 billion market for communications infrastructure. Lucent provided products and services that included voice network switching products, fiber optic networking, wireless equipment, and network design and services. Revenues, profits, and the company's stock price soared as demand for high-speed networks seemed limitless (Waters 2000).

During this rapid growth period, Lucent's capital expenditures continued to climb as the company tried to keep up with rising demand. However, in 2001 the global telecommunications market deteriorated as established service providers significantly reduced capital spending after building far too much capacity in the previous years. By 2001, the many telecommunications companies racing to build new fiber optic networks had installed over 39 million miles of fiber, enough to circle the earth 1,500 times (Bearden, August 31, 2001). Lucent had been one of the key beneficiaries of the race to wire the US with high-speed fiber optic networks, but in 2001 demand for the company's products dried up and Lucent's sales collapsed as network capacity far outstripped demand.

This telecommunications bust intensified during 2002 and the market deterioration continued into 2003. New orders for equipment were lackluster, but even worse was that Lucent had approved US$8.4 billion of loans for customers to buy their equipment. Many of the young telecommunications companies that received loans from Lucent went bankrupt and never repaid the loans (Waters 2001). As shown in Figure 2.2(a–d), the results for Lucent were plunging revenues, mounting losses, and imploding stock prices. The company posted losses for 2001, 2002, and 2003, and accordingly the stock price fell 99 percent from the record high and reached a low of 55 cents in 2002. At its peak, Lucent had a workforce of over

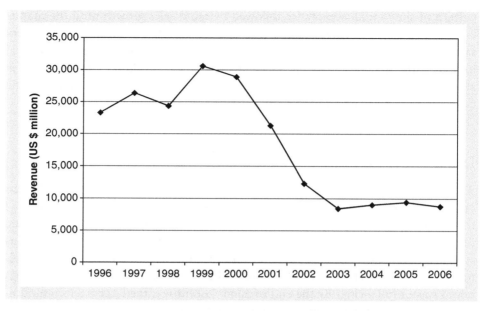

Fig. 2.2a Revenue (US$ million) for Lucent Technologies, 1996–2006.
Source: Bloomberg.

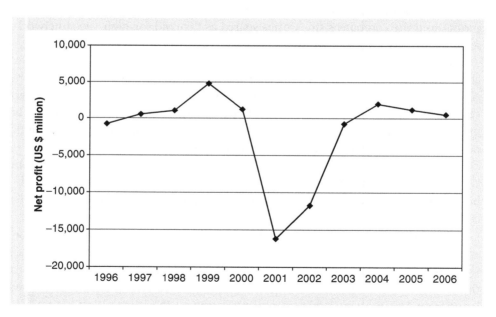

Fig. 2.2b Net profit (US$ million) for Lucent Technologies, 1996–2006.
Source: Bloomberg.

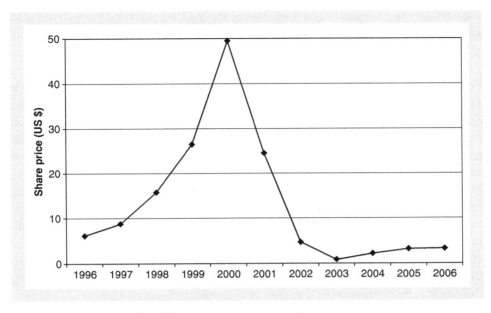

Fig. 2.2c Stock price (US$) for Lucent Technologies, 1996–2006.
Source: Bloomberg.

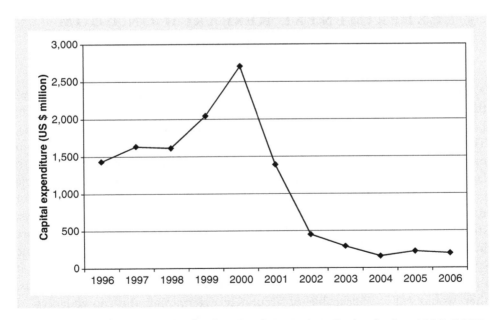

Fig. 2.2d Capital expenditure (US$ million) for Lucent Technologies, 1996–2006.
Source: Bloomberg.

160,000, but in 2001 made plans to shed more than 60 percent of employees and initiated mass layoffs. After limping along for several years while the global telecommunications market slowly recovered, Alcatel acquired Lucent in 2006.

The EMI and Lucent Technologies examples illustrate a pattern of dynamic behavior that is quite widespread. In fact, the evidence indicates that across a large range of industries, the product lifecycle exhibits a pattern characterized by rapid demand and output growth in the introduction phase, followed by market saturation in the mature phase (Klepper and Graddy 1990; Bass 1969; Klepper 1996). Correspondingly, there are a large number of case studies documenting B&B dynamics across a wide range of industry sectors. A few example industries where boom and bust has been prevalent include chainsaws (Porter 1985), commercial (Bakken et al. 1992; Kummerow 1999) and domestic (Hodgkinson 1997, 2005) real estate, agricultural commodities (Meadows 1970), oil tankers and bulk shipping (Bakken et al. 1992; Doman et al. 1995), chemicals (Sharp 1982), and airlines (Lyneis 2000; Liehr et al. 2001). The natural question to ask is: "Why does senior management fall prey to the B&B trap so often?" The next section begins to answer this question by reviewing the findings from experimental studies of dynamic decision making.

EXPERIMENTAL RESEARCH ON BOOM AND BUST

A number of experimental studies on dynamic decision making have investigated the nature of the behavioral rules yielding B&B dynamics (Sterman 1987, 1989a, b; Bakken et al. 1992; Paich and Sterman 1993; Diehl and Sterman 1995; Moxnes 1998). The findings from these studies suggest that individuals and groups suffer from misperceptions of feedback between decisions and the environment, in turn leading to boom and bust. This phenomenon has two components: (1) people typically have incomplete and inaccurate mental models or cognitive maps of complex decision environments and generally tend to ignore feedback, time delays, stock accumulation processes, and non-linearities; and (2) decision makers are incapable of accurately inferring the dynamics of even relatively simple dynamic systems (Sterman 2000). The implication of the second component is that even if managers had perfect mental models of their complex decision environments, they would still be incapable of accurately determining the consequences of their decisions. Both components of misperceptions of feedback are a direct consequence of "bounded rationality" in a broad sense.

In an experimental study examining boom and bust dynamics using a simulated new product launch task, participants made quarterly decisions for price and investments in production capacity (Paich and Sterman 1993). The participants' goal was to maximize cumulative profit from the sales of their product through a forty-quarter simulation. Varying the strength of key feedback loops in the simulated market enabled the experimenters to test whether increasing feedback effects, non-linearities and delays would affect participants' performance. Participants performed the task repeatedly, encouraging learning. However, typical participants' decisions led to boom and bust. Moreover, rising feedback complexity dramatically diminished performance relative to potential and accentuated the B&B dynamics.

Paich and Sterman (1993) estimated the capacity investment decision rules participants adopted when managing a new product launch. The information cues and parametric form of the decision rules were based on: "participants written reports of their strategies, prior models of similar decisions in the literature, and the feedback structure of the task" (Paich and Sterman 1993: 1450). The decision rules identified through this analysis indicated participants in the simulated management environment: (1) selected the share of the market they sought to capture; (2) estimated future demand from information about current demand and recent demand growth; and (3) invested to balance capacity (supply) with demand. Estimated cue weights of the decision rules over trials suggested participants did not gain insight into the dynamics of the system, and experience did not mitigate the misperceptions of feedback, which resulted in B&B behavior. In short, despite repetition of the game, participants did not learn.

Another recent experimental study using a modified version of Paich and Sterman's (1993) simulated new product launch task, investigated the role of mental models on performance (Gary and Wood 2011). After an initial learning phase, participants' completed a knowledge test as an assessment of their mental models of the task. One set of questions tested participants' recall of the bivariate causal relationships between pairs of variables from the management simulation. A second set of questions tested participants' ability to infer the dynamics of small sets of interdependent variables from the new product launch simulator. The knowledge test confirmed that participants had inaccurate and incomplete mental models of the environment that did not accurately account for feedback. On average, participants earned cumulative profits that were roughly 50 percent of the benchmark. The results also indicated that mental model accuracy is a significant predictor of performance. Participants with more accurate mental models of the new product launch simulator achieved higher performance levels and mitigated the B&B dynamics.

Gary and Wood (2011) further explored the implicit cue weights for the decision rules identified by Paich and Sterman (1993). The three cues in the target capacity decision rule included actual demand, demand growth rate, and the ratio of order backlog to actual production capacity.[1] Participants also made quarterly pricing decisions in the new product launch simulation, and the two cues for the pricing decision rule included unit variable cost and a markup based on the

Table 2.1 Estimated Information Weights for Price and Target Capacity Decision Heuristics

Parameter	Mean reported by Paich and Sterman (1993)	Mean	Std Dev	Median p-value	% NS
Capacity investment					
Decision rule:					
Intercept (c)	8.414	3.8701	3.4409	0.0000	0.1318
Industry demand (a_0)	0.383	0.0617	0.2994	0.0896	0.5698
Demand growth rate (a_1)	0.036	0.1286	0.2859	0.1388	0.5891
Backlog/capacity (a_2)	0.318	0.2207	0.3828	0.0265	0.4574
Lag Target Capacity (ρ_{TC})	0.560	0.6532	0.2480	0.0000	0.0891
Adj. R^2	0.872	0.8340			
Pricing decision rule:					
Intercept (b_0)	3.125	−0.0790	0.7252	0.0498	0.4979
Unit variable cost (b_1)	0.259	0.3692	0.2919	0.0057	0.2675
Backlog/capacity (b_2)	0.016	0.0053	0.0299	0.0809	0.5597
Lag Price (ρ_{Pr})	0.781	0.6750	0.1802	0.0000	0.0247
Adj. R^2	0.947	0.9511			

Notes: [1] The model estimated for the target capacity heuristic was:
$$log(C_t^*) = c + a_0 log(D_{t-1}) + a_1 log(1 + g_{t-1}) + a_2 log(B_{t-1} / C_{t-1}) + \rho_{TC}C_{t-1}^* + \varepsilon_1$$
[2] The model estimated for the price heuristic was:
$$log(P_t) = b_0 + b_1 log(UVC_{t-1}) + b_2 log(B_{t-1} / C_{t-1}) + \rho_{Pr}P_{t-1} + \varepsilon_2$$

ratio of order backlog to current production capacity. Information weights were estimated for the capacity and pricing decision rules separately for each trial block for each participant. Table 2.1 presents the results, averaged across 360 decision trials, along with the results reported by Paich and Sterman (1993) for comparison.

Across both studies, the estimated decision rules captured the bulk of the variance in the participants' observed behaviors for each trial. On average, participants' target capacity decisions were primarily based on their prior expectations of market demand captured in the intercept term. This intercept term was a significant predictor of target capacity decisions in more than 86 percent of the instances ($c = 3.870$, $p<.000$). Actual industry demand had a weaker effect on participants' capacity decisions ($a_0 = .062$, $p<.10$) and was not significant in over 56 percent of the cases. Information about the ratio of backlog/capacity had a significant impact on target capacity decisions in almost 65 percent of the cases and was given moderate weight in the decision rule ($a_2 = .221$, $p<.05$). Surprisingly, participants were insensitive to the demand growth rate in setting target capacity decisions ($a_1 = .129$, ns). Given the time delays associated with adjusting capacity, such information weights in the decision rules guaranteed that capacity fell far short of actual demand in the boom phase and resulted in excess capacity in the bust phase when the market saturated and demand declined down to the equilibrium replacement level.

For the pricing decision rule, unit cost was a significant predictor of participants' pricing decisions. In contrast, the backlog/capacity ratio had little effect on pricing behaviors. During the rapid growth phase of the product lifecycle—when demand often exceeded production capacity—decreasing price as unit costs fell only served to exacerbate the imbalance between demand and capacity and ensured a more painful bust phase when the market saturated.

In summary, participants' decision rules reflected "mental models" that were typically incomplete and dynamically deficient. In particular, participants' mental models did not incorporate time delays in adjusting capacity or feedback effects for market diffusion or saturation (Paich and Sterman 1993; Gary and Wood 2011).

In another experimental study of B&B dynamics in a completely different context, two different sets of managers with many years of experience in either commercial real estate development or the oil tanker industry have been shown to adopt myopic decision rules leading to B&B (Bakken et al. 1992). This study involved experienced managers making decisions in their own domains of expertise. Such results are important in that they highlight the fact that inaccurate and incomplete mental models can persist even after extensive experience and training (see also Hodgkinson 1997, 2005).

The bottom line is that the widespread deficiencies of incomplete and inaccurate mental models are typically associated with the absence of accurate accounts of: (1) feedbacks between decision variables and state variables (that is the variables describing the environment in which agents operate); (2) time lags (3) possible non-linearities. Learning in dynamically complex environments is very difficult and, as a result, deficient mental models continue to serve as the basis for poor decision making. In addition, these deficient mental models interact with equally widespread (and partly overlapping) biases and heuristics in decision-making processes. We discuss the role these biases and heuristics play in decisions leading to boom and bust in the next section.

ROLE OF DECISION BIASES IN BOOM AND BUST

It is now widely accepted that cognitive processing limitations prevent human beings from making objectively rational or optimum decisions when operating in complex decision environments for at least two reasons. First, decision makers cannot generate or identify all possible feasible alternative courses of action. Second, even for the alternative courses of action identified, decision makers are generally not likely to access and process all the information needed to value anticipated consequences accurately and to select among them (Cyert and March 1963; Simon 1976, 1979; Morecroft 1985; Sterman 2000). As a result, decision makers employ, consciously and unconsciously, a wide range of simple rules of thumb, routines and heuristics to make decisions in complex environments (Forrester 1961; Allison 1971; Nelson and Winter 1982; Simon 1982; Kahneman and Tversky 2000). In fact, decision makers adopt such simple rules and heuristics even when provided with "full" information and when the decision tasks are not too difficult (cf. also the discussion in Dosi et al. 2005).

Although some decision heuristics work reasonably well under some conditions, they generally yield systematic biases into decision processes (for discussions of different biases see, for example, Tversky and Kahneman 1974; Hogarth 1987; Kahneman and Lovallo 1993; Camerer and Lovallo 1999; Dosi and Lovallo 1997; Kahneman and Tversky 2000). Such biases play important roles in B&B dynamics. Here we shall discuss in particular how two cognitive biases, *attribution errors* and *the inside view* frame, tend to both foster behaviors resulting in boom and bust, and, relatedly, act as impediments to learning.

Attribution Errors

Decision makers operating in complex and uncertain environments tend not to attribute negative outcomes to their own decision-making errors or management ability. The typical response is for decision makers to take too much credit for positive outcomes and to attribute negative outcomes to the environment (Nisbett and Ross 1980; Repenning and Sterman 2002). For example, in a firm that experiences boom and bust dynamics over several years, managers typically attribute firm success in the boom phase to their own decisions and actions. On the other hand, managers tend to point at exogenous factors in order to explain unexpected busts. It is easy to find external forces to blame for negative, unintended outcomes (e.g., fickle customers, overaggressive competitors, or a downturn in the macro economy). Conversely, attributing success in the boom phase to management decision making ensures that the same decisions and behaviors continue after the boom. For instance, continued aggressive capacity expansion, based on extrapolated demand forecasts, worsen the bust when capacity surpasses demand and utilization falls. Moreover, managers attributing the bust to exogenous or external forces out of their control miss the opportunity to learn how their decision-making errors contribute to the bust.

The Inside View

The *inside* view is a mindset decision makers commonly adopt when facing complex problems. Decision makers have a strong tendency to consider problems as unique and thus focus on the particulars of the case at hand when generating solutions (Kahneman and Tversy 1979; Kahneman and Lovallo 1993). They draw mainly on knowledge about the specific characteristics of the current situation, focus on obstacles to the pursuit of the intended strategy and typically extrapolate from current trends (Kahneman and Tversky 1979; Kahneman and Lovallo 1993).

By adopting an inside view, managers in a firm struggling to meet growing demand in the boom phase may build bottom–up forecasts of future demand. Managers typically construct such forecasts by anchoring on the firm's sales from the most recent year, extrapolating the growth in firm sales from the previous year, and often factoring in additional demand growth expected from their own managerial decisions such as new marketing efforts. Subsequently, in the throws of the bust phase, managers using an inside view would typically look for the unique factors of the problem situation responsible for the bust. For example, executives at EMI re-organized their CT scanner manufacturing and marketing operations in the bust phase in the belief that this could restore the division's health—it did not. They did not recognize that the CT scanner market, like so many other markets with pronounced product lifecycles, was approaching saturation. Instead, they believed specific problems in the manufacturing and marketing functions were driving the company's performance downturn.

Adopting an inside view activates numerous cognitive biases (Lovallo and Kahneman 2003). Perhaps, the most relevant to boom and bust dynamics is anchoring and adjustment—the tendency to insufficiently adjust estimates away from a salient (frequently meaningless) anchor (Tversky and Kahneman 1974). There is strong empirical support indicating that the anchor and adjustment heuristic is incorporated into a wide range of decision rules such as expectation formation, forecasting, aspiration and goal adaptation, and updating of perceptions (Sterman 1988; Lant 1992). As a concrete example, when setting the price of a product or service each month or quarter, marketing managers are likely to anchor on the previous price level and make insufficient adjustments around that value. Also, in forecasting demand, the planning or marketing department will likely base their forecast on simple extrapolations anchored on the most recent demand levels as in the decision rule identified in Paich and Sterman (1993) discussed previously. Using the anchor and adjustment heuristic for forecasting demand is particularly insidious in markets where boom and bust is possible, since the anchoring process ensures managers will form expectations that future demand will continue growing without end while they are in the boom phase of rapid growth. If managers respond to such forecasts by investing aggressively in expanding capacity, the hazard of ending up with excess capacity and the associated financial bust becomes far more likely.

It is also important to notice that cognitive biases, which are identified at the level of individual behaviors, tend to "scale up" to the collective organizational level. Part of the reason for this is that relatively few people make the largest firm decisions. A recent McKinsey survey reports that only one or two people make nearly 40 percent of all large firm decisions. While it is beyond the scope of this work to examine the vast literature on individual and organizational decision making, there are good reasons to believe that organizations, in many instances, reinforce rather than mitigate individual decision biases (see, for example, March and Shapira 1987; Kahneman and Lovallo 1993). Escalation situations are well studied examples of a "scale free" phenomenon applying at widely different units of analysis, ranging from individual choices under experimental conditions all the way to enormous collective tragedies such as the Vietnam War (cf., Staw and Ross 1978; Janis 1982). More broadly, organizations are not simple aggregations of independent individuals but rather hierarchically nested structures that often tend to amplify cognitive and behavioral biases throughout their hierarchical layers. Indeed, this is likely to apply even more so when the decision process occurs top–bottom, as typically in strategic commitments (e.g., investment/production capacity decisions).

We have discussed the role of both inaccurate mental models and cognitive biases in strategic decision making resulting in B&B dynamics. These factors also impede learning. Next, we discuss additional impediments to learning that may partially explain the widespread nature of boom and bust.

IMPEDIMENTS TO LEARNING

The widespread and repeated incidences of B&B dynamics across a wide range of firms and industries suggest there are strong underlying impediments to learning at work. The lack of learning is particularly surprising in chronically cyclical industries that repeatedly experience boom and bust episodes (e.g., almost all basic materials industries). Together with the cognitive and behavioral factors discussed above, this section discusses two additional (even if related) barriers to learning. The low frequency of B&B episodes within a particular executive's career is one such obstacle. In addition, causal ambiguity in understanding the reasons for boom and bust is another obstacle (clearly overlapping with the inaccurate and incomplete mental models and cognitive biases discussed above) discussed in this section.

The long length of time between boom and bust cycles probably act as an impediment to learning. Quick, high frequency feedback cycles facilitate learning, while delayed, low frequency feedback cycles impair learning. Boom and bust cycles typically operate on a time period of at least several years if not a decade or more in some industries (Sterman 2000). Managers who make the decisions resulting in B&B dynamics may not immediately recognize their decision making errors were responsible for the unintended behavior. In order to learn that decision errors are causing the problem and to discover how to avoid B&B behavior, repeated observations are likely to be necessary (although possibly not sufficient; cf., the earlier discussion of the *inside view*). However, the low frequency of B&B episodes implies that managers may well move to a different company, move to a different industry, or even leave the workforce altogether before they can experience several B&B cycles. In addition, when there are long lags between B&B cycles, individual decision makers or the organization as a whole may well forget the lessons learned several years or a decade or more before even if they participated in them. Managerial turnover within organizations just augments the problem in that the institutional memory about B&B episodes in the company's history may well walk out the door when key managers involved depart the company.

Conditions for learning are best when there is also clear feedback about how to improve performance and avoid mistakes. However, the feedbacks between actions, environmental responses and payoffs, are typically ambiguous for managers going through a boom or bust. Clear, unambiguous feedback is not readily available during either the boom or the bust phase. For example, in the bust phase it is often very difficult to disentangle the real causal factors responsible for the decline. This *causal ambiguity* makes it very difficult for managers to learn how their sequence of decisions contributes to B&B dynamics (cf., Powell et al. 2006).

The well-known B&B story of Atari in home video games and the subsequent repeated boom and busts of Worlds of Wonder in toys illustrate the damaging effects of failing to learn how decision errors contribute to B&B dynamics. In the six years from 1976 to 1982, Atari's revenues streaked from US$35 million to nearly US$2 billion (WarnerCommunications, 1976–83). However, by 1983 the console market had reached saturation point and the company's operating income fell from a healthy US$300 million at the end of 1982, to US$536 million in losses by the end of 1983. Everyone who wanted a home video game system had bought one, and yet Atari and their rivals kept churning out units. Worlds of Wonder (WoW) was an American toy company founded in 1985 by former Atari employees including Donald Kingsborough, the former President of Atari. WoW achieved one of the fastest two-year growth spurts of any major US manufacturing start-up. The company's talking bear, Teddy Ruxpin, and Lazer Tag, a gun game, were among the toy industry's biggest hits during 1985 and 1986. The high-tech, high priced Teddy Ruxpin was selling so fast, toy stores could not keep him on the shelves:

"We're building them as fast as we can build them. We certainly can't meet demand. Even if we had six more factories, we still can't meet demand." (Paul Rago, vice president of Worlds of Wonder Inc., interview quote in New York Times article on December 20, 1985).

WOW had shown explosive growth, going from zero sales to US$93 million in just a year and to more than US$300 million at the end of its second year. However, sales of Teddy Ruxpin and Lazer Tag began to collapse in 1987 turning the boom to bust, and the company posted a US$43 million quarterly loss in mid-1987. Battered by high inventories swollen by unexpectedly poor sales, the company tried unsuccessfully to obtain additional funds from investors. By the end of 1987, WoW filed for bankruptcy protection. Many of WOW's senior managers had also been part of Atari's senior management, but they failed to learn from the previous experiences, and had repeated their mistakes a few short years later at Worlds of Wonder.

Clearly, if strategic behaviors resulting in B&B dynamics are so endemic one can hardly imagine a "magic bullet" remedy. However, it is worth investigating prescriptions aimed at mitigating such episodes.

Tentative Strategies for Moderating Boom and Bust Behavior

How can management practices be refined in order to overcome the cognitive and behavioral biases leading to overshoot and collapse? Let us consider two possible (partial) remedies entailing, firstly, the construction of *schemata* of the common structure underlying B&B dynamics and, secondly, a greater reliance on the "outside view" (as opposed to the "inside view" discussed above). If developed, schemata of the high level causal structure underpinning B&B dynamics guide decisions instead of deficient mental models. The outside view focuses on a set of reference cases similar to the case at hand and derives forecasts based on the statistics of similar past cases.

Building Schemata of the Underlying Structures of Boom and Bust

While it is common to think about different classes of problems in natural sciences, engineering, and medicine and to identify the similarities of problems and solutions within the same class, it has not been common in management practice.

However, findings from a large body of research in psychology and cognitive science suggest that developing schemata identifying different classes of management problems could dramatically improve managerial decision making. Research findings across a range of problem domains indicate that experts develop schemata to organize their knowledge of different classes of problems within the domain and use these schemata to represent problems at a deeper, "structural" level.

For example, in the domain of medicine, research indicates that experienced physicians diagnose routine cases using knowledge organized in schemata of different illness categories to accurately diagnose and treat patients (Schmidt and Boshuizen 1993). These illness schemata emerge from continuing exposure to patients and are, therefore, largely the result of extended practice. Novice physicians and students do not have these knowledge structures. Schmidt and Boshuizen (1993) found that the illness schemata used by experienced physicians consisted of high level, simplified causal models explaining signs and symptoms of different illness categories combined with a "script" for how to effectively treat an illness in different categories.

In the management domain, recent research indicates managers often use analogical reasoning to make strategic choices, but are typically not aware they are reasoning by analogy (Gavetti and Rivkin 2005) and they often do so in rather undisciplined ways. Drawing on prior experience and applying relevant insights to solve similar problems can be a powerful approach for solving complex problems. Barnett and Koslowski (2002) compared problem-solving approaches and solutions of management consultants, restaurateurs, and novices (non-business undergraduates) in solving a common problem about a change in road conditions that would affect the patronage of a restaurant. Despite a lack of restaurant experience, the consultants performed better than the restaurateurs and undergraduates, who did not differ significantly from one another. Barnett and Koslowski (2002) attributed the consultants' higher performance to a wide repertoire of schemata of managerial problems developed through the substantive variability in their career experiences. Consultants work on different problems in different companies and—so it seems—are accustomed to applying insights gained from previous projects to similar problems encountered in other firms or industries. These findings hint at the efficacy of structured, disciplined analogical reasoning involving schemata of simplified causal models germane to entire classes of phenomena or problems.

Enduring causal models underpin many recurring managerial problems and challenges such as product lifecycle diffusion (Bass 1969; see also the survey in Dosi 1992), commodity production cycles (Meadows 1970)[2] and inventory management in supply chains (Sterman 1989b). The causal models of these common managerial problems display sufficient invariance across different instantiations to allow for formation of schemata identifying crucial state variables and relationships between system variables and the high leverage control (or strategic) variables in the hands of the decision makers. Based on substantial evidence from other problem domains, we suggest managers armed with schema of these and other managerial problems would probably make better decisions when faced with such challenges.

For example, schemata of product lifecycle diffusion could easily guide managers to collect and consider information about the potential number of customers in the total market, the industry growth rate, competitors' aggregate capacity investments, and the average useful lifetime of the product. Managers possessing a schema for logistic product lifecycle diffusion would understand that as new customers purchase the product, fewer potential customers remain and that when most potential customers have purchased the product, demand tends to approach the level of replacement purchases determined by the average useful lifetime of the product. Fundamental uncertainties would remain about, for example, the rate of technical progress, which in turn affects the number of future potential customers, their preferences, and rates of substitution of new for old products. Such uncertainties would imply significant forecasting errors. Still, our claim is that using any naive logistic product lifecycle schemata instead of grossly deficient mental models might reduce errors even by an order of magnitude. Yet the disciplined use of schemata composed of high level causal models is not a "natural" part of decision making in business. So for example, if EMI's and Lucent Technologies' managers had applied even utterly simple schemata of the product lifecycle diffusion model they may have recognized earlier that the markets for CT scanners and telecommunications networking equipment, respectively, could not expand exponentially forever. Staying alert for signals of market saturation, EMI's and Lucent's managers might have curtailed aggressive capacity expansion.

Adopting the "Outside View"

Developing schemata of the underlying structure for classes of phenomena and managerial problems involves explicit efforts aimed to form *reference classes* of similar problems. In turn, this very process facilitates the adoption of an *outside view*. In contrast to the inside view discussed above, managers adopting an outside view ignore the details of the case at hand and simply focus on understanding the historical statistics and patterns of similar phenomena. For example, awareness of logistic product lifecycle diffusion dynamics might have straightforwardly led managers to an attempt to estimate the near-saturation level of demand in CT scanners by drawing on the diffusion patterns of other medical devices (e.g., X-ray machines, sonograms, etc.) Similarly, an appreciation of the short and pronounced lifecycles in toy demand should have sent loud warnings of potential boom and bust dynamics to Atari's management.

Using the statistical history of analogous situations to predict not just the quantity of next quarter's demand but the structure of demand over time is not immediately intuitive. Adopting an outside view takes deliberate effort, but the rewards for predictive accuracy can be substantial. For instance, EMI's executives could have responded differently to the decline in unit sales and financial results. At the time, management responded by allocating resources to reorganize the company's manufacturing and marketing operations. Instead, adopting an outside view may have helped executives at EMI understand that the CT scanner market was approaching saturation. Armed with an understanding that the market was saturating, EMI may have been able to either sell the firm at an optimal time or change their strategy to one more compatible with their firm's skills. Instead, they sustained substantial losses before selling out for a minimal sum once GE and Siemens became dominant.

Conclusions

Strategic decisions leading to boom and bust dynamics are widespread and persistent. The cases we have briefly discussed are just a few out of an enormous number of examples including both individual companies and whole industries. As experimental evidence shows, decisions resulting in B&B dynamics are rooted in grossly incomplete and inaccurate mental models of the problem domain and pervasive cognitive biases. One important bias leads managers to frame the decision setting as involving a unique problem (the "inside view"), even though it actually belongs to a whole category of decision problems sharing the same basic features.

We have identified two tentative strategies for overcoming B&B behavior. The first strategy focuses on developing schema of commonly recurring management problems or challenges. In other domains, expert knowledge is organized through schemata composed of simplified but powerful causal models linking underlying reference categories for information processing and decision making. Such schemata replace deficient mental models of the problem/challenge and provide guidance about the high leverage points of the system and decisions for effective management in such situations. We propose that developing schemata of logistic demand growth in managing product lifecycles may well mitigate boom and bust behaviors. A second tentative strategy for overcoming boom and bust decisions is to ensure managers adopt an outside view by paying attention to historical time series of similar cases of diffusion/capacity building in order to detect inflection or turning points. These two strategies would probably offer remarkable performance improvements. What is surprising is that they are not part of the standard "tool box" of managers and management training. As a result, problems such as boom and bust persist and are repeated, many times over.

Over 250,000 telecommunications workers lost jobs as part of the telecoms bust during 2001. At the time, the telecommunications industry as a whole had an estimated US$500 billion in outstanding loans that could have gone into default. In fact, the decision errors yielding the fiber optic boom and bust are not new. In the nineteenth century, a US railroad boom began in 1869 with the completion of the Transcontinental Railroad spanning east to west across the country. A railroad building frenzy ensued and rival railroads laid four additional routes to the Pacific financed by large loans from the bond market. The bust arrived just four years later and 90 heavily indebted railroads went bankrupt.

However, there may be a collective brighter side to boom and bust. In fact, what is likely to be a catastrophe from the point of view of individual or company level returns might well correspond to a *collective bonanza* in the accumulation of knowledge and infrastructure development. As Perez (2006) convincingly argues, the establishment of all major infrastructures associated with dominant techno-economic paradigms has been intimately linked to major *technological bubbles* entailing the euphoric and reckless build up of overcapacities of various kinds. This applies to canals, and later, railroads, to fiber optic networks and the dot.com bubble. Prior research suggests that cognitive biases may, under some circumstances, lead to collective social gains such as the collective value of overconfidence that often drives individual entrepreneurial decisions (Dosi and Lovallo 1997). Similarly, it may well be that collectively boom and bust behaviors, at least in some circumstances, drive private investors to develop externalities and collective physical infrastructures that no sober exclusively profit-motivated actor would have done otherwise. We all enjoy cheaper phone calls due to the boom in fiber optic infrastructure and, more importantly, the expansive race in medical diagnostic imaging has saved countless lives.

ENDNOTES

1 Paich and Sterman's (1993) decision rule for target capacity was: $C_t^* = s^* [D_0^{e(1-\alpha_0)} D_{t-1}^{\alpha_0}](1 + g_{t-1})^{\alpha 1}(B_t / C_t)^{\alpha 2}$. Where s^* is a constant target market share of 50 percent, D^e is the prior estimate of market demand, D_{t-1} is the actual demand lagged by one time period, g_{t-1} is lagged demand growth, and the ratio of backlog/capacity. In both studies, the decision rule was estimated as:
$$\log(C_t^*) = c + a_0\log(D_{t-1}) + a_1\log(1 + g_{t-1}) + a_2\log(B_t / C_t) + \varepsilon_1.$$

2 Meadows (1970) expanded the original Cobweb model (Ezekiel 1938) to provide a more comprehensive endogenous explanation for commodity cycles and recent research on cyclical industries continue to use this model (Aramburo 2006).

REFERENCES

ALLISON, G. T. (1971). *Essence of Decision*. Boston, MA: Little, Brown and Company.

ARAMBURO, S. A. (2006). *Essays on Commodity Cycles Based on Expanded Cobweb Experiments of Electricity Markets*. Bergen: University of Bergen.

BAKKEN, B. E., GOULD, J. M. and KIM, D. H. (1992). 'Experimentation in Learning Organizations: A Management Flight Simulator Approach.' *European Journal of Operations Research*, 59/1: 167–82.

BARNETT, S. M. and KOSLOWSKI, B. (2002). 'Adaptive Expertise: Effects of Type of Experience and the Level of Theoretical Understanding it Generates.' *Thinking and Reasoning*, 8/4: 237–67.

BARTLETT, C. A. (1983a). *EMI and the CT Scanner (A)*. Boston, MA: Harvard Business School Publishing.

—— (1983b). *EMI and the CT Scanner (B)*. Boston, MA: Harvard Business School Publishing.

—— (1983c). *EMI and the CT Scanner Teaching Note*. Boston, MA: Harvard Business School Publishing.

BASS, F. M. (1969). 'A New Product Growth Model for Consumer Durables.' *Management Science*, 15/5: 215–27.

BEARDEN, T. (2001). 'Boom and Bust.' *Online NewsHour: PBS Broadcasting*, August 31.

CAMERER, C. and LOVALLO, D. (1999). 'Overconfidence and Excess Entry: An Experimental Approach.' *The American Economic Review*, 89/1: 306–18.

COUGHLAN, P. J. (2001). *Competitive Dynamics in Home Video Games (A): The Age of Atari*. Boston, MA: Harvard Business School Publishing.

—— (2004). *The Golden Age of Home Video Games: From the Reign of Atari to the Rise of Nintendo*. Boston, MA: Harvard Business School Publishing.

CYERT, R. M. and MARCH, J. G. (1963). *A Behavioral Theory of the Firm* (2nd edn.). Cambridge, MA: Blackwell Publishers Inc.

DIEHL, E. and STERMAN, J. D. (1995). 'Effects of Feedback Complexity on Dynamic Decision Making.' *Organizational Behavior and Human Decision Processes*, 62/2: 198–215.

DOMAN, A. M., GLUCKSMAN, N., and SASPORTES, M. (1995). 'The Dynamics of Managing a Life Insurance Company.' *System Dynamics Review*, 11/3: 219–32.

DOSI, G. (1992). 'Research on Innovation Diffusion: An Assessment,' in N. Nakicenovic (ed.), *Innovation Diffusion and Social Behaviors*. Heidelberg/Berlin/New York: Springer Verlag.

—— LOVALLO, D. (1997). 'Rational Entrepreneurs or Optimistic Martyrs? Some Considerations on Technological Regimes, Corporate Entries and the Evolutionary Role of Decision Biases,' in R. Garud, P. R. Nayyar, and Z. B. Shapira (eds.), *Technological Innovation Oversights and Foresights*. Cambridge/New York: Cambridge University Press.

—— MARENGO, L., and FAGIOLO, G. (2005). 'Learning in Evolutionary Environments,' in K. Dopfer (ed.), *The Evolutionary Foundations of Economics*. Cambridge: Cambridge University Press.

EMI (1973–80). *EMI Limited Annual Reports*.

EZEKIEL, M. (1938). 'The Cobweb Theorem.' *The Quarterly Journal of Economics*, 52/2: 255–80.

FORRESTER, J. W. (1961). *Industrial Dynamics*. Cambridge, MA: MIT Press.

GARY, M. S., and WOOD, R. E. (2011). 'Mental Models, Decision Rules, and Performance Heterogeneity.' *Strategic Management Journal*, 32: 569–594.

GAVETTI, G. and RIVKIN, J. W. (2005). 'How Strategists Really Think. Tapping the Power of Analogy.' *Harvard Business Review*, April, 83/4: 54–63.

GREENWALD, J., FRANK, S., and TAYLOR, C. (2001). 'Busted By Broadband Fiber-Optic Suppliers were at the Center of NASDAQ's Boom. But a Too-Good Technology and Frantic Overbuilding Triggered a High-Speed Collapse.' *Time*, March 26: 157.

HODGKINSON, G. P. (1997). 'Cognitive Inertia in a Turbulent Market: the Case of UK Residential Estate Agents.' *Journal of Management Studies*, 34/6: 921–45.

—— (2005). *Images of Competitive Space: A Study of Managerial and Organizational Strategic Cognition*. Basingstoke: Palgrave Macmillan.

HOGARTH, R. M. (1987). *Judgment and Choice* (2nd edn.). Chichester: John Wiley and Sons.

JANIS, I. L. (1982). *Groupthink: Psychological Studies of Policy Decisions and Fiascoes*. Boston, MA: Houghton Mifflin.

KAHNEMAN, D. and LOVALLO, D. (1993). 'Timid Choices and Bold Forecasts: A Cognitive Perspective on Risk Taking.' *Management Science*, 39/1: 17–31.

—— TVERSKY, A. (1979). 'Intuitive Predictions: Biases and Corrective Procedures.' *TIMS Studies in Management Science*, 12: 313–27.

—— —— (2000). *Choices, Values, and Frames*. Cambridge: Cambridge University Press.

KLEPPER, S. (1996). 'Entry, Exit, Growth, and Innovation over the Product Life Cycle.' *The American Economic Review*, 86/3: 562–83.

—— GRADDY, E. (1990). 'The Evolution of New Industries and the Determinants of Market Structure.' *The RAND Journal of Economics*, 21/1: 27–44.

KUMMEROW, M. (1999). 'A System Dynamics Model of Cyclical Office Oversupply.' *The Journal of Real Estate Research*, 18/1: 233–55.

LIEHR, M., GRÖßLER, A., KLEIN, M., and MILLING, P. M. (2001). 'Cycles in the Sky : Understanding and Managing Business Cycles in the Airline Market.' *System Dynamics Review*, 17/4: 311–32.

LOVALLO, D. and KAHNEMAN, D. (2003). 'Delusions of Success: How Optimism Undermines Executives' Decisions.' *Harvard Business Review*, 81/7: 62–72.

LYNEIS, J. M. (2000). 'System Dynamics for Market Forecasting and Structural Analysis.' *System Dynamics Review*, 16/1: 3–25.

MARCH, J. G. and SHAPIRA, Z. (1987). 'Managerial Perspectives on Risk and Risk Taking.' *Management Science*, 33/11: 1404–18.

MEADOWS, D. L. (1970). *Dynamics of Commodity Production Cycles*. Cambridge, MA: Productivity Press.

MORECROFT, J. D. W. (1985). 'Rationality in the Analysis of Behavioral Simulation Models.' *Management Science*, 31/7: 900–16.

MOXNES, E. (1998). 'Not Only the Trajedy of the Commons: Misperceptions of Bioeconomics.' *Management Science*, 44/9: 1234–48.

NELSON, R. R. and WINTER, S. G. (1982). *An Evolutionary Theory of Economic Change*. Cambridge, MA: Harvard University Press.

NISBETT, R. E. and ROSS, L. (1980). *Human Inference: Strategies and Shortcomings of Social Judgment*. Englewood Cliffs, NJ: Prentice-Hall.

PAICH, M. and STERMAN, J. D. (1993). 'Boom, Bust, and Failures to Learn in Experimental Markets.' *Management Science*, 39/12: 1439–58.

PEREZ, C. (2006). 'The Nature and Consequences of Major Technology Bubbles.' *CERF Working Paper*, Judge Business School, Cambridge University.

PINSON, C. (1987). *Swatch: Case Study*. Fontainebleau: INSEAD.

PORTER, M. E. (1985). *Competitive Advantage: Creating and Sustaining Superior Performance*. New York: The Free Press.

POWELL, T. C., LOVALLO, D., and CARINGAL, C. (2006). 'Causal Ambiguity, Management Perception, and Firm Performance.' *Academy of Management Review*, 31/1: 175–96.

REPENNING, N. P. and STERMAN, J. D. (2002). 'Capability Traps and Self-Confirming Attribution Errors in the Dynamics of Process Improvement.' *Administrative Science Quarterly*, 47/2: 265–95.

SALTER, M. (1969). *Tensor Corporation: Case 370–041*. Boston, MA: Harvard Business School Publishing.

SCHMIDT, H. G. and BOSHUIZEN, H. P. A. (1993). 'On Acquiring Expertise in Medicine.' *Educational Psychology Review (Historical Archive)*, 5/3, 205–21.

SHARP, J. A. (1982). 'The Dynamics of the UK Chemical Plant Investment Cycle.' *European Journal of Operational Research (Netherlands)*, 9/3: 238–47.

SIMON, H. A. (1976). *Administrative Behavior*. New York: The Free Press.

—— (1979). 'Rational Decision Making in Business Organizations.' *American Economic Review*, 69: 493–513.

—— (1982). *Models of Bounded Rationality Volume 2: Behavioral Economics and Business Organization*. Cambridge, MA: MIT Press.

STAW, B. M. and ROSS, J. (1978). 'Commitment to a Policy Decision: A Multi-Theoretical Perspective.' *Administrative Science Quarterly*, 23/1: 40–64.

STERMAN, J. D. (1987). 'Testing Behavioral Simulation Models by Direct Experiment.' *Management Science*, 33/12: 1572–92.

—— (1989a). 'Misperceptions of Feedback in Dynamic Decision making.' *Organizational Behavior and Human Decision Processes*, 43/3: 301–35.

—— (1989b). 'Modeling Managerial Behavior: Misperceptions of Feedback in a Dynamic Decision Experiment.' *Management Science*, 35/3: 321–39.

—— (2000). *Business Dynamics: Systems Thinking and Modeling for a Complex World*. New York: McGraw-Hill/Irwin.

—— HENDERSON, R., BEINHOCKER, E. D., and NEWMAN, L. I. (2007). 'Getting Big Too Fast: Strategic Dynamics with Increasing Returns and Bounded Rationality.' *Management Science*, 53/4: 683–96.

'Toy Maker Finds a Buyer.' (1989). *New York Times*, February 22.

TVERSKY, A. and KAHNEMAN, D. (1974). 'Judgement Under Uncertainty: Heuristics and Biases.' *Science*, 185: 1124–31.

WARNER COMMUNICATIONS (1976–83). *Warner Communications Annual Reports*.

WATERS, R. (2000). 'The Big Explosion of the Revenue Growth Factor—What Went Wrong at Lucent Technologies.' *Financial Times*, December 22.

—— (2001). 'Reinvention at the Speed of Light: Telecommunications is Struggling not Only with a Boom–Bust Cycle but also New Technology.' *Financial Times*, June 4.

3

INFORMATION OVERLOAD REVISITED

KATHLEEN M. SUTCLIFFE

KARL E. WEICK

INTRODUCTION

DURING morning rush hour on March 11, 2004, near simultaneous blasts hit a commuter train station in Spain's capital of Madrid, killing 191 people and injuring 2000. In the aftermath, Interpol Washington[1] asked a team of United States FBI personnel to analyze a set of latent fingerprints found by Spanish police on a plastic bag of detonators left at the crime scene. Within two weeks FBI examiners had analyzed a digital photograph of the fingerprints received electronically from the Spanish national police and reported a match with a candidate print from an integrated automated fingerprint identification (IAFIS) computer search (Stacey 2004). That led to a decision in early May to arrest, jail, and label as a terrorist, Brandon Mayfield—an Oregon lawyer. Mayfield's prints were on file as he had been arrested as a juvenile and had served in the Army (Heath 2004). Two weeks after Mayfield's arrest Spanish national police fingerprint examiners verified that the prints actually matched a foreign terrorist. The FBI quickly released Mayfield. Nonetheless, they could not avert attacks on the fingerprint lab's credibility or stop an investigation into the root causes of the mistake.

This erroneous identification and the decision to arrest an innocent victim could easily have been attributed to poor evidence: the electronic images of the latent prints found at the crime scene were of "low resolution and without a scale" (Stacey 2004: 708). But the case is not that simple. In fact, Mayfield had never traveled to Madrid, which should have been evidence enough—at least a red flag to investigators that things were not as they seemed (Heath 2004). But there is more. After the FBI team identified a match (and before Mayfield's arrest), they sent their findings to Spanish national police who had been conducting a concurrent analysis. When Spanish police compared the evidence to the subject's fingerprints (i.e., Mayfield's prints), instead of seeing a match, they arrived at an inconclusive finding (Stacey 2004). This precipitated face to face meetings between FBI fingerprint unit personnel and Spanish fingerprint examiners, a US court appointed independent examination (which confirmed the original FBI analysis), and an additional review by personnel from the FBI Laboratory Quality Assurance and Training Unit. Following a face to face meeting with Spanish officials in Madrid, FBI personnel returned to the US and after an all night discussion, recognized their error. A secondary team of FBI examiners under the direction of a different unit chief convened to review the case concurred with the Spanish national police that the latent fingerprints indeed belonged to a different suspect (Stacey 2004: 711).

The subsequent examination revealed the following sequence (see Stacey 2004: 712–14). The initial fingerprint examination was made by a highly respected and experienced supervisory fingerprint examiner. The examiner initially encoded seven identifying characteristics of the latent fingerprint, initiated a search of the automated information system (IAFIS), received a list of possible candidates from the search, compared the existing print to the candidates' prints, and identified the subject. The existing rule at the time required that a supervisor verify every latent print analysis with less than 12 characteristics; moreover, it was routine for verifiers to know the previous examiner's results. Thus, the original examiner notified the unit chief who reviewed the on-screen images and who concurred. The unit chief then assigned the case to a second verifier (a retired supervisory fingerprint examiner working as a contractor) who requested original fingerprint cards from another FBI division, and after three days, also verified the original fingerprint examiner's identification.

While the FBI may not resemble a "typical" organization, this event is typical of organization events because it involves a high stakes, high profile decision coupled with performance pressures, time pressures, role pressures, and distributed information all of which can trigger a regression to a less expert stage (Barthol and Ku 1959) and subsequently increase the likelihood of flawed decision making. In the Madrid case, pressures overloaded "expert" decision makers and transformed them into "advanced beginners" who were more easily overwhelmed and made a high profile decision "by the rules" (Dreyfuss and Dreyfuss 1986). Specifically "the power of the IAFIS correlation [candidate match], coupled with the inherent pressure of working an extremely high-profile case, was thought to have influenced the examiner's initial judgment and subsequent examination . . ." (Stacey 2004: 713) and led decision makers to see what they expected to see. Such influence would have been less marked had less regression occurred.

There are additional symptoms of overload visible in the Madrid episode. For example, information search and retrieval became less systematic and less thorough (Eppler and Mengis 2004: 333). The analysis and organization of information became more arbitrary which is evident in a lack of critical evaluation. When people become credulous they are more likely to make superficial analyses. The investigators lost differentiation as the relationship between details and overall perspective weakened and as they "overestimated" the importance of peripheral cues (Eppler and Mengis 2004: 333). There was more abstraction in the interest of more meaning and that abstraction led to more misinterpretation. There were problems of workload bottlenecks in that the FBI examiners had too many inputs and too many cases to examine in the time available (Woods et al. Roth 2002: 25; Stacey 2005, personal communication). And finally, there were covert production pressures on personnel to place production and not "reliability" as their primary priority (Stacey 2004: 714–16).

Overload might have been less of a problem for the FBI if the examiner and the people who checked the work, had been more resilient and more accustomed to daily pressures and media visibility. Fingerprint examiners routinely have heavy caseloads, but they work most of the time by themselves in relative isolation and obscurity. In the Madrid case overload led decision makers to omit consideration of some data, restrict attention to other portions of the data, filter out discrepant information, and seek to confirm their initial expectations that a match existed.

While the FBI problems are organizational problems and system problems, it is not obvious that they are information processing problems. They are that, but they are more. And it is the "more" that this chapter is about.

Conventional Definitions of Overload

Individuals typically describe information overload[2] as the situation of receiving too much information. Organizational scholars define overload as a state induced when the amount of input to a system exceeds its processing capacity (Speier et al. 1999) or when information processing capabilities and the information loads[3] encountered are mismatched (O'Reilly 1980: 684). Perception plays a key role in overload as in this definition: overload is the "perceived inability to maintain a one to one relationship between input and output within a realizable future with an existing repertoire of practices and desires" (Weick 1970: 68). The readily available Wikipedia definition of overload reads, overload "involves large amounts of currently available information, a high rate of new information being added, contradictions in available information, a low signal to noise ratio, and inefficient methods for comparing and processing different kinds of information."

Prevailing treatments of overload posit that when a system (individual or organization) is no longer able to process information and becomes overloaded, primary and secondary symptoms are manifested (Schneider 1987). For example primary symptoms of overload include a general lack of perspective, an inability to select out relevant information, and increasing "distraction by irrelevant and interfering cues" (Schneider 1987: 148), which lead to cognitive strain and stress and a feeling of lack of control (Lipowski 1975). These changes prompt a variety of coping strategies (Wright 1974) and mechanisms of adjustment (Miller 1960). Mechanisms of adjustment may mitigate immediate pressures but they often result in increasing errors or negative affect (stress, frustration, and confusion), and under certain conditions can negatively affect the timeliness and quality of decisions (see Speier et al. 1999; Eppler and Mengis 2004). These adjustments can lead to a set of secondary symptoms such as reduced scanning, narrowed and internally focused attention, increased control and centralization, and rationalization and legitimation (Schneider 1987: 145) that can exacerbate the very problems they are trying to fix.

The idea that inputs are excessive and increasingly overwhelm individuals and organizations is not surprising. There are continuing organizational and institutional pressures for decision makers to collect information to demonstrate a commitment to rational decision making and to justify decisions (Feldman and March 1981), to validate information already acquired, to have it on hand in case it is useful, to keep up with colleagues, or to use it as currency (Edmunds and Morris 2000). In addition, as Sparrow notes (1999: 144; see also Hodgkinson and Sparrow 2002), the information decision makers face is increasingly problematic in that it is of low quality, low value, highly ambiguous, and has a short period of relevance (i.e., a short half-life). These four qualities compound both the mental effort and the time required to make sense of the information, which can divert decision makers' attention to irrelevant issues or blind them to more important matters (Sparrow 1999: 144).

Although load can become excessive as inputs increase, it also can become excessive when capacity is limited. Increasing task demands, competing task demands, increasing complexity of tasks, too few resources (i.e., skills or knowledge that exceed requirements), hallmarks of today's organizational contexts, can limit capacity and thereby increase overload. Capacity is also limited when time is short; when production or performance pressures exist, when there is too little control over the processing of inputs (Hahn et al. 1992), and too little time to process inputs (Kock 2000).

In fact, the issue of time as it pertains to overload has become more explicit and more prominent. This is evident in recent descriptions suggesting that overload occurs when "the demands on an entity for information processing time exceed its supply of time (Schick et al. 1990: 315), when the time needed to meet decision makers' processing requirements exceeds the time available for processing (Speier et al. 1999: 339; Kock 2000), or "when the attentional system is no longer able to allocate its resources in a manner which results in adequate performance" (Hahn et al. 1992: 366).

Time pressures also increase as a result of distractions and interruptions (Perlow 1998; Speier et al. 1999; Jett and George 2003). But distractions and interruptions in and of themselves do not constitute overloads. It depends on how one interprets them. Furthermore, distractions lead to the buildup of queues which can lead directly to overload, or can lead indirectly to overload by decreasing the amount of time to work on something and increasing time pressure. Interruptions break the flow of work and often bring it to a halt. As interruptions take time away from present activity, they fuel feelings of time pressure. Interruptions also increase information processing demands by forcing decision makers to shift attention to the interruption, to contemporaneously attend to competing inputs, or to focus or narrow attention on one task at the expense of others. There are costs to refocusing and returning to the primary task. Decision accuracy may decrease as decision makers lose or forget cues, and decision time may increase as decision makers take time to get back up to speed (Speier et al. 1999). As the information load increases and a decision maker experiences less control over the processing system, arousal and stress elevate, and consequent coping adjustments such as narrowing attention are the result (Speier et al. 1999).

Still there are occasions when time pressures are not all bad—time pressures act like a double-edged sword. Laboratory studies show that under some conditions, such as when the task is simple, time pressures can actually improve decision quality in terms of decision time and decision accuracy (Hahn et al. 1992; Speier et al. 1999; see also Chajut and Algom 2003). Time pressures can help decision makers narrow their attention and focus on the most relevant information (i.e., as attention is narrowed decision makers dismiss or ignore irrelevant cues). But after a certain point as the information load is increased (when time pressures are high and a task gets more complex), the speed and quality of decisions decline (Hahn et al. 1992; Speier et al. 1999).

OVERLOAD: ASSUMPTIONS AND THE INFORMATION PROCESSING PERSPECTIVE

Overload has been subject to much speculation and conceptual attention for decades, yet empirical research on overload, particularly in organizational theory (and as it pertains to organizational decision making), is surprisingly sparse.

The few empirical studies that have been conducted in organization studies over the past four decades mainly "focus on the satisfaction of the person experiencing the overload" (Eppler and Mengis 2004: 338).

Conventional views of overload in organization theory originate in the information processing approach to organization design (e.g., Thompson 1967; Galbraith 1974), an approach that Lant and Shapira (2001a, b) call a computational perspective as contrasted to an interpretive perspective. From a computational perspective, the problem decision makers and organizations face is "one of searching and processing relevant information when such search is costly and decision makers are boundedly rational" (Lant and Shapira 2001a: 2). Herbert Simon's (1971) summary description of overload is an uncommonly rich statement of this perspective and begins to bridge computation and interpretation.

Whether a computer will contribute to the solution of an information-overload problem, or instead compound it, depends on the distribution of its own attention among four classes of activities: listening, storing, thinking, and speaking. A general design principle can be put as follows: An information processing subsystem (a computer or new organization unit) will reduce the net demand on the rest of the organization's attention only if it absorbs more information previously received by others than it produces—that is, if it listens and thinks more than it speaks.

Recall James Thompson's (1967) claim that the key "problem for complex organizations is one of coping with uncertainty," which is reduced through information. Organization scholars typically define uncertainty as the difference between the amount of information an organization needs to possess for task performance and the amount that it possesses (Galbraith 1974; Tushman and Nadler 1978). Organizations must determine how best to organize to process the information they do possess that decision makers confront. This raises the issue of processing capacity. From the information processing perspective, organization design matters; that is, the information processing capacity depends on the organization's goals, hierarchy, relational infrastructure and patterns of interaction. An organization's design can increase or reduce the information processing requirements and affect capacity (Hodgkinson and Sparrow 2002). For example, changes due to centralization or interdisciplinary teams increase information processing requirements (and decrease capacity) by increasing the need for intensive coordination and communication (Eppler and Mengis 2004: 330). In contrast, better coordination through standard operating procedures, rules, and other coordination processes can decrease information processing requirements and increase capacity (Eppler and Mengis 2004: 330).

Several assumptions underlie the view that overload is a problem in information processing. The first is that representation and computation rather than construction and interpretation are the primary organizational activities (from a computation standpoint there are too many separate objects to attend to). The second is that the organization is a finite container that is overfilled with demands.

The third is that communication channels are conduits with fixed information limits (i.e., channel capacity). The fourth is that the goal of a transformation process is a one to one correspondence between input and output (i.e., quick response). The fifth is that output must be formulated in response to input within a fixed time interval. The sixth is that short-term storage is limited. The seventh is that attention is a scarce resource (e.g., Simon 1973). And the eighth is that overload is a disease that ought to be fought (Eppler and Mengis 2004).

Rethinking the Information Processing Assumptions

Computational information processing perspectives tend to neglect the more interpretive aspects of information processing or the idea that part of organizational information processing necessitates the creation of "meaning around information in a social context" (Lant 2002: 345). When scholars view organizations as interpretation systems (Daft and Weick 1984), the problem of overload takes on a different meaning. Overload is not necessarily a case of too much data, rather it is an inability to make sense of demands, capabilities, and context as well as data. In fact, some have argued that the issue of significance is at the heart of the information overload problem (Woods et al. 2002: 25); that assessing "the significance of data when it is not known a priori what data from a large data field will be informative" is vital.

This suggests that overload is a problem of interpretation as much as it is a problem of computation and information processing. Overload is a particular way of bracketing a stream of experience. This means that overload is not a discrete, discontinuous, sudden event. Instead, it waxes and wanes, comes and goes. It is embedded in the experiences of becoming (Tsoukas and Chia 2002) and thrownness (Weick 2004) and ready to hand (Heidegger 1962) and making sense of these experiences. Taking interpretation more seriously brings a different set of assumptions to the forefront.

John Dewey provides the basic infrastructure for our ideas. His analysis enables us to recast the setting of overload as a normal part of living rather than as a disease or something extraordinary.

Present activity is not a sharp narrow knife-blade in time. The present is complex, containing within itself a multitude of habits and impulses. It is enduring, a course of action, a process including memory, observation and foresight, a pressure forward, a glance backward, and a look outward. It is of moral moment because it marks a transition in the direction of breadth and clarity of action or in that of triviality and confusion. Progress is present reconstruction adding fullness and distinctness of meaning, and retrogression is a present slipping away of significance, determinations, grasp. (Dewey 1922: 281)

When individuals increase present meaning, they multiply sensed directions and they complicate and extend the significance they find within their experience. Dewey expresses this in the form of a categorical imperative: "So act as to increase the meaning of present experience" (p. 283). Thus, complexity and perplexity increase hand in hand with an increase in significance and meaning. What discussions of overload often miss is that apparent setbacks are actually complications, extensions, and growth in complexity resulting from new interpretations. Thus, no matter how much any moment reflects sense and meaning, that same moment of accomplishment is also a moment of complication (p. 285). In Dewey's (1922) words, each achievement

creates a new distribution of energies which then has to be employed in ways for which past experience gives no exact instruction. Every important satisfaction of an old want creates a new one; and this new want has to enter upon an experimental adventure if it is to find its satisfaction. From the side of what has gone before achievement settles something. From the side of what comes after, it complicates, introducing new problems, unsettling factors. There is something pitifully juvenile in the idea that "evolution," progress, means a definite sum of accomplishment which will forever stay done, and which by an exact amount lessens the amount still to be done, disposing once and for all of just so many perplexities and advancing us just so far on our road to a final stable and unperplexed goal. (p. 285)

To make progress is also to increase the intricacy of the problems an entity must deal with and the amount of instability it must face in subsequent situations. Said differently, whenever wants, tools, and possibilities are multiplied this increases: "the variety of forces which enter into relations with one another and which have to be intelligently directed" (p. 286). Such increases are what some have labeled overload.

This emerging complication creates a crucial moment of interpretation. Dewey observed:

The facts are not the kind that yield unthinking optimism and consolation because new struggles and failures are inevitable. The total scene of action remains somewhat as it did before except that is has become more complex and more subtly unstable. But this very situation of greater complexity and instability is the result of the expansion of power, not its contraction, and the expansion comes from the success, not the failure, of power. When this is grasped and admitted it becomes a challenge to intelligence. Instruction in what to do next can never come from an infinite goal, which for us is bound to be empty. It can be derived only from study of the deficiencies, irregularities and possibilities of the actual situation. (Dewey 1922: 288–9)

Complication and instability are hallmarks of human activity, sensemaking, and meaning. Another way to label these same complications is as excess load. But to settle for this label is to miss their significance for learning. Information overload "is a transitory sensation that is experienced by individuals developing schemas that will allow them to upgrade their performance in job-related tasks" (Kock 2000: 261).

OVERLOAD THROUGH
A SENSEMAKING LENS

When people act in the world portrayed by Dewey, their circumstance may be one of projects, action in context, or concerns that shift as their needs shift. Heidegger (1962) refers to this "absorbed coping" as a *ready-to-hand* mode of engagement. When people act in this engaged mode, they are aware of the world holistically as a network of interrelated projects rather than as an arrangement of separate physical objects such as tools. It is this holistic awareness that forestalls overload. If one of those projects is interrupted, then people shift to an *unready-to-hand* mode of experience. Even though problematic aspects of the interruption stand out, people still do not become aware of context-free objects nor do they report feelings of overload. Instead, they and the objects they work with remain situated but they treat them as temporarily unusable. As Heidegger puts it:

The modes of conspicuousness, obtrusiveness, and obstinacy all have the function of bringing to the fore the characteristics of presence-at-hand in what is ready-to-hand. But the ready-to-hand is not thereby just *observed* [italics in original] and stared at. Such equipment still does not veil itself in the guise of mere Things. It becomes "equipment" in the sense of something which one would like to shove out of the way... *[W]hen an assignment has been disturbed* [italics in original]—when something is unusable for some purpose—then the assignment becomes explicit[4]... The context of equipment is lit up,[5] not as something never seen before, but as a totality constantly sighted beforehand in circumspection. (Heidegger 1962: 103–5)

It is only when people step back from the interrupted project into a *present-at-hand* mode that they engage in reflection using analyses that are general, abstract, and context-free. In a present-at-hand mode, tools, artifacts, and objects appear as independent entities, removed from tasks, endowed with distinct measurable properties of mass and weight, and manipulated by distinct subjects. Most important, it is not until people step back and separate themselves from the world, that sensations of overload are experienced. Detached inspection creates more overload than does immersion in ongoing activity. Thus, overload is a present-at-hand moment, not a ready-to-hand moment or an unready-to-hand moment. Overload is partly an act of reflecting on an interrupted, detached moment of thrownness rather than an immersion in and acceptance of thrownness. To disassemble a flow into separate objects creates more things to notice, more detached observing, more data points, less clustering, and more likelihood of overload.

When people step back either partially (unready-to-hand) or fully (present-at-hand), they try to make sense. What they face is something like William James's description: "The world is a buzzing, pulsating, formless mass of signals, out of which people try to make sense, into which they attempt to introduce order, and from which they construct against a background that remains undifferentiated" (cited in Patriotta 2003). What James describes as a "formless mass of signals" is true more for present-at-hand moments than for unready-to-hand moments, and more for novices than for experts. This is the core of the argument that interpretation plays a more significant role in overload than has been acknowledged.

When people introduce "order," there is no guarantee that it will persist. Typically, order is transient and people must recreate it repeatedly. These transitions are occasions of overload. As an example of the close ties between sensemaking and overload, consider Schulman and colleagues' (Schulman et al. 2004) finding that electricity dispatchers often reset the criteria of adequate performance in order to preserve a sensible task. "Reliability becomes that bar that the operators can actually jump" (p. 22). Operators redefine the standards (e.g., "Who said we had to recover in 10 minutes, why 10, why not 15 minutes?", p. 22). People in the control room "adapt reliability criteria to meet circumstances that they can actually manage, where those circumstances are increasingly real time in their urgency" (p. 21). Although these adjustments may sacrifice efficiency, they improve comprehension. A network with fixed performance criteria run by confused dispatchers is replaced by a network with malleable criteria run by knowledgeable dispatchers.

Notice also that sensemaking facilitates action and the resumption of ready-to-hand functioning (see Weick et al. 2005). A direction for the next period that takes the form of a temporary synthesis, pattern, or plausible story reduces excess load and enables people to keep going. Sensemaking that is focused on interpretation and meaning mitigates overload whereas computation and choice associated with decision making often amplify overload. As an expert wildland fire crew chief said: "A decision is something you polish" (Weick 2002: S9), polishing eats up time, investments of time build pressures to justify the time expenditure, and justification makes it harder to drop the decision or revise it and harder to handle information that could undo it.

Sensemaking skills are a means to manage excess load. Part of the reason the load is excessive is because it seems inexplicable, irrelevant. If context makes it more relevant, then the overload is lowered. Making something more relevant is primarily an issue of context in the sense that: "the meaning of a particular piece of data depends on what else is going on, what else could be going on, what has gone on, and [what] the observer expects or intends to happen" (Woods et al. 2002: 27). The same datum can change meaning as context changes, which means that it is fruitless to mount a search for the "important stuff." Meaning is sensitive to some but not all details of the current situation. For example, alarm codes in control rooms mean different things depending on what else is occurring (Woods et al. 2002: 27). Depending on the context, an alarm may be unimportant, unimportant even if it goes off repeatedly, needs immediate attention, or needs immediate attention but only if other alarms are going off repeatedly, etc.

The contexts for sensemaking often resemble what Heidegger has described as "the prereflective experience of being thrown into a situation of acting without the opportunity or need to disengage and function as detached observers" (Winograd and Flores 1986: 97). As an example, Rhona Flin (1996: 105) argues that the challenge for the incident commander at an unfolding disaster is to continually make sense of an unexpected and dynamic situation that is characterized by unfamiliarity, scale, and speed of escalation. Incident commanders have to deal with: (1) extremely difficult decisions; (2) ambiguous and conflicting information; (3) shifting goals; (4) time pressure; (5) dynamic conditions; (6) complex operational team structures; (7) poor communication; and (8) courses of action that all carry significant risks (Flin 1996: 37). These same eight characteristics, albeit scaled down, show up in less disastrous situations of thrownness. Thrownness is one way to describe situations where people are engaged and subject to moments of overload.

EXPERTISE AS AN ANTIDOTE
TO OVERLOAD

The effects of thrownness on sensemaking and overload depend on the expertise of the individuals and system that are thrown into disordered situations. Consider the case of variations in expertise among nurses.

Advanced beginners [in nursing] seldom have sufficient experience to manage rapidly changing critical care situations smoothly. Consequently, in situations that call for rapidly changing priorities for patient's management, they miss cues and continue care in a relatively unchanging and rule-governed way... Without an experientially learned sense of salience, the care of critically ill patients can become a flat landscape of anxiety-producing tasks to be accomplished. Advanced beginners speak of 'prioritizing' their actions, but the basis for their judgments about what to do first seems most driven by what they know how to do (physical care procedures) and by what, in their limited experience, seems most important. (Benner et al. 1996: 63–4)

Notice this description references issues of significance, attention, and expertise. This brings us back to the idea that significance is at the heart of the information overload problem, particularly "when it is not known a priori what data from a large data field will be informative" (Woods et al. 2002: 25). Significance and expertise go hand in hand which suggests that overload is predominantly a phenomenon of novices and advanced beginners, less so those whose functioning is competent, and least so for those whose functioning is proficient and expert. It also raises the possibility that overload can become an issue for anyone, including experts, if under pressures for regression to less expert stages of functioning. Just such regression is a strong possibility in the Madrid case discussed at the beginning of this chapter.

RECONCEPTUALIZING OVERLOAD

Adding the variable of differences in expertise to the rethinking done so far brings together various concepts. The work of Dreyfus and Dreyfus (1986) and others (e.g., Ericsson et al. 2006) who explore the nature of expertise facilitates much of this convergence. Dreyfus and Dreyfus (1986) propose that skilled performance passes through five levels of proficiency (i.e., novice, advanced beginner, competent, proficient, and expert). The move from novice to expert reflects changes particularly in three aspects (see Benner 1984: 13–14): The first is a move from relying on abstract principles (rule-based behavior) to using past concrete experience as paradigms; the second is a change in the perception of the demand situation such that the situation is seen less as a compilation of bits and more as a complete whole with certain relevant parts; the third is a move from being an observer outside the situation to being an involved performer engaged in the situation. Classifying gradations in the expertise of individuals and systems enables prediction of the duration and intensity of overload (see Box 3.1 for representative descriptions of each stage that have been selected for their relevance to issues of overload).

Several propositions follow from this line of thinking. First, the progression from novice to expert suggests a progression from more time in a present-at-hand mode to less time in this mode and a growth of meaning and significance in what people observe and respond to. Second, as people progress from novice to expert they experience longer periods of ready-to-hand functioning that are subject to fewer interruptions and unready-to-hand moments. Third, overload is predominantly a phenomenon of present-at-hand functioning and limited response repertoires.

Overload is an interpretation that people make in response to breakdowns, the interruption of ongoing projects, or an imbalance between demand and capability. For example, in the nursing scenario noted earlier: "anxiety is generated when . . . patients' changing needs and concerns are experienced as an interruption in the flow of the nurse's care, rather than the focus of that care" (Benner et al. 1996: 62). A novice nurse interprets procedures as the salient project and the interruption of that project by changes in patient needs, as the threat. The shift from procedures as the project to caring for patient needs directly relates to experience, repertoire, and stage of expertise.

The ability to remain focused on the project that was interrupted influences the content of interpretations in the face of breakdowns. Other influences include: the ability to make sense of the interruption without detaching from and dissecting the event, familiarity with related events, and capability to discriminate among similarities and differences between the current event and previous related events, and capabilities for recovery from the interruption.

Box 3.1. Descriptions of Five Stages of Expertise

Novice: "The instruction process [in skill acquisition] begins with the instructor de-composing the task environment into context-free features which the beginner can recognize without benefit of experience, The beginner is then given rules for determin-ing actions on the basis of these features, like a computer following a program. Through instruction, the novice acquires rules for drawing conclusion or for determining actions, based upon facts and features of the situation that are recognizable without experience in the skill domain being learned" (p. 37).

Advanced beginner: "Performance improves to a marginally acceptable level only after the novice has considerable experience coping with real situations. While this encourages the advanced beginner to consider more objective facts and to use more sophisticated rules, it also teaches the learner an enlarged conception of what is relevant to the skill ... With the addition of many new elements now known by the learner to be relevant to the skill, the task appears to become more difficult, and the advanced beginner often feels overwhelmed by the complexity of the skill and exhausted by the effort required to notice all relevant elements and to remember an increasing number of more and more complicated rules" (p. 38).

Competence: "With more experience, the number of potentially relevant elements of a real-world situation that the learner is able to recognize becomes overwhelming. At this point, since a sense of what is important in any particular situation is missing, perform-ance becomes nerve-wracking and exhausting ... To cope with this problem and to achieve competence, people learn through instruction or experience to adopt a hier-archical perspective. First they must devise a plan, or choose a perspective, which then determines which elements of the situation are to be treated as important and which ones can be ignored. By restricting themselves to only a few of the vast number of possibly relevant facts and features, decision making becomes easier ... The problem is that there are a vast number of different situations that the learner may encounter, many differing from each other in subtle, nuanced ways, and in each a plan or perspective must be determined. There are, in fact, more situations than can be named or precisely defined, so no one can prepare for the learner a list of what to do in each possible situation. Thus, competent performers have to decide for themselves what plan to choose without being sure that it will be appropriate in the particular situation. Now coping becomes frightening rather than exhausting, and the learner feels great responsibility for his or her actions" (p. 39).

Proficient: As the "performer acquires the ability to discriminate between a variety of situations entered into with concern and involvement, plans are intuitively evoked and certain aspects stand out as important without the learner standing back and choosing those places or deciding to adopt that perspective. Action becomes easier and less stressful as the learner simply sees what needs to be achieved rather than deciding, by a calculative procedure, which of several possible alternatives should be selected. There is less doubt that what one is trying to accomplish is appropriate when the goal is simply obvious rather than the winner of a complex competition. In fact, at the moment of involved intuitive response there can be no doubt, since doubt comes only with detached evaluation of performance ... The proficient performer simply has not had enough experience with the wide variety of possible action in each of the situations he or she can now discriminate to have rendered the best response automatic. For this reason, the proficient performer, seeing the goal and the important features of the situation, still must *decide* what to do. To do this, he or she falls back on detached, rule-based determination of actions" (p. 41).

Expert: "The expert not only knows what needs to be achieved, based on mature and practiced situational discrimination, but also knows how to achieve the goal. A more subtle and refined discrimination ability is what distinguishes the expert from the proficient performer. This ability allows the expert to discriminate among situations all seen as similar with respect to the plan or perspective, distinguishing those situations requiring one action from those demanding another... [T]he expert not only sees what needs to be achieved, but also how to achieve it. When things are proceeding normally, experts don't solve problems and don't make decisions, they simply do what experience has shown normally work, and it normally works" (p. 42).

Source: Excerpts are from Benner et al. 1996.

When ongoing projects are interrupted by an imbalance between demand and capability there are four increasingly effortful ways to handle it (see Schulman et al. 2004: 19–21). Individuals rebalance demands and capabilities initially by activating responses that they have developed previously "just in case" an imbalance occurs. If the imbalance persists, they activate responses "just in time" to handle instabilities (e.g., queue). If instabilities still persist despite just-in-time adjustments, then they make more extreme adjustments "just for now" (e.g., they filter demands according to a priority scheme). And if those just-for-now adjustments fail, then the last resort is to activate an extreme response that is executed "just this way" (e.g., they change criteria for what constitutes an acceptable performance). The smaller the response repertoire, the faster a system will move through this sequence to "just this way" functioning. Novices will move through this sequence faster than advanced beginners who will move through faster than competent performers who will move through faster than proficient performers who will move through faster than expert performers.

Interruption can produce either an unready-to-hand or a present-at-hand mode of engagement. The perception of overload is greater in the present-at-hand mode than in the unready-to-hand mode. Higher levels of overload occur in present-at-hand engagement because individuals must attend to more separate elements, know fewer patterns to connect the elements, and, as a consequence, feel more pressure to rely on what they already know. There are limits to what novices and advanced beginners know, which means they miss or intentionally ignore more clues. Missed clues mean that subsequent action may make things worse and lead to more frequent and more intense subsequent breakdowns. By contrast lower levels of overload occur in unready-to-hand engagement, because experts preserve the context of the interrupted project. And this preservation provides a meaningful frame for what they then notice. Noticing occurs in the service of resumption, recovery, and resilience. And the size and content of the response repertoire determines noticing.

The larger and more heterogeneous the response repertoire, the more that a person, a team, or an organization can afford to see (Sutcliffe and Vogus 2003). And the more one sees, the more ways one can see to recover from an interrupted project. And the more options for recovery the lower the likelihood that one will detach in a present-at-hand mode and experience more unconnected elements and more overload. Stated differently, the larger the repertoire, the lower the likelihood that unready-to-hand will be converted into present-at-hand, and the higher the likelihood that unready-to-hand will be converted into ready-to-hand.

The more limited the response repertoire, the greater the likelihood that decision makers will treat interruptions as present-at-hand rather than unready-to-hand. In the case of a limited response repertoire, there are fewer ways to recover from an interruption that preserve the project (i.e., less likelihood of converting unready-to-hand to ready-to-hand), hence, decision makers are more likely to disassemble the project in the interest of a detached analysis to determine what caused the interruption. Disassembling and detached analysis (present-at-hand) create separate parts, and separate parts without connections or context place greater demands on attention and therefore induce greater load. Thus, a present-at-hand mode of engagement creates more imbalance than does an unready-to-hand mode of engagement.

As experience develops people are able to stay in ready-to-hand and unready-to-hand modes of engagement for longer periods of time and over a greater variety of conditions. Consequently, they spend less time in present-at-hand modes of engagement, which means that they experience fewer occasions of overload. It may not be simply amount of experience that matters since generalists may be in better positions to moderate overload than are specialists. Generalists tend to have larger and more varied response repertoires (Bunderson and Sutcliffe 2002) that enable them to stay in a ready-to-hand mode for longer periods of time, to bounce back more quickly from an unready-to-hand interruption, and to be less overloaded when they experience a present-at-hand mode.

IMPLICATIONS AND CONCLUSION

Although this volume is devoted to the topic of organizational decision making, our treatment of overload seldom mentions decision making. There are two reasons for that omission. First, we take seriously the observation that: "To 'decide' presupposes previous consideration of a matter causing doubt, wavering, debate, or controversy and implies the arriving at a more or less logical conclusion that brings doubt or debate to an end" (*Webster's New Dictionary of Synonyms*

1984: 215). Overload, treated as an issue of interpretation rather than computation, has its effects on "previous consideration of matters causing doubt" and therefore affects what is bracketed as being in need of deciding and what resources are available for the deciding and its aftermath. Second, overload is about action, interpretation, and sensemaking. And, as we have mentioned elsewhere (Weick et al. 2005: 409), when action is the central focus, interpretation, not choice, is the core phenomenon. Scott Snook (2001) made a similar point in his analysis of a friendly fire tragedy. Reflecting on his research, Snook says:

I could have asked, "why did they *decide* to shoot?" However, such a framing puts us squarely on a path that leads straight back to the individual decision maker, away from potentially powerful contextual features and right back into the jaws of the fundamental attribution error. "Why did they decide to shoot?" quickly becomes "Why did they make the *wrong* decision?" Hence, the attribution falls squarely onto the shoulders of the decision maker and away from potent situation factors that influence action. Framing the individual-level puzzle as a question of meaning rather than deciding shifts the emphasis away from individual decision makers toward a point somewhere "out there" where context and individual action overlap.... Such a reframing—from decision making to sensemaking—opened *my* eyes to the possibility that, given the circumstances, even *I* could have made the same "dumb mistake." This disturbing revelation, one that I was in no way looking for, underscores the importance of initially framing such senseless tragedies as "good people struggling to make sense," rather than as "bad ones making poor decisions". (pp. 206–7)

Previous literature reviews make it clear that there is scant empirical work on which to build an inductive picture of overload. To encourage more empirical work, we have come at the problem of overload from a perspective other than the prevailing perspective of information processing. By mixing the complexities of everyday activity, the situation of thrownness, sensemaking of interruptions, and levels of expertise, we position overload as transitory, commonplace, embedded, influenced by experience, and driven by diverse interpretations of demand–capability imbalances. The research questions that flow from such an analysis mainly fall into the domain of learning. Overload links to learning in two different ways. First, overload is high at the novice and advanced beginner stage of learning since present-at-hand and unready-to-hand modes of engagement prevail at these stages. Second, the activity of learning itself, whatever the stage of expertise, initially involves novice-like moments when elements prevail and when a "big picture" is difficult to achieve. This suggests that a learning organization is an overloaded organization. It also suggests that a learning orientation is an invitation to overload (Bunderson and Sutcliffe 2002, 2003).

The proposed conceptualization of overload also has implications for practice. For example, decision makers will want to develop capabilities that enable people to move out of an unready-to-hand moment swiftly and to resume action. Important capabilities that further this movement are resilience, intuition, and improvization (Weick and Sutcliffe 2001). Furthermore, decision makers may want to encourage sensemaking that focuses on plausibility rather than accuracy (Weick et al. 2005). The pursuit of accuracy may increase overload to debilitating levels. Plausibility preserves the framework provided by the ongoing project and holds the performer in a state of unready-to-hand engagement, whereas the pursuit of accuracy tends to generate a present-at-hand way of operating, which may fracture the project, increase the difficulty of subsequent sensemaking, and make it harder to reassemble a coherent big picture.

In many ways our analysis boils down to the conclusion, overload just is. People interact, do what is ready to hand, bracket portions of flowing events, get interrupted by what they bracket and by their efforts to learn, sometimes detach from the flow to take a closer look, but always keep going. Moments of overload arise from the way in which people handle fluctuating demands with fluctuating resources. This is not to trivialize the topic of overload. Far from it. Instead, it is an effort to reposition overload in the context of everyday practice. Thus, we want to animate Herbert Simon's four present participles—listening, storing, thinking, and speaking—by contextualizing them amid ongoing thrownness, sensemaking, complicating, recovering, and learning. It is only by adding in these parameters of interpretation that we can assure a system that listens and thinks more than it speaks.

ENDNOTES

1 The USNCB (United States National Central Bureau) for INTERPOL (international police organization) is an office under the control and direction of the Departments of Justice and Homeland Security. The US authority for INTERPOL functions rests by law with the US Attorney General. The USNCB serves as a point of contact for both American and foreign police seeking assistance in criminal investigations that extend beyond their national boundaries. Known within the international community as INTERPOL Washington, the USNCB brings together US police at all levels, providing a neutral territory where jurisdictions and mandates are interwoven to permit cooperation and assistance to the fullest extent possible.

2 Other labels for overload include cognitive overload, sensory overload, communication overload, knowledge overload, data smog, information fatigue, overkill, overabundance, breakdown, explosion, deluge (see Eppler and Mengis 2004: 329). The claim that overload is both a recent and growing phenomenon (see Kock 2000) belies its prominence in the literature for at least a century. For example, the information glut in the 1880s led manufacturers to advertise a particular desk as a solution for filing books and papers (Noyes and Thomas 1995; Edmunds and Norris 2000). In the 1920s, H. G. Wells pondered over how to organize the large mass of knowledge that was being collected by civilized man (Wells 1921, 1933).

3 The amount of data to be processed per unit of time is generally conceived of as the information load accompanying the work.

4 John Dewey (1922: 178–9) makes a similar point: "In every waking moment, the complete balance of the organism and its environment is constantly interfered with and as constantly restored... *Life is interruptions and recoveries*... At these moments of a shifting in activity, *conscious feeling and thought arise and are accentuated*."

5 See also David Woods et al.'s (2002) use of spotlight as a positive selectivity in dealing with overload.

References

BARTHOL, R. P. and KU, N. D. (1959). 'Regression Under Stress to First Learned Behavior.' *Journal of Abnormal Psychology*, 59: 134–6.

BENNER, P. (1984). *From Novice to Expert: Excellence and Power in Clinical Nursing Practice*. Upper Saddle River, NJ: Prentice Hall.

—— TANNER, C. A., and CHESLA, C. A. (1996). *Expertise in Nursing Practice: Caring, Clinical Judgment, and Ethics*. New York: Springer.

BUNDERSON, J. S. and SUTCLIFFE, K. M. (2002a). 'Comparing Alternative Conceptualizations of Functional Diversity in Management Teams: Process and Performance Effects.' *Academy of Management Journal*, 45/5: 875–93.

—— —— (2002b). 'Why Some Teams Emphasize Learning More than Others: Evidence from Business Unit Management Teams', in M. Neal, E. Mannix, and H. Sondak (eds.), *Research on Managing Groups and Teams*. New York: Elsevier Science Ltd., 49–84.

—— —— (2003). 'Management Team Learning Orientation and Business Unit Performance.' *Journal of Applied Psychology*, 88/3: 552–60.

CHAJUT, E. and ALGOM, D. (2003). 'Selective Attention Improves Under Stress: Implications for Theories of Social Cognition.' *Journal of Personality and Social Psychology*, 85: 231–48.

DAFT, R. L. and WEICK, K. E. (1984). 'Toward a Model of Organizations as Interpretation Systems.' *Academy of Management Review*, 9/2: 284–95.

DEWEY, J. (1922/2002). *Human Nature and Conduct*. Mineola, NY: Dover.

DREYFUS, H. L. and DREYFUS, S. E. (1986). *Mind Over Machine*. New York: Free Press.

EDMUNDS, A., and MORRIS, A. (2000). 'The Problem of Information Overload in Business Organizations: A Review of the Literature.' *International Journal of Information Management*, 20: 17–28.

EPPLER, M. J. and MENGIS, J. (2004). 'The Concept of Information Overload: A Review of Literature from Organization Science, Accounting, Marketing, MIS, and Related Disciplines.' *The Information Society*, 20: 325–44.

ERICSSON, K. A., CHARNESS, N., FELTOVICH, P. J., and HOFFMAN, R. R. (2006). *The Cambridge Handbook of Expertise and Expert Performance*. New York: Cambridge University Press.

FELDMAN, M. S., and MARCH, J. G. (1981). 'Information as Signal and Symbol.' *Administrative Science Quarterly*, 26: 171–86.

FLIN, R. H. (1996). *Sitting in the Hot Seat: Leaders and Teams for Critical Incident Management*. New York: Wiley.

GABA, D. M., HOWARD, S. K., and JUMP, B. (1994). 'Production Pressure in the Work Environment.' *Anesthesiology*, 81: 488–500.

GALBRAITH, J. R. (1974). 'Organization Design: An Information Processing View.' *Interfaces*, 3: 28–36.

HAHN, M., LAWSON, R., and LEE, Y. G. (1992). 'The Effects of Time Pressure and Information Load on Decision Quality.' *Psychology and Marketing*, 9/5: 365–78.

HEATH, D. (2004). 'FBI's Handling of Fingerprint Case Criticized.' *Seattle Times*. June 1, online version.

HEIDEGGER, M. (1962). *Being and Time*. New York: Harper and Row.

HODGKINSON, G. P. and SPARROW, P. R. (2002). *The Competent Organization: A Psychological Analysis of the Strategic Management Process*. Philadelphia, PA: Open University Press.

JETT, Q. R. and GEORGE, J. M. (2003). 'Work Interrupted: A Closer Look at the Role of Interruptions in Organizational Life.' *Academy of Management Review*, 28: 494–507.

KOCK, N. (2000). 'Information Overload and Worker Performance: A Process-Centered View.' *Knowledge and Process Management*, 4: 256–64.

LANT, T. K. (2002). 'Organizational Cognition and Interpretation,' in J. A. C. Baum (ed.), *The Blackwell Companion to Organizations*. Oxford, UK: Blackwell, 344–62.

—— SHAPIRA, Z. (2001a). 'Introduction: Foundations of Research on Cognition in Organizations,' in T. K. Lant and Z. Shapira (eds.), *Organizational Cognition: Computation and Interpretation*. Mahwah, NJ: Lawrence Erlbaum Associates, Inc., 1–12.

—— —— (2001b). 'New Research Directions on Organizational Cognition,' in T. K. Lant and Z. Shapira (eds.), *Organizational Cognition: Computation and Interpretation*. Mahwah, NJ: Lawrence Erlbaum Associates, Inc., 367–76.

LIPOWSKI, Z. J. (1975). 'Sensory and Information Inputs Overload: Behavioral Effects.' *Comprehensive Psychiatry*, 16/3: 199–221.

LORD, R. G. and FOTI, R. J. (1986). 'Schema Theories: Information Processing and Organizational Behavior,' in H. P. Sims and D. A. Gioia (eds.), *The Thinking Organization*. San Francisco, CA: Jossey-Bass, 20–48.

MILLER, J. G. (1960). 'Information Input Overload and Psychopathology.' *American Journal of Psychiatry*, 116: 695–704.

O'REILLY, C. A. (1980). 'Individuals and Information Overload in Organizations: Is More Necessarily Better?' *Academy of Management Journal*, 23: 684–96.

PATRIOTTA, G. (2003). 'Sensemaking on the Shop Floor: Narratives of Knowledge in Organizations.' *Journal of Management Studies*. 40/2: 349–76.

PERLOW, L. A. (1999). 'A Time Famine: Toward a Sociology of Work Time.' *Administrative Science Quarterly*, 44: 57–81.

SCHNEIDER, S. C. (1987). 'Information Overload: Causes and Consequences.' *Human Systems Management*, 7: 143–53.

SCHICK, A. G., GORDON, L. A., and HAKA, S. (1990). 'Information Overload: A Temporal Approach.' *Accounting, Organizations and Society*, 15: 199–220.

SCHULMAN, P., ROE, E., van EETEN, M., and DE BRUIJNE, M. (2004). 'High Reliability and the Management of Critical Infrastructures.' *Journal of Contingencies and Crisis Management*, 12/1: 14–28.

SIMON, H. (1971). 'Designing Organizations for an Information-Rich World,' in M. Greenberger (ed.), *Computers, Communications and the Public Interest*. Baltimore, MD: Johns Hopkins Press, 37–72.

SIMON, H. A. (1973). 'Applying Information Technology to Organization Design.' *Public Administration Review*, 33/3: 268–78.

SPARROW, P. R. (1999). 'Strategy and Cognition: Understanding the Role of Management Knowledge Structures, Organizational Memory, and Information Overload.' *Creativity and Innovation Management*, 8: 140–8.

SPEIER, C., VALACICH, J. S., and VESSEY, I. (1999). 'The Influence of Task Interruption on Individual Decision Making: An Information Overload Perspective.' *Decision Sciences*, 30: 337–59.

STACEY, R. B. (2004). 'A Report on the Erroneous Fingerprint Individualization in the Madrid Train Bombing Case.' *Journal of Forensic Identification*, 54/6: 706–18.

—— (2005). *Personal Communication*, Washington, DC.

SUTCLIFFE, K. M. and VOGUS, T. (2003). 'Organizing for Resilience,' in K. S. Cameron, J. E. Dutton, and R. E. Quinn (eds.), *Positive Organizational Scholarship*. San Francisco, CA: Berrett-Koehler, 94–110.

THOMPSON, J. D. (1967). *Organizations in Action*. New York: McGraw-Hill.

TSOUKAS, H. and CHIA, R. (2002). 'On Organizational Becoming: Rethinking Organizational Change.' *Organization Science*, 13/5: 567–82.

TUSHMAN, M. L. and NADLER, D. A. (1978). 'Information Processing as an Integrating Concept in Organization Design.' *Academy of Management Review*, July: 613–24.

WEICK, K. E. (1970). 'The Twigging of Overload,' in H. B. Pepinsky (ed.), *People and Information*. New York: Pergamon Press, 67–131.

—— (2002). 'Puzzles in Organization Learning: An Exercise in Disciplined Imagination.' *British Journal of Management*, 13(Special Issue): S7–S17.

—— (2004). 'Designing for Thrownness,' in R. J. Boland, and F. Collopy (eds.), *Managing as Designing*. Palo Alto, CA: Stanford University Press, 74–8.

—— SUTCLIFFE, K. M. (2001). *Managing the Unexpected: Assuring High Performance in and Age of Complexity*. San Francisco, CA: Jossey-Bass.

—— —— OBSTFELD, D. (1999). 'Organizing for High Reliability: Processes of Collective Mindfulness,' in R. Sutton and B. Staw (eds.), *Research in Organizational Behavior*. Greenwich, CT: JAI, 81–124.

—— —— —— (2005). 'Organizing and the Process of Sensemaking.' *Organization Science*, 16: 409–21.

WELLS, H. G. (1921). *The Salvaging of Civilization*. New York: Macmillan, 141–66.

—— (1933). *The Shape of Things to Come*. New York: Macmillan, 420.

WINOGRAD, T. and FLORES, F. (1986). *Understanding Computers and Cognition*. Norwood, NJ: Ablex.

WOODS, D. D., PATTERSON, E. S., and ROTH, E. M. (2002). 'Can We Ever Escape from Data Overload? A Cognitive Systems Diagnosis.' *Cognition, Technology and Work*, 4: 22–36.

WRIGHT, P. (1974). 'The Harassed Decision Maker: Time Pressures, Distractions, and the Use of Evidence.' *Journal of Applied Psychology*, 59/5: 555–61.

4

DECISION MAKING WITH INACCURATE, UNRELIABLE DATA*

JOHN M. MEZIAS

WILLIAM H. STARBUCK

INTRODUCTION

IN 1996, Royal Dutch Shell (RDS) negotiated control of Russia's Sakhalin Island oil and natural gas development project, which is the world's largest integrated oil and gas project (*Fortune* 2007). At that time, observers lauded this agreement as a major achievement that would provide RDS with control of strategic reserves far into the future. However, a series of poor decisions over the next decade cost RDS billions of dollars and control over this critical asset. Early on, RDS infuriated locals by falling behind its commitment to road and school building. Pipeline design flaws caused damaging landslides. Other incidents of mismanagement included an oil spill, routing the pipeline through a protected nature reserve, and illegally dredging the

* This chapter has benefited from suggestions by Philip Bromiley and Gerard Hodgkinson.

bay during salmon spawning. In August 2006, Russia's Ministry of Natural Resources announced a lawsuit against RDS for billions of dollars to hold it accountable for these disasters at Sakhalin Island. Although some accused the Ministry of "shaking down" RDS as part of a Russian strategy to wrest natural resource control from foreign firms, most analysts and environmental groups believed RDS's mismanagement warranted the lawsuit (Lustgarten 2007). RDS's missteps in this project were not limited to community relations and environmental affairs, however; RDS had also underestimated costs, which doubled the US$10 billion estimate. In February 2007, RDS sold its controlling interest in the project at a steep loss.

Given this project's magnitude and potential importance, one wonders how RDS's decision making and perceptions could repeatedly have been so error filled. However, this is only one example of executives making poor decisions that lead to huge losses. Indeed, a survey of more than 200 firms across various industries in 30 countries found that more than half of all business projects failed and businesses judged only 2.5 percent of the 10,640 projects to have been fully successful (Price-Waterhouse Coopers 2004). Why do the world's top business firms have such high failure rates? This chapter reviews some evidence that decision makers often rely on inaccurate or unreliable data. The chapter also points out ways decision makers react when they realize their data are inaccurate or unreliable. Lastly, it examines some options for coping more effectively with inaccurate, unreliable data.

THE INACCURACY OF PERCEPTIONS

Business and political journalists generally interview people who participated in decision making. The participants explain their goals, situations faced, and the logic behind their decisions. Likewise, research about decision making and sensemaking usually assumes managers are aware of and understand their organizations and their organizations' environments. Some studies obtain almost all of their data about decision inputs and premises from the decision makers. Other studies correlate data about firms' actions with managers' perceptions of their organizations or business environments. However, almost no research has examined the accuracy of such perceptions (Starbuck and Mezias 1996).

Perception errors result from both noticing and sensemaking (Schwenk 1984; Salgado et al. 2002). Noticing errors is more likely when stimuli are unfamiliar, changing slowly, or buried amid voluminous data, and stimuli foster erroneous sensemaking when data are inaccessible, changing very rapidly, or distorted by subordinates (Starbuck and Milliken 1988a, b; Wagner and Gooding 1997). Perceivers make noticing errors because they tend to see data that confirm prior beliefs, because they become too involved in courses of action to observe stimuli accurately, because their cultures blind them to some stimuli, or because they do not perceive stimuli to be relevant to their jobs (Singer and Benassi 1981). Behavioral decision theorists have remarked various heuristics that distort human perceptions. Perceivers make sensemaking errors because of their biases, vested interests, hierarchical positions, illusions of expertise, social environments, or strong needs to believe they made correct decisions (Bazerman 1997; Ragins et al. 1998).

A few studies during the 1970s compared perceptual data with supposedly "objective" data, and these studies found large errors and biases in managers' perceptions, both of their organizations and their organizations' environments. One series of such studies began in the 1960s, when Lawrence and Lorsch inferred that organizations with properties matching their market environments earn higher profits than do firms with properties inconsistent with their market environments. Lawrence and Lorsch (1967) got their data about organizational properties and environmental properties by interviewing managers, and the key variable they discussed was an abstract concept they called "environmental uncertainty." Their study stimulated two later studies that attempted to use questionnaires to measure managers' perceptions of environmental uncertainty (Tosi et al. 1973; Downey et al. 1975). Both studies compared top managers' perceptions of their firms' markets with "objective" financial reports and industry statistics, and both studies found correlations between subjective and "objective" measures that were near zero and were as likely to be negative as positive.

Around that same time, Grinyer and Norburn (1975) examined relations between profitability and explicit strategic planning activities. They found a low correlation between profitability and formal strategic planning as well as inconsistent and meaningless correlations between profitability and consensus among executives about their firms' goals or their personal responsibilities.

Payne and Pugh's (1976) review of more than 100 studies marshaled further evidence about misperceptions of organizational properties. After analyzing subjective and "objective" measures of organizational structures and climates, they drew three conclusions: (1) workers in the same organization disagree so strongly that it makes no sense to talk about average perceptions of their organization, "Perceptual measures of each of the structural and climate variables have varied so much among themselves that mean scores were uninterpretable" (1976: 1168); (2) except for organizational size, workers' perceptions of organizational properties correlate weakly with 'objective' measures of those properties; and (3) differences among workers' perceptions of organizational properties correlate with workers' jobs and hierarchical statuses. For instance, higher status workers view their organizations more favorably.

These early studies showed that perceptual data correlate with each other even though the perceptual data correlate very weakly with "objective" data. Lawrence and Lorsch (1967) observed that managers' perceptions of their organizations mesh logically with their perceptions of their organizations' environments. Payne and Pugh (1976) found that perceptions of different organizational properties fit together logically. Thus, although people make sense of their organizations' properties and organizations' environments, the sense they make corresponds weakly to 'objective' measures. The sense that people make could result from (1) human brains imposing logic on ambiguous stimuli or (2) collective sensemaking among coworkers (Weick 1995).

Mezias and Starbuck (2003) conjectured that these early studies had to be misleading because so many managers could not possibly be succeeding with very erroneous perceptions. Because these studies had not aimed specifically to assess perceptual accuracy, the "objective" measures had been rather ad hoc, and so unreliable measures might have undermined relations between perceptual and "objective" data. Therefore, convinced they would find much smaller perception errors, Mezias and Starbuck made two studies of perceptual accuracy.

Their first study, using data from managers in several companies, revealed one reason why perceptions of organizational properties are so heterogeneous. When researchers tried to operationalize various organizational properties that appear in academic writings, they found that almost all of these concepts are social constructions that exist only in people's minds. When Mezias and Starbuck asked clusters of close colleagues to state their perceptions of these social constructs, the colleagues gave very disparate estimates.

Mezias and Starbuck's first study also found large differences between subjective and "objective" data. In the best case, only 39 percent of managers' perceptions of a given variable were within 50 percent of the "objective" measure. In the worst case, 31 percent of managers' perceptions exceeded 200 percent of the "objective" value. Especially surprising, managers' perceptions of variables related to their areas of expertise were no more accurate than the perceptions of managers who had no expertise in those areas. For instance, managers with sales experience made as inaccurate estimates of sales related variables as did managers without sales experience. Likewise, managers with more work experience made as inaccurate estimates as did their less experienced colleagues. The only strong and prevalent perceptual bias was that managers greatly underestimated the change in their business environments over the previous five years.

In their second study, Mezias and Starbuck observed senior managers' perceptions of quality performance in four divisions of a company in which quality improvement had top priority. The company trained all managers in quality improvement, and each business unit had a quality improvement department. The company was distributing quality measurements to all managers frequently, and managers met frequently to discuss quality performance in their divisions. Yet 49 to 91 percent of managers reported, "I don't know," when asked about current measures of quality performance, and managers who said they did not know the quality measures offered qualitative assessments of quality as often as did the managers who thought they knew the measures. Perceptions incorporated halo effects in that managers offered similar qualitative assessments of quality on different dimensions even though the numeric measures across the different dimensions varied considerably.

Although Mezias and Starbuck's studies asked about different kinds of variables and questioned different kinds of managers, both studies generated similar overall statistics. About three-eighths of managers had fairly accurate perceptions that fell between 50 percent and 150 percent of "objective" measures. About five-eighths of managers had less accurate perceptions; these errors averaged 200 percent and ranged up to 5,000 percent. In both studies, perceptions of specialists had roughly the same accuracy as those of nonspecialists. If managers are making decisions that accord with their perceptions, then most managers are basing decisions on inaccurate perceptions.

Managers do receive distorted, error-filled information. Many studies have noted that organizational reports attempt to mislead their readers. For instance, reports emphasize financial and numerical data, highlight successes and rationalize failures, and give senior executives credit for good results (Hofstede 1967; Altheide and Johnson 1980; Boland 1982; Bettman and Weitz 1983;). However, even accurate information makes inadequate impressions on managers. Specialists receive more information about their areas than do non-specialists, and experienced managers have more opportunities than inexperienced ones to receive information, yet specialists and non-specialists, experienced and inexperienced, exhibit similar perceptual inaccuracies. Moreover, managers receive much more information than they can possibly process. Corporate information systems generate reports whether or not the reports bear on current issues, and reports give data that are easy to collect even if these are irrelevant to the receivers, so managers learn to ignore nearly all reports they receive. Indeed, managers often feel they are drowning in data. An average manager in a Fortune 1000 company is sending and receiving about 180–200 documents a day through various media. According to the Institute for the Future (1997): "Today's corporate staffs are inundated with so many communications tools—fax, electronic mail, teleconferencing, postal mail, interoffice mail, voice mail—that sometimes they don't know where to turn for the simplest tasks."

THE INACCURACY OF PREDICTIONS

People have different perceptions for many reasons and subjective data differ from "objective" data for many reasons (Salgado et al. 2002). However, large as they are, discrepancies between subjective and "objective" data actually understate the unreliability of the data going into decision making. Perceptual data are retrospective because people can only observe what happened. Yet, the entire purpose of decision making is to affect the future so people have to translate their perceptions of past events into predictions about future events. If one thinks of perception errors as creating probability distributions for data that enter into decision making, prediction adds more variance to these distributions.

One indication of how much uncertainty people associate with the future comes from research about the value of information concerning the consequences of decisions. Studies suggest that people lack effective heuristics for deciding how much data to acquire before making a decision (Beach 1966; Phillips et al. 1966). Many people also have difficulty placing values on information they do not have but could obtain. For example, Starbuck and Bass (1967) asked 785 diverse people how much money they would be willing to pay for information from a test market about a potential new product. The answers had extreme dispersion and only 15 percent of people were willing to spend a near-optimum amount.

Retrospection gives inferences too much credibility, partly because history affords a sample of one. Events, even engineered ones, never replicate previous events exactly. Moreover, observers cannot discover exactly what might have happened; they can only speculate about possibilities. When thinking about possible futures, many overestimate likelihoods of more probable events and underestimate likelihoods of more improbable events (Kahneman and Tversky 1973; Lichtenstein et al. 1982), and many overestimate values of seemingly more valuable options and underestimate values of seemingly less valuable options (Weinstein 1980; Massey and Thaler 2006). Furthermore, people normally assume that what did happen had a high probability. As Fischhoff (1980: 83) remarked, people "not only tend to view what has happened as having been inevitable but also to view it as having appeared 'relatively inevitable' before it happened."

Sequences of observations over time form "time series" and statisticians call correlations between successive observations "autocorrelations." Autocorrelations induce errors in retrospective studies, and the great majority of social and economic time series have high autocorrelations. Ames and Reiter (1961) examined 100 series that they picked at random from 3000 series in *Historical Statistics for the United States*. Five-sixths of the series had autocorrelations between successive years that were above 0.80. Autocorrelations generally decline as longer intervals separate correlated values. Ames and Reiter found mean autocorrelations of 0.60 for a three-year interval and 0.45 for a five-year interval. These high autocorrelations allow linear extrapolations of past events to make reasonable forecasts about short-run futures.

People do, however, risk large errors if they base predictions on complex theories (Pant and Starbuck 1990). Autocorrelations often exist because past events influence current events. Such self-dependence amplifies effects of random perturbations by making effects persistent. For example, an earthquake or flood does not merely affect earnings and capital expenditures during the period when it occurs; it continues to have effects for several periods because economic activities in each period influence those in the following period (Wold 1965). Furthermore, whether or not autocorrelation results from self-dependence, autocorrelation produces correlations between series that have nothing whatever to do with causal links between those series (Ames and Reiter 1961). Hence, autocorrelations create the appearance of relationships among variables even though such relationships are absent from the actual causal processes that generated the variables.

Additional variance also comes from future actions of colleagues, competitors, or neighbors. Cohen et al. (1972) argued that decisions result from interactions among streams of problems, potential actions, participants, and choice opportunities. These streams change continuously while decision-making processes are going on. Participants inject their pet problems and propose actions that are unrelated to any visible problems. Some injections occur because different participants have different perceptions, and differences arising from different perceptions influence participants' post-decision actions. After a decision becomes visible externally, competitors and neighbors react and take steps that are difficult to predict. Neighbors may disclose preferences or goals that were not visible earlier. Competitors may try to counteract strategic moves, and they often make responses that surprise their competitors and take advantage of their competitors' weaknesses. In extreme cases, competitive reactions redefine environmental structures in ways that are difficult to anticipate but likely to undermine effectiveness of long-standing policies and strategies (Farjoun and Starbuck 2007).

Yet more variance arises from managers' efforts to manipulate and conceal outcomes. Those who advocated actions seek to portray outcomes as more desirable than "objective" evidence indicates. When they can portray decisions as successful, they trumpet these successes. When others might see decisions as producing failures, managers conceal or obfuscate disappointing outcomes (Nystrom and Starbuck 1984).

Baumard and Starbuck (2005) studied the aftermaths of 14 strategic ventures by a large telecommunications company. Managers in the company nominated these ventures as strategic failures. However, managers saw little evidence that large failures involved faulty decision making. They explained that large failures had idiosyncratic and largely exogenous causes, either unpredictable societal trends or involvement of outsiders. The larger the failure, the more idiosyncratic or exogenous causes they saw. They also said larger failures had occurred in ventures to which the company had weaker commitments and over which it had weaker control. Because large failures developed slowly over long periods, their high social and monetary costs were not immediate. Failures that later appeared large seemed to be only having complications while in process, so large failures were always past events and accountability was always ex post. Managers did attribute some small failures to experiments that deviated from the company's traditional core beliefs. When such interpretations seemed implausible, they described the situations as idiosyncratic or experimental, as if one should expect experiments to fail. Like many large, divisionalized companies, senior managers competed for promotions, resources, and political advantage. Managers can gain individually even if the company loses, or they can lose individually even if the company gains. One result seems to be weak communication. In only eight of the 14 ventures did managers report problems upward before top managers ruled that the ventures had failed. The managers of small ventures did not report problems that might imply ventures had been ill-advised, and managers of large ventures did not report problems that they thought might diminish over time. All the managers who reported problems portrayed these as involving only implementation issues.

How People React to Inaccuracy and Unreliability

Decision makers should be skeptical about data affecting their decisions. Apparent facts surrounding decisions are actually distributions of possible facts, and these distributions have wide variances. Uncertainty due to these distributions obviously makes people very uncomfortable. One major proposition advanced by Cyert and March (1963) was that organizations pursue "uncertainty avoidance." Cyert and March said that organizations avoid having to anticipate accurately by reacting quickly and by negotiating with and controlling their environments. However, few subsequent studies have observed what organizations do to avoid uncertainty. The term "uncertainty avoidance" has survived mainly as a cultural property. Hofstede (1980) used this term when he observed that tolerance for uncertainty and ambiguity seems to be a fundamental difference among societal cultures, and many studies have used Hofstede's concepts to describe national cultures. As well, many studies have used questionnaires to ask managers about their "perceived environmental uncertainty," the concept created by Lawrence and Lorsch. However, "environmental uncertainty" is only a fraction of the uncertainty associated with decision making, and managers' perceptions of uncertainty are subject to at least as much inaccuracy as their other perceptions.

In real-world decisions, prevalent reactions to unreliable data include seeking more data, collapsing probability distributions into certainties, reverting to ideology, acting incrementally, and playing to the audience. Although these reactions can be beneficial or harmful or both, depending on circumstances, some seem more likely to yield benefits and others more likely to be fruitless or dysfunctional.

Seeking More Data

Feldman and March (1981) pointed out that even though organizations gather more information than they use, they also routinely ask for more information. People act as if they can reduce or eliminate uncertainties in data by gathering more data.

However, people tend to seek data that reinforce their current perceptions, and seeing additional data tends to give people more confidence in their expectations and perceptions even when additional data do not make their expectations and perceptions more accurate (Oskamp 1965; Slovic and Corrigan 1973).

Such behavior played an influential role in the decision making preceding the US invasion of Iraq in 2003. Pillar (2006: 20), who was working in the CIA during the pre-invasion decision making, has written:

... the Bush administration repeatedly called on the intelligence community to uncover more material that would contribute to the case for war. The Bush team approached the community again and again and pushed it to look harder at the supposed Saddam-al-Qaeda relationship—calling on analysts not only to turn over additional Iraqi rocks, but also to turn over ones already examined and to scratch the dirt to see if there might be something there after all. The result was an intelligence output that—because the question being investigated was never put in context—obscured rather than enhanced understanding of al-Qaeda's actual sources of strength and support.

In addition to the CIA, the US had several other agencies gathering and analyzing information about Iraq, including the Defense Intelligence Agency, the National Security Agency, and the Department of State. However, these agencies did not always agree with each other and they were reporting alternative interpretations of data and offering equivocal estimates of Iraq's capabilities and intentions. Therefore, Paul Wolfowitz and Donald Rumsfeld created a new intelligence agency within the Department of Defence: the Office of Special Plans (Hersh 2003). This unit used the same data that were available to other agencies, but it also received data from the Iraqi National Congress, an exile group headed by Ahmad Chalabi. One person in this office said, "We were providing information to Wolfowitz that he hadn't seen before." Hersh (2003: 45) reported:

According to the [anonymous] Pentagon adviser, Special Plans was created in order to find evidence of what Wolfowitz and his boss, Defense Secretary Donald Rumsfeld, believed to be true—that Saddam Hussein had close ties to al-Qaeda, and that Iraq had an enormous arsenal of chemical, biological, and possibly even nuclear weapons that threatened the region and, potentially, the United States.

Of course, Chalabi gave them what they had told him they were seeking—false information about Iraq's arsenal.

An obvious corollary of the yearning for more data is vulnerability to manipulation by those who supply the additional data.

Collapsing Probability Distributions into Certainties

People can dispel their discomfort when facing uncertainty in only one way, by attaining certainty. One common way to do this is to ignore contingencies. When people predict the outcome of a sequence of probabilistic events, they assume that actual events at each stage will be the most likely ones (Bar-Hillel 1973; Tversky and Kahneman 1974). Similarly, social science researchers usually transform probability distributions that attend their data analyses into binary statements about statistical significance, and then they discuss their findings as if only statistically significant numbers have substantive importance. Although people tend to exaggerate both high probabilities and low probabilities under diverse conditions, these propensities seem to become more extreme when people are aware that impending decisions are going to be very important.

Again, decision making before the US invasion of Iraq provides an example. Russell (2004) pointed out that intelligence gathering and analyses naturally generate probability distributions of possible interpretations. Russell observed that it was impossible to state conclusively whether Iraq possessed weapons of mass destruction (WMDs) because most "evidence" was subject to error and interpretation. Indeed, one of analysts' interpretations was that Iraq must have WMDs because their behavior implied that they did not have them.

Woodward (2004: 247–9) reported that CIA Director, George Tenet, and his top deputy, John McLaughlin, briefed President Bush and Vice-President Cheney on Iraq's weapons of mass destruction on December 21, 2002. According to Woodward, after McLaughlin presented satellite photographs and intercepted messages, the President opined that the presentation would not "convince Joe Public." The President said that he challenged, "I've been told all this intelligence about having WMD and this is the best we've got?" Woodward said that Tenet then raised his arms and replied, "Don't worry, it's a slam-dunk!" that Iraq had WMDs. During an interview on CBS, Woodward said he "asked the President about this, and he said it was very important to have the CIA director say this, 'Slam-dunk' is, as I interpreted it, a sure thing, guaranteed" (CNN 2004).

Several years later, Tenet (2007) wrote that although he had no doubt at that time that Saddam Hussein had unconventional weapons, Bush had misrepresented the foregoing conversation: "There was never a serious debate that I know of within the administration about the imminence of the Iraqi threat...the administration's message was: Don't blame us. George Tenet and the C.I.A. got us into this mess."

Reverting to Ideology

Although prescriptions assert that beliefs should rest upon evidence, they often do not, especially when facts are scarce or unavailable. Bayes' theorem states that modified beliefs should combine prior beliefs with evidence; prior beliefs create what Tversky and Kahneman (1974) called "anchoring." However, when there is little or unreliable evidence, Bayes' theorem says prior beliefs should remain unmodified, making subjectivity dominant.

In the case of the US invasion of Iraq in 2003, the lack of reliable evidence and disagreement among intelligence agencies allowed President Bush's prior beliefs to dominate his decisions. During an interview on television, Bob Woodward reported the following conversation between himself and the President:

Woodward: [The President] said, explicitly, he believes we have a duty to free people, to liberate people. And I asked him directly, I said, "Is this not kind of a dangerous paternalism where people are going to say, now, wait a minute, where's the United States coming in and liberating us?" And he said, quite directly, he said, "That's an elite view," and that people who are liberated are delighted and happy with it. And he wants to fix things. I think it is a moral determination, which we've not seen in the White House maybe in 100 years . . . as he has said publicly and he recounted for me, he believes that freedom is God's gift to humanity, and that we as the instruments of that need to help people along when we can. And Iraq . . . the drive in Bush is this notion of liberating people as much as protecting the country. (PBS 2004)

Playing to the Audience

Someone who realizes that decisions are going to have unreliable foundations should also anticipate that resulting decisions are likely to be wrong, or at least that retrospective analyses are going to find errors. Thus, one aspect of the decision-making agenda becomes building a public case that actions had substantial justifications when the decisions occurred. Exemplifying this tactic, Doug Harvey, a former major league baseball umpire, noted that with close plays in which he could not be certain he made the right decision, he would "sell his call." For example, when calling a player "out," Harvey recommended giving "a little bit more to your motion—bingo!—so that they can see the action, and it makes you look more sure of yourself, that you've nailed it" (Useem et al. 2005: 114). So too do managers dramatize their decision-making behavior to instill confidence and to engender commitment to chosen courses of action.

The Bush administration clearly recognized that their decision making about Iraq would have to appear to have strong justification. Pillar (2006), who was the CIA's senior intelligence officer for the Near East and South Asia from 2000 to 2005, has claimed that the Bush administration disregarded the expertise of the intelligence community, politicized the intelligence process, and selected unrepresentative raw intelligence to make its public case. Pillar (2006: 18) wrote:

the greatest discrepancy between the administration's public statements and the intelligence community's judgments concerned not WMD (there was indeed a broad consensus that such programs existed), but the relationship between Saddam and al-Qaeda. The enormous attention devoted to this subject did not reflect any judgment by intelligence officials that there was or was likely to be anything like the "alliance" the administration said existed. The reason the connection got so much attention was that the administration wanted to hitch the Iraq expedition to the "war on terror" and the threat the American public feared most, thereby capitalizing on the country's militant post-9/11 mood.

Another example concerns aluminum tubes the Bush administration characterized as components of centrifuges used to produce nuclear weapons. This notion
originated with a junior analyst at the CIA in April 2001. However, in the fall of
2001, senior nuclear scientists declared that the tubes were inappropriate for
nuclear development and speculated that Iraq probably intended to use them
in small artillery rockets. This judgment was forwarded to the White House.
Nevertheless, a year later in September 2002, Vice President Cheney cited the
tubes as "irrefutable evidence" of Iraq's nuclear weapons program, and Ms Rice,
the President's national security adviser, stated that the tubes were "only really
suited for nuclear weapons programs" (Barstow et al. 2004: A1). Later, in February 2003, Secretary of State Powell showed photos of these tubes to the United
Nations Security Council as evidence of Iraq's nuclear weapons program.

Moving Incrementally

Another logical reaction to awareness that decisions are going to have unreliable
foundations might be caution. When their data finally convinced them that most
managers have very inaccurate perceptions, Mezias and Starbuck were quite surprised
to observe that this condition seemed to cause little concern in the managers'
companies. Most of the studied managers came from the world's best-known companies. If perceptual errors were causing serious problems, these companies had the
resources to eliminate them. However, these companies were not devoting significant
resources to error correction, so these errors must not have been causing them serious
problems. Eventually, the researchers realized that people can usually act effectively
without having accurate perceptions: They need only pursue general, long-term goals.
Because people usually get prompt evidence about the effectiveness of their actions, at
least in gross terms, their misperceptions cause only small errors. For example,
managers' ability to improve product quality depends hardly at all on their knowledge
of current quality measures. The managers mainly need to accept the idea that they
should improve quality. Many actions are likely to produce such improvements, and
it does not matter whether chosen actions offer the greatest improvements. If a
controversy develops that measurements might resolve, such as which aspects of
quality are most deficient, managers can then make measurements or examine
measurements that already exist. Furthermore, in many domains, managerial performance is comparative. Managers have to perform as well or better than their
competitors do. They need not take optimal actions, unless their competitors are
taking optimal actions, which is very unlikely. Managers do not even have to present
rationales for actions that resemble those taken by competitors.

Of course, the foregoing argument assumes a benign form of competition. Aggressive competition and warfare are not benign, and they always elicit surprising
responses. Opponents try to make surprising responses that exploit their competitors'

weaknesses. Aggressive competition and warfare also polarize public opinion and they spill over into adjacent industries or regions. These effects redefine environmental structures in ways that are difficult to anticipate but likely to undermine effectiveness of long-standing policies and strategies.

For instance, the US's attack on Iraq brought several reactions that surprised the Bush administration and the Pentagon. Because the US's leaders had anticipated an easy victory and a complaisant populace in Iraq, they provided far too few soldiers to control the country and they did not prepare for long-term occupation of a hostile populace (Woodward 2004). Insurgents or opportunists stole armaments that Iraq had stored, and they destroyed oil pipelines and refining equipment. The invasion polarized opinions. People who had previously been rather neutral decided to support either invaders or insurgents, with one result being many newly active insurgents. Angry Moslems from around the world went to Iraq to participate in attacks on US and British military forces, and they attacked in ways for which invaders were unprepared, especially roadside bombs and suicide attacks. The invasion reactivated long-standing animosities among Kurds, Shiites, and Sunnis, and Shiites and Sunnis began kidnapping and killing each other in an escalating civil war. Former allies that advised against invasion refused to enter the war. Some invaders committed crimes that made them look despicable. The actual costs of warfare vastly exceeded pre-attack estimates. Perhaps hoping to distract public attention from Iraq, President Bush proposed domestic legislation about retirement savings, medical costs, flag burning, and marriage between homosexuals—all of which failed. As the US populace gradually realized how badly the invasion had turned out, the President's popularity plummeted to previously unseen lows and his political party lost control of Congress. Iran and North Korea went ahead with development of nuclear weapons and missiles to deliver them; when the US threatened to respond militarily, Iran and North Korea seemed to scoff at the US's threats.

How People ought to React to Inaccuracy and Unreliability

Creating Robust Organizations that can Endure Unreliable Data

Perhaps the most interesting challenge is to design organizations and decision processes that act effectively despite inaccurate and unreliable data, just as aircraft designers try to anticipate pilots' errors. Since data errors are not causing widespread alarm, it seems likely that many organizations are already doing some of these things. This section reviews some elements that make organizations robust.

One element fostering organizational robustness is anticipation of inaccuracy and unreliability when allocating data-gathering resources. Data gathering resources and educational efforts should focus on crucial variables, and extra resources and backup systems should go where errors are most likely and consequences of error harshest. However, these allocation problems need sophisticated analyses because of the likelihood of errors when judging what variables are crucial and what consequences would be harshest. Financial investment models offer a fitting analogy. One wants to invest the largest amounts where expected returns are highest and risks smallest. However, forecasts about returns and risks are often very wrong, so one needs to mitigate risks and hedge bets through diversification.

A second element is to seek multifaceted feedback about performance outcomes. People who expect to make mistakes not only realize the value of information about their performances: they also recognize that the most useful information may relate to unpredicted outcomes, side-effects, or neglected effects. Thus, they have to obtain information bearing on different aspects of their performances, not merely information about basic measures such as profitability or output quantity. Grinyer and Norburn (1975) found that less profitable firms focus their strategic planning on information in formal reports, whereas strategic planning by more profitable firms considers information from diverse sources.

A third element is to concentrate on incremental moves, avoiding drastic innovations. To remain effective amid changing social and economic environments, organizations must depart from their familiar domains. Smaller innovations entail smaller risks because they place less reliance on understanding of environments, and outcomes from smaller innovations are more likely to resemble predictions. Of course, it takes more small innovations to match any given rate of environmental change, so smaller innovations have to occur more frequently. This, in turn, implies that organizations need cultures that support experimentation and change (Hedberg et al. 1976; Quinn 1980; Nystrom and Starbuck 1984).

Some academic writers have advocated that organizations should pursue portfolios of incremental "real options" (Bowman and Hurry 1993; Brown and Eisenhardt 1997; McGrath 1999). This real-options perspective proposes that organizations should undertake many simultaneous projects on small scales to obtain information before deciding what projects to develop fully. However, exploratory options evoke cognitive and political processes that misrepresent the options' effectiveness (Barnett 2003, 2005; Adner and Levinthal 2004).

Widely heralded as a master of innovation, 3M Company shows how organizational culture can support experimentation and change: 3M asks each division to generate 25 percent of revenue from recently introduced products; managers can devote up to 15 percent of their time to new product development, and 3M makes product-development grants of up to $75,000. Compensation and promotions reflect successful development; and successful product champions get the opportunity and autonomy to manage new products as separate businesses. Consequently, the corporate culture tolerates inaccurate or unreliable data that arise from exploratory activities (Russell 1989).

A fourth element in robust organizations is an ability to recognize and correct errors. However, Mezias and Starbuck's interviews with managers suggest that willingness to acknowledge error is quite unusual. Many managers worry about the security of their positions and fear consequences of being wrong, and many managers anticipate punishment if they reveal superiors' errors. When Mezias and Starbuck asked managers of data-gathering projects to tell about instances in which their analyses had corrected misperceptions, many responded by saying that they feared such stories would anger superiors who would not want to admit that past actions left large room for improvement. Thus, organizations have widespread opportunities to foster candor and encourage error correction. Organizations should explicitly acknowledge the likelihood of mistakes and emphasize efforts to improve rather than to cover up mistakes. Managers should reward personnel who discover mistakes or needed changes.

Eisenhardt's (1989) research suggests that more effective decision making considers more alternatives, incorporates a two-tiered advice process, and provides for conflict resolution. Where risks are high and investments substantial, organizations may find it worthwhile to use a Devil's Advocate or Dialectic approach to performance analysis (Cosier and Schwenk 1990). Brown (1966) reported that ITT Corporation used Devil's Advocate methods extensively during Harold Geneen's tenure as CEO. However, Mason and Mitroff (1981) argued that Devil's Advocate methods place too much emphasis on what is wrong rather than what would be better, so they advocated a dialectic approach instead. Later empirical studies indicated that both methods can improve decision making and both can degrade implementation, depending on participants and circumstances (Schweiger et al. 1986; Schwenk and Cosier 1993).

In his discussion of battlefield decision making, General Peter Pace, Vice Chairman of the US Joint Chiefs of Staff, argued that the correctness of specific decisions ought to be secondary to longer-run organizational development. "You have to assess the environment and make a decision based on your experience and training. You react instinctively. What I have learned is that if you're collaborative when you can be, it builds trust" (Useem et al. 2005: 107). Pace added that if managers are open with subordinates when mistakes occur, it facilitates learning and allows subordinates to feel more comfortable admitting their own mistakes. Thus, although mistakes happen and decisions or projects may be suboptimal, the process engenders the trust, learning, and candor that provide longer-term benefits for organizations.

Educating and Informing

Robust organizational designs provide protection mainly for everyday actions taken in response to immediate problems. Strategic planning and policy development call for more emphasis on correcting misperceptions. Managers need good understandings of their situations when making decisions with lasting effects.

However, Mezias and Starbuck's second study of managers' perceptions shows how difficult it is to convey accurate information. The studied managers worked in one of the world's most respected firms, which has superb education, information, and human-resources functions. The study focused on a quality initiative that had the very highest priority at the corporate level. Yet after two years of this initiative, most of the divisional senior managers remained uninformed about quality performance in their divisions.

It seems even very wealthy organizations with excellent human resources are unable to disseminate information effectively. Managers receive too much data, most of which has no action implications. As a result, they fail to notice some data and they may not believe other data. Although objective data become more valuable as managers' perceptions become less realistic, people become less willing to accept information as it diverges more from their expectations. Not only do people tend to interpret nearly all information as confirming their existing perceptions, but also many people may share perceptions, with the result that social support rigidifies and blurs perceptions (Daft and Weick 1984). Presumably, organizations subject their personnel to floods of information because organizations are unable to make useful judgments about relevance and importance.

Strategic-planning consultants report that many organizations have turned away from managers' pooling judgments and developing strategies collectively. Instead, organizations are using planning activities to educate managers about actual properties of firms and market environments. Thus, management practice seems to recognize that organizations can gain from educating and informing. This recognition has propelled the SAS Institute to 19 straight years of double-digit growth. The Institute's product integrates an Executive Information System with data warehousing, data analysis, client–server computing, applications development, graphics, report writing, project management, and decision support (Taylor 1996).

More generally, information systems generate problems as well as solutions. Most managers could benefit by relying less on beliefs and more on data-based analyses. However, automatic periodic reports dull senses and divert managers' attentions from what is important by inundating them with irrelevant, obsolete, or misleading data (Nystrom and Starbuck 1984). Modern information technology could help make perceptions more objective and up to date. The fact that technological innovations are introducing new data and different viewpoints offers managers a rationale for abandoning past perceptions.

Some uses of "data warehouses" illustrate opportunities offered by information technology. Data warehouses are massive databases that describe past transactions. Plummeting costs of data storage now allow firms to record everything, without having to decide in advance what information to gather and keep, so prior decisions about what to record do not limit future analyses. There can be more objectivity, less subjectivity. For example, a data-warehouse analysis kept Helene Curtis from making a costly pricing blunder. When Unilever introduced Rave shampoo, Helene Curtis' managers expected Rave to compete with their higher priced line, Salon Selectives. They contemplated a preemptive price reduction to keep Rave from taking too much business from Salon Selectives. However, Helene Curtis buys data recorded by the checkout scanners in chain stores. Helene Curtis also gets daily reports from its field sales personnel, who record data from about 40,000 retail outlets in palmtop computers and transmit these to headquarters each night. Analyses of these data revealed that Unilever was positioning Rave to compete with Helene Curtis' lower priced shampoo, Suave. Therefore, cutting the price of Salon Selectives would have lowered margins without hindering the success of Unilever's Rave.

Can Managers Gain Competitive Advantages from or Despite Inaccurate, Unreliable Data?

One possibility is that managers might by-pass limitations of rational decision making and develop skills and experience for operating in ambiguous, fast-cycle environments. Baumard (1999) asserted that some managers have exceptional abilities to operate effectively in environments they view as ambiguous and uncertain. He argued that these exceptional managers forgo attempting rational problem solving and instead engage in a pragmatic, creative cunning that generates new sensemaking frameworks. "Strategy sometimes consists in establishing temporary articulations to avoid fossilizing knowledge into restrictive statements, and so as to take tactical advantage of their unfinished or mutable character" (Baumard 1999: 228). Thus, in addition to traditional strategizing process of appraising the present realistically and forecasting the future accurately, a second mode of strategizing has managers using creativity to exploit unfamiliar environments that nurture data errors. Barry Cunningham's decision to publish the first Harry Potter book provides an example of this. Although a dozen other publishers had turned the manuscript down primarily because it did not conform to the traditional notion of a children's book, Cunningham felt this well written and interesting tale would defy conventional wisdom and appeal to children.

Whereas some people benefit by creating uncertainty in their competitors, other people lose by hesitating in the face of uncertainty. Indecision can allow growing problems to escalate and lower the likelihood of success for an eventual course of action. Conversely, decisive managerial actions, even if based on erroneous data, can sometimes make success more likely by engendering enthusiasm and mobilizing critical resources. Indeed, Porac and Rosa (1996: 35) argued that any sensemaking framework can be effective: "A frame's fit with the external environment is largely irrelevant because a firm succeeds by imposing its frame on its environment...". "Success", they said, "is more a function of energy and persistence than of repeating cycles of belief and discrediting." (1996: 40). Sarasvathy (2001) proposed that entrepreneurship uses imagination to create and exploit opportunities that lurk in ambiguity. Creating the future involves creating goals and values, not merely pursuing them. Wiltbank et al. (2006) described "non-predictive" strategies as employing social networks not only to gather data about environments but also to decide what environments ought to exist. Wiltbank et al. (2007) studied early-stage investors in new firms and inferred that investors experience fewer failures if they place less reliance on predictions, make smaller investments, and try harder to shape the future.

However, when they depend on noisy, unreliable data, efforts to shape futures and decisive actions are highly likely to yield disappointing results... as the Bush administration amply demonstrated in Iraq. The Bush administration experienced both success and failure in forcing their environment to conform to their perceptions. They failed insofar as they did not find WMDs and their declaration of "mission accomplished" on May 1, 2003, proved very premature. They succeeded insofar as they created an Iraq filled with terrorists, some of whom had links to al-Qaeda.

REFERENCES

ADNER, R. and LEVINTHAL, D. (2004). 'What is Not a Real Option: Considering Boundaries for the Application of Real Options to Business Strategy.' *Academy of Management Review*, 29: 74–85.

ALTHEIDE, D. L. and JOHNSON, J. M. (1980). *Bureaucratic Propaganda*. Boston: Allyn and Bacon.

AMES, E. and REITER, S. (1961). 'Distributions of Correlation Coefficients in Economic Time Series.' *Journal of the American Statistical Association*, 56: 637–56.

BAR-HILLEL, M. (1973). 'On the Subjective Probability of Compound Events.' *Organizational Behavior and Human Performance*, 9: 396–406.

BARNETT, M. (2003). 'Falling off the Fence? A Realistic Appraisal of a Real Options Approach to Corporate Strategy.' *Journal of Management Inquiry*, 12: 185–96.

—— (2005). 'Paying Attention to Real Options.' *R&D Management*, 35: 61–72.

BARSTOW, D., BROAD, W. J. and GERTH, J. (2004). 'How the White House Embraced Disputed Arms Intelligence.' *New York Times*, October 3, 2004.

BAUMARD, P. (1999). *Tacit Knowledge in Organizations*. London: Sage.

—— STARBUCK, W. H. (2005). 'Learning from Failures: Why It May Not Happen.' *Long Range Planning*, 38: 281–98.

BAZERMAN, M. H. (1997). *Judgment in Managerial Decision Making* (2nd edn.). New York: Wiley.

BEACH, L. R. (1966). 'Accuracy and Consistency in the Revision of Subjective Probabilities.' *IEEE Transactions on Human Factors in Electronics*, HFE-7: 29–37.

BETTMAN, J. R. and WEITZ, B. A. (1983). 'Attribution in the Board Room: Causal Reasoning in Corporate Annual Reports.' *Administrative Science Quarterly*, 28: 165–83.

BOLAND, R. J., Jr. (1982). 'Myth and Technology in the American Accounting Profession.' *Journal of Management Studies*, 19: 109–27.

BOWMAN, E. and HURRY, D. (1993). 'Strategy Through the Option Lens: An Integrated View of Resource Investments and the Incremental-Choice Process.' *Academy of Management Review*, 18: 760–82.

BROWN, S. H. (1966). 'How One Man Can Move a Corporation.' *Fortune*, 74/1.

BROWN, S. and EISENHARDT, K. M. (1997). 'The Art of Continuous Change: Linking Complexity Theory and Time-Paced Evolution in Relentlessly Shifting Organizations.' *Administrative Science Quarterly*, 42: 1–34.

CNN (2004). Woodward: Tenet Told Bush WMD Case a 'Slam Dunk': Says Bush Didn't Solicit Rumsfeld, Powell on Going to War (www.cnn.com/2004/ALLPOLITICS/04/18/woodward.book/).

COHEN, M. D., MARCH, J. G., and OLSEN, J. P. (1972). 'A Garbage Can Model of Organizational Choice.' *Administrative Science Quarterly*, 17: 1–25.

COSIER, R. A. and SCHWENK, C. R. (1990). 'Agreement and Thinking Alike: Ingredients for Poor Decisions.' *Academy of Management Executive*, 4/1: 69–74.

CYERT, R. M. and MARCH, J. G. (1963). *A Behavioral Theory of the Firm*. Englewood Cliffs, NJ: Prentice-Hall.

DAFT, R. L. and WEICK, K. E. (1984). 'Toward a Model of Organizations as Interpretation Systems.' *Academy of Management Review*, 9: 284–95.

DOWNEY, H. K., HELLRIEGEL, D., and SLOCUM, J. W., Jr. (1975). 'Environmental Uncertainty: The Construct and its Application.' *Administrative Science Quarterly*, 20: 613–29.

EISENHARDT, K. M. (1989). 'Making Fast Strategic Decisions in High-Velocity Environments.' *Academy of Management Journal*, 32: 543–76.

FARJOUN, M. and STARBUCK, W. H. (2007). 'Organizing at and Beyond the Limits.' *Organization Studies*, 28/4: 1–26.

FELDMAN, M. S. and MARCH, J. G. (1981). 'Information in Organizations as Signal and Symbol.' *Administrative Science Quarterly*, 26: 171–86.

FISCHHOFF, B. (1980). 'For Those Condemned to Study the Past: Reflections on Historical Judgment', in R. A. Shweder and D. W. Fiste (eds.), *New Directions for Methodology of Behavioral Science*. San Francisco, CA: Jossey-Bass, 79–93.

GRINYER, P. H. and NORBURN, D. (1975). 'Planning for Existing Markets: Perceptions of Executives and Financial Performance.' *Journal of the Royal Statistical Society, Series A*, 138819: 70–9.

HEDBERG, B. L. T., NYSTROM, P. C., and STARBUCK, W. H. (1976). 'Camping on Seesaws: Prescriptions for a Self-Designing Organization.' *Administrative Science Quarterly*, 21: 41–65.

HERSH, S. M. (2003). 'Selective Intelligence.' *New Yorker*, May 12.

HOFSTEDE, G. H. (1967). *The Game of Budget Control*. Assen: Van Gorcum.

—— (1980). *Culture's Consequences: International Differences in Work-Related Values*. Newbury Park, CA: Sage.

INSTITUTE FOR THE FUTURE (1997). *Managing Corporate Communications in the Information Age*, Menlo Park, CA: The Institute for the Future, SR-619.

Kahneman, D. and Tversky, A. (1973). 'On the Psychology of Prediction.' *Psychological Review*, 80: 237–51.

Lawrence, P. R. and Lorsch, J. W. (1967). *Organization and Environment*. Boston: Graduate School of Business Administration, Harvard University.

Lichtenstein, S., Fischhoff, B., and Phillips, L. (1982). 'Calibration Probabilities: The State of the Art to 1980', in D. Kahneman, P. Slovic, and A. Tversky (eds.), *Judgment under Uncertainty: Heuristics and Biases*. Cambridge: Cambridge University Press, 306–33.

Lustgarten, A. (2007). 'Shell Shakedown.' *Fortune*, February 1.

Mason, R. O. and Mitroff, I. I. (1981). *Challenging Strategic Planning Assumptions*. New York: John Wiley.

Massey, C. and Thaler, R. H. (2006). 'The Loser's Curse: Overconfidence vs. Market Efficiency in the National Football League Draft.' Manuscript, Duke University.

McGrath, R. (1999). 'Falling Forward: Real Options Reasoning and Entrepreneurial Failure.' *Academy of Management Review*, 22: 974–96.

Mezias, J. M. and Starbuck, W. H. (2003). 'Studying the Accuracy of Managers' Perceptions: A Research Odyssey.' *British Journal of Management*, 14: 3–17.

Nystrom, P. C. and Starbuck, W. H. (1984). 'To Avoid Organizational Crises, Unlearn.' *Organizational Dynamics*, 12/4: 53–65.

Oskamp, S. (1965). 'Overconfidence in Case-Study Judgments.' *Journal of Consulting Psychology*, 29: 261–5.

Pant, P. N. and Starbuck, W. H. (1990). 'Innocents in the Forest: Forecasting and Research Methods.' *Journal of Management*, 16: 433–60.

Payne, R. L. and Pugh, D. S. (1976). 'Organizational Structure and Climate,' in M. D. Dunnette (ed.), *Handbook of Industrial and Organizational Psychology*. Chicago: Rand McNally, 1125–73.

PBS (2004). Online Focus: Plan of Attack. Online NewsHour (www.pbs.org/newshour/bb/middle_east/jan-june04/woodward_4-21.html).

Phillips, L. D., Hays, W. L., and Edwards, W. (1966). 'Conservatism in Complex Probabilistic Inference.' *IEEE Transactions on Human Factors in Electronics*, HFE-7: 7–18.

Pillar, P. R. (2006). 'Intelligence, Policy, and the War in Iraq.' *Foreign Affairs* (March/April), 85/2: 15.

Porac, J. and Rosa, J. A. (1996). 'In Praise of Managerial Narrow-Mindedness.' *Journal of Management Inquiry*, 5: 35–42.

PriceWaterhouse Coopers (2004). *Boosting Business Performance through Programme and Project Management: A First Global Survey on the Current State of Project Management Maturity in Organizations Across the World*. London: PriceWaterhouse Coopers.

Quinn, J. B. (1980). *Strategies for Change: Logical Incrementalism*. Homewood, IL: Irwin.

Ragins, B. R., Townsend, B. and Mattis, M. (1998). 'Gender Disparity in the Executive Suite: CEOs and Female Executives Report on Breaking the Glass Ceiling.' *Academy of Management Executive*, 12/1: 28–42.

Russell, K. (2004). 'The Subjectivity of Intelligence Analysis and Implications for U.S. National Security Strategy.' *SAIS Review*, 24/1: 147–63.

Russell, M. (1989). 'Masters of Innovation: How 3M Keeps Its New Products Coming.' *Business Week*, April 10: 58–63.

Salgado, S. R., Starbuck, W. H. and Mezias, J. M. (2002). 'The Accuracy of Managers' Perceptions: A Dimension Missing from Theories about Firms,' in M. Augier and J. G. March (eds.), *The Economics of Choice, Change, and Organizations: Essays in Memory of Richard M. Cyert*. Cheltenham: Edward Elgar, 168–85.

SARASVATHY, S. D. (2001). 'Causation and Effectuation: Toward a Theoretical Shift from Economic Inevitability to Entrepreneurial Contingency.' *Academy of Management Review*, 26: 243–63.

SCHWEIGER, D., SANDBERG, W., and RAGAN, J. (1986). 'Group Approaches for Improving Strategic Decision Making: A Comparative Analysis of Dialectical Inquiry, Devil's Advocacy, and Consensus.' *Academy of Management Journal*, 29: 51–71.

SCHWENK, C. (1984). 'Cognitive Simplification Processes in Strategic Decision Making.' *Strategic Management Journal*, 5: 111–28.

—— COSIER, R. (1993). 'Effects of Consensus and Devil's Advocacy on Strategic Decision Making.' *Journal of Applied Social Psychology*, 23: 126–39.

SINGER, B. and BENASSI, V. A. (1981). 'Occult Beliefs.' *American Scientist*, 69: 49–55.

SLOVIC, P. and CORRIGAN, B. (1973). *Behavioral Problems of Adhering to a Decision Policy*. Napa, CA: Institute for Quantitative Research in Finance.

STARBUCK, W. H. and BASS, F. M. (1967). 'An Experimental Study of Risk-Taking and the Value of Information in a New Product Context.' *Journal of Business*, 40: 155–65.

—— MEZIAS, J. M. (1996). 'Opening Pandora's Box: Studying the Accuracy of Managers' Perceptions.' *Journal of Organizational Behavior*, 17/2: 99–117.

—— MILLIKEN, F. J. (1988a). 'Executives' Perceptual Filters: What They Notice and How They Make Sense,' in D. C. Hambrick (ed.), *The Executive Effect: Concepts and Methods for Studying Top Managers*. Greenwich, CT: JAI Press, 35–65.

—— —— (1988b). 'Challenger: Changing the Odds until Something Breaks.' *Journal of Management Studies*, 25: 319–40.

TAYLOR, P. (1996). 'Survey—FT IT: R&D Keeps Software at the Leading Edge.' *Financial Times*, May 1.

TENET, G. (2007). *At the Center of the Storm: My Years at the CIA*. New York: Harper Collins.

TOSI, H., ALDAG, R., and STOREY, R. (1973). 'On the Measurement of the Environment: An Assessment of the Lawrence and Lorsch Environmental Uncertainty Subscale.' *Administrative Science Quarterly*, 18, 27–36.

TVERSKY, A. and KAHNEMAN, D. (1974). 'Judgment under Uncertainty: Heuristics and Biases.' *Science, New Series*, 85: 1124–31.

USEEM, J., SCHLOSSER, J., GIMBEL, B. et al. (2005). 'How I Make Decisions.' *Fortune* (June 27), 151(13): 106.

WAGNER, J. A., III and GOODING, R. Z. (1997). 'Equivocal Information and Attribution: An Investigation of Patterns of Managerial Sensemaking.' *Strategic Management Journal*, 18: 275–86.

WEICK, K. E. (1995). *Sensemaking in Organizations*. Thousand Oaks CA.: Sage.

WEINSTEIN, N. D. (1980). 'Unrealistic Optimism about Future Life Events.' *Journal of Personality and Social Psychology*, 39/5: 806–20.

WILTBANK, R., DEW, N., READ, J. S., and SARASVATHY, S. D. (2006). 'What to Do Next? The Case for Non-Predictive Strategy.' *Strategic Management Journal*, 27: 981–98.

—— READ, J. S., DEW, N., and SARASVATHY, S. D. (2007). 'Prediction and Control Under Uncertainty: Outcomes in Angel Investing.' Manuscript, Willamette University.

WOLD, H. O. A. (1965). 'A Graphic Introduction to Stochastic Processes,' in H. O. A. Wold (ed.), *Bibliography on Time Series and Stochastic Processes*. Edinburgh: Oliver and Boyd, 7–76.

WOODWARD, B. (2004). *Plan of Attack*. London: Simon and Schuster.

5

BORGS IN THE ORG? ORGANIZATIONAL DECISION MAKING AND TECHNOLOGY*

TERRI L. GRIFFITH

GREGORY B. NORTHCRAFT

MARK A. FULLER

INTRODUCTION

THE Merriam-Webster Dictionary (Anon. 1974) defines technology as "a technical means for achieving a practical outcome." In common parlance, technology means tools, and humankind is a prodigious user of tools. In the decision-making arena, we might think of technology as any physical tool exogenous to human cognition

* Many of the ideas presented were developed during the Sea Ranch Workshop on Technology and Organizational Decision Making. We send our thanks to all the participants.

used to assist human cognition. To the extent that decision-making is about thinking, then decision-making technology is about tools used to assist that thinking.

The idea of using physical tools to assist human thinking has a long and distinguished history. The Goseck Circle (Mukerjee 2003), for example, was 75 meters wide and consisted of four concentric circles (see Figure 5.1). It was used as early as 4900 B.C. for "astronomical observation combined with calendar calculations to coordinate an easily-judged lunar calendar with the more demanding measurements of a solar calendar" (http://en.wikipedia.org/wiki/Goseck_circle). Around 320 B.C., the kleroterion was used in ancient Greece to randomly assign jurors to cases in the Athenian courts (see Figure 5.2). Prospective jurors names were inscribed on tickets and placed in slots. Black and white balls were dropped down a thin tube; jurors were selected if a white ball landed next to the ticket bearing their name.

In contrast, today the use of the term technology in the decision-making realm almost always refers to computerized information technology, specifically, the use of computers as a tool for assisting decision making by managing information. These days some tasks—such as flying an F-14 Tomcat fighter plane—are not even possible without computerized decision making assistance (for a general discussion, see Stengel 1993). Regardless of the application, the appearance of any technology in the decision making process highlights the same question: Does it help? Does the use of a particular tool improve, enhance, facilitate, or otherwise augment (Engelbart 1968)[1] human intellect as the foundation for decision making?

Engelbart's (1962) theory of augmentation—assisting the development of greater human intellect by allowing machines to perform the mechanical part of thinking and idea sharing—can be accomplished in two distinct ways, either through supplementing an entity's decision-making ability, or by supplanting (replacing)

Fig. 5.1 Goseck Circle (Image captured from: www.fh–augsburg.de/~harsch/museum/Chronologia/C_a0700/Goseck/goseck.html).

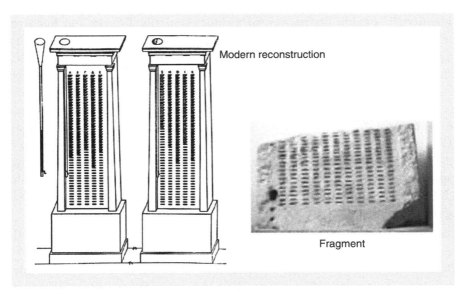

Fig. 5.2 Kleroterion (Images captured from: http://mkatz.web.wesleyan.edu/grk201/GRK201.Dikastai.html).

human intellect as the basis for decision making. We explore this augmenting role for technology in two realms: individual decision making and group decision making. In both realms, we explore what technology has to offer, as well as the limitations inherent in using tools to augment cognitive processes.

INDIVIDUAL DECISION MAKING

Most scholars (e.g., Simon 1957; Mintzberg et al. 1976) seem to agree that individual decision making consists of three distinct phases: identification and clarification of the decision to be made; development of alternatives from which to choose; and analysis and selection among alternatives. This characterization of individual decision making highlights two specific activities in which individual decision makers must engage: (1) information *gathering* (or search); and (2) information *use* (including information integration, analysis, and choice).

Most scholars also agree that individual decision making "rationality"—in the sense of making fully informed and computationally correct decisions—is unattainable for many, if not most real world decisions. Simon (1957) coined the phrase "bounded rationality" to reflect inherent limitations in individual decision making, such as the inability of any individual to gather all relevant information, or to identify all possible alternatives for a choice scenario. Tversky and Kahneman later (e.g., 1974) built on this foundation by identifying a number of heuristics that individual decision makers use that bias their information gathering (e.g., availability: Wilson et al. 1985) or analysis (e.g., anchoring: Northcraft and Neale 1988) attempts. In light of the concept of bounded rationality, a reasonable question to ask is to what extent technology augments decision making, removing the limits on rationality suggested by the work of Simon, and that of Tversky and Kahneman?

The use of computers to augment individual decision making emerged in the mid-1970s (e.g., Keen and Scott Morton 1978). The formal concept of Decision Support Systems (DSS) was introduced by Gorry and Scott Morton (1971). Shim et al. (2002) identify four technology developments that have influenced decision support more recently:

- Data warehousing: The collection and storage of integrated data (e.g., transaction records from a bank or retail store).
- On-line analytical processing: the assessment of "warehoused" data by analysts or management using software for to help them see different views, reports, and the like.
- Data mining: a more sophisticated form of on-line analytical processing using statistical and artificial intelligence methods. The goal is to identify patterns and then develop rules of action. For example, analysts might discover that ice cream and bananas are often purchased at the same time and so should be shelved near one another in a grocery store.
- Web: the World Wide Web (www) (via the Internet) provides both a development and delivery platform for the use of technology in decision making. Shim et al. note that the www can make it both easier and less costly to make information and model-driven decision tools available around the world.

We discuss these four technological advancements in terms of their ability to support activities related to the two primary decision making activities of information gathering and information use.

Information Gathering

Data warehousing and the development of the World Wide Web both augment information gathering (search) processes in individual decision making by increasing the availability of required information. Imagine, for example, that one wanted to buy new golf clubs. Thirty years ago, the cost of information gathering would likely have limited an individual's search process to geographically proximal vendors and the golf clubs they stocked. Today, a prospective purchaser can log onto the World Wide Web to find out what types of golf clubs are available anywhere; consult databases, chat rooms, and bulletin boards (e.g., epinions.com) to gather product information and user opinions; and compare prices across vendors around the world.

Paradoxically, the technological augmentation of information availability for individual decision making might also eventually reduce the need for comprehensive information search. The possibility of making a poor decision (for example, overpaying for a product) is to some extent premised on the existence of inefficient markets. Consumers overpay only if they don't know they don't have to do so. The heightened availability of information offered by information technology developments probably reduces the information asymmetry typical of seller–buyer relationships (Akerloff 1970; Baron and Besanko 1987) and in doing so decreases the likelihood of uninformed consumers. Ultimately technology-mediated increases in information availability might drive markets to be more efficient (something that seems to have already occurred to some extent with on-line airfares), and thus (paradoxically) reduce the need for consumers to be informed. After all, if consumers are fully informed, attempts at opportunistic pricing will only cost a vendor sales. Anyone who regularly shops on the web knows that most markets certainly have not yet reached that point of efficiency—witness the variance in prices one can still find for the same golf clubs from different on-line vendors.

Part of the reason that technology advancements have not necessarily created completely efficient markets is the distinction between information availability and information *possession*. The fact that a piece of information is available does not mean any particular individual decision maker can find it. In the context of the web, the fact that an on-line vendor has the lowest price for a product doesn't mean an individual decision maker can find that vendor on the web. In fact, the more information that is available, the *less* likely it should be that any particular—critical—piece of information will be found during a search. This reality reflects the fact that storage and search are both enacted processes. In many instances, the creators of information must characterize that information in order to store it on sites that use indexed search engines, much as historically file folders in a file cabinet had to be labeled. Characterizations of information—the labels or descriptions attached by its creators—limit the ability of searchers to find that information, if the searchers are using different terminology. On the other side of the coin, information search is also limited by the searcher's characterization of the target of the search. "Googling" a product requires an individual decision maker to decide how to characterize the product, and a poor choice of characterization (e.g., inadequate search terms) can lead to a less than satisfactory search outcome. Thus, the decision to characterize information—either at the level of storage or search—is itself subject to "bounded rationality," thus bounding the augmentation of individual decision making by technology-increased information availability.

Information Use

The availability of more information raises the specter of having more information to analyze in order to reach an appropriate choice. The ideas of information overload and "paralysis of analysis" (Baumgartner 2005) reflect an abundance problem (Brody 1998; Horowitz 1999), whereby "lightning-quick online searches typically lead Web users into piles of documents that are, to be kind, of dubious reliability" (Brody 1998: 26). Thanks to technology, our ability to collect data far exceeds our ability to make sense of it (Horowitz 1999: 55). For example, a web search for "golf clubs" generates over 42 million "hits."

Information integration technologies (including on-line analytical processing and data mining) reflect the ability of technology advancements to assist individual decision makers in the use (integration and analysis) of information they have gathered. Integration technologies thereby go beyond information gathering and take part in the analysis and choice processes. For example, TiVo, iTunes, Netflix, Amazon, and eBay all use a database of past customer searches and purchases to identify additional products customers might like, thereby simplifying the customer's future information search process. Similarly, Walmart is a leader with their extensive inventory tracking and control systems (using a set of computer systems described by CNBC as second only to the United States Pentagon's, CNBC, 2004). Beyond just storing every purchase ever made and using a real-time tracking system that looks like NASA's mission control, Wal-Mart is taking the lead in RFID[2] and vendor integration:

Much of the data collected during RFID reads [Walmart will track cases of inventory from stockroom to floor to when the case boxes go to the trash] will be passed on to Retail Link, Wal-Mart's Web-based software that lets the retailer's buyers and some 30,000 suppliers check inventory, sales, and more. The company is developing software for Retail Link that will leverage that data and trigger a business process—for example, creating a purchase order. (Sullivan 2004)

We distinguish between systems intended to technologically supplement human decision making and systems intended to supplant human decision making with computerized information systems. However, even in systems intended to supplant human decision making (e.g., expert systems), the systems themselves must be adaptable to changes in the environment or decision making needs (Beynon et al. 2002: 130). As Davenport and Harris point out (2005: 84), "even the most automated systems rely on experts and managers to create and maintain rules and monitor the results." Thus, to the extent that such systems employ algorithms that integrate available information to either recommend or make a decision, these algorithms are still designed by humans, and therefore also raise the bounded rationality concerns raised by Simon. Even expert systems that can learn are still limited by the information they have been programmed—by their human architects—to learn from.

Decision Types and the Effectiveness of DSS

Some decisions may be more amenable to technological automation than others. Researchers have focused on examining the match between the decision being made, and the technology being used to support that decision. Perhaps this approach is best exemplified by the literature on Task-Technology Fit (Goodhue and Thompson 1995; Zigurs and Buckland 1999). When a decision is routine—when the parameters of the decision and possible choice options are well known a priori—a decision is said to be well "structured" and thereby a good candidate for automation (Simon 1960).

Unfortunately for technology, not all decisions are so well structured, and not all decision environments allow even structured decisions to remain so for long. Yates et al. (2003) note that the use of systems to support decision making has been disappointing in some cases because the technology is not able to capture "quality dimensions" that are of importance to users. The ability of organizations to delegate routine decisions to DSS can alter the fundamental nature of work, by allowing decision makers to focus more of their attention on those decisions that are not amenable to automation (Chase et al. 1984). The benefits, however, depend on the joint structuring of the work, the technology, and the particular people involved (for example, their knowledge, skills, and abilities).

Arnold and Sutton (1998) suggest that DSS may be most useful in those circumstances where expert tacit knowledge is least accessible to novice decision makers, so that the DSS provides the maximum advantage over the decision maker's own intuitions or calculations. Unfortunately, this assumes that the DSS has faithfully captured the expert's tacit knowledge, and further raises concerns that a (novice) decision maker under those circumstances will be least able to understand whether current circumstances render the DSS recommended choice inappropriate, or perhaps even how to implement the DSS output (Rochlin 1997). Decision automation may also prove unfortunate for the novice in that DSS use may decrease learning (Brody et al. 2003) in much the same way that many parents now fear that overreliance on calculators or computers hinders the development of math skills or writing skills in their children.

Another problem suggested by the mixed results of DSS implementations is that technology may give rise to unwarranted confidence (Alpert and Raiffa 1982). Xia (citing Koriat et al. 1980; Sniezek et al. 1990) suggests that "research has shown that effort and extensiveness of information processing could increase choice confidence although not necessarily increase decision correctness" (Xia 1999: 271). The use of a DSS might create an "aura of objectivity" as a function of the unbiased information processing it represents. Inappropriate deferral to a DSS without critical consideration of its limitations may result—a problem complicated by the fact that such overconfidence may be more likely to occur when task expertise is low (Arnold et al. 1998). More generally, turning over control of decisions to technology begs the question of the extent to which decision making can faithfully adjust to the changes and challenges of a dynamic environment.

The bottom line is that while DSS can relax some of the limitations on individual decision making implied by Simon's concept of "bounded rationality," technology-assisted decision making falls far short of being "un-bounded" rationality, and is perhaps more accurately described as "less bounded" rationality. Not surprisingly, then, meta-analyses of DSS impacts by McLeod (1992) and Benbasat and Lim (1993) generally have shown equivocal results. In the end, decision aids (like DSS) necessarily reflect some of the limitations of their creators. Some bounds on individual rationality will always remain (such as the inherent limitations imposed by the very human process of information characterization), no matter how sophisticated the technology involved. When it comes to DSS, there is always a "ghost in the machine" (Ryle 1949) and woe to the decision maker who fails to bear that limitation in mind.

Beynon et al. (2002) propose that the impossibility of absolutely rational individual decision making suggests that the goal of DSS design ultimately should not be the supplanting of human decision makers, but instead to understand, "how can we substantially improve the quality of interaction, and the degree of flexible engagement, between humans and computers" (p. 127). In other words, how can we augment human decision making by supplementing and supplanting only where appropriate (Schwartz 2001)?

GROUP DECISION MAKING

Changing the level of analysis from individual to group decisions raises a host of new issues in understanding an appropriate role for technology. Group decision support systems (GDSS), like DSS, are systems developed to augment human decision making, although within the specific context of groupwork. DeSanctis and Gallupe (1987: 589) defined a GDSS as a technology designed,

> to improve the process of group decision making by removing common communication barriers, providing techniques for structuring decision analysis, and systematically directing the pattern, timing, or content of discussion.

They further introduced a categorization scheme identifying levels of features, where level 1 systems facilitate information exchange through technical features, level 2 systems provide additional decision modeling and automated planning tools, and level 3 systems "are characterized by machine-induced group communication patterns and can include expert advice" (DeSanctis et al. 1987: 594).

Broader Group Support System (GSS) technologies focus on within group processes rather than individual impediments to effective decision making. For example, a key concern for group decision making is process loss. In the context of group decision making, process loss is the inability of a group to take advantage of all the information at its disposal to make a decision (e.g., Steiner 1972; Pinsonneault et al.

1999). For example, the inability of a group to access all of the information available among its members to make a decision invites the possibility of missing critical information, and thereby making a suboptimal decision. In addition to their effects on the core processes of information gathering and information use, GSS technologies also influence process loss via group configuration.

Group Configuration

Shim et al. (2002: 116) note that: "One of the more significant trends over the past 20 years has been the evolution from individual stand-alone computers to the highly interconnected telecommunications network environment of today." Griffith and Neale (2001) argue that technology broadens the possible pool of group members. In effect, the existence of GSS technologies has created new opportunities for interaction, so some decisions can now be group-based that previously might have needed to be individual-based.

In many respects, virtual groups have different dynamics than their face-to-face counterparts. Chidambaram (1996), for example, suggests that virtual groups tend to be more task oriented and exchange less social–emotional information, slowing the development of relational links (Chidambaram 1996). Others (e.g., Griffith et al. 2003) show virtual groups having greater procedural conflict (conflict about how the work will be done) than face-to-face groups, but similar goal focused or relationship focused conflict. There is also evidence that conflict goes undiscovered longer in more virtual groups (Chase 1999) and that such groups may communicate less effectively (Hightower and Sayeed 1995; Northcraft et al. 2006). Despite these drawbacks, many of which can be alleviated through training or facilitation, the use of groupware to allow geographically distributed participation in decision making increases the probability that a group will have access to critical information needed to make a high quality decision. The broad-based virtual participation in decisions allowed by GSS also promotes better understanding of decisions, and potentially more investment and ownership of those decisions during implementation.

Information Gathering

Regardless of configuration, a key, but difficult, first step in groups is to access all the information available in the group (e.g., Stasser and Titus 1985). One major feature of GSS design is the possibility of increasing the airtime available to individual group members by allowing everyone to electronically "talk" simultaneously, rather than having to wait and "take turns" (Pinsonneault et al. 1999; Potter and Balthazard 2004). Increased airtime increases the probability that everyone who has critical information will find an opportunity to surface it.

Increased opportunities for contribution don't necessarily translate into better information, however (Pinsonneault et al. 1999). For example, more airtime presents another version of the abundance problem noted earlier (Brody 1998). If everyone in a group can electronically talk at once, there will be more ideas to sort through to find the most decision-critical information.

Furthermore, social influence (Festinger 1954) is an ever-present force in group discussions. Social influence refers to the willingness of individuals to use others as a primary source of information about how they should be feeling or thinking (Asch 1956; Latane and Darley 1970). In group settings, social influence processes can convince an individual that critical information she or he possesses is in fact unimportant, or too disruptive to volunteer, leading that individual to not share that critical information with the group. In more virtual settings, co-located subgroups may be similarly hampered, with the subgroups not sharing information with their distant counterparts (Northcraft et al. 2006). Group decision making quality suffers accordingly.

On the other hand, technology can enhance a group's ability to surface particularly diverse and potentially disruptive information. For example, a GSS can be structured to collect ideas from participants electronically before anyone in the group knows what anyone else thinks, thus forestalling the possibility that conformity pressures will inhibit initial idea contributions. GSS can also render ongoing idea exchange during group discussions anonymous, thus increasing the willingness of participants to be controversially critical of ideas that have been surfaced. Significantly, these benefits are obviously available even to groups that do not use technological intermediation for their discussions (e.g., everyone could write down their ideas on paper and submit them anonymously). However, the increased psychological distance among group members created by technological intermediation—particularly when it enables anonymous contribution—may significantly lower conformity pressures in groups, thereby increasing the probability that unique critical information is shared in the group.

Perhaps one key to accessing all the information available in a group is understanding who knows what in the group. Transactive memory (Wegner 1986; Moreland 1999; Hollingshead 2001) refers to a group's understanding of the experience and expertise represented among its membership. Groups that have good transactive memory typically outperform groups that don't (e.g., Lewis 2004; Lewis et al. 2006) because they know where to seek out critical information among their members for high quality decision making. In effect, it is harder for process loss to occur if the group knows where (in which member) the critical information resides. (This can also provide a means for overcoming the abundance problem by prioritizing search around the comments of the most expert group members.) Although transactive memory is typically thought of as something in the heads of group participants (e.g., Hollingshead 2001), the idea of a technologically mediated transactive memory or (TM)[2] refers to a people-focused database (such as personal profiles of community of practice members) that captures physically (electronically) a representation of a group's transactive memory. In this vein, technology offers the possibility of creating an electronic expertise/experience directory that can be searched by the group, and is NOT reliant on particular group members' physical memory (though still reliant on human characterizations of particular individuals' experience and expertise). This sort of database can also assist groups at the composition level, by increasing understanding of who needs to be participating in order to maximize the probability that critical information sources will be represented among the discussion participants.

Information Use

GSS provide opportunities for information processing that differ from those available in face-to-face environments. These differences are tied to the features (Griffith and Northcraft 1994) that the GSS provides, such as parallelism (the ability to allow decision-making participants to exchange, and thus start to use, information at the same time), group memory (the recording and ability to recall information shared related to decision making), and anonymity (the ability to exchange and use information without knowing the source of the information). Each of these features can potentially influence information use by groups.

Some researchers argue that GSS features such as group memory may reduce the cognitive blocking associated with decision making. Cognitive blocking occurs when current information can't be processed concurrently with the assimilation of new information and vice versa (Lamm and Trommsdorff 1973). The group memory features of a GSS—where past information shared can be retrieved for current information use—may help decision-making groups by-pass this cognitive blocking, and thus enhance group decision making.

Similarly, features like anonymity may also help groups make better decisions (e.g., Baltes et al. 2002). Normative influence effects may, for example, cause opinions in the minority to be suppressed, even if those opinions are correct. Public commitment to a position reduces the likelihood that group members will change their positions downstream. From an information influence standpoint, creating an environment where minority opinions persist may stimulate additional information processing. These sorts of normative and information influences may be affected by features such as anonymity embedded in GSS.

Research has shown that GSS may not always demonstrate these desired benefits on information use (Dennis 1996; Baltes et al. 2002). Dennis posits four possible reasons for the limited effects we observe when using information in GSS environments. First, given that GSS have the technical ability to enhance the information gathering and exchange process (discussed earlier), perhaps the additional information provided in a GSS environment may distract from higher quality information use. Second, GSS come in a variety of flavors and configurations. While this flexibility may be useful under the control of expert users or facilitators, in average settings the GSS may not be appropriately configured to the task— basically an issue of task-technology fit (Zigurs et al. 1999; Dennis et al. 2001). Third, features like anonymity may have a very different effect on decision making than anticipated. Information provided anonymously may lack credibility and accountability; thus, even if a GSS facilitates the provision of more information, the information may be of lower perceived quality. Further, anonymity may also reduce the ability to clarify or challenge information provided by a contributor. Fourth and finally, a GSS may make it harder to identify important information, given that more information is exchanged, and the social cues that may be tied to "important" information in a face-to-face interaction may be missing in technology mediated environments. In essence, information may get lost in the shuffle if not appropriately managed through proactive facilitation, training, or some other method that lets the group adapt their methods and tools.

This is not to say that such systems are without hope. Software is now available that allows groups to model their decision making (Chen et al. 2002). Such technologies may allow us to quickly identify the strengths and weakness of strategies (through the use of stakeholder analysis tools), or to quickly assess group attitudes towards particular decision options (for example, through voting tools and multicriteria analysis tools). Furthermore, new research on capturing decision makers' mental models— using GSS—may provide decision makers with new opportunities for learning through conceptualization, discussion, and experimentation, which in turn may support a group's integration of knowledge (Kivijarvi and Tuominen 2001). Perhaps more importantly, we will get better at how to adaptively structure (DeSanctis and Poole 1994) the combined strengths of the technology, the people, and the process.

IMPLICATIONS IN A RAPIDLY EVOLVING WORLD

Reminiscent of an old children's math riddle: if each succeeding generation of technology decreases the remaining bounds on rational decision making by 50 percent, how soon will decision making be completely rational? Answer: Never—technology can continually improve decision making but never can it completely overcome the cognitive limits of its architects.

Our review paints a picture of uncertainty regarding the interactions between technology and decision making. As noted by Weick (1990), there is a technology in the head—the one that matters—that is related to, but generally not the same as, the one on the floor. People *enact* technologies, based on human sensemaking, which renders the moderating role of technology in decision making dynamic.[3] The enactment of technology is particularly critical in groups since it is unlikely that group members will homogeneously enact the same technology (e.g., Griffith 1999). In the early years of Doug Engelbart's career, individuals were more likely to know when they were interacting with technology. The adjustments people made as they used technological tools were often concrete and so likely to trigger sensemaking and adaptive structuration (Griffith 1999).

Today's landscape is quite different. The best knowledge management systems, for example, are largely passive (Griffith and Sawyer 2006). Systems such as that provided by Tacit (www.tacit.com) are designed to work in the background without human intervention, until someone needs to find an answer or someone who can provide an answer. Sensemaking about these more passive (from the human perspective) technologies may be more varied given there are less concrete features on which to base sensemaking and ultimately, adaptive structuration.

We are moving from technology playing a signal role in decision making to a pervasive one. Hansmann et al. (2003) outline these pervasive/ubiquitous computing principles:

- Decentralization—synchronized computing, everywhere.
- Diversification—possession and use of several specialized devices (for example, a laptop computer, a mobile phone, and an iPod (p. 19).
- Connectivity—Lou Gerstner of IBM described his version of connectivity as "Everybody's software, running on everybody's hardware, over everybody's network" (pp. 19–20).
- Simplicity—seamless integration across these devices. "Complex technology is hidden behind a friendly user-interface" (p. 22).

This future computing landscape is a necessary, but not sufficient, condition for what we call Pervasive Decision Support (PDS). PDS additionally implies that individuals and groups are engrained with a predilection to take on new capabilities. We aren't arguing for "Borgs in the org" with a deterministic refrain of "you will be assimilated,"[4] but rather an extension of human skill sets to include methods of adaptive structuration—decisions about how to integrate with technology for the most efficient and effective decision making in a given context.

Users aren't there yet. Jasperson et al. (2005) recently took on the task of modeling the "post-adoptive" behaviors of IT users. They found that IT users apply a limited set of technology features and "rarely initiate technology or task-related extensions of the available features" (p. 526) if left to their own devices.

It will take continued development of organizational practices and technological tools to fully reap the benefits of technology for organizational decision making. Jasperson et al. (2005) argue for a research stream to address how to motivate users to "[continuously] exploit and extend the functionality built into IT applications" (p. 525). It seems critical to help users understand that availability and implementation of technology is just the beginning of effective use.

An explicit approach is needed for:

1. Teaching users to be flexible with their adaptive structuration. Users need to understand that how they are working today may not be the way they should work tomorrow given ever increasing capabilities—and they should embrace the opportunity for these adjustments. The PDS landscape is in constant flux and so users need to be able to make explicit choices about adapting their decision-making approach. What new capabilities should be incorporated? What new capabilities are not worth the transaction cost? Expectations, technology features, and implementation approaches all may affect the likelihood that people are willing to evolve their use of technology systems. Expectations that adjustments in use are likely may prevent users from "anchoring" (Tversky et al. 1974) on the initial form of use. Technology features such as SIM cards and transferable phone numbers in cell phones reduce some switching costs. Implementation built around simulation and/or virtual reality (e.g., Ottosson 2002) may also provide avenues for users to discern better combinations of technology and decision practice before settling into a particular pattern of use.

2. Grasping the organizational realities. Decision-making functions in an organizational context. Currently this means that a camera-capable smartphone may be taken away at the front desk of a firm concerned about data leakage (or a health club); the National Science Foundation may scan a PC for viruses before it can be brought inside their offices; a wireless-enabled laptop may be cut off from the Internet at a vendor's site given security protocols. These organizational realities need to be factored into the decision-making approach. For example, decision makers need to make appropriate choices about what information to carry on a hard drive, versus what can be accessed via an Internet-based source; plans must be made for conference calls with an understanding of the network's capabilities (e.g., number of calls that can be connected via one phone).

3. Presenting systems integration as a life skill—at least until the fully integrated view of pervasive computing (Hansmann et al. 2003) is a reality. For modern decision makers to take full advantage of the current level of PDS, they need to realize that there are integration costs. While Apple markets its Mac personal computer based on a model of full integration (for example, limited effort needed on the part of the user to integrate digital cameras and photo-editing capabilities), that is not the reality of IT today. Users need a basic level of literacy around the integration of various information sources. At a minimum level this means understanding that electronic data can be moved from application to application, though it may not be obvious. For example, www.melissadata.com/ ssl/HomeSales.asp provides data on home sales by zip code. This information

can be useful for tracking trends in a local real estate market, if the information can be moved into an application such as Excel. It would be nice if there were a "download" button on the website, but there is not. The minimum skill of being able to cut and paste the data from the screen, into an application which can put it into a column and row structure, is key to getting the most out of available data.[5]

4. Setting boundaries about where to stop with the integration of technology and decision making. This last point again highlights the difference between technologies that supplement versus supplant human activities in decision making. Decision-support systems vary in their design for supplementing versus supplanting, as well as in their form of use (either supplementing or supplanting). If PDS supplements decision making, there is the opportunity to learn from the experience; the decision maker is still involved in the process and receives feedback about the inputs, processes, and outcomes. If there is tacit information that the system doesn't know, the decision maker can adjust. If the environment changes, the decision maker can adjust. If the PDS *supplants* human decision-making activity the decision maker loses out on the opportunity to make real-time adjustments and to learn from the cause and effect of the process. A decision has been made, but the decision maker may have no idea about the decision's quality. This then begs the question of the form that monitoring and control of the supplanting PDS should take.

These last four points highlight the parameters for effectively enacting technologically augmented decision making. Ancient technologies and even early computer-based decision tools were more likely to trigger the thoughtful consideration necessary to get the most from the technology while maintaining control of the process. Technologies were more physical and/or obtrusive. Now the biggest questions may be how to effectively and mindfully incorporate technology in decision making and what to do in the situations where technology is not available, where decision makers have to effectively revert to less enabled approaches.

ENDNOTES

1 Doug Englebart is the inventor of the mouse, hypertext, and a winner of the National Medal of Technology in 2000.

2 RFID: radio frequency identification. Minimally, RFID is a wireless/radio-based barcode (for more, see www.rfidjournal.com/article/gettingstarted/).

3 Organizational and management information systems scholars have built a solid foundation in this area. For examples, please see Carlson and Zmud (1999), DeSanctis and Poole (1994), Griffith (1999) and, Orlikowski (1992).

4 See for example: Episode #75, *Star Trek: The Next Generation,* "The Best of Both Worlds, Part II."

5 The speed of technology change was brought home to us by a recent Wall Street Journal article (Mossberg and Boehret 2006). In between the first and second drafts of this chapter, Zillow.com was reviewed. Zillow.com provides a satellite image-enabled database of housing prices by zip code, street, or street corner—a dramatic increase in the ease of information gathering.

REFERENCES

AKERLOFF, G. (1970). 'The Market for Lemons.' *Quarterly Journal of Economics,* 89: 488–500.

ALPERT, M. and RAIFFA, H. (1982). 'A Progress Report on the Training of Probability Assessors,' in D. Kahneman, P. Slovic, and A. Tversky (eds.), *Judgment Under Uncertainty: Heuristics and Biases.* Cambridge: Cambridge University Press.

ANON. (1974). *The Merriam-Webster Dictionary.* New York: Simon and Schuster.

ARNOLD, V. and SUTTON, S. G. (1998). 'The Theory of Technology Dominance: Understanding the Impact of Intelligent Decision Aids on Decision Makers' Judgments.' *Advances in Accounting Behavioral Research,* 1: 175–94.

ASCH, S. E. (1956). 'Studies of Independence and Conformity: A Minority of One Against a Unanimous Majority.' *Psychological Monographs,* 70: 1–70.

BALTES, B. B., DICKSON, M. W., SHERMAN, M. P., BAUER, C. C., and LaGANKE, J. S. (2002). 'Computer-Mediated Communication and Decision Making: A Meta-Analysis.' *Organizational Behavior and Human Decision Processes,* 87: 156–79.

BARON, D. and BESANKO, D. A. (1987). 'Monitoring, Moral Hazard, Asymmetric Information, and Risk Sharing in Procurement Contracting.' *Rand Journal of Economics,* 18: 509–32.

BAUMGARTNER, J. (2005). 'Avoiding Analysis Paralysis.' *Communications Engineering and Design,* 31/6: 20–6.

BENBASAT, I. and LIM, L. H. (1993). 'The Effects of Group, Task, Context, and Technology Variables on the Usefulness of Group Support Systems: A Meta-Analysis of Experimental Studies.' *Small Group Research,* 24: 430–62.

BEYNON, M., RASMEQUAN, S., and RUSS, S. (2002). 'A New Paradigm for Computer-Based Decision Support.' *Decision Support Systems,* 33: 127–42.

BRODY, H. (1998). 'Untangling Web Searches.' *Technology Review,* July/August: 26.

BRODY, R. G., KOWALCZYK, T. K., and COULTER, J. M. (2003). 'The Effect of a Computerized Decision Aid on the Development of Knowledge.' *Journal of Business and Psychology,* 18/2: 157–74.

CARLSON, J. R. and ZMUD, R. W. (1999). 'Channel Expansion Theory and the Experiential Nature of Media Richness Perceptions.' *Academy of Management Journal,* 42/2: 153–70.

CHASE, N. 'Training Trend' (www.qualitymag.com).

CHASE, R. B., NORTHCRAFT, G. B., and WOLF, G. (1984). 'Designing High Contact Service Systems: Applications to a Savings-and-Loan.' *Decision Sciences,* 5/4: 542–56.

CHEN, C.-K., GUSTAFSON, D. H., and LEE, Y.-D. (2002). 'The Effect of a Quantitative Decision Aid—Analytic Hierarchy Process—On Group Polarization.' *Group Decision and Negotiation,* 11/4: 329–44.

CHIDAMBARAM, L. (1996). 'Relational Development in Computer-Supported Groups.' *MIS Quarterly*, 20/2: 143–63.

CNBC (2004). 'The Age of Walmart: Inside America's Most Powerful Company.' 1: 29.

DAVENPORT, T. H. and HARRIS, J. G. (2005). 'Automated Decision Making Comes of Age.' *Sloan Management Review*, 46/4: 83–9.

DENNIS, A. R. (1996). 'Information Exchange and Use in Group Decision Making: You Can Lead Group to Information, But You Can't Make it Think.' *MIS Quarterly*, 20/4: 433–45.

—— WIXOM, B. H., and VANDENBERG, R. J. (2001). 'Understanding Fit and Appropriation Effects in Group Support Systems Via Meta-Analysis.' *MIS Quarterly*, 25/2: 167–93.

DESANCTIS, G. and GALLUPE, R. B. (1987). 'A Foundation for the Study of Group Decision Support Systems.' *Management Science*, 33/5: 589–609.

—— POOLE, M. S. (1994). 'Capturing the Complexity in Advanced Technology Use: Adaptive Structuration Theory.' *Organization Science*, 5/2: 121–47.

ENGELBART, D. C. (1962). 'Augmenting Human Intellect: A Conceptual Framework.' Palo Alto, CA: Stanford Research Institute.

—— (1968). *Study for the Development of Human Intellect Augmentation Techniques*. Palo Alto, CA: Stanford Research Institute.

FESTINGER, L. A. (1954). 'A Theory of Social Comparison Processes.' *Human Relations*, 7: 117–40.

GOODHUE, D. L. and THOMPSON, R. L. (1995). 'Task-Technology Fit and Individual Performance.' *MIS Quarterly*, 19/2: 213–36.

GORRY, G. A. and SCOTT MORTON, M. S. (1971). 'A Framework for Management Information Systems.' *Sloan Management Review*, 13/1: 50–70.

GRIFFITH, T. L. (1999). 'Technology Features as Triggers for Sensemaking.' *Academy of Management Review*, 24/3: 472–88.

—— NEALE, M. A. (2001). 'Information Processing in Traditional, Hybrid, and Virtual Teams: From Nascent Knowledge to Transactive Memory,' in B. M. Staw and R. I. Sutton (eds.), *Research in Organizational Behavior*, Vol. 23. Stamford, CT: JAI Press, 379–421.

—— NORTHCRAFT, G. B. (1994). 'Distinguishing Between the Forest and the Trees: Media, Features, and Methodology in Electronic Communication Research.' *Organization Science*, 5/2: 272–85.

—— SAWYER, J. E. (2006). 'Supporting Technologies and Organizational Practices for the Transfer of Knowledge in Virtual Environments.' *Group Decision and Negotiation*, 15: 407–23.

—— MANNIX, E. A., and NEALE, M. A. (2003). 'Conflict in Virtual Teams,' in C. B. Gibson and S. G. Cohen (eds.), *Virtual Teams that Work*. San Francisco, CA: Jossey-Bass, 335–52.

HANSMANN, U., MERK, L., NICKLOUS, M. S., and STOBER, T. (eds.) (2003). *Pervasive Computing: The Mobile World* (2nd edn.). Berlin: Springer.

HIGHTOWER, R. and SAYEED, L. (1995). 'The Impact of Computer Mediated Communication Systems on Biased Group Discussions.' *Computers in Human Behavior*, 11/1: 33–44.

HOLLINGSHEAD, A. B. (2001). 'Cognitive Interdependence and Convergent Expectations in Transactive Memory.' *Journal of Personality and Social Psychology*, 81/6: 1080–9.

HOROWITZ, A. S. (1999). 'The End of Intuition.' *Intelligent Enterprise*, 4/20: 55–6.

JASPERSON, J., CARTER, P. E., and ZMUD, R. W. (2005). 'A Comprehensive Conceptualization of the Post-Adoptive Behaviors Associated with IT-Enabled Work Systems.' *MIS Quarterly*, 29/3: 525–57.

KEEN, P. G. W. and SCOTT MORTON, M. S. (1978). *Decision Support Systems: An Organizational Perspective*. Reading, MA: Addison-Wesley Publishing Company.

KIVIJARVI, H. and TUOMINEN, M. (2001). 'A Dynamic and Multicriteria Group Support System.' Paper presented at the 34th Hawaii International Conference on System Sciences.

KORIAT, A., LICHTENSTEIN, S., and FISCHHOFF, B. (1980). 'Reasons for Confidence.' Journal of Experimental Psychology: Human Learning and Memory, 6/2: 107–18.

LAMM, H. and TROMMSDORFF, G. (1973). 'Group Versus Individual Performance on Tasks Requiring Ideational Proficiency (Brainstorming): A Review.' European Journal of Social Psychology, 3: 361–87.

LATANE, B. and DARLEY, J. (1970). The Unresponsive Bystander: Why Doesn't He Help? New York, NY: Appleton-Century-Crofts.

LEWIS, K. (2004). 'Knowledge and Performance in Knowledge-Worker Teams: A Longitudinal Study of Transactive Memory Systems.' Management Science, 50/11: 1519–33.

—— LANGE, D., and GILLIS, L. (2006). 'Transactive Memory Systems, Learning, and Learning Transfer.' Organization Science, 16/6: 581–98.

McLEOD, P. L. (1992). 'An Assessment of the Empirical Literature on Electronic Support of Group Work: Results of a Meta-Analysis.' Human–Computer Interaction, 7: 257–80.

MINTZBERG, H., RAISINGHANI, D., and THÉORÊT, A. (1976). 'The Structure of "Unstructured" Decision Process.' Administrative Science Quarterly, 21: 246–75.

MORELAND, R. L. (1999). 'Transactive Memory: Learning Who Knows What in Work Groups and Organizations,' in L. L. THOMPSON, J. M. Levine, and D. M. Messick (eds.), Shared Cognition in Organizations: The Management of Knowledge. Mahwah, NJ: Lawrence Erlbaum Associates, 3–31

MOSSBERG, W. S. and BOEHRET, K. (2006). 'A New Web Site for Real-Estate Voyeurs.' The Wall Street Journal, D1.

MUKERJEE, M. (2003). 'Circles for Space: German "Stonehenge" Marks Oldest Observatory.' Scientific American, 289/6: 32–4.

NORTHCRAFT, G. B. and NEALE, M. A. (1988). 'Experts, Amateurs, and Real Estate: An Anchoring-and-Adjustment Perspective on Property Pricing Decisions.' Organizational Behavior and Human Decision Processes, 39: 84–97.

—— GRIFFITH, T. L., and FULLER, M. A. (2006). 'Virtual Study Groups: A Challenging Centerpiece for "Working Adult" Management Education', in S. P. Ferris (ed.), Teaching and Learning with Virtual Teams. Hershey, PA: Idea Group.

ORLIKOWSKI, W. J. (1992). 'The Duality of Technology: Rethinking the Concept of Technology in Organizations.' Organization Science, 3: 398–427.

OTTOSSON, S. (2002). 'Virtual Reality in the Product Development Process.' Journal of Engineering Design, 13/2: 159–72.

PINSONNEAULT, A., BARKI, H., GALLUPE, R. B., and HOPPEN, N. (1999). 'Electronic Brainstorming: The Illusion of Productivity.' Information Systems Research, 10/2: 110–33.

POTTER, R. E. and BALTHAZARD, P. (2004). 'The Role of Individual Memory and Attention Processes During Electronic Brainstorming.' MIS Quarterly, 28/4: 621–43.

ROCHLIN, G. I. (1997). Trapped in the Net: The Unanticipated Consequences of Computerization. Princeton, NJ: Princeton University Press.

RYLE, G. (1949). The Concept of Mind. London: Hutchinson.

SCHWARTZ, A. (2001). 'A Larger Role in the Public Policy Process for User Control.' Communications of the ACM, 44/3: 106–7.

SHIM, J. P., WARKENTIN, M., COURTNEY, J. F. et al. (2002). 'Past, Present, and Future of Decision Support Technology.' Decision Support Systems, 33: 111–26.

SIMON, H. (1957). *Models of Man: Social and Rational.* New York: Wiley.

SIMON, H. A. (1960). *The New Science of Management Decision.* New York: Harper and Row.

SNIEZEK, J. SNIEZEK, J. A., A., PAESE, P. W., and SWITZER, F. S. I. (1990). 'The Effect of Choosing on Confidence in Choice.' *Organizational Behavior and Human Decision Processes,* 46: 264–82.

STASSER, G. and TITUS, W. (1985). 'Pooling of Unshared Information in Group Decision Making: Biased Information Sampling During Discussion.' *Journal of Personality and Social Psychology,* 48/6: 1467–78.

STEINER, I. A. (1972). *Group Processes and Productivity.* New York: Academic Press.

STENGEL, R. F. (1993). 'Toward Intelligent Flight Control.' *IEEE Transactions on Systems, Man, and Cybernetics,* 23/6: 1699–717.

SULLIVAN, L. 'Walmart's Way: Heavyweight Retailer Looks Inward to Stay Innovative in Business Technology,' *InformationWeek* (www.informationweek.com).

TVERSKY, A. and KAHNEMAN, D. (1974). 'Judgment Under Uncertainty: Heuristics and Biases.' *Science,* 185: 1124–31.

WEGNER, D. (1986). 'Transactive Memory: A Contemporary Analysis of the Group Mind.' in G. Mullen and G. Goethals (eds.), *Theories of Group Behavior.* New York: Springer-Verlag, 185–208.

WEICK, K. E. (1990). 'Technology as Equivoque: Sensemaking in New Technologies,' in P. S. Goodman and L. S. Sproull (eds.), *Technology and Organizations.* San Francisco, CA: Jossey-Bass, 1–44.

WILSON, M. G., NORTHCRAFT, G. B., and NEALE, M. A. (1985). 'The Perceived Value of Fringe Benefits.' *Personnel Psychology,* 38: 309–20.

XIA, L. (1999). '*Consumer Choice Strategies and Choice Confidence in the Electronic Environment.*' Paper presented at the American Marketing Association, Chicago.

YATES, F. J., VEINOTT, E. S., and PATALANO, A. L. (2003). 'Hard Decisions, Bad Decisions: On Decision Quality and Decision Aiding,' in S. Schneider and J. Shanteau (eds.), *Emerging Perspectives on Judgment and Decision Research, Cambridge Series on Judgment and Decision Making.* New York: Cambridge University Press.

ZIGURS, I. and BUCKLAND, B. K. (1999). 'A Theory of Task/Technology Fit and Group Support Systems Effectiveness.' *MIS Quarterly,* 22/3: 313–34.

6

MAKING THE DECISION TO MONITOR IN THE WORKPLACE: CYBERNETIC MODELS AND THE ILLUSION OF CONTROL*

DAVID ZWEIG

JANE WEBSTER

KRISTYN A. SCOTT

INTRODUCTION

A control mode which depends heavily upon monitoring, evaluating and correcting in an explicit manner is likely to offend people's sense of autonomy and self-control and, as a result, will probably result in an

* We thank Bradley Alge and Jeffrey Stanton for their comments on an earlier version of this chapter and the Social Sciences and Humanities Research Council of Canada for financial support.

> unenthusiastic, purely compliant response . . . the more obvious and expli-
> cit the measurement, the more noxious it is to employees and thus, the
> greater cost to the organization employing such methods. (Ouchi 1979)

Management control theory suggests that managers must rely on control procedures such as monitoring to ensure efficient and consistent production of goods and services. For decades, managers have depended on the tenets of cybernetic control theory as a model of organizational control (e.g., Mintzberg 1979; Daft 1983; Strank 1983). At its core, actions in the cybernetic control model depend on rationality. Operating as a closed feedback loop, a cybernetic approach involves the careful measurement of inputs, process, and outputs and a comparison of these measures to a standard. The system reveals discrepancies and implements interventions to restore balance. This is a rational and mechanistic process. However, humans are not always rational and do not operate as machines. As Ouchi (1979) and many others have noted (e.g., Hofstede 1978, 1981; Dunbar 1981; Dermer and Lucas 1986; Snell and Youndt 1995), the application of cybernetic models to control behaviors may be destined to fail.

A key form of organizational decision making concerns the monitoring of employee performance. Nowhere has the application of cybernetic models of control to decision making been more evident than in the sphere of electronic performance monitoring. In this context, one stereotypically thinks of the deskilled call center agent being continuously monitored by her supervisor, but peers also monitor their highly skilled colleagues for availability (Zweig and Webster 2002). Whether monitored for performance or for availability, research has been documenting the negative implications for employees over the past 30 years. For instance, a multitude of studies has found that electronic monitoring leads to perceptions of privacy invasion and injustice, higher stress, lowered job satisfaction and increased turnover (e.g., Turner and Karasek 1984; Chalykoff and Kochan 1989; Aiello and Kolb 1995; Stanton 2000; Alge 2001). Ironically, despite the clear evidence pointing to the deleterious effects of electronic monitoring, managers and organizations continue to rely on monitoring to enact control (Zweig 2005).

Recent statistics suggest that electronic monitoring in the workplace is growing at an alarming rate. Beyond traditional forms of electronic monitoring such as telephone or keystroke surveillance, a recent American Management Association survey (2005) found that 76 percent of companies monitor employees' website connections, 55 percent monitor employees' email, and 50 percent store and review employees' computer files. Further, organizations continue to explore the use of real-time employee location tracking using technologies such as radio frequency identification tags and digital mapping (e.g., Perreault et al. 2006). This occurs even though these technologies trigger privacy concerns and have little useful application except for security purposes (Perreault et al. 2006)—as it is the availability of and communication with employees that is generally of importance, not their physical locations.

This chapter explores the reliance on cybernetic control models by managers and organizations when making decisions by investigating the desire for people to establish and maintain control. Further, we argue that applying cybernetic models of control to decision making might be inappropriate when applied to humans. Establishing control via the application of cybernetic models is illusory and can lead to a repetitive spiral of increased control. In contrast, research on leadership offers a different paradigm of control. It considers how a manager's behavior can trigger the appropriate response in an employee by activating the employee's working self-concept for how he or she should behave in the workplace. That is, this chapter examines how employees' desired behaviors and performance can be realized without the need to engage in electronic monitoring.

CYBERNETIC CONTROLS

It has been argued that one of the greatest human fears is losing control and that one of the strongest human motivations and most basic needs is to have control over one's life. (Shapiro et al. 1996: 1224)

Control is a cybernetic, regulatory process that directs or constrains an iterative activity to some standard or purpose (Green and Welsh 1988). In their simplest form, cybernetic models of control operate like a thermostat. Inputs into the system affect its outputs. For example, an agent raises the desired temperature and the thermostat turns the furnace on. When the building reaches the desired temperature, the furnace turns off. The system notes and corrects any deviation from the desired temperature (see Figure 6.1). Although simplistic, this model of

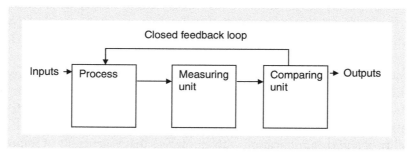

Fig. 6.1 Traditional cybernetic model of control (adapted from Hofstede (1978)).

control has dominated management research and practice since the early twentieth century (Hofstede 1978).

A fundamental tenet of cybernetic control paradigms is that increased monitoring and control can reestablish control that has been lost. Thus, feedback loops are created by the system to detect deviations, analyze, and act upon them. The system identifies any environmental disturbances that threaten to diminish control and implements new processes and procedures to limit any future deviations. When applied to mechanistic processes, the cybernetic control model is a useful paradigm. It is elegant and straightforward and this is likely why it is so popular. However, cybernetic control systems do not learn (Hofstede 1981); they merely react to data.

Many scholars have used the metaphor of control systems to describe the self-regulation of behavior (e.g., Carver and Scheier 1998; Klein 1989). However, the focus is on regulating one's own behavior. When this focus shifts from internal to external regulators of behavior, applying the cybernetic paradigm can lead to difficulties (e.g., Hofstede 1981; Argyris 1990). Specifically, when the mechanistic process is applied as an external regulator of behavior, such as when tasks are monitored by the system and deviations from task completion are regulated, the effects of interventions are unknown (Hofstede 1981). Maintaining stasis is elusive because the system engages in a series of trial and error attempts at re-establishing control. Despite this, managers attempt to reduce the behavior of people into binary-like activities that can be fed into the system and regulated. Repeatedly, these efforts have resulted in failures (e.g., Argyris 1990; Mulholland 2002).

Hofstede (1981) and others (e.g., Dermer and Lucas 1986) argue that there are four basic assumptions underlying the successful use of cybernetic control models. Firstly, objectives are unambiguous and standards are clear. Secondly, accomplishments are measured perfectly. Thirdly, there is a perfect knowledge of cause and effect relationships. Fourthly, activities are repetitive. According to Hofstede, a cybernetic control model will operate effectively only when these four conditions are satisfied.

Although the conditions for cybernetic control and electronic monitoring may not be suitable for the equivocal jobs of professionals, applying electronic monitoring to deskilled positions such as call center agents might seem more appropriate. Call center agents operate in a closely monitored environment and managers encourage agents not to deviate from detailed scripts for customer interactions. Management collects detailed information such as phone-based logs, keystrokes, and mouse activities, while supervisors routinely "listen in" on agent's conversations with customers (Davies 2005a). In these jobs, managers set clear standards for employee performance. For example, management establishes benchmarks for call waiting times and the times required to address customer concerns. Furthermore, call monitoring technologies perfectly measure employee performance against these benchmarks. These technologies, which presumably allow for complete behavioral control, identify cause and effect relationships. Finally, the activities of call center staff are quite repetitive in nature. Employees pick up phone calls, address customer issues relying on scripts, and move on to the next call. In practice, however, the call center context violates each of the basic assumptions of the cybernetic model.

Numerous studies have documented the discrepant objectives of call centers. Although management places an emphasis on customer satisfaction, this outcome is rarely measured (Grant and Higgins 1991; Mulholland 2002; Thompson and Davies 2005). Rather, managers use call waiting time and call resolution time as the standards for performance evaluation and as proxies for customer satisfaction. For employees, these discrepant objectives create confusion and mask the true measurement of outputs. However, employees will engage in rewarded activities. As Grant and Higgins (1991) demonstrated, if organizations reward quantity over quality, employees will respond by increasing the quantity of their work while reducing quality. Thus, the first two conditions necessary for the successful application of cybernetic control models are not met.

If managers believe that there is a clear relationship between incentives and results, then the data gathered from electronic monitoring techniques should provide concrete evidence of the third condition, the effects of rewards and punishments on employee behaviors. For example, employees are rewarded for demonstrating low call waiting times and are punished for engaging in off-task behaviors. In this way, the cause and effect relationships between incentives and results are clear. However, evidence suggests that electronically monitored employees will seek out ways to undermine monitoring and that invasive forms of electronic monitoring might actually serve as a catalyst for employee resistance (e.g., Bain and Taylor 2000). Specifically, call center employees can engage in activities such as picking up calls and immediately hanging up on customers to increase their call response statistics. Thus, call center employees can cut off customers to reduce their call handling times. As well, the monitoring system rarely measures customer satisfaction directly. Both of these examples suggest that the relationship between incentives and results is not altogether clear.

Finally, although call center employees are trained to engage in repetitive behaviors (i.e., the fourth condition of effective cybernetic model use) customer issues do not always fall into predetermined scripts. Whereas employees can be trained to address routine issues, there are many situations in which call center employees are required to address customer complaints that fall outside of the expected parameters. In these situations, call center employees must act in ways that are not proscribed or scripted. However, addressing these issues successfully will often place call center agents at a disadvantage because they are sacrificing their call handling times to resolve customer concerns successfully (Mulholland 2002). This has resulted in some organizations "insourcing" their previously outsourced call centers. In this case, agents use their local knowledge to handle ambiguous calls, while computers using speech recognition technologies address routine inquiries (MacNeela 2005).

In sum, the call center context violates all of the four conditions necessary for the successful application of cybernetic control models (as identified by Hofstede 1981). Although we focus our argument here to the call center context, we suggest that cybernetic models of control may not be appropriate in any organizational setting where managers can choose to implement strict monitoring and surveillance practices. So the question is, why do organizations and managers insist that cybernetic models of control are successful? The answer may lie in our need to establish, maintain, and preserve the illusion of control over our environments.

ELECTRONIC MONITORING AND THE ILLUSION OF CONTROL

Gaining and maintaining control is essential for evolutionary survival (Averill 1973; Bandura 1989). In fact, achieving control over one's environment has been identified as one of the most critical variables involved in an individual's psychological health and well being (Bandura 1989) and decades of research have demonstrated the importance of control to physical and mental well-being (Skinner 1996). Further, individuals tend to hold very strong beliefs about their capacity to exercise control over their own behavior and the environment (Bandura 2001). Thus, to protect their sense of control, people will attribute negative outcomes to situational, as opposed to dispositional, factors (Seligman 1991). Given this drive to establish and maintain control, it is little wonder that cybernetic control models are so enticing.

Thompson, Armstrong, and Thomas (1998) suggest that people will use a control heuristic to judge their degree of influence over an outcome. Two elements drive this control heuristic. First, people assess their intentionality to achieve the outcome and second, they evaluate the connection between actions and the outcomes. Intentionality is driven by the ability to produce a positive outcome. People establish connections when they associate particular actions with that outcome. In an electronic monitoring context, people may form intentionality beliefs if they trust that a desired positive outcome will occur and when they make subjective judgments that associate an action with a positive outcome. In this way, people strengthen the connection between actions and outcomes. In other words, if people believe that performance targets can be set and met, and that achieving those performance targets is of value to them, their intentionality beliefs will be strengthened. Furthermore, as people tend to see themselves as effectual agents, it is not necessary for people to observe a large number of behavior–outcome pairings to establish a connection. In fact, people can make judgments about control with no direct observations of behavior and outcomes simply because of prior expectations for success (Langer 1975; Thompson et al. 1998). Thus, people create an illusion about their ability to establish and maintain control over their environments. It is this illusion that may promote the reliance on cybernetic models of monitoring.

The illusion of control fosters the belief that conventional controls such as concrete performance standards and targets will accurately measure and thereby determine behavior (Dermer and Lucas 1986). This illusion also suggests that managers can intervene when necessary and successfully effect change by altering a given mix of existing controls (Rosanas and Velilla 2005). Although a higher illusion of control can have advantages such as confidence and motivation, it can also result in the discounting of key information as well as concomitantly rigid and retrospectively focused cognition (Dunbar 1981).

Illusions of control can deceive managers (Dunbar 1981). Managers who adopt a cybernetic approach know that any deviations from the prescribed inputs, throughputs and outputs demand increasing control or modifications to the control paradigm. A division of labor often characterizes organizational control processes associated with cybernetic paradigms (Hofstede 1978). One way to achieve this control is via the strict specialization of tasks and the routinization of behavior. This "Tayloristic" approach to control is endemic in call center environments (Mulholland 2002; Brannen 2005). Staff personnel measure and compare behavior according to standards set by higher management, break down behavior, and set time-based performance targets. Management introduces discipline and/or new control procedures to address deviations from scripts or from timed performance criteria. Workers' responses to the control process determine whether the control has been effective.

Although cybernetic models would predict that this action and reaction sequence should result in complete control, decades of mounting evidence suggests the opposite is true (e.g., Argyris 1990; Mulholland 2002). Further, we know from decades of research on deskilling tasks that employees will demonstrate higher turnover, absenteeism, and counterproductive behaviors (Kerr and Slocum 1981). Adding close monitoring on top of deskilling can further exacerbate negative outcomes. As stated by Hofstede (1978), Taylorism and the division of labor can go too far. Workers are better educated, expect more from their jobs and want more than merely extrinsic rewards. Workers also want to experience control over their environments. Of course, there are individual differences in the degree to which people desire control over their environments (e.g., growth need strength, Hackman and Oldham 1980; external locus of control, Spector 1988); however, the desire to maintain control is universal. In other words, not only do organizations and managers strive to maintain control, but so do employees.

When people feel that they lack control, a number of different outcomes are possible. People can respond with passive behaviors. For example, people can develop a sense of learned helplessness (Seligman 1991) in which they relinquish all control and accept their fate, or they can experience lowered self-efficacy

(Bandura 1989). Another response to a lack of control is active. People can actively engage in behaviors designed to re-establish control. However, they may express this desire as deviance (Dunbar 1981). As noted earlier, call center employees may seek to re-establish control over their environments by looking for ways to avoid monitoring, or by tricking the system to enhance their performance outcomes (e.g., Bain and Taylor 2000). In essence, the illusion that managers can control the behavior of others with a mix of reward and punishments can trigger a spiral of increasing control (Hofstede 1981; Dermer and Lucas 1986) and deviance.

This increasing spiral of action and reaction has been called pseudo control (Hofstede 1981), defensive routines (Argyris 1990), and dysfunctional behavior (Birnberg et al. 1983). Regardless of the label, people tend to react to methods of establishing and maintaining control with suspicion and resistance (Henri 2006). According to Hofstede (1978), achieving pseudo-control via correcting standards (rather than the process) and adjusting one element of the process at the expense of others (i.e., increasing call answer targets at the expense of customer satisfaction) expresses the belief that people are robots. People are not robots, so what should managers do?

We argue that the root of the issue lies in the maintenance of the illusion of control described earlier. Of course, organizations and managers do need to control the activities of their employees. However, it is the scope and the depth of control required that becomes fundamental in determining how organizations will direct the activity of their employees. If the illusion of control is strong, then managers will adopt a strict cybernetic approach to control that will flow downwards throughout the organization. Thus, holding true to a cybernetic approach, policies and procedures will be determined at higher levels of the organization that clearly stipulate inputs, throughputs, and outputs to maintain control. Regardless of whether or not the organization requires this mode of control, it is adopted.

SUBSTITUTES FOR AND ALTERNATIVES TO CYBERNETIC CONTROL

Ultimately, the purpose of control in an organization is to accomplish goals. However, there are many routes to goal accomplishment of which cybernetic control is only one possibility. Green and Welsh (1998) extend the cybernetic perspective by incorporating resource dependence. They propose two alternative "quasi-control" strategies—resource dependence reduction and restructuring. Deskilling jobs (as in call centers) is the classic response to resource dependence, thus making these jobs more amenable to cybernetic controls (Green and Welsh 1998). At the extreme, machines replace employees, as in the case of speech recognition systems that handle routine enquiries at call centers (MacNeela 2005).

Dunbar (1981) suggests that employees receive the wrong type of feedback in cybernetic systems. Specifically, these systems provide feedback about outcomes. However, this feedback may be confusing because employees do not know the underlying causal relations between actions and outcomes. Instead, he proposes that employees receive feedback on relations between variables as substitutes for controls. Others propose more diverse measures because firms that value flexibility over control exhibit more diversity in measurement of performance (Henri 2006). Consequently, some suggest that multiple performance indices as tools of diagnosis are preferable to fewer performance indicators used as records of achievement (e.g., Rosanas and Velilla 2005). For example, to promote self-management, Davies (2005b) suggests that multiple indicators of an employee's call center performance be visible on his desktop. Although useful, all of these efforts serve to maintain the fundamental tenets of cybernetic models. In each, managers correct deviations by increasing control within a closed feedback loop. Perhaps organizations require a different model, one that frees organizations, managers, and employees from the shackles of monitoring and breaks the illusion of control cycle.

Moving away from a Tayloristic approach to management control, Hofstede (1978) argues that the most promising way to avoid the illusion of control is to push control downward to those who are involved in the process. Thus, self-control replaces external control. This does not involve relinquishing all management control; rather, employees must regulate their own behaviors in response to clearly and jointly established performance goals. Doing so requires a leap of faith and a measure of trust.

As noted earlier, the illusion of control is universal, easily established, and difficult to break. People strive for cognitive consistency in their environments and try to develop their own models of the world that make sense. To do so, they often trick themselves into believing that they have control where none exists. Thus, to suggest that we should alter our thinking to reject the need to maintain an illusion of control is naïve. However, we can alter how we organize our activities in ways that can preserve the illusion of control and still achieve organizational goals. This requires a different approach to control, one that rejects cybernetic principles and adopts a more balanced perspective.

Many researchers have called for different models of control that downplay cybernetic approaches and have documented mixed support for alternative control models. For example, Snell and Youndt (1995) explored the relationships between traditional cybernetic controls, output controls, and input controls on firm performance and found that cybernetic controls have the strongest positive relationship with overall firm performance. Conversely, Henri (2006) found that flexible, as opposed to more control-oriented firms, promote greater diversity of measurement, attention focusing, and strategic decision making. Leifer and Mills (1996) suggest that reliance on traditional, objective controls limits an organization's capability to address environmental uncertainty. Further, they argue that allowing for normative control mechanisms and self-management, in addition to cybernetic controls, positions an organization to address uncertainty and ambiguity more effectively. Leifer and Mills also explore the implications of different control models and identify loss of control as a key impediment to any rejection of cybernetic approaches. Similar to our discussion of the illusion of control above, Leifer and Mills acknowledge that offering employees more flexibility in regulating their own behaviors can threaten organizational and managerial perceptions of control. Their solution is to use a combination of control mechanisms and to build trust. Indeed, evidence from recent investigations of trust in organizations support Leifer and Mill's propositions.

Deutsch-Salamon and Robinson (2002) examined over 3,600 employees working in 88 locations of a major retail organization that engaged in electronic monitoring activities. All locations had the same surveillance systems in place to control theft and absenteeism. Results indicated that employees who worked in locations with higher expressed levels of trust in management—a high trust climate—exhibited higher responsibility norms and less deviance (e.g., property and production losses). The researchers concluded that managers should consider refocusing their efforts away from monitoring and control and move toward fostering a trust climate to reduce deviance. The interesting thing to note is that the researchers do not suggest the elimination of all forms of electronic monitoring. Rather, they suggest that monitoring efforts can co-exist successfully with employee desires for respect and trust. In other words, employees will accept some level of monitoring as long as they feel that their employers trust and respect them.

In addition to the effects of trust climate on the acceptance of supervisory monitoring by employees, McKnight and Webster (2001) proposed that a climate of organizational trust is important to the acceptance of peer monitoring for availability. In a trusting environment, the employee feels that the system is fair, ethical, and protecting. In contrast, a climate of control may lead to unethical behaviors (McKnight and Webster 2001).

Building trust is crucial in moving away from strict cybernetic models of control. Without trust, it is unlikely that any efforts at relinquishing control or moving control downwards would be successful. But, how does an organization promote the development of trust, especially in a call center context?

Although not examining trust directly, Alge et al. (2006) proposed that monitoring elicits perceptions of privacy invasion and unfairness because the activity itself raises questions about one's self-identity. Employee may construe perceived discrepancies between how they see themselves in general and how they see themselves in a monitored environment as a threat to their personal identity that trigger negative attitudes and behaviors. Specifically, viewing themselves as independent agents whose behavior is self-determined is incongruent with being monitored electronically under the rubric of a cybernetic control paradigm. This violation of the "ideal self" can trigger negative evaluations of the entity that is engaged in monitoring (i.e., the organization and supervisors), leading in turn to negative attitudes and behaviors. Similar to Zweig and Webster (2002) who suggested that monitoring system characteristics be designed to be as benign as possible to avoid privacy and fairness concerns, Alge et al. suggest that electronic monitoring systems should be as transparent as possible and only as intense as is required to accomplish organizational goals. These are useful guidelines to follow if organizations decide to implement or continue to monitor their employees electronically or otherwise. But again, these suggestions only apply within the framework of cybernetic models of control. We need a new approach. From the perspective of managers, we need an approach that preserves the illusion of control without relying on strict adherence to cybernetic models to achieve this control. Further, we need to offer the targets of monitoring opportunities to self-regulate their own behaviors in an effort to achieve and succeed.

DEVELOPING MEASURES OF TRUST AND DEDICATION, NOT CALL ANSWER TIMES

Electronic monitoring reduces employees' "moral autonomy" or the control that they have over their own self-concepts (Brey 1999). In contrast, Ashby's Law of Requisite Variety (1956) suggests that a major source of variety in outcomes is due to the people who execute the processes and only these people possess the variety that can regulate processes. Ashby's law implies that the group that engages in the production of outcomes must have control. In the call center or monitored environment, this means that management must allow front-line staff to control their own performance. However, for employees to have control, leaders must first relinquish this control to them. The question is how to get leaders to relinquish operational control without perceiving this act as surrender of control. Perhaps the answer to this question lies in helping leaders understand how handing over operational control is perceived by subordinates as maintaining, and not losing control. If a leader can demonstrate trust by relinquishing control over tasks, employees may reciprocate by triggering the relevant aspects of their self-concepts that elicit the desired outcomes, namely, high quality job performance.

Self-concepts are representations of the self organized into schemas that encompasses beliefs about who the individuals are, their personalities, and the traits that best represent them (Markus and Wurf 1987). People form schemas through experience and these schemas serve as organizational structures that guide the processing of self-related information in daily social interactions (Markus 1977). These self-representations can take a variety of forms including current self-views and beliefs about what the self could (ideal) and should (ought) be (Markus and Nurius 1986; Markus and Wurf 1987). Moreover, the self-concept is multifaceted and dynamic, involved in all aspects of social information processing. Specifically, it serves as a mediator between the environment and behavior (Markus and Wurf 1987).

A comprehensive review of the leadership and self-identity literature (van Knippenberg et al. 2004) suggests that leadership influences many aspects of follower self-concepts. For example, Shamir et al. (1993) describe the effects of leaders on followers as one of self-concept activation. Specifically, they posit that charismatic leaders cause transformational effects on followers. Similarly, Lord and Brown (2004) have theorized that effective leaders motivate and inspire their subordinates by activating the relevant structures in employees' working self-concepts. That is, leaders make salient the constructs required to carry out a task. As a consequence, the construct becomes more accessible in the working self-concept of subordinates, thus influencing their behaviors. Their model suggests that a subordinate first observes leader behavior and then encodes the behavior into the underlying trait implied by the behavior (see Figure 6.2). In so doing, the subordinate activates these same traits in her mind. Thus, subordinate behavior is influenced through the process of behavioral encoding and working self-concept activation. Thus, leaders may exert influence through activities designed to make various subordinate self-schemas more accessible (Lord et al. 1999). Stated differently, effective leaders are able to bring the relevant self-structures into the working self-concept of the subordinate, thus bringing about the desired behavior

Leaders who demonstrate trust in their employees by eschewing electronic monitoring and entrusting operational control to subordinates are sending a strong message, namely that employees are trusted to accomplish their goals and thus there is no need for the organization to monitor their actions. Therefore, rather than triggering self-identity concerns by engaging in electronic monitoring (Alge et al. 2006), the goal of leaders in the organization should be to activate the desire for performance as a key element of the employee's self-concept.

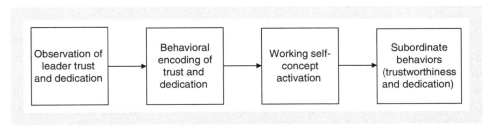

Fig. 6.2 Activation of working self-concept (adapted from Lord and Brown (2004)).

Along with demonstrating trust, it is possible that leaders who behave in a dedicated manner may help make the trait of dedication more accessible in their employee's working self-concept. Indeed, Scott and Brown (2006) asked participants to form an impression of a leader who was exhibiting behaviors consistent with many agentic aspects of the leader prototype (e.g., dedicated, goal oriented). Although they found that certain leader characteristics (e.g., gender) may influence the extent to which changes in the working self-concept occur, their results were consistent with the Lord and Brown (2004) model discussed previously. That is, under certain conditions, simply forming an impression of a leader engaging in certain prototypical behaviors led to activation of those same traits, such that participants indicated their self-perceptions were similar. Extending these results, Scott (2005) found that the impression formation process also affected the behavior of participants, such that engaging in this process resulted in greater persistence on an impossible task. Interestingly, Scott (2005) found this effect of working self-concept activation on behavior simply by asking participants to read a description of a leader who was exhibiting prototypical leadership behaviors. If merely reading about leaders' behaviors in a laboratory setting can activate the relevant traits in employees' working self-concepts and elicit the desired behaviors, it is not difficult to imagine the effects on employees who work for a dedicated and trusting leader.

Of course, if employees do not know what managers expect of them or how to achieve organizational goals, activating their relevant working self-concepts will not be successful. As Snell and Youndt (1995) suggest, cybernetic controls should be replaced with substitutes when standards are ambiguous—substitutes such as, selection, socialization, training, increased autonomy, improved career paths, leadership, and reskilling (Kerr and Slocum 1981; Green and Welsh 1998; Davies 2005b). For example, rigorous selection and training help employees understand the values and goals of the organization. Realistic job previews might also help establish expectations (Premack and Wanous 1985). Organizations can provide clear performance guidelines but employees are ultimately responsible for reaching them. There might be less need for strict control when expectations and outcomes are clear, and when leaders demonstrate the appropriate behaviors to their employees. Leaders are not surrendering control, they are establishing the framework for real control, as opposed to the illusory control resulting from their reliance on cybernetic models.

Pitted against the lure of control offered by engaging in electronic performance monitoring, it may be difficult to accept the notion that leaders might be able to influence the behavior of subordinates by making salient the pertinent aspects of the working self-concept. However, Hofstede (1978) stated that a vague model that corresponds to reality is still preferable to a precise model that does not (such as the cybernetic models discussed in this chapter). Application of the self-concept to leadership is a relatively recent theoretical and empirical proposition (e.g., Lord et al. 1999; Lord and Brown 2004; Scott and Brown 2006). As such, more research needs to further elucidate the effects of working self-concept activation in real-world settings. But, if future investigations are supportive, there is hope for a real alternative to cybernetic models of control, especially in electronic monitoring contexts.

DISCUSSION AND CONCLUSIONS

In this chapter, we have reviewed the literature on cybernetic control and proposed that adopting a cybernetic model to control the behaviors of employees is ineffective. Specifically, we drew upon numerous studies conducted in a multitude of different organizational contexts that suggest that the use of cybernetic models results in an illusion of control (e.g., Snell and Youndt 1995; Leifer and Mills 1996). With few exceptions (e.g., Alge et al. 2004), very little research has considered *why* managers engage in electronic monitoring. We posited that it is this illusion of control that has triggered the growth of electronic performance monitoring in the workplace.

Building upon research offering alternatives to cybernetic models of control (e.g., Snell and Youndt 1995; Leifer and Mills 1996), we offered a new approach to management control. Rather than attempting to maximize outcomes under a cybernetic control paradigm by altering the characteristics of monitoring systems to avoid triggering privacy and fairness concerns (e.g., Alge et al. 2006), we have suggested that managers and leaders can maintain control and accomplish their objectives by changing their behaviors and thereby influencing the behaviors of their employees.

In essence, we are advocating a shift away from cybernetic models of control and the removal of externally driven behavior control systems. Managers who demonstrate trust and dedication can activate these same traits in the working self-concepts of their employees. Managers may not need to electronically monitor workers who feel trusted and are dedicated. If managers ensure that employees have the required knowledge, skills, and abilities to conduct their jobs effectively, train these employees well, and offer clear performance expectations, employees will encode trust and dedication from their leaders and demonstrate appropriate behavioral responses.

Is working self-concept activation a solution or are we just being naive? Call centers generate feelings of individual insecurity: they constantly lower targets for customer contact times and, more importantly, they hold over employees the threat of off-shoring their jobs (Brannen 2005). Given the current workplace environment employees infer that if they want to keep their jobs, they need to accept close monitoring (Brey 1999).

What we are proposing is more akin to a homeostatic process (Hofstede 1978) in which leader behavior activates relevant traits in employees' working self-concepts. Employees engage in desired behaviors and are responsible for all decision-making activity themselves. Supervisors intervene only when required. Obviously, this type of system is more vulnerable than a cybernetic one. It takes time to train employees, establish norms for performance, build trust, and demonstrate dedication. Organizations must make a considerable commitment of effort to adopt this framework. In contrast, it is cheap and easy to implement an electronic monitoring system. When jobs are deskilled, selecting employees with the right mix of knowledge, ability, and personality becomes less important. However, the long-term negative effects of electronic performance monitoring (EPM)—for organizations and employees—are clear. EPM results in increased stress, which can lead to increased illness (Cohen et al. 1991) rising health costs and absenteeism, dissatisfaction, and turnover (Cascio 1991). Monitoring technologies that collect and distribute too much personal information will lead to perceptions of privacy invasion, unfairness, result in negative attitudes toward the organization, and possibly increase deviant behavior (e.g., Bain and Taylor 2000; Stanton 2000; Alge 2001; Zweig and Webster 2002). Adler et al. (2001) reported alarmingly high levels of turnover among monitored employees in some organizations (estimates suggest turnover rates ranging from 30–60 percent). The existing paradigm of electronic monitoring control as a closed-loop feedback system that closely regulates, monitors and adjusts behavior does not work. It is time for a new approach.

As discussed earlier, the self-concept serves as a mediator between the environment and behavior (Markus and Wurf 1987). Working within an electronically monitored environment activates traits such as distrust and fear in an employee's self-concept. Activation of these traits, in turn, can elicit behaviors (e.g., deviance) that perpetuate the need for increased monitoring. If leaders activate a different set of traits, a different set of behaviors will emerge. A great deal of research on leadership suggests that leaders can exert positive influences on employees' behaviors (e.g., van Knippenberg et al. 2004). Furthermore, preliminary evidence suggests that through a process of behavioral encoding, leaders may be able to activate the working self-concepts of subordinates (e.g., Scott and Brown 2006). This is a promising avenue for future research, specifically relating to the effects of leader behaviors in electronically monitored environments. For if changing the behaviors of leaders to elicit desired trait activation in employees results in better outcomes than does the use of electronic performance monitoring, perhaps we can replace the illusion of control offered by cybernetic models with real controls, for both organizations and employees alike.

References

ADLER, S., NELSON, M. T., BUTZ, R. et al. (2001). 'Predictors of Cognitive and Affective Service Performance.' Paper presented at the 16th Annual Conference of the Society of Industrial and Organizational Psychology, San Diego, CA.

AIELLO, J. R. and KOLB, K. J. (1995). 'Electronic Performance Monitoring and Social Context: Impact on Productivity and Stress.' *Journal of Applied Psychology*, 80: 339–53.

ALGE, B. J. (2001). 'Effects of Computer Surveillance on Perceptions of Privacy and Procedural Justice.' *Journal of Applied Psychology*, 86: 797–804.

—— BALLINGER, G. A., and GREEN, S. G. (2004). 'Remote Control: Predictors of Electronic Monitoring Intensity and Secrecy.' *Personnel Psychology*, 57: 377–410.

—— GREENBERG, J., and BRINSFIELD, C. T. (2006). 'An Identity-Based Model of Organizational Monitoring: Integrating Information Privacy and Organizational Justice,' in J. J. Martocchio (ed.), *Research in Personnel and Human Resources Management*, Vol. 25. Greenwich, CT: JAI Press.

AMERICAN MANAGEMENT ASSOCIATION (2005). *Electronic Monitoring and Surveillance Survey*. New York: AMA/ePolicy Institute (www.amanet.org) (accessed April 20, 2006).

ARGYRIS, C. (1990). 'The Dilemma of Implementing Controls: The Case of Managerial Accounting.' *Accounting, Organizations and Society*, 15: 503–12.

ASHBY, W. R. (1956). *Introduction to Cybernetics*. New York: Wiley.

AVERILL, J. R. (1973). 'Personal Control Over Aversive Stimuli and its Relationship to Stress.' *Psychological Bulletin*, 80: 286–303.

BAIN, P. and TAYLOR, T. (2000). 'Entrapped by the "Electronic Panopticon"? Worker Resistance in the Call Center.' *New Technology, Work and Employment*, 15: 2–16.

BANDURA, A. (1989). 'Human Agency in Social Cognitive Theory.' *American Psychologist*, 44: 1175–84.

—— (2001). 'Social Cognitive Theory: An Agentic Perspective.' *Annual Review of Psychology*, 52/1: 1–26.

BIRNBERG, J. G., TUROPOLEC, L., and YOUNG, S. M. (1983). 'The Organizational Context of Accounting.' *Accounting, Organizations and Society*, 8: 111–29.

BRANNEN, J. (2005). 'Time and the Negotiation of Work-Family Boundaries: Autonomy or Illusion?' *Time and Society*, 14: 113–31.

BREY, P. (1999). 'Worker Autonomy and the Drama of Digital Networks in Organizations.' *Journal of Business Ethics*, 22/1: 15–25.

CARVER, C. S., and SCHEIER, M. F. (1998). *On the Self-Regulation of Behavior*. Cambridge: Cambridge University Press.

CASCIO, W. F. (1991). *Costing Human Resources* (3rd edn.). Boston, MA: PWS-Kent.

CHALYKOFF, J. and KOCHAN, T. A. (1989). 'Computer-Aided Monitoring: Its Influence on Employee Job Satisfaction and Turnover.' *Personnel Psychology*, 42: 807–34.

COHEN, S., TYRELL, D. A. J., and SMITH, A. P. (1991). 'Psychological Stress and Susceptibility to the Common Cold.' *New England Journal of Medicine*, 325: 606–12.

DAFT, R. L. (1983). *Organization Theory and Design*. St. Paul, MN: West.

DAVIES, J. (2005a). 'The Six Building Blocks of Contact Center Workforce Optimization.' *Gartner Research*, February 1, ID# G00123457.

—— (2005b). 'Agent Esteem and Self-Actualization are Key to Customer Satisfaction.' *Gartner Research*, August 26, ID# G00129449.

DERMER, J. D. and LUCAS, R. G. (1986). 'The Illusion of Managerial Control.' *Accounting, Organizations and Society*, 11: 471–82.

DEUTSCH-SALOMON, S. and ROBINSON, S. L. (2002). 'Does Trust Climate Deter *Organizational Deviance? An Organizational Level Analysis*.' Paper presented at the 2002 annual Academy of Management Meetings, Denver, CO.

DUNBAR, R. L. M. (1981). 'Designs for Organizational Control,' in P. C. Nystrom and W. H. Starbuck (eds.), *Handbook of Organizational Design*, Vol. 2. Oxford: Oxford University Press, 85–115.

GRANT, R. A. and HIGGINS, C. A. (1991). 'The Impact of Computerized Performance Monitoring on Service Work: Testing a Causal Model.' *Information Systems Research*, 2: 116–42.

GREEN, S. G. and WELSH, M. A. (1988). 'Cybernetics and Dependence: Reframing the Control Concept.' *Academy of Management Review*, 13: 287–301.

HACKMAN, J. R., and OLDHAM, G. R. (1980). *Work Redesign*. Reading, MA: Addison-Wesley.

HENRI, J.-F. (2006). 'Organizational Culture and Performance Measurement Systems.' *Accounting, Organizations and Society*, 31: 77–103.

HOFSTEDE, G. (1978). 'The Poverty of Management Control Philosophy.' *Academy of Management Review*, 3: 450–61.

—— (1981). 'Management Control of Public and Not-for-Profit Activities.' *Accounting, Organizations and Society*, 6: 193–211.

KERR, S. and SLOCUM, J. W., Jr. (1981). 'Controlling the Performances of People in Organizations,' in P. C. Nystrom and W. H. Starbuck (eds.), *Handbook of Organizational Design*, Vol. 2. Oxford: Oxford University Press, 116–34.

LANGER, E. J. (1975). 'The Illusion of Control.' *Journal of Personality and Social Psychology*, 32/2: 311–28.

LEIFER, R. and MILLS, P. K. (1996). 'An Information Processing Approach for Deciding Upon Control Strategies and Reducing Control Loss in Emerging Organizations.' *Journal of Management*, 22: 113–37.

LORD, R. G., and BROWN, D. J. (2004). *Leadership Processes and Follower Self-Identity*. Mahwah, NJ: Lawrence Erlbaum Associates.

—— —— FREIBURG, S. J. (1999). 'Understanding the Dynamics of Leadership: The Role of Follower Self-Concepts in the Leader/Follower Relationship.' *Organizational Behavior and Human Decision Processes*, 78: 167–203.

MacNEELA, A. (2005). 'For Bet Direct, Insourcing Reduces Costs and Increases Productivity.' *Gartner Research*, November 14, ID# G00131270.

MARKUS, H. (1977). 'Self-Schemata and Processing Information about the Self.' *Journal of Personality and Social Psychology*, 35: 63–78.

—— NURIUS, P. (1986). 'Possible Selves.' *American Psychologist*, 41: 954–69.

—— WURF, E. (1987). 'The Dynamic Self-Concept: A Social Psychological Perspective.' *Annual Review of Psychology*, 38: 299–337.

McKNIGHT, H. and WEBSTER, J. (2001). 'Collaborative Insight or Privacy Invasion? Trust Climate as a Lens for Understanding Acceptance of Awareness Systems,' in C. Cooper, S. Cartwright, and C. Earley (eds.), *Handbook of Organizational Culture and Climate*. Chichester: Wiley, 533–55.

MINTZBERG, H. (1979). *The Structuring of Organizations*. New York: Prentice-Hall.

MULHOLLAND, K. (2002). 'Gender, Emotional Labor and Teamworking in a Call Center.' *Personnel Review*, 3: 283–303.

OUCHI, W. (1978). 'A Conceptual Framework for the Design of Organizational Control Mechanisms.' *Management Review*, 25/9: 833–48.

PERREAULT, L., LAPIERRE, C., PLANTE, M., BACHY, D., and CARON, C. (2006). 'MicroGeomatics: A New Paradigm for Mobile Workforce Management.' (www.geoplace.com/uploads/featurearticle/0603fm.asp) (accessed March 24, 2006).

PREMACK, S. L. and WANOUS, J. P. (1985). 'A Meta-Analysis of Realistic Job Preview Experiments.' *Journal of Applied Psychology*, 70/4: 706–19.

ROSANAS, J. M. and VELILLA, M. (2005). 'The Ethics of Management Control Systems: Developing Technical and Moral Values.' *Journal of Business Ethics*, 57: 83–96.

SCOTT, K. A. (2005). 'Female First, Leader Second? Examining the Role of Leader Gender in the Categorization of Leader Behavior.' Unpublished doctoral dissertation, University of Waterloo, Waterloo, ON.

—— BROWN, D. J. (2006). 'Female First, Leader Second? Gender Bias in the Activation of Prototypical Leadership Traits.' *Organizational Behavior and Human Decision Processes*, 101: 230–42.

SELIGMAN, M. (1991). *Learned Optimism*. New York: Knopf.

SHAMIR, B., HOUSE, R. J., and ARTHUR, M. B. (1993). 'The Motivational Effects of Charismatic Leadership: A Self-Concept Based Theory.' *Organization Science*, 4/4: 577–94.

SHAPIRO, D. H., Jr., SCHWARTZ, C. E., and ASTIN, J. A. (1996). 'Controlling Ourselves, Controlling Our World.' *American Psychologist*, 51: 1213–30.

SKINNER, E. A. (1996). 'A Guide to Constructs of Control.' *Journal of Personality and Social Psychology*, 71: 549–70.

SNELL, S. A., and YOUNDT, M. A. (1995). 'Human Resource Management and Firm Performance: Testing a Contingency Model of Executive Controls.' *Journal of Management*, 21: 711–37.

SPECTOR, P. E. (1988). 'Development of the Work Locus of Control Scale.' *Journal of Occupational Psychology*, 61/4: 335–40.

STANTON, J. M. (2000). 'Reactions to Employee Performance Monitoring: Framework, Review and Research Directions.' *Human Performance*, 13: 85–113.

STRANK, R. (1983). *Management Principles and Practice: A Cybernetic Approach*. New York: Gordon and Breach Science Publishers.

THOMPSON, E. and DAVIES, J. (2005). 'Define the Role of the Customer Service Agent in Customer Experience Management.' *Gartner Research*, August 26, ID# G00129511.

THOMPSON, S. C., ARMSTRONG, W., and THOMAS, C. (1998). 'Illusions of Control, Underestimations, and Accuracy: A Control Heuristic Explanation.' *Psychological Bulletin*, 123: 143–61.

TURNER, J. and KARASEK, R. A. (1984). 'Software Ergonomics: Effects of Computer Application Design Parameters on Operator Task Performance and Health.' *Ergonomics*, 27: 663–90.

VAN KNIPPENBERG, D., VAN KNIPPENBERG, B., De CREMER, D., and HOGG, M. A. (2004). 'Leadership, Self, and Identity: A Review and Research Agenda.' *Leadership Quarterly*, 15: 825–56.

ZWEIG, D. (2005). 'Beyond Fairness and Privacy Concerns: Examining Psychological Boundary Violations as a Consequence of Electronic Performance Monitoring', in J. Weckert (ed.), *Electronic Monitoring in the Workplace: Controversies and Solutions*. London: Idea Group.

—— WEBSTER, J. (2002). 'Where is the Line Between Benign and Intrusive? An Examination of Psychological Barriers to the Acceptance of Awareness Monitoring Technologies.' *Journal of Organizational Behavior*, 23: 605–33.

7

CULTURE AND DECISION MAKING

JACQUES ROJOT

INTRODUCTION

LONG ago, Montesquieu theorized about the impact of climates on human behavior and Pascal remarked that what is true on one side of the Pyrenees is wrong on the other. Yet, the relationships between culture and decision making are simultaneously obvious, puzzling, and irritating. No matter how one defines it, culture seems to influence both decision-making processes and decision outcomes. However, when one tries to delve into the details of cultural influence, multiple and contrary interpretations arise. Also, the notion of culture has long been ideologically loaded. The eighteenth-century German theoreticians, for example, contrasted the German national "Kultur" with the French "civilization." German Kultur, they said, represented the genius of the German people, a spontaneous, living knowledge shared by all Germans (Valade 1992), whereas French civilization exemplified the empty and artificial universalism of the Enlightenment.

This chapter argues that the primary effects of cultures in decision making take the form of limitations on decision makers' rationality. Simon pointed out that decision making reflects the limitations of human brains. Subsequently, scholars have written many words about the psychological limitations on rationality. However, rationality also confronts cultural limitations that both augment and dominate the psychological ones.

The chapter begins by summarizing some of the writing about national, occupational, and organizational cultures. It then considers the implications of these writings for organizational decision making.

NATIONAL CULTURE: THE FRENCH EXAMPLE

There are nearly as many interpretations of culture as observers of it. For example, Kluckhohn and Strodtbeck (1961) identified six dimensions along which cultures differ: relationship to nature, human relationships, truth and reality, human nature, human activity and attitudes toward time and change. Based on an extensive experimental study, Hofstede (1980) inferred that cultures differ along four dimensions: power versus distance, uncertainty versus avoidance, individualism versus collectivism and masculinity versus femininity. He later (1991) added a fifth dimension: long-term versus short-term orientation. Trompenaars and Hampden Turner (1997) identified value orientations along seven continua: universalism versus particularism, individualism versus communitarianism, neutral versus emotional, defuse versus specific, achievement versus ascription, human–time relationship versus human–nature relationship.

Perhaps, observers have such diverse perceptions because cultures are complex and contradictory. For instance, Crozier (1963) described some contradictions within French culture. It lacks cooperative activities and informal groups, and there is little communication and much distance between social strata. However, threats evoke a latent defensive solidarity that enforces a strict egalitarianism. These inconsistent characteristics lead to difficulties in facing conflict and developing leadership because conflict and leadership challenge the concept that authority should be absolute, omnipotent, and universal, a concept that reflects French cultural values about social class and education. French culture does not accommodate the ideas of checks and balances, due process, countervailing power, or substantive limitations. Superiors must avoid the face to face conflict in order to protect their absolute authority from challenges or perceived challenges. Yet, subordinates feel threatened by such authority and they strenuously avoid direct exposure to it, as it would require either abject submission or direct confrontation.

The French organizational solution relies on impersonal rules. Power gathers at the top, above strata of subordinates with precisely defined rights and duties. The result fits Crozier's model of the French bureaucratic vicious circle, which he contrasts with the American organizational model. The American model, based on functional divisions and procedural rules, does not require centralization of power, and results in relatively frictionless groups and many face to face interactions.

D'Iribarne (1989) described France as a country that continues to observe traditions that started in the middle ages. One's beliefs and behavior relate to one's position in society. The social hierarchy compares not only the haves and the haves not, but also the noble and the vile, and these distinctions still strongly influence the desire for autonomy, the sense of duty, and workplace relationships. Nowadays, it is not so much birth as other factors such as formal degrees, education, seniority, and initiation ceremonies. Privileges, duties, and responsibilities attach to each social condition. Membership in a specific social group, especially at work, defines honorable treatment and honorable behavior. It influences what individuals consider acceptable or unacceptable for persons in their positions. Individuals perform the duties of their positions and feel responsible for carrying these out. Individuals do not object to rules, regulations, orders, or instructions insofar as they perceive these to be compatible with their work duties. On the other hand, individuals do resent controls, particularly narrow controls on work quality and procedures, that imply that they are unable to perform honorably on their own. Finally, when good personal relationships abound, individuals often perform beyond expectations and job descriptions. Again, the French model contrasts with the American one, in which free and fair contracts between equals provide for control and due process.

Maurice et al. (1982) noted intriguing differences between similar enterprises in France and Germany. In France, average wages for blue collar workers were lower compared to white collar workers, there were more white collar workers, fewer workers held vocational degrees, and there were more foremen, who enjoy less autonomy and prestige. These differences reflect Germany's system of continuing vocational education, which alternates classroom and plant training and allows workers to continue training throughout their professional lives and to gain nationally recognized degrees as high graduate engineer. In Germany, acquiring degrees helps to assure promotion, whereas in France, promotions depend on seniority, individuals' "potential," and initial training. French training is enterprise-specific and focuses on internal mobility and enterprise-specific skills. Thus, French training hampers interenterprise mobility whereas German training allows interenterprise mobility. In turn, both training and mobility affect organizational properties with larger spans of control for German supervisors and more multiskilling for German workers.

OCCUPATIONAL AND ORGANIZATIONAL CULTURES

Other researchers have focused on occupational cultures that cross national borders. Sainsaulieu (1977) surmised that workers share rules, values and practices that help them manage relationships such as solidarity, mutual help, technical complementarity, dependence, authority, on the job training, information, control, and appraisal. They build communities around occupations such as metalworkers, sailors, miners, railway workers. These communities significantly influence the day to day running of organizations, labor conflicts, and decisions reached by its members. At both a national level and an enterprise level, occupational cultures span across organizations and produce similarities among them. During the economic growth of the 1960s, four types of occupational cultures arose among industrial workers: a fusion culture among unskilled labor, a negotiation culture among highly skilled blue collar employees and technical staff, an affinity culture among internally promoted supervisors, and a withdrawal culture among minorities.

Gregory (1983) studied professionals working in Silicon Valley and found "occupational communities" having distinctive cultures that are not simply subcultures, but cross-cut organizational boundaries and provide employees with significant reference groups both inside and outside their companies. Such cultures include computer scientists, software engineers, and marketers.

Finally, a new wave of scholarly work has focused attention on organizational properties and direct influences on decision making. Martin (2002) and Martin and Frost (1996) identified three theoretical perspectives, that both interfere with each other. The integration perspective stresses aspects of culture that unify and unite an organization by focusing on management and decisions by leaders (for example, Schein 1985). This perspective asserts that managers can control organizational culture and even make it their most important tool. Accordingly, a strong culture is healthy for an organization; everyone should share this culture and use it to guide decision making. The differentiation perspective focuses on inconsistencies, differences, and persistent subcultures within organizations; and it acknowledges that organizational cultures have permeable and ill-defined boundaries. Culture reflects many outside factors and combines shared elements, truly unique elements, elements that are not really unique although people believe them to be so (Martin 2002). Culture is something an organization is, not something that an organization has (Smircich 1983), thus it is not susceptible to managerial manipulation. Consequently, culture conditions decision making and is not an outcome of planned decisions. The segmentation perspective is complex and difficult to put into words because it emphasizes the ambiguity of culture. Weick's (1979) concept of loose coupling illustrates how ambiguity implies uncertainty and complexity. Cultural artifacts and rules of behavior have multiple and divergent interpretations (Schein 1985) and links between actions and outcomes are unclear. Employees do not really know what others expect from them; they see different behaviors sanctioned in similar ways and similar behaviors sanctioned in different ways. Double binds prevail (Watzlawick 1963), and the organizations' external relations use hypocrisy (Brunsson 1989). Facing many contradictory demands, an organization operates as a collection of decoupled units, and oversight by top management emphasizes ceremonial inspection and evaluation (Meyer and Rowan 1977). This segmentation perspective sees an organization as having three fully decoupled levels. The top echelon specializes in discourse about the properties of a "good" organization according to prevailing values. The managerial and functional hierarchy produces policies, rules, and strategies according to occupational and managerial requirements and fashions. Although managers used these in their own communications and interactions, other parts of the organization ignore them. Finally, the operating or technical core does work in the most efficient ways, with little regard for discourses or policies.

IMPLICATIONS FOR UNDERSTANDING ORGANIZATIONAL DECISION MAKING

The foregoing ideas about culture make very elusive and unstable foundations for discussions of decision making. National cultures seem to be diffuse and volatile. Individuals in any country differ greatly in the extent to which they share beliefs and values. For instance, the more Anglophile of the Japanese will be much closer to the English average on a given trait than a randomly selected English person. In other words, what is the practical use of a mean with an enormous standard deviation? Furthermore, mysteries shroud the processes by which national cultures change. Direct experience indicates that national traits do change and sometimes quickly. For instance, before 1976, abortion in France was illegal and theoretically could result in the death penalty. In 1976, France legalized abortion and soon after began to reimburse patients through the national health system. Similarly, during the late 1960s and early 1970s, traditional "Anglo-Saxon Puritanism" gave way in the US to the "summer of love," and the social outcomes that were visible on the streets, shops, and bookshop windows. Then in the late 1980s, Puritanism returned to such an extent that the same bookshops veiled magazines featuring topless models. If any fashion can mold very flexible cultural traits, culture becomes an explanation that explains nothing.

Occupational and organizational cultures raise questions of dominance. How can occupational culture co-exist with national culture? Or with organizational culture? Which dominates the other and under what conditions? Do they merge? Do they generate conflict?

Recent writing about organizational culture poses additional issues. The integration perspective suggests that unitary and strongly shared beliefs and culture may be dangerous for sound decision making. For example, a strong culture may foster group think (Janis 1982). The integration perspective also says little about how to integrate diverse employees into a unified cultural mold, although Schein (1985) recommended Lewin's (1947) model of unfreezing, introducing change, and refreezing. The differentiation perspective speaks to these issues, but it does not help to explain how organizational culture is shaped and by what process it emerges. The segmentation perspective offers a more complex framework that lends itself to the analysis of cultural change. For instance, Bartunek (1984) described a "second order" change in the interpretive schemes of a religious order when the order adopted a dialectical process of resolving conflict between groups holding different perspectives. Brunsson (1985, 1989) contrasted an ideology of action (monolithic and simple) with an ideology of decision (complex and rational); he said organizations decouple the two ideologies to allow the efficient operation of an organization. Brunsson also noted that characteristics of organizational culture such as conclusiveness, consistency, and complexity favor change. Meyerson and Martin (1987) and Martin (2002) applied the three perspectives to analyses of cultural changes in the Peace Corps in Africa and in a start-up company. Hatch (1993) offered the most comprehensive framework for the analysis of cultural changes with a model of the dynamics of organizational culture.

These scholarly works, however, need augmentation. They describe and/or illustrate changes in culture, but do not explain fully the processes of change. Indeed, a "deus ex machina" often appears to be operating. For Bartunek, it is the relative, but undefined, power of the groups in conflict. For Brunsson and Martin, change comes from external shocks that move individuals in and out of organizations. Although Hatch outlined elements that motivate the dynamics of corporate culture, she did not attempt to explain the change processes but called for field studies. Interestingly, she introduced Giddens's theory of structuration (Giddens 1976, 1984), but limited it to the importation of "artifacts" from other organizations. Similarly, Johnson's (1988) concept of cultural web, accurately describes the importance of corporate culture, but de-emphasizes the introduction of change. The discussion below draws on Giddens.

LIMITATIONS ON ORGANIZATIONAL RATIONALITY

The central argument of this chapter is that the concept of culture becomes much more useful if one interprets cultures as sets of limitations on rationality. This interpretation addresses some of the issues that other cultural theories ignore. The next section of this chapter briefly reviews the literature about limitations on rationality, and then the ensuing section argues the merits of interpreting cultures as such limitations.

Simon (1955: 104) proposed "that there is a complete lack of evidence that, in actual human choice situations of any complexity," human brains are unable to make the complex calculations that would be necessary in order to choose optimal actions. Simon (1955: 113–14) said that humans have "limited" or "approximate" rationality: they do not know all possible outcomes of their potential actions, they engage in limited searches to investigate such outcomes, and they categorize outcomes crudely as satisfactory or unsatisfactory. The limitations of rationality certainly do not mean that individuals act randomly or irrationally. Within the frameworks of their limited knowledge, capabilities, and means of action, humans try to select preferred alternatives. Therefore, they remain rational but within limits. Their decisions are almost always rational from decision makers' points of view, but may not appear so to outside observers because decision makers using limited capabilities in the context of a too rich and too complex world.

Limitations on rationality occur at two levels. First, perfect rationality demands synoptic perception and a desire to maximize. A decision maker weighs all costs and benefits, considers all possible alternative courses of action together with all their potential consequences, and then selects the one that maximizes satisfaction. Obviously, this cannot be the case because there is not enough information and not enough time to consider all possible courses of action and the human mind is too limited to analyze them even it they were they available. Additionally, the world is too uncertain and turbulent to allow a decision maker to assess all the potential consequences of a course of action with any degree of foresight. Thus, instead of being synoptic, consideration of alternatives is sequential and decisions satisfice rather than maximize. Second, limitations to rationality occur at a second, more complex, level that Simon (1976) called the internal environment of the decision maker. A decision maker does not simply perceive an objective environment; the decision maker actively constructs or enacts an environment. In addition to objective outside information that a decision maker may ignore or perceive inaccurately, decision making incorporates subjective inputs. Situation and process interact.

Because each situation is unique—a combination of a given individual in a given situation—typologies are useful. Several categories of limitations on rationality appear to be rich in operational consequences for decision making. Of course, the types of limitations affect each individual differently, but similarities are sufficient to allow scholars to generalize.

Research on decision making in situations of uncertainty (Kahneman et al. 1982) suggests that humans define situations by using simplified models of reality based on biases and "cognitive heuristics." Heuristics are systematically applied rules of thumb for simplifying reality. Without them, each decision would require reprocessing of all the circumstances of a situation, the environment, and all the consequences that may follow even the simplest decision. They are therefore helpful and their use is unavoidable. However, heuristics may also oversimplify reality and create errors and decision makers are unaware that they are using them. Bazerman (2002) provided useful examples and conveniently summarized research on this topic (see also Shapira, Chapter 15 in this volume). He outlined three general heuristics that are at the root of common biases, and he described how the availability, representativeness, and anchoring and adjustment heuristics cause biases in decision making: Recall of events is based on vividness and recency and not only on actual frequency, and retrieval of events from memory biases the assessment of their frequency. People overestimate the probability of co-occurrence of events. They ignore base rates in estimating the likelihood of events in favor of sometimes irrelevant information. They ignore statistics in overestimating the representativeness of small samples as well as regression to the mean of extreme events and the likelihood of co-occurrence of events. Available irrelevant information anchors estimates of the value of uncertain events without sufficient adjustment. People also overestimate the probability of events that must occur jointly and underestimate the probability of events that must occur independently and they demonstrate overconfidence in their judgment, capacities, or knowledge. Other biases include systematic search for confirming evidence, not looking for disconfirming evidence, assuming that whatever happened was what had to happen, and assuming that others share our knowledge when we deal with them. Drawing on Kahneman and Tversky's prospect theory, Bazerman complemented the list of biases by describing the impact of framing the dimensions of a problem at hand, notably regarding risk. For instance, individuals will take risks to avoid a loss that they would not take to obtain an equivalent gain. He also outlined various motivational biases: positive and unrealistic illusions of optimism, of control on random events, of self-attribution for success and other-attribution for failure, egocentrism, and regret avoidance. Finally, he drew on Staw's work (1976, 1997) to describe the causes of the irrational escalation of commitment to an unsatisfactory course of action.

Another type of limitation on rationality issues from the unreliability of human memory. It is in fact "fallible, incomplete, malleable and susceptible to external factors" (Offer and al. 2000: 737). In a longitudinal study, Offer and al. (2000) interviewed 73 14-year-old males in 1962, and interviewed 67 of them again when they were 48. The researchers found such significant differences between adult memories of adolescence and what was actually reported 34 years later that accurate memory could generally be considered doing no better than what could be expected by chance. For instance, in 1962, only 14 percent of the respondents said they were their mother's favorite, but 30 percent remembered being the favorite 34 years later. Twenty-eight percent of the teenagers said that they did not like school and homework, but as adults 58 percent remembered not liking school and homework. Eighty-two percent of the boys reported being disciplined with physical punishment while only 33 percent of the men reported such punishment. Memories that affect many decisions are not accurate but are mental reconstructions that incorporate beliefs, prejudices and subsequent experience.

Building on Simon's work, Shapira (1997) contrasts the traditions of behavioral decision theory and organizational decision making. He points out that even though individuals make decisions, organizational membership alters the decision-making contexts. Factors that separate organizational decision making from decision making by isolated individuals include pervasive ambiguity, a longitudinal context that includes history, other participants with expectations, deep-reaching incentives including survival, the repetitive character of many decisions with the development of routines and ubiquitous conflict, power and authority. A fully isolated individual, taken out of context, left alone in a simplified and no-risk situation with a well defined task meets few relevant limitations on rationality because the situation evokes very few pressures or routines. On the other hand, an individual deeply embedded in an interactive, ongoing, hierarchical, complex, ambiguous, conflict ridden and risky organizational situation faces multiple and complex limitations.

At a simple level, limitations on the rationality of individual people influence organizational decisions. For instance, Loftus and Loftus (1993) demonstrated that a jury is deeply influenced by witnesses in the decisions it reaches in court. However, they also demonstrated that witnesses' memories not only change over time, but are subject to influence, fragile, and suggestible. Repressed memories, often of sexual abuse, for example, can in fact be totally invalid but may neverthe-less bring a jury to convict an innocent individual (Loftus and Ketcham 1996).

At a more complex level, Cyert and March (1963) pointed out that organizations do not have goals, only individuals do. Similarly, only individuals make decisions, organizations cannot. However, decisions taken by individuals within organiza-tional contexts differ from decisions taken by isolated individuals. Just as a goal set through complex bargaining within a dominant coalition of organization members becomes roughly analogous to an organization goal (Cyert and March 1963), decisions taken by individuals in positions of responsibility become analogous to organizational decisions. March and Simon (1958) outlined the "cognitive limits on rationality" that organizations bring to bear on decision making by members, resulting in repertories of loosely coupled action programs in which members engage without further deliberation when relevant stimuli occur.

Perrow (1979) described organizational "unobstrusive controls" that frame individual decision making. He pointed to the

> specialization of activities and roles so that attention is directed to a particular set of values; attention directors that channelize attention ... rules that limit choice in recurring situa-tions ... a restrictive range of stimuli and situations that narrow perception; training and indoctrination that allow the individual to make decisions by himself as the organization would like him to decide. (1979: 145)

One can see these features, unlike Perrow, not as the results of deliberate and almost conspiratorial planning by top management but as unavoidable outcomes of organizational structure. Following March and Simon, one can consider that they result from division of work, modes of communication, and uncertainty absorption. Although top management designs the organizational structure, this takes place within unacknowledged conditions and brings forth unforeseen consequences, which in turn become new unacknowledged conditions of further action (Giddens 1984). Recursively, employees react within these conditions and influence each other. Thus, limitations emerge from an interactive processes rather than intentional design. In a similar line of thought, March and Olsen (1976, 1979: 12) described the ambiguity and multiple pressures surrounding decision making in organizations: "decisions are a stage for many dramas." Limitations on the rationality of the participants come from the many other organizational activities into which they are simultaneously involved. According to March and Olsen, they include executing standard operating procedures, discovering what has happened to the organization, distributing glory and blame, the play of friendship, trust, and power and status relationships.

Limitations on rationality form a continuum with an increasing degree of complexity that includes nationality, occupation, and organization. The simplest limitations on rationality may be the physical and biological ones. Psychology has demonstrated that perception takes place through the simultaneous operation of selection, structuration, and interpretation (Hirst 1965). Hence, even at the most basic levels, different individuals perceive different realities. When an individual interacts with others in situations that are more complex, additional limitations on rationality come into action. In a way, the next basic level of limitations is made of rules (national laws, occupational customs, organizational regulations). These rules place very visible and obvious limitations on the rationality of members of collectivities. Whether they obey the rules or not is irrelevant because in any case, they influence decision making, even when decision makers seek to escape their influence or to circumvent them. As well, people in collectivities build shared stocks of knowledge and they construct reality by typifing habitual actions (Berger and Luckmann 1966). These shared typifications mean that members of a group share views of reality and develop accepted ways to do things. These typifications influence not so much the process of decisions as their premises. The results include, for instance, the recognition or not of decision opportunities as well as the decisionless choices and choiceless decisions reported by Salancik and Cooper Brindle (1997).

Social psychologists have studied how social influence or situational determinants place strong limitations on rationality. Festinger (1962) defined cognitive dissonance as a tension felt by people whose cognitions are inconsistent. Inconsistency among cognitive elements such as between beliefs and perceptions creates tension and people strive to resolve such tension. Obviously, a possible solution is to change one's beliefs or one's perceptions. Festinger pointed out that some beliefs are easy to change and others hard to change; and likewise, some perceptions are easy to change and others hard to change. Human brains, he proposed, adopt the easier alternatives. Staw (1977, 1997) argued that people become committed to their situations or their prior acts, and tend to behave as they have been behaving even when continuation and escalation may be irrational. Salancik (1977) and Beauvois and Joule (1987, 1998) developed the psychology of commitment originally proposed by Kiesler (1971). It holds that only one's acts commit one, not one's decisions. Salancik (1977: 26) neatly summarized its basis by evoking the possibility that "a good deal of what we think and feel follows from our behavior" and not the other way around. In other words, attitudes follow behavior instead of the commonly held view that behavior derives from attitudes. This implies that one does not have direct access to the knowledge of what one thinks, feels, or wants. One must draw inferences from one's own behavior and the circumstances within which it occurred. Therefore, the determinant of decisions and behavior is not rationality but the circumstances of a situation within which one is involved. Within this theoretical framework, limitations on rationality and other decisive factors in decision making rest in organizational circumstances that include organizational culture.

The latter line of thought introduces another perspective on decision making that supports an even stronger case for viewing culture as limitations on rationality. This point of view finds its philosophical roots in phenomenology and support in recent work by biologists. It implies that the traditional mechanism of rational action preceded by deliberate decision is at least partly misleading. Some students of the activity of the brain hold that action is decision and decision is action (Berthoz 2003) or that action is often indistinguishable from emotions and precedes deliberation and decision (Damasio 1994). Merleau-Ponty (translation by Mingers 2006: 156) stated, "When we are engaged in acting in the world, we neither control our bodies, nor do we 'think of' an intention... Rather the doing of the action is synonymous with the intention itself...". Such a framework gives situational factors greater roles in organizational decision making. Decisions or actions are immersed within the interactions of individuals and their organizational environments and merge with these. The location of a decision maker in the time and space of an organization (Giddens 1976, 1984) induces the decision maker to enact an organizational decision.

Viewing Cultures as Limitations on Rationality

To consider cultures as sets of limitations on the rationality of decision makers would speak to several issues: cultural change, the shaping of connections among national, occupational and corporate cultures, and cultures' diverse effects on decision making.

One should not view limitations on rationality only in a negative sense. For instance, Bazerman (2002) noted that heuristics can lead to more efficient cognitive processing and decision making. Giddens' (1976) remark that structure is both enabling and constraining applies to limitations on rationality that come from culture. More generally, one can consider organizational routines as the memory of an organization. Routines are certainly organizational limitations on the rationality of individual members, but most times they are helpful by providing clear guidelines for choice and action in confusing circumstances. Actually, business has deemed routines important to the point of enshrining them into processes certificated by outside agencies, such as the ISO. This has immensely eased, for instance, subcontracting and the establishment of networks of suppliers. Even more generally, "the way we do things around here" is an indisputable consequence of organizational culture and has both negative and positive consequences. In some circumstances, "the way we do things around here" can constitute a competitive advantage, such as the profit-sharing and participative human resource policies of Marriott and Nordstrom.

Culture consists of shared limitations on the rationality. Of course, individuals share those limitations differently, depending on the collectivities to which they belong and particulars of specific situations. Usually, a larger collectivity allows for more deviations from shared limitations. Hence, national culture will tend to be looser than occupational culture, which tends to be looser than organizational culture. A powerfully inclusive collectivity exerting pressure on its members places limitations that are more similar on its members' rationality than does a looser one. The smaller the group, the easier it is for a strong culture to develop. Mutual interactions are be more numerous, deviants are more visible. In addition, a given collectivity may exert different amounts of pressure in different circumstances. For instance, national culture has a more powerful influence and places more stringent limits on citizens while the country is at war than after the country has been at peace for a long time.

National culture creates general national limitations on rationality, even if they are rather loose, and allows for much individual deviation from the average. The common understanding of rules is an example: in Germany and Switzerland, most pedestrians wait at a red light until it turns green, even with no incoming cars insight; whereas in France, pedestrians hasten to cross the street against the light even with cars coming. Driving habits in the UK and France afford another concrete example: "asocial driving" is, without further legal definition, a driving offense in the UK, whereas in France, courtesy at the wheel of a car is almost non-existent. Even medicine shares these biases: a "liver crisis" is unknown to physicians outside of France. On a more scientific level, Hofstede's ranking of nations on four dimensions seeks to describe behaviors that reflect shared perceptual biases.

Cultures, or shared limitations on rationality, are not limited to nations, occupations and organizations. Several partly distinct cultures may co-exist within a collectivity. For instance, researchers have identified how individuals use broad categories of social reality to interpret and act (Littlejohn et al. 1994). They apply broad views of the world that "deep philosophical principles which define what it means to be a person and [to] lead a life...basic moral assumptions" (Littlejohn et al. 1994: 70). Bellah et al. (1985) said these principles include four models: the Biblical or authoritarian, based on God's authority; the republican, based on civic rights and duties; the utilitarian, based on the pursuit of individual interests; and the expressivist, based on the pursuit of individual rights and free expression. Within each of these views of the world, the proper ways to act seem obvious and evident; yet these same people are unable to see the world from another standpoint, at least spontaneously.

Boltanski and Thevenot (1991) described how relationships among individuals rest on systems of shared meanings based on commonly held values. The shared meanings allow one to find social relationships, guide one's attitude toward others, characterize situations, and coordinate interactions. These values are consistent within each of six "worlds" that define coherent universes of situations and relations:

1. *The world of inspiration* values creative geniuses, artists, researchers, and creators and emphasizes creativity and inspiration, in the lab, office, studio, or marketing agency's creative department.

2. *The domestic world* values those who respect superiors and peers, and the rules of honorable conduct and emphasizes tradition, precedent, lineage, seniority, family, ancestors, and elders.

3. *The world of opinion* values the opinion of others, recognition by the largest possible audience, or fame that an action can bring its actor, the promotion of one's personal image. Acknowledgement of behavior by as many as possible and public opinion are emphasized, whether for a movie or rock "star," a successful "charismatic" businessman, teen "idol," news anchor, jet-set or TV "personality."

4. *The civic world* values public service and democratic operation of institutions and organizations, collective good over individual interests. It emphasizes equity, citizenship, solidarity, and law that rules democratic collectivities.

5. *The merchant world* values the market laws. It emphasizes profit, competition, gaining customers or market share, gaining the best price, successful business ventures, closing deals, getting the best of a bargain, even if opportunism is involved.

6. *The industrial world* values technical performance, efficiency and science. It emphasizes a scientific approach to industrial production, high technology, capital intensive enterprises, plant and technical training, scientific improvement engineering and measurement of productivity, machine objective rationality.

These worlds are surprisingly similar to the moral realities that Bellah et al. (1985) perceived. Specifically, their republican world is similar to the civic world, their traditional world is similar to the domestic one, their utilitarian world is comparable to the merchant one, and their expressive one is similar to the inspiration one. The additional opinion and industrial worlds appear to be frequent combinations of some separable features that warrant their addition as distinct categories. Each world uses preferred principles, subjects, objects, figures that shape decision making and correspond both to limitations on rationality and to features attributed to cultures.

At a corporate level, collectivities are more inclusive and tighter than at a national level, at least within the managerial group. There is less room for variations among cultures or shared limitations on rationality. Johnson (1988) outlined a "cultural web" of organizational action consisting of reciprocally reinforcing elements, "myths, rituals, symbols, control systems and formal and informal power structures which support and produce relevance to core beliefs." The cultural web establishes strongly constraining "cognitive bounds" within which management operates. Again, culture is identical to socially constructed limitations on rationality that shape on corporate decision making. March and Simon (1957) identified in terms of cognitive limitations on individual rationality, subtle and "unobtrusive" influences that an organization's structure and communications exert on employees' decisions, resulting in a set unique, to some extent, to each organization.

Culture understood as limitations on rationality has direct effects on decision making, as classic examples illustrate. In the early 1970s IBM specialized in research and design of big powerful computers that it rented to clients. These orientations influenced the people IBM hired, the training it gave to employees, and the values that top managers espoused. IBM's resulting cognitive limitations in its research, engineering, and marketing conspired to make its forecasting ignore elements present in the technological and market environment that were allowing the design of a personal computer. It thus lost ground that was almost impossible to make up. The "talent mindset" developed at Enron consisted of overpaying the brightest young "stars" and promoting them to the highest positions. This mindset pervaded the organization and some commentators deemed it to have played a major part in the company's demise (Gladwell 2002). Because of a defeat in 1870, the French military general headquarters developed an aversion to defensive tactics and an emphasis on attack in all circumstances. In 1914, this heuristic permeated the doctrine taught at the War College and probably influenced the selection of personnel for promotions. The heuristic also resulted in huge human losses during the first year of World War I. The "attack" heuristic prevented search for alternative tactics and drove to further reliance on offensive ones.

Changes in culture become evident when enough individuals start to share a new limitation. Giddens (1976, 1984) explained how repeated day to day interactions gradually turn into accepted and shared behaviors and cognitions. Thus, reproduction is also production in that it contains germs of social change. When enough people, through interactions in context, partake of a new perception or belief, it becomes a more generalized limitation on cognition, in other words, a cultural trait.

Behavior in the Paris "metro" (subway) is a case in point. In the 1960s and 1970s, at rush hour, when a train paused at a station, passengers would dig their way into a car, crushing as many people as possible, helping themselves by hand and foot pressure on the sides of the open door. In turn, they were crushed by other fellow passengers waiting behind on the platform until a solid block of bodies inside the car prohibited any further entrance. The automatic doors then huffed and puffed until they closed with difficulty. Fellow riders told any protester, old, young, nimble, or with stiff joints, either to shut up and accept the common fate or to take a cab. Nowadays, the behavior is the opposite. Even when cars could accommodate more passengers and occupants block the doorways, travelers nevertheless wait on the platform for the next train. The few individuals who try to force their way in become the objects of general scorn, negative comments, and possibly of physical retaliation.

Another example comes from the sunny southern beaches, where female topless sun bathing was prohibited. Police strictly enforced this prohibition by local ordinances adopted by virtually every local authority, and the few guilty parties were sentenced for offenses to public decency. The very few exceptions consisted of fenced private naturist "reserves" for fully nude practitioners and were closed to the general public. Nowadays, topless sunbathing on the beach has become the general rule and what has become the exception, if not yet a scandal, is the covered body top.

In the business world also, examples exist. For instance personal experience demonstrates that in a large multinational where a strict male dress code and a prohibition of drinking on duty, whether on company premises or on outside business, were unanimously observed, open shirts collars and consumption of wine are now fully accepted, if not yet prevalent.

These changes occurred gradually. Presumably, some individuals had opposed the former behaviors but yielded silently to the majority's pressure. Gradually, more individuals came to share this opposition. The silent minority became vocal. Reflexivity brought more individuals bending back on their past behavior to consider the new one as acceptable and drove some of them to adopt it. Finally, the minority became the majority. Numbers, of course, were not the only factor. The media, rumors, exemplary famous cases very likely played major roles by publicly demonstrating the growing social acceptability of the new practices. The change process ends (provisionally) when the new limitations (the new rational way to behave on a beach, in the subway, at work) drive to taken for granted decisions—the decisionless choices, according to Salancik and Cooper Brindle (1997).

Analysis of culture as limitations on rationality can harmonize national, occupational, and corporate cultures in a single coherent set of connections. The limitations have similar effects, but come from different sources. Differences in between individuals come from how people immersed in national, occupational, and organizational environments reconcile organizationally accepted behavior and cognitive limitations with the other sets of limitations that come from other sources as well as from personal experience and cultures.

The academic world provides an example: in more and more research and teaching institutions worldwide, academics gather, coming from very different backgrounds: ethnic, national, religious, socio-economic and familial, training and research. Their only common set of limits on their rationality is their occupational choice of the academic profession including notably the ones issuing from training for and obtaining a PhD. An organizational culture puts limitations on rationality. It is visible in decisions taken by individuals either as organization members or in their personal lives. It shapes organizational and individual decisions regarding who gets or does not get tenure, who gets promoted, what is acceptable in terms of time devoted to consulting, teaching standards, preferred outlets for publication, campus residence, and the like. However, within that organizational culture, other limitations on the rationality of members do exist and come from either cultural influences having other sources or from individual experience. For instance, academics trained in finance may share a "physics envy." Nationals from other countries may be inclined toward international work. Relations with the students may be influenced by religious limitations. Socio-economic backgrounds, at least in Europe, separate individuals who socialize outside work and those who do not.

CONCLUSION

The primary effects of cultures in decision making take the form of limitations on decision makers' rationality. This applies to individual decision making as well as organizational decision making but sheds a new light on the latter. The concept of limitations of rationality, complemented with elements of Giddens' theoretical framework, facilitates understanding of individual differences and changes in culture. It replaces rather vague definitions of culture with a notion that is well grounded in theory, experimentally verified, and particularly relevant for decision making.

REFERENCES

BARTUNEK, J. (1984). 'Changing Interpretitive Schemes and Organizational Restructuring: The Example of a Religious Order.' *Administrative Science Quarterly*, 29: 365–92.

BAZERMAN, M. (2002). *Judgment in Managerial Decision Making* (5th edn.). Hoboken: Wiley.

BEAUVOIS, J.-L. and JOULE, R. V. (1987). *Petit traité de manipulation à l'usage des honnêtes gens*. Grenoble: Presses Universitaires de Grenoble.

BELLAH, R. N., MADSEN, R., SULLIVAN, W. M., SWIDLER, A., and TIPTON, S. M. (1985). *Habits of the Heart: Individualism and Commitment in American Life*. Berkeley, CA: University of California Press.

BERGER, P. L. and LUCKMANN, T. (1966). *The Social Construction of Reality.* New York: Doubleday.

BERTHOZ, A. (2003). *La decision.* Paris: Odile Jacob.

BOLTANSKI, L. and THEVENOT, L. (1991). *De la justification.* Paris: Métaillé.

BRUNSSON, N. (1989). *The Organization of Hypocrisy: Talks, Decisions and Actions in Organizations.* New York: Wiley.

CROZIER, M. (1963). *Le phénoméne bureaucratique.* Paris: Editions du Seuil.

CYERT, R. M. and MARCH, J. G. (1963). *A Behavioral Theory of the Firm.* Englewood Cliffs, NJ: Prentice Hall Inc.

DAMASIO, A. R. (1994). *Descartes' Error: Emotions, Reason and the Human Brain.* New York: Putnam.

D'IRIBARNE, P. (1989). *La Logique de l'honneur.* Paris: Editions du Seuil.

FESTINGER, L. (1962). *A Theory of Cognitive Dissonance.* Palo Alto, CA: Stanford University Press.

GIDDENS, A. (1976). *New Rules of the Sociological Method.* New York: Basic Books.

—— (1984). *The Constitution of Society.* Cambridge: Polity Press.

GLADWELL, M. (2002/2003). 'Management: la chasse aux bons éléves'. *Commentaire* (Winter), 100 (translated from the *New Yorker*, July 22, 2002).

GREGORY, K. (1983). 'Native Views Paradigms: Multiple Cultures and Culture Conflicts in Organizations.' *Administrative Science Quarterly,* 28: 359–76.

HATCH, M.-J. (1993). 'The Dynamics of Organizational Change.' *Academy of Management Review,* 18, 657–93.

HIRST, R. (1965). *Perception of the External World.* New York: Macmillan.

HOFSTEDE, G. H. (1980). *Culture's Consequences: International Differences in Work Related Values.* Beverley Hills, CA: Sage Publications.

JANIS, I. L. (1982). *Groupthink: Psychological Studies of Policy Decisions and Fiascoes.* Boston, MA: Houghton Mifflin.

JOHNSON, G. (1988). 'Rethinking Incrementalism.' *Strategic Management Journal,* 9: 75–91.

KAHNEMAN, D., SLOVIC, P., and TVERSKY, A. (1982). *Judgment Under Uncertainty: Heuristics and Biases.* New York: Cambridge University Press.

KIESLER, C. A. (1971). *The Psychology of Commitment: Experiments Linking Behavior to Belief.* New York: Academic Press.

LEWIN, K. (1947). 'Group Decision and Social Change,' in T. Newcomb and E. Hartley (eds.), *Readings in Social Psychology,* New York: Holt.

LITTLEJOHN, S. W., SHAILOR, J., and BARNETT PEARCE, W. (1994). 'The Deep Structure of Reality in Mediation,' in J. P. Folger and T. S. Jones (eds.), *New Directions in Mediation.* Thousand Oaks, CA.: Sage Publications.

LOFTUS, E. F. and KETCHAM, K. (1996). *The Myth of Repressed Memories.* New York: St Martin's Griffin.

—— LOFTUS, G. R. (1980). 'On the Permanence of Stored Information in the Human Brain.' *American Psychologist,* 35/5: 409–20.

MARCH, J. G. and OLSEN, J. P. (eds.) (1976). *Ambiguity and Choice in Organizations.* Bergen, Oslo, Trömso: Universitetsforlaget.

—— GUETZKOW, H. and SIMON, H. A. (1958). *Organizations.* New York: Wiley.

MARTIN, J. (2002). *Organizational Culture: Mapping the Terrain.* Thousands Oaks, CA: Sage.

—— FROST, P. (1996). 'The Organizational Culture War Games: A Struggle for Intellectual Dominance,' in S. CLEGG, C. Hardy and W. Nord (eds.), *Handbook of Organization Studies*. London: Sage, 599–621.

MAURICE, M., SELLIER, F., and SILVESTRE, J. J. (1982). *Politique d'education et organisation industrielle en France et en Allemagne*. Paris: Presses Universitaires de France.

MERLEAU-PONTY, M. (1945). *Phénoménologie de la perception*. Paris: Gallimard.

MEYER, J. W. and ROWAN, B. (1977). 'Institutional Organizations: Formal Structures as Myth and Ceremony.' *American Journal of Sociology*, 83: 940–69.

MEYERSON, D. and MARTIN, J. (1987). 'Cultural Change: An Integration of Three Different Views.' *Journal of Management Studies*, 24/6, 623–47.

MINGERS, J. (2006). *Realising Systems Thinking*. New York: Springer Science.

OFFER, D., KAIZ, M., HOWARD, K., and BENNET, E. (2000). 'The Altering of Reported Experiences.' *Journal of the Academy of Child and Adolescent Psychiatry*, 39/6: 735–42.

PERROW, C. (1979). *Complex Organizations: A Critical Essay* (2nd edn.). Glenview, IL: Scott, Foresman and Co.

SAINSAULIEU, R. (1977). *L'identité au travail*. Paris: Presses de la Fondation Nationale des Sciences Politiques.

SALANCIK, G. R. (1977). 'Commitment and the Control of Organizational Behavior and Belief,' in B. M. Staw and G.R. Salancik (eds.), *New Directions in Organizational Behavior*. Chicago, IL: Saint Clair Press.

—— COOPER BRINDLE, M. (1997). 'The Social Ideology of Power in Organizational Decisions,' in Z. Shapira (ed.), *Organizational Decision Making*. Cambridge: Cambridge University Press.

SCHEIN, E. (1985). *Organizational Culture and Leadership*. San Francisco: Jossey-Bass.

SHAPIRA, Z. (1997). 'Introduction and Overview,' in Z. Shapira (ed.), *Organizational Decision Making*. Cambridge: Cambridge University Press.

SIMON, H. A. (1955). 'A Behavioral Model of Rational Choice.' *Quarterly Journal of Economics*, 69: 99–118.

—— (1965). *Administrative Behavior* (2nd edn.). New York: The Free Press.

—— (1976). 'From Substantive to Procedural Rationality,' in S. Latsis (ed.), *Method and Appraisal in Economics*. London: Cambridge University Press, 129–48.

SMIRCICH, L. (1983). 'Concepts of Culture and Organizational Analysis.' *Administrative Science Quarterly*, 28: 339–58.

STAW, B. M. (1976). 'Knee Deep in the Big Muddy: A Study of Escalating Commitment to a Chosen Course of Action.' *Organization Behavior and Human Performance*, 16: 27–44.

—— (1997). 'The Escalation of Commitment: An Update and Appraisal,' in Z. Shapira, (ed.), *Organizational Decision Making*. Cambridge: Cambridge University Press.

TROMPENAARS, F. and HAMPDEN TURNER, C. (1997). *Riding the Waves of Culture: Understanding the Cultural Diversity in Business*. London: Nicholas Brearley.

VALADE, B. (1992). 'Culture,' in Boudon (ed.), *Traité de Sociologie*. Paris: Presses Universitaires de France.

WATZLAWICK, P. (1963). 'A Review of the Double Bind Theory.' *Family Process*, 2: 132–53.

WEICK, K. (1979). *The Social Psychology of Organizing*. Reading: Addison Wesley.

PART II

DECISION MAKING DURING CRISES AND HAZARDOUS SITUATIONS

FACING THE THREAT OF DISASTER: DECISION MAKING WHEN THE STAKES ARE HIGH

MICHAL TAMUZ
ELEANOR T. LEWIS

INTRODUCTION

THE stakes are high for managers when their decisions can precipitate industrial accidents or intensify the damages wrought by natural forces. Confronted with the possible consequences of their choices, organizational decision makers plan for what could go wrong by interpreting the present and making sense of the past. They reflect on previous disasters, but often have sparse experience from which to learn. The prohibitive costs of failure reduce the feasibility of learning from trial and error. To avert or mitigate possible disaster, managers can choose from an array of decision-making routines: they can plan how to respond, scan for warnings, study past errors and close calls, and imagine future threats.

Applying the term "disaster" broadly, this chapter examines decision making that could result in (or avert) high negative consequences, including events that cause loss of lives and property in the organization or community. High stakes decision making usually occurs during natural disasters or in industries using high hazard technologies, such as aviation, nuclear power, and chemical manufacturing. However, it can also occur in organizations operating in high benefit industries. For example, healthcare policy makers have called attention to the dangers of hospitalization, where medical errors can cause harm rather than heal (e.g., Kohn et al. 2000). Similarly, food safety regulators make decisions about infrequent, but extremely damaging events linked with vegetable farming, such as the choice to implement a "lettuce safety initiative" in response to fatal E. coli contaminations (Grady 2007). The chapter identifies common constraints that characterize high stakes decision making in different contexts and considers how organizations address these constraints.

Disasters, accidents, and near accidents punctuate and propel research on high stakes decision making. These include natural disasters such as the impact of Hurricane Katrina on New Orleans; high risk technology failures such as the *Columbia* shuttle explosion; industrial accidents such as the release of poisonous gas in Bhopal; transportation accidents such as the capsizing of the *Estonia* ferry; terrorist threats and attacks; and medical technology failures such as radiation overdoses. Researchers apply their theories to decipher these events; they also use these events to expand their understanding of high stakes decision making. Detailed investigations of disasters offer insights into decision-making patterns that remain largely invisible to outsiders under routine conditions.

Studies of high stakes decision making appear in disparate research literatures that focus on specific types of events with high negative consequences and on particular levels of analysis. These studies build their conceptual frameworks on the foundations of various disciplines including management, social psychology, sociology, and political science. Some research streams focus on the public arena, where administrators and elected officials are key decision makers. These decision makers prepare for and respond to natural disasters or regulate aviation and other hazardous technologies. Other research literatures concentrate on private industry, where decision makers may huddle together in nuclear power plants or confer while conducting patient rounds in hospitals. Disasters have spurred the development and refinement of theories of organization and cognition; however, organizational level decision making plays a peripheral role in these theories that alternatively focus on the organizational (e.g., Turner 1978), industry (e.g., Perrow 1984), and individual (e.g., Weick 1990) levels of analysis.

When organizations engage in high stakes decision making, common decision-making practices emerge across organizational contexts. To illustrate these practices, the chapter includes examples from recent events and from social science research. The review focuses on organizational rather than individual high stakes decision-making (e.g., Kunreuther et al. 2002), but is not a comprehensive review (see Marcus et al. 1993 and Vaughan 1999 for related reviews). It excludes cases of malfeasance and deliberate harm, such as fraud and sabotage, focusing instead on decision making in situations where things go wrong despite the efforts by organizations and their members. The chapter concentrates on high stakes decision making in situations that could have negative outcomes; however, the stakes are also high when organizations anticipate extremely positive outcomes and further research is needed in this area.

The first part of this review examines decision making under the threat of disaster; the second part concentrates on decision making in the midst of disaster; and the third focuses on the choices made during post-disaster investigations. For ease of presentation, the chapter considers these disaster-related phases separately, but in practice, they circle back and interlink in a mesh of feedback loops. Often only a post-disaster investigation, for example, clarifies what occurred in the midst of disaster. The chapter concludes with a discussion of several decision-making practices that organizations have developed to help address some of the challenges for decision makers identified throughout the review.

DECISION MAKING UNDER THE THREAT OF DISASTER

This section examines how organizations plan for expected, but unpredictable disasters; struggle to interpret warning signals; learn from errors, small failures, and near misses; and, despite the obstacles, seek to gather data to support their learning efforts.

Planning for the Expected but Unpredictable

Preparing for disaster is complicated because it involves planning and prevention. Immediate problems distract decision makers' attention from future concerns (Levinthal and March 1993). Decision makers also must weigh the certain costs of investing resources in the present against uncertain payoffs at an undetermined future time (March 1981). Moreover, it is difficult to demonstrate that investments in prevention were successful. These decision-making constraints are particularly salient for elected officials: the voters are likely to hold them accountable if they neglect immediate needs, but they may no longer be in office when disaster hits.

Decision makers lack reliable information on how to predict the timing, location, and potential damage of some future events. Long-term predictions of impact remain uncertain, even for inevitable natural disasters such as tornadoes and hurricanes, where short-term forecasts are relatively accurate. Unusual and, perhaps, unimaginable events, such as nuclear accidents or terrorist acts, raise even greater uncertainties for decision makers (Clarke 2005).

Decision makers face paradoxical constraints when they plan for expected—albeit temporally unpredictable—disasters. On the one hand, it may be difficult to mobilize scarce resources to prevent damages that have not occurred in recent history (if ever). An example is the series of decisions that led the Army Corps of Engineers to build the levees in New Orleans to obsolete standards (Marshall 2006).

On the other hand, given the lack of reliable predictions, decision makers can also focus on worst case scenarios to the exclusion of more likely negative events. For instance, the government has failed to complete the controversial national repository for nuclear waste in Nevada (now on hold indefinitely), because it must build the repository to last for a million years (Vastag 2004). Meanwhile, low level nuclear waste remains stored on site at nuclear facilities across the country, where it may be more likely to cause problems. When decision makers base their plans on the worst case, they not only tend to overestimate the likelihood of extreme cases, but also their ability to cope with them, leading to overconfidence and a misplaced sense of security. Clarke (1999) describes disaster response plans as "fantasy documents," such as the wildly unrealistic plan for a mass evacuation of Long Island in case of a nuclear plant accident.

To augment their limited experience with disasters, decision makers construct exercises and simulations. Like the planning process, disaster response simulations enable decision makers from different organizations to establish personal and professional relationships that they can rely on in actual emergencies (Kapucu 2006). Some high reliability organization theorists argue that decision makers working in high hazard industries can use simulations to overcome some of the constraints of a lack of reliable predictive information (e.g., La Porte 1982; Marone and Woodhouse 1986). Simulations enable participants to imagine circumstances beyond their immediate experience and to anticipate what could go wrong when they execute response plans. This experience can be valuable to front-line responders (e.g., firefighters or air traffic controllers) who go through realistic simulation scenarios; however, organizational decision makers cannot necessarily substitute simulations for actual or vicarious experience (Sagan 1993).

Simulations can yield ineffective decision-making guidelines. Even the most detailed simulations cannot anticipate and incorporate all of the ways in which complex systems can interact to produce a "normal accident" (Perrow 1984). Simulations based on incomplete or inaccurate information can be misleading. Politicians can also claim that plans are in place and they are prepared even if the simulations were unrealistic (Clarke 1999). Finally, decision makers may not act on conclusions from an exercise, even when they consider the exercise effective. A year before Hurricane Katrina, a federally funded exercise called "Hurricane Pam" accurately foreshadowed the effects of Katrina, but decision makers did not use the exercise results to improve hurricane disaster response (*House Report* 2006: 109–377).

Interpreting Warning Signals

In contrast to natural disasters, industrial accidents and other technological failures defy prediction and their warning signals can be difficult to discern. Decision makers can overlook warning signs because of the language they use to frame and classify their experiences. Warnings may also become lost in a fog of ambiguous signals, go unnoticed in the noise of routine performance deviations, or be disregarded after too many false alarms.

Language influences how decision makers attend to and interpret information. For example, the vocabulary that NASA staff used to frame discussions about the tendency of chunks of foam insulation shielding the space shuttle to fall off and strike the shuttle during takeoffs allowed them to dismiss this as a critical problem (Ocasio 2005). Different groups also can develop distinct vocabularies for talking about and engaging in "sensemaking" about disasters leading to divergent approaches to handling hazards (Gephart 1997). Similarly, organizational definitions of medication errors can lead health care providers to label some mishaps as errors and classify identical mishaps as non-events. The language used to classify errors contributes to underreporting, and thus reduces available data (Tamuz et al. 2004).

Even decision makers who proactively seek warning signals can overlook them in the streams of performance feedback. Turner (1978) posited that a precondition of industrial accidents was a "failure of foresight," in which organizations overlooked or ignored warnings. However, Gephart (1984) argued that some warnings only become self-evident in hindsight and managers can find it difficult to sort out potential warning signals from the noise of other signals. The difficulty in identifying warnings is illustrated by nuclear power plant managers and engineers who struggle to identify anomalous events because the plant drifts "within a safety border, which is influenced by error signals, feedback loops, and imperfect watchfulness" (Marcus and Nichols 1999: 496). At NASA, managers did not see the shedding of the insulating foam as a threat so they denied engineers' requests for additional information that could clarify potential damage to the *Columbia* (Weick 2005).

False alarms can also be a source of danger. Before making choices on the basis of warning signals, decision makers must first determine if the warnings are credible. False alarms have led to close calls in firing nuclear missiles (Sagan 1993) and delayed the response to actual warning signals (Perrow 1984).

Learning from Reported Errors, Small Failures, and Near Misses

When organizations have limited experience with disasters, they gather information about and seek to learn from small failures (Sitkin 1992; Edmondson 2004) and near accidents (March et al. 1991). Near accidents are events in which no damages or injuries occurred, but under slightly different circumstances the events could have caused harm. This section discusses how decision makers can benefit from analyzing these safety-related events in depth.

Studies in the aviation and nuclear power industries suggest that in-depth, inductive analyses of potentially dangerous events can assist organizations in drawing useful conclusions from particular near accidents or precursor events (e.g., Carroll et al. 2002). For example, in the airline-based Aviation Safety Action Partnership (ASAP) a decision making team made up of representatives of management, pilots and regulators informally discusses pilot reports until they reach a consensus on how to respond to the hazardous event or situation. The airlines have adopted their ASAP recommendations to change particular operating procedures and enhance pilot training materials (Ganter et al. 2000).

In nuclear power plants in contrast, regulations require a structured event review process. The plant gathers hazard reports and sorts them by their safety significance, multidisciplinary plant representatives engage in a standard root cause analysis,

---

Box 8.1 Near Misses Identify Threats to Patient Safety

In a Neonatal Intensive Care Unit (NICU) at an Indianapolis hospital three infants died after receiving adult doses of heparin, a drug routinely used to prevent clotting in intravenous drug lines. A veteran pharmacy technician placed a vial with the wrong concentration of heparin in the drawer of an automated drug cabinet. The nurses who removed the vial subsequently failed to double check the concentration before administering the heparin.

On the surface, the event was a tragedy involving human error: highly experienced personnel performing routine actions they had done before without incident in a hospital that correctly administers heparin hundreds of times a day. Clearly multiple factors converged to allow this to happen, including the purchase of similar looking vials that had different concentrations of the same drug and the error occurring with patients vulnerable to overdoses.

The tragedy of the infants' death was intensified because this hospital had reportedly experienced "near misses" involving heparin previously. However, following the near misses, the hospital decided to make limited changes that were insufficient to prevent future fatal errors. Near misses present the opportunity to learn from experience, i.e. how to prevent future negative events, but decision makers may draw disparate conclusions from these ambiguous events.

Sources: Rodriguez, September 19, 2006; Webber, September 18, 2006.

and they prescribe corrective actions (Carroll 1998; Perin 2005). However, Perin found that event review participants actually drew on their experience and judgment, not necessarily quantifiable data, to "arrive at a coherent image out of the collage of evidence," and to generate hypotheses that could account for the evidence (Perin 2005: 215).

Data-Gathering Complications

Organizations face difficulties in gathering information about safety-related events and relaying it from front-line employees to organizational decision makers. Decision makers interpret away potential dangers; the politics of blame generate disincentives for reporting errors and system breakdowns; and professional norms are not always consistent with relaying information upwards to managers. Studies have also identified conditions under which national regulators and unit level supervisors successfully fostered event reporting.

Interpreting Away Potential Dangers and Errors

Near accidents are open to alternative interpretations, in part, because they do not result in negative consequences. Decision makers can choose to "emphasize how close the organization came to a disaster, thus the reality of danger in the guise of safety, or the fact that the disaster was avoided, thus the reality of safety in the guise of danger" (March et al. 1991: 10). They can interpret near accidents either as a warning (e.g., in aviation see Tamuz 2001) or as reassurance that the system remains robust (e.g., in the *Challenger* space shuttle explosion, see Starbuck and Milliken 1988).

When decision makers explain away errors, organizations cannot gather valid data about their experience. For example, near-launchings of nuclear weapons, caused by poor design and unsafe behavior, were "explained away as 'operator error' " and the information about the actual underlying causes was thus overlooked (Sagan 1993: 224). In contrast, to avoid potential individual culpability, managers in air traffic control towers (Tamuz 2001) and teaching hospitals (Tamuz et al. 2004) "defined away dangers" by classifying hazardous situations into technically correct, but non-reportable categories. In their study of multiple, often fatal errors at the UK's Bristol Royal Infirmary, Weick and Sutcliffe (2003) found that clinical and bureaucratic decision makers at multiple levels were not trying to cover up their errors. Instead, they explained away preventable deaths by attributing them to the complexity of patient cases rather than to the poor performance of physicians, thereby precluding individual and organizational learning (Weick and Sutcliffe 2003: 81). Baumard and Starbuck (2005) also found that managers in a European telecommunication firm explained away large failures by ascribing them to idiosyncratic or external conditions beyond the control of the organization. Whether the processes underlying the explaining away of error are political or cognitive (or both), these processes reduce the amount of valid data available to decision makers.

Disincentives for Reporting

An organization depends on its employees to disclose problems so that the organization can learn from its experience. But front-line employees are often reluctant to report negative information (e.g., Morrison and Milliken 2000), in particular when supervisors could use the information for disciplinary purposes (e.g., Lawler and Rhode 1976). Organizational politics also provide disincentives for managers to disclose their own or their employees' possible failures. The effects of this widespread phenomenon are intensified in high hazard environments, such as the military (e.g., Sagan 1993), nuclear power (e.g., Perin 2005), and aviation (e.g., Tamuz 2001). In these contexts employees can be the sole source of information about hazards, and supervisors hold their employees strictly accountable for compliance to rules and regulations.

Professional Norms

Organizations in high hazard industries sometimes rely on professional norms rather than bureaucratic rules to guide behavior and these norms can inadvertently hinder gathering information about threats to safety. Professionals pride themselves on being innovative, independent problem solvers; yet this very behavior can keep potential warning signals from surfacing. Tucker and Edmondson (2003) found that nurses improvised "work-arounds" to temporarily solve system-based problems (such as shortages of critical equipment or services), but nurses rarely brought these "solved" problems to the attention of their managers.

In teaching hospitals, administrators may not hear about errors and small failures, in part because of the professional norms governing the relationship between residents (physicians in training) and the hospital. Physician training norms have stifled opportunities for both individual and organizational learning from errors (Hoff et al. 2006). In an Emergency Department, for instance, residents regularly discussed their errors with other physicians on their team. But because little information reached the department, these residents' experience could not inform departmental decisions about preventing errors (Schenkel et al. 2003). The physicians were aware of threats to patient safety, and sometimes willing to talk about them, but the hospital was not ready to listen.

Fostering Reporting

To overcome some of the internal organizational barriers to gathering information about safety related events, a few industry associations and regulators have developed industry wide reporting systems designed to collect data about these events. In aviation, safety analysts have found that event reports can provide valid information about potential dangers. These reports have proved instrumental in changing airline procedures as well as air traffic regulations (e.g., Mewhinney 2006). However, fluctuations in the number of events that pilots report are not reliable safety indicators (e.g., Tamuz 2001). Other industries, such as chemical manufacturing (e.g., Phimister et al. 2003) and health care (e.g., Leape 1994), have sought to follow aviation safety models with mixed results (Fernald 2004; Etchegary et al. 2005;). This suggests that although industries may confront common obstacles to gathering information about threats to safety, policies that promote reporting may be industry specific.

Supervisors can personally create conditions that promote error reporting within their units. Edmondson (1999) found that high performing nursing units had higher incident reporting rates, reflecting the nurses' perceptions that supervisor support created an environment of "psychological safety." Research in aviation and health care suggests that the organizational structure and the mix of bureaucratic and professional procedures used to control employee behavior may generate different methods for fostering the reporting of safety related events.

DECISION MAKING IN THE MIDST OF DISASTER

Despite the predicament of obtaining data on real-time decision making during disaster response, researchers have sought to understand the decisions that organizations make as they respond to the unfolding events. Disaster response typically demands coordination among many organizations and this section considers studies of interorganizational communication as well as decision making. It also presents research that documents how specific decision-making practices have contributed to catastrophic outcomes and studies recommending how to avert them.

Coordinating Decision Making During a Disaster

The nature of crises means that disaster investigators and researchers often must depend on reconstructions based on survivors' recollections and incomplete records. The 9/11 Commission report (2004), for example, used both sources in its meticulous reconstruction of the communications between the New York City police and fire departments during their response to the September 11 attacks. Detailed disaster investigations can provide reconstructions of the sequence of organization

---

Box 8.2 The Disastrous Response to Hurricane Katrina

Freudenburg and his colleagues (2006) argue that the massive destruction and loss of life that followed Hurricane Katrina resulted from four separate disasters:

- the powerful storm itself;
- the failure of the levees and other protection systems;
- the way decision makers modified the environment in New Orleans over the last 50 years;
- the failed organizational response to the hurricane and the flooding.

The choices that decision makers made as they planned for or responded to the hurricane contributed to each of these disasters.

Hurricane Katrina's aftermath illustrates both the key role of interorganizational communication and decision making during disaster response as well as previous points about disaster planning:

1. Decision makers had focused on more visible solutions to New Orleans' vulnerable geography. For example, they built levees rather than rebuilding wetlands, which would have reduced the huge storm surge (von Heerden and Bryan 2006).
2. Local decision makers delayed making evacuation mandatory because their previous experience led them to believe that a complete evacuation would be unnecessary.
3. Disaster response decision makers failed to learn from the simulated disaster of "Hurricane Pam" (*House Report* 2006: 109–377).

---

members' real-time disaster response decisions that are invaluable to scholars. Research is now beginning to emerge on the response to Hurricane Katrina (e.g., Daniels et al. 2006; Freudenburg et al. 2006; von Heerden and Bryan 2006) and detailed studies of decision making may follow as researchers sift through the available data.

The dynamic nature of a crisis response requires "interorganizational and interjurisdictional coordination" (Tierney 1985: 77). This was evident in Bhopal India, for example, where an industrial accident at a chemical plant released a cloud of poisonous gas that killed thousands of people in the surrounding community (Shrivastava 1987). The lack of coordinated decision making between the corporation and government agencies responsible for protecting the community exacerbated the harm to people and property. Studies have also captured how organizational decision makers establish this critical interorganizational coordination, for example, by examining the links that organizations establish during a disaster (e.g., Topper and Carley 1999; Kapucu 2006).

Disasters can require both immediate responses and actions staggered over months or years. How organizations make decisions can undermine their efforts to respond effectively to both these acute events and slowly evolving events. Acute events include natural disasters such as Hurricane Katrina, the 9/11 attacks, and the toxic contamination of a state office building (Clarke 1989). Slowly evolving events include those at the Bristol Royal Infirmary (Weick and Sutcliffe 2003) and the massive oil spill at Guadalupe Dunes in California, which developed over 38 years (Beamish 2002). Clarke (1989) studied both the immediate response to the toxic contamination and the protracted response to its cleanup; he characterized coordination decisions as following an "interorganizational garbage can" decision making model. The study illustrates how the plans for centralized command and control decision making often differ from the choices that organizations actually make as they attempt to coordinate disaster response efforts with others.

Government agencies in particular have difficulty making decisions requiring interorganizational coordination during disaster response. As Daniels et al. (2006: 8) note, natural disasters, such as Hurricane Katrina, "do not respect the boundaries defining governmental or organizational missions and responsibilities." Indeed, the failure of interjurisdictional coordination among all levels of government agencies is a recurring theme in studies of Hurricane Katrina (e.g., Bier 2006).

Decision Making as the Culprit (or Hero)

Researchers have long studied how decision making contributes to high negative consequence events, both to understand how organizations operate when things are going wrong, as well as when they are going as expected. These studies have identified misguided decision making practices that have contributed to or directly caused negative outcomes. For example, during the decision-making processes that led to the launch of the space shuttle *Columbia*, time and production pressures distracted decision makers' attention from risk (Buljan and Shapira 2005) and they focused on meeting deadlines as a goal in itself (Blount et al. 2005).

Analyses of the space shuttle *Challenger* disaster vividly illustrate how decision making can generate negative consequences. In his first-hand account, former Thiokol engineer, Roger Boisjoly, focused on the critical choices that immediately preceded the launch decision (Boisjoly et al. 1989). Enlarging the focus, subsequent analyses shifted attention to decision making in the months and years that preceded the ill-fated launch (Vaughan 1996). According to these analyses, engineers and managers at NASA and Thiokol routinely used decision-making practices that eventually contributed to the shuttle's destruction. Starbuck and Milliken (1988) argue that a history of successfully coping with high-risk endeavors shaped how NASA and Thiokol decision makers interpreted the data from previous shuttle flights. They "fine tuned" the odds of future success by interpreting the results of real-life experiments in a complex and incompletely understood technical and political system and became gradually acclimated to the results.

Vaughan's (1996) analysis of the *Challenger* also drew her attention to the recurring, incremental decision-making practices in the years preceding the launch. Drawing on interviews with participants and archival documents, she concluded that recurring signals of potential danger lost their salience to decision makers as they assessed the risks of variations in performance. The normalization of deviance was the outcome of cultural factors in the organization and its environment, including the culture of the engineers' workgroup, the professional engineering culture, and restricted access to the data used by the engineering workgroup.

Both *Challenger* analyses emphasize the importance of understanding how decision makers interpret and assess risks of future endeavors based on historical technical data and do so in the context of cultural assumptions and political pressures. These analyses illustrate how incremental changes in decision-making practices can result in disaster, particularly when organizations make decisions based on incomplete information about technologies they do not fully understand. Tragically, as Vaughan's (2005) analysis of the *Columbia* space shuttle accident suggests, understanding these processes does not necessarily prevent their recurrence.

Research on High Reliability Organizations (HRO) highlights distinctive decision making practices in organizations that routinely manage complex and dangerous technologies with few major disruptions. For example, decision makers maintain "mindfulness" when categorizing ambiguous information that helps them notice warnings of unexpected events (e.g., Weick and Roberts 1993). HRO researchers also stress the benefits of decentralized decision making, where managers defer to the expertise of lower ranking employees, especially when identifying hazards, and give them decision making authority to respond to emergent threats (e.g., Rochlin et al. 1987). Again, the *Challenger* studies emphasize that these decision making practices may not be universally effective, particularly when the organization confronts complex technology operating under unknown parameters.

DECISION MAKING DURING
POST-DISASTER INVESTIGATIONS

Disasters tend to be complex and it is difficult for decision makers to untangle their causes. Accident investigations have high stakes for individuals and organizations—reputations and reparations are on the line—and stakeholders have incentives to deflect blame onto others. Perhaps the most difficult obstacle is to avoid hindsight bias: the tendency to believe that decision makers could have foreseen the causes of events when there were structural or other barriers to prevent such foresight. When looking back and attempting to explain what caused an accident, decision makers impose structure on situations that they originally experienced as ill-formed and confusing (Turner 1978). Decision makers who know that a negative result occurred tend to look for the flawed perceptions that led to it (Starbuck and Milliken 1988), which, in hindsight, makes behaviors and outcomes appear more tightly linked than they were at the time of occurrence.

Given the complexity of events, the politics of decision making, and hindsight bias, investigations may yield unreliable assessments of the causes of disasters. For example, Tasca's (1990) study of parallel investigations of marine accidents by the National Transportation Safety Board (NTSB) and the courts found that the separate investigations produced strikingly different conclusions about the ship owners' responsibility. Tasca's findings notwithstanding, the tendency more generally for disaster investigations to "blame the operator" distracts attention from the responsibility of those higher in the organization (e.g., Perrow 1984) and stops the search for further explanations that could reveal faulty system design or inadequate procedures (e.g., Sagan 1993). Haunschild and Sullivan (2002) suggest that airlines that generate heterogeneous explanations for accidents (rather than simply blaming the pilot) dig deeper into their causes, and thus learn how to reduce the number of accidents. For some accidents, investigators may simply be unable to ascertain what occurred or why it happened (e.g., see the NTSB Report 2000 about TWA flight 800).

Accident investigations can reveal needed changes in technical specifications, organizational procedures, and industry practices. They can also generate new methods for gathering safety related data, inform organizational level decision making, and create new industry level associations. For example, the creation of the Institute of Nuclear Power Operation following Three Mile Island has increased information sharing about hazardous events in the nuclear power industry (e.g., Perin 2005). Similarly, the results of an aviation accident investigation helped mobilize political support for the founding of the Aviation Safety Reporting System (Reynard et al. 1986).

Yet many lessons learned from investigations are later forgotten. Organizational decision makers may make decisions, then fail to implement them (e.g., Pfeffer 1992), but when the stakes are high the consequences of such failures can be deadly. For example, investigations of New York City's response to the attacks of 9/11 found that the lack of interoperable communication equipment hindered inter-agency coordination, and contributed to the deaths of firefighters and police (9/11 Commission 2004). This finding was widely publicized; communities across the US accepted it, but many still have not updated their communication equipment (US Conference of Mayors 2006).

CONCLUSION: DEVELOPING
DECISION-MAKING PRACTICES

Decision makers must make difficult choices before, during, and after a disaster, all under conditions of ambiguity and uncertainty and often constrained by a lack of valid and reliable information. Researchers have identified decision making practices that lead to failure, such as "fine-tuning the odds" (Starbuck and Milliken

1988) and the "normalization of deviance" (Vaughan 1996, 2005; Beamish 2002), but it has been more difficult to identify comparable decision-making practices that produce safety. The generalizations drawn from research on high reliability organizations are not sufficient to assure positive outcomes, as their originators would recognize. Furthermore, such broad prescriptions cannot incorporate the subtle and incremental interpretive biases that shape how decision makers make sense of the organization's experience and use these interpretations to guide their decisions.

Research findings from diverse literatures suggest that despite the constraints and challenges decision makers face when the stakes are high, managers have developed decision-making practices to support their efforts to avert or mitigate the effects of disasters. Organizations collect and analyze data about small failures and near misses, mobilize support from other organizations in their environment, and draw on local expertise to generate and test working hypotheses regarding how to recognize and remove hazards.

Data Gathering and Analysis

Organizations can gather and analyze information about near accidents, errors, and small failures to supplement their sparse experience with disastrous events and thus reduce hindsight bias. Cannon and Edmondson (2005) argue that organizational learning from failure is feasible when organizations actively identify and analyze small and large failures. Knowing about near misses allows decision makers to consider alternative near histories that could result from a particular set of circumstances (March et al. 1991). Near miss reporting systems routinely provide data to decision makers concerned with aviation safety in industry and government, however, there are mixed results on the implementation of such reporting systems in other industries, such as health care.

Seeking Support in the Organizational Environment

The politics of blame (Sagan 1994) produce disincentives for front-line employees to report potential problems and for managers to relay information higher up in the organization. These disincentives reduce the valid information available about emerging threats. Organizations seek to counteract the internal politics of blame. In hospitals, the Joint Commission on Accreditation of Health-care Organizations (the major accrediting body for US hospitals) has implemented a policy of not blaming individuals for medical errors. It exerts external pressure on hospitals to change their behavior towards health care providers who make mistakes. For example, Joint Commission representatives cautioned against blaming the health care providers involved in deaths at an Indianapolis hospital (Webber 2006).

Decision makers can also turn to other organizations and professional associations in their environment. For example, pharmacy management teams in hospitals rely on the Institute for Safe Medication Practices to learn about others' experience with harmful medication errors. The Institute collects hazard reports, compiles information, and disseminates warnings about potentially dangerous situations (i.e., look alike drug vials) and actual adverse drug events (for examples, see www.ismp.org). The air transportation industry also supports an array of aviation safety organizations that gather reports of hazards and near accidents from pilots and issue warnings to the aviation community. In both of these examples, decision makers cultivate relationships with other organizations in their environment to counteract disincentives to report potential dangers. Information from external sources may make it easier for organizational decision makers to ask if a similar event could happen in their organization, and to decide whether to change their procedures.

Internal Experimentation

Warning signals before a disaster can be ambiguous and difficult to identify among the noise of benign errors and deviations from expected performance. Organizations draw on the experience of front-line employees and local experts to try to make sense of these signals. As part of the event review process in nuclear power plants, local experts seek to discover what actually led to potentially dangerous events, interpret the evidence, and propose hypotheses to explain them (Perin 2005). Similarly, in a hospital, managers encouraged pharmacists to generate and test simple hypotheses based on their experience with medication errors or "work-around" situations (Tamuz et al. 2004). When organizations engage in such deliberate experimentation, Cannon and Edmondson (2005) posit that it fosters organizational learning from small failures. As the *Challenger* case illustrates, generating hypotheses about the meaning of potential dangers does not guarantee positive outcomes. It does, however, reflect organizations' efforts to make sense of warnings that may be embedded in small failures and near misses.

Natural disasters are inevitable and complex technologies yield their share of disasters; and when the stakes are high, organizations struggle to make decisions under difficult cognitive and political constraints. Despite these constraints organizations have developed decision-making practices to guide their choices under these difficult conditions. Researchers have a stake in learning from organizations' experience with these events and, in turn, informing managers' understanding of organizational decision making.

References

BAUMARD, P. and STARBUCK, W. H. (2005). 'Learning from Failures: Why it May Not Happen.' *Long Range Planning*, 38: 281–98.

BEAMISH, T. (2002). *Silent Spill: The Organization of an Industrial Crisis.* Cambridge, MA: MIT Press.

BIER, V. (2006). 'Hurricane Katrina as a bureaucratic nightmare,' in R. J. DANIELS, D. F. Kettl, and H. Kunreuther (eds.), *On Risk and Disaster Lessons from Hurricane Katrina.* Philadelphia, PA: University of Pennsylvania Press, 243–54.

BLOUNT, S., WALLER, M. J., and LEROY, S. (2005). 'Coping with Temporal Uncertainty: When Rigid, Ambitious Deadlines Don't Make Sense,' in W. H. Starbuck and M. Farjoun (eds.), *Organization at the Limit: Management Lessons from the Columbia Disaster.* Oxford: Blackwell Publishers, 122–39.

BOISJOLY, R.P., Curtis, E.F., and MELLICAN, E. (1989). 'Roger Boisjoly and the Challenger Disaster.' *Journal of Business Ethics*, 8: 217–30.

BULJAN, A. and SHAPIRA, Z. (2005). 'Attention to Production Schedule and Safety as Determinants of Risk-Taking in NASA's Decision to Launch the Columbia Shuttle,' in W. H. Starbuck and M. Farjoun (eds.), *Organization at the Limit: Management Lessons from the Columbia Disaster.* Oxford: Blackwell Publishers, 140–56.

CANNON, M. D. and EDMONDSON, A. C. (2005). 'Failing to Learn and Learning to Fail (Intelligently): How Great Organizations Put Failure to Work to Innovate and Improve.' *Long Range Planning*, 38: 299–319.

CARROLL, J. S. (1998). 'Organizational Learning Activities in High-Hazard Industries: The Logics Underlying Self-Analysis.' *Journal of Management Studies*, 35: 699–717.

—— RUDOLPH, J. W., and HATAKENAKA, S. (2002). 'Learning from Experience in High-Hazard Industries'. *Research in Organizational Behavior*, 24: 87–137.

CLARKE, L. (1989). *Acceptable Risk?* Berkeley, CA: University of California Press.

—— (1999). *Mission Improbable.* Chicago, IL: University of Chicago Press.

—— (2005). *Worst Cases: Terror and Catastrophe in the Popular Imagination.* Chicago, IL: University of Chicago Press.

DANIELS, R. J., KETTL, D. F., and KUNREUTHER, H. (eds.) (2006). *On Risk and Disaster Lessons from Hurricane Katrina.* Philadelphia, PA: University of Pennsylvania Press.

EDMONDSON, A. (1999). 'Psychological Safety and Learning Behavior in Work Teams.' *Administrative Science Quarterly*, 44/4: 350–83.

—— (2004). 'Learning from Failure in Health Care: Frequent Opportunities, Pervasive Barriers.' *Quality and Safety in Health Care*, 13/Suppl. 2: 3–9.

ETCHEGARAY, J. M., THOMAS, E. J., GERACI, J. M., SIMMONS, D., and MARTIN, S. K. (2005). 'Differentiating Close Calls from Errors: A Multidisciplinary Perspective.' *Journal of Patient Safety*, 1/3: 133–7.

FERNALD, D. H., PACE, W. D., HARRIS, D. M. et al. (2004). 'Event Reporting to a Primary Care Patient Safety Reporting System: A Report From the ASIPS Collaborative.' *Annals of Family Medicine*, 2: 327–32.

FREUDENBURG, W. R., GRAMLING, R. LASKA, S., and ERIKSON, K. (2006). 'Come Hell and High Water: Learning the Lessons of Katrina.' Paper presented at Annual Meeting of American Sociological Association, Montreal, Canada, August 12.

GANTER, J., DEAN, C., and CLOER, B. (2000). 'Fast Pragmatic Safety Decisions: Analysis of an Event Review Team of the Aviation Safety Action Partnership.' USDOE, SAND2000–1134.

GEPHART, R. P. (1984). 'Making Sense of Organizationally Based Environmental Disasters.' *Journal of Management*, 10/2: 205–25.

—— (1997). 'Hazardous Measures: An Interpretive Textual Analysis of Quantitative Sensemaking during Crises.' *Journal of Organizational Behavior*, 18: 583–622.

GRADY, D. (2007). 'When Bad Things Come from "Good" Food.' *New York Times*, January 2.

HAUNSCHILD, P. and SULLIVAN, B. (2002). 'Learning from Complexity: Effects of Accident/Incident Heterogeneity on Airline Learning.' *Administrative Science Quarterly*, 47: 609–43.

HOFF, T., POHL, H., and BARTFIELD, J. (2006). 'Teaching But Not Learning: How Medical Residency Programs Handle Errors.' *Journal of Organizational Behavior*, 27/7: 869–96.

HOUSE REPORT (2006). 'A Failure of Initiative: Final Report,' H.Rpt. 109–377, March (http://a257.g.akamaitech.net/7/257/2422/27mar20061546/www.gpoaccess.gov/serialset/creports/pdf/hr109–377/pam.pdf) (accessed on January 15, 2007).

KAPUCU, N. (2006). 'Interagency Communication Networks During Emergencies—Boundary Spanners in Multiagency Coordination.' *American Review of Public Administration*, 36/2: 207–25.

KOHN, L., CORRIGAN, J., and DONALDSON, M. (eds.) (2000). *To Err Is Human: Building A Safer Health System*. Institute of Medicine. Washington, DC: National Academy Press.

KUNREUTHER, H., MEYER, R., ZECKHASUER, R. et al. (2002). 'High Stakes Decision Making: Normative, Descriptive, and Prescriptive Considerations.' *Marketing Letters*, 13/3: 259–68.

LaPORTE, T. (1982). 'On the Design and Management of Nearly Error-Free Organizational Control Systems,' in D. SILLS, V. Shelanski, and C. Wolf (eds.), *Accident at Three Mile Island*. Boulder, CO: Westview.

LAWLER, E. and RHODE, J. (1976). *Information and Control in Organizations*. Santa Monica, CA: Goodyear.

LEAPE, L. L. (1994). 'Error in Medicine.' *Journal of the American Medical Association*, 272/23: 1851–7.

LEVINTHAL, D. A. and MARCH, J. G. (1993). 'The Myopia of Learning.' *Strategic Management Journal*, 14: 95–112.

MARCH, J. G. (1981). 'Footnotes to Organizational Change.' *Administrative Science Quarterly*, 26/4: 563–77.

—— SPROULL, L.S., and TAMUZ, M. (1991). 'Learning from Samples of One or Fewer.' *Organization Science*, 2/1: 1–13.

MARCUS, A. and NICHOLS, M. (1999). 'On the Edge: Heeding the Warnings of Unusual Events.' *Organization Science*, 10/4: 482–99.

—— McAVOY, E., and NICHOLS, M. (1993). 'Economic and Behavioral Perspectives on Safety,' in S. Bacharach (ed.), *Research in Organizational Behavior*, Vol. 15. Greenwich, CT: JAI Press.

MARONE, J. and WOODHOUSE, E. (1986). *Averting Catastrophe: Strategies for Regulating Risky Technologies*. Berkeley, CA: University of California Press.

MARSHALL, B. (2006). 'Levees Built Using Obsolete Standards.' *New Orleans Times-Picayune*, May 1 (www.nola.com/newslogs/tpupdates/index.ssf?/mtlogs/nola_tpupdates/archives/2006_05_01.html) (accessed on January 15, 2007).

MORRISON, E. W. and MILLIKEN, F. J. (2000). 'Organizational Silence: A Barrier to Change and Development in a Pluralistic World.' *Academy of Management Review*, 25/4: 706–25.

MEWHINNEY, M. (2006). 'NASA Aviation Safety Reporting System Celebrates 30th Anniversary.' National Aeronautics and Space Administration Ames Research Center November 21.

(www.nasa.gov/centers/ames/research/2006/aviation_anniversary.html) (accessed on January 15, 2007).

NATIONAL TRANSPORTATION SAFETY BOARD. (2000). *In-Flight Breakup Over the Atlantic Ocean, Trans World Airlines Flight 800, Boeing 747-131, N93119, Near East Moriches, New York, July 17, 1996.* Aircraft Accident Report NTSB/AAR-00/03, Washington, DC.

OCASIO, W. (2005). 'The Opacity of Risk: Language and the Culture of Safety in NASA's Space Shuttle Program,' in W. H. Starbuck and M. Farjoun (eds.), *Organization at the Limit: Management Lessons from the Columbia Disaster.* Oxford: Blackwell Publishers.

PERIN, C. (2005). *Shouldering Risks: The Culture of Control in the Nuclear Power Industry.* Princeton, NJ: Princeton University Press.

PERROW, C. (1984). *Normal Accidents: Living with High Risk Systems.* New York: Basic Books.

PFEFFER, J. (1992). *Managing with Power: Politics and Influence in Organizations.* Boston, MA: Harvard Business School Press.

PHIMISTER, J. R., OKTEM, U., KLEINDORFER, P. R., and KUNREUTHER, H. (2003). 'Near-Miss Incident Management in the Chemical Process Industry.' *Risk Analysis,* 23/3: 445–59.

REYNARD, W. D., BILLINGS, C. E., CHEANEY, E. S., and HARDY, R. (1986). *The Development of the NASA Aviation Safety Reporting System.* National Aeronautics and Space Administration, Scientific and Technical Information Branch (NASA Reference Publication 1114), US Government Printing Office, Washington, DC.

ROBERTS, K., MADSEN, P., DESAI, V., and VAN STRALEN, D. (2005). 'A Case of the Birth and Death of a High Reliability Healthcare Organisation.' *Quality Safety and Health Care,* 14, 216–20.

ROCHLIN, G. I., LA PORTE, T. R., and ROBERTS, K. H. (1987). 'The Self-Designing High-Reliability Organization: Aircraft Carrier Flight Operations at Sea.' *Naval War College Review,* 40: 76–90.

RODRIGUEZ, G. (2006). 'Methodist Hospital Admits to Previous Heparin Overdoses'. WISH-TV, September 19 (www.wishtv.com/Global/story.asp?S=5429788) (accessed January 16, 2007).

SAGAN, S. D. (1993). *The Limits of Safety: Organizations, Accidents and Nuclear Weapons.* Princeton, NJ: Princeton University Press.

—— (1994). 'Toward a Political Theory of Organizational Reliability.' *Journal of Contingencies and Crisis Management,* 2/4: 228–40.

SCHENKEL, S., KHARE, R., ROSENTHAL, M., SUTCLIFFE, K., and LEWTON, E. (2003). 'Resident Perceptions of Medical Errors in the Emergency Department.' *Academic Emergency Medicine,* 10: 1318–24.

SHRIVASTAVA, P. (1987). *Bhopal: Anatomy of a Crisis.* Cambridge: Ballinger Publishing Company.

SITKIN, S. (1992). 'Learning through Failure: The Strategy of Small Losses.' *Research in Organizational Behavior,* 14: 231–66.

STARBUCK, W. H. and MILLIKEN, F. (1988a). 'Challenger—Fine-Tuning the Odds Until Something Breaks.' *Journal of Management Studies,* 25/4: 319–40.

—— —— (1988b). 'Executives' Perceptual Filters: What They Notice and How They Make Sense,' in D. C. Hambrick (ed.), *The Executive Effect: Concepts and Methods for Studying Top Managers.* Greenwich, CT: JAI Press.

TAMUZ, M. (2001a). 'Defining Away Dangers: A Study in the Influences of Managerial Cognition on Information Systems,' in T. K. Lant and Z. Shapira (eds.), *Organizational Cognition: Computation and Interpretation*. Mahwah, NJ: Lawrence Erlbaum, 157–83.

—— (2001b). 'Learning Disabilities for Regulators: The Perils of Organizational Learning in the Air Transportation Industry.' *Administration and Society*, 33: 276–302.

—— THOMAS, E., and FRANCHOIS, K. (2004). 'Defining and Classifying Medical Error: Lessons for Reporting Systems.' *Quality and Safety in Health Care*, 13: 13–20.

TASCA, L. (1990). 'The Social Construction of Human Error.' Unpublished doctoral dissertation, State University of New York, Stonybrook, NY.

THE 9/11 COMMISSION. (2004). *Final Report of the National Commission on Terrorist Attacks Upon the United States*. New York: W. W. Norton and Company.

TIERNEY, K. J. (1985). 'Emergency Medical Preparedness and Response in Disasters: The Need for Interorganizational Coordination.' *Public Administration Review*, 45: 77–84.

TOPPER, C. M. and CARLEY, K. M. (1999). 'A Structural Perspective on the Emergence of Network Organizations.' *The Journal of Mathematical Sociology*, 24/1: 67–96.

TUCKER, A. and EDMONDSON, A. (2003). 'Why Hospitals Don't Learn from Failures: Organizational and Psychological Dynamics That Inhibit System Change.' *California Management Review*, 45/2: 55–72.

TURNER, B. A. (1978). *Man-Made Disasters*. London: Wykeham.

US CONFERENCE of MAYORS (2006). 'Interoperable Communications Still Major Challenge Across America.' US Conference of Mayors, March 6 (www. usmayors.org/uscm/us%5Fmayor%5Fnewspaper/documents/03_06_06/interoperable.asp) (accessed on January 15, 2007).

VASTAG, B. (2004). 'Federal Ruling Requires Million-Year Guarantee of Safety at Yucca Mountain Nuclear Waste Site.' *Journal of the National Cancer Institute*, 96/22: 1656–7.

VAUGHAN, D. (1996). *The Challenger Launch Decision*. Chicago, IL: University of Chicago Press.

—— (1999). 'The Dark Side of Organizations: Mistake, Misconduct, and Disaster.' *Annual Review of Sociology*, 25: 271–305.

—— (2005). 'System Effects: On Slippery Slopes, Repeating Negative Patterns, and Learning from Mistakes,' in W. H. Starbuck and M. Farjoun (eds.), *Organization at the Limit: Management Lessons from the Columbia Disaster*. Oxford: Blackwell Publishers.

VON HEERDEN, I. and BRYAN, M. (2006). *The Storm: What Went Wrong and Why During Hurricane Katrina—The Inside Story from One Louisiana Scientist*. New York: Viking.

WEBBER, T. (2006). 'Infants' Doses Were 1,000 Times Too Strong.' *Indianapolis Star*, September 18 (www.indystar.com/apps/pbcs.dll/article?AID=/20060918/LOCAL/609180457&SearchID=73257342423461) (accessed on September 20, 2007).

WEICK, K. (1990). 'The Vulnerable System: An Analysis of the Tenerife Air Disaster.' *Journal of Management*, 16/3: 571–93.

—— (2005). 'Making Sense of Blurred Images: Mindful Organizing in Mission STS-107,' in W. H. Starbuck and M. Farjoun (eds.), *Organization at the Limit: Management Lessons from the Columbia Disaster*. Oxford: Blackwell Publishers.

—— ROBERTS, K. (1993). 'Collective Mind in Organizations—Heedful Interrelating on Flight Decks.' *Administrative Science Quarterly*, 38/3: 357–81.

—— SUTCLIFFE, K. (2003). 'Hospitals as Culture of Entrapment: A Reanalysis of the Bristol Royal Infirmary'. *California Management Review*, 15/2: 73–84.

9

THE FIT BETWEEN CRISIS TYPES AND MANAGEMENT ATTRIBUTES AS A DETERMINANT OF CRISIS CONSEQUENCES

TERI JANE URSACKI-BRYANT
CAROLYNE SMART
ILAN VERTINSKY

INTRODUCTION

CRISIS management scholars and practitioners have struggled with the notion of what exactly constitutes a crisis (see, for example, Quarantelli 1998). The term is often confused with related concepts such as disaster. Boin (2005: 163) draws the distinction that a crisis involves a "process of perceived disruption," while the term disaster "applies to a collectively-arrived-at appraisal of such a process in negative terms...a disaster is a crisis with a bad ending." The notion of disruption is a strong, recurring element in crisis definitions. Rosenthal et al. (2001: 6), for example, refer to crises as "periods of upheaval and collective stress disturbing everyday patterns and threatening core values and structures of a social system in unexpected, often inconceivable, ways" (see also Shrivastava 1987; Shrivastava et al. 1988; Weick, 1988). Other key elements are urgency and uncertainty (Rosenthal Charles and 't Hart 1989; Rosenthal and Kouzmin 1993). Recent work on crises has emphasized the social construction of the crisis: "authorities decide whether an event or process indicates progress or disruption of normality," and hence whether it constitutes a crisis (Boin 2005). In this chapter we define a crisis to be a situation where: (1) there is a threat or a realization of a discontinuity in the organizational environment, its institutions and/or processes, that threatens key organizational values; (2) there is recognition that an urgent response is needed; (3) decision makers perceive a high level of risk; and (4) there is a consensus, at least among key decision makers and stakeholders, that the situation constitutes a crisis. This definition excludes routine emergency situations as well as those where key stakeholders and decision makers have not socially constructed a crisis because they do not perceive the threat or misinterpret its nature or potential impact. We also exclude "pseudo-crises" that decision makers manufacture as part of their political strategies (e.g., attempts to draw attention to an issue by constructing it as a crisis).

Threatening discontinuities in the system are triggers that may set crisis management decision processes in action. Similar triggers (i.e., events or states of the system) may result in different types of emergent crisis situations in different organizations, depending on their attributes and their environments. For example, an organizational environment that is complex and in flux may slow the social construction of a crisis, as organization members may be unable to perceive critical discontinuities against the background noise of a rapidly changing environment. An organization in such an environment, however, may have more flexible operating procedures and abilities to spontaneously re-organize and mobilize resources once it recognizes the need to respond.

Organizations with specialized crisis management knowledge (e.g., a center for disease control) and other resources (e.g., hospitals and public health services) may anticipate and unambiguously interpret a particular trigger event (e.g., epidemic contagion) as a crisis and employ standard operating procedures (e.g., quarantine) to deal with it, while an organization without such specialized knowledge and resources may meet such an event with surprise, confusion, and disorientation. Munificent environments, large endowments of slack resources, and diversification generally dampen the impacts of threats and provide a wider range of options to mitigate their negative impacts and/or amplify some of the positive consequences that may be obtained as a result of the threat (e.g., learning, organizational reform).

In contrast, a highly specialized, tautly efficient organization may have little room to maneuver or capacity to absorb the impacts of the threat.

Emergent crises may set in motion different types of crisis management decision processes. The attributes of the decision processes that are invoked reflect not only the type of emergent crisis but also organizational institutions that evolved in response to "normal organizational life," and past organizational experience with crises and "sense-making processes" that incorporated them into organizational institutions and knowledge.

The "fit" between crisis management decision processes and the type of emergent crisis is the subject of this chapter. We explore how different decision process characteristics may lead to different consequences of the crisis management process. We also explore the vulnerabilities of the different decision processes to perceptual and cognitive biases.

We start in the second section by exploring some key environmental and organizational characteristics that may influence the type of crisis management system that an emergent crisis type activates. In the third section we provide a typology of crises and the decision system attributes that may reduce their negative consequences or amplify their positive consequences. In the fourth section we explore the "fit" of alternative crisis management decision processes with some specific crisis types. In this section, we also explore some of the immediate consequences of crisis decision making. The fifth section deals with the longer term consequences of the crisis as a function of the decision processes and the types of crisis the system has faced. In the sixth section we summarize our conclusions.

ORGANIZATIONAL AND ENVIRONMENTAL ATTRIBUTES: ANTECEDENTS OF CRISIS MANAGEMENT

The attributes of an organization and its environment determine to a large extent not only the type and frequency of threatening disruptions (i.e., crisis triggers) it faces but also the way the problem situations are constructed and the decision processes that are activated to cope with them. Volatility and complexity are among the most important of these environmental attributes.

Volatile environments reduce the ability to predict the onset of disruptions and thus increase the element of surprise. Volatility slows the process of institutionalization. Environments in flux may constrain the development of standard operating procedures (SOPs) or increase the likelihood of suboptimal application of

SOPs. Experience with discontinuities and disruptions may, however, help develop different kinds of institutions. It may lead to the emergence of higher level SOPs that emphasize search and adaptability (Holling 1978; March 1991). It may affect organizational values, reducing the value placed on efficiency and increasing the value of preparedness. In volatile environments maintaining slack and diversification are not sources of vulnerability and constraints on organizational performance but a means of achieving resilience. Indeed experiences with volatility reduce the temptation to focus and put slack to some "productive use" when there is no crisis at hand (Ellis 1998).

Complex environments encourage the evolution of complex organizations where the information to know what to do and the means to do it (if either even exist) often reside in separate departments. Small breakdowns in one system can cascade into major problems in seemingly only tangentially related ones when there is strong coupling of environments (La Porte and Consolini 1991; Boin et al. 2003).

The scope and scale of the organizational environment affect the contingencies that it may face, the horizons that the organization scans, the dimensions considered and the types and diversity of other organizations that may share the effort to cope with the interruptions. For example, in dealing with the SARS epidemic the need to contain the disease's spread in all countries simultaneously was paramount as international travel was a potential vehicle for renewed contagion (WHO 2006). International dimensions imply involvement of multiple domestic governments and their networks and institutions for managing bilateral and multilateral relationships. Each domestic government must manage its unique political environment, the distinct patterns of interests that the disruption triggers and the responses of the stakeholders involved (WHO 2005a, b). Large scale and diversity of interests often imply a highly political environment within which stakeholders construct the crisis and activate decision processes to cope with it (Shrivastava et al. 1988).

Environments are sources of organizational experiences. Organizational sense-making processes translate these experiences into "histories" that organizations incorporate into their institutions. Histories tend to mold problem definitions through the lens of old experiences. This is a source of efficiency in the response system but also a potential source of bias stemming from the tendency to force a new problem into the mold of an old one, even when it really requires different coping mechanisms (Brandstrom et al. 2004). Repeated experiences with similar disruptions tend to lead to the evolution of specialized standard operating procedures and specialized organizational units to deal with them. If an organization routinizes coping with disruptions, it may not construct the onset of disruption as a crisis: it may become an "emergency" for which the organization is ready. The existence of specialized emergency units may, however, increase the likelihood that such emergency organizations become gatekeepers that narrow the range of information searched and consequently the way problems are defined or solved. Indeed, emergency organizations tend to see restoration of a system to normality as the prime objective of crisis management. The existence of emergency units may also lead to organizational overconfidence or complacency.

More generally, the institutional capacity of the organization and its resources to deal with disruptions of different kinds affect the way it constructs crises, the options open for dealing with them and the likelihood of choosing particular crisis management mechanisms in preference to others. For example, organizations with communication infrastructure that can accommodate peak load flows of information may be better able to coordinate the mobilization of resources and maintain a more decentralized response system than one that must cope with overloaded channels that lead to miscommunication (Liang and Hue 2004). Organizations with high levels of social capital may be able to use a more efficient command and control system that maintains security of the information it possesses than an organization with a low-trust culture (Pearson and Clair 1998). In such organizations, post-crisis learning may become easier: effort not needed to ensure confidence in the system and deflect blame can be used to provide an account that allows optimal learning. In such organizations, leaders are more likely to listen to dissent and experiment (Nystrom and Starbuck 1984).

TYPES OF CRISES

Given the wide variety of crises, it is useful to identify types of crises and how they may generate certain types of consequences in specific organizational environments and/or require certain types of decision processes for their effective resolution. As La Porte (2005: 7) observes, each mix of conditions "suggests different organizational dynamics, perhaps different emphases of skills, and very likely relations with stakeholding groups."

One important distinction is whether the trigger event arises from natural causes or human action, whether due to error or intention (Pearson and Mitroff 1993). Where the trigger is of natural origin, there is often relevant past experience. Efficiency and speed in the mobilization of known types of resources are the primary objective. When the trigger is human error, there may be active efforts to obscure the identity of those responsible. Avoiding such cover-ups requires a transparent process for ensuring accountability, not only to prevent a recurrence, but also to restore or preserve confidence in the institutions involved. Where the trigger results from human intention, the event is what La Porte (2005: 10) refers to as a "predatory crisis," such as a terrorist attack. Here there are likely to be active efforts by those responsible to thwart remedial action.

Addressing such crises may require a delicate balance between providing the information necessary to deal with the incident at hand (e.g., apprehend the individuals responsible) and preserving the confidentiality of information that must remain secret for longer term or broader social goals (e.g., the weakening of a terrorist network). If the integrity of this mechanism is suspect, there may either be dangerous leaks (if too much information flows out) or a flowering of counter-productive conspiracy theories and resulting social fragmentation (if too little information flows out). The quality of much of the available information is also suspect, requiring a fine procedural balance between ensuring reliability and not dismissing information that may prove vital but cannot be definitively confirmed. This type of crisis is likely to be particularly traumatic for society and require some form of healing process.

Triggers vary in the degree to which decision makers understand the mechanism through which they affect the system. For example, when a bomb goes off, they know in medical terms exactly what has caused the deaths. However, when an unknown disease strikes, they may know only that people are dying. It may not even be apparent that the cause of death is the same across the cases noted, if indeed they are at first even distinguished as deviations from normal mortality. In the former case, the initial response at least is clear: mobilization of resources to provide known forms of medical care. In the latter, considerable epidemiological work may be necessary before decision makers even know whether they are dealing with one or many agents, what the vector of transmission is, etc. Without an understanding of what is happening, decision pathologies such as panic are more likely, placing a premium on communication to convey what decision makers know and what progress they are making, and to counteract rumors and social disintegration. Decision processes must emphasize openness to new information and ideas and tolerance of uncertainty, yet at some point they must bring order to the confusion and decide on a course of action, even if the state of the information is still far from perfect.

Crises differ in the speed of their arrival and development. 't Hart and Boin (2001: 31–5) distinguish four combinations. The "fast-burning" crisis is "short, sharp, and decisive', for example, a hostage-taking. In this case speed of response is critical, and there may be little or no time to consult with other relevant parties. The "cathartic crisis," consists of an "abrupt termination following long and gradual onset," for example, the stand-off at Waco. Here there may appear to be time for wide involvement in decisions, yet when the critical moment comes, it may be over in the blink of an eye. The development of multiparty consultation must leave open the option to override consultative processes when the need for immediate decisive action suddenly crystallizes. The "slow-burning crisis...creeps up rather than bursts out, and fades away rather than being resolved," for example, the Vietnam War. This combination poses challenges of identifying the crisis early enough to take effective action, and of deciding when and how to declare the crisis over and return to normalcy. The "long shadow" crisis can "occur suddenly and raise critical issues of much wider scope and significance," for example, Three Mile Island. Here resolution of the trigger itself is only the beginning: full resolution must involve long-term mobilization of efforts for major social change. Such change requires a process that maintains momentum even in the face of resistance of entrenched interests and a decline in the perceived salience of the issue.

Crises come in all sizes. Where a disaster is vast, it requires not only large scale resource mobilization, but also a decision process that can incorporate the massive amount of local information about the distribution of needs and resources while also providing central coordination. When the effects are purely local, there may be little outsiders can profitably do other than to provide resources and let the local authorities (assuming they have survived) do their jobs. Large crises are likely to become politically charged, as the stakes become large enough to have noticeable distributive effects (e.g., who will pay for massive aid, and who will get it?) These stakes may re-ignite underlying political, ethnic, religious, or geographical conflicts. They also draw the attention of the media and of policy actors seeking to advance their agendas of reform or preservation of the status quo. Many analysts have also argued that the scope of crises has broadened over time. The "modern" crisis is likely to be complex, prolonged, span borders, and be deeply enmeshed with other problems (Boin 2005). All of these tendencies require decision processes that include a larger number of actors, often from different sectors and/or nations. Such processes must respect cultural and institutional differences, and must also be flexible enough to accommodate a sudden expansion of parties to the issue if the problem cascades through previously unforeseen channels.

Some degree of conflict is inherent in most crises, since at a minimum there may be differences of opinion about how to proceed. However, in some crises the conflictual element is incidental and unifying tendencies overcome it. For example, citizens' propensity to "rally round the flag" as an initial response to an enemy attack has often been noted. In such cases a key challenge is to maintain this overall sense of unity and its mobilization-enhancing effects as long as possible, while not disregarding potentially useful dissident voices and falling prey to groupthink (Janis 1972). Many crises provoke conflicts of interest due to the distributional consequences of alternative solutions. Here the legitimacy of the dispute resolution mechanism must be impeccable or it may perpetuate bitterness and a sense of grievance. Typically this requires that consultation processes be broadly and genuinely inclusive of all those who may receive compensation (to ensure it is adequate) or have to pay for it (to ensure they perceive their share of the burden to be fair). Perhaps the most difficult crises are those that have at their root a serious dispute between two parties (e.g., the genocide in Rwanda). In such cases, where forceful intervention may be the only feasible option, it is essential to have in place processes that can quickly and convincingly establish the legitimacy of the action required, however painful or bitterly resisted.

In some cases, the near total uncertainty surrounding the nature of a problem and how to deal with it can lead to paralyzing social fragmentation. When "both understanding and procedures for sensemaking collapse together" (Weick 1993: 637–8), groups disintegrate. The result is "the cessation of all the feelings of consideration that the members of the group otherwise show one another" (Freud 1959: 8–9), and a *sauve qui peut* in which the only consideration is individual salvation. Where such a risk is implicit in a crisis, decision processes must emphasize confidence building and create some sense that a resolution is, if not at hand, at least conceivable.

The "Fit" Between Decision Processes and Crisis Types

Crises do not occur in a vacuum: they affect pre-existing organizations with existing decision processes and modes of operation. Even if other entities later displace them, the initial reaction typically occurs within an existing organization. A crisis triggers an organization's SOPs for dealing with its perceived impacts. As a clearer understanding of the magnitude and nature of the problem emerges, the organization is likely to modify these SOPs. As noted above, crises combine uncertainty, urgency, and threat. Depending on the extent to which the existing organization's design gives it inherent capabilities to deal with these challenges, the crisis may overwhelm the organization's normal routines and resources, creating stress and leading to pressure to reconfigure its processes. These adaptations may enhance crisis-coping capabilities or become pathological depending on how well they fit the requirements of the crisis being faced.

In this chapter thus far we have identified four key aspects of decision processes: degree of centralization of decision making; legitimacy and trust; diversity of information sources used; and speed in reaching conclusions and taking action. Here we elaborate further on where each aspect is likely to be most critical.

Centralization involves both the concentration of power in the hands of a few people and concentration of power in higher organizational levels (e.g., national government versus provincial or local). Christensen and Kohls (2003: 334) suggest that "the literature that has focused on decision-making under uncertainty, threat or crisis is nearly unanimous in finding that under such conditions there is a tendency for decision-making to move to the top of the hierarchy in the organization." Hermann (1963) identified centralization as the key adaptation of bureaucratic structures to the demands of a crisis. Numerous studies of international and corporate crisis decision making have reported that the dominant decision structure is a small group of usually top decision makers in the organization and their advisors (Hermann and Hermann 1982; 't Hart et al. 1993). 'T Hart et al. (1993) explain the tendency to centralize as a result of time pressure. Centralization appears to offer increased control, coordination and fast response. Thus, whatever the organization's initial level of centralization, it is likely to increase under the pressure of a crisis.

Centralization is likely to be helpful where those at ground level are unable to appreciate the full scale of the problem, where there is a serious locational mismatch between needs and resources, where local decision-making capability is weak, or where there is a strong risk of spin-off effects cascading through other related systems. It may be counter-productive where communication links are poor, where the situation is developing so rapidly that there is no time to transmit information to a central location and await a response, or where local decision-making capacity is well developed.

A crisis can test and challenge the legitimacy of agencies involved in responding to it (Quarantelli 1988; 't Hart et al. 1993). At the extreme, a crisis "can put to the test the viability of the political regime and challenge the capacity of ruling elites or incumbent authorities to withstand formidable and acute threats to the legitimacy of the political system" (Rosenthal and 't Hart 1990: 358). As Boin and 't Hart (2003: 544) observed in reviewing the experience of 9/11: "Successful performance in times of a collective stress turns leaders into statesmen. But when the crisis fails to dissipate and 'normality' does not return, leaders are obvious scapegoats."

Crises involving high levels of conflict, such as those with major distributional consequences, are most likely to bring issues of legitimacy and trust to the forefront. "Long-shadow" crises, where an event reveals a serious but previously ignored long-term issue such as racism or organizational malfeasance, bring a serious risk of accusations of a cover-up. Decision processes in these cases require careful attention to the development and maintenance of trust in the fairness of the system. An important element of such social capital preservation is communication and consultation. The dilemma facing crisis managers is the need to balance requirements for transparency and information sharing to maintain trust with the need to avoid panic and short circuit attempts at gaming the system. Culture-bound expectations with respect to the need and right to be informed or consulted and the degree of immediate threat and uncertainty experienced by the public clearly affect the optimal balance.

Perceptions of outcomes must also be managed carefully: perceived failure can fatally weaken an organization's legitimacy, while perceived success, particularly where it is perceived to have occurred against long odds, can create a mythology of near invincibility (Rosenthal et al. 2001: 35). Crises that draw intensive media attention thus also raise the profile of legitimacy and trust issues.

The role of the media in framing and interpreting crises has been the subject of several studies. The media tend to reinforce and build upon existing public attitudes (Douglas and Wildavsky 1982; Nelkin 1988). To preserve trust and legitimacy, decision processes must devote attention to developing positive relationships with media representatives and endeavouring to appear honest, cooperative and forthcoming with information (Pearson and Clair 1988: 73; Susskind and Field 1996). To the impact of the mass media one must add the ever-growing presence of internet communications and the impact of NGOs as well as unorganized individuals (e.g., bloggers) on shaping public opinion, disseminating information, and spreading rumors. There is little research on the effects of these new patterns of communication on crisis management.

Decision processes vary widely in the diversity of information sources used. In crisis situations time pressure narrows the attention span of decision makers and intensifies cognitive biases (Svenson and Maule 1993). Time pressure also reduces the access of decision makers to other stakeholders and information sources (Smart and Vertinsky 1977; Ashmos et al. 1997; Christensen and Kohls 2003). In deriving priorities salient stakeholders and issues dominate and broad segments of stakeholders and issues are ignored (Christensen and Kohls 2003).

Group dynamics, centralization, and this individual narrowing of cognitive abilities contribute to many possible crisis decision pathologies. Brown and Miller (2000) note that research on small group decision making under stress reveals the following: (1) a decrease in the number of communication channels during information exchanges; (2) deference of members of small groups to their leaders; and (3) reduced consultation by those higher in the organization with those in lower levels, blocking feedback from the field. The tendency to centralize does not, however, extend to small groups that often form at the top to manage a crisis. Driskell and Salas (1991) found that within-group information sharing increases during a crisis.

The empirical relationships associated with crisis management theories focus largely on the consequences of the stress induced by the crisis decision environment and time pressure (see, e.g., Smart and Vertinsky 1977; George 1986; Dror 1988;). Stress induced destructive group dynamics, where a small group of key decision makers suppresses disconfirming information and dissident opinions and shelters itself from reality and the rational judgment of alternative options, is a widely cited example of a group decision pathology (Janis 1972; 't Hart 1990). Stress avoidance mechanisms that are triggered lead to selective attention, favoring information that confirms prior beliefs and avoiding unpleasant, threatening information (Janis and Mann 1977).

Parker and Stern (2005: 305) identify six pathologies associated with information processing:

overvaluation of past success; overconfidence in current policy; insensitivity to policy failures and warnings critical of existing policy; wishful thinking; cognitive overload and ambiguity associated with high signal to noise ratios; and receptivity fatigue.

Holsti (1978), on the basis of a review of the literature, indicates that persons under intense stress suffer increased cognitive rigidity and erosion of general cognitive abilities, including creativity and ability to cope with complexity. Often they transfer and maintain past experience and assumptions and beliefs inappropriately despite contradictory information. Brandstrom et al. (2004: 206), for example, suggest that historical analogies are more likely to be chosen when they "are readily available (for example, because they refer to very recent or very vivid events—even when these are unlikely to recur) and seemingly representative (that is, morphologically 'fitting' the present situation—even when this ignores maxims of statistical probability)."

Given the tendency to develop these pathologies, it is important to ensure that robust mechanisms are in place to counteract them. The composition of the top management group, for example, makes a difference. Research has found that heterogeneity does not increase conflict or reduce communications among top crisis management teams, but rather allows the introduction of different perspectives and alternative strategic options to the deliberations of the team. "Teams with heterogeneous functional backgrounds are more likely to represent multiple stakeholder interests during a crisis" (Greening and Johnson 1997: 352). The ability of individuals to cope with stress varies also as a function of the orientation of managers. D'Aveni and MacMillan (1990) found that managers who pay more attention to the external environment of the firm are more able to cope with stress and attend to a broader array of environmental factors, which improves their ability to adapt. Managers with a high need for structure are more likely to rely on stereotypical thinking and tend to define their problems as one dimensional (Kaplan et al. 1993).

Attention to the information processing aspect of the decision process is particularly important in crises where the mechanisms driving the problem are ill-understood, since in this case the downside of lost or overlooked information is especially severe. It is also critical where there are tight linkages that risk the problem cascading into other domains, or where there are major distributional impacts. A narrow focus may lead decision makers to miss these ripple effects or ignore distributional side effects of alternatives that can undermine social acceptance. Conflict dominated crises and those triggered by human error may lead participants to withhold or distort information, again emphasizing the need for a process that is robust not just in analyzing arriving information, but also in identifying gaps and seeking out needed information.

"Predatory crises" have special information processing requirements in that the information available is likely to come from sources of dubious credibility, often little better than those who have committed the acts triggering the crises. Sifting through conflicting and unreliable information poses unique challenges.

Speed of response is both a consequence of other decision process characteristics, such as degree of centralization, and an independent process attribute. It is likely to be particularly important in the case of "fast-burning" and "cathartic" crises (Rosenthal et al. 2005). In the "fast-burning crisis," the entire course of events occurs at a high pace, and speed is essential throughout. Failure to act quickly (even immediately) may mean failing to act at all. This may not only result in a poor problem outcome, but also have political costs of appearing indecisive.

In the case of a "cathartic crisis," there is a sudden turning point that requires the ability to switch instantly into an immediate response mode. The key here is identifying the critical point, since overriding established processes too soon carries considerable political risk, while doing so too late forfeits the opportunity to intervene. Crises with a strong "contagion" element, such as virulent disease outbreaks and financial panics, also require a rapid response, since every delay makes the ultimate resolution of the problem more difficult. Where human intent has triggered a crisis, as with terrorist incidents, speed of response may be essential in order to act before evidence disappears and the perpetrators escape.

Speed is not always necessary, however, or even beneficial. In "slow-burning crises," there may be ample time for making decisions at a contemplative pace. Deciding on a course of action too quickly in these cases may result in a poor decision because the full nature of the crisis may not yet have revealed itself. This is especially true if decision makers have a poor understanding of the causal mechanism driving events or the distributional consequences are not immediately apparent.

As the crisis winds down, staying in crisis mode keeps leaders in the public eye and provides an opportunity to influence and reframe the political agenda, but staying too long risks neglecting other important issues (and losing the political capital associated with their resolution) and generating dependency and unrealistic expectations among those being helped. On the other hand, returning to "normal" management and policy making too soon exposes leaders to the risk of being caught off guard if the crisis re-emerges, and of appearing to have cynically paid attention to it only when the attention it attracted provided political gains. (Rosenthal et al. 2001: 30–1). The public may also interpret such actions as not taking the issue seriously, or as an attempted cover-up if the matter is one with the potential for serious political consequences.

THE CONSEQUENCES OF CRISES

The consequences of a crisis begin during the crisis itself, as the trigger event stimulates certain psychological and organizational reactions. How decision makers handle these reactions has a major impact on the processes that begin when the crisis is over and on the degree of conflict, learning, change, and trauma that result.

During the crisis, there are likely to be high levels of confusion and stress. If these reactions are not addressed by institutions and measures that reassure and reduce levels of stress, an atmosphere of negativity and recrimination may develop that can be hard to dispel. The threat at the core of a crisis can generate either conflict or solidarity; the former is much more likely if there is a perception that existing institutions are failing to cope, and/or there is a lack of trust and confidence among the participants. Fault finding behaviour in subsequent phases of a crisis increases when decision makers are blamed for failing to prevent the crisis in the first place or for an inadequate initial response; when there is a high level of friction among people and organizations during the crisis; when constructive media relations are not maintained; when expectations are heightened by communication but then not fulfilled; and when there is a perception that justice has not been done in response to a shock or wrongdoing (Hansen and Stern 2001). Such problems are also more likely when pre-existing conflicts among those affected by the crisis lead to accusations of inequity in the distribution of assistance. In such cases, aid may actually exacerbate existing problems and leave recipients worse off overall (Rosenthal et al. 2001).

Crises, with their increased flow of information and heightened scrutiny of actions, create circumstances that may either promote or impede learning (Stern 1997). Evaluation of outcomes is both a "transition ritual" marking the end of a crisis, and a "crucial input to organizational learning." This evaluation phase provides a basis for prescriptions or lessons aimed at preventing crises, reducing their impacts or managing them more effectively. However, it can easily become a ritual in which leaders gain credibility by appearing to take responsibility while in actuality shifting the consequences of failure onto underlings. It is also a phase during which, in bureaucratic organizations, "framing and blaming" provides scope for departmental gains in power and resources, leading to the misrepresentation of events and misdirection of the learning process (Rosenthal et al. 2001). The development of a blame-free culture within an organization is an important precursor to post-crisis learning (Elliot et al. 2001).

The occurrence of the crisis may lead to a shift in the power structure in the system and lead those involved to re-evaluate their values, attitudes, and key beliefs with regard to the system and its vulnerability. There are numerous barriers to learning both during and after a crisis. These include: rigidity of core beliefs, values, and assumptions; ineffective communication and information difficulty; failure to recognize similar or identical situations that happen elsewhere ("isomorphic" properties); maladaptation; threat minimization and environmental shifts; cognitive narrowing and event fixation; centrality of expertise; denial and disregard of outsiders; and focus upon "single-loop" or single cause learning (Elliot et al. 2001).

The quest for certainty and stability may inhibit "unlearning" that must precede the learning from the crisis (Nystrom and Starbuck 1984; Scheaffer and Mano-Negrin 2003). The search for scapegoats in making sense of the crisis and the incentives created for key actors to cover up failures, shift blame, and claim credit threaten any process of sober post-crisis analysis. Opportunistic actors who seek to rewrite history to serve their own objectives may also complicate the construction of post-crisis reality.

An important aspect of learning is changes to values and priorities.

Crisis stress may force decision-makers to confront issues of value complexity and face trade-offs that, under other circumstances, they might prefer to avoid. As a result, decision-makers may succeed in establishing clear value hierarchies that may facilitate the realignment of policy. (Stern 1997: 74)

As both participants in the crisis decision-making process and the general public are exposed to a barrage of similar information through the media,

the common experience of crisis may produce convergence of lay and expert belief systems and provide an impetus to collective action in the domestic and international realms that may overcome tendencies toward inertia in [a] variety of political settings. (Stern 1997: 76)

Ideally the outcome of learning is some degree of reform that improves the preparedness of the system to prevent, absorb and contain new threats that could create crises. Crises open "policy windows" (Kingdon 1984: 99–103) by bringing problems to the fore and creating a sense of urgency. Decision-making structures put in place to deal with the crisis may also provide a concentration of power that facilitates overcoming previous impasses. The ability of leaders to introduce reforms that reflect the lessons learned depends in part, on their leadership performance during the crisis. Maintenance of both public confidence during the crisis and trust in its aftermath is difficult given "the intricate interplay of objective and constructed features in contemporary crises" (Boin and t'Hart 2003: 551). Without trust, the public is likely to view proposals for reform as cynical opportunism unless decision makers nurture support for them before and during the crisis. While crisis induced reforms may find easy acceptance at first, they face implementation challenges when politics as usual return and crisis rhetoric is out of place. Only crisis leaders that cultivate implementation units during the crisis can rely on their support after the crisis.

The opportunity for post-crisis reform is further limited by the fact that "the imperatives of effective crisis containment conflict with the imperatives of reform craft" (Boin and t'Hart 2003: 549). Reformers must portray a crisis as the result of serious flaws in the system that must lead to major changes, while crisis managers must reassure and restore confidence in the system. While reformers must secure the early support of implementing actors for their plans, crisis managers must override routines and procedures to speed up decision making. Implementing the lessons derived from the crisis experience takes time and resources. Often new threats divert the attention of policy makers from the reform agenda created by a crisis before implementation. Indeed, policy makers often forget commitments made immediately after a crisis, particularly when the proposed reforms would threaten existing power structures or result in the replacement of elites. Threatened elites may propose "pre-emptive reforms" to take the wind out of reformers' sails, or engage in fear-mongering about the possible ramifications of dramatic change. For reform to succeed, reformers must keep the sense of crisis alive, speed up reform decision-making processes so that resolution occurs while reform momentum is still strong, and circumvent deadlocks through flexibility and adept bargaining (Rosenthal et al. 2001).

The long-term effects on a community affected by a crisis may include trauma that results in a high and continuing level of distress. This may affect the community as a whole, or an element of it that feels its interests were not given due consideration. The fact that the "unimaginable" has actually happened may disrupt the confidence in the future so necessary to the smooth functioning of society, where much activity relates to planning for the future or making intertemporal trade-offs that become difficult to accept (or even conceptualize) if there is uncertainty as to whether there will be a future for an individual or collective (Erickson 1994; Hansen and Stern 2001). Healing such trauma requires "emergence of a relatively broad and stable consensus about what has happened and how it has been handled" (Rosenthal et al. 2001: 194).

Groups that feel they have been inadequately consulted, inadequately compensated, unfairly burdened, or made a scapegoat for a problem not of their making may suffer a severe and long-lasting loss of confidence in the system, a feeling that when the chips were down, their interests were unfairly treated. It is not easy to redress such a loss of confidence, and it may generate unease in other groups that reason by analogy that their interests may similarly be short changed in a future crisis. Thus the evaluation, learning and reform phases are as much about reassuring the members of the organization or society affected as they are about selecting a theoretically "optimal" response. Justice must be seen to be done, both in the treatment of individuals and more broadly in the way society is perceived to function.

SUMMARY AND CONCLUSION

It is well-established in the management literature that the optimal managerial approach varies with the conditions faced by the organization. Organizational approaches to management thus evolve in response to the environment in which

Table 9.1 Summarizing the Fit Between Crisis Characteristics and Crisis Management Attributes

Crisis characteristic		Key performance dimensions	Facilitating process features	Pathology if absent
Trigger	Natural	Efficency, speed	Routinization, coordination, mobilization	Loss of opportunity to minimize/mitigate impact, criticism for indecisiveness
	Human	Trust, confidentiality, accountability	Transparency	Loss of confidence, trauma
	Known	Efficiency, speed	Routinization, coordination, mobilization	Loss of opportunity to minimize and mitigate impact, criticism for indecisiveness
	Unknown	Diversity of information sources and methods of interpretation	Heterogeneity and external orientation of crisis management team, open communication, large processing capacity	Groupthink, other information processing pathologies
Speed of arrival	Fast-burning	Speed	Unity of command	Loss of opportunity to minimize/mitigate impact, criticism for indecisiveness
	Cathartic	Rapid transition from consultation to action	Delegation to front-line managers	Loss of opportunity to minimize/mitigate impact, criticism for indecisiveness
	Slow-burning	Comprehensive info search, identification of optimal time to intervene	Participation	Drift, bogged down without direction
	Long shadow	Long-term mobilization for reform	Transparency, consultation	Failure to address underlying causes if trapped by inertia
Scale (large)		Diversity of information sources, central coordination	Centralization if time and mechanisms for communication exist; high peak load capacity	Lack of coordination, waste, inability to contain crisis
Conflict (high)		Legitimacy, trust, confidentiality	Transparency that balances security and trust, participation	Social fragmentation, loss of legitimacy
Uncertainty (high)		Diversity of information, confidence-building	Participation and appropriate risk communication strategy	Social fragmentation

the organization finds itself and the resources it has at its disposal. When a crisis strikes, it elicits reactions from the organization that depend on the organization's prior experiences, and that may or may not be appropriate to the special challenges that arise during the crisis. In fact, the longer and the more successfully the organization has coped with its prior environment, the more difficulty it may face in deviating from practices that have always worked well in the past.

Our analysis points to the importance of fit in crisis management: the process adopted should have certain features likely to result in high performance on the dimensions critical in the particular type of crisis the organization faces. If it does not, a variety of sub-optimal outcomes are likely. These linkages between crisis types, key performance dimensions, process features and the pathologies that may result if fit is poor are summarized in Table 9.1.

The five analytically distinguishing characteristics of crises we have examined are listed in the far left column of the table. The middle columns highlight some of the most critical performance dimensions necessary for the effective resolution of each type as identified in the discussion above, as well as the process features likely to lead to such performance. The far right column summarizes the pathologies likely to result if the fit between the crisis type and the approach to managing it is poor.

Adopting a managerial approach that "fits" is essential to an organization not just surviving the crisis, but emerging from it with a strengthened ability to cope with the newly normalized environment and greater resilience to future crises.

References

Ashmos, D. P., Duchon, D., and Bodensteiner, W. D. (1997). 'Linking Issues Labels and Managerial Actions: A Study of Participation in Crisis vs. Opportunity Issues.' *Journal of Applied Business Research*, 13/4: 31–45.

Boin, A. (2005). 'From Crisis to Disaster: Towards an Integrative Perspective,' in R. W. Perry and E. L. Quarantelli (eds.), *What is a Disaster? New Answers to Old Questions*. Philadelphia, PA: Xlibris Books.

—— 't Hart, P. (2003). 'Public Leadership in Time of Crisis Mission Impossible?' *Public Administration Review*, 63/5: 544–53.

—— Lagadec, P., Michel-Kergan, E., and Overdijk, W. (2003). 'Critical Infrastructures Under Threat: Learning from the Anthrax Scare.' *Journal of Contingencies and Crisis Management*, 11/3: 99–104.

Brandstrom, A., Bynander, F., and t'Hart, P. (2004). 'Governing by Looking Back: Historical Analogies and Crisis Management.' *Public Administration*, 82/1: 191–210.

Brown, T. M., and Miller, C. E. (2000). 'Communication Networks in Task Performing Groups: Effects of Task Complexity, Time Pressure and Interpersonal Dominance.' *Small Group Researchers*, 31/2: 131–57.

CHRISTENSEN, S. L. and KOHLS, J. (2003). 'Ethical Decision Making in Times of Organizational Crisis: A Framework for Analysis.' *Business and Society*, 42/3: 328–58.

COMFORT, L. K. (2005). 'Risk, Security and Disaster Management.' *Annual Review of Political Science*, 8: 335–56.

D'AVENI, R. A. and MacMILLAN, I. C. (1990). 'Crisis and the Content of Managerial Communication: A Study of the Focus of Attention of Top Managers in Surviving and Failing Firms.' *Administrative Science Quarterly*, 35: 643–57.

DOUGLAS, M., and WILDAVSKY, A. (1982). *Risk and Culture*. Berkeley, CA: University of California Press.

DRISKELL, J. E. and SALAS, E. (1991). 'Group Decision Making Under Stress.' *Journal of Applied Psychology*, 76/3: 473–78.

DROR, Y. (1988). 'Decision Making Under Disaster,' in L. K. Canfort (ed.), *Managing Disaster*. Durham, NC: Duke University Press.

ELLIOTT, D., SMITH, D., and McGUINNESS, M. (2001). 'Exploring the Failure to Learn: Crises and the Barriers to Learning.' *Review of Business*, fall: 17–24.

ELLIS, P. (1998). 'Chaos in the Underground: Spontaneous Collapse in a Tightly-Coupled System.' *Journal of Contingencies and Crisis Management*, 6/3: 137–53.

ERICKSON, K. T. (1994). *A New Species of Trouble: Explorations in Disaster, Trauma and Community*. London: W.W. Norton and Company.

FREUD, S. (1959). *Group Psychology and the Analysis of the Ego*. New York: Norton.

GEORGE, A. L. (1986). 'The Impact of Crisis Induced Stress on Decision Making.' *Medical Implications of Nuclear War*. Washington, DC: National Academy Press.

GREENING, D. W. and JOHNSON, R. A. (1997). 'Managing Industrial and Environmental Crises: The Role of Heterogeneous Top Management Teams.' *Business and Society*, 36: 334–7.

HANSEN, D. and STERN, E. (2001). 'From Crisis to Trauma: The Palme Assassination Case,' in U. Rosenthal, A. Boin, and L. K. Comfort (eds.), *Managing Crises: Threats, Dilemmas, Opportunities*. Springfield, IL: Charles C. Thomas.

HERMANN, C. F. (1963). 'Some Consequences of Crisis which Limit the Viability of Organizations.' *Administrative Science Quarterly*, 8: 61–82.

—— HERMANN, M. G. (1982). 'A Look Inside the "Black Box": Building Upon a Decade of Research,' in G. W. Hopple (ed.), *Biopolitics, Political Psychology and International Politics*. London: Pinter, 1–36.

HOLLING, C. S. (1978). 'Myths of Ecological Stability: Resilience and the Problem of Failure.' *Journal of Business Administration*, 9/2: 97–109.

HOLSTI, O. R. (1978). 'Limitations of Cognitive Abilities in the Face of Crisis,' in C. F. Smart and W. T. Stanbury (eds.), *Studies on Crisis Management*. Halifax, Nova Scotia: Institute for Research on Public Policy.

JANIS, I. L. (1972). *Victims of Groupthink*. Boston: Houghton Miffler.

—— MANN, L. (1977). *Decision Making: A Psychological Analysis of Conflict, Choice and Commitment*. New York: Free Press.

KAPLAN, M. F., WANSHULA, L. T., and ZANA, M. P. (1993). 'Time Pressure and Information Integration in Social Judgment: The Effect of Need for Structure,' in O. Svenson and A. J. Maule (eds.), *Time Pressure and Stress in Human Judgment and Decision Making*. New York: Plenum Press, 255–67.

KINGDON, J. W. (1984). *Agendas, Alternatives and Public Polices*. Boston: Little, Brown and Company.

LA PORTE, T. R. (2005). 'Anticipating Rude Surprises: Reflections on "Crisis Management" Without End.' Paper presented in Biennial Research Workshop, Communicable Crises: Prevention, Management and Resolution in an Era of Globalization, International Public Management Network, August 15–17, Vancouver, B.C., Canada.

—— CONSOLINI, P. M. (1991). 'Working in Practice But Not in Theory: Theoretical Challenges of "High-Reliability Organizations."' *Journal of Public Administration Research and Theory*, 1/1: 19–48.

LIANG, H. and HUE, Y. (2004). 'Investigating Public Health Emergency Response Information System Initiatives in China.' *International Journal of Medical Informatics*, 73: 675–85.

MARCH, J. G. (1991). 'Exploration and Exploitation in Organizational Learning.' *Organization Science*, 2/1: 71–87.

NELKIN, D. (1988). 'Risk Reporting and the Management of Industrial Crises.' *Journal of Management Studies*, 25: 341–51.

NYSTROM, P. C. and STARBUCK, W. H. (1984). 'To Avoid Organizational Crises, Unlearn.' *Organizational Dynamics*, 12: 53–65.

PARKER, C. F. and STERN, E. K. (2005). 'Bolt from the Blue or Avoidable Failure? Revisiting September 11 and the Origins of Strategic Surprise.' *Foreign Policy Analysis*, 1: 301–31.

PEARSON, C. M., and CLAIR, J. A. (1988). 'Reframing Crisis Management.' *Academy of Management Review*, 23/1: 59–76.

QUARANTELLI, E. L. (1988). 'Disaster Crisis Management: A Summary of Research Findings.' *Journal of Management Studies*, 25: 373–85.

—— (1998). *What is a Disaster? Perspectives on the Question*. London: Routledge.

ROSENTHAL, U. and KOUZMIN, A. (1993). Globalizing an Agenda for Contingencies and Crisis Management.' *Journal of Contingencies and Crisis Management*, 1/1: 1–12.

ROSENTHAL, R. and 'T HART, P. (1990). 'Experts and decision makers in crisis situations'. *Knowledge: Creation, Diffusion, Utilization*, 12/4: 350–72.

—— CHARLES, M. T., and 'T HART, P. (1989). *Coping with Crisis: The Management of Disasters, Riots and Terrorism*. Springfield, IL: Charles C. Thomas.

—— BOIN, R. A., and COMFORT, L. K. (2001). *Managing Crises: Threats, Dilemmas, Opportunities*. Springfield, IL: Charles C. Thomas Publishers Ltd.

SCHEAFFER, Z. and MANO-NEGRIN, R. (2003). 'Executives Orientation as Indicators of Crisis Management Policies and Practices.' *Journal of Management Studies*, 40/2: 573–606.

SHRIVASTAVA, P. (1987). *Bhopal: Anatomy of a Crisis*. Cambridge, MA: Ballinger.

—— MITROFF, I., MILLER, D., and MIGLANI, A. (1988). 'Understanding Industrial Crises.' *Journal of Management Studies*, 25: 285–303.

SMART, C. and VERTINSKY, I. (1977). 'Decisions for Crisis Decision Units.' *Administrative Science Quarterly*, 22/4: 640–59.

STERN, E. (1997). 'Crisis and Learning: A Conceptual Balance Sheet.' *Journal of Contingencies and Crisis Management*, 5/2: 69–86.

SUSSKIND, L. and FIELD, P. (1996). *Dealing with an Angry Public*. New York: Free Press.

SVENSON, O. and MAULE, A. J. (eds.) (1993). *Time Pressure and Stress in Human Judgment and Decision Making*. New York: Plenum Press.

'T HART, P. (1990). *Groupthink in Government: A Study of Small Groups and Policy Failure*. Swets and Zeilinger: Rockland, MA and Amsterdam.

—— BOIN, A. (2001). 'Between Crisis and Normalcy: The Long Shadow of Post-Crisis Politics,' in U. Rosenthal, R. A. Boin, and L. K. Comfort (eds.), *Managing Crises: Threats, Dilemmas, Opportunities*. Springfield, IL: Charles C. Thomas Publishers Ltd.

'T HART, P., ROSENTHAL, U. and KOUZMIN, A. (1993). 'Crisis Decision Making: The Centralization Thesis Revisited.' *Administration and Society*, 25/1: 12–45.

WEICK, K. E. (1988). 'Enacted Sensemaking in Crisis Situations.' *Journal of Management Studies*, 25/4: 305–18.

—— (1993). 'The Collapse of Sensemaking in Organizations: The Mann Gulch Disaster.' *Administrative Science Quarterly*, 38: 628–52.

WHO (2005a). *WHO Outbreak Communication Guidelines*. Geneva: WHO.

—— (2005b). *Outbreak Communication: Best Practices for Communicating with the Public During an Outbreak*. Geneva: WHO.

—— (2006). *SARS: How a Global Epidemic was Stopped*. Geneva: WHO.

10

EMPLOYING ADAPTIVE STRUCTURING AS A COGNITIVE DECISION AID IN HIGH RELIABILITY ORGANIZATIONS

KARLENE H. ROBERTS

KUO FRANK YU

VINIT DESAI

PETER M. MADSEN

INTRODUCTION

SATURDAY, June 15, 1996, was a seemingly normal day for Greater Manchester Police (GMP), UK. At 9:41 AM, however, a local television station reported a bomb threat tip. Suddenly, GMP faced a major crisis. Police officers immediately began searching for the alleged bomb while evacuating about 80,000 people in Manchester city center. At 10:00 AM, police located the bomb and called the bomb squad to the scene while simultaneously evacuating citizens. The bomb squad arrived 15 minutes before the bomb was set to detonate, but unfortunately failed to deactivate it, resulting in a catastrophic explosion. The city suffered major damage—an estimated 50,000 square meters of retail space and nearly 25, 000 square meters of office space were destroyed. The blast site included parts of the Arndale shopping center, the Corn Exchange, and the Royal Exchange. The Royal Insurance building is no more. The shockwaves affected structures over eight kilometers from the epicenter. Miraculously no one died, although 220 people sustained injuries (mainly glass related) and the city suffered total damage equal to an estimated US$700 million.

Although GMP could not stop the impending explosion, they successfully evacuated 80,000 people from a highly populated area in very little time and prevented any loss of life. The GMP organization responded decisively to the threat because they could effectively integrate information from two seemingly unrelated sources. Firstly, the local television station aired the breaking news about a bomb in Manchester city center (but not giving its location). Police remained oblivious of the situation until they saw it on the news. Secondly, the police had issued a parking ticket to an unusually placed truck in the center of town. Upon hearing about the bomb threat, the police were able to associate the two events and immediately suspected that the truck played a role in the overall scheme. In 20 minutes, police pinpointed and confirmed the exact location of the bomb, thus leaving enough time for citizens to vacate the city. The combination of two pieces of seemingly unrelated information allowed GMP to understand and handle the situation in the most effective way.

Unlike GMP, not all organizations are successful in preventing such catastrophes. Because key errors can interact, snowball, and cascade to catastrophic outcomes, some organizations strive for nearly error-free operation (Weick and Roberts 1993). High Reliability Organizations (HROs) are an example of organizations that succeed in achieving low error rates in the face of potentially catastrophic loss (Roberts 1990). GMP is an HRO because of its adaptive responses to novel information using appropriate cognitive integration in a distributed decision-making context.

One argument that criticizes this work describes HROs as an exceptional subcategory of organizations that do not necessarily generalize to the broader class of organizations. Weick and Roberts (1993), for instance, suggest that HROs focus mainly on their reliability while overlooking qualities such as efficiency that are high priority to other organizations. However, recent research, finds that many organizations increasingly operate in potentially hazardous environments with widely differing reliability ratings (e.g., Marcus and Nichols 1999; Ciavarelli et al. 2001; Gaba et al. 2003; Madsen et al. 2006). Pool (1997: 276) suggests that more organizations must focus on achieving high reliability because of their reliance on advanced technologies. This suggests that HRO research has the potential to make important contributions because it examines organizations that successfully handle challenging crises. Organizations that desire to achieve more reliable practices and outcomes can learn lessons learned in HROs that achieve reliability in hazardous environments.

Research on HROs identified several structural and cognitive mechanisms that support rapid and effective decision-making in crises (e.g., Weick and Roberts 1993 Klein et al. 1995; Bigley and Roberts 2001; Roberts et al. 2005;). However, HRO research rarely touches upon how specific methods fare across organizations that are successful and unsuccessful in achieving highly reliable operations. This chapter begins to fill this gap through an analysis of three organizations that operate in crisis prone environments.

In each case, *organizational structures* and *group mental models* were adapted to facilitate effective decision making in the high-risk incidents. Each organization experienced different success rates in its attempt to attain high reliability. The first organization effectively structures and facilitates decision making in highly hazardous situations. The second organization went from low to high reliability and then reverted to lower reliability. The third organization created a structure to foster high reliability decision making in crisis prone situations. Each organization operates in environments with examples of both high and low reliability decision making.

The chapter begins by discussing processes contributing to high and low reliability decision making. It then discusses the three cases, covering the similar processes used in the three situations and notes what managers can take from this. Finally, the chapter argues for research that does not concentrate on a single organization but examines interactions among geographically distributed units addressing the same problem.

Decision-Making Contexts of Disaster Prone Environments

There are many examples of bad decisions in organizations that should have been highly reliable: the Titanic; space shuttles Challenger and Columbia; Chernobyl; and a vast number of medical accidents. There are also a number of successful cases, some of which include organizations that use structured activities to facilitate decision making, leading members to re-organize their norms, values, and rules, to search for latent errors, and to build slack to eliminate errors. Organizations in this group include US commercial nuclear power plants, the US Navy carrier aviation program, and some health care settings. To illustrate, Wilson (1986: 21) states, that although naval aircraft carriers "represent 'a million accidents waiting to happen' almost none of them do."

Successful and unsuccessful organizations share similar operating environments. Many organizations operate in dangerous situations with high levels of uncertainty and risk. Members of each organization perform in situations requiring a high degree of reliability because of the risk of poor outcomes. What, then, determines success versus failure? Perrow (1984) classifies organizations and systems based on their degree of complexity and on the degree to which organizational elements are integrated. Interactively complex systems, according to Perrow, are those in which two or more discrete failures can interact in unexpected ways that potentially have a complex and unpredictable effect on the overall system. When parts of these systems are tightly joined or lack slack to minimize errors, problems tend to increase and may be complicated by operator intervention.

Turner's (1978) Disaster Incubation Model (DIM) gives one explanation of how poor decisions occur and accumulate in these organizations. Four of Turner's six steps in the DIM refer to the emergence of poor decision making: (1) starting point; (2) incubation period; (3) precipitating event; and (4) onset. The starting point involves culturally accepted views associated with an organization's processes, rules, laws, codes, and procedures designed to ensure safety against danger. The incubation period is a time in which small mistakes add up to something greater. The incubation period is a series of events that are at odds with the organization's norms and beliefs. These discrepant events represent times during which organizations could detect and change the flaws of their models and procedures.

In organizations headed for crises, however, these incubating events are neglected, noticed but misunderstood or noticed but not taken care of adequately. They indicate latent failures in an organization's system. Latent failures weaken an organization's defense system before any significant accident transpires. They usually go unnoticed until they interact with some precipitating event, an event in which conditions that normally pose little threat begin to act in unexpected ways. Precipitating events are small errors, a set of abnormal situational conditions, or technical problems. However, in concert with latent failures, precipitating events can lead to regrettable disaster.

Turner's (1978) DIM suggests that a cyclical process takes place in organizations facing hazardous situations. This sometimes recursive, and unstructured process deals with error incubation and detection, decision making involving potential solutions, and disastrous or mitigated outcome events. The process model suggests that not all tightly linked, highly complex systems are accident prone as Perrow (1984) indicates. Instead, organizations may build redundant structures, build up slack resources, and create other processes to improve error rates and overall decision making in situations demanding high reliability.

Employing Adaptive Structuring
as a Cognitive Decision Aid

Research on HROs identifies structures and processes that guide cognitive evaluation and decision making in cases requiring high reliability. In resorting to structural adaptations and procedures, organizations as systemic entities can scan their environments expansively, examine their operations microscopically, and respond to changing contingencies rapidly. Structural adaptations allow organizations to become more than the sum of their parts. When the organization as a system compensates for inevitable myopia that an individual decision maker suffers it achieves enhanced cognitive coherence. Providing some cognitive theoretical underpinning behind the HRO research helps illustrate how decision makers rely on structural processes as cognitive decision aids to achieve systemic advantages.

Weick and Daft (1983) see organizations as connected networks, where members congregate and share information, or engage in sensemaking, to interpret and understand what transpires. Sensemaking is the process by which organizational members create mental models of the organization and its environment (Weick 1995). All organizational members do not hold the same mental models of the organization, though they share some similarity and compatibility from constant interaction with one another (O'Connor 1987).

The overlapping mental models facilitate decision making in high reliability situations by letting members cooperate in the pursuit of similar goals. By sensemaking, organizational decision makers can interpret their environments in ways that reduce uncertainty because they draw from information across varied intra- and interorganizational networks. Therefore, decision makers can artificially stretch time and shorten reaction time by reducing the time required to gather, interpret, and verify information regarding situational understandings (Roberts 1990).

Organizational decision makers usually develop overlapping mental models of their technological environments slowly through environmental interactions that fit conditions they normally face (Weick 1995). Slow and familiar changes in the environment can be reconciled with these mental models, while rapid and unfamiliar changes, and particularly changes to the nature of crises posed by the task environment, cannot be reconciled (Weick 1993). For this reason, organizational members experience dangers as stunning, scary, and incomprehensible and may become rigid (Perrow 1984; Staw et al. 1984).

Effective decision making in huge crises begs people to develop quickly new mental models of situations as they evolve. However, due to the difficulty of the task, people cling to existing models as long as possible, selectively processing information that confirms and updates them (Louis and Sutton 1991; Weick 1995). Cognitive rigidity not only leads to delay in decision making but also misinterpretations of information due to erroneous mindsets. When subject to extreme rigidity, people abandon existing mental models, give up hope of understanding the threat, and (sometimes literally) run for their lives (Weick 1993).

Effective decision making that achieves high reliability depends on recognizing anomalies or latent errors before the crisis begins (Marcus and Nichols 1999; Ramanujam and Goodman 2003). When encountering anomalies, successful decision makers reconsider or revise their understanding of the situation. In the Manchester bombing, the bomb threat forced the police to re-appraise the anomalous, illegally parked van as a potential bomb location, instead of as another common instance of illegal parking. The ability to reexamine anomalous events as the situation changed illustrates heedful sensemaking during crisis.

Despite the importance of sensemaking, most organizations are poorly equipped to find and use information in ways that enhance decision-making reliability (Weick 1995). Over time they adapt to the demands of their environments. As part of this process, organizational members learn which sources of information about their environments are most useful in performing their daily functions. People usually monitor useful information sources closely while ignoring other information. This process is adaptive because monitoring information sources is costly and organizations are more efficient by paying attention only to information sources that are most useful under normal conditions (Starbuck and Milliken 1988). With time, people become used to ignoring most information about the environment, especially information suggesting that radical or discontinuous changes are transpiring (Audia et al. 2000).

While selective information processing is efficient under normal conditions, it is very *in*effective for decision making when situations with probable catastrophic outcomes arise. These situations push organizations toward more unfamiliar environments (Dutton 1988). Information gathering routines that previously brought high efficiency under normal conditions no longer provide organizations with enough information to make sense of the unfolding scenario. When organizational decision makers do not understand that the environment is changing, they become increasingly decoupled from reality and fail to change the way they make decisions until disasters strike. The reactive mode rather than the preemptive decision-making mode substantially increases the likelihood of mistakes.

Although sensemaking is usually an unconscious process, leaders can structure their organizations and train employees to make rapid sensemaking possible when confronted with a dangerous situation (Weick 1995). Organizational members must create new mental models and discover ways to integrate their individual mental models to coordinate action and avoid rigid and selective information processing (Roth 1997). They must readily abandon one model in favor of another upon the discovery of new information or a change in environmental conditions (Bigley and Roberts 2001).

Weick and Roberts (1993) developed the idea of "collective mind" to elucidate how some organizations can successfully maintain shared mental models in dangerous and quickly changing conditions. Collective mind is

a pattern of heedful interrelations of actions in a social system. Actors in the system construct their actions (contributions), understanding that the system consists of connected actions by themselves and others (representation), and interrelate their actions within the system (subordination). (Weick and Roberts 1993: 357)

To establish collective mind in an organization, members must understand that their actions are connected. They must also create their mental models and select their actions with connectedness in mind. This connectedness allows people to mitigate hazardous conditions as they unfold. Weick and Roberts point out that "As heedful interrelating and mindful comprehension increases organizational errors decrease" (1993: 357).

Often organizations are not effectively structured to develop collective mind and continuous sensemaking in dangerous situations. The next section discusses three examples of organizations that operate in hazardous environments and were not all together successful in incorporating procedures to help decision making in incidents requiring high reliability.

THREE APPROACHES OF ADAPTIVE STRUCTURING IN HROS

The first example describes how firefighters use the Incident Command System (ICS) to assemble and control complex temporary systems (Bigley and Roberts 2001). This system effectively combines information to facilitate decision making, expanding in scope as incidents escalate in complexity, and resetting as situations change or are resolved. The second example is a pediatric intensive care unit (PICU) that tried to achieve highly reliable operations by spreading decision-making authority, and was successful until the unit changed its strategy (Madsen et al. 2006). The third example is a police department's emergency (911) call system. Although routinely effective, the system experiences both failures and successes. The system's structural design decreases the consequences of failure by retaining flexibility as situations evolve (Roberts et al. 2007).

The Incident Command System (ICS) in a Large County Fire Department

Bigley and Roberts (2001) investigated the operation of the Incident Command System (ICS) in a large county fire department that serves the county government and its constituent cities. Serving a population of over 1.2 million and a jurisdictional area that covers more than 560 square miles, the department contains sixty plus fire stations located in the county's major geographic divisions. Each division consists of a number of battalions that in turn are broken down into stations. In total, the fire department hires over 800 full-time firefighters and has 700 firefighters on call.

The ICS builds a very rigid structure on site at each emergency. To respond effectively to any emergency though, it has to retain a sense of internal and external malleability as circumstances unfold and change. This organization faces several challenges: (1) how to make the ICS more malleable; (2) how to get away from centralized decision making to meet the challenges of a constantly changing situation; and (3) how to provide tools that assist in developing a decision-making fabric similar to that of heedful interrelating. To perform these tasks, the ICS developed four structural processes that Bigley and Roberts (2001) label "structure elaborating," "role switching," "authority migration," and "system resetting."

Incident commanders need to be vigilant to the likelihood that the system they create might fail to conform to the situation's needs (that is, being too complex or not complex enough). As the emergency abates, commanders can disengage parts of the system as they become excessive. They breathe malleability into the system in many ways. One way involves considerable role switching, where team members take on different positions during different times in the crisis. Role switching involves the assignment and reassignment of personnel to different roles within the organization depending on the organization's needs. Role switching complements structure elaboration.

Authority migration also builds in flexibility and takes place when the incident demands it. Different emergency responders are experts in emergency medicine, hazardous materials handling, urban search and rescue, as well as construction or chemical processing. Informal decision-making authority is often explicitly unlinked from the official hierarchy and travels quickly across ICS positions to individuals who have the expertise to solve particular problems.

To respond to quickly changing situations, the entire structure may have to reset itself to regain hierarchical flexibility. Sometimes incident commanders discover that their initial organizational form is not solving the problem, or they are confronted with "nasty surprises." The prudent thing to do is to disengage and reset the structure to confront the new or changing problem effectively.

These structural processes are implemented to inject fluidity into the decision making process. According to Bigley and Roberts (2001), constrained improvization and cognitive management methods aid structural fluidity. Supervisors may not understand enough about the contingencies of local situations facing subordinates to provide sufficient direction. In addition, since each emergency is unique, task environments often outstrip the experience base of those people in the ICS. Thus, supervisors often have considerable discretion in the extent to which they give detailed instructions to subordinates. When subordinates gain sufficient experience, training, and resourcefulness to adapt to local conditions, the supervisor frequently leaves the task partially unstructured, and provides subordinates with enough discretion to improvise. This strategy increases the chance that the decision will be specifically appropriate to the problem.

To address emergencies effectively team members spend much time developing cognitive representations of the situation and altering those representations as the world changes. They engage in ongoing "size ups" that are communicated across team members. Developing high fidelity models and communicating them assists people in coordinating decision making that reflects the nature of the problem. Accurate and timely communication is integral to reaching this goal.

Representations are developed, communicated, and embedded within the system in terms of scope and detail. This embedding is frequently consistent with the lines of authority such that people at the top of the organization have more scope and those closer to the bottom have more detail. Detail and scope are enmeshed, resulting in "having the big picture," or "having the bubble." This is synonymous with Weick and Roberts' (1993) notion of collective mind since leadership is able to amalgamate details from across the organization to arrive at a comprehensive understanding of the environment as crises unfold, and use this understanding to mold decision making under uncertainty, time pressure, and complexity.

The Pediatric Intensive Care Unit (PICU)

Madsen et al. (2006) discuss the creation of a Pediatric Intensive Care Unit (PICU) to treat severe and chronically ill youth in a metropolitan area. Both complex and unpredictable, pediatric intensive care performs a myriad of delicate procedures, some as minor as injections or intravenous line insertions that could cause patients to become agitated and move in unpredictable ways. To meet the challenges of treating critically ill children, a metropolitan hospital created a new PICU in 1988 that serves a population of 2.5 million with 20 percent under the age of 15 and a geographic size of Vermont tripled. Initially the hospital employed a pediatric intensivist as the director of the new PICU, with a second intensivist joining the unit a year later. These two physicians lead the unit until 2000, when they both left the hospital. During their tenure, the PICU grew considerably in terms of beds, equipment, patients, and admissions to become one of the biggest PICUs in the United States.

The first intensivist noticed a sharp distinction between the bedside caregiver, typically a resident nurse who monitors small groups of patients within close proximity, and the physician who attends to a larger group of patients but allocates less time to each. Since bedside caregivers spend more time with patients, they are the first organizational members to notice changes in patients that may signal health problems. On the other hand, the intensivist noticed that physicians relied on information from laboratory values, radiographic findings, and physician colleagues as resources to make effective decisions, but often neglected information from nurses.

The intensivist wanted to design an ideal unit that involved nurses in making patient care decisions and avoided mistakes that potentially emerge from selective information processing. When the PICU began admitting patients, the intensivist began asking nurses for their insights on patient treatment options, inviting them to perform some tasks usually assigned to doctors. At first, nurses disliked this approach because their responsibilities seemed to increase; furthermore, they thought the approach implied that the physicians were incompetent. This initial reaction surprised the new PICU director persuading him that instituting his desired participative organizational design in the unit needed a long-term commitment and evolving effort.

As the intensivist continued encouraging nurses to help make patient care decisions, many dedicated nurses (and later the dedicated respiratory care practitioners) began warming to his proposal. At this point, participative decision making in the unit was not formal and largely involved queries by staff members, observations about patients and requests for their views about effective treatment routes. Several nurses and respiratory care practitioners working in the unit reported that the intensivist's approach made them feel valued, yet under qualified to give suggestions on patient treatment options. In response, the intensivist started assisting staff members in medical decision making. He introduced information through conversations with care staff and continued to invite staff members to attend the physicians' rounds.

Calling on his prior experience with a decentralized approach in other workplaces, the second intensivist enthusiastically supported the PICU director's push to delegate care decisions to nurses, respiratory care practitioners, and residents. When the second intensivist arrived training became more formalized. The intensivists started showing staff members how to identify medical problems that brought children to the PICU. They taught caregivers how to spot and treat symptoms that could arise because of disease or inappropriate medical care. The intensivists also gave staff members formalized decision-making aids to help them know when to treat a patient themselves and when to ask for help. They taught staff members to categorize patients' symptoms, assess the severity of the category, and begin treating the most acute symptoms while calling for additional help if necessary.

Both intensivists taught informally when opportunities arose, but also started formal in-service training lessons for all staff members. The intensivists encouraged everyone to read medical journals and textbooks to enhance their education. Some former nurses and respiratory care practitioners said they became so interested in what they learned in these sessions that they decided to return to school for advanced degrees. With more training, staff members felt more comfortable accepting responsibility and the two intensivists delegated more authority to them. However, specialists from other hospital departments were not used to such a degree of decentralization. Despite this, the PICU directors created a policy to support staff members' decisions in these situations. While their decisions were far from infallible, the two PICU intensivists felt that their decentralized design improved response times and decision quality on average because staff with more direct information about critical situations made more effective care decisions. They felt that distributing decision-making authority reduced the need for information to flow through the chain of command and back to the bedside caregivers, substantially enhancing response speed.

The unit's decentralization met with some staff opposition. Most of the staff at least cooperated with the decentralized approach, but it needed their commitment to learn how to carry out new duties. However, internal opposition to the decentralized design was not nearly as strong as resistance from other hospital departments. Those from other departments increasingly discussed the PICU's design and processes with the intensivists, at times to advise the intensivists of resistance from administration, and at other times to argue that staff members made poor care decisions. Hospital administrators and some physicians in other departments also saw the decentralization approach as a waste of time and resources.

With the implementation of decentralized decision making, the PICU experienced a noticeable decrease in the mortality rate for a PICU of its size even while the unit was growing rapidly. By 1993, the PICU's mortality rate was 4.6 percent compared to the average rate of 7.8 $\pm$ 0.8 percent for PICUs of relative size (Madsen et al. 2006). In 1999, the last year the original intensivists remained at the unit, its mortality rate was 3.5 percent. Several other indicators of patient medical outcomes also appeared to improve, such as the introduction of several medical innovations that improved health care. An innovation that yielded such improvements involved respiratory care practitioners, who changed the treatment for severe asthma through altering the blend of helium and oxygen when administering gas to patients. Such innovations would not have been possible without the medical training employed by the PICU intensivists' decentralized decision-making approach. Bedside caregivers reported more satisfaction among staff in the decentralized unit compared with other medical settings.

More doctors were hired as the unit grew until it stabilized with a total complement of five. Until 1997, the only physicians assigned to the PICU were supporters of the decentralized approach, an unorthodox yet effective design. Beginning in 1997, intensivists trained elsewhere were hired. Some of these externally trained intensivists failed to see the value of the PICU's approach and thought that the unit's design might constitute malpractice because physicians were not always in control of patient treatment. The new intensivists advocated strict physician authority and one-way, downward communication, expressed concern for malpractice liability on the part of physicians in the PICU, and possessed generally negative feelings about the unit that resonated with physicians' feelings in other hospital departments. Some hospital administrators even argued against allocating resources to support the unit's expansion. In such a resistant environment, both original intensivists left the hospital to accept positions elsewhere.

According to remaining staff members in the PICU, the structure of decision making changed after the departure of the two original intensivists. Decision making eventually took the path of tradition, whereby physician authority overruled bedside caregiver suggestions and patient care decisions. The new physicians did not encourage staff members to participate in rounds and no longer used rounds as an opportunity to train nurses. Although current staff members do not doubt the competence of current PICU intensivists, they suggest that health outcomes have generally declined since 1999. Statistics show that the annual mortality rate at the unit has increased. Staff turnover increased during the same period. The PICU seems to have lost some measure of reliability since its departure from the decentralization approach advocated by the original intensivists.

Big City Police Department

Roberts et al. (2007) examined the interactions between sensemaking and decision making in a large police department they dub Big City Police Department (BCPD). BCPD serves a large urban metropolis inhabited by about 380,000 people, investigating in excess of 100 homicides annually (one of the highest totals per capita in the United States). In 2000, each of this department's emergency response phoneline (911) operators responded to an average of 17,000 calls, the highest level of emergency operator activity of any large US city.

BCPD is a paramilitary organization. However, emergency dispatchers and police officers have great discretion in handling emergencies. Information coming into the communication center travels across at least four different individuals. Citizens make emergency calls to report a crime or to request police assistance. Complaint operators respond to and evaluate citizen calls. If a call requires police assistance, they note pertinent details in a computerized format and electronically transmit important information, such as the level of urgency priority, to dispatchers.

Upon receiving information from complaint operators, dispatchers re-evaluate the calls and may change a call's priority level if deemed appropriate. Dispatchers allocate available resources to handle the calls, communicate with officers through primary police radio channels to make assignments, and monitor police response to the calls. In emergency situations, complaint operators send preliminary information to dispatchers while continuing to question callers for further information. Thus, complaint operators and dispatchers are in constant contact through the communication center's computer system. Dispatchers also maintain contact with police officers through the event's duration. Call takers and dispatchers are responsible for making sense of incoming 911 calls and letting police officers know what to expect when they arrive at the scene. The two primary goals at BCPD are citizen and police safety.

Roberts et al. (2007) conducted an archival review of 32 adjudicated homicide cases transmitted through the 911 system. Homicides are delicate situations that are handled reliably by the police, or result in further death. This review illustrates, through the portrayal of cases in which callers minimized or withheld valuable information, the complexity of the call taker's job. Other callers explained their understandings of the calls based on incomplete information; these callers often gave accounts that made sense of what they witnessed about the situation, but did not suggest that a homicide had transpired. Reports of the same incident by a number of people from different perspectives, the changing nature of the incident over time, and the increasing number of first responders can make call takers' jobs more complex.

Roberts et al. (2007) noted a number of regularities in the way police addressed calls. They call these "practices": "early model adoption," "model migration and resetting," and "having the bubble." First, even if there is vague and confusing information from the beginning of a call, call takers assign a priority code and an identifying code to the situation as they handle the call. This practice provides an integrative framework police use to coordinate information and facilitate comprehension. It creates a working shared model that can evolve over time. This early model adoption, however, became problematic in several cases where the initial model was incorrect but adopters kept it beyond its usefulness. While early model adoption is usually a heuristic that aids problem solving, it can be deceiving if it leads observers to generate inaccurate conclusions about the incident. Therefore, although BCPD developed a procedure to facilitate the early sharing of mental models this procedure sometimes made mental models hard to revise.

On the other hand, early adopted models are often customized with updated situational understandings. This is referred to as model migration and resetting. Model migration is the process through which each individual contributes information to the working mental model and then transmits it to others, who may integrate that information with their own to modify situational awareness further. Model resetting materializes when the model is either revised or abandoned based on further understanding the unfolding situation. Although the adoption of a model allows people to share information and coordinate actions in an integrative effort, each person has unique information that can assist in sensemaking.

Roberts et al. (2007) proposed that a key structural design exists at BCPD that allows the adoption of early mental models yet helps with model migration and resetting when situations escalate or change. This flexibility in modifying shared mental models emerged because dispatchers were centrally located and primarily responsible for receiving, interpreting, and sharing information across the organization, as situations unfold. In any potential crisis, each organizational member has a unique perspective of what the crisis is and how it is changing. These local views are important, and their integration with an outsider's view (particularly one who can see the overall picture) is paramount.

Heath and Staudenmeyer (2000) propose that organizations decrease effectiveness when their participants focus on partitioning complex tasks and concentrate on their individual components with tunnel-like vision but fail to pay attention to reintegrating the tasks, taking a step back, and taking in the entire picture. As hazardous situations develop, environments change so rapidly that decision makers constantly lack information from disparate areas of the organization. One individual must be able to see the big picture or have the bubble in order to coordinate courses of action successfully. In most large US police departments like BCPD, dispatchers must have the bubble because they have central positions in the crisis response hub. Call takers direct information from callers electronically to dispatchers so that dispatchers gain access to relevant information from bystander reports. This is more efficient than directly placing callers in touch with dispatchers, since call takers carefully screen out pertinent knowledge from often ambiguous and uncertain calls. Conversely, dispatchers work with police officers via radio to relay information from callers regarding developing incidents. Dispatchers are therefore in a position to collect information from call takers and police officers, and to utilize this information to coordinate police officer movements and facilitate organizational sensemaking as events transpire.

CONCLUDING REMARKS

Adaptive structuring processes, as illustrated in the three examples, provide many lessons organizations can use to achieve more reliable practices and outcomes. These lessons should not be blindly applied because organizations operate in different decision environments, face varying hazard levels, and cope with changing resource constraints. Comprehension is crucial: people need to understand how mistakes are made and how adaptive structuring can mitigate them in disaster prone contexts.

All three cases describe contexts characterized by hierarchical structures, but each case describes adaptive structuring processes designed to remove the rigidity originally associated with its hierarchical nature. Adaptive structuring thereby facilitates malleable decision-making processes.

The ICS first elaborates its structure to suit the size of the emergency; larger emergencies generally demand more elaborate structures. However, the ICS insures various skills held by different people will come to the fore by encouraging role switching and migrating decision making to experts. To control against going too far down an incorrect path, the system includes a resetting mechanism. The PICU realizes similar high reliability outcomes by using lower level people to make decisions usually made at higher levels. It underscores this process by giving care givers formal decision making aids to help them decide when to treat and when to ask for help. BCPD accomplishes high reliability decision making through a similar process. The structure connects one or many citizen callers with one or many call takers who try to separate relevant from irrelevant information, passing relevant information along in the organizational network.

All three reliability enhancing approaches have built in mechanisms to integrate information across organizational networks. The ICS does this through its three structural mechanisms. Structure elaboration and its opposite, structure degeneration, pertain to the need to be responsive to local condition changes, as do role switching and resetting. The PICU operates in much the same was as US Navy aircraft carriers (Roberts 1990) ensuring that the decision-making structure has in it someone with the "big picture" who can allocate resources with broad discretion. BCPD has a decision-making structure that allows for information re-interpretation over time with call takers and dispatchers acting as tier one and tier two in the information filtration process. Sometimes the information is still misinterpreted as it reaches the police officer on the beat. His or her knowledge of the local situation can add important data to the interpretation process. Meaning is negotiated continuously and activities are accommodated according to changing situations.

The three field studies offer insights about how decisions are made in situations in which people in the same geographic region respond to critical events. Decision makers use similar processes in each situation and modify them to meet the situation's special constraints. We advise managers that achieving high reliability operations requires tailor-making management practices to their situations. Managers must remain flexible to meet changing situational contingencies whatever processes they use.

Examples like Hurricane Katrina and the Southeast Asian tsunamis illustrate the fact that geographical distribution puts additional stress on decision makers. The world not only faces more natural disasters that must be addressed from geographically disparate locations, organizations themselves are spreading everywhere in a global economy. Some research points to the role of interorganizational relationships in creating and attenuating disasters. For instance, Turner's (1976) DIM argues that potential accidents begin as minor failures that are complicated unknowingly through relationships among multiple and often dispersed organizations, until a triggering event (often the accident itself) causes direct intervention. Understanding how people in such distributed situations can best amalgamate information to make decisions in constantly changing and potentially hazardous situations.

References

AUDIA, P. G., LOCKE, E. A., and SMITH, K. G. (2000). 'The Paradox of Success: An Archival and a Laboratory Study of Strategic Persistence Following Radical Environmental Change.' *Academy of Management Journal*, 43: 837–53.

BIGLEY, G. A., and ROBERTS, K. H. (2001). 'Structuring Temporary Systems for High Reliability.' *Academy of Management Journal*, 44: 1281–300.

CIAVARELLI, A., FIGLOCK, R., SENGUPTA, K., and ROBERTS, K. H. (2001). 'Assessing Organizational Safety Risk Using Questionnaire Survey Methods.' Paper presented at the 11th International Symposium on Aviation Psychology, Columbus, OH.

DUTTON, J. E. (1988). 'Understanding Strategic Agenda Building and its Implications for Managing Change,' in L. R. PONDY, R. J. Boland, and H. Thomas (eds.), *Managing Ambiguity and Change*. Chichester, UK: Wiley.

GABA, D. M., SINGER, S. J., SINAIKO, A. D., BOWEN, J. D., and CIAVARELLI, A. P. (2003). 'Differences in Safety Climate Between Hospital Personnel and Naval Aviators.' *Human Factors*, 45: 173–85.

HEATH, C. and STAUDENMAYER, N. (2000). 'Coordination Neglect: How Lay Theories of Organizing Complicate Coordination in Organizations,' in B. M. Staw and R. I. Sutton (eds.), *Research in Organizational Behavior*. Amsterdam: Elsevier Science, 153–91.

KLEIN, R. L., BIGLEY, G. A., and ROBERTS, K. H. (1995). 'Organization Culture in High Reliability Organizations: An Extension.' *Human Relations*, 48: 771–93.

LOUIS, M. and SUTTON, R. I. (1991). 'Switching Cognitive Gears: From Habits of Mind to Active Thinking.' *Human Relations*, 44: 55–76.

MADSEN, P., DESAI, V., ROBERTS, K. H., and WONG, D. (2006). 'Designing for High Reliability: The Birth and Evolution of a Pediatric Intensive Care Unit.' *Organization Science*, 17: 239–48.

MARCUS, A. A., and NICHOLS, M. L. (1999). 'On the Edge: Heeding the Warnings of Unusual Events.' *Organization Science*, 10: 482–9.

POOL, R. (1997). *Beyond Engineering: How Society Shapes Technology*. New York: Oxford University Press.

PERROW, C. (1984). *Normal Accidents: Living with High Risk Technologies*. New York: Basic Books.

RAMANUJAM, R. and GOODMAN, P. S. (2003). 'Latent Errors and Adverse Organizational Consequences: A Conceptualization.' *Journal of Organizational Behavior*, 24: 815–36.

ROBERTS, K. H. (1990). 'Some Characteristics of One Type of High Reliability Organization.' *Organization Science*, 1: 160–76.

—— MADSEN, P., and DESAI, V. (2005). 'The Space Between in Space Transportation: A Relational Analysis of the Failure of STS 107,' in M. Farjoun and W. H. Starbuck (eds.), *Organization at the Limit: Lessons from the Columbia Disaster*. Malden, MA: Blackwell, 81–98.

—— —— —— (2007). 'Organizational Sense Making During Crisis,' in C. Pearson, C. Roux-Dufort, and J. Clair (eds.), *International Handbook of Organizational Crisis Management*. Thousand Oaks, CA: Sage.

ROTH, E. M. (1997). 'Analysis of Decision Making in Nuclear Power Plant Emergencies: An Investigation of Aided Decision Making,' in C. Zsambok and G. Klein (eds.), *Naturalistic Decision Making*. Mahwah, NJ: Erlbaum, 175–82.

STARBUCK, W. H. and MILLIKEN, F. J. (1988). 'Challenger: Fine Tuning the Odds Until Something Breaks.' *Journal of Management Studies*, 25: 319–40.

STAW, B. B., SANDELANDS, L. E., and DUTTON, J. (1981). 'Threat Rigidity Effects in Organizational Behavior: A Multi-Level Analysis.' *Administrative Science Quarterly*, 26: 501–24.

TURNER, B. M. (1978). *Man Made Disasters*. London: Wykeham Press.

WEICK, K. E. (1993). 'Organization Re-Design as Improvisation,' in G. Huber and W. Glick (eds.), *Organizational Change and Re-Design*. New York: Oxford University Press.

—— (1995). *Sensemaking in Organizations*. Thousand Oaks, CA: Sage.

—— DAFT, R. L. (1983). 'The Effectiveness of Interpretation Systems,' in K. S. Cameron, and D. S. Whetton (eds.), *Organizational Effectiveness: A Comparison of Multiple Models*. New York: Academic Press.

—— ROBERTS, K. H. (1993). 'Collective Mind in Organizations: Heedful Interrelating on Flight Decks.' *Administrative Science Quarterly*, 38: 357–81.

WILSON, G. (1986). *Super Carrier: An Inside Account of Life Aboard the World's Most Powerful Ship the U.S.S. John F. Kennedy*. New York: Berkley Books.

11

EXPERTISE AND NATURALISTIC DECISION MAKING IN ORGANIZATIONS: MECHANISMS OF EFFECTIVE DECISION MAKING*

MICHAEL A. ROSEN

EDUARDO SALAS

REBECCA LYONS

STEPHEN M. FIORE

INTRODUCTION

SEVERAL years ago the United States and allied forces mounted the Millennium Challenge '02—the largest wargame ever at the time. The purpose of this exercise

* This research was supported by the Office of Naval Research Collaboration and Knowledge Interoperability (CKI) Program and ONR MURI Grant #N000140610446 (Dr Michael Letsky, Program Manager).

was to evaluate new technologies, organizational structures, and approaches to conducting warfare. The outcome of the first day of this exercise illustrates some critical issues for modern organizations. The simulated enemy consisted of an undermanned, underequipped force that used motorcycle messengers to relay communications, and World War II era signal light technologies to manage aircraft. This simulated enemy bested the blue forces (i.e., the allied forces), a force far superior in numbers utilizing some of the most advanced information collection, communication, and integration technology in the world. Clearly, amassing information superiority over an opponent does not directly translate into better outcomes. Possessing the right information at the right time is obviously key to making good decisions. But what are the mechanisms that enable an organization to leverage an information advantage into effective decision making in complex environments such as war fighting? What are the characteristics of expert decision makers that enable rapid and adaptive performance? The importance of this issue is not limited to the military. Medical, aviation, oil, nuclear and financial (to name a few) organizations also face the problem of integrating large amounts of information into rapid decision making. Additionally, decision making in many of these organizations is constrained by a set of contextual factors similar to those present in military organizations (e.g., time pressure, high stakes outcomes, uncertain information).

The purpose of this chapter is to address the types of issues raised above as seen through the naturalistic decision making (NDM) perspective, a relatively nascent yet vibrant research tradition that seeks to understand how professionals are able to translate their experience into quality decisions within complex "real-world" environments. We will document the types of adaptations that experts make within organizations that enable decision-making effectiveness in the face of complexity. To this end, we first provide an overview of the NDM movement. Secondly, we explore the role of individual expertise in decision making in NDM environments. Thirdly, we explore the issue of expert teams. This chapter draws from NDM investigations of individual and team decision making within organizations from a variety of domains as well as basic research on the nature of expertise (e.g., Cannon-Bowers and Salas 1998; Salas and Klein 2004).

What is NDM?

Cohen (1993) divides the long history of decision-making research into three general paradigms: the formal–empiricist, the rationalist, and the naturalistic. The classical decision making (CDM) approach of Bernoulli (1738) and others typify the *formal–empiricist* paradigm. Researchers working in this tradition sought to use formal normative models of choice between concurrently available options. CDM researchers tested their formal models against behavioral data and attempted to refine their models to account for the behavior of people in artificial tasks, culminating in the idea that decision makers attempt to maximize their subjectively expected utility (SEU) in decision tasks (Savage 1954). The *rationalist* approach, exemplified by the judgment and decision making (JDM) and behavioral decision theory (BDT) traditions, shares many commonalities with its predecessor, the formal–empiricist approach. Whereas the formal–empiricists attempted to adjust their models to account for misalignments with behavioral data, the rationalists counted these deviations from "optimal" normative models as error on the part of the decision maker. This line of research led to the cataloging of various heuristics and biases, and drew an essentially pessimistic picture of the nature of human decision making. Both the formal–empiricist and the rationalist perspectives proved to be impossible to apply to many real world problems (Orasanu and Connolly 1993) as they failed to account for the experience of the decision maker, the complexity of the task, and environmental constraints (Cannon-Bowers et al. 1996). Instead of focusing on normative models of optimization, the *naturalistic* paradigm places the decision maker at the center of the investigation and seeks to understand how professionals make quality decisions in complex situations where time and other resources are extremely limited. NDM and organizational decision making (ODM; Simon 1955) are examples of this tradition. ODM and NDM share many similarities including a focus on what decision makers actually do, a rejection of a conceptualization of decision making as a choice between multiple options, and origins in descriptive and observational methodologies (Lipshitz et al. 2006).

Defining the NDM Approach

NDM is concerned with "the way people use their experience to make decisions in field settings" (Zsambok 1997: 4). This definition contains two explicit factors. Firstly, it emphasizes the importance of expertise within a decision-making domain; the experience of the decision maker is an integral component of NDM research (Salas and Klein 2001). Secondly, NDM highlights the importance of understanding decision making in context; decision making is bound with task constraints (Klein 1998). The following sections expand on the above definition of NDM by outlining the core features of NDM research.

NDM Environment

As NDM focuses on decision making in field settings, some NDM researches have used descriptions of task environments to frame the emerging approach. Orasanu and Connolly (1993) provide a list of eight such characteristics: (1) ill-structured problems; (2) uncertain dynamic environments; (3) shifting, ill-defined, or competing goals; (4) action/feedback loops; (5) time stress; (6) high stakes; (7) multiple players; and (8) organizational goals and norms. Cannon-Bowers and colleagues

(1996) contributed several other task characteristics such as information quantity, decision complexity, and the level of expertise of the decision maker. Not all of these variables need be present in high degrees to be of interest to NDM researchers; however, most NDM research involves more than one of these variables.

Essentials of NDM Research

Lipshitz and colleagues (2001) provide five essential characteristics that define NDM research: (1) an emphasis on proficient decision makers; (2) an orientation toward the *process* of decision making (not just outcomes); (3) the development of situation–action matching decision rules; (4) context-bound informal modeling; and (5) empirical-based prescription. NDM focuses on understanding expertise in decision making; the decision maker's use of prior knowledge and skill is at the center of inquiry (Pruitt et al. 1997). Additionally, NDM is process oriented: it seeks to provide a description of the information decision makers seek, how this information is interpreted, and what decision rules people apply and how they are applied (Lipshitz et al. 2001; Pliske and Klein 2003). The emphasis on expertise and description leads to an understanding of decision making as a matching process between situations and actions instead of the generation of, and choice from, the set of all possible options (Klein 1998). This view emphasizes the importance of context in expert decision making (e.g., Ericsson and Lehman 1996). Consequently, NDM models tightly couple the decision maker and the context of decision making. Finally, NDM research derives all prescriptions for improving decision making from the analysis of descriptive models of how expert decision makers function and not from abstract models of optimization that can not be practically implemented. Thus, regardless of action choices that are "better" in theory, NDM researchers prescribe only realistic actions and strategies. Although NDM models are generally very specific to a particular context, the next section discusses a high level model that illustrates how experts make effective decisions without employing analytical strategies and serves as a framework for more context rich models of decision making in many domains.

An Exemplar NDM Model

Klein (1998) developed the recognition primed decision (RPD) model to explain the ability of fireground commanders to make rapid and effective decisions without generating and evaluating a large set of options. The RPD model describes expert decision making with two general processes: (1) retrieval of a course of action based on pattern recognition; and (2) the evaluation of this course of action through mental simulation. Firstly, the decision maker perceives environmental cues and attempts to detect patterns in the environment. When the decision maker is able to match the present situation with a similar situation that has occurred before, she or he retrieves from memory: expectancies that are associated with the situation, a possible course of action that has been successful in the past, information about the cues that are most important in this situation, and goals for the situation. If the pattern matching process does not produce a reasonable match, the decision maker seeks more information and performs a more detailed and exhaustive diagnosis of the current situation. After the decision maker finds a reasonable match, she or he evaluates the course of action via mental simulation to determine the fit between the recalled course of action and the present situation. This results in either the adoption (either unchanged or modified) or rejection of the course of action. If the decision maker rejects a course of action, she or he recalls and evaluates another possible course of action or engages in more information gathering.

In sum, to a large extent, NDM is a research tradition sharing common goals and methodological approaches with ODM; that is, both approaches use a descriptive technique to investigate decision making in real world environments with the aim of understanding and improving performance in these environments. In the following section, we detail the types of mechanisms developed by decision makers to adapt to these constraints and make effective decisions in complex environments.

Mechanisms of Individual Expertise and Decision-Making Effectiveness

NDM emphasizes the importance of a decision maker's knowledge and experience; therefore, NDM draws on and contributes to the scientific understanding of expertise. Two high level features characterize the current understanding of expertise. First, expertise is a function of extensive domain specific knowledge, accumulated by the expert over years of experience—the knowledge-based view of expertise (e.g., de Groot 1946/1978; Chase and Simon 1973). Second, psychological and physiological adaptations to the task constraints enable expertise (Ericsson and Lehman 1996). Experts achieve superior performance via specialized knowledge, performance strategies, and inference patterns while novices use more generalized strategies.

Despite this domain specificity, researchers have synthesized the empirical findings to form an understanding of the types of adaptations that enable consistently superior performance across different domains (see Glaser 1987; Glaser and Chi 1988; Bedard and Chi 1992; Hoffman et al. 1997; Chi 2006; Feltovich et al. 2006). Sternberg (1997) characterized this collection of mechanisms of expert performance as a "prototype" of expertise, with each mechanism's role dictated by the demands of the task environment. In the following sections, we present the mechanisms that experts use to excel at decision making in a NDM-like environment (adapted from Salas and Rosen 2009) and discuss their implications for decision making in naturalistic contexts. These mechanisms are summarized in Table 11.1.

Table 11.1 Mechanisms of Expertise and Individual Decision Making

Expert decision makers:

1. *Are tightly coupled to cues and contextual features of the environment.*
   - They develop psychological and physiological adaptations to the task environment.
   - They are sensitive to and leverage contextual patterns of cues in decision making.

2. *Have a larger knowledge base and organize it differently from non-experts.*
   - They have a more conceptually organized knowledge base.
   - They have more robust connections between aspects of their knowledge.
   - They have a more abstracted and functional knowledge base.

3. *Engage in pattern recognition.*
   - They perceive larger and more meaningful patterns in the environment.
   - They are able to detect subtle cue configurations.
   - They are able to retrieve courses of action based on situation/action matching rules.

4. *Engage in deliberate and guided practice.*
   - They devote time and effort to improving knowledge and skills.
   - They have high motivation to learn and long term learning goals.

5. *Seek diagnostic feedback.*
   - They seek out input from other experts.
   - They self-diagnose their performance, identify weaknesses in their knowledge and processes, and correct them.

6. *Have better situation assessment and problem representations.*
   - They spend more time evaluating the situation.
   - They create deeper, more conceptual, more functional, and more abstracted situation representations.

7. *Have specialized memory skills.*
   - They functionally increase their ability to handle large amounts of information.
   - They anticipate what information will be needed in the decision making.

8. *Automate the small steps.*
   - They quickly and effortlessly do what requires large amounts of attention for non-experts.
   - They have more cognitive resources available for dealing with more complex aspects of decision making.

9. *Self-regulate and monitor their processes.*
   - They evaluate their own understanding of a situation.
   - They judge the consistency, reliability, and completeness of their information.
   - They make good decisions about when to stop evaluating the situation.

Expert Decision Makers are Tightly Coupled to Cues and Contextual Features of the Environment

As an adaptation to a task, expertise is limited to that task and does not readily transfer to other tasks or domains. However, within their domain of expertise, expert decision makers are able to take advantage of contextual cues to increase decision-making effectiveness (Chi 2006). Over time, expert decision makers develop sensitivity to patterns of cues that relate both causally and correlationally to decision-making tasks. This increases their effectiveness in familiar contexts (Feltovich and Barrows 1984). Certain task characteristics afford the development of expertise more readily than others. For example, Shanteau (1992) notes that experts in domains with static tasks, more predictable and decomposable problems, and available feedback generally exhibit more reliable decision-making effectiveness than experts in domains without these characteristics.

Expert Decision Makers Have a Larger Knowledge Base and Organize it Differently from Non-Experts

Although this general point is obvious, there are important subtleties to the issue. First, experts not only have a larger knowledge base (i.e., a larger semantic network consisting of more nodes; Quillian 1969) to draw on in the course of decision making (de Groot 1946/1978; Chase and Simon 1973); they also organize knowledge in a more conceptual manner (Chi et al. 1981; Bordage and Zacks 1984). Additionally, in comparison to novices, experts have more robust interconnections between concepts (i.e., more and stronger links; Feltovich et al. 1984). The knowledge advantage of an expert is not only a matter of degree (i.e., more knowledge), but one of knowledge organization. This enables pattern recognition, a central mechanism of expert decision making.

Expert Decision Makers Engage in Pattern Recognition

The RPD model emphasizes the importance of pattern recognition in expert serial and non-analytic decision making. The first general theory of expertise, known as "chunking theory" (Simon and Chase 1973), similarly highlighted the importance of pattern recognition abilities in expertise. According to chunking theory, expertise is a product of years of experience with a particular domain that allows an expert to develop a repository of "chunks" (Miller 1956), a collection of complex patterns. Experts use this repository of chunks to perceive larger and more meaningful patterns in the environment. For example, expert radiologists are able to make better decisions because they are sensitive to subtle cue configurations in X-ray films that more novice radiologists are unable to detect (Lesgold et al. 1988). Experts do not achieve this increased pattern recognition via superior psychophysical properties of their perceptual systems, but through a superior knowledge base. By storing a larger number of patterns of greater complexity than novices, expert decision makers are able to rapidly perceive and select responses to a greater variety and complexity of situations without time consuming forward and deliberative thinking (Gobet and Simon 1996).

Expert Decision Makers Engage in Deliberate and Guided Practice

Practice is central to the development of expertise. However, general experience or unstructured practice alone is not enough. Practice episodes must be engineered so that they are optimal for learning (see Ericsson et al. 1993). Within modern organizations with shifting or ill-defined task constraints, these practice episodes can include an array of activities such as "extensive preparation of task accomplishment, gathering information from domain experts, or seeking feedback" (Sonnentag and Kleine 2000: 89). Experts engage in these task supporting behaviors to develop performance abilities in a global or long-term sense, in addition to increasing immediate performance levels.

Expert Decision Makers Seek Diagnostic Feedback

Developing experts must receive feedback in order to adjust their performance processes and improve their decisions. Sonnentag (2000) found that expert performers in organizational contexts actively sought more feedback from colleagues in comparison to moderate performers in technical jobs (e.g., software design and engineering). Developing expert decision makers must proactively seek input from individuals with higher levels of expertise. This is especially true in environments where the effects of decisions are not immediately available due to temporal lags or spatial distribution.

Expert Decision Makers Have Better Situation Assessment and Problem Representations

Expert decision makers form better representations of situations, problems, and environments. Summarizing much the NDM literature to date, Orasanu and Connolly (1993) state that "experts are distinguished from novices mainly by their situation assessment abilities, not their general reasoning skills" (p. 20). In relation to novices whose representations are more superficial, experts are able to represent available information about a situation in a deeper, more conceptual, more functional, and more abstract manner (Glaser and Chi 1998; Feltovich et al. 2006). This facilitates expert decision making by: (1) supporting recall of relevant information; (2) easing the integration of information; (3) focusing attention on the critical aspects of the situation; and (4) aiding analogical reasoning and the evaluation of courses of action (Zeitz 1997). The difference in quality between expert and novice representations increases as the definition of the problem decreases (Bedard and Chi 1992). Expert decision makers spend more time evaluating the situation while novice decision makers spend more time generating and evaluating courses of action (Chi et al. 1981; Randel et al. 1996; Van Gog et al. 2005). Representing the situation is a critical step for an expert decision maker as this representation forms the basis of the pattern recognition and mental simulation processes.

Expert Decision Makers Have Specialized Memory Skills

In many organizations, the amount of information relevant to a decision far exceeds the basic limitations of human information processing (i.e., the fixed capacity of working memory; Hodgkinson and Sparrow 2002). However, specialized memory skills enable experts to increase the amount of information they can store in working memory by rapidly storing information into and retrieving information from their long-term memories (Ericsson and Kintsch 1995). Because the memory demands for different tasks vary greatly, the experts develop different types of memory skills in response to the constraints of the task. Therefore, these memory skills are tightly bound to the domain of expertise and do not provide increased memory abilities in tasks unrelated to this domain.

Expert Decision Makers Automate the Small Steps

Automaticity is a term used to describe changes in aspects of processes used during task performance as skill increases. Specifically, automaticity comprises: (1) a decrease in the attention needed for performance; (2) a decrease in the conscious control of performance; and (3) an increase in the speed and accuracy of performance (Moors and De Houwer 2006). An important mechanism of expertise is the development of automaticity for the basic or low level skills of a domain (Lesgold et al. 1988). In this way, experts quickly and effortlessly accomplish what requires effortful exertion on the part of the novice (Sternberg 1997). By automating these basic elements of performance, experts can focus on more complex aspects of performance (Feltovich et al. 2006). That is, as the small steps begin to require less effort, an expert has more cognitive resources available for more complex cognition (e.g., Shaffer 1975; Wagner and Stanovich 1996). This, like memory skill, is a means to overcome information processing limitations (Salthouse 1991).

Expert Decision Makers Self-Regulate and Monitor Their Processes

Even though experts develop automaticity in the low level components of task performance, they consciously monitor their own performance when needed. This self-monitoring and metacognition—knowledge about one's own knowledge, cognitive processes, and performance (Flavell 1979)—are key to both the development of expertise and expert performance in general (Glaser and Chi 1988; Feltovich et al. 2006). By monitoring their own performance, expert decision makers can evaluate how well they understand the present situation. They can make judgments about the consistency, reliability, and completeness of their information. Additionally they can make decisions about when to stop analyzing and when to search for additional information (Cohen et al. 1996). Metacognition is critical to the development of expertise as the learner must be aware of his or her performance processes in order to make adjustments and improvements.

Team Effectiveness in NDM-like Settings

In today's work environments, decision makers do not operate in isolation. Often times, teams perform distributed decision making tasks, where the complexity of the problem or environment exceeds the capacity of one person to comprehend and address the necessary aspects of the decision (Brehmer 1991). Therefore, decision making in coordinated groups is a critical issue for organizations, and as we will show: "it takes more than a set of experts to make an expert team" (Salas et al. 2006: 439). The following section is devoted to mechanisms of expert team performance that enable effective decision making at the team level in organizational settings.

What are Expert Teams?

Individual expertise is a necessary but insufficient condition to realize effectiveness in larger organizational units. Decision making in many modern work domains involves combining inputs from multiple decision makers. In this situation, individual expertise must be recognized (Bonner 2004) and coordinated (Faraj and Sproull 2000) in order to make expert decisions at the team level (Salas et al. 2006). A team is "a distinguishable set of two or more people who interact, dynamically, interdependently, and adaptively toward a common and valued goal/objective/mission, who have been assigned specific roles or functions to perform" (Salas et al. 1992: 4). Decision making at the team level involves the integration or pooling of information, the identification of possible courses of action, the selection of a solution, and the evaluation of consequences (Cannon-Bowers et al. 1995). Just as decision making occurs at the team level, so does expertise. An expert team is "a set of interdependent team members, each of whom possesses unique and expert level knowledge, skills, and experience related to task performance, and who adapt, coordinate, and cooperate as a team, thereby producing sustainable, and repeatable team functioning at superior or at least

Table 11.2 Prototypical Mechanisms of Expert Team Performance and Decision Making

Members of expert teams:

1. *Develop shared mental models.*

   - They anticipate each other's needs and actions.
   - They can communicate implicitly.
   - They interpret cues in a complimentary manner.

2. *Learn and adapt.*

   - They self-correct.
   - They learn from past decision-making episodes.
   - They adapt coordinating processes to dynamic environments.
   - They compensate for each other.

3. *Maintain clear roles and responsibilities.*

   - They manage expectations.
   - They understand each others' roles and how they fit together.
   - They maintain clarity of roles while maintaining flexibility.

4. *Possess clear, valued, and shared vision.*

   - They develop their goals with a shared sense of purpose.
   - They guide their decisions with a common set of values.

5. *Develop a cycle of pre-brief → performance → debrief.*

   - They regularly provide individual and team level feedback to one another
   - They establish and revise team goals and plans.
   - They dynamically set priorities.
   - They anticipate and review issues/problems of members.
   - They periodically diagnose team decision making "effectiveness," including its results, and its processes.

6. *Are led by strong team leaders.*

   - They are led by someone with good leadership skills and not just technical competence.
   - They believe the leaders care about them.
   - Leaders of expert teams provide situation updates.
   - Leaders of expert teams foster teamwork, coordination, and cooperation.
   - Leaders of expert teams self-correct first.

7. Have a strong sense of "collective," trust, teamness, and confidence.

   - They manage conflict well; they confront each other effectively.
   - They have a strong sense of team orientation.
   - They trust other team members' "intentions."
   - They strongly believe in the team's collective ability to succeed.

8. *Cooperate and coordinate.*

   - They identify teamwork and task work requirements.

(Continued)

Table 11.2 (*Continued*)

- They ensure that, through staffing and/or development, the team possesses the right mix of competencies.
- They consciously integrate new team members.
- They distribute and assign work thoughtfully.
- They examine and adjust the team's physical workplace to optimize communication and coordination.

Source: Adapted from Salas et al. 2006.

near-optimal levels of performance" (Salas et al. 2006: 440). We discuss the characteristics of expert team performance that enable expert team decision making below. Table 11.2 summarizes these characteristics. As with individual expertise, these mechanisms of reliably superior team performance are a prototype. That is, the degree to which each mechanism contributes to expert team decision making varies with the constraints of the team task.

Expert Teams Develop Shared Mental Models

Mental models are knowledge structures that enable people to integrate and make sense of the informational cues they receive from the environment (Johnson-Laird 1983). To be a member of an effective team, each individual must possess an accurate mental model of taskwork (i.e., a representation that enables them to make the appropriate decisions about their individual task), and a mental model of teamwork (i.e., a representation of how the team functions as a unit). Additionally, team members must share mental models; there must be a common understanding of the team and taskwork. Shared has two meanings in this context (Cooke et al. 2004). Firstly, team members can share a mental model in the sense that they hold the same representations of the task, team, and environment. This is the case with highly homogenous teams functioning in relatively simple environments. Secondly, team members can share a mental model in the sense they distribute these representations throughout the team. Each member possesses different aspects of the entire model of the task or system. This is often the case in teams with heterogeneous expertise. Environments that are too complex for any one person to comprehend at any one point in time necessitate this type of distributed arrangement (Brehmer 1991). By sharing mental models, team members are able to form complementary or congruent explanations of environmental cues and implicitly coordinate their responses (Orasanu 1990; Weick and Roberts 1993).

Expert Teams Learn, Adapt, and Shift Strategies as Needed

In many organizations, task constraints change frequently. This highlights the importance of continuous learning and adaptation at both the individual and team levels. Researchers have conceptualized team learning as both an outcome (e.g., a change in the behavioral repertoire of a team; e.g., Ellis et al. 2003) and a process (e.g., a set of learning behaviors the team uses to produce learning outcomes; e.g., Edmondson 1999). Team adaptation focuses on the team's ability to adjust its performance processes in response to salient changes in the environment. Burke and colleagues (2006) present a model of team adaptation consisting of four phases: (1) situation assessment (wherein team members build a coherent understanding of the current situation); (2) plan formulation (wherein the team members generate and decide upon the most effective course of action); (3) plan execution (wherein the team carries out the selected course of action through coordinated team performance); and (4) team learning (wherein the team evaluates its own performance and forms/integrates lessons learned). In this way emergent states (e.g., shared mental models) and affects (e.g., mutual trust) generated in one decision-making episode influence how the team performs in future episodes.

Expert Teams Have Clarity of Roles and Responsibilities

Members of expert teams are aware of their responsibilities and roles as well as the roles and responsibilities of their teammates. Because of this mutual understanding of team roles and responsibilities, expert team members are better able to anticipate the actions and needs of their fellow team members (i.e., knowledge about what a team member is supposed to be doing facilitates sharing of task relevant information). However, unwavering adherence to predefined roles can be deleterious to a team's ability to adapt. Expert teams strike a balance between defining roles and flexibly adapting to changes in the task. Eisenstat and Cohen (1990) review studies of top management teams from several work domains. Their research highlights the importance of clear definitions of team roles and responsibilities to team decision making effectiveness, concluding that: "team members could accept whatever boundaries the executive established as long as they were clear" (p. 85).

Expert Teams Have a Clear, Valued, and Shared Vision

Vision and values enable expert team decision making in two general ways (Campion et al. 1993; Pearce and Ensley 2004). First, possessing a clear vision—an understanding of the team's mission, objectives, and overall purpose—helps team members dynamically generate goals in complex and changing environments, essentially translating the global understanding of the team's purpose into action in a specific setting. Second, shared values guide the team members' decisions about appropriate methods for reaching these goals. Well articulated and understood goals and vision are necessary for giving effective feedback as well as integrating feedback into future performance episodes. A clear vision of the team's purpose helps teams to manage conflicting goals. For example, Perkins and colleagues (1990) report on teams that struggle with the competing goals of efficiency and quality (operating room teams, mental health treatment teams, teams of correctional officers). The expert teams in these domains managed these competing goals by focusing on one or the other as the situation allowed (e.g., when time pressure was low, quality was the focus and efficiency was the goal when time pressure was high). The team's vision of its purpose as a unit drove this process.

Expert Teams Maintain Performance by Engaging in a Cycle or Discipline of Pre-brief → Performance → Debrief

Feedback is critical to the development of expertise; it drives a team's self-correction, learning, and adaptation of performance processes. In addition to retrospectively learning from experience, feed-forward or prospective feedback is useful for managing expectations and establishing goals and priorities, as well as establishing performance strategies. Expert teams have mechanisms in place to ensure that this anticipatory and retrospective analysis of performance occurs and ensure that the results are leveraged into increased performance outcomes. High performance teams use a pre-brief, performance, debrief cycle. The pre-brief provides an opportunity for the leader to articulate goals, roles, expectations, and other preparatory information found to increase performance in high stress conditions (Inzana et al. 1996). Debriefs consist of review and critique of the performance episode. In this way, expert teams maximize learning from experience (Smith-Jentsch et al. 1998).

Expert Teams Have Strong Team Leadership

Leaders of expert teams posses expertise in team leadership in addtioin to expertise in their task roles (Zaccaro et al. 2001; Salas et al. 2004). Specifically expert teams have leaders who: (1) solicit ideas and observations from team members; (2) explain why team member input is rejected when possible; (3) seek out opportunities to reinforce effective teamwork; (4) are receptive to and request feedback on their own performance as a team leader; (5) provide behavior oriented rather than person oriented feedback; (6) provide specific solution oriented feedback; (7) restate others' feedback to make it constructive; (8) voice satisfaction when improvements are noted; and (9) give situational updates. Team leaders who have received training on these behaviors are able to increase team performance levels (Tannenbaum et al. 1998).

Expert Teams Have a Strong Sense of Collective, Trust, Teamness, and Confidence

Emotion is a critical factor in individual decision making (e.g., Damasio 2000). Team level affects are similarly essential to the cooperation and coordination that drives team decision making. Several of the more fundamental team level affects include mutual trust (Bandow 2001), collective efficacy (Gibson 2003), collective orientation (Driskell and Salas 1992), and a team learning orientation (Bunderson and Sutcliffe 2003). Expert teams have members that trust the abilities and intentions of their fellow team members, believe in the importance of teamwork, are confident in the ability of the team to reach its goals, and are motivated to learn how to work as a team more effectively.

Expert Teams Cooperate and Coordinate

Cooperation and coordination are the hallmarks of expert teams (see Wilson et al. 2007). To produce high levels of performance, team members must be able to organize the team's effort by directing team resources and responses so that they complete the task successfully and in a timely manner (Cannon-Bowers et al. 1995). By coordination, we are specifically referring to the process of managing the interdependencies within a team. That is, coordination involves the behavioral and cognitive mechanisms and strategies needed to complete the team's task (e.g., mutual performance monitoring, back-up behavior; Wilson et al. 2007). Cooperation is the affective component, the motivational forces described above that bind the team together and drive it to higher levels of performance. Team decision making involves the integration of individual contributions to the development of shared situational understanding, course of action selection, and implementation. Teams that reach consistently superior decision outcomes do so through qualitatively different coordination and cooperation processes than less effective teams, especially under high stress conditions (Salas et al. 1997; Serfaty et al. 1998).

In sum, expert teams fluidly coordinate their responses to what is oftentimes a dynamic and uncertain environment. Information is distributed and synthesized by means of the behavioral, cognitive, and affective mechanisms discussed above. These mechanisms that enable expert team decision making are separate from the mechanisms of individual expertise. Forming a team of individuals with decision-making expertise at the individual level does not guarantee expert decision making at the team level. Expertise must be recognized, coordinated, and leveraged to the demands and constraints of the task and organizational setting.

CONCLUDING REMARKS

NDM is "the effort to understand and improve decision making in field settings, particularly by helping people more quickly develop expertise and apply it to the challenges they face" (Salas and Klein 2001: 3). As such, NDM contributes to ODM in the development of practical methods based on contextually driven models for improving decision-making effectiveness and reducing error (Gore et al. 2006; Lipshitz et al. 2006). By delineating the essential mechanisms of expert performance in decision making in naturalistic environments at the individual and team levels, we have outlined the "prototype" of expert decision making—the types of adaptations that expert decision makers develop to deal with the complexity of real-world decision tasks. Researchers have much work to accomplish in the pursuit of a complete understanding of how individuals and teams are able to exhibit reliably and repeatedly superior decision-making effectiveness. However, with an understanding of the types of adaptations individuals and teams make coupled with information about the nature of the decision-making environment and task, researchers can make predictions about how best to support decisions and how to best prepare decision makers for specific contexts.

References

BANDOW, D. (2001). 'Time to Create Sound Teamwork.' *The Journal for Quality and Participation,* 24: 41–7.

BEDARD, J. and CHI, M. T. H. (1992). 'Expertise.' *Current Directions in Psychological Science,* 1/4: 135–9.

BERNOULLI, D. (1738). 'Specimen Theoriae Novae de Mensura Sortis.' *Commentarii Academiae Scientrum Imperialis Petropolitanae,* 5: 175–92.

BOAS, S., ZAKAY, E., ESTHER, B., and POPPER, M. (2000). 'Leadership and Social Identification in Military Units: Direct and Indirect Relationships.' *Journal of Applied Social Psychology,* 30/3: 612–40.

BORDAGE, G. and ZACKS, R. (1984). 'The Structure of Medical Knowledge in the Memories of Medical Students and General Practitioners: Categories and Prototypes'. *Medical Education,* 18: 406–16.

BREHMER, B. (1991). 'Distributed Decision Making: Some Notes on the Literature,' in J. Rasmussen, B. Brehmer, and J. Leplat (eds.), *Distributed Decision Making.* Chichester: Wiley, 3–14.

BUNDERSON, J. S. and SUTCLIFFE, K. M. (2003). 'Management Team Learning Orientation and Business Unit Performance.' *Journal of Applied Psychology,* 88/3, 552–60.

BURKE, C. S., STAGL, K., SALAS, E., PIERCE, L., and KENDALL, D. (2006). 'Understanding Team Adaptation: A Conceptual Analysis and Model.' *Journal of Applied Psychology,* 91/6: 1189–207.

CAMPION, M. A., MEDSKER, G. J., and HIGGS, A. C. (1993). 'Relations Between Work Group Characteristics and Effectiveness: Implications for Designing Effective Work Groups.' *Personnel Psychology,* 46: 823–47.

CANNON-BOWERS, J. A. and SALAS, E. (eds.) (1998). *Making Decisions Under Stress.* Washington, DC: American Psychological Association.

—— TANNENBAUM, S. I., SALAS, E., and VOLPE, C. E. (1995). 'Defining Competencies and Establishing Team Training Requirements,' in R. Guzzo and E. Salas (eds.), *Team Effectiveness and Decision Making in Organizations*. San Francisco, CA: Jossey-Bass.

—— SALAS, E., and PRUITT, J. S. (1996). 'Establishing the Boundaries of a Paradigm for Decision-Making Research.' *Human Factors*, 38/2: 193–205.

CHASE, W. G. and SIMON, H. A. (1973). 'Perception in Chess.' *Cognitive Psychology*, 4: 55–81.

CHI, M., FELTOVICH, P., and GLASER, R. (1981). 'Categorization and Representation of Physics Problems by Experts and Novices.' *Cognitive Science*, 5: 121–52.

CHI, M. T. H. (2006). 'Two Approaches to the Study of Experts' Characteristics,' in K. A. Ericsson, N. Charness, R. Hoffman, and P. Fletovich (eds.), *The Cambridge Handbook of Expertise and Expert Performance*. New York: Cambridge University Press, 21–30.

COHEN, M. S. (1993). 'Three Paradigms for Viewing Decision Biases,' in G. Klein, J. Orasanu, R. Calderwood, and C. E. Zsambok (eds.), *Decision Making in Action*. Norwood, NJ: Ablex, 36–50.

—— FREEMAN, J. T., and WOLF, S. (1996). 'Meta-Recognition in Time Stressed Decision Making.' *Human Factors*, 38: 206–19.

COOKE, N. J., SALAS, E., KIEKEL, P. A., and BELL, B. (2004). 'Advances in Measuring Team Cognition,' in E. Salas and S. M. Fiore (eds.), *Team Cognition*. Washington, DC: APA.

DAMASIO, A. R. (2000). 'A Second Chance for Emotion,' in R. D. Lane and L. Nadel (eds.), *Cognitive Neuroscience of Emotion*. Oxford: Oxford University Press, 12–23.

DE GROOT, A. (1946/1978). *Thought and Choice in Chess* (2nd edn.). The Hague: Mouton De Gruyter.

DRISKELL, J. E. and SALAS, E. (1992). 'Collective Behavior and Team Performance.' *Human Factors*, 34: 277–88.

EDMONDSON, A. C. (1999). 'Psychological Safety and Learning Behavior in Work Teams.' *Administrative Science Quarterly*, 44: 350–83.

EISENSTAT, R. A. and COHEN, S. G. (1990). 'Summary: Top Management Groups,' in J. R. Hackman (ed.), *Groups That Work (and Those That Don't)*. San Francisco, CA: Jossey-Bass, 78–86.

ELLIS, A. P. J., HOLLENBECK, J. R., ILGEN, D. R. et al. (2003). 'Team Learning: Collectively Connecting the Dots.' *Journal of Applied Psychology*, 88/5: 821–35.

ERICSSON, K. A. and KINTSCH, W. (1995). 'Long-Term Working Memory.' *Psychological Review*, 102/2: 211–45.

—— LEHMANN, A. C. (1996). 'Expert and Exceptional Performance.' *Annual Review of Psychology*, 47: 273–305.

—— KRAMPE, R. T., and TESCH-ROMER, C. (1993). 'The Role of Deliberate Practice in the Acquisition of Expert Performance.' *Psychological Review*, 100/3: 363–406.

FARAJ, S. A. and SPROULL, L. (2000). 'Coordinating Expertise in Software Development Teams.' *Management Science*, 46: 1554–68.

FELTOVICH, P. J. and BARROWS, H. S. (1984). 'Issues of Generality in Medical Problem Solving,' in H. G. Schmidt and M. L. De Volder (eds.), *Tutorials in Problem-Based Learning*. Assen: Van Gorcum, 128–42.

—— JOHNSON, P. E., MOLLER, J. H., and SWANSON, L. C. S. (1984). 'The Role and Development of Medical Knowledge in Diagnostic Expertise,' in W. J. Clancey and E. H. Shortliffe (eds.), *Readings in Medical Artificial Intelligence*. Reading, MA: Addison-Wesley.

FELTOVICH, P. J., PRIETULA, M. J., and ERICSSON, K. A. (2006). 'Studies of Expertise from Psychological Perspectives,' in K. A. Ericsson, N. Charness, P. J. Feltovich, P. J., and R. R. Hoffman (eds.), *Cambridge Handbook of Expertise and Expert Performance*. New York: Cambridge University Press, 41–67.

FLAVELL, J. H. (1979). 'Metacognition and Cognitive Monitoring.' *American Psychologist*, 34/10, 906–11.

GIBSON, C. B. (2003). 'The Efficacy Advantage: Factors Related to the Formation of Group Efficacy.' *Journal of Applied Social Psychology*, 33/10, 2153–86.

GLASER, R. (1987). 'Thoughts on Expertise,' in C. Schooler and K. W. Schaie (eds.), *Cognitive Functioning and Social Structure over the Life Course*. Norwood, NJ: Ablex, 81–94.

GLASER, R. and CHI, M. T. H. (1988). 'Overview,' in M. T. H. Chi, R. Glaser, and M. Farr (eds.), *The Nature of Expertise*. Hillsdale, NJ: Erlbaum, xv–xxviii.

GOBET, F. and SIMON, H. A. (1996). 'Templates in Chess Memory: A Mechanism for Recalling Several Boards.' *Cognitive Psychology*, 31: 1–40.

GORE, J., BANKS, A., MILLWARD, L., and KYRIAKIDOU, O. (2006). 'Naturalistic Decision Making and Organizations.' *Organization Studies*, 27/7: 925–42.

HODGKINSON, G. P. and SPARROW, P. R. (2002). *The Competent Organization: A Psychological Analysis of the Strategic Management Process*. Buckingham: Open University Press.

HOFFMAN, R. R., FELTOVICH, P. J., and FORD, K. M. (1997). 'A General Conceptual Framework for Conceiving of Expertise and Expert Systems,' in P. J. Feltovich, K. M. Ford, and R. R. Hoffman (eds.), *Expertise in Context*. Menlo Park, CA: AAAI Press/MIT Press, 543–80.

HOLYOAK, K. J. (1991). 'Symbolic Connectionism: Toward Third-Generation Theories of Expertise,' in K. A. Ericsson and J. Smith (eds.), *Toward a General Theory of Expertise*. Cambridge: Cambridge University Press, 301–35.

INZANA, C. M., DRISKELL, J. E., SALAS, E., and JOHNSTON, J. H. (1996). 'Effects of Preparatory Information on Enhancing Performance Under Stress.' *Journal of Applied Psychology*, 81/4: 429–35.

JOHNSON-LAIRD, P. N. (1983). *Mental Models*. Cambridge, MA: Harvard University Press.

KLEIN, G. (1998). *Sources of Power*. Cambridge, MA: MIT Press.

LESGOLD, A. M., RUBINSON, H., FELTOVICH, P. J. et al. (1988). 'Expertise in a Complex Skill: Diagnosing X-ray Pictures,' in M. T. H. Chi, R. Glaser, and M. Farr (eds.), *The Nature of Expertise*. Hillsdale, NJ: Erlbaum, 311–42.

LIPSHITZ, R., KLEIN, G., ORASANU, J., and SALAS, E. (2001). 'Taking Stock of Naturalistic Decision Making.' *Journal of Behavioral Decision Making*, 14/5: 331–52.

—— —— CARROLL, J. S. (2006). 'Naturalistic Decision Making and Organizational Decision Making: Exploring the Intersections.' *Organization Studies*, 27/7: 917–23.

MILLER, G. (1956). 'The Magical Number Seven, Plus or Minus Two: Some Limits on Our Capacity for Processing Information.' *Psychological Review*, 63/2: 81–97.

MOORS, A. and DE HOUWER, J. (2006). 'Automaticity: A Theoretical and Conceptual Analysis.' *Psychological Bulletin*, 132/2: 297–326.

ORASANU, J. (1990). *Shared Mental Models and Crew Decision Making*, No. 46. Princeton, NJ: Cognitive Sciences Laboratory, Princeton University.

—— CONNOLLY, T. (1993). 'The Reinvention of Decision Making,' in G. Klein, J. Orasanu, R. Calderwood, and C. E. Zsambok (eds.), *Decision Making in Action*. Norwood, CT: Ablex, 3–20.

PEARCE, C. L. and ENSLEY, M. D. (2004). 'A Reciprocal and Longitudinal Investigation of the Innovation Process.' *Journal of Organizational Behavior*, 25: 259–78.

PERKINS, A. L., SHAW, R. B., and SUTTON, R. I. (1990). 'Summary: Human Service Teams,' in J. R. Hackman (ed.), *Groups that Work (and Those That Don't)*. San Francisco, CA: Josey-Bass, 349–60.

PLISKE, R. and KLEIN, G. (2003). 'The Naturalistic Decision-Making Perspective,' in S. L. Schneider and J. Shanteau (eds.), *Emerging Perspectives on Judgment and Decision Research*. New York: Cambridge University Press, 559–85.

PRUITT, J. S., CANNON-BOWERS, J. A., and SALAS, E. (1997). 'In Search of Naturalistic Decisions,' in R. Flin and E. Salas et al. (eds.), *Decision Making Under Stress: Emerging Themes and Applications*. Aldershot, UK: Ashgate, 29–42.

QUILLIAN, M. R. (1969). 'The Teachable Language Comprehender: A Simulation Program and Theory of Language.' *Communications of the ACM*, 12/8, 459–76.

RANDEL, J. M., PUGH, H. L., and REED, S. K. (1996). 'Differences in Expert and Novice Situation Awareness in Naturalistic Decision Making.' *International Journal of Human–Computer Studies*, 45/5: 579–97.

SALAS, E., and KLEIN, G. (eds.) (2001). *Linking Expertise and Naturalistic Decision Making*. Mahwah, NJ: Erlbaum.

—— ROSEN, M. A. (2009). 'Experts at Work: Principles for Developing Expertise in Organizations,' in S. W. J. Kozlowski and E. Salas (eds.), *Learning, Training, and Development in Organizations*. Mahwah, NJ: Erlbaum, 99–134.

—— DICKINSON, T., CONVERSE, S., and TANNENBAUM, S. (1992). 'Toward an Understanding of Team Performance and Training,' in R. Swezey and E. Salas (eds.), *Teams: Their Training and Performance*. Norwood, NJ: Ablex Publishing.

—— CANNON-BOWERS, J. A., and JOHNSTON, J. H. (1997). 'How Can You Turn a Team of Experts into an Expert Team? Emerging Training Strategies,' in C. E. Zsambok and G. Klein (eds.), *Naturalistic Decision Making*. Mahwah, NJ: Erlbaum, 359–70.

—— BURKE, C. S. and STAGL, K. C. (2004). 'Developing Teams and Team Leaders: Strategies and Principles,' in D. Day, S. J. Zaccaro, and S. M. Halpin (eds.), *Leader Development for Transforming Organizations: Growing Leaders for Tomorrow*. Mahwah, NJ: Lawrence Erlbaum Associates, Inc., 325–55.

—— ROSEN, M. A., BURKE, C. S., GOODWIN, G. F., and FIORE, S. (2006). 'The Making of a Dream Team: When Expert Teams do Best,' in K. A. Ericsson, N. Charness, P. J. Feltovich, and R. R. Hoffman (eds.), *Cambridge Handbook of Expertise and Expert Performance*. New York: Cambridge University Press, 439–53.

SALTHOUSE, T. A. (1991). 'Expertise as the Circumvention of Human Processing Limitations,' in K. A. Ericsson and J. Smith (eds.), *Toward a General Theory of Expertise*. Cambridge: Cambridge University Press, 286–300.

SAVAGE, L. J. (1954). *The Foundations of Statistics*. New York: Wiley.

SERFATY, D., ENTIN, E. E., and JOHNSTON, J. H. (1998). 'Team Coordination Training,' in J. Cannon-Bowers and E. Salas (eds.), *Making Decisions Under Stress*. Washington, DC: APA, 221–45.

SHAFFER, L. H. (1975). 'Multiple Attention in Continuous Verbal Tasks,' in P. M. Rabbitt and S. Dornic (eds.), *Attention and Performance* Vol. 5, London: Academic Press, 157–67.

SHANTEAU, J. (1992). 'Competence in Experts: The Role of Task Characteristics.' *Organizational Behavior and Human Decision Processes*, 53: 252–66.

SIMON, H. A. (1955). 'A Behavioral Model of Rational Choice.' *Quarterly Journal of Economics*, 69: 99–118.

—— CHASE, W. G. (1973). 'Skill in Chess.' *American Scientist*, 61: 393–403.

SMITH-JENTSCH, K., ZEISIG, R. L., ACTON, B., and MCPHERSON, J. A. (1998). 'Team Dimensional Training: A Strategy for Guided Team Self-Correction,' in J. A. Cannon-Bowers and E. Salas (eds.), *Making Decisions under Stress*. Washington, DC: APA, 271–97.

SONNENTAG, S. (2000). 'Excellent Performance: The Role of Communication and Cooperation Processes.' *Applied Psychology: An International Review*, 49/3: 483–97.

—— KLEINE, B. M. (2000). 'Deliberate Practice at Work: A Study with Insurance Agents.' *Journal of Occupational and Organizational Psychology*, 73: 87–102.

STERNBERG, R. J. (1997). 'Cognitive Conceptions of Expertise,' in P. J. Feltovich, K. M. Ford, and R. R. Hoffman (eds.), *Expertise in Context*. Menlo Park, CA: AAAI Press/MIT Press, 149–62.

TANNENBAUM, S. I., SMITH-JENTSCH, K. A., and BEHSON, S. J. (1998). 'Training Team Leaders to Facilitate Team Learning and Performance,' in J. Cannon-Bowers and E. Salas (eds.), *Making Decisions Under Stress*. Washington, DC: APA, 247–70.

VAN GOG, T., PAAS, F., and VAN MERRIENBOER, J. J. G. (2005). 'Uncovering Expertise-Related Differences in Troubleshooting Performance: Combining Eye Movement and Concurrent Verbal Protocol Data.' *Applied Cognitive Psychology*, 19: 205–21.

WAGNER, R. K. and STANOVICH, K. E. (1996). 'Expertise in Reading,' in K. A. Ericsson (ed.), *The Road to Excellence*. Mahwah, NJ: Erlbaum, 189–225.

WEICK, K. E., and ROBERTS, K. H. (1993). Collective Mind in Organization: Heedful Interrelating on Flight Decks.' *Administrative Science Quarterly*, 38: 357–81.

WILSON, K. A., SALAS, E., PRIEST, H. A., and ANDREWS, D. (2007). 'Errors in the Heat of Battle: Taking a Closer Look at Shared Cognition Breakdowns Through Teamwork.' *Human Factors*, 49/2: 243–56.

ZACCARO, S. J., RITTMAN, A. L., and MARKS, M. A. (2001). 'Team Leadership.' *Leadership Quarterly*, 12: 451–83.

ZEITZ, C. M. (1997). 'Some Concrete Advantages of Abstraction: How Experts' Representations Facilitate Reasoning,' in P. J. Feltovich, K. M. Ford, and R. R. Hoffman (eds.), *Expertise in Context*. Menlo Park, CA: AAAI Press/MIT Press, 43–65.

ZSAMBOK, C. E. (1997). 'Naturalisitc Decision Making: Where are We Now?' in C. E. Zsambok and G. Klein (eds.), *Naturalistic Decision Making*. Mahwah, NJ: Erlbaum, 3–16.

PART III

DECISION-MAKING PROCESSES

12

COGNITIVELY SKILLED ORGANIZATIONAL DECISION MAKING: MAKING SENSE OF DECIDING

JULIA BALOGUN

ANNIE PYE

GERARD P. HODGKINSON*

INTRODUCTION

Having lost its market dominance, the board of a FTSE100 retail company was under pressure from shareholders to improve perform- ance. Eighteen months later, the Chief Executive appointed to bring

* The authors gratefully acknowledge financial support from the following sources in the preparation of this chapter: Pye (ESRC grant numbers R000237467 and WF 29250020 [with Mangham]); Balogun (UK ESRC/EPSRC Advanced Institute of Management (AIM) Research, grant number RES-331-25-3014); Hodgkinson (UK ESRC/EPSRC Advanced Institute of Management (AIM) Research, grant number RES-331-25-0028). We are also grateful to Bill Starbuck for his valuable editorial encouragement and advice.

about this agenda of cost cutting, reorganizing and downsizing, resigned. He explained how the board had also embraced change in this turn-around time by making its systems and processes more professional, in part through formalizing its decision making processes: there were now clear guidelines and protocols as to how proposals went through committee prior to reaching the main board.

After a lengthy explanation of the details of these changes, he summarized and said: "...that was a change, a formalization of decisions. [Pause] To be honest with you, *it's bullshit* [laughs loudly] because what really happened was that the decisions would be made and discussions would be had and if there was anything controversial, the Deputy Chair would talk to the Chairman and if the Chairman didn't agree with it, then something would change."

This example characterizes the colorful picture of people doing their jobs in organizational contexts: there are structures, systems, and processes, and also frontstages and backstages, where different people with different agendas and personal interests use their differing power resources to influence and shape meaning, leading to a particular definition of the situation at a particular moment in time. And so it goes on. In this case, the Chief Executive (CE) recognized that for all he had the role, responsibility and in his view, the right ideas as to what had to change and how, ultimately he did not have sufficient power and influence nor eventually, the personal desire to persist: his reputation was worth more than this, so he resigned while he still could.

The authors of this chapter have many such examples in their studies of senior managers and change in organizations[1], which stand in stark contrast to the more static, two dimensional, colorless, and people-less examples that characterize much of the decision-making literature. The aim of this chapter is to bring the organizational cognition approach to decision making together with a sensemaking perspective on deciding, in an endeavor to bring real people and processes into the picture to develop a more integrative understanding of how people "do decision making"—an enterprise which has both academic and practical relevance. The chapter begins by positioning this approach within decision-making research. It then explains the concepts of sensemaking and deciding, and sensereading and sensewrighting; explores why such skills are critical to processes of organizational decision making; and finally, why this is an important area for future research.

DECISION-MAKING RESEARCH

Much research has investigated decision making from an "information processing" perspective. Most of this is lab-based and experimental, with a focus on the individual decision maker, enabling a greater understanding of the role of the individual decision makers' initial judgments and preferences in decision making (Hodgkinson and Maule 2002). In particular, it has informed understanding of managers' cognitive strategies for handling the mass of complex information available to them. There has been a focus, for example, on the role of heuristics and biases (Kahneman et al. 1982; Gigerenzer et al. 1999; Maule and Hodgkinson 2002). With the exception of research investigating processes of strategy development and strategic change (see, for example, Ranson et al 1980; Bartunek 1984; Smircich and Stubbart 1985; Johnson 1987), less attention has been paid to developing a more sociological or sensemaking perspective, concerned with how managers socially construct their organizational worlds and their competitive environments.

A sensemaking perspective points to the importance of understanding the conversational and social practices through which people constantly negotiate and renegotiate their social worlds (Gephart 1993; Pye 1993; Weick 1995; Balogun 2003; Balogun and Johnson 2004; Maitlis 2005). It pays attention to how people "deal with" (whether unconsciously or otherwise) constraints imposed by their information processing limitations and their organizational context, delving into the socio-political nature of organizations to show that the answer to better decision making does not necessarily lie with the provision of greater quantities of "more accurate," "objective" and timely data, but rather requires an understanding of the social processes of negotiation involved in deciding.

Some research on managerial and organizational cognition has sought to connect these two different traditions. Lant and Shapira (2001a, b), for example, distinguish computational and interpretive perspectives on organizational cognition, arguing that both are ultimately necessary in order to generate a more comprehensive account of organizational decision making and other cognitive processes. Yet little research actually does this. Since the computational perspective tends to focus on the individual decision maker, it remains limited. Of course, people enter group arenas with their own agendas and biases that can kick start political behaviors (Schwenk 1989). However, people do very often resolve these issues and do move on to make decisions. So how does this happen? This chapter argues that, to appreciate how people do or do not get their views accepted when competing logics collide requires greater understanding of the interaction between sensemaking and cognition, thus making sense of deciding.

SENSEMAKING AND DECIDING

"Sensemaking is what it says it is, namely, making something sensible" (Weick 1995: 16). It is a social process of meaning construction and reconstruction that enables individuals through interacting with others to collectively create, maintain and interpret their world (Gioia and Chittipeddi 1991; Pye 1995; Balogun and Johnson 2004; Maitlis 2005). However, although the sensemaking perspective puts more emphasis on processes of social negotiation, much of the work on sensemaking and decision making focuses on disaster and inquiry sensemaking (Gephart 1993, 1997; Weick and Roberts 1993; Brown 2000). In addition, despite Weick's (1995) warning that sensemaking involves a power effect in which some voices are more privileged than others, there is still a lack of empirical study of the power dynamics which underlie the sensemaking process (Willmott 2002; Pye 2003; Weick et al. 2005).

While there might be little work on sensemaking and deciding per se, Brown's (2000) and Gephart's (1993, 1997) work on disaster and inquiry sensemaking does show how people and stakeholder groups position themselves to have their account of events accepted over the accounts of others, revealing the importance of understanding the role of agency in decision making. It supports other research (Gigerenzer et al. 1999) that suggests people do not just learn to overcome biases when they use heuristics, they innovate their own improvement heuristics that work for them. They learn to reconcile competing viewpoints in a way that enables them to re-interpret reality and reframe issues in situ.

However, to achieve this, individuals within groups engage in skilful sensegiving (Gioia and Chittipeddi 1991; Corley and Gioia 2004; Maitlis 2005), stage management and front and backstage activity (Goffman 1959; Mangham 1979, 1986; Pye 2002), so they can refashion the signals coming from other players and draw others into their agenda (Balogun et al. 2005). Hence, the distinction between sensemaking and sensegiving (Gioia and Chittipeddi 1991: 442), which defines sensegiving as a "process of attempting to influence the sensemaking and meaning construction of others toward a preferred redefinition of social reality," is useful because it introduces agency, adding a political dimension. Purely cognitive perspectives on sensemaking, with a focus on mental representation and modeling (e.g., Huff and Schwenk 1990) and a lesser concern for agency, cannot capture this much richer process. Integration with more sociological approaches, however, introduces a focus on the processes of social interaction that show how at times of change and uncertainty, people act in less preprogrammed ways, actively interpreting and shaping outcomes collectively. There is, in fact, an array of work that supports the need to understand more about how people are able to shape and influence the interpretations of others: ranging from strategic issue selling (Jackson and Dutton 1988; Dutton and Ashford 1993), through managerial agenda framing (Pitt et al. 1997), and framing as a leadership skill (Fairhurst 2005), to improvization (Mangham 1986) and the management of meaning (Pfeffer 1981; Smircich and Morgan 1982). An appreciation of this body of work is, therefore, central to developing understanding of how individuals work within groups to shape and influence organizational deciding.

The concept of framing is defined by Fairhurst and Sarr (1996: 3) as

the ability to shape the meaning of a subject, to judge its character and significance. To hold the frame of a subject is to choose one particular meaning (or set of meanings) over another. When we share our frames with others (the process of framing), we manage meaning because we assert that our interpretations should be taken as real over other possible interpretations.

This is a broader definition of framing than is usually the case in the decision-making literature and brings to the fore the political aspect often silently subsumed within the act of sensemaking. In so doing, it highlights the political nature of meaning construction and presentation (Hensmans 2003; Fiss and Zajac 2006) which is not just the prerogative of leadership. Many different stakeholders engage in "thought leadership" activity (Hodgkinson and Sparrow 2002), attempting to upwardly influence or in some cases contest the sensegiving of managers and offer alternative meanings or visions of reality; hence, intertwined and mutually reinforcing leader and stakeholder sensemaking shapes the processes and outcomes of organizational sensemaking (Maitlis and Lawrence 2007).

The sensemaking perspective also ensures attention to process; hence, this chapter is not concerned with decision making per se, but also the process of deciding, since this brings into play a "crucial set of elements, including self, action, interaction, interpretation, meaning and joint action" (Weick 1995: 41). It describes sensemaking as a dual, cyclical and ongoing process of sensereading and sensewrighting to better portray the aspect of skilled practice that is the focus of attention here and to clarify the relationship between sensemaking and sensegiving. When people are sensemaking, they are also sensegiving by giving off cues and interpretations they have made through their behavior and orientation towards action. It is not necessarily the case that others actually "pick up," "receive," or "accept" the sense that another is seeking to give: indeed, through their actions, people may give sense, both intentionally and unintentionally. As this chapter moves on to discuss, power relationships have an important role to play here.

SENSEREADING AND SENSEWRIGHTING AS MUTUALLY CONSTITUTIVE PROCESSES

Mangham and Pye (1991) developed the metaphor of sensewrighting in their analysis of the behavior of top management teams running large organizations:

We settled, finally, upon the notion of the executive as artist/scientist/craftsperson, someone who "reads" the circumstances in which he or she finds himself/herself and someone who "wrights" in the sense that a playwright "wrights" and a shipwright "wrights". Someone, that is, who shapes the material with which he or she works; someone who inherits and is shaped by a tradition and yet remains capable of going beyond that tradition and of shaping *it*, someone whose work reflects his or her understanding of the world at a particular moment in time, someone whose work, however, is never finished, always evolving... enterprises are not usually haphazard arrangements of offices and people; the way they are set up and the people who are selected to occupy the offices communicate the wrighter's perspective on the world, his or her explanations of the way things are (or should be). (27–8)

The executives here were mostly FTSE 100 directors, skilled in the arts of intentional sensewrighting. However, there were occasions when even these practitioners could be seen to take action without awareness of sense given or the unintended side of sensewrighting. On such occasions they might act simply on the basis of routine or taken-for-granted assumptions about what is expected or is taken to be commonsense behavior around here, and in so doing, cultural norms or social mores. The classic phrase "dearly beloved, we are gathered here today..." illustrates this point. Anyone with a Christian upbringing or who has ever watched a classic US western film need only hear this phrase to know the context and the types of behaviors expected of people in this setting. Users of this phrase can perform with confidence since they know with some certainty that it triggers a particular reaction from recipients. The giving of sense in circumstances where people are acting within existing social norms is not necessarily the kind of leadership and direction setting type of sensegiving described by Gioia and Chittipeddi (1991).

It is also important not to overlook the unintended consequences that arise from people operating on the basis of different sets of taken for granted world views that obscure power effects hidden in the relationships between individuals and that triggering particular responses to action and behavior. For example, Victor (a pseudonym) was the new CEO of a FTSE100 consumer goods multinational with a mandate from the board to effect a turnaround. An internal appointee who already knew many of the ills that needed curing, he spent the first three months talking to colleagues to gain their views and to get them on-side with a change program. He then tested some proposals with executive colleagues and found they were supportive of these ideas. The board also agreed with the proposed actions and so he set about implementing the plan. Progress was slower than intended but people seemed to know what was expected—after all, the CEO had heard people referring to "Victor's vision," so they knew there was a plan. However, after six months of progress which did not live up to ambition, Victor realized that despite his early consultations with executive colleagues, they essentially saw it as *his* plan and hence it did not have their full commitment.

So he started again, this time with a facilitated, three-day away day for the top 30 executives in the company to develop a new vision, one to which they could all sign up. Although the structural power positions and resources had not changed between these two change endeavors, the way the CEO enacted power changed significantly as he effected a shift of power balance: more than simply being encouraged to believe their views were important, now power to write the future was literally and metaphorically vested with the senior management team. The sequence of events, the actions taken and interpretations made together shaped the responses of participants, which in turn helped create a particular collective view (Pye 2005).

Interestingly, it is often the more accidental "unintended" aspect of sensewrighting that receives more attention than the intentional skilful aspect, in which the sensegiver may unwittingly (a) give a different sense to that intended, as in Victor's case; or (b) like Gerald Ratner, give sense in addition to that which was intended. Ratner's infamous speech to a meeting of the Institute of Directors in London in 1991 unintentionally wiped millions off the value of his high street retail company almost over night. In response to a suggestion of a colleague to add in a few jokes, he explained to the audience that he could sell jewelry and other items cheaply because it was "total crap": the press took this to mean that everything Ratner's sold was rubbish, and this ultimately cost Ratner his job as well as a significant chunk of his personal wealth.

The Ratner case illustrates the mutually constitutive aspect of sensewrighting and sensereading. When using terms like "sensegiving" or "managing meaning," there is an implication of actor intentionality and recipient passivity. That is, it implies that those in charge are able to engage in a series of actions that have a particular and intended impact on those on the receiving end: in other words, that leaders can "place" meanings on the recipients. In reality, the intent of the person attempting to "do" sensegiving and the interpretations and response of those on the receiving end remain only loosely coupled, unless participants make use of what are normative behaviors for that particular context. Thus to understand how the cognitively skilled practitioner shapes processes of deciding requires not only getting to grips with processes of sensewrighting but also acknowledging how these efforts are shaped and limited by processes of sensereading (Pye 1995). Clearly, sensereading is an active process, not a passive one, intimately intertwined with sensewrighting which in turn is located in a particular context where particular norms pertain at a particular time. Cognitively skilled practitioners know they are acting within limitations and, at best, can only limit the range of "random response" (Peckham 1979; Sederberg 1984). In other words, they aim to reduce the number of different interpretations that might arise. As Mangham and Pye (1991: 28) observed:

we know roughly what to expect from others in the enterprise in which we work and they know, roughly, what to expect from us. What they do and what we do, therefore, is shaped by these mutual expectations. The entire enterprise is created and sustained through a dialectical process with our responses both creating and being created by the responses of others.

Hence the sense made of an action or utterance depends on the context of recipients and their existing understandings and interpretations. Change research in particular is increasingly revealing the limitations of senior management hegemony and control. Balogun and Johnson (2005) argue:

> Those lower down in organizations are active shapers of the way initiatives develop. Senior managers may be institutionally empowered to introduce novel templates in an attempt to redirect understandings, but their hegemony may be constrained by alternative recipient narratives.

It is, therefore, more appropriate to talk of attempting to "align interpretations" (Balogun and Johnson 2004; Balogun 2006) than managing meaning.

Skilful Practitioners: Influencing Meaning and Aligning Interpretations

To understand the relevance of viewing the way chief executives or others behave during deciding in terms of limiting the range of random responses through ongoing sensewrighting and sensereading, it is important to stay with the argument that people cannot *give* sense, per se. The next illustration is of a chief executive appointed to a FTSE 100 manufacturing company, to head a much-needed phase of strategic renewal, building on a period of radical change, with shareholders and the annual results calendar driving much of the timing. However, within a few weeks of taking up his appointment, he set off to Australia for a fortnight, to complete a series of outstanding engagements from his previous employment, leaving his new team to come up with a strategic plan by the time of his return. For some, this could be seen as a complete abdication of his responsibility as leader of the enterprise; for others, it could be seen as maximizing the wealth of corporate experience and insight embodied in the senior management team. His actions and the responses of his team together sustained the latter view, consistently defining his role as facilitator rather than director of change and with hindsight, team members expressed how empowered and valued they felt in taking forward strategic change within the company.

While leaders may not be able to land a particular "sense" on an individual's desk, depending on their power resources and the quality of their relationships, leaders may be able to limit the range of alternative senses available to others, so as to increase the likelihood that they can ultimately achieve some alignment in interpretations. Framing a position or argument is important, and some senior decision makers do it very skilfully, sometimes almost without knowing or noticing and sometimes with a lot of forethought and stage management—almost game playing. For example, the chairman who says, "Let's pool our views on this one.

I think we should do...how about you?" probably knows exactly how she or he is limiting and shaping the response of others. In our experience, skilled practitioners, like this chairman, appreciate the subtleties of power and influencing.

Hardy (1996) offers some theorizing to help make sense of influencing occurs by drawing on Lukes (1974), distinguishing between three types of power—resource, process, and meaning. Resource power is to do with overt decision making, enacted through the use of resources, such as funds, information, or credibility; for example, the capacity to hire, fire, reward, punish, provide funds, expertise, and so on. In addition, those who control the agendas of meetings, for example, are able to draw on process power so that other actors are effectively prevented from participating and, therefore, influencing decision making.

The third dimension—meaning—is to do with symbolic power and the use of symbols, rituals, language, and co-option, for example, to shape perceptions, cognitions, and preferences (Pfeffer 1981). Symbolic power involves an unobtrusive "ability to define reality, not only for oneself, but for others" (Hardy 1985: 390). As such, it is more about inhibiting opposition or getting cooperation through a process of symbol construction designed to legitimize one's own actions and delegitimize those of opponents (Pettigrew 1992) than it is about defeating declared opponents. It is less about agenda setting, for example, than shaping the language and thought processes through which any agenda item is constructed and examined. Symbolic power is similar to the notion of dramaturgical power (Mangham 1986; Clark 1995) that conceives of individuals as performers or actors on a stage, presenting a (different) character to various audiences, inviting them to believe in the reality of the performance. This is where the skills of improvizational artistry can create opportunities for sensewrighting (Mangham 1986). It places a focus on the process through which people seek to work with props, scripts, norms, resources, language, characters, and characterization to shape meaning.

All three types of power are closely interrelated and interwoven in daily life such that it is unhelpful to seek to distinguish them. However, it is the third type of power that is most interesting for studies of deciding—not just because of its obvious relevancy to framing, sensereading, and sensewrighting, but also because the idea of power as creating legitimacy warrants greater attention (Hardy and Clegg 1996). This is in part because despite the fact that writers have paid attention to the concept of meaning power, they still tell us little about how skilled practitioners actually work with it. How those with resource and process power at their disposal act to influence is fairly well understood and transparent to both to academics and practitioners. For example, if someone can affect materially others' interests (e.g., promotion chances and future pay rises), they are unlikely to be challenged by such potentially vulnerable individuals. Yet how skilful people shape meanings and interpretations to suppress evident conflict and inhibit potential conflict through the more subtle and hidden means of symbolic power, limiting the range of responses, is less clear to both of these communities.

Bringing together the notion of the power of meaning with the concept of framing highlights the need for decision makers to operate within dynamic and shifting power relations, since the exercise of this third aspect of power is a skill available to both leaders and others (Pye 2005). Power can no longer be conceived of just in terms of a (relatively) autonomous subject (e.g., a leader or a senior manager) mobilizing different dimensions of power in the form of resources, processes and meaning. Individual managers become an effect of power constructed by resources, processes and meanings (Balogun et al. 2005). This systemic view sees power as diffused throughout the organizational social system (Clegg 1989; Lawrence et al. 2007), exists relationally, as something that rather than as a property vested in or possessed by individual, autonomous actors. Mangham (1986) draws on a boardroom dialogue to illustrate this point. In the conversation two characters, Paul (Managing Director) and George (Finance Director) are locked in a debate about the financial situation of their company. Paul becomes increasingly annoyed with George as he refuses to back down in response to Paul's "cues" suggesting that George should adopt Paul's interpretation of the figures (we are doing OK) as opposed to his own (we are heading for "a thumping great loss"). George does give in—but the point is that there is only a power relation between Paul and George because George is prepared to yield. The consequences of not yielding could be bad for George but he could choose not to do so if he were prepared to go against the established and taken for granted norms of interaction within the senior management team.

Power needs to be studied as a socially situated activity, since even those who are skilful manipulators of different power dimensions are subject to the taken-for-granted or naturalized acceptance of received wisdom, both within and beyond their own organizations (Hardy 1996). To be skilled at sensewrighting, it is also necessary to be skilled at sensereading—in other words, to be able to understand the social order in one's particular sphere of operation, and to use it to good effect. In this way, some people who may not be nominally as powerful as others may still exercise significant influence.

Balogun et al. (2005) show how change agents adept at sensereading use their knowledge and skill to exercise greater sensewrighting ability. One of their change agents described his organization as run by "money men", in other words, an organization with a culture that places priority on the bottom line, and then explained how he got their attention for his programs,

The issue with pensions, for example, is for us a couple of hundred million pound impact and the value of the pension fund is about the same as the market capitalisation of the fund. So that gets senior management attention...In the US you have very high medical costs...25% of the profits were related to a cost you need to control.

He also described how he manipulated a meeting to get support from (resistant) others,

I think this time I had a pretty strong and clear message and one of my managers was great and played "good cop, bad cop". I was the bad cop. I gave the tough message and set her up to be more consulting and help people get through it.

This research into change agents shows the importance of activities such as stage management, agenda aligning and selling, gathering intelligence, and managing up: the more constrained people perceive themselves to be from their reading of their context of action (in the sense that they are not vested with more overt resource and process power), the more they need to rely on backstage activity and improvisation (Mangham and Pye, 1991). Like other research, it shows the role of language is critical in developing shared action, if not shared meaning, through alignment with a common goal; although coordinated action is not necessarily underpinned by shared meaning (Pye 1993), it can result from shared communication mechanisms (Donnellon et al. 1986). Those in charge can exercise managerial hegemony, in as far as it exists, through goal alignment towards the support of a particular set of actions that would not have received support otherwise. However, a focus on supposedly "privileged voices" (Weick 1995) may obscure the complete story of deciding (Gore et al. 2006).

Individual actors must not be overlooked in this analysis as identity affects improvisation. "From the perspective of sensemaking, who we think we are (identity) as organizational actors shapes what we enact and how we interpret, which affects what outsiders think we are (image) and how they treat us, which stabilizes or destabilizes our identity." (Weick et al. 2005: 22). Pattriotta and Spedale (2006) draw on this argument to illustrate how deciding is shaped by processes of identity construction. They present a case study of a task force comprising different groups of experts convened by an oil company to develop a framework for a full field development study. The case shows how the task force was distracted from its convened purpose, into a struggle between the different experts as to the identities they wanted to portray (and the roles they therefore wanted to take in the task force). Each expert jockeyed for position by challenging the identities presented by the other experts, whilst simultaneously presenting themselves as an expert in their particular field, but also as able to cover the range of activity required in the task force. So, for example, one member challenged the strategist about his relevance to the group given the remit of the task force. They sometimes resorted to direct attacks on the competence of other task force members to legitimize themselves and simultaneously delegitimize others. Pattriotta and Spedale also show how task force members drew on their identities as "experts" to legitimize their definition of particular terms above the interpretations of others.

As these case examples illustrate, the study of deciding must not be divorced from consideration of the decision makers involved: it must consider not just the information processing focus on, for example, an individual's personal preferences, biases and heuristics, but also decision makers' identities (projected and imposed) and their social skills and capabilities. Each decision maker is working within a tangled web of individual and collective cycles of sensereading and sensewrighting. Cognitively skilled decision makers usually negotiate and seek to shape this jumbled net of meanings and shifting power relations in such a way as to broadly gain acceptance for their position and get some form of shared support for action or a particular point of view from the different parties involved. However, as the opening case of the FTSE 100 retail CEO illustrated, there are occasions when competing logics do not get resolved or reconciled and the range of responses becomes too random and widespread, such that shared meaning or support for action is not sustained. At this point, the cognitively skilled actor who lacks strong allies (a key power resource) may decide to walk away and ultimately, as happened in this case, watch the identities of the chairman and the deputy chair change dramatically as the power balance shifted further towards shareholders, leading to a very different definition of the situation.

In Conclusion: Researching Deciding

Although computational and interpretive perspectives on organizational cognition are both necessary in order to generate a more comprehensive account of organizational decision making and other cognitive processes (Lant and Shapira 2001a, b), presently these perspectives remain largely disconnected from one another. This chapter has argued that drawing on sociological insights is one way of achieving the integration that is much needed to advance understanding and the practice of organizational deciding; providing a conception that is both more inclusive (i.e. putting the organization and the manager into organizational cognition and decision making) and injecting greater agency and process orientation into the equation. The aim has been to highlight an oft-overlooked aspect of decision-making research—the aligning of interpretation and influencing processes, conceived here in terms of sensereading and sensewrighting, as exercised by skilled practitioners. It is only in following the shifting dynamics of sensereading and sensewrighting over time and in context that it is possible to observe and monitor skilful practice, and its impacts and outcomes. Conventional analyses of decision making are not only more static, they lose the significance of time and context that are crucial to sense made and lack the colorful characters, who breathe life into the processes of deciding. Thus this chapter has argued the focus should be on making sense of deciding rather than decision making, acknowledging the inter-relationship between cognitively skilled practitioners and continuing organizational processes rather than as a series of separate decision-making episodes.

The inclusion of a sociological lens on decision making is consistent with the broader practice turn in sociology and management research, and in particular, the growing strategy as practice perspective (Whittington 2006; Balogun et al. 2007; Jarzabkowski et al. 2007; Johnson et al. 2007). This perspective argues for a return to a study of strategists, their day to day activities and practices, and how these activities influence strategic outcomes. It builds on the practice turn and the interest in "rehumanising management" to conceive of strategizing as a situated social activity. This places a focus on strategic practitioners (their skills, knowledge, identities, personalities, etc), their practices (the resources, concepts, and discourses on which strategists draw from within their organizations but also more broadly institutionally and socially), and their praxis (the day to day activities of strategists).

Reviews of research within this perspective to date (Balogun et al. 2007; Jarzabkowski et al. 2007) reveal that it is hard to maintain all three of these aspects in simultaneous focus during research. The area in which there is least understanding is probably the practitioner and the impact of themes such as, their identities or their skills and knowledge, on what they do. This is a challenge that research on deciding also faces. Yet as this chapter highlights, to understand deciding, researchers need to grasp not only such aspects as an individuals' levels of self-awareness about what he or she projects but also how others read those individuals and the outcomes this creates. There is a difference between "naive" practitioners who do not understand what images they project on to others, and skilled practitioners who not only understand but are able to manipulate such images as and when required. This observation returns us to our point of departure—to individual people—the skilled decision makers who often have to work as a collective, within a mesh of dynamic and shifting power relationships. It also accords with the underlying ethos of research on naturalistic decision making (Lipshitz et al. 2006). While simulations can and do reveal certain aspects of the decision-making process, and provide more detail on particular aspects of that process, understanding the cognitively skilled decision maker also requires more studies of deciding and those doing that deciding in "real world settings." This in turn points to studying deciding as situated practice through ethnographic or ethnomethodological approaches (Alby and Zucchermaglio 2006) also common in studies of naturalistic decision making. The authors of this chapter hope the case made here for making sense of deciding will provide some much needed lifeblood for nurturing such future research.

ENDNOTE

1. These include: a study of top management teams and board members of large UK listed plcs (Pye 2002); a study of a top management team managing change in an NHS acute hospital (Bate et al. 2000); a study of change agency (Balogun et al. 2005); and a study of strategy making based on scenario planning (Hodgkinson and Wright 2002, 2006).

REFERENCES

ALBY, F. and ZUCCHERMAGLIO, C. (2006). ' "Afterwards We Can Understand What Went Wrong, But Now Let's Fix It": How Situated Work Practices Shape Group Decision Making.' *Organization Studies*, 27/7: 943–66.

BALOGUN, J. (2003). 'From Blaming the Middle to Harnessing its Potential: Creating Change Intermediaries.' *British Journal of Management*, 14/1: 69–84.

—— (2006). 'Managing Change: Steering a Course between Intended Strategies and Unanticipated Outcomes.' *Long Range Planning*, 39/1: 29–49.

—— JOHNSON, G. (2004). 'Organizational Restructuring and Middle Manager Sensemaking.' *Academy of Management Journal*, 47/4: 523–49.

—— —— (2005). 'From Intended Strategy to Unintended Outcomes: The impact of change recipient sensemaking'. *Organization Studies*, 26/11: 1573–602.

—— Hope HAILEY, V., GLEADLE, P., and WILLMOTT, H. (2005). 'Managing Change Across Boundaries: Boundary Shaking Practices.' *British Journal of Management*, 16: 261–78.

—— JARZABKOWSKI, P., and SEIDL, D. (2007). 'Strategy as Practice Perspective,' in V. Ambrosini, M. Jenkins, and N. Collier (eds.) *Advanced Strategic Management*. Basingstoke: Palgrave MacMillan.

BATE, S. P., KHAN, R., and PYE, A. J. (2000). 'Towards a Culturally Sensitive Approach to Organization Structuring: Where Organization Design Meets Organization Development.' *Organization Science*, 11: 197–211.

BARTUNEK, J. M. (1984). 'Changing Interpretive Schemes and Organizational Restructuring: The Example of a Religious Order.' *Administrative Science Quarterly*, 29: 355–72.

BROWN, A. D. (2000). 'Making Sense of Inquiry Sensemaking.' *Journal of Management Studies*, 37/1: 45–75.

CLARK, T. (1995). *Managing Consultants: Consultancy as the Management of Impressions*. London: Sage.

CLEGG, S. (1989). *Frameworks of Power*. London: Sage.

CORLEY, K. G. and GIOIA, D. A. (2004). 'Identity Ambiguity and Change in the Wake of a Corporate Spin-off.' *Administrative Science Quarterly*, 49: 173–208.

DUTTON, J. E. and ASHFORD, S. J. (1993). 'Selling Issues to Top Management.' *Academy of Management Review*, 18/3: 397–428.

—— ASFORD, S. J., O'NEILL, R. M., and LAWRENCE, K. A. (2001). 'Moves that Matter: Issue Selling and Organizational Change.' *Academy of Management Journal*, 44/4: 716–36.

ELBANNA, S. (2006). 'Strategic Decision Making: Process Perspectives.' *International Journal of Management Reviews*, 8/1: 1–20.

FISS, P. C. and ZAJAC, E. J. (2006). 'The Symbolic Management of Strategic Change: Sensegiving via Framing and Decoupling.' *Academy of Management Journal*, 49/6: 1173–93.

FAIRHURST, G. T. (2005). 'Reframing the Art of Framing: Problems and Prospects for Leadership.' *Leadership*, 1/2: 165–85.

—— SARR, R. A. (1996). *The Art of Framing: Managing the Language of Leadership*. San Francisco, CA: Jossey-Bass.

FLOYD, S. W. and WOOLDRIDGE, B. (1997). 'Middle Management's Strategic Influence and Organizational Performance.' *Journal of Management Studies*, 34/3: 465–85.

GEPHART, R. P. (1993). 'The Textual Approach: Risk and Blame in Disaster Sensemaking.' *Academy of Management Journal*, 36/6: 1465–514.

—— (1997). 'Hazardous Measures: An Interpretive Textual Analysis of Quantitative Sense-making During Crises.' *Journal of Organizational Behavior,* 18: 583–622.

GIOIA, D. A. and CHITTIPEDDI, K. (1991). 'Sensemaking and Sensegiving in Strategic Change Initiation.' *Strategic Management Journal,* 12: 433–48.

GIGERENZER, G., TODD, P. M., and the ABC Research Group (eds.) (1999). *Simple Heuristics That Make Us Smart.* New York: Oxford University Press.

GORE, J., BANKS, A., MILLWARD, L., and KYRIAKADOU, O. (2006). 'Naturalistic Decision Making and Organizations: Reviewing Pragmatic Science.' *Organization Studies,* 27/7: 925–42.

HARDY, C. (1985). 'The Nature of Unobtrusive Power.' *Journal of Management Studies,* 22/4: 384–99.

—— (1996). 'Understanding Power: Bringing About Strategic Change.' *British Journal of Management,* 7/Special Issue: S3–S16.

HARDY, C. and CLEGG, S. R. (1996). 'Some Dare Call it Power,' in S. R. CLEGG, C. Hardy, and W. R. Nord (eds.), *Handbook of Organization Studies.* London: Sage.

HENSMANS, M. (2003). 'Social Movement Organizations: A Metaphor for Strategic Actors in Institutional Fields.' *Organization Studies,* 24: 355–81.

HODGKINSON, G. P. and MAULE, A. J. (2002). 'The Individual in the Strategy Process: Insights from Behavioral Decision Research and Cognitive Mapping,' in A. S. Huff and M. Jenkins (eds.), *Mapping Strategic Knowledge.* London: Sage.

—— SPARROW, P. R. (2002). *The Competent Organization: A Psychological Analysis of the Strategic Management Process.* Buckingham: Open University Press.

—— WRIGHT, G. (2002). 'Confronting Strategic Inertia in a Top Management Team: Learning from Failure.' *Organization Studies,* 23: 949–77.

—— —— (2006). 'Neither Completing the Practice Turn, nor Enriching the Process Tradition: Secondary Misinterpretations of a Case Analysis Reconsidered.' *Organization Studies,* 27: 1895–1901.

HUFF, A. S. and SCHWENK, C. R. (1990). 'Bias and Sensemaking in Good Times and Bad,' in A. S. Huff (ed.), *Mapping Strategic Thought.* Chichester: Wiley.

KAHNEMANN, D., SLOVIC, O., and TVERSKY, A. (eds.) (1982). *Judgment under Uncertainty: Heuristics and Biases.* Cambridge: Cambridge University Press.

JACKSON, S. E. and DUTTON, J. E. (1988). 'Discerning Threats and Opportunities.' *Administrative Science Quarterly,* 33/3: 370–88.

JARZABKOWSKI, P., BALOGUN, J., and SEIDL, D. (2007). 'Strategizing: The Challenges of Practice Perspective.' *Human Relations,* 60/Special Issue: 5–27.

JOHNSON, G. (1987). *Strategic Change and the Management Process.* Oxford: Basil Blackwell.

—— LANGLEY, A., MELIN, L., and WHITTINGTON, R. (2007). *Strategy as Practice: Research Directions and Resources.* Cambridge: Cambridge University Press.

LANT, T. K. and SHAPIRA, Z. (eds.) (2001a). *Organizational Cognition: Computation and Interpretation.* Mahwah, NJ: Lawrence Erlbaum Associates.

—— —— (2001b). 'Introduction: Foundations of Research on Cognition in Organizations,' in T. K. Lant and Z. Shapira (eds.), *Organizational Cognition: Computation and Interpretation.* Mahwah, NJ: Lawrence Erlbaum Associates.

LAWRENCE, T. B., MAUWS, M. K., DYCK, B., and KLEYSEN, R. F. (2005). 'The Politics of Organizational Learning: Integrating Power into the 4I Framework.' *Academy of Management Review,* 30/1: 180–91.

LIPSHITZ, R., KLEIN, G., and CARROLL, J. S. (2006). 'Introduction to the Special Issue: Naturalistic Decision Making and Organizational Decision Making: Exploring the Intersections.' *Organization Studies,* 27/7: 917–23.

LUKES, S. (1974). *Power: A Radical View.* London: Macmillan.

MAITLIS, S. (2005). 'The Social Processes of Organizational Sensemaking.' *Academy of Management Review,* 48/1: 21–49.

—— LAWRENCE, T. B. (2007). 'Triggers and Enablers of Sensegiving in Organizations.' *Academy of Management Journal,* 50: 57–84.

MANGHAM, I. (1978). *Interactions and Interventions in Organizations.* Chichester: Wiley.

—— (1979). *The Politics of Organizational Change.* Westport, CT: Greenwood Press.

—— (1986). *Power and Performance in Organizations.* Oxford: Blackwell.

—— PYE, A. (1991). *The Doing of Managing.* Oxford: Blackwell.

MAULE, A. J. and HODGKINSON, G. P. (2002). 'Heuristics, Biases and Strategic Decision Making.' *The Psychologist,* 15/2: 68–71.

PATTRIOTTA, G. and SPEDALE, S. (2006). 'Between Controversies and Face Games: Senesemaking and Decision Making in a Consultancy Task Force.' EGOS Conference, Strategy as Practice Track, Bergen, July.

PECKHAM, M. (1979). *Explanation and Power.* Minneapolis, MN University of Minnesota Press.

PETTIGREW, A. (1992). 'The Character and Significance of Strategy Process Research.' *Strategic Management Journal,* 13: 5–16.

PFEFFER, J. (1981). *Power in Organizations.* Marshfield, MA: Pitman.

PITT, M., McAULEY, L., DOWDS, N., and SIMS, D. (1997). 'Horse Races, Governance and the Chance to Fight: On the Formation of Organizational Agendas.' *British Journal of Management,* 8/Special Issue: S19–S30.

PYE, A. (1993). '"Organizing as Explaining" and the Doing of Managing: An Integrative Appreciation of Processes of Organizing.' *Journal of Management Inquiry,* 2/2: 157–68.

—— (1995). 'Strategy through Dialogue and Doing: A Game of Mornington Crescent?' *Management Learning,* 26/4: 445–62.

—— (2002). 'The Changing Power of "Explanations": Directors, Academics and their Sensemaking from 1989 to 2000.' *Journal of Management Studies,* 39/7: 907–26.

—— (2003). 'Making Sense of (the Explanatory Function of) Strategizing.' European Group on Organization Studies, Annual Conference, Business in Organizing—Organizing in Business, Copenhagen, Denmark.

—— (2005). 'Leadership and Organizing: Sensemaking in Action.' *Leadership,* 1/1: 31–50.

RANSON, S., HININGS, B., and GREENWOOD, R. (1980). 'The Structuring of Organizational Structures.' *Administrative Science Quarterly,* 25/1: 1–17.

SCHWENK, C. R. (1989). 'Linking Cognitive, Organizational and Political Factors in Explaining Strategic Change.' *Journal of Management Studies,* 26/2: 177–87.

SEDERBERG, P. C. (1984). *The Politics of Meaning: Power and Explanation in the Construction of Social Reality.* Tucson, AZ: University of Arizona Press.

SMIRCICH, L. and MORGAN, G. (1982). 'Leadership: The Management of Meaning.' *Journal of Applied Behavioral Science,* 18/3: 257–73.

—— STUBBART, C. (1985). 'Strategic Management in an Enacted World.' *Academy of Management Review,* 10/4: 724–36.

WEICK, K. E. (1995). *Sensemaking in Organizations.* Thousand Oaks, CA: Sage.

—— ROBERTS, K. H. (1993). 'Collective Mind in Organizations: Heedful Interrelating on Flight Decks.' *Administrative Science Quarterly,* 38: 357–81.

—— SUTCLIFFE, K. M., and OBSTFELD, D. (2005). Organizing and the Process of Sensemaking.' *Organization Science,* 16/4: 409–21.

WHITTINGTON, R. (2006). 'Completing the Practice Turn in Strategy Research.' *Organization Studies*, 1/1: 117–25.

—— MOLLOY, E., MAYER, M., and SMITH, A. (2006). 'Practices of Strategising/Organising: Broadening Strategy Work and Skills.' *Long Range Planning*, 39: 615–29.

WILLMOTT, H. (2002). 'Strategy as Practice.' Presentation to 3rd Strategy as Practice Workshop, Cranfield, November 18 (www.strategy-as-practice.org).

13

LINKING RATIONALITY, POLITICS, AND ROUTINES IN ORGANIZATIONAL DECISION MAKING

ISABELLE ROYER

ANN LANGLEY

INTRODUCTION

SINCE Allison's (1971) classic study of the Cuban missile crisis, researchers have generally agreed that organizational decision making has rational, political, and routine elements (e.g., Mintzberg et al. 1976; March 1997). Each of these elements constitutes a partial analytic paradigm that concentrates on one type of explanation (Allison 1971). For example, while the rationality paradigm describes decision as a goal directed but satisficing choice among alternatives bounded by cognitive limitations (Simon 1957), political approaches consider decision to be the result of interactions among powerful people (Allison 1971). In turn, the approach based on routines (Nelson and Winter 1982)—also called programs (March and Simon 1958), rules (e.g., Zhou 1997) or organizational processes (Allison 1971)—indicates that action results from following normatively appropriate behavior (March and Olsen 1989). Although one paradigm may be sufficient to explain a particular situation, the three paradigms complement each other to better explain—and consequently predict—"strategic" decisions (Allison 1971). Strategic decisions are those decisions that are "important in terms of actions taken, the resources committed, or the precedents set" (Mintzberg et al. 1976: 246). They are typically made under uncertainty, involve several decision makers, and do not have preprogrammed solutions.

In line with Allison's (1971) work, this chapter aims to integrate the three paradigms in order to improve understanding of strategic decision making. However, while Allison contrasted the three approaches in order to highlight their distinctive contributions, we focus here on the possible linkages between them.

Few studies have previously attempted to link all three elements together,[1] but several authors have considered the relationships between rationality and politics. These writings have been somewhat inconsistent however. Rationality and politics have been variously described as mutually exclusive alternatives whose efficacy is contingent on context (e.g., Nutt 2002), as independent process variables (e.g., Dean and Sharfman 1993, 1996), or as interdependent processes (e.g., Langley 1989). Because these inconsistencies are partly due to different concept definitions, we first specify the definitions and perspectives adopted in this chapter. The chosen definitions focus on organizational *processes* and *behaviors* rather than on intentions or outcomes. They are also intended to be value neutral (e.g., rationality is not intrinsically "good" and politics is not intrinsically "bad"), and the nature of the goals being pursued (personal vs. organizational) is not included in the definition of the behavior.

Rationality refers here to *procedural rationality*, which is the process of information search and analysis associated with organizational issues, regardless of the precise use of the information collected or the goals driving it. This definition is consistent with Langley's (1989) definition of analysis, but is broader than that suggested by Dean and Sharfman (1993, 1996) who define "rationality" in terms of the degree to which decisions are driven by organizational goals and are grounded in information. In contrast, the key element in the current definition is that the decision process involves some kind of information search and analysis. The use of that information, though important, is for us a separate question.

Politics refers here to *socio-political processes*, which are social interactions between people around organizational issues, regardless of the nature of the goals sought, or of the overt or covert nature of the processes. This definition is close to Fahey's (1981) definition of behavioral/political decision making, and is thus broader than those associating politics only with bargaining (e.g., March and Simon 1958; Thompson and Tuden 1959; Nutt 2002) or those reducing it to illegitimate or covert actions to influence decisions (e.g., Eisenhardt and Bourgeois 1988). It is also broader than definitions assuming that political processes always imply the domination of self-interest (e.g., Dean and Sharfman 1996).

Routines refer here to *patterned processes* in the treatment of organizational issues regardless of whether these patterns derive from explicit policies and procedures or from implicit values and norms. A routine is thus a pattern that places boundaries around who does *what, how,* and *when* within an organizational decision process. This definition excludes the types of routines that imply ready-made answers to problems, but focuses instead on decision practices (Sutcliffe and McNamara 2001) that channel the paths of organizational decision making. Strategic planning cycles with predefined document formats and meeting schedules are typical routines that an organization may engage in during the production of strategic decisions, but specific routines or practices exist for all kinds of decisions.

Based on these definitions, this chapter develops arguments about how procedural rationality, socio-political processes, and decision routines link together in the production of strategic decisions. It also considers how organizations might mobilize these linkages to improve organizational decision making. In fact, we shall argue that both procedural rationality and socio-political processes are critical elements in strategic decision making, and that efficient and effective decision processes will tend to combine them. Yet organizations do not necessarily achieve ideal combinations naturally and may develop decision pathologies such as groupthink (Janis 1972), escalating commitment (e.g., Staw 1997), and decision paralysis (Langley 1989). Drawing on the earlier contributions of the Carnegie School, we shall also show how *decision routines* can significantly shape the weight of socio-political and procedurally rational processes.

The argument proceeds in three sections. The first section introduces a "static" perspective on decision making that views rationality and politics as alternatives whose appropriateness depends on a key contingency: uncertainty. This section considers classic prescriptions from the literature and shows how and why descriptive decision behavior may diverge from them. The second section takes a more "dynamic" perspective, viewing uncertainty no longer as a fixed contingency, but as a contextual variable that evolves over time. The third section adds consideration of the role of routines from both a prescriptive and a descriptive angle, drawing on recent contributions that discuss their "ostensive and performative" dimensions. The chapter concludes with implications for future research and practice.

A Static View: Rationality and Politics as Alternatives, Uncertainty as a Critical Contingency

Classic Prescriptions for Organizational Decision Making Under Uncertainty

In an early contribution, Thompson and Tuden (1959; reformulated in Thompson 1967) proposed a model associating specific decision approaches with two contingencies: uncertainty about goals (preferences about outcomes) and uncertainty about means (beliefs about cause–effect relations). According to these authors, decision making by "calculation" (close to this chapter's notion of "procedural rationality") is only possible and appropriate when both objectives and means are clear. This is so because calculation demands a priori criteria and the ability to collect unambiguous information about alternatives. The authors argue that when objectives are clear but the means for producing results are ambiguous, collective judgment based on the majority opinion of experts is more appropriate because it takes into account experiential knowledge. When goals are ambiguous but means are clear, the authors recommend compromise based on bargaining since the concern is to arrive at an agreement that will satisfy all stakeholders (Thompson and Tuden 1959). They view the situation of unclear goals and unclear means (called "anomie") as problematic, offering "inspiration" or the intervention of a charismatic leader as a possible fit. Note that the last three contingencies all involve some form of socio-political processes as defined in this chapter. However, while the use of majority judgment implies social interaction based on collegiality, bargaining often implies power differentials and conflict, while inspiration implies the effective use of persuasion by talented leaders.

In an interesting empirical study, Nutt (2002) used data on 376 strategic decisions to test Thompson's (1967) contingency model. He found that the fit between decision context and process predicted decision success (in terms of degree of adoption, decision value and time to implementation), confirming Thompson's (1967) model as a sound prescriptive guide. However, Nutt's study (2002: 83) also revealed discrepancies between the behavior of organization members and the prescriptions of the model ("Decision makers in this study were prone to using the wrong decision approach"). Other literature helps elucidate these discrepancies.

Prescriptions vs. Reality: Organizational Decision Making and Uncertainty in Practice

There is considerable evidence that people do not naturally behave according to the prescriptive contingency model. For example, the cognitive psychology literature has generally portrayed individuals as poor information processors who "avoid mental procedures that require sustained attention, concentration, or computing power" (Tetlock 1983: 74). Rather, the literature suggests that people tend to apply heuristics that simplify decision making but that diverge from normative recommendations (Einhorn and Hogarth 1981; Kahneman et al. 1982). If left to themselves, many people will tend to make decisions without undertaking any major effort to analyze information (Frederick 2005).

However, this "information processor" view of individuals ignores the social context in which decision making occurs. Individuals are also interested in the approval and status conferred by others. For example, research by Tetlock (1985) has shown that accountability to others changes the extent to which people engage in formal information search. When people are accountable to others whose views are known (i.e., low uncertainty about goals), they tend to take positions that are most readily acceptable to their interlocutors—the "acceptability heuristic" tends to drive decisions. However, when people are accountable to others whose views are *un*clear (i.e., high uncertainty about goals), they tend to increase information search and analysis in order to be able to defend their position in the face of possible disagreement, or to explain their decisions if they turn out poorly (Tetlock 1985; Doney and Armstrong 1996).

Tetlock's (1985) research thus suggests that procedural rationality and socio-political processes are interdependent. Indeed, other authors have shown that people use procedural rationality to support political processes, for example, to justify decisions to others (Bower 1970; Feldman and March 1981; Meyer 1984), to contribute to adversarial debate (Lindblom and Cohen 1979), to exert control (Dalton 1959), or to deflect attention away from issues (Meltsner 1976). Based on an empirical study of the role of formal analysis in organizations, Langley (1989: 609) argued that procedural rationality and socio-political processes are in fact symbiotic:

Formal analysis would be less necessary if everybody could execute their decisions themselves, and nobody had to convince anybody of anything. In fact, one could hypothesize that the more decision making power is shared between people who do not quite trust one another, the more formal analysis will be important. (1989: 609)

Langley (1995) went on to describe several decision situations where organizations became involved in paralytic sequences of analysis and counter-analysis that failed to converge. These were often associated with divergent goals and a high degree of uncertainty—exactly the situations where Thompson would have advised against the use of procedural rationality. An interview quotation from Langley's (1995: 66) empirical work is revealing of this dynamic: "Studies were simply the ammunition in a battle."

Langley (1995) also identified situations where organizations converged too rapidly on a choice. These situations included cases where powerful leaders had known views that were not questioned by subordinates, cases where particular individuals could act alone without sanction, and cases where everyone appeared to instantaneously share the same goals. This last phenomenon is similar to what Janis (1972) calls "groupthink"—a situation in which decision makers develop a high degree of solidarity that discourages them from expressing doubts about proposed courses of action. Thus, certainty about goals does not necessarily encourage procedural rationality. It may instead be associated with one-sided political processes that produce rapid commitment with little serious reflection.

In summary, while the prescriptive contingency model proposed by Thompson and Tuden (1959) has empirical support, real decision making behavior does not always follow its prescriptions. In addition, this model treats different modes of decision making as mutually exclusive. Yet, procedural rationality and socio-political processes are often interdependent in practice. Finally, Thompson and Tuden's (1959) model views uncertainties as static exogenous conditions. Yet, as Stinchcombe (1990) observed, uncertainty evolves over the course of a decision and may be reduced in part by information derived from decision-making activities themselves. This suggests the need for a more dynamic view.

A Dynamic View: Rationality and Politics as Complementary, Uncertainty as Evolving Over Time

Descriptive studies have shown that strategic issues tend to generate streams of interlinked decisions that may or may not converge (Quinn 1980; Langley et al. 1995). Indeed, in their study of 25 strategic decisions, Mintzberg et al. (1976) observed that 22 of them included repeated episodes of evaluation and choice and that all the strategic decisions they studied were constituted of a series of subdecisions (see also Simon 1957). However, while Mintzberg et al. (1976) noted that three different modes of evaluation were possible (called analysis, judgment, and bargaining), they did not examine whether there might be some progression in their use over time. In this section, we first present a prescriptive model that considers how the use of procedural rationality and socio-political processes might evolve during organizational decision-making processes. We then contrast the prescriptive model with certain observed patterns that appear quite common despite their negative consequences.

A Prescriptive Dynamic Model of Organizational Decision Making Under Uncertainty

As noted, Thompson and Tuden's (1959) prescriptive *contingency* model suggests that procedural rationality is only effective when goals are known and when means are clear. Taking a temporal perspective, this situation seems unlikely to exist at the earliest stages of a major strategic decision when uncertainty and ambiguity are highest. Contingencies may, however, evolve during the decision process (Stinch-combe 1990). In particular, one could argue that effective decision processes should gradually reduce uncertainties about goals and about means until procedural rationality can be used appropriately (i.e., moving from cell 1 to cell 4 in Figure 13.1). According to Thompson and Tuden's (1959) model, any change in uncertainties would require changes in decision modes to maintain fit with uncertainties.

Daft and Lengel (1986) who also frame decision contingencies according to uncertainties provide a way to render Thompson and Tuden's model more dynamic. They indicate that different types of uncertainty require different ap-proaches to uncertainty reduction. The accumulation of data to answer specific

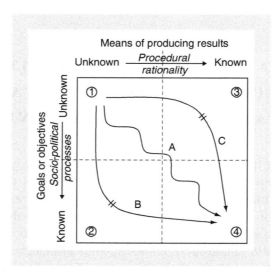

Fig. 13.1 Evolution of contingencies over time through socio-political processes and procedural rationality.

Notes: A: Incrementalism; B: Focus on socio-politics; C: Focus on rationality; // Possible Pathologies: either paralysis or over commitment.

questions (i.e., procedural rationality) is necessary for the reduction of uncertainty about means while face to face interaction, debate, clarification, and enactment (i.e., socio-political processes) enable the development of mutual understanding and the reduction of uncertainty about goals. As a result, moving from cell 1 to cell 4 in Figure 13.1 implies both a socio-political process to reduce uncertainty about goals, and procedural rationality to reduce uncertainty about means. Further, since procedural rationality requires certainty about goals to be efficient (Simon 1957; Thompson and Tuden 1959), it follows that the process consisting of reducing both types of uncertainties logically starts with a domination of socio-political processes before moving towards a domination of procedural rationality.

Beyond this logical general statement, decision makers may follow various paths to reduce both uncertainties. The prescriptive path (Path A in Figure 13.1) involves a cyclical reduction of both uncertainties. Alternate paths B and C are associated with certain decision pathologies described later.

Recommendations for cyclical paths that involve the complementary uses of procedural rationality and socio-political processes appeared in some of the earlier literature on decision making. For example, Cyert and March (1963) suggested that effective managers artfully blend formal analytical behavior and political techniques to bring about cohesion and step by step movement toward broadly conceived ends, which are then constantly refined and reshaped as new information appears. Viewing decision processes as chains of subdecisions allows us to consider appropriate ways of blending socio-political processes and procedural rationality over time. We argue that these processes may co-evolve in a reinforcement process where reduction of uncertainty about goals helps reduce uncertainties about means that in turn favors additional reduction of uncertainties about goals.

Starting from a highly uncertain situation, any active organizational process aimed at reducing uncertainty involves enactment (Daft and Weick 1984). Following Daft and Lengel (1986), since uncertainty about goals is high, initial enactment will first imply engaging in a socio-political process. This will create commitment, which favors the implementation of certain activities (Nutt 2002) including experimentation and testing that will allow learning (Daft and Weick 1984). The implementation of these activities provides solution designs and concrete data that can nurture procedural rationality.

Such activities further nurture socio-political processes in two ways. First, since some goal conflicts are based on different bets about the future (Allison 1971), reducing uncertainty about the future can help reduce these conflicts (March and Simon 1958). Second, enactment per se favors a reduction of uncertainty about goals since participation in action helps develop preferences for this action (Weick 1979; March and Olsen 1982). In both cases, reduction of uncertainty about means engages opponents in cognitive revision that reduces uncertainty about goals (Meyer 1984).

Following this reinforcement process, uncertainties about goals and means decline step by step in a process of mutual adjustment until both are low enough to make a final decision (see the zigzag path A from cell 1 to cell 4 in Figure 13.1). Fahey (1981) and Feldman (1989) observed such cyclical processes in their research. Quinn (1980: 16)[2] further prescribed similar ones. His study of ten large firms showed that the most effective strategies tend to follow a "process in which the organization probes the future, experiments, and learns from a series of partial commitments." He called this process "logical incrementalism" because it both "utilizes the global analyses inherent in formal strategy formulation models" and "embraces the central tenets of the political behavior approach."

The Prescribed Dynamic Model vs. Pathological Paths

However, people may tend not to follow the prescriptive path for at least two reasons. Firstly, as we indicated earlier, people tend to collect more information precisely in situations where others' opinions are unknown and where goals are unclear (situations where socio-political processes are appropriate), and less information when others' opinions are known and goals are shared (situations where procedural rationality is appropriate). Because, the process starts with high levels of both uncertainties, this may result in considerable investment in procedural rationality at first that will decrease over time as goals become clearer. This is precisely opposed to the prescribed pattern of evolution from socio-political processes to procedural rationality. Secondly, the need for closure that induces a need for immediate and permanent answers (Kruglanski 1989) can lead to a search for quick solutions rather than careful scrutiny (Blount et al. 2002), ignoring the required balance between the two components. A focus on a single dimension is detrimental to the reduction of uncertainty in the other dimension later on, potentially generating pathologies of decision making, including two that are well known: escalation of commitment (path B) and paralysis (path C).

Path B: Focusing on Uncertainty About Goals First

An approach that favors reducing uncertainties about goals first (cell 1 to cell 2) may tend to produce convergence on means that have been insufficiently analyzed. As we argue below, this may result in the persistence of weak solutions and escalation of commitment.

As Langley (1995) noted, once everybody agrees on goals, decision makers are not inclined to engage in procedural rationality because it is not necessary to convince others. Thus, early agreement favors early reduction in analysis and consequently increases the risk of ineffective means. Later, it favors persistence and reduces adjustments because of high commitment. High commitment occurs because participants have publicly agreed to their decision and their participation implies volition—two of the four characteristics that increase commitment in addition to explicitness and irreversibility according to Salancik (1977). As research in cognitive psychology has suggested, committed people tend not to reevaluate adopted behavior (Goodman et al. 1980) and to ignore disconfirming information (Kiesler and Sproull 1982). Negative feedback in such situations tends to favor escalation of commitment (e.g., Staw 1997) and groupthink (Janis 1972).

Groups who display groupthink symptoms not only tend to ignore disconfirming evidence, but they also tend to reduce the number of alternatives considered (usually two), and to make little or no attempt to obtain additional information (Janis 1983). Such limited analytical processes impede the invention of relevant solutions and may result in a downward spiral toward fiascos. Such phenomena occur in both private companies (Ross and Staw 1993) and in public organizations (Janis 1972; Esser and Lindoerfer 1989; Starbuck and Farjoun 2005).

Path C: Focusing on Uncertainty About Means First

Conversely, focusing first on the reduction of uncertainty about means through procedural rationality (cell 1 to 3) could lead to a carefully considered decision that might be extremely logical, but hard to implement because of lack of commitment. Delaying the reduction of uncertainty about goals through socio-political processes (cell 3 to cell 4) may result in blockages later. Because people have not had the opportunity to develop preferences towards a proposed decision through enactment and interactions, the risk of incompatible preferences is high, and decision paralysis may ensue (Langley 1995).

Indeed, persistent divergence on goals may generate the sequences of contradictory analyses described earlier as different participants engage in procedural rationality to justify competing proposals, while failing to address the more fundamental goal and value differences that lie at the root of their disagreement. Some writers have viewed the production of analysis by competing groups as a potentially constructive way to improve decisions (e.g., Braybrooke and Lindblom 1963). However, if such disagreements are based on goals rather than facts, the production of more "facts" may not be helpful. Additional facts may become an obstacle to decision-making because the evaluation of several alternatives lowers confidence and commitment (Brunsson 2000) and can generate unacceptably high levels of decisional stress when these options have negative consequences (Hodgkinson and Wright 2002). In addition, the production of competing analyses that come to different conclusions may actually confuse those who are most open to logical argument (Langley 1995).

In summary, from a prescriptive perspective, path A that consists of cyclical reductions of both uncertainties looks the most promising. Other paths involving imbalanced reduction seem to be relatively ineffective because of their potential for groupthink or escalation (path B), or because of lack of commitment or paralysis and divergence (path C). Thomas and Trevino's (1993) three contrasting case studies of alliance development offer support for these ideas. Based on Daft and Lengel's (1986) model, they showed that early insistence on procedural rationality to the exclusion of socio-political processes (path C) derailed an otherwise potentially productive alliance because the rational arguments used failed to cope with fundamental goal ambiguities. Meanwhile, another collaboration failed because the political processes used failed to resolve concrete uncertainties that required information (path B). The most successful collaboration combined both procedural rationality and socio-political processes to reduce gradually both uncertainty about goals and uncertainty about means (path A).

Ironically, however, people and organizations may naturally tend towards the ineffective patterns. Routines may offer a way to modulate these tendencies.

THE INFLUENCE OF ROUTINES ON THE ROLE AND EVOLUTION OF PROCEDURAL RATIONALITY AND SOCIO-POLITICAL PROCESSES

Simon (1957) argues that two key administrative routines are involved in any composite decision: "procedural planning" and "review." "Procedural planning" constructs the environment that will influence decision. It includes the attribution of tasks, standard practices, authority, channels of communication, and values. "Review" completes the process by controlling alignment between activities and goals. The aggregate of the two preceding processes corresponds essentially to our definition of "decision routines." Decision routines may manifest themselves in formally prescribed rules or in informal but generally accepted practices. They usually take the form of a logical succession of phases and partial decisions that specify who does what when and how during decision making.

The management literature is replete with proposals for normative decision routines. Some of these normative recommendations are rather general, such as Quinn's (1980) model of "logical incrementalism." Others are specific to a particular type of strategic decision such as innovation decisions (e.g., Stage-Gate process, Cooper 1994), or acquisitions (Haspeslagh and Jemison 1991). Even when these routines are not formalized, external observers may still describe them using maps or flow-charts that capture their regularities (e.g., Fahey 1981; Meyer 1984).

For example, in a study of medical equipment budgeting in hospitals, Meyer (1984) found that respondents used a cartographic metaphor to describe the way medical equipment decisions "traveled" through the organization (Meyer 1984: 7). They were able to chart itineraries showing the different types of activities to be carried out, with indications of who would participate and how. An example of a composite chart from his study appears in Figure 13.2.

Meyer (1984) describes this generic process as composed of four rather different subprocesses. The decision journey first involves the use of clinical judgment among colleagues (socio-political processes), then emphasizes the computation of fiscal benefits and costs (procedural rationality), and ends with negotiation among members of a budget committee (socio-political processes), and strategic deliberations among members of the governing board (combining elements of rationality and politics). This "routine" thus structures the intervention of procedural rationality and socio-political processes over time. Others, including Fahey (1981) and Grant (2003) have drawn up similar charts, describing different decision routines. To the extent that organizations can impose such routines, they can thus at least partially channel the pattern and ordering of episodes of procedural rationality and socio-political processes in ways that more closely reflect the prescriptive patterns we described earlier.

To elaborate on how decision routines influence rationality and politics over time, we distinguish between the two aspects of organizational routines introduced by Feldman and Pentland (2003): the ostensive aspect and the performative aspect. The ostensive aspect of a routine is its prescribed form, representing an abstract ideal procedure. The performative aspect is its descriptive manifestation, which consists of the specific actions taken by specific people at specific times in executing the routine. Although the performative dimension often deviates from the ostensive dimension, the latter can still exert a powerful influence on decision making.

Prescription and the Ostensive Aspect of Routines

The ostensive aspects of routines are the loci for prescription. They tend to correspond to managerial interests since managers are officially empowered to modify routines (Feldman and Pentland 2003) or to introduce new ones (Sutcliffe and McNamara 2001). Managers may further have the power to monitor performances and enforce compliance (Feldman and Pentland 2003). Thus, managers may attempt to use the ostensive aspect of a routine to favor the prescriptive evolution of decision processes as described earlier: in other words, the production of a cyclical reduction of both types of uncertainties involving both rationality and politics. We propose here two basic design principles for decision routines. The first suggests that managers should attempt to incorporate a balanced set of rational

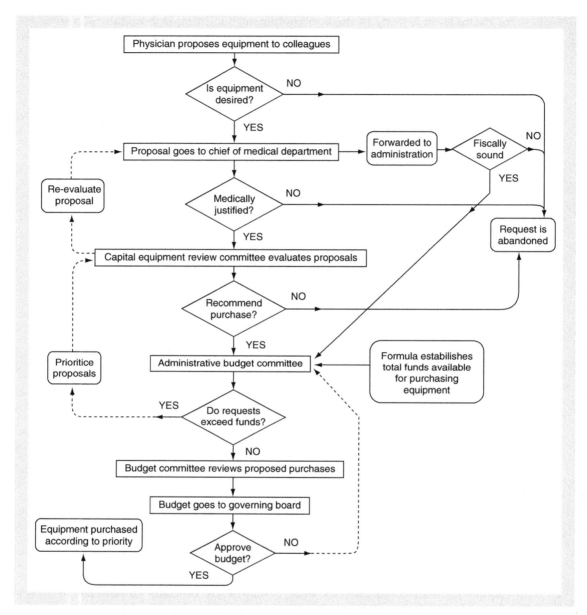

Fig. 13.2 A decision routine for capital investment.

Source: Meyer, 1984: 9; reprinted with permission.

and political components into the ostensive routine. The second deals with the modulation of routines over time.

Balancing Rational and Political Components

Routines have two types of components according to their major influence either on procedural rationality or on socio-political processes. The first set involves activities that provide information such as design, search, analysis, budgets, and schedules as well as experimentation and testing. The second set involves participation through assignments, interactive forums, consultative or decision-making committees, and monitoring of goals. Like means and goals, these two sets of routine components are never completely separate. For instance, experiments aimed at providing data about the potential of an idea may require the collaboration of a variety of people and may thus come to involve socio-political processes. Similarly, participation may be viewed not only as an arena for socio-political interaction, but as a way to increase the number of alternatives considered and may therefore contribute to procedural rationality.

However, generally, the close association of different routine components with rationality on one hand and politics on the other hand suggests that prescriptive routines should normally integrate both sets of components. In addition, the media used should evolve with the evolution of uncertainties. Thus, Daft and Lengel (1986) would suggest starting with elements such as group meetings, the use of intermediaries, and direct contact (i.e., socio-political processes) that are the most effective in reducing uncertainty about goals and then continue with media more effective in reducing uncertainty about means such as planning and special reports (i.e., closely associated with procedural rationality). Failure to integrate both rational and political components into the decision routine will tend to be detrimental.

The stage-gate process for product innovation developed by Cooper (e.g., 1994) illustrates the potential problems of a lack of balance between rational and political components of a decision routine. The stage-gate process splits the product development process into stages and gates before the final commitment to market launch. It stipulates the design, resolution, test, and study activities in each phase. When the tasks of a phase are complete, managers compare achievements with requirements set during the previous gate. Depending on the results, they may enter the next stage, hold the project to favor a better one, stop it, or recycle to better adjust means and goals. This decision routine thus provides useful guidelines for reducing uncertainty about means, essentially through procedural rationality. However, although most authors call for the use of multifunctional teams, the model does not incorporate explicit attention to socio-political processes. Thus, initial goals remain unquestioned leaving little room for adjustment and renegotiation. If this happens, the stage-gate process can easily result in paralysis (path C Figure 13.1).[3]

Modulating Participation and Formalization Over Time to Avoid Premature Closure

While prescriptive decision routines need to begin by favoring socio-political processes, this does not mean that such processes have no role to play later on. As noted earlier, instantaneous convergence on goals naturally leads to reduced interest in procedural rationality, and may generate escalation of commitment to a failing course of action. To sustain evaluation and adjustment of means, there are advantages to the partial renewal of participation throughout the process. Changing participants stimulates the questioning of goals, and reduces cohesiveness, which is one of the ingredients of groupthink (Janis 1972). It also helps avoid escalation (Simonson and Staw 1972) and favors de-escalation (Ross and Staw 1993). Pinfield (1986) suggests monitoring the access of participants to different stages of an evolving decision process in order to maintain the match between the issues and participants' interests and expertise. Such modulations of participation have, however, to be contained in order to avoid the opposite pitfall, that is a return to high uncertainty about goals with potential conflict that may lead to paralysis.

Similarly, routines that begin with extensive early formalization may sometimes cut off alternatives and induce premature convergence. For example, proforma budget requirements ensure consideration of the financial outcomes of a project. However, they may be problematic if imposed too early (Simon 1957). Early evaluations are provisional and based on inaccurate estimates, but they are semantically precise (Meyer 1984) and thus tend to absorb uncertainties. Formality tends to generate an illusion of control (Hogarth and Makridakis 1981) so re-evaluation is less probable, increasing the chances of escalation of commitment (Staw 1997). Thus, effective decision routines will modulate formalization throughout the process.

We have pointed out that the ostensive aspect of routines enables managers to orient decision making deliberately toward the prescribed balance of rationality and politics and to avoid the pathological paths. However, in practice, it is not the ostensive aspect of a routine that determines outcomes, but its performative aspect, in other words, the way the routine is actually performed.

Performative Aspects of Decision Routines

The performative aspect of a routine always deviates from the ostensive aspect. Because routines cannot be comprehensive and because the context for enactment varies, strict replication is impossible (Nelson and Winter 1982). Further, people who enact routines can choose to deviate from them. Deviations from the ostensive aspect of routines may be problematic when relevant analyses or people are omitted. However, they may also be sensible when they respond to unanticipated situations and incorporate improvements (Feldman and Pentland 2003). Paradoxically, given that routines are intended to optimize decision-making patterns, there is evidence that blind adherence to ostensive routines can sometimes have negative consequences. Sutcliffe and McNamara (2001) observed that people who stuck too closely to an analytical routine for credit decision making tended to produce poor assessments because they performed the process automatically, favoring conformative rather than relevant behavior.

Feldman and Pentland (2003) suggest that the ostensive aspect of a routine may serve three different purposes when performed by participants: it can serve prospectively as a guide to action ("guiding"), it can serve as justification of previous action ("accounting"), and it can serve as a reference term that organizes understanding ("referring"). Meyer's (1984) study illustrates these different purposes.

For example, the "map" of how decisions proceed, shown in Figure 13.2 (Meyer 1984), illustrates the way in which the ostensive aspect of the routine acts as a guide. It is in this role that it prescribes the intervention of procedural rationality and socio-political processes. However, Meyer (1984) and others (e.g., Brunsson 2000) also draw attention to the use of the different subprocesses in a symbolic rather than instrumental mode. Once there is some clarity about which choice is likely to emerge, there will be temptations to take shortcuts in performing the rest of the routine. However, there will often remain a need to display appropriate analyses and to show that appropriate people were consulted in appropriate forums. Thus, people may produce analytical information retrospectively, and consensus and participation in decisions may appear to be ceremonial rather than substantive. Here, the ostensive routine serves an "accounting" purpose, contributing legitimacy to decisions and facilitating their implementation.

This "accounting" purpose cannot, however, exist unless the routine has become invested with intrinsic value and meaning, reflecting how things "should" and indeed "must" be done. In this sense, the ostensive routine becomes a short-hand for a whole range of taken for granted activities (its "referring" role). This also means that although managers may indeed have, in theory, the ability to impose or modify ostensive routines, change may be more difficult than it appears. Firstly, because existing routines are invested with meaning (e.g., participative routines imply rights to decision influence), change may be perceived as illegitimate. Secondly, any changes proposed will tend to interact with existing decision routines. For example, Lozeau et al.'s (2002) study of the introduction of strategic planning in hospitals showed how the socio-political processes that had traditionally regulated decision making tended to capture and divert the ostensibly "rational" planning procedures.

In summary, by predefining who is expected to do what how and when, decision routines can shape the weight of socio-political and procedurally rational processes in decision making and influence the extent to which any particular decision may reflect the prescribed patterns. However, since routines are neither instantaneously adaptable nor identically reproduced each time they are used, there is no easy recipe for adjustment. Rather, routines are channeling devices whose influence is significant, though only partly predictable.

Conclusion

Our synthesis of the relationships between procedural rationality, socio-political processes and decision routines suggested that the decision-making patterns naturally favored by individuals and by organizations tend to be opposed to prescriptive models. In particular, we noted that procedural rationality and socio-political processes are more symbiotic than contingent. Further, individuals tend to freeze means or goals early on rather than adjust them over time. We then described how decision routines might influence both procedural rationality and socio-political processes. The precise effect of a component of an ostensive routine is complex since managers may perform it instrumentally, ceremonially or not at all. Further, the symbiotic relationship between rationality and political processes can reinforce, cancel or reverse this influence.

Despite the complexity, the capacity of routines to shape the relative weights of procedural rationality and socio-political processes makes them particularly interesting. Their relevance is particularly important when one considers that people may naturally tend to behave in ways that are contrary to prescriptive theory. This leads us to reinstate decision routines as a key component of organizational decision making and as an (albeit delicate) path to improving effectiveness. This conclusion is consistent with the work of classic decision theorists (March and Simon 1958) and with recent developments on routines (Feldman and Pentland 2003), and dynamic capabilities (Eisenhardt and Martin 2000).

The symbiotic relationship between procedural rationality and socio-political processes and the complex influence of routines on these two components opens up opportunities for further research. We focused here on the main relationships between the three components of decision making. More fine-grained research is necessary to improve understanding of how these processes occur as well as to detail prescriptively how organizations can successfully mobilize routines to generate both commitment and ensure sensible decisions. Specific routines designed for a variety of organizational decisions such as capital budgeting, innovation, acquisitions, and venturing offer opportunities for applied research.

The process of modifying routines is also an interesting research problem and practical concern in its own right and may constitute a particular challenge. In certain cases, attempts to modify the ostensive aspects of routines may themselves be subject to the decision routines that are under modification, generating a non-linear, dynamic, and partly endogenous process of change.

The complex relationships described also have several consequences for research methods. Firstly, the symbiotic relationship between procedural rationality and socio-political processes implies that even research focusing on understanding one component has to integrate the other, or at least control for it in order to generate valid conclusions. Secondly, the evolution of procedural rationality and socio-political processes over time suggests a need for longitudinal research designs. Finally, studying the relationships between routines and decision making demands multilevel research designs since ostensive routines are generally located at a higher organizational level than the decisions they channel.

The inclusion of multiple levels of analysis to capture the relationships between rationality, politics, and routines over time makes both research and theorizing more complex. However, Mitchell and James (2001) recently argued that organization theories tend to suffer from oversimplification and called for thinking that is more sophisticated. This chapter supports that call. Moreover, we believe that existing methods can deal with multilevel and temporal complexity, both qualitatively (Langley 1999; Yin 2003) and quantitatively (e.g., HLM methods proposed by Bryk and Raudenbausch 1992).

Endnotes

1 But see Meyer (1984), to be discussed in some depth later, and Fahey (1981).

2 Lindblom's (1959) earlier notion of "disjointed incrementalism" inspired Quinn's (1980) work. However, Lindblom saw incrementalism as a much less deliberate and managerially controlled process than Quinn.

3 Indeed, Wind and Mahajan (1997) indicate that the stage-gate process often tends to be used merely as a screening process, forgetting the recycling and suspending options. As described by Wind and Mahajan (1997: 7), "The stage gate process has been referred to, tongue in cheek but quite often accurately, as "exultation → disenchantment → confusion → search for the guilty → punishment of the innocent → distinction of the uninvolved."

References

ALLISON, G. T. (1971). *Essence of Decision: Explaining the Cuban Missile Crisis.* Boston, MA: Little, Brown.

BLOUNT, S., WALLER, M. J., and LEROY, S. (2005). 'Coping with Temporal Uncertainty: When Rigid, Ambitious Deadlines Don't Make Sense,' in W. H. Starbuck and M. Farjoun (eds.), *Organization At The Limit: Lessons From The Columbia Disaster.* Malden, MA: Blackwell, 122–39.

BOWER, J. L. (1970). *Managing the Resource Allocation Process: A Study of Corporate Planning and Investment.* Boston, MA: Harvard University Press.

BRAYBROOKE, D. and LINDBLOM, C. E. (1963). *A Strategy of Decision: Policy Evaluation as a Social Process.* New York: Free Press.

BRUNSSON, N. (2000). *The Irrational Organization: Irrationality as a Basis for Organizational Action and Change.* Bergen: Fagbokforlaget.

Bryk, A. and Raudenbush, S. (1992). *Hierarchical Linear Models: Applications and Data Analysis Methods*. Newbury Park, CA: Sage.

Cooper, R. G. (1994). 'Third-Generation New Product Processes.' *Journal of Product Innovation Management*, 11/1: 3–14.

Cyert, R. M and March, J. G. (1963). *A Behavioral Theory of the Firm*. Englewood Cliffs, NJ: Prentice-Hall.

Daft, R. L. and Lengel, R. H. (1986). 'Organizational Information Requirements, Media Richness and Structural Design.' *Management Science*, 32/5: 554–71.

—— Weick, K. E. (1984). 'Toward a Model of Organizations as Interpretation Systems.' *Academy of Management Review*, 9/2: 284–93.

Dalton, M. (1959). *Men Who Manage*. New York: Wiley.

Dean, J. W. and Sharfman, M. P. (1993). 'The Relationship Between Procedural Rationality and Political Behavior in Strategic Decision Making.' *Decision Sciences*, 24/6: 1069–83.

—— —— (1996). 'Does Decision Process Matter? A Study of Strategic Decision-Making Effectiveness.' *Academy of Management Journal*, 39/2: 368–96.

Doney, P. M. and Armstrong, G. M. (1996). 'Effects of Accountability on Symbolic Information Search and Information Analysis by Organizational Buyers.' *Journal of the Academy of Marketing Science*, 24/1: 57–65.

Einhorn, H. J. and Hogarth, R. M. (1981). Behavioral Decision Theory: Processes of Judgment and Choice.' *Annual Review of Psychology*, 32: 53–88.

Eisenhardt, K. M. and Bourgeois III, L. J. (1988). 'Politics of Strategic Decision Making in High-Velocity Environments: Toward a Midrange Theory.' *Academy of Management Journal*, 31/4: 737–70.

—— Martin, J. A. (2000). 'Dynamic Capabilities: What Are They?' *Strategic Management Journal*, 21/10/11 Special Issue: 1105–21.

Esser, J. K. and Lindoerfer, J. S. (1989). 'Groupthink and the Space Shuttle Challenger Accident: Toward a Quantitative Case Analysis.' *Journal of Behavioral Decision Making*, 2: 167–77.

Fahey, L. (1981). 'On Strategic Management Decision Processes.' *Strategic Management Journal*, 2/1: 43–60.

Feldman, M. S. (1989). *Order Without Design: Information Production and Policy Making*. Stanford, CA: Stanford University Press.

—— March, J. G. (1981). 'Information in Organizations as Signal and Symbol.' *Administrative Science Quarterly*, 26/2: 171–85.

—— Pentland, B. T. (2003). 'Reconceptualizing Organizational Routines as a Source of Flexibility and Change.' *Administrative Science Quarterly*, 48/1: 94–118.

Frederick, S. (2005). 'Cognitive Reflection and Decision Making.' *Journal of Economic Perspectives*, 19/4: 25–42.

Goodman, P. S., Bazerman, M., and Conlon, E. (1980). 'Institutionalization of Planned Organizational Change,' in B. M. Staw and L. L. Cummings (eds.), *Research in Organizational Behavior*. Greenwich, CT: JAI Press, 215–46.

Grant, R. M. (2003). 'Strategic Planning in a Turbulent Environment: Evidence from the Oil Majors.' *Strategic Management Journal*, 24/6: 491–517.

Haspeslagh, P. C. and Jemison, D. B. (1991). *Managing Acquisitions: Creating Value through Corporate Renewal*. New York: Free Press.

Hodgkinson, G. P. and Wright, G. (2002). 'Confronting Strategic Inertia in a Top Management Team: Learning from Failure.' *Organization Studies*, 23/6: 949–77.

HOGARTH, R. M. and MAKRIDAKIS, S. (1981). 'Forecasting and Planning: An Evaluation.' *Management Science*, 27/2: 115–38.

JANIS, I. L. (1972). *Victims of Groupthink: A Psychological Study of Foreign-Policy Decisions and Fiascoes*. Boston, MA: Houghton Mifflin.

—— (1983). 'Groupthink,' in R. W. Allen and L. W. Porter (eds.), *Organizational Influence Processes*. Glenview, IL: Scott, Foresman, 270–80.

KAHNEMAN, D., SLOVIC, P., and TVERSKY, A. (1982). *Judgement Under Uncertainty: Heuristics and Biases*. Cambridge: Cambridge University Press.

KIESLER, S. and SPROULL, L. (1982). 'Managerial Response to Changing Environments: Perspectives on Problem Sensing from Social Cognition.' *Administrative Science Quarterly*, 27/4: 548–70.

KRUGLANSKI, A. W. (1989). *Lay Epistemics and Human Knowledge: Cognitive and Motivational Bases*. New York: Lenum Press.

LANGLEY, A. (1989). 'In Search of Rationality: The Purposes Behind the Use of Formal Analysis in Organizations.' *Administrative Science Quarterly*, 34/4: 598–631.

—— (1995). 'Between "Paralysis by Analysis" and "Extinction by Instinct."' *Sloan Management Review*, 36/3: 63–76.

—— (1999). 'Strategies for Theorizing from Process Data.' *Academy of Management Review*, 24/4: 691–710.

—— MINTZBERG, H., PITCHER, P., POSADA, E., and SAINT-MACARY, J. (1995). 'Opening Up Decision Making: The View from the Black Stool.' *Organization Science*, 6: 260–79.

LINDBLOM, C. E. (1959). 'The Science of Muddling Through.' *Public Administration Review*, 19/2: 79–88.

—— COHEN, D. K. (1979). *Usable Knowledge: Social Science and Social Problem Solving*. New Haven, CT: Yale University Press.

LOZEAU, D., LANGLEY, A., and DENIS, J.-L. (2002). 'The Corruption of Managerial Techniques by Organizations.' *Human Relations*, 55/5: 537–64.

MARCH, J. G. (1997). 'Understanding How Decisions Happen in Organizations,' in Z. Shapira (ed.), *Organizational Decision Making*. New York: Cambridge University Press, 9–32.

—— OLSEN, J. P. (1982). *Ambiguity and Choice in Organizations* (2nd edn.). Bergen: Universitetsforlaget.

—— —— (1989). *Rediscovering Organizations: The Organizational Basis of Politics*. New York: Free Press.

—— SIMON, H. A. (1958). *Organizations*. New York: Wiley.

MELTSNER, A. J. (1976). *Policy Analysts in the Bureaucracy*. Berkeley, CA: University of California Press.

MEYER, A. D. (1984). 'Mingling Decision Making Metaphors.' *Academy of Management Review*, 9/1: 6–17.

MINTZBERG, H., RAISINGHANI, D., and THÉORÊT, A. (1976). 'The Structure of "Unstructured" Decision Processes.' *Administrative Science Quarterly*, 21/2: 246–75.

MITCHELL, T. and JAMES, L. (2001). 'Building Better Theory: Time and the Specification of When Things Happen.' *Academy of Management Review*, 26/4: 530–47.

NELSON, R. R. and WINTER, S. G. (1982). *An Evolutionary Theory of Economic Change*. Cambridge, MA: Belknap Press.

NUTT, P. C. (2002). 'Making Strategic Choices.' *Journal of Management Studies*, 39/1: 67–96.

PINFIELD, L. T. (1986). 'A Field Evaluation of Perspectives on Organizational Decision Making.' *Administrative Science Quarterly*, 31/3: 365–88.

QUINN, J. B. (1980). 'Strategies for Change: Logical Incrementalism.' Homewood, IL: Irwin.

ROSS, J. and STAW, B. M. (1993). 'Organizational Escalation and Exit: Lessons from the Shoreham Nuclear Power Plant.' *Academy of Management Journal*, 36/4: 701–32.

SALANCIK, G. R. (1977). 'Commitment and the Control of Organizational Behavior and Belief,' in B. M. Staw and G. R. Salancik (eds.), *New Directions in Organizational Behavior*. Malabar, FL: Robert E. Krieger, 1–54.

SIMON, H. A. (1957). *Administrative Behavior: A Study of Decision-Making Processes in Administrative Organization* (2nd edn.) New York: Free Press.

SIMONSON, I. and STAW, B. M. (1992). 'Deescalation Strategies: A Comparison of Techniques for Reducing Commitment to Losing Courses of Action.' *Journal of Applied Psychology*, 77/4: 419–26.

STARBUCK, W. H. and FARJOUN, M. (eds.) (2005). *Organization At The Limit: Lessons From The Columbia Disaster*. Malden, MA: Blackwell.

STAW, B. M. (1997). 'The Escalation of Commitment: An Update and Appraisal,' in Z. Shapira (ed.), *Organizational Decision Making*. Cambridge: Cambridge University Press, 191–215.

STINCHCOMBE, A. (1990). *Information and Organizations*. Berkeley, CA: University of California Press.

SUTCLIFFE, K. M. and MCNAMARA, G. (2001). 'Controlling Decision-Making Practice in Organizations.' *Organization Science*, 12/4: 484–501.

TETLOCK, P. E. (1983). 'Accountability and Complexity of Thought.' *Journal of Personality and Social Psychology*, 45/1: 74–83.

—— (1985). 'Accountability: The Neglected Social Context of Judgment and Choice,' in L. L. Cummings, and B. M. Staw (eds.), *Research in Organizational Behaviour*. Greenwich, CT: JAI Press, 297–332.

THOMAS, J. B. and TREVINO, L. K. (1993). 'Information-Processing in Strategic Alliance Building—A Multiple-Case Approach.' *Journal of Management Studies*, 30/5: 779–814.

THOMPSON, J. D. (1967). *Organizations in Action*. New York: McGraw-Hill.

—— TUDEN, A. (1959). 'Strategies, Structures and Processes of Organizational Decision,' in J. D. Thompson (ed.), *Comparative Studies in Administration*. Pittsburgh, PA: University of Pittsburgh Press.

WEICK, K. E. (1979). *The Social Psychology of Organizing*. New York: Random House.

WIND, J. and MAHAJAN, V. (1997). 'Issues and Opportunities in New Product Development: An Introduction to the Special Issue.' *Journal of Marketing Research*, 34/1: 11–12.

YIN, R. K. (2003). *Case Study Research: Design and Methods* (3rd edn.). Thousand Oaks, CA: Sage.

ZHOU, X. (1997). 'Organizational Decision Making as Rule Following,' in Z. Shapira (ed.), *Organizational Decision Making*. New York: Cambridge University Press, 257–81.

14

SUPERSTITIOUS BEHAVIOR AS A BYPRODUCT OF INTELLIGENT ADAPTATION*

JERKER DENRELL

INTRODUCTION

AN anthropologist once visited a remote tribe. She observed that each morning, before sunrise, members of the tribe sacrificed a goat in order to make the sun rise. Since the tribe was poor, the anthropologist believed that this was a wasteful practice. As a result, the anthropologist proposed that the members of the tribe should avoid sacrificing a goat for one day, to see if the sun would nevertheless rise. In response, one of the older tribe members told her, "In these matters one cannot afford to experiment."

Because the tribe repeatedly sacrificed a goat in the morning, their behavior will be associated with the desired outcome: the rise of the sun. The only way to find out whether there is a causal link between the behavior and the outcome is to

* I am grateful for comments and advice from Christina Fang, James March, and Udo Zander.

experiment. However, the tribe considers experimentation as too costly, exactly because it believes that sacrificing the goat may be responsible for producing the desired outcome.

I argue that this story illustrates an important mechanism that perpetuates superstitious behavior in organizations and elsewhere. Superstitious behavior occurs when an individual repeats a behavior that is associated with the desired results but the causal connection between the behavior and the desired result is missing (Levitt and March 1988). In the above story, sacrificing the goat had no causal influence on the desired outcome.[1] Because the tribe sacrificed the goat before the sun rises, however, the members of the tribe will observe a positive but spurious correlation between the action and the desired outcome.

The logic of superstitious behavior is such that tribe members or managers can only learn whether the link between their behavior and the desired outcomes is spurious or causal if they stop engaging in this behavior and observe the resulting outcome. However, as the story illustrates, such experimentation can be costly. The reason is that experimenting to find out whether alternative approaches are superior often requires that individuals try out activities they believe are inferior (Einhorn and Hogarth 1978; Klayman and Ha 1987; March 1991; Denrell 2005, 2007); For instance, in order to evaluate whether a rule for how to select employees is effective, managers need to employ individuals who do not conform to the rule (Einhorn and Hogarth 1978; Einhorn 1986). If managers believe that their current rule is likely to be valid, managers believe that employees that do not conform to the rule are likely to perform poorly.

More generally, if performance is satisfactory, an intelligent policy of adaptation implies that experimentation should be limited (Berry and Fristedt 1985; Brezzi and Lai 2000; Winter 2000; Denrell 2007). Rather than experimenting with alternative approaches, managers should often stick to the established approach. A by-product of such limited experimentation is superstitious behavior. By repeating actions associated with satisfactory performance consequences, managers will not obtain the information that is required to assess whether the link between their activities and the results is causal. As a result, managers may perpetuate superstitious behavior.

To develop my argument, I first review the literature on superstitious behavior in psychology. I then illustrate why limited experimentation is a necessary feature of an intelligent learning policy and why limited experimentation can explain why individuals and organizations perpetuate superstitious behavior. I subsequently discuss several sources of superstitious behavior in organizations. Finally, I note that an implication of my analysis is that innovations will emerge from managers who are inclined to, or forced by stakeholders, to make unreasonable decisions that ignore the costs of experimenting.

Superstition and the Costs
of Experimentation

In 1948, B. F. Skinner published one of his most cited articles ever. The title was "'Superstition' in pigeons" (Skinner 1948). Skinners article described the result of a single experiment. In this experiment, Skinner placed a hungry pigeon in a chamber (a "Skinner Box"). Occasionally food pellets would drop into the chamber. The pigeon's actions did not influence when food pellets dropped into the chamber. Rather, every 15 seconds, food would appear. Although one might have expected the pigeons to wait in front of the feeder, Skinner's pigeons became very active. A pigeon would begin by walking around the box. Eventually, some food would drop in. At this moment, the pigeon might have been picking at a wall. Because the food pellet dropped in when the pigeon picked at the wall, the probability that the pigeon would pick at the wall increased. When the next piece of food dropped in, the pigeon was even more likely to pick at the wall. Eventually, each pigeon developed a distinctive ritual. Some would pick at a wall. Others would walk in circles or rapidly thrust their heads into one of the upper corners of the chamber. Still others bobbed their heads up and down. According to Skinner, these behaviors were the result of conditioning. The accidental pairing between of some random act of the pigeon with the presentation of the food was enough to reinforce these idiosyncratic behaviors.

Researchers later repeated the same experiment with both children and adults as participants. Results were similar: superstitious behavior emerged as the result of an accidental pairing between actions and results (cf., Vyse 1997). In one experiment (Ono 1987), subjects would sit in front a small table that contained three response levers and a device to keep track of points. The researcher instructed the participants to earn as many points as possible. Points appeared on the counter at irregular or regular intervals, but always completely independent of anything the participants did. A number of repetitive behaviors soon emerged, some lasting throughout the session, others being transitory. For example, one participant made four rapid pulls on a single lever and then held the lever for several seconds. Participants in the experiments started to engage in such superstitious behavior when they coincidentally received several points while performing the behavior.

Skinner (1948) defined such repetitive behavior, triggered by a coincidental pairing with reinforcers, as "superstitious." Although the term "superstitious" generally connotes unfounded beliefs, typically containing supernatural and magical elements, the meaning of superstitious is, in the context of these experiments, narrower. Superstitious behavior refers to repeated behavior that developed by being reinforced by rewards causally unrelated to the behavior. Superstitious learning is then the process by which superstitious behavior develops in a series of trials as a response to observations of the outcomes following the behavior. Actions that results from false beliefs are not necessarily declared superstitious. Rather research on superstitious behavior focus on cases where individuals or animals repeat an activity in spite of the fact the activity has no, or perhaps even a negative, effects on desired outcomes.

Several scholars have argued that such superstitious behaviors can develop in organizations in situations when "the subjective experience of learning is compelling, but the connections between actions and outcomes are misspecified" (Levitt and March 1988: 151). Making use of computer simulations of experiential learning, Lave and March (1975) and Levinthal and March (1981) illustrated how organizations in beneficial environments may develop superstitious beliefs connecting their activities to their success. Suppose the performance of an organization is high but independent of the actions of its managers. In this setting, anything that managers do will seem to be associated with high performance. As a result, through a process similar to that Skinner illustrated, managers may come to believe that the activities they are engaging in lead to high performance (Lave and March 1975).

One explanation for such superstitious behavior is that humans and animals are subject to a confirmation bias. Like the behavior of the participants in Wason's (1960) classical experiment on rule discovery, individuals fail to see the significance of subjecting their hypothesis to tests that would make it possible to falsify them. They believe that the behavioral sequence they have discovered is a necessary condition for the outcome, when it may only be a sufficient condition or when the outcome may be unrelated to their activities.

In discussing the classical experiment of Skinner, Killeen (1977, 1982) suggested an interesting alternative explanation. Killeen argued that the behavior of pigeons was rational. Specifically, he argued that it was rational for the pigeons to reproduce an action that seemingly produces a valued outcome. The pigeons in Skinner's experiment were hungry because Skinner had starved them (Skinner reduced their weight to about 75 percent of the normal). Because the pigeons were hungry, Killeen argued that it was rational for the pigeons to try out any action that could produce food. Thus, according to this interpretation, the pigeons might have continued their idiosyncratic movements just in case their actions really made a difference.

Killeen's interpretation would also seem to apply to the experiments conducted with humans. Not only pigeons but also humans face a trade-off between the benefits and costs of experimenting with alternative actions. If one never deviates from the practices believed to be the best, there is no way of finding out whether alternative practices are in fact better. Nevertheless, it is possible that one believes that the costs of experimenting are greater than the benefits. In such cases, one should stick with actions although it is possible that they are less than optimally effective. As emphasized by Vyse (1997: 75), people often provide a similar justification for their use of charms or superstitious rituals. Although aware of their potential inefficiency, they justify their use by saying, like the tribe members in the above story, "I don't want to take any chances."

Although this argument may be unsatisfactory as an explanation of the details of the above experiments, it suggests the interesting possibility that far from being stupid, some superstitious behavior may reflect intelligent adaptation. Specifically, in situations where individuals have found an activity that generates satisfactory performance, it may be optimal to avoid experimenting with alternative actions. As a result, individuals will not find out whether the association between the activity and the observed performance is causal or merely spurious.

THE OPTIMALITY OF LIMITED EXPERIMENTATION

To illustrate when and why experimentation should be limited, consider the following situation. You can choose between two alternatives: A and B. Alternative A always offers a payoff of zero. Alternative B offers a payoff of 1 with probability p and a payoff of -1 with probability $1-p$. The value of p is constant and lies between 0 and 1 (it is drawn from a uniform distribution), but the specific value of p is unknown. You want to maximize the total sum of the payoffs realized in a series of 25 choices.

This is a version of the so called "one-armed bandit problem" (Thompson 1933; Bellman 1956; DeGroot 1970). In this problem, there is a trade-off between exploring the unknown alternative B versus exploiting the known alternative A. Because the value of p is unknown, it is useful to choose alternative B to see if it is better than A. If you choose B, however, and the outcome is -1, you need to decide whether to continue to explore B or switch to A. The dilemma is that by choosing A, you gain no further information about the possible value of B. Because one sample does not provide much information about the value of B, it seems useful to continue to sample B. On the other hand, based on past outcomes, B seems to be worse than A.

An optimal policy in this problem needs to specify when past outcomes justify that you will abandon B even if abandoning B implies that you will not get any new information about the value of p. As has been demonstrated in mathematical work on the one-armed bandit problem, the optimal policy implies that exploration will be limited. If past outcomes have been sufficiently negative, it is best to switch to the known alternative (A) even if this implies that you will not get any additional information about the value of p (DeGroot 1970; Holland 1975; Berry and Fristedt 1985; March 1991; Sutton and Barto 1998; Denrell 2007).

A similar result holds if a decision maker can choose repeatedly between several unknown alternatives. For example, suppose that a decision maker could choose in

25 periods between two alternatives, B and C. Alternative B offers a payoff of 1 with probability p and a payoff of -1 with probability $1-p$. Alternative C offers a payoff of 1 with probability q and a payoff of -1 with probability $1-q$. The values of p and q are constant and lie between 0 and 1 (they are drawn from a uniform distribution), but are otherwise unknown. In this setting, an optimal policy implies that the decision maker will eventually converge upon one alternative and then stop exploring the other alternative (Rotschild 1974; Brezzi and Lai 2000). With positive probability, however, the chosen action may not be the best. Thus, the learning process may converge to an inferior action and then stop.

The optimal policy in these problems is very difficult to compute and experiments show that people seldom conform to it (Meyer and Shi 1995). Nevertheless, this work on the optimal policies in bandit problems provides an illustration of why it may be adaptive to stop experimenting. It shows that limited learning may be optimal even if such a policy occasionally results in persistence with suboptimal practices. Far from stupid, such behavior is a result of intelligent adaptation in an uncertain world. From the perspective of an omniscient observer, such as the anthropologist in the above story, the resulting behavior may seem to be unsatisfactory. However, from the perspective of the learner, such as the members of the tribe in the above story, there can be no guarantee that exploring alternative actions will generate higher payoffs.

LIMITED EXPERIMENTATION AND SUPERSTITION

To illustrate how superstitious behavior can emerge as a by-product of intelligent adaptation and limited experimentation, consider again the behavior of the pigeons in Skinner's experiment. The critical feature of this experiment is that a valued outcome occurs with equal frequency when the pigeon picks at a wall or when the pigeon does nothing. In most settings, this is unusual. Food usually does not just drop in. Similarly, firm performance is seldom high regardless of the actions taken. Decision makers usually expect that they need to take an action to reach an outcome. In examples where superstitious behavior develop this expectation is false. Unaware of this, the decision maker may reasonably attribute the observed level of performance to the action taken. If so, it may be reasonable to repeat the action. In situations where performance is high regardless of the action taken, this may result in the false belief that the chosen action leads to high performance.

To make the underlying mechanism behind such superstitious learning more precise, consider an individual who can choose between two activities: A and B.

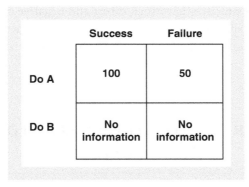

Fig. 14.1 The payoff information available to an individual repeatedly engaging in activity A.

The individual starts by trying out activity A. Suppose that activity A has a surprisingly high success rate. Figure 14.1 illustrates the information that such an individual would have. The individual knows that activity A is associated with success, but has not tried B. In situations where superstitious behavior occurs, however, both activities have an equally high success rate, because neither A nor B influence performance. The individual may not be certain that the situation he or she faces has this feature, however. If a high success rate is unusual, the individual may reasonably believe that activity A may have a causal influence on performance. If so, it makes sense for this individual to stick to activity A, even if this implies that the individual will not get any information about the possible value of activity B.

Although the circumstances in which such superstitious beliefs develop may seem special, the argument of this chapter is that they are typical of complex systems, such as organizations. Consider a successful firm. Generally, it is difficult to know exactly what contributes to its success. There are numerous activities going on simultaneously in any reasonable complex organization. Any of these activities may contribute to success. For example, the recent marketing campaign may or may not be important. To find out whether the marketing campaign is important, managers need to experiment. A marketing researcher might suggest an elaborate experiment that would require management to change the marketing campaign in some regions and keep it in other regions. If the firm has been surprisingly successful, however, management may consider such experimentation as too risky. After all, perhaps the marketing campaign is the source of the success of the firm. If management does not experiment, however, they will not be able to find out whether the marketing campaign contributes to their success or not.

In contrast to the view that learning from experience will eventually eliminate false causal beliefs (Friedman 1953), the perspective advanced in this chapter suggests that researchers should view organizational learning as a coarse grained filter that only eliminates practices with a direct and severely negative impact on performance. Unless practices have such direct and negative consequences, organizations may avoid experimenting with alternative approaches. The result is that a non-significant fraction of organizational behavior is likely to be superstitious.

Sources of Organizational Superstition

To suggest hypotheses about when and where superstitious behavior is likely to occur in organizations, here I examine various reasons for why an activity may be associated with high performance, in the absence of a genuine causal link. I argue that in many of these cases, the experimental design that would enable organizations to learn whether such activities have a causal effect on performance is too costly and risky.

Confounding Variables

Many things happen simultaneously in organizations. Management may increase marketing expenditures at the same time as they increase the sales force. If the larger sales force increases sales, marketing expenditures will correlate strongly with sales. If the marketing campaign were useless, the correlation would be spurious.

Complex organizations spontaneously produce many such spurious correlations and these spurious correlations are a fertile source of superstitious learning. (Lounamaa and March 1987). Consider an organization with five managers, each responsible for one department (such as sales, marketing, operations, etc). Imagine that each manager can control some decision variables. For example, the vice president for marketing can increase marketing expenditures, etc. It is possible that only some of these decision variables have a positive causal effect on total performance. Nevertheless, all managers may try to change the decision variables under their control, to increase the performance of the organization. Suppose performance increases, because the manager responsible for the decision variable with a positive causal effect on performance makes the right decisions. Each manager may attribute the increase in performance to the changes he or she introduced. As a result, all managers become more confident that the changes they introduced are beneficial to the organization. If the manager responsible for the decision variable with a positive causal effect on performance continues to make the right decisions, performance will continue to be high, and the confidence of all managers may continue to increase.

The managers in this organization could avoid this problem of misplaced confidence if they adopted a careful experimental design. Instead of making several simultaneous changes, they could experiment with making incremental changes in single activities (Lounamaa and March 1987). It is possible to disentangle the contributions of individual activities in this way, but it would take a long time. If there were n activities in the organizations, managers would need to explore all combinations of these n activities. Except for areas such as research and development and quality control, organizations seldom make such extensive tests of their beliefs about the links between actions and outcomes. If they do not, it is likely that several of their behaviors are superstitious.

Trends

Management makes a change and observes that performance increases. Performance might have increased anyway if there was an upward trend in performance. Such trends are common in time series of organizational performance. Due to external factors, such as change in demand, supply, exchange rates, and competition, performance tends to be auto-correlated. It may increase or decrease for a given period. It follows that any actions taken during these periods will seem to have positive or negative effects.

How can managers identify whether a given activity has a causal effect on performance if there is a trend in performance driven by external factors? Ideally, managers should postpone the activity and observe whether performance still increases. If performance is high, managers may consider such experimentation too risky. After all, perhaps the activity is responsible for the increase in performance.

If managers avoid experimentation, they are likely to pick up many superstitious behaviors during periods when external events improve performance (Lave and March 1975). Any activity adopted by managers during such periods will be associated with high performance. Superstitious behaviors are especially likely to emerge in new industries where there is considerable uncertainty about the determinants of performance. Early entrants in such industries may become very successful. Consultants and the business press may associate the successes of these firms with several peripheral activities these firms engage in, that may have little to do with their success.

An interesting way in which this may happen is if a new generation of managers dominates successful firms in a new industry. These managers may adopt a management style in line with the values of the new generation. As an example of this, consider Internet firms during the Internet boom. Individuals in these firms were typically quite young and tended to have certain ways of dressing, interacting, and certain beliefs about leadership, that were quite common for people in their age group. The business press often attributed the success of these firms to their corporate culture and human resource practices. In an alternative and possibly more reasonable interpretation, the successes of these firms and their adoption of practices congruent with the values of a younger generation merely occurred at the same time.

Regression to the Mean

Suppose you toss a dice and the outcome is one. If you toss the dice again, it is likely that you will get a higher outcome. If you had obtained an outcome of six, however, it is likely that the outcome on the next toss would be lower. This is the phenomenon of regression to the mean. Regression to the mean can generate systematic trends in performance. An organization with poor performance in the current period, for example, is likely to have higher performance in the next period. This occurs whenever chance factors have some influence on organizational performance (Harrison and March 1984).

Regression to the mean can also generate spurious correlations. Activities initiated when performance is low will seem to contribute to increased performance. Activities initiated when performance is high will seem to contribute to decreased performance. Since many activities in organizations are contingent on the level of performance, regression to the mean will produce several superstitious behaviors in organizations. In particular, because managers are take action when performance is low (Cyert and March 1963), managers can easily develop superstitious beliefs about the value of such activities. Consider, for example, management by exception (Cohen and March 1986). The idea is that management will decentralize decisions and only intervene if performance falls below a certain threshold. Due to regression to the mean, any intervention on the part of management will seem to increase performance. If the intervention of management consists of replacing the head of the unit with low performance, management will learn that this strategy is successful. If the intervention of management consists of supporting the unit with low performance, management will learn that this strategy is successful (Cohen and March 1986).

Empirical research has demonstrated that most people are unaware of the effects of regression to the mean (Kahneman and Tversky 1973; Schaffner 1985). Even if they were aware of them, however, identifying such effects can be difficult and costly. To identify if an activity has a genuine causal effect on performance, or if the change in performance is simply due to regression to the mean, managers should do nothing and see if performance regresses to the mean. If managers believe that the action may have some effect, however, they many consider the option of doing nothing as too risky.

Treatment Effects

If a manager believes that technology A is more likely to be successful than technology B, it makes sense for this manager to allocate more resources to technology A. For example, the manager may assign his or her best researchers to work on technology A. Suppose that technology A turns out to be more successful than technology B. For example, the manager may observe the payoff information depicted in Figure 14.2. The fact that technology A appears to be more successful, however, does not demonstrate that technology A had a higher underlying potential. It is possible that technology B would have been equally successful if the manager had allocated the same amount of resources to developing technology B (Einhorn and Hogarth 1978; Brehmer 1980; Arthur 1989). The association between success and the use of technology A is then spurious.

It is reasonable for managers to allocate more resources to products or technologies managers believe are more promising. When such preferential treatment of products and technologies influence the observed rate of success, it becomes very difficult for managers to learn about the underlying potential of different products, technologies, and management practices. To learn, managers need to allocate an even amount of resources to all possible products or technologies. However, doing so is risky, precisely because it is most profitable to allocate most resources to the most promising products and technologies.

Sorenson and Waguespack (2006) provide an interesting illustration of how such treatment effects can complicate learning in the motion picture industry. In the motion picture industry, distributors provide a link between production companies, which produce movies, and theaters, which display movies. The revenues of the movies they distribute determine the profit of distributors. The revenue of movies, in turn, depends on marketing efforts, the release date, and the quality of the movie. It is usually difficult to predict the quality of a movie. Thus, movie distributors have to

	Success	Failure
Technology A	100	50
Technology B	60	50

Fig. 14.2 The payoff information available to a manager who believes that technology A is the best and thus spends more time and resources on developing technology A.

select movies based on some indicators of its quality and attraction. One such indicator is whether the distributor knows and has previously worked with the individuals involved in the production of the movie (i.e., the actors, producers, etc.).

Sorenson and Waguespack (2006) show that distributors are more likely to select a movie if the distributor knows several of the individuals involved in the production of this movie. There is also evidence that such movies also generate more revenue. Nevertheless, this evidence does not necessarily imply that selecting movies involving actors that the distributor has worked with previously is a winning strategy. The problem is that distributors also spend more money marketing such movies and release them at dates that are more favorable. Thus, it is not clear whether the higher revenues from movies that involve individuals that distributors have worked with previously are due to the selection rule (choosing movies involving known individuals) or to the fact that distributors market such movies more extensively and release them on dates that are more favorable.

To find out whether it would be more profitable to focus on movies that involve unknown actors and producers, distributors would have to experiment with alternative approaches. Distributors would have to market movies that involve unknown actors and producers more extensively. Distributors would also have to release such movies at dates that are more favorable. Given the current evidence, however, shifting priorities in such a way would be risky. After all, movies that involve individuals that distributors have worked with previously are currently generating higher revenues. It is thus possible that such movies are of higher quality. Trying out alternative approaches would then generate lower revenues. Suspecting this, distributors might avoid experimentation with alternative approaches.[2]

SOURCES OF INCIDENTAL EXPERIMENTATION

Reasonable managers limit experimentation with alternative approaches when current performance is satisfactory. It follows that it will be managers who are inclined to make unreasonable decisions, or forced by stakeholders to make unreasonable decisions, who are likely to discover the potential value of alternative approaches (Denrell and March 2001; Denrell et al. 2003).

The government and other stakeholders can force organizations to adopt alternative practices. If the government forces a manager to adopt an approach the manager believes is inferior, the manager may sometimes discover that the consequences were not as bad as the manager thought (Denrell 2005). Sometimes the manager may even discover that the new approach is superior. An interesting example of this occurred when legislators forced the University of Texas Medical School to enlarge its class size from 150 to 200 students (Dawes 1994). The medical school typically invited 800 students to come to interviews. Based on the interviews, the school ranked all 800 students and selected the best 150 students. One year, the legislator forced the medical school to admit 50 additional students. To handle this, the school had to admit 50 students among those that had performed the worst on the interviews (the hospital had ranked these students between 700 and 800). Nevertheless, these students did as well in school and afterwards as the other students. They received similar grades, similar jobs, and similar evaluations after their first year in residency. Thus, it seemed like the interview process, as a selection device, was a complete waste of time. The hospital only found out about this because the legislation forced the hospital to admit students the hospital believed were inferior.

Non-economic motives provide another source of deviations from efficiency concerns that can stimulate discoveries of the economic value of alternative practice. For example, managers might adopt fashionable organizational practices without much regard for their efficiency implications (Abrahamson 1996). It is possible that such managers will discover that the practice they adopted is more efficient than established practices. The managers would not have made this discovery if they had evaluated the practice only based on its estimated contribution to efficiency (Denrell and March 2001).

More generally, ideology is a source of incidental experimentation. Individuals embracing ideological beliefs are typically willing to experiment with alternatives that are consistent with their ideologies but seem inferior to most. Ideologues may also persist with new approaches even if the initial results are poor. In this sense, ideology provides a shield against reason and efficiency concerns (Hirschman 1967; Denrell and March 2001). The Polish philosopher Lezek Kolakowski, made a similar point when he noted that ideology acts like

... a Fata Morgana which makes beautiful lands arise before the eyes of the members of a caravan and thus increases their efforts to the point where, in spite of all their sufferings, they reach the next tiny waterhole. Had such tempting mirages not appeared, the exhausted caravan would inevitably have perished in the sandstorms, bereft of hope. (Kolakowski 1961: 127–8, translated in Hirschman 1967: 32)

This suggests that ideologically motivated individuals and organizations will be more likely to explore new approaches and to persist with them long enough to discover their potential advantages, if any. Fanatical individuals and organizations, driven by a logic of ideological appropriateness rather than by a logic of consequences (March 1994), will be more likely to persist in exploring alternative approaches that are consistent with their ideology but initially generate poor performance. They will also be more likely to persist with alternatives that turn out to be false hopes. However, since they are more likely to explore alternatives that seem poor to others, they will sometimes be the first to discover valuable innovations.

CONCLUSION

Organizations learn from experience (Cyert and March 1963; Nelson and Winter 1982; Levitt and March 1988; Huber 1991; Miner and Mezias 1996). Some researchers have suggested that such organizational learning will eventually eliminate false causal beliefs (Friedman 1953). Other researchers have emphasized that bounded rational individuals will often fail to learn from experience (Brehmer 1980; Nisbett and Ross 1980; Levinthal and March 1981; Gilovich 1991; Dawes 1994). The perspective on organizational learning sketched in this chapter suggests a different view on why and when organizations will persist in using suboptimal practices.

Organizations may engage in less than optimal practices because those practices are spuriously associated with high performance. This is not necessarily an indication of stupidity or cognitive biases. Even if managers followed an optimal policy of learning, they may fail to test the counter-factual, because experimentation with alternative practices is costly. By examining the conditions under which such superstitious behavior is likely to occur, I have tried to develop a theory of organizational superstitions. I have also suggested hypotheses about when organizations will discover the value of alternative approaches, through incidental experimentation.

Practically, this perspective suggests that managers or researchers should not view experience as a source of wisdom. Consultants, business students, and researchers often view experienced executives as reservoirs of insight. However, given the scope for spurious correlation in organizations and the limits of experimentation, practical experience does not necessarily produce insight into causal relations. Rather, experience produces a set of satisfactory rules of thumb. Typically, these fail to identify the precise nature of causal links. However, such identification may not be necessary in order to produce adequate performance. Identifying causal links may simply be a too costly task for managers to engage in. Managers should leave the task of identifying causal links to individuals and organizations with little concern for current performance, such as academics and universities.

ENDNOTES

1 However, a colleague of mine once remarked that it is possible that the members of this tribe do us all a big favor.
2 Sorenson and Waguespack (2006) find that controlling for the money spent on marketing and the release date, movies involving unknown actors and producers actually generate more revenue. Such estimates may not convince distributors, however, because the estimates rely on statistical assumptions that may or may not be correct.

REFERENCES

ABRAHAMSON, E. (1996). 'Management Fashions.' *Academy of Management Review,* 21: 254–85.

ARTHUR, B. W. (1989). 'Competing Technologies, Increasing Returns, and Lock-in by Historical Events.' *Economic Journal,* 99: 116–31.

BELLMAN, R. (1956). 'A Problem in the Sequential Design of Experiments.' *Sankhya,* 16: 221–9.

BERRY, D. A. and FRISTEDT, B. (1985). *Bandit Problems.* London: Chapman and Hall.

BREHMER, B. (1980). 'In One Word: Not From Experience.' *Acta Psychologica,* 45: 223–41.

BREZZI, M. and LAI, T. L. (2000). 'Incomplete Learning from Endogenous Data in Dynamic Allocation.' *Econometrica,* 68: 1511–16.

COHEN, M. and MARCH, J. (1986). *Leadership and Ambiguity* (2nd edn.). Boston: Harvard Business School Press.

CYERT, R. D. and MARCH, J. G. (1963). *A Behavioral Theory of the Firm.* Englewood Cliffs, NJ: Prentice-Hall.

DAWES, R. (1994). *House of Cards: Psychology and Psychotherapy Built on Myth.* New York: Free Press.

DEGROOT, M. H. (1970). *Optimal Statistical Decisions.* New York: McGraw-Hill.

DENRELL, J. (2003). 'Vicarious Learning, Under-Sampling of Failure, and the Myths of Management.' *Organization Science,* 14/3: 227–43.

—— (2005). 'Why Most People Disapprove of Me: Experience Sampling in Impression Formation.' *Psychological Review,* 112/4: 951–78.

—— (2007). 'Adaptive Learning and Risk Taking.' *Psychological Review,* 114/1: 177–87.

—— MARCH, J. G. (2001). 'Adaptation as Information Restriction: The Hot Stove Effect.' *Organization Science,* 12/5: 523–38.

—— FANG C., and WINTER, S. (2003). 'The Economics of Strategic Opportunity.' *Strategic Management Journal,* 24/10: 977–90.

EINHORN, H. J. (1986). 'Accepting Error in Order to Make Less Error.' *Journal of Personality Assessment,* 50/3: 387–95.

EINHORN, H. J. and HOGARTH, R. M. (1978). 'Confidence in Judgement: Persistence of the Illusion of Validity.' *Psychological Review,* 85: 395–416.

FRIEDMAN, M. (1953). 'The Methodology of Positive Economics.' *Essays in Positive Economics.* Chicago, IL: Chicago University Press.

FURUSTEN, S. (1999). *Popular Management Books.* London: Routledge.

GARVIN, D. A. (2000). *Learning in Action.* Boston, MA: Harvard Business School Press.

GILOVICH, T. (1991). *How We Know What isn't So.* New York: Free Press.

HARRISON, R. J. and MARCH, J. G. (1984). 'Decision-Making and Postdecision Surprise.' *Administrative Science Quarterly,* 29: 26–42.

HIRSCHMAN, A. O. (1967). *Development Projects Observed.* Washington, DC: Brookings Institution.

HOLLAND, J. H. (1975). *Adaptation in Natural and Artificial Systems.* Cambridge, MA: MIT Press.

HUBER, G. P. (1991). 'Organizational Learning: The Contributing Processes and the Literatures.' *Organization Science,* 2/1: 88–115.

KAHNEMAN, D. and TVERSKY, A. (1973). 'On the Psychology of Prediction,' *Psychological Review,* 80: 237–51.

KLAYMAN, J. and HA, Y.-W. (1987). 'Confirmation, Disconfirmation, and Information in Hypothesis Testing.' *Psychological Review,* 94/2: 211–28.

KILLEEN, P. R. (1977). 'Superstition: A Matter of Bias, not Detectability.' *Science*, 199: 88–90.

—— (1982). 'Learning as Causal Inference,' in M. L. Commons and J. A. Nevin (eds.), *Quantitative Analyses of Behavior: Discriminative Properties of Reinforcement Schedules.* Cambridge, MA: Ballinger, 89–112.

KOLAKOWSKI, L. (1961). *Die Mensch One Alternative.* Munich: R. Piper.

LAVE, C. A. and MARCH, J. G. (1975). *An Introduction to Models in the Social Sciences.* New York: Harper and Row.

LEVINTHAL, D. A. and MARCH, J. G. (1981). 'A Model of Adaptive Organizational Search.' *Journal of Economic Behavior and Organization*, 2: 307–33.

LEVITT, B. and MARCH, J. G. (1988). 'Organizational Learning.' *Annual Review of Sociology*. 14: 319–40.

LOUNAMAA, P. and MARCH, J. G. (1987). 'Adaptive Coordination of a Learning Team.' *Management Science*, 33/1: 107–23.

MARCH, J. G. (1991). 'Exploration and Exploitation in Organizational Learning.' *Organization Science*, 2: 71–87.

—— (1994). *A Primer on Decision Making.* New York: Free Press.

MEYER, R. J. and SHI, Y. (1995). 'Sequential Choice Under Ambiguity: Intuitive Solutions to the Armed-Bandit Problem.' *Management Science*, 41/5: 817–34.

MINER, A. S. and MEZIAS, S. J. (1996). 'Ugly Duckling No More: Pasts and Futures of Organizational Learning Research.' *Organization Science*, 7/1: 88–99.

NELSON, R. R. and WINTER, S. G. (1982). *An Evolutionary Theory of Economic Change.* Cambridge, MA: Harvard University Press.

NISBETT, R. E. and ROSS, L. (1980). *Human Inference: Strategies and Shortcomings of Social Judgment.* Englewood Cliffs, NJ: Prentice-Hall.

ONO, K. (1987). 'Superstitious Behavior in Humans.' *Journal of the Experimental Analysis of Behavior*, 47: 261–71.

ROTSCHILD, M. (1974). 'A Two-Armed Bandit Theory of Market Pricing.' *Journal of Economic Theory*, 9: 185–202.

SCHAFFNER, P. E. (1985). 'Specious Learning About Reward and Punishment.' *Journal of Personality and Social Psychology*, 48: 1377–86.

SKINNER, B. F. (1948). '"Superstition" in Pigeons.' *Journal of Experimental Psychology*, 38: 168–72.

SORENSON, O. and WAGUESPACK, D. (2006). 'Social Structure and Exchange: Self-Confirming Dynamics in Hollywood.' *Administrative Science Quarterly*, 51/4: 560–89.

SUTTON, R. S. and BARTO, A. G. (1998). *Reinforcement Learning: An Introduction.* Cambridge, MA: MIT Press.

THOMPSON, W. R. (1933). 'On the Likelihood that One Unknown Probability Exceeds Another in View of the Evidence of Two Samples.' *Biometrika*, 25: 285–94.

VYSE, S. A. (1997). 'Believing in Magic: The Psychology of Superstition.' Oxford: Oxford University Press.

WINTER, S. (2000). 'The Satisficing Principle in Capability Learning.' *Strategic Management Journal*, 21/Special Issue: 981–96.

15

ON THE IMPLICATIONS OF BEHAVIORAL DECISION THEORY FOR MANAGERIAL DECISION MAKING: CONTRIBUTIONS AND CHALLENGES

ZUR SHAPIRA

INTRODUCTION

THE roots of behavioral decision theory (Kahneman 1991) include Edwards' (1954) studies of probability revision, Meehl's (1954) analysis of clinical judgment, Luce and Raiffa's (1957) landmark essay on game theory and Simon's (1947, 1955) treatise on decision making in organizations. The last 50-plus years of research on the psychology of probability estimation and choice behavior led to the development of the "heurisitcs and biases" paradigm in the study of judgment under uncertainty (Kahneman et al. 1982), as well as to the development of prospect theory and framing in individual choice behavior (Kahneman and Tversky 1984). Research in the behavioral decision theory tradition has relied mainly on lab experiments, and focused on the cognitive aspects of individual choice behavior. Over the past 50 years, behavioral decision theory has produced a remarkable set of findings on individual choice behavior although it neglected the effects of social and emotional factors as well as the conflict inherent in decisions (Kahneman 1991).

Over the same period, the pioneering work by Simon (1947) has led to a paradigmatic development in organization theory. The Carnegie approach led to numerous studies that examined the role of information processing and decision making as the basic elements in analyzing decision making in and by organizations. Two books from the golden period of the Carnegie school, March and Simon's (1958) *Organizations*, and Cyert and March's (1963) *A Behavioral Theory of the Firm*, are landmarks in the field of organization theory. In the period that followed the Carnegie School era, scholars who developed formal theories of organizations, with the exception of March, did not treat decision making as the central element of their framework. For example, Thompson's (1967) influential book on organization theory had many propositions related to decision making by organizations but without a focus on information processing as a unifying concept. Other research trends were pursued by various scholars on topics related to organizational decision making, such as the analysis of power (Pfeffer 1981), escalation processes (Staw 1981), commitment (Salancik 1977), and sensemaking (Weick 1994) to name a few. March subsequently extended the analyses of his 1958 and 1963 books on organizational decision making in several directions, such as alternative notions of rationality (March 1978), analysis of decisions as random processes or "garbage cans" (Cohen et al. 1972), and the role that attention allocation, search, rules, obligations, and myths play in organizational decision making (March 1988, 1994).

The relations between the two traditions are intriguing. Simon's initial work served as an impetus for further studies both in the field of behavioral decision theory and organizational decision making. Even though organizational processes are not the mere aggregation of individual activities, Simon treated them similarly and his approach appeared to be relevant for both levels of analysis. As March (1978) noted, "He [Simon] obscured a distinction one might make between individual and organizational decision making proposing for the most part the general ideas for both." Yet, despite the fact that the two traditions share common roots the research agendas of behavioral decision theory and organizational decision making in the last 50 years or so reflect few similarities and many differences. This chapter discusses the implications of behavioral decision theory to managerial decision making by looking at the contributions made and the challenges its findings pose in attempting to contribute more to decision making in and by organizations.

Behavioral Decision Theory: Its Goals and Some Major Achievements

The main development of behavioral decision theory rose from the collaboration of Daniel Kahneman and Amos Tversky in the 1970s. Three classical articles on heuristics (Tversky and Khaneman 1974), prospect theory (Kahneman and Tversky 1979), and framing (Tversky and Kahneman 1981) mark the major impact of their joint work. While the original work on heuristics and biases had a large impact on research in fields such as marketing and social psychology, it was the publication of prospect theory that caught the attention of economists. Initially prospect theory met with strong resistance but evidence accumulated in support of prospect theory over the years and economists acknowledged the theory and the paradigm of behavioral decision theory, eventually leading to the winning of the Nobel Prize in Economic Sciences by Kahneman in 2002.

This chapter does not survey behavioral decision theory because extensive reviews of the literature exist that describe the major findings of this research field (see Payne et al. 1992; Mellers et al. 1998). The heuristics and biases paradigm shows that in estimating probabilities and frequencies under uncertainty, people use heuristics (rules of thumb) such as availability, representativeness, and anchoring and adjustment. The use of such heuristics is natural for human beings because in many cases such as the prediction of future stock prices people do not have all the information needed to make proper estimates according to established quantitative models. In other situations, such as in weather forecasting, the information is so vast that people cannot process all the available information and hence should rely on decision aids or refrain from making predictions. If people are still required or interested in making predictions, they often look for short cuts to help them come up with estimates. Although there are arguments that people are poor users of quantitative modeling (Paulos 1990) the argument of the heuristics and biases paradigm is not that people are inherently stupid, a comment that was made often to sort of mock the work in behavioral decision theory (see Kahneman 2003a). Rather, the argument is that in using heuristics people make judgments that end up being at odds with predictions of normative decision models such as Bayes rule. If people deviate from Bayes rule, they commit a bias; and if one equates the use of this rule with rationality then one opens the door for a discussion as to whether the empirical findings of the heuristics and biases paradigm show that people are not rational. It is important to note though that the use of heuristics is a natural element of human judgment, and judgments are considered biased only in comparison against a certain normative model such as Bayes rule.

It is true that testing the validity of Bayes rule as describing judgment was the major building block leading to the development of the heuristics and biases paradigm. Edwards (1954), one of the pioneers of the field used the Bayesian paradigm as a cornerstone of his research on human inference in the context of judgment under uncertainty. Researchers who use the Bayesian paradigm argue that people can hold different initial estimates of future events to start with but updating them in light of additional data needs to follow Bayes rule. Since it sets a normative rule of updating beliefs, many researchers consider it to be a fundamental requirement of rationality. The failure of people to use Bayes rule properly was a major force that helped push the development of behavioral decision theory (Kahneman 2003a), but the purpose of the paradigm was not to demonstrate that people are not intuitive statisticians, as was the argument of Peterson and Beach (1967), but to learn how people actually come up with estimates of the likelihood of uncertain events.

When faced with the initial gap between predictions according to Bayes rule and the actual predictions made by participants in numerous experiments (cf., Edwards 1954), decision theorists argued that people should be taught the rule and then those gaps would disappear. The truth was far from that since even trained professionals make consistent statistical inference errors (Tversky and Kahneman 1971). In attempting to account for the reasons why people do not follow Bayes rule, researchers working in the behavioral decision theory paradigm set out to find what models people were actually using in estimating the probability of future events. The idea was therefore, to develop a descriptive model of human judgment. The thought was that when such a descriptive model becomes available, comparing its aspects with those of normative models would help develop prescriptive procedures for improving judgment. Researchers in behavioral decision theory felt strongly that fighting erroneous judgment by merely teaching people the rules of normative decision theory would not work, but that the actual comparison of normative and descriptive approaches may yield a valuable prescriptive approach. Figure 15.1 presents this idea.

Note that the change program adopted by behavioral decision theory researchers was not different from approaches that other change agents were taking in say medicine. It is clear that helping people quit smoking or fight obesity is not easily achieved by merely providing people with information that demonstrates, very clearly, that smoking and obesity are bad habits, even if such information are supported by a lot of data. Rather, understanding the reasons that lead people to smoke or over eat, namely, building a descriptive model of their behavior is necessary in order to develop prescriptions that will help people give up those habits.

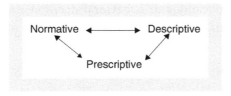

Fig. 15.1 Three models involved with changing decision behavior.

The above point is of importance in understanding that the major goal of behavioral decision theory was to construct a descriptive model of human judgment and decision making, that is, to find how people go about developing estimates and making decisions, and not to come up with a list of biases. True, in many cases where one develops a new scientific paradigm, which contrasts with findings of an accepted paradigm (i.e., Bayes rule) demonstrating biases with respect to the reining paradigm help highlight the uniqueness of the new paradigm. Nevertheless, those researchers in management who believe that behavioral decision theory intends merely to highlight the biases in judgment and decision making are simply wrong. While the demonstration of biases captured a lot of attention and helped muster more support for the growing field in its battles with existing strong paradigms (such as the expected utility paradigm) the primary goal of behavioral decision theory was and still is the attempt to arrive at a descriptive model of human judgment. The comparison of such a model with normative decision models would help the development of prescriptive procedures that will help improve human judgment and decision making.

In brief, the main areas of research in behavioral decision theory include judgment, choice, and decision. The first decision heuristic was most likely Simon's (1955) satisficing principle; new heuristics defined by Tversky and Kahneman (1974) include: availability, representativeness (see also Kahneman and Frederick 2002), and anchoring and adjustment. Over the years additional heuristics were identified, such as the hindsight heuristic (Fischhoff 1975), the simulation heuristic (Tversky and Kahneman 1982), and the affect heuristic (Finucane et al. 2000). Concepts pertaining to biases people use or are prone to include several others, such as the confirmation trap and the overconfidence bias (see Bazerman 2005 for a review of these and other relevant biases). In research on choice behavior and decision making, behavioral decision theory had to battle and is still battling very strong frameworks, such as the expected utility paradigm. Today, prospect theory and the concepts of framing and loss aversion are the major building blocks for an alternative framework to the expected utility paradigm.

To examine the implications of behavioral decision theory to organizational decision making, the main feature of the latter field need to be specified.

Some Aspects of Managerial Decision Making

There are a few characteristics that exemplify the nature of organizational decision making which differs from the phenomenon of individual decision making as studied in lab experiments (cf., Shapira 1997). First, unlike most lab studies of individual decision making, *ambiguity* is pervasive in organizational decisions. Information in organizational decisions is often ambiguous, and there is ambiguity about interpreting the history of decisions. In contrast, in most experimental studies of individual decision making in the behavioral decision theory tradition, participants are presented with clear information, even if it is posted in the form of a probability distribution, and often with monetary payoffs that "direct" their preferences.

Second, decision making within and by organizations is embedded in a *longitudinal* context. That is, participants in organizational decision making are a part of ongoing processes. Even if they do not take on active roles in all phases of a decision, they are a part of decision processes and their consequences. Decisions in organizations are made in a longitudinal manner, and commitment may be more important in some of these processes than judgmental accuracy. This aspect calls for a history dependent analysis of organizational decision making, and highlights the role of sensemaking in organizational life. In addition, the longitudinal nature of many managerial decisions suggests that managers often participate only in certain parts of a decision process but not in others (cf., Cohen et al. 1972). In contrast, most lab studies of individual decision making are conducted in artificial settings (i.e., laboratory experiments) that are not connected to the participants' ongoing activities.

Thirdly, *incentives* play an important role in organizational decision making. Incentives, penalties, and their ramifications are real and may have long lasting effects (Shapira 1995). These effects are even stronger because of the longitudinal nature of decisions in organizational contexts. Furthermore, survival is a real aspect of life in organizations, but it is almost impossible to reproduce a feeling of survival in an experimental setting. One implication of the quest for survival is that managers may be more concerned with their ability to justify their decisions than with arriving at the best quality decisions. In contrast, incentives used in experimental studies of individual choice behavior are meager and do not have a potential for lingering effects. This does not mean that incentives eliminate judgmental biases; in fact they may even aggravate them. However, considerations of incentives and penalties are very salient in organizations, they command managerial attention, and may have a larger impact on decisions in comparison with cognitive aspects of the decision process.

Fourthly, many executives especially in middle levels of management make *repeated* decisions on the same issues and within the same domain. Consider for instance a bank loan officer who reviews requests for consumer car loans. Such an officer may develop a sense of a proper use of skills (which may be erroneous) and a sense of having control on the situation (which may also be faulty). The beliefs of having control and using one's skills are pervasive in managerial thinking about risk taking (Shapira 1995). In addition, several repeated decisions such as decisions on new loans are made by rule following rather than by pure information processing modes (March 1994). The idea of a "decision" in this context may take on a different meaning.

Fifthly, *conflict* is pervasive in managerial decision making. Many times, power considerations, and agenda setting determine actual decisions rather than calculations based on the decisions' parameters (cf., Cohen et al. 1972). Further, organizations are hierarchical systems where people report to superiors. The nature of authority relations may have a large impact on the way decisions are made in organizations bringing into the process a different layer relating to the fact that organizations are inherently political systems.

IMPLICATIONS OF BEHAVIORAL DECISION THEORY FOR MANAGERIAL AND ORGANIZATIONAL DECISION MAKING

Researchers in managerial and organizational decision making who do not subscribe to behavioral decision theory raise two major criticisms against behavioral decision theory. The first claim is that behavioral decision theory deals almost exclusively with individuals and the second is that its findings are based on laboratory experiments with undergraduate students and the generalizability of such findings to real life decision making, and in particular in organizations, is questionable.

These criticisms have their merit. While individuals such as CEOs make many decisions in organizations, committees or groups of decision makers also make a significant chunk of organizational decisions. The argument therefore is that behavioral decision theory research is not relevant to many managerial decision making situations. On the other hand, there are derivations from prospect theory for example that hold very well in describing decisions in real business contexts. For instance, the well-known disposition effect (Shefrin and Statman 1985; Shapira and Venezia 2001) points at an inclination of investors to sell stocks which are considered to be winners early, and hold on to losing stocks much longer. This is a direct corollary from the principle of loss aversion saying that the absolute pain from certain losses is larger than the absolute joy associated with identical gains. Numerous lab experiments as well as data on actual purchase and sale of stocks in different stock markets demonstrate this argument. However, there are hardly any studies that examine whether the same effect influences committees and groups of managers.

The problem of generalizability of lab experiments' findings to real life situations is also not clear and requires more elaboration. To begin with, it is worthwhile to note that the so called "Kahneman and Tversky experiments" are not really experiments in the strict sense of the word but are mainly demonstrations. It is not that they did not run proper experiments, they ran many of them, but much of the data presented in their articles are simple demonstrations that gain their strength from being simple and realistic so that everyone can relate to from their own real life experience. They are not tasks that can be carried only in the lab. The questions that Kahneman and Tversky gave their participants can be easily generalized to other individuals. Yet not much has been done with respect to generalizing such questions to groups of people such as managers who are holding a meeting, say, to decide whether to invest in a new plant. Such study questions are likely to affect managerial decisions in a similar way but demonstrations in empirical research will help set the stage for it.

In the next section, the contributions of behavioral decision theory to managerial decision making are demonstrated with regards to forecasting and planning.

CONTRIBUTIONS OF BEHAVIORAL DECISION THEORY: PREDICTION AND PLANNING

A famous Chinese proverb says that forecasting is difficult especially with regard to the future. However, in business organizations forecasting demand for products and services is necessary for planning future operations and schedules. In addition, in variety of engineering projects, where one stage depends on the completion of a prior stage, planning is important for scheduling the following phases as well as for budgeting decisions. It is commonplace that engineering projects often end up in time overruns that lead to cost overruns. The question as to why companies and governments continue to fund projects based on estimates given to them is intriguing. Recent studies show that despite the need for more accurate estimates of engineering design costs, especially in competitive bidding for fixed price design contracts, estimates are still off the mark (Hudgins and Lavalle 1995). There are many large scale projects that get continued funding despite such problems (Eurochannel and the Denver Airport are such examples). In other cases, such as the Texas Supercollider, immense projected costs lead to their cancellation.

Companies who bid for projects tend to submit rosy forecasts with underestimates of completion time and costs so as to increase their chances of winning the bidding process. However, this motivational bias can be minimized if those who grant the projects are aware of this bias and engage in a careful due diligence. In addition, they better set some schedule of fines to make sure that companies who make rosy forecasts regarding project duration think harder about not deviating from such schedules. Regardless of this motivational bias, cognitive aspects play a major role in making forecasts and the longer the project duration, the larger the bias is likely to be. Some cognitive and organizational aspects involved in the prediction of long term engineering construction projects are described in the next section.

Cognitive Aspects of Prediction

The question about forecasting in construction engineering is reminiscent of a similar puzzle about entrepreneurship. The US Small Business Administration (1991) claimed that about 95 percent of small businesses fail within five years of their founding. When asked why entrepreneurs still start new businesses, the answers provided are generally that entrepreneurs suffer from cognitive biases (Kahneman and Lovallo 1993) or that they are risk-seeking, as they are described in the economics literature.

The seeds of the psychological study of prediction were laid in Kahneman and Tversky's (1973, 1979b) work on prediction and on the "the planning fallacy," and were elaborated on in a beautiful article by Kahneman and Lovallo (1993) who pointed out the difficulties that managers have in making predictions. The tendency to focus on a particular set of variables was defined by Kahneman and Lovallo as the tendency to take the "inside view." They argued that in adopting this view, managers usually end up with rosy forecasts and that the remedy should be a focus on the "outside view," that is, on the aggregate data that can be collected to determine the statistical base rate for the question at hand (see Lovallo and Kahneman 2006).

Busenitz and Barney (1994), suggested that the overconfidence bias is the more likely answer to the entrepreneurial puzzle, and Hayward et al. (2006). acknowledged overconfidence as a major concept in developing a new, "hubris" theory of entrepreneurship.

Managerial Predictions

Research in management has also pointed out that managers have a hard time making accurate predictions and that their perceptions about several elements involved with forecasts are flawed. Mezias and Starbuck (2003) ran a few studies to examine the accuracy of managerial perceptions regarding prior year's results such as sales of their own business units in the prior year and found out that managers had erroneous responses to such questions. They commented though that managers are aware of the fact that they miss many data points that eventually lead them to make such errors. Mezias and Starbuck argue however that studying managers' perceptions with large samples using statistical measures may be misleading because situations where managers' inaccurate perceptions lead to serious consequences are rare (see also Maule and Hodgkinson 2003; Winter 2003). The next section discusses predictions in one such context.

Predictions, Time and Cost Overruns in Grand Scale Engineering Projects

When people make predictions about long-term projects, overconfidence may run high but it is hard to imagine that all members of a certain organization are biased in the same way. Indeed, one characteristic of groups and organizations is that there is a diversity of opinions on many issues, and predicted durations of projects is likely to be one of them. In analyzing grand scale engineering projects, Shapira and Berndt (1997) analyzed the time and cost overruns of three types of grand scale projects: bridges, skyscrapers, and canals. In particular, they compared the Brooklyn and the Golden Gate bridges, the Empire State building with the World Trade Center and the Erie and Cape Cod canals. They did not select a random sample but picked up projects that ended up as either being over- or underbudget to illustrate a framework that combined cognitive and organizational perspectives. Of course, they did not expect forecasts to be on target but the fact that the completion of huge projects such as the Golden Gate Bridge, the Empire State building, and the Erie canal were on budget, suggest that one cannot focus solely on overconfidence in explaining the deviation from target schedules in the completion of large scale projects. Part of the success of the completion of the Empire State building and the Golden Gate Bridge is the fact that they were constructed immediately after the great depression and labor was much cheaper than anticipated. In addition, many innovations were applied in the construction of these three grand scale projects that eventually helped their completion on target and even under budget, as was the case of the Golden Gate bridge.

The analysis of these cases does not imply that overconfidence does not play a role but that there are organizational mechanisms that may help rein in overconfidence and may correct the errors it generates. Shapira and Berndt (1997) based their framework on Kahneman and Lovallo's (1993) framework as well as March and Shapira's (1992) risk-taking model. Their thesis was that different champions take on the lead role in different periods of an engineering grand scale project. These roles include the initiator, the person in charge of construction, and the person in charge of maintenance of the completed project. Shapira and Berndt (1997) argued that each of these champions may suffer from overconfidence but they see themselves as champions who have a mission to pursue their project in a politically charged decision-making environment. Thus, in addition to over-confidence, the tendency of managers to be overfocused on their mission may also constitute a bias. Shapira and Berndt (1997) developed a framework based on the ideas of overconfidence, narrow framing, and the use of the inside perspective by champions who anticipate that their opponents would use the outside perspective. According to their analysis, the degree of success of such projects may vary with time, hence people may evaluate the same project as successful at some points in time and as failure at others as has been the case with the evaluation of projects such as the Sydney Opera house (Hall 1980).

The above analysis suggests that behavioral decision theory can contribute to the analysis of managerial decision making. It is not that behavioral decision theory fully explains managerial decision processes but its robust findings regarding such constructs as overconfidence, the tendency to use narrow frames and the inside perspective in forecasting, can be combined with the political aspects of organizational decision making that eventually yield a framework with greater explanatory power.

CHALLENGES: DECISION MAKING IN LOW PROBABILITY, HIGH CONSEQUENCE EVENTS

The previous section dealt with cases in which the implications of behavioral decision theory contributed to the understanding of managerial decision making in organizational contexts. This section describes a different situation, one where judgmental heuristics and biases cannot explain the fiascos that occur in situations of high consequence, low probability events (cf., Kunreuther et al. 1997). Such situations pose a challenge to the ability of behavioral decision theory to contribute to the understanding of organizational decision making because context variables play a more central role than judgmental variables.

Several disasters have been analyzed from organizational perspectives including the Three Miles Island accident (Perrow 1984), the Challenger (Starbuck and

Milliken 1986), and the Columbia (Starbuck and Farjoun 2005) disasters. Most of those analyses looked at organizational and systemic levels of analyses varying from the effects of managerial attention to goals (Buljan and Shapira 2005) to system wide aspects of the organization as a whole (cf., Starbuck and Farjoun 2005).

To compare levels of analyses employed by behavioral decision theory and organizational decision making in the context of disasters, consider the case of hurricanes. Those are one of nature's most powerful forces as demonstrated by Hurricane Katrina that hit the Gulf States on August 29, 2005, and did more damage than any previous weather event anywhere (*Economist* 2006). In battling the severe consequences of hurricanes, sophisticated instruments are being continuously constructed and improved. While the increase in precision of estimates helps forecasters and officials prepare for dealing with hurricanes, the issue of risk management is very complex and involves many additional aspects. Numerous studies concentrate on improving forecasts of the path and intensity of a storm. The goal is to develop a forecasting system that integrates previously independent models for predicting wind, wave, and storm surge, and will allow officials to decide, based on the five-day forecast, how to appropriately evacuate the public far in advance of the storm and with ample evacuation time. Note that currently, the National Hurricane Center issues a hurricane warning for a community 24 hours before it expects the storm to hit land. However, the time to evacuate a large community, such as Miami, takes 84 hours. Hence, officials often have to make evacuation decisions prior to an official hurricane warning, while basing such evacuation decisions on storm forecasts that are extremely unreliable. This was evident in August 2004 when the NHC predicted that Hurricane Charley would make land fall near Tampa, but Charley quickly intensified and changed its course to a more easterly path. While officials decided to evacuate most of Tampa, the storm eventually hit land near Fort Myers, catching many residents off guard in the area that had not chosen to evacuate.

Chinander and Shapira (2005) analyzed the evacuation decision process from the perspective of the top authority in a county, who is the person deciding whether to issue an evacuation order in Florida. Consider the case of the mayor of Miami who in 1999 was pondering whether to call for an evacuation when Hurricane Floyd approached Miami, and was 100 miles off shore. The National Hurricane Center advised the mayor that Floyd would turn north and would not hit Miami. Nevertheless, the potential devastation of a category 4 hurricane hitting Miami were so enormous that the mayor decided to call for a partial evacuation. Eventually the hurricane did not hit land in Florida; it turned north where it caused a lot of damage.

Chinander and Shapira (2005) used signal detection theory to describe the potential errors confronting a decision maker who is facing uncertainty. The model was developed in electrical engineering and Einhorn and Hogarth (1978) utilized it to examine personnel selection decisions, and Lampel and Shapira (2001) used it to analyze strategic surprises between buyers and suppliers. While researchers developed the original model to help decision makers make inferences about moving targets detected on Sonar or radar screens, it has since then been utilized in many domains (see Swets et al. 2000). Chinander and Shapira focused on the potential costs associated with type I and type II errors a mayor faces in deciding whether to evacuate or not. While the default of calling for an evacuation is the preferred call, since the ultimate goal is saving life, there are increasing costs associated with such decisions if it turns out to be a false alarm. It has been rumored that within the two days before Katrina hit New Orleans, Max Mayfield the head of the National Hurricane Center called Ray Nagins, the Mayor of New Orleans, and Kathleen Blanco, the Louisiana Governor, and told them that the chances of Katrina hitting New Orleans were very high and that they should take all necessary precautions. However, in the aftermath of Katrina, it appears that one of the reasons that prevented Nagins from issuing a mandatory evacuation was his worry that the business community would sue him if the evacuation turned out to be a false alarm.

If this was the case in the wake of Hurricane Katrina, imagine what would be the situation should a more "normal" hurricane have led a mayor to call for an evacuation, and later turned out to be a false alarm. When Hurricane Ernesto approached Florida in August 2006, people prepared for its consequences. After it was gone, leaving much smaller damage than anticipated, Broward's county residents were looking to get the federal government to pay for their county's and all of South Florida's preparation costs, which amounted to a figure somewhere in the region of US$10–15 million (Schultz 2006).

In comparing the role of judgmental errors and organization wide factors in situations of low probability, high consequence events, it appears that the latter carry more weight in determining the eventual outcomes. Furthermore, progress in the technology of forecasting of hurricanes is enormous and even though hurricanes are largely unpredictable, the National Hurricane Center is issuing more accurate predictions every year. It appears that the disaster following Hurricane Katrina was caused by faulty organizational decision processes than by erroneous predictions. As Chinander and Shapira (2005) argue, the costs associated with making either a type I or type II errors in such situations can be enormous and they are going up all the time since the population of southern Florida is increasing and the near future is holding increased hurricane activity in comparison to the last 40 years or so (*Economist* 2006). It is not that predictions play no role in such situations, they definitely do, but the National Hurricane Center is relying much less on human intuition and much more on instrumentation, which is not susceptible to judgmental biases. Furthermore, even though the particular location where a hurricane makes a land fall is a low probability event, the National Hurricane Center has many data points from the past to create more accurate models that will help make better predictions about hurricanes. Current research on human judgment may not be a major factor in helping improve managerial decision making in such situations. To improve our understanding of managerial decision making in low probability, high consequence events research should focus on the many different aspects of organizational decision processes.

CONCLUDING REMARKS

Behavioral decision theory has had a huge impact on the social sciences; it has affected research in social psychology, marketing, economics, and finance. Its contributions to managerial decision making are evident mainly in contexts of prediction (Kahneman and Lovallo 1993) and strategic planning and decision making (Schwenk 1984; Bateman and Zeithaml 1989a, b; Zajac and Bazerman 1991; Das and Teng 1999; Hodgkinson et al. 1999; Maule and Hodgkinson 2002, 2003). It has been lacking in studying the effects of emotions on decisions in organizational contexts, the consideration of motivation and incentives in managerial decision making (cf., Shapira 1981), and the study of group decision making. In looking at the potential cross pollination between the two fields, March and Shapira (1982) noted that the field of organizational decision making can use a variety of findings from behavioral decision theory in its quest to study the role of attention, search, and decision simplifications on managerial decisions. They also suggested that the other direction of learning could also be fruitful if behavioral decision theorists were to look at the issues of conflict, history dependent processes, and the ways managers shape and construct their preferences in organizational settings. The potential cross-pollination between the two fields did not materialize although more behavioral decision theorists are interested in real-life problems and more organization theorists who study managerial decision making are aware of the major findings of behavioral decision theory.

Given the fact that that the two fields share a common root (e.g., Simon's work) the paucity of cross-pollination is intriguing. Why have the two fields failed to produce more joint work? One obstacle has definitely been the methodologies used in their research. Behavioral decision theory was developed in psychology and its findings have mostly been based on lab experiments, while studies of organizational decision making have been carried in field settings. Many researchers in organization theory have long been convinced that one should conduct longitudinal research to understand organizational phenomena and view lab experiments as limited in this respect. In addition, many of them conceive of behavioral decision theory as work done within the rational actor framework, thereby missing a lot of real action that exists in real organizational processes. Furthermore, lab studies appear to some to be based on superficial settings in comparison to the messy but realistic organizational settings. Finally, the notion that most researchers in the area of managerial cognition hold is that cognition should not be limited to the study of statistical reasoning. The pervasive use of ideas such as sensemaking and social construction in organizational studies points at the different emphases of the two fields.

It is interesting to note that some cognitive psychologists are also critical of the fact that studies of cognition focused on calculation more than on interpretation (see, e.g., Lant and Shapira 2001). For example, Jerome Bruner, one of the early and longstanding contributors to the study of human cognition comments that work following the cognitive revolution shifted from studying "... meaning to information, from construction to the processing of information." He added that those are profoundly different matters (1990: 4). Bruner also said that he initially expected that the study of cognition would lead to collaboration between psychology and its sister disciplines in the humanities and social sciences such as anthropology, linguistics, and even law. For him cognition is the study of meaningmaking that must be embedded in the context of culture.

Bruner's words are strong and he claims that the study of cognition has been to some degree a victim of its own success. Even though he does not mention the study of managerial decision making in his essay, it is clear that his ideas have implications for this field as well. The study of organizational decision making has vacillated back and forth from computation to interpretation for a long time. However, as Lant and Shapira (2001) suggested, one needs to look for ways to encourage researchers from these two streams of research to combine forces and examine common questions and issues. Joint work on interpretation and computation may shed more light on major concepts such as ignorance, ambiguity (Shapira 1993; Kunreuther and Meszaros 1997), and meaning, in a way that can prove more beneficial than work undertaken solely within one discipline.

References

BATEMAN, T. S. and ZEITHAML, C. P. (1989a). 'The Psychological Context of Strategic Decisions: A Model and Convergent Experimental Findings.' *Strategic Management Journal*, 10: 59–74.

—— —— (1989b). 'The Psychological Context of Strategic Decisions: A Test of Relevance to Practitioners.' *Strategic Management Journal*, 10: 587–92.

BAZERMAN, M. (2005). *Judgment in Managerial Decision Making* (6th edn.). New York: Wiley.

BRUNER, J. (1990). *Acts of Meaning*. Cambridge, MA: Harvard University Press.

BULJAN, A. and SHAPIRA, Z. (2005). 'Attention to Production Schedule and Safety as Determinants of Risk Taking in NASA's Decision to Launch the Columbia Shuttle,' in

W. H. Starbuck and M. Farjoun (eds.), *Organizations at the Limit: Management Lessons from the Columbia Disaster.* Oxford: Blackwell.

BUSENITZ, L. and BARNEY, J. (1994). 'Biases and Heuristics in Strategic Decision Making: Differences Between Entrepreneurs and Managers in Large Organizations.' *Academy of Management Best Papers Proceedings*, 85–9.

CHINANDER, K. and SHAPIRA, Z. (2005). 'The Hurricane Evacuation Decision Process: Is Strategic Learning Possible?' Paper presented at the Annual Meeting of the European Group on Organization Studies, Berlin.

COHEN, M., MARCH, J., and OLSEN, J. (1972). 'A Garbage Can Model of Organizational Choice.' *Administrative Science Quarterly*, 17: 1–25.

CYERT, R. and MARCH, G. (1963). *A Behavioral Theory of the Firm.* Englewood Cliffs, NJ: Prentice-Hall.

DAS, T. K. and TENG, B.-S. (1999). 'Cognitive Biases and Strategic Decision Processes.' *Journal of Management Studies*, 36: 757–78.

Economist (2006). 'Reaping the Whirlwind: Hurricanes Used to be Thought Unconnected to Climate Change. Now a Link is Emerging.' September 9: 10.

EDWARDS, W. (1954). 'The Theory of Decision Making.' *Psychological Bulletin*, 51: 380–417.

EINHORN, H. and HOGARTH, R. (1978). 'Confidence in Judgment: Persistence of the Illusion of Validity.' *Psychological Review*, 85: 395–416.

FINUCANE, M. L., ALHAKAMI, A., SLOVIC, P., and JOHNSON, S. M. (2000). 'The Affect Heuristic in Judgments of Risks and Benefits.' *Journal of Behavioral Decision Making*, 13/1: 1–17.

FISCHHOFF, B. (1975). 'Hindsight? Foresight: The Effects of Outcome Knowledge on Judgment Under Uncertainty.' *Journal of Experimental Psychology: Human Perception and Performance*, 1: 288–99.

HALL, P. (1980). *Great Planning Disasters.* Berkeley, CA: University of California Press.

HAYWARD, M., SHEPHERD, D., and GRIFFIN, D. (2006). 'A Hubris Theory of Entrepreneurship.' *Management Science*, 52: 160–72.

HILLER, N. and HAMBRICK, D. C. (2005). 'Conceptualizing Executive Hubris: The Role of (Hyper-) Core Self-Evaluations in Strategic Decision-Making.' *Strategic Management Journal*, 26: 297–319.

HODGKINSON, G. P., BOWN, N. J., MAULE, A. J., GLAISTER, K. W., and PEARMAN, A. D. (1999). 'Breaking the Frame: An Analysis of Strategic Cognition and Decision Making Under Uncertainty.' *Strategic Management Journal*, 20: 977–85.

HUDGINS, D. and LAVALLE, P. (1995). 'Estimating Engineering Design Costs.' *Engineering Management Journal*, 7: 17–23.

KAHNEMAN, D. (1991). 'Judgment and Decision Making: A Personal View.' *Psychological Science*, 2: 142–5.

—— (2003a). 'A Perspective on Judgment and Choice: Mapping Bounded Rationality.' *American Psychologist*, 58: 697–720.

—— (2003b). 'A Psychological Perspective on Economics.' *American Economics Review: Papers and Proceedings*, 93: 162–68.

—— FREDERICK, S. (2002). 'Representativeness Revisited: Attribute Substitution in Intuitive Judgment,' in T. Gilovich, D. Griffin, and D. Kahneman (eds.), *Heuristics and Biases: The Psychology of Intuitive Judgment.* New York: Cambridge University Press.

—— LOVALLO, D. (1993). 'Timid Choices and Bold Forecasts: A Cognitive Perspective on Risk Taking.' *Management Science*, 39: 17–31.

—— TVERSKY, A. (1979a). 'Prospect Theory: An Analysis of Decision Under Risk.' *Econometrica*, 47: 263–91.

—— —— (1979b). 'Intuitive Prediction: Biases and Corrective Procedures.' *TIMS Studies in Management Sciences*, 12: 313–27.

—— —— (1982). 'The Simulation Heuristic,' in D. Kahneman, P. Slovic, and A. Tversky (eds.), *Judgment Under Uncertainty: Heuristics and Biases*. New York: Cambridge University Press.

—— —— (1984). 'Choices, Values and Frames.' *American Psychologist*, 39: 341–50.

KAHNEMAN, D., SLOVIC, P., and TVERSKY, A. (1982). *Judgment Under Uncertainty: Heuristics and Biases*. New York: Cambridge University Press.

KUNREUTHER, H. and MESZAROS, J. (1997). 'Organization Choice Under Ambiguity: Decision Making in the Chemical Industry Following Bhopal,' in Z. Shapira (ed.), *Organizational Decision Making*. Cambridge: Cambridge University Press.

LANT, T. K. and SHAPIRA, Z. (2001). 'New Research Directions on Organizational Cognition,' in T. K. Lant and Z. Shapira (eds.), *Organizational Cognition: Computation and Interpretation*. Mahwah, NJ: Erlbaum, 367–76.

LUCE, D. and RAIFFA, H. (1957). *Games and Decisions*. New York: Wiley.

LOVALLO, D. and KAHNEMAN, D. (2003). 'Delusions of Success.' *Harvard Business Review*, July: 29–36.

MARCH, J. (1978). 'Bounded Rationality, Ambiguity, and the Engineering of Choice.' *Bell Journal of Economics*, 9: 588–608.

—— (1988). *Decisions and Organizations*. Oxford: Basil Blackwell.

—— (1994). *A Primer on Decision Making*. New York: Free Press.

—— (1997). 'Understanding How Decisions Happen in Organizations,' in Z. Shapira (ed.), *Organizational Decision Making*. Cambridge: Cambridge University Press.

—— SHAPIRA, Z. (1982). 'Behavioral Decision Theory and Organizational Decision Theory,' in G. Ungson and D. Braunstein (eds.), *New Directions in Decision Making*. Boston, MA: Kent Publishing Co.

—— —— (1987). 'Managerial Perspectives on Risk and Risk Taking.' *Management Science*, 33, 1404–18.

—— —— (1992). 'Variable Risk Preferences and the Focus of Attention.' *Psychological Review*, 99, 172–83.

—— —— (1958). *Organizations*. New York: Wiley.

MAULE, A. J. and HODGKINSON, G. P. (2002). 'Heuristics, Biases and Strategic Decision Making.' *The Psychologist*, 15: 68–71.

—— —— (2003). 'Re-appraising Managers' Perceptual Errors: A Behavioural Decision Making Perspective.' *British Journal of Management*, 14: 33–7.

MEEHL, P. (1954). *Clinical vs. Statistical Prediction: A Theoretical Analysis and a Review of the Evidence*. Minneapolis, MN: University of Minnesota Press.

MELLERS, B., SCHWARTZ, A., and COOKE, A. (1998). 'Judgment and Decision Making.' *Annual Review of Psychology*, 49: 447–77.

MEZIAS, J. and STARBUCK, W. H. (2003). 'Studying the Accuracy of Managers' Perceptions: A Research Odyssey.' *British Journal of Management*, 14: 3–17.

PAULOS, J. (1990). *Innumeracy: Mathematical Illiteracy and its Consequences*. New York: Vintage.

PAYNE, J., BETTMAN, J., and JOHNSON, E. (1992). 'Behavioral Decision Research: A Constructive Processing Perspective.' *Annual Review of Psychology*, 43: 87–131.

PERROW, C. (1984). *Normal Accidents*. New York: Basic Books.

PETERSON, C. and BEACH, L. (1967). 'Man as an Intuitive Statistician.' *Psychological Bulletin*, 68: 29–46.

PFEFFER, J. (1981). *Power in Organizations*. Marshfield, MA: Pitman.

SALANCIK, G. (1977). 'Commitment and Control of Organizational Behavior and Belief,' in B. Staw and G. Salancik (eds.), *New Directions in Organizational Behavior*. Chicago, IL: St Clair Press.

SCHULTZ, J. (2006). 'South Florida Counties Push for Ernesto Aid.' *Palm Beach Post. Com*, September 1.

SCHWENK, C. (1984). 'Cognitive Simplification Processes in Strategic Decision Making.' *Strategic Management Journal*, 5: 111–28.

SHAPIRA, Z. (1981). 'Making Tradeoffs Between Job Attributes.' *Organizational Behavior and Human Performance*, 28: 331–55.

—— (1993). 'Ambiguity and Risk Taking in Organizations.' *Journal of Risk and Uncertainty*, 7: 89–94.

—— (1995). *Risk Taking: A Managerial Perspective*. New York: Russell Sage Foundation.

—— BERNDT, D. (1997). 'Managing Grand Scale Engineering Projects: A Risk Taking Perspective.' *Research in Organizational Behavior*, 19: 303–60.

—— VENEZIA, I. (2001). 'Patterns of Behavior of Professionally Managed and Independent Investors.' *Journal of Banking and Finance*, 25: 1573–87.

SHEFRIN, H. and STATMAN, M. (1985). 'The Disposition to Sell Winners Too Early and Ride Losers Too Long: Theory and Evidence.' *Journal of Finance*, 40: 777–90.

SIMON, H. (1947). *Administrative Behavior*. New York: Free Press.

—— (1955). 'A Behavioral Model of Rational Choice.' *Quarterly Journal of Economics*, 69: 99–118.

STARBUCK, W. H. and MILLIKEN, F. (1989). 'Challenger: Fine-Tuning the Odds Until Something Breaks.' *Journal of Management Studies*, 25: 319–40.

—— M. FARJOUN (eds.) (2005). *Organizations at the Limit: Management Lessons from the Columbia Disaster*. Oxford: Blackwell.

STAW, B. (1981). 'The Escalation of Commitment to a Course of Action.' *Academy of Management Review*, 6: 577–87.

SWETS, J., DAWES, R., and MONAHAN, J. (2000). 'Psychological Science Can Improve Diagnostic Decisions.' *Psychological Science in the Public Interest*, 1: 1–26.

THOMPSON, J. (1967). *Organizations in Action*. New York: McGraw-Hill.

TVERSKY, A. and KAHNEMAN, D. (1971). 'Belief in the Law of Small Numbers.' *Psychological Bulletin*, 76: 105–10.

—— —— (1974). 'Judgment Under Uncertainty: Heuristics and Biases.' *Science*, 185: 1124–31.

—— —— (1981). 'The Framing of Decisions and the Psychology of Choice.' *Science*, 211: 453–8.

WEICK, K. (1994). *Sensemaking in Organizations*. Thousand Oaks, CA: Sage.

WINTER, S. G. (2003). 'Mistaken Perceptions: Cases and Consequences.' *British Journal of Management*, 14: 39–44.

ZAJAC, E. and BAZERMAN, M. (1991). 'Blind Spots in Industry and Competitor Analysis: Implications of Interfere (Mis)perceptions for Strategic Decisions.' *Academy of Management Review*, 16: 37–56.

16

INTUITION IN ORGANIZATIONAL DECISION MAKING

EUGENE SADLER-SMITH
PAUL R. SPARROW

INTRODUCTION

THE concept of intuitive judgment is traditionally associated with the heuristics and biases research of Kahneman, Tversky, and others (see, for example, Kahneman et al. 1982). Within this paradigm, subjective probabilities are numerical expressions of beliefs concerning uncertain events that may be assessed using heuristics that reduce complex computational tasks to simpler judgmental ones. Such intuitive judgments can be economical and effective, but they accrue negative outcomes when rules for inference are used which are founded on false assumptions or when errors of logic are used which have attendant biases. Intuitive judgments based upon the heuristics of representativeness, availability, and anchoring and adjustment can be useful, but they may also lead to severe and systematic errors (Kahneman et al. 1982). However, as well as the "heuristics and biases" perspective, intuition has been viewed from a variety of different standpoints, some of which are summarized in Table 16.1. The study of intuition and intuitive judgment has not been confined merely to the heuristics and biases field of inquiry; it is a much more eclectic area.

Recently a number of management researchers have drawn upon developments in cognitive and social psychology, as well as from neuroscience, to reach a broad consensus that portrays intuition as an experiential phenomenon based upon implicitly stored knowledge and in which there is a complex interplay of cognitive and affective processes operating below the level of conscious awareness (Klein 1998 2003; Burke and Miller 1999; Khatri and Ng 2000; Hogarth 2001; Dane and Pratt 2007; Davis and Davis 2003; Sadler-Smith and Shefy 2004; Sinclair and Ashkanasy 2005; Hodgkinson et al. 2008; Sadler-Smith 2008). The process of intuiting involves rapid, holistic information processing of which the recipient is unaware. In conscious awareness affect ('hunch' or 'gut feel') and a degree of certitude are the manifestations of an intuition.

Table 16.1 Approaches to Defining Intuition

Perspective	Description	Source
Heuristics and biases	Intuitive judgments based upon the heuristics of representativeness, availability, and anchoring and adjustment can be useful, but they may also lead to severe and systematic errors.	Kahneman, Slovic, and Tversky (1982).
Intuition-as-ability	Ability to appraise a situation holistically and pull patterns together.	Showers and Chakrin (1981).
	A questioning outlook on certain types of data and situations; the ability to judge when normative analyses break down.	Blattberg and Hoch (1990).
	Innate problem solving ability; visualizing the causes of a situation.	Swink (1995).
	Ability to recognize patterns and interpret cues.	Klein (2003).
	Ability to judge stimulus properties on the basis of information that is activated in memory but not consciously retrieved.	Bolte and Goschke (2005).
	"Non-logical processes" known through judgment, decision, and action, and consisting of "good sense," intuition, inspiration, or even "genius."	Barnard (1938).
	Willingness to make decisions when all the facts are not currently available, and the ability to have such decisions validated with probability higher than chance.	Simon (1947).
Information processing	Unconscious process. Preliminary perception of coherence (pattern, meaning, structure) guiding thought and inquiry toward a hunch or hypothesis (a novel recombination of knowledge and information precipitated out of memory) about the nature of that coherence.	Bowers et al. (1990).

(Continued)

Table 16.1 (*continued*)

Perspective	Description	Source
	Synthesizing unconnected memory fragments into a new information structure.	Mintzberg et al. (1998).
	A means of complex data processing.	Payne et al. (1993).
Dual processing	Cognitive experiential self theory (CEST): two parallel information processing systems—cognitive (rational analytical) and experiential (equivalent to intuitive).	Epstein (1994).
	System 1 (intuitive) / System 2 (analytical).	Stanovich and West (2000).
Cognitive-affective /neuro-scientific	Immediate judgements based on feeling and the adoption of a global perspective.	Allinson and Hayes (1996).
	Using "soft," personal information and "gut-feel."	Molloy and Schwenk (1995).
	Awareness of thoughts, feelings, or bodily sense connected to a deeper perception, understanding, and way of making sense of the world (i.e., a system of processing that is synthetic and integrative).	Sadler-Smith and Shefy (2004).
	Non-sequential, holistic, and comprises both cognitive and affective elements, and results in direct knowing without any use of formal reasoning.	Sinclair and Ashkanasy (2005).
	Affectively charged judgments that arise through rapid, non-conscious, and holistic associations.	Dane and Pratt (2007).
	Somatic markers and the role of emotion in decision making.	Damasio (1999).
	Automatic, reflexive social cognition with neural correlates in the ventro-medial pre-frontal cortex, basal ganglia, and amygdala.	Lieberman, Jarcho and Satpute (2004).
Intuitionist and alternative epistemology	Irreducibility of intuitive knowledge. "Moral" things are intrinsically "good," they cannot be further defined and analyzed because a moral thing (like "good" or "bad") is a simple idea that cannot be broken down into smaller ideas and cannot (or need not) be proved empirically.	Moore (1903).
	Knowledge derived from inward illumination—a beam of light cast upon a chaotic confusion.	Amabile (1983).
	An alternative, competing, and inductive way of knowing.	Davis-Floyd and Arvidson (1997).

Note: The categories are not mutually exclusive; they are intended to indicate the variety of perspectives and interpretations of the term "intuitive."

RATIONALITY AND INTUITIVE JUDGMENT

Early discussions of intuition in management decision making may be traced to the Appendix of Chester Barnard's *The Functions of the Executive* (1938). Barnard argued that there are two separate mental processes: "logical processes" that are conscious and expressible in words, and "non-logical processes" known through judgment, decision, and action, and consisting of "good sense," intuition, inspiration, or even "genius" (and not equivalent to illogicality or irrationality). Barnard, himself an AT&T executive, noted that although intuition is error prone, managers cannot operate without it to the extent that intuition accounts for much business decision making, which managers rationalize after the fact. Intuition is supported by "organic" (implicit) knowledge "impressed upon us unconsciously or without conscious effort on our part" (1938: 302).

Simon (1947, 1987) considered the work of Barnard as too optimistic about the contribution of intuition in management but nonetheless accommodated it in his theory of decision making as "analyses frozen into habit." Simon coined the term "bounded rationality" to refer to the limits imposed by human information processing capacity upon rational decision making. Rationality is limited by "a vast maze of possibilities, a maze that describes the environment" (Simon 1982: 66) and confronted by this managers must rely on subconscious pattern recognition processes. The trait of intuition is associated with a willingness to make decisions when not all the facts are "in," with a higher than chance "batting average" of success serving as a validation (see Sadler-Smith and Shefy 2004: 84–5). These deliberations lead to a number of inferences: a rational action is feasible if decision makers in agreement about goals and cause and effect relationships, and if they are cognisant of the environmental and other constraints, under which decision makers take action (Dean and Sharfman 1993). Conversely, if decision makers cannot come to consensus on goals and cause and effect relationships, and are not fully cognisant of environmental constraints (including uncertainty) they cannot rely exclusively upon rational methods. Hence, the limits of rationality may be all too apparent in uncertain environments where it is difficult to identify, to measure and predict key variables and their interrelationships (Priem et al. 1995). Rational analysis and intuitive judgment are complementary components of effective decision making (see Louis and Sutton 1991; Hodgkinson and Clarke 2007) to the extent that, as noted by Herbert Simon:

...it is a fallacy to contrast "analytic" and "intuitive" approaches to problems. Intuition and judgment—at least good judgment—are simply analyses frozen into habit and into the capacity for rapid response through recognition...Behaving like a manager means having command of the whole range of management skills and applying them as they become appropriate. (Simon 1987: 61–3)

In Simon's theory, intuition describes a sophisticated way of reasoning and decision making which becomes possible where, after years of experience and mastery of a task or domain, managers can compress their learning and "chunk" together information, thereby further honing their expertise and decision-making skills, leading in turn to greater accuracy.

Empirical evidence sheds some light upon the effects that dynamism and uncertainty can have upon the effectiveness of particular decision-making behaviors. For example, rationality was found to be related positively to performance in stable industries (Frederickson 1984), and negatively to performance in dynamic industries (Frederickson and Iaquinto 1989). Dean and Sharfman (1993) observed that decision makers engage in a less rational process of strategic decision making when faced with problems characterized by high degrees of uncertainty. Daake et al. (2004) explored the type of information used by experienced and highly educated professionals making major strategic decisions in a US hospital. They used survey, focus groups, observations, and interviews with stakeholders and 21 strategic planning group decision makers over a 16-month period. Their study revealed a greater reliance on informal data (opinion, stories, illustrations, analogies, and metaphors) than on facts and formal data, and upon tacit, experience-based information over formal data at a ratio of 10:3. Khatri and Ng (2000) surveyed senior managers across a variety of industrial sectors in the US and found that not only are intuitive processes used often in decision making by senior managers, but that the use of intuitive decision making was found to be positively associated with organizational performance in an unstable environment, but negatively so in a stable environment. In a replication and extension of this work in a UK small business context Sadler-Smith (2004) observed that there was a positive relationship between intuitive decision style and contemporaneous financial and non-financial performance but this did not appear to be moderated by environmental instability. Furthermore, a statistically significant relationship between intuitive decision style and subsequent financial performance was observed.

Some studies that have compared the accuracy of a individuals' intuitive judgments, as opposed to the application of external, rational, rule-based analyses of the problem at hand, have found rational analysis to be more accurate than intuitive analysis (Cooksey 2000; Dunwoody et al. 2000). However, Hammond et al. (1997) found that in terms of its accuracy, analytic cognition was not uniformly superior to intuitive and quasi-rational cognition, and that the latter may enable people to draw upon substantive knowledge (possibly non-verbal) that was otherwise unavailable when processing analytically. Moreover, when they compared the use of intuitive versus rational judgments *within* individuals (a group of expert highway engineers) they found that an intuitive reasoning strategy performed as well as, or better than, rational analysis. A reliance on analytical reasoning was more likely to produce extreme errors or failures, which was not the case with intuitive reasoning. Intuition was found to be adaptive when information presented to the manager required a reliance on perceptual processes to interpret it (it required the manager to sense it by relying on vision, hearing, etc.), cues were multiple and appeared in parallel (rather than in a simple, linear sequence), or when many of the cues were redundant or irrelevant. A number of the studies referred to above suffer from the limitation of self-reported measures of intuition (for example, Khatri and Ng 2000; Sadler-Smith 2004). There is a need for more research that uses experimental designs and which focuses upon direct observations, rather than self-reports, of intuitive behavior under different sets of task conditions.

Heuristics and Intuition

Heuristics and biases researchers such as Kahneman and Tversky, as well as seeing the downside to intuitive judgments due to biases, also saw some benefits to heuristic processing. It is indeed the case that newer conceptions of bounded rationality have increasingly emphasized its "up-side" (Hodgkinson and Sparrow 2002: 305). The term "ecological rationality" (meaning "designed" to fit with reality) is used by Gigerenzer and Todd (1999: 5; Gigerenzer 2004) to describe heuristics that are components of an "adaptive toolbox". The rationally bounded mind can reach into its toolkit for a fast (i.e., computationally simple) and frugal (i.e., sparing in their information requirements) means of solving a problem or making a decision. From the perspective of ecological rationality, heuristics have the potential to improve reasoning and decision making.

Gigerenzer's view is that fast and frugal heuristics are a way in which the human mind can take advantage of the structure of information to arrive at a reasonable judgment. Research by Gigerenzer and his colleagues has investigated the nature of those environments where heuristics work well. They have also identified meta-heuristics (i.e., rules that people use to decide which heuristic to use) and whether or not people actually use these in specific environments. Heuristics have varying degrees of complexity and include "take the best" (answer according to the single most valid cue that discriminates between objects); "minimalist" (take cues in random order and answer according to the first one that discriminates between objects); and "take the last". By examining actual judgment processes, Gigerenzer and Todd (1999) have argued that individuals have a repertoire of heuristics available to them and that the effectiveness of these is domain specific. Fast and frugal heuristics solve certain classes of problems; they are not generically effective or ineffective but rather they are ecologically rational contingent upon their match with the demands of the task and environment. Fast and frugal heuristics have an experiential basis. The initial understanding of which information to generalize (and therefore enable a robust heuristic to be devised), and the conscious choice of knowing which heuristic to use is often guided by unconscious, experience-based intuition.

Smith (Chapter 24 of this volume) equates fast and frugal heuristics with intuition. Although heuristics share some of the features of intuition (they are a fast and cognitively economical response, in terms of conscious processing, to a complex problem), they are not equivalent to intuitions. Sinclair and Ashkanasy (2005) argued that intuition implies an absence of awareness of the process used to arrive at a decision; hence, there is a difference between the direct knowing associated with intuition and the deliberative approach associated with heuristics. As Dane and Pratt (2007) note, heuristics may lack domain sensitivity and be applied (inappropriately) across various domains resulting in accuracies and biases. Novices are especially prone to the context free application of "rules of thumb" (Dreyfus and Dreyfus 1986). Heuristics are predetermined rules applied volitionally and consciously in response to a specific decision scenario, intuition on the other hand is:

> ...based on a broad constellation of past experiences, knowledge, skills, perceptions and emotions. Intuition is not a formulated action plan predicated upon predetermined meta-rules, but rather is knowledge constructed whole-cloth in sudden shift from subconscious to conscious awareness [although the rules of inference used may not enter conscious awareness]. (Davis and Davis 2003: 59)

Moreover, unlike heuristics, intuitions are non-volitional, they occur as an involuntary response to implicitly or explicitly perceived stimuli. Managers may be able to influence the likelihood of their making an accurate intuitive response (for example, through the acquisition of domain specific expertise) but they cannot necessarily "force" an intuition to happen or block its occurrence.

DUAL-PROCESSING PERSPECTIVES

Dual-processing theories hypothesize parallel systems of perception and cognitive processing (see Chaiken and Trope 1999). Dual-process theories differ in terms of the general properties distinguished for each system, and in relation to the relative independence of each system. Dual-process theories share the common view that two separate processes are involved in reasoning. Within Epstein's cognitive experiential self theory (CEST) the experiential system (which has much in common with what other researchers have called "intuitive") functions independently of the rational system that underpins the analytic mode of processing. Separate systems serve cognitive and experiential processing. Emotions are "almost invariably" the outcomes of pre-conscious interpretations of previously experienced events (Epstein and Pacini 1999: 473) derived from automatic searching by the experiential system of long-term memory for related events. Epstein et al. (1996) observed that heuristic responses to vignettes are determined primarily by experiential (intuitive) processing, but influenced to a lesser extent by rational processing.

Recent studies using functional magnetic resonance imaging (fMRI) techniques have identified the neural geographies of effortful, reflective social cognition (associated with brain regions referred to as the C-system) and automatic, reflexive social cognition (associated with regions referred to as the X-system). X-system processing resulted in heightened neurological activity in the basal ganglia, ventromedial pre-frontal cortex, and the amygdala (a component of the brain's limbic system associated with affect and emotion) (Lieberman et al. 2004). Gioia and Ford (1996) distinguished between an active consciousness that stores data currently perceived by the senses (and acts as a gateway to both the decision-making environment and the rest of the mind) and a pre-consciousness that is accessible through processes such as intuition, incubation, the use of metaphor, or mental imagery. According to this view, after initial capture, information is stored either as tacit knowledge (which can be back translated into conscious awareness) or subconsciously (and hence of which we are unaware). Tacit knowledge is stored in a perceptual format and has to be back-translated by the active conscious in order for it to be accessible. Working memory is the most likely site at which the "back translation" manifests, in other words, where tacit knowledge becomes conscious and explicit (see also Le Doux 1996: 280).

COGNITION AND AFFECT

One reason dual-processing theories are especially relevant in any discussion of intuition is because of the significance they attach to affect. Although a number of scholars, including Simon, have tended to see emotions as detrimental to the intuitive process, Simon acknowledged "in order to have anything like a complete theory of human rationality, we have to understand what role emotion plays in it" (Simon 1983: 29). Much of human information processing occurs automatically and outside of consciousness (Wilson and Schooler 1991) based upon rules and inferences acquired implicitly and held tacitly (Reber 1993). As a result people may know more than they can tell (Polanyi 1996) and may be unable to verbalize how they arrived at a particular judgment (Haidt 2001). Intuitions are automatic, involuntary responses to particular configurations of environmental cues.

Simon argued that to be focused on analytical thought, powerful motivational forces (including emotions) are required, but overly strong emotions (especially in stressful situations) may narrow attention to very specific and perhaps transient goals (1997: 90). Emotion, imagination, and memories, which occasionally combine to form insights, drive decision-making processes (Langley et al. 1995). By combining ideas from evolutionary psychology and neuroscience, Muramatsu and Honoch (2005) argued that emotion and cognition link in terms of attentional resources and memory processes. Emotions divert attentional mechanisms to important pieces of information in the environment, thereby enabling the deployment of the necessary resources (Holland and Gallagher 1999; Faucher and Tappolet 2002). Emotions activate and regulate many of the activities involved in the encoding, storing, and retrieval of information about important events and so have an effect upon the way that people reconstruct previously experienced situations (Bower 1981; Christianson 1992; Dolcos and Cabeza 2002). Historically, cognitions and emotions are seen sometimes as competing explanations, but this need not be the case. As Muramatsu and Hanoch (2005: 209, 214) noted "emotions can be viewed as information-processing systems just like memory and perception" and that with recent advances cognitive neuroscientists are beginning to identify the neural pathways through which emotion modulates judgment and decision making.

Researchers examining the non-conscious nature of problem solving have explored the cognitive and neural mechanisms underpinning intuition and the related process of insight. Bowers et al. (1990) found that in experimental settings people could respond discriminatively to coherences that they could not explicitly identify. Their tacit perception guided participants towards a conscious representation of these coherences in the form of a "hunch" or "gut feeling." Bowers et al. explained this in terms of the creation of an activation in mnemonic and semantic networks that spreads through neural pathways and eventually reaches a level sufficient to cross the threshold into conscious awareness and generate a hunch. In subsequent replications, these judgments improved significantly when participants were induced into a positive rather than neutral or negative mood (Bolte et al. 2003). When participants had only brief opportunities to respond (thus requiring rapid intuitive judgment), they were still able to make above-chance judgments within 1.8 seconds, though not within one second (Bolte and Goschke 2005). The spreading activation explanation posits that neural activation spreads from "clue" words to related concepts in memory. These converge on a common associate where there is a perception of coherence. The activation of a new common associate gives rise to the intuition, and biases judgments even though activation is not sufficient to support conscious retrieval of the concept that supported the solution (Dorfman et al. 1996; Bowden and Jung-Beeman 1998). An alternative explanation is multiple trace memory theory (Hintzman 1988), which presumes that clue words activate all memory traces in parallel and these traces respond simultaneously by creating a single "echo." The intensity of this activation is the sum of all activation levels of traces and interpreted as a familiarity signal. More recently, findings suggest that coherence judgments which eventually yield insights have a physical location in the anterior superior temporal gyrus (aSTG) brain region (Jung-Beeman et al. 2004).

Other researchers concerned with the role of affect have focused upon the somatic (from the Greek *soma*, meaning "body") facets of intuitive decision making (Damasio 1994). Bechara et al. (1996) compared the performance on a high-risk gambling task of normal participants and patients with damage to the ventro-medial pre-frontal cortex (implicated in inducing emotions). Damage to this region can result in the impoverishment of "decision-making apparatus to a dramatic degree" (Damasio 1999: 280 and 302). In the experiment, Bechara and his colleagues observed that normal participants began to choose advantageously before they were consciously aware which strategy worked best; moreover, they generated anticipatory skin conductance responses (SCRs) before they exercised a risky choice and before they became consciously aware of the strategy. Patients with pre-frontal cortex damage continued to choose disadvantageously even after they realized the correct strategy; they also failed to demonstrate any anticipatory SCRs (Damasio 1999). The amygdala and ventromedial pre-frontal cortex are involved in processing that is automatic, fast, and involuntary, in processing of emotionally arousing tasks, but also in higher order cognitive activities such as planning and decision making (Adolphs and Damasio 2001). These findings indicate that the autonomic responses associated with intuitions based upon previous experiences and emotional states guide decision making and outcomes in advance of conscious awareness. The intuitive system underpinning such processes may have evolved earlier in humans than did the rational system (Epstein 1994). The pattern of somatic and visceral signals from the body (Le Doux 1996) acts as a warning, referred to by Damasio (1994, 1999) as a "somatic marker," which allows the decision maker to anticipate the "pain" or "pleasure" of outcomes (Shafir and LeBouef 2002).

The influence of the unconscious system is likely to be more compelling and difficult to control than the rational system for two reasons: firstly, it is associated with affect; and secondly, it is beyond immediate control because the person "does not know there is anything to control" (Epstein 1994: 716). The opportunity for conscious control, however, may exist when any insight eventually occurs (see Epstein 1994). Verbalizing (for example, by "thinking aloud") can result in the disruption of the non-reportable memory retrieval processes such as spreading activation (Bowers et al. 1990) which are crucial to achieving insightful solutions (Schooler et al. 1993). The mode of representation and encoding of information (for example, as images) may also be an important contributory factor to these mechanisms. The positive and negative feelings associated with images are retrievable more quickly, they require less effortful processing and may serve to override or guide rational decision processes. The anticipatory emotions generated by the intuitive system may influence and compete with cognitive appraisals from the rational system in uncertain situations (Loewenstein et al. 2001) and the responses generated by the limbic system may over-ride the functioning of 'higher' brain regions (Le Doux 1996).

INTUITIVE JUDGMENT, DOMAIN SPECIFICITY, AND PROBLEM STRUCTURE

Cognitive continuum theory (Hammond et al. 1997) argues that the use of intuitive judgment strategies in decision making varies according to the characteristics of the task in terms of an analytic–intuitive continuum (Goldstein 2004). There is an assumption that there is "good" intuitive decision making (portrayed as intelligent processing of complex data) and "bad" intuitive decision making (portrayed as unvigilant, biased, or lazy processing of information). Some see intuiting as an irrational mental function that operates on a lower plane of intellectuality (Osbeck 1999). Recent research shows that rather than being irrational, intuition involves cognition (albeit of a particular kind) and affect, and in certain contexts can yield decision outcomes that are as effective as rationality (Khatri and Ng 2000). Intuition, derived from experiences and prior learning, draws upon and associationistic processes based upon elaborate and complex domain-specific schemas (Klein 1998, 2003) and is context-dependent (Dane and Pratt 2007). Whereas the fast and frugal heuristics discussed earlier involve a consideration of predetermined rules of inference (such as A → B → C), experts exercise intuitive judgments in ways that are appropriate to the dynamics of the problem and its context. Effective intuitive judgment is not context-free or formulaic, moreover, the context-dependent use of intuition is one means of distinguishing between expert and novice performance. As Davis and Davis (2003: 44) noted, many simple problems require programmed decisions, but programmed decisions and heuristics are only as successful as the quality and amount of information available to the model upon which they are based. The decisions which managers are faced with in workplace settings are often characterized by problem structures which are ambiguous, dynamic, data poor, and time pressured (Schön 1983; Klein 1998, 2003). Context and problem structure plays a crucial role in determining the appropriateness and efficacy of intuitive judgments (Klein 1998, 2003; Burke and Miller 1999).

Shapiro and Spence (1997: 67) offered a continuum of problem structuredness ranging from "well" (tightly) structured problems (examples being accounts receivable, order entering, and inventory control) to "ill" (loosely) structured problems (examples being mergers and acquisitions, new product planning, and R&D planning). Dane and Pratt (2007) equate well structured problems to Laughlin's (1980) notion of "intellective" tasks characterized by objective criteria for success within the definitions, rules, operations, and relationships of a particular conceptual system. Dane and Pratt equate ill-structured problems to Laughlin's "judgmental" tasks (political, ethical, aesthetic, or behavioral judgments for which there is no objective criterion or demonstrable solution—to which might be added moral judgments, see Haidt 2001, as well as creative and entrepreneurial judgment, see Sadler-Smith 2008). Intuition may be neither necessary nor effective in tightly structured situations (such as those where computational complexity is to the fore). On the other hand, in loosely structured situations experts may rely upon their intuitive judgments in ways that take into account the unique features, subtleties, novelties, nuances, and demands of the local context. In spite of its perceived risks, managers may have intuition as the only option available when time is too short for a comprehensive assessment and key aspects of a situation are difficult or impossible to quantify (see Schoemaker and Russo 1993).

Tight Structures—Decision Situations Not Favoring Intuition

As the problem structure associated with a task becomes "tighter" and more intellective, the effectiveness of rational decision making is likely to increase; conversely, intuitive judgments are likely to become more effective relative to rational analysis as a problem becomes increasingly unstructured (Klein 2003). Shafir and LeBouef (2002) argue that in certain situations individuals often make counter-rational judgments based on "intuitions," at the root of which is a failure to make use of well defined or accurate reasoning (Slovic 1972: 789). Consequently, such judgments are "bad" when compared with outcomes accruing from the rigorous and accurate application of a statistical model (see Meehl 1954). In tightly structured, intellective tasks in data rich, objectively quantifiable, and computationally complex domains, statistical models perform better than human judges do. Statistical models accurately predict the relationship between cues or indicators when provided with exactly the same information as human judges (for example, a résumé, a financial spreadsheet, or an X-ray image) and well defined criterion variables (for example, performance in a prescribed and well defined job role). Objective statistical and quantitative procedures have the advantage of being able to apply the same formulae consistently and rapidly over large numbers of cases without physical or emotional fatigue (see Hogarth 2001: 144–50). Nor are they—if designed correctly—prone to misconceptions, fallacies, or cognitive load limitations that restrict human performance.

Table 16.2 Tight vs. Loose Decision Structures

Tight decision structure (favouring analysis)	Loose decision structure (favouring intuition)
Intellective: objective criteria for success within the definitions, rules, operations, and relationships of a particular conceptual system (Laughlin 1980).	Judgemental: political, ethical, aesthetic, or behavioural judgments for which there is no objective criterion or demonstrable solution (Laughlin 1980). Moral judgments (Haidt 2001).
Well-structured problems such as accounts receivable, order entering and inventory control (Shapiro and Spence 1997).	Ill-structured problems such as mergers and acquisitions, new product planning and R&D planning (Shapiro and Spence 1997).
Analysis: conflict resolution; optimization; justification; computational complexity (Klein 2003).	Intuition: time pressure; ill-defined goals; dynamic conditions; experienced participants (Klein 2003).

The situations that favor analytical approaches are characterized by computational complexity, a need for justification, requiring optimization, and where objective criteria for success exist (Laughlin 1980; Klein 2003). In situations where it is possible to identify explicit criterion variables and there are reliable and valid procedures available, statistical models on average will out-perform humans (Hogarth 2001). Hogarth also notes, however, that experts often have to decide what criteria to include in a model (such as what to look for in an X-ray image) and how to build such a model (since there may be no alternative to a human judge or designer for such a task). Moreover, when an environment is complex and individuals have specific, relevant expertise with which they can interpret contextual cues, intuitions lead to valid judgments (Yaniv and Hogarth 1993). (See Table 16.2.)

Loose Structures—Decision Contexts Favoring Intuition

In dynamic environments or those in which the criterion variable is not known (for example, a new business venture or the performance of an new hire in a newly created job role) human beings' ability to sense changes and detect faint signals, or to move beyond statistical models in foresightful ways can be advantageous. While models and computers may be good at aggregating and analyzing data, intuition (since it derives from integrative pattern recognition and holistic judgments) may be the only avenue open to managers to weigh, aggregate, and make sense of intangibles involved in judgments where there are "deeper core values that underlie a decision" (see Schoemaker and Russo 1993: 28). Furthermore, although models and computers are efficient in handling objective data quickly and consistently, intuition may serve as a check on solutions derived through statistical modeling and other rationally analytic procedures. It is also possible for intellective problems that have been solved by rational analyses to be screened intuitively by an expert to sense whether the calculated solution looks and feels like it "ought to" (Burke and Sadler-Smith 2006).

Among the characteristics of loosely structured decision contexts are task demands which are judgmental in nature and that cannot be solved only by computational means, including include time pressured scenarios, ill-defined goals, dynamic conditions, and where there are experienced participants (Klein 2003). Dijksterhuis et al. (2006) in their unconscious thought theory (UTT) tested a "deliberation-without-attention" hypothesis and found in their study of consumer behavior that that simple choices produce better results after conscious thought, but that "choices in complex matters (such as between different houses or different cars) should be left to unconscious thought" (2006: 1005). Dane, Rockman, and Pratt (2005) found that analytical decision making works better in highly structured tasks, although intuition is most effective compared to analysis when decision makers are domain experts who are facing tasks that are poorly (loosely) structured. Expertise exercised in loosely structured situations is likely to foster effective intuitive decision outcomes. In Burke and Miller's (1999: 95) study the benefits of this type of intuitive decision making clustered in four areas: expediting of decisions; improvement in quality of decision; development of a more complete set of personal and professional skills; and making decisions that are consistent with company culture and values. Wagner (2002) argued that management competence requires the ability to "imagine a more desirable future and invent ways of reaching it", and since they are based more on intuition rather than rationality, many of the judgmental aspects of management competence are inherently difficult to describe (Wagner 2002: 50).

CONCLUSIONS AND FUTURE RESEARCH

Intuition should not be seen as a substitute for rational analysis (and vice versa), nor should intuition and rationality be treated as mutually exclusive opposites. Rather, intuition and analysis are qualitatively different facets of human information processing that may operate in parallel and interact depending upon the subject's expertise, the demands of the task, and the social setting. The relationship between the problem domain and the decision maker's expertise is critical. Domain is an important factor in relation to creativity and decision making (Ford and Gioia 2000), and this understanding may be applied to intuition. However, whereas novelty and value of a creative act clearly requires subjective and domain specific judgment (the unit of analysis is the decision itself), intuition is more concerned with the front-end aspects of creativity and the issues of interpretation and alternative generation (the unit of analysis is the individual). Given the distinction between loose and tight problem structures, in future it will be important to examine the looser and more judgmental side of the equation and focus upon the actual behaviors that managers use in such situations as well as on self-reported behaviors.

Simon (1982) warned that in describing various forms of intuition researchers should beware of simply developing ever more complex labels for the process, and should focus instead on developing explanations of it. In decision-making research, intuitive judgments have most often been associated with the traditional heuristics and biases work, and researchers continue to explore related issues in areas such as the use of fast and frugal heuristics. The emphasis has recently shifted and many decision-making researchers interpret intuition as affectively charged, holistic judgments based upon unconsciously executed expertise (Sinclair and Ashkanasy 2005; Sadler-Smith and Shefy 2004; Dane and Pratt 2007), a view which differs from models of purely heuristic processing which focus more narrowly upon fallacies, inferential logic, and predetermined rules. Intuition is based upon deep knowledge structures and mental simulations derived from past experiences (Klein 1998), and knowledge, skills, perceptions, and feelings held tacitly and often arrived at by an implicit and holistic perception of the problem before conscious awareness takes hold (Davis and Davis 2003). Indeed, Kahneman (2003: 1452) argued himself that:

Intuitive judgments occupy a position... between the automatic operations of perception and the deliberate operations of reasoning. All the characteristics that students of intuition have attributed to System 1 are also properties of perceptual operations... the operations of System 1 [also] deal with stored concepts as well as with percepts. This view of intuition suggests that the vast store of scientific knowledge available about perceptual phenomena can be a source of useful hypotheses about the workings of intuition.

Intuition reflects knowledge held tacitly and not expressed in words or other symbols and acquired through perceptual and other non-symbolic mental processes (Sadler-Smith and Shefy 2004). Intuitive knowing is based upon a number of mechanisms that need to be integrated into a coherent theory of intuition (Hodgkinson et al. 2008). Such a conceptualization is likely to encompass the access mechanisms associated with the separate processes of incubation, insight, and intuition, the representation of intuitive and subconscious expertise in schemata, attentional mechanisms, meta-cognition and self-regulation, emotional memories, and the various neurological correlates of these processes.

Future development of the field requires a synthesis of work on creative perceptual processes and intuitive judgments, and to model the links between these, cognitive systems, and neurological structures (see Lieberman et al. 2004). There is a need to synthesize work on rapid perceptual framing, implicit learning, and mastery of complex performance tasks into models of intuition. There also needs to be a clearer understanding of the link between cognition, emotions, and feeling states, and decision making and risk (see Slovic et al. 2002), based upon the significant developments in cognition, neurology, and neuroscience which have taken place over the last decade (see Le Doux 1996; Damasio 1999). The intellectual challenge of developing these new syntheses is daunting, but given the recent resurgence of interest in the topic of intuition and the rapid developments in cognitive neuroscience (see Churchland 2002; Gazzinga, Ivry, and Mangun 2002) and social cognitive neuroscience (Lieberman 2007), important research questions are being identified and explored and new avenues and new possibilities opened up. The future holds the prospect of fruitful dialogue between intuition researchers from disparate fields of inquiry; their findings are likely to have significant implications for decision-making research and management practice.

REFERENCES

ADOLPHS, R. and DAMASIO, A. (2001). 'The Interaction of Affect and Cognition: A Neurobiological Perspective,' in J. Forgas (ed.), *Handbook of Affect and Social Cognition*. Hillsdale, NJ: Erlbaum, 27–49.

ALLINSON, C. W. and HAYES, J. (1996). 'The Cognitive Style Index: A Measure of Intuition-Analysis for Organizational Research.' *Journal of Management Studies*, 33/1: 119–35.

AMABILE, T. M. (1983). 'The Social Psychology of Creativity: A Componential Conceptualisation.' *Journal of Personality and Social Psychology*, 45: 357–76.

BARNARD, C. I. (1938). *The Functions of the Executive*. Cambridge, MA: Harvard University Press.

BECHARA, A., TRANEL, H., DAMSIO, H., and DAMSIO, A. R. (1996). 'Failure to Respond Autonomically to Anticipated Future Outcomes Following Damage to Prefrontal Cortex.' *Cerebral Cortex*, 6: 215–25.

BLATTBERG, R. C. and HOCH, S. J. (1990). 'Database Models and Managerial Intuition: 50 Percent Model and 50 Percent Manager.' *Management Science*, 36/8: 887–99.

BOLTE, A. and GOSCHKE, T. (2005). 'On the Speed of Intuition: Intuitive Judgements of Semantic Coherence Under Different Response Deadlines.' *Memory and Cognition*, 33/7: 1248–55.

—— —— KUHL, J. (2003). 'Emotion and Intuition: Effects of Positive and Negative Mood on Implicit Judgements in Semantic Coherence'. *Psychological Science*, 14/5: 416–21.

BOWDEN, E. M. and JUNG-BEEMAN, M. (1998). 'Getting the Right Idea: Semantic Activation in the Right Hemisphere May Help Solve Insight Problems.' *Psychological Science*, 9: 435–40.

BOWER, G. H. (1981). 'Mood and Memory.' *American Psychologist*, 36: 129–233.

BOWERS, K. S., REGEHR, G., BALTHAZARD, C., and PARKER, K. (1990). 'Intuition in the Context of Discovery.' *Cognitive Psychology*, 22: 72–110.

Burke, L. and Sadler-Smith, E. (2006). 'Instructor Intuition in the Educational Context.' *Academy of Management Learning and Education*, 5/2: 169–81.

Burke, L. A. and Miller, M. K. (1999). 'Taking the Mystery Out of Intuitive Decision-Making.' *Academy of Management Executive*, 13/4: 91–9.

Chaiken, S. and Trope, Y. (eds.) (1999). *Dual-Process Theories in Social Psychology*. New York: Guilford Press.

Christianson, S. A. (1992). 'Emotional Stress and Eyewitness Memory: A Critical Review.' *Psychological Bulletin*, 112: 284–309.

Churchland, P. S. (2002). *Brain-Wise: Studies in Neurophilosophy*. Cambridge, MA: MIT Press.

Cooksey, R. W. (2000). 'Commentary on "Cognitive Adaptation and its Consequences: A Test of Cognitive Continuum Theory."' *Journal of Behavioural Decision-Making*, 13: 55–9.

Daake, D., Dawley, D. D., and Anthony, W. P. (2004). 'Formal Data Use in Strategic Planning: An Organizational Field Experiment.' *Journal of Managerial Issues*, 16/2: 232–47.

Damasio, A. R. (1994). *Descartes' Error: Emotion, Reason and the Human Brain*. New York: Harper Collins.

—— (1999). *The Feeling of What Happens: Body, Emotion and the Making of Consciousness*. London: Vintage.

Dane, E. I. and Pratt, M. G. (2007). 'Exploring Intuition and Its Role in Managerial Decision-Making.' *Academy of Management Review*, 32/1: 33–54.

—— Rockman, K. W., and Pratt, M. G. (2005). 'Should I Trust My Gut? The Role of Task Characteristics in Intuitive and Analytical Decision-Making.' *Academy of Management Annual Meeting, Best Paper Proceedings*, Hawaii, August.

Davis, S. H. and Davis, P. B. (2003). *The Intuitive Dimensions of Administrative Decision-Making*. Lanham: Scarecrow.

Davis-Floyd, R. and Arvidson, P. S. (eds.) (1997). *Intuition: The Inside Story*. New York: Routledge.

Dean, J. W. and Sharfman, M. P. (1993). 'Procedural Rationality in the Strategic Decision-Making Process.' *Journal of Management Studies*, 30/4: 587–620.

Dijksterhuis, A., Bos, M. W., Nordgren, M. F., and Van Baaren, R. B. (2006). 'On Making the Right Choice: The Deliberation Without Attention Effect.' *Science*, 311: 1005–7.

Dolcos, F. and Cabeza, R. (2002). 'Event-Related Potentials of Emotional Memory: Encoding Pleasant, Unpleasant and Neutral Pictures.' *Cognitive, Affective and Behavioral Neurosciences*, 2: 252–63.

Dorfman, J., Shames, V. A., and Kihlstrom, J. F. (1996). 'Intuition, Incubation and Insight: Implicit Cognition in Problem Solving,' in G. Underwood (ed.), *Implicit Cognition*. Oxford: Oxford University Press, 257–96.

Dreyfus, H. L. and Dreyfus, S. E. (1986). *Mind over Machine: The Power of Human Intuitive Expertise in the Era of the Computer*. New York: Free Press.

Dunwoody, P. T., Haarbaur, E., Mahan, R. P., Marino, C., and Tang, C. (2000). 'Cognitive Adaptation and its Consequences: A Test of Cognitive Continuum Theory.' *Journal of Behavioural Decision-Making*, 13: 55–9.

Epstein, S. (1994). 'Integration of the Cognitive and the Psychodynamic Unconscious.' *American Psychologist*, 49: 709–24.

—— Pacini, R. (1999). 'Some basic issues regarding dual process theories from the perspective of cognitive-experiential self theory', in S. Chaiken and Y. Trope (eds.), *Dual Process Theories in Social Psychology*. New York: Guilford Press, 462–82.

EPSTEIN, S. PACINI R., DENES-RAJ, V., and HEIR, H. (1996). 'Individual Differences in Intuitive-Experiential and Analytical-Rational Thinking Styles.' *Journal of Personality and Social Psychology*, 71: 390–405.

FAUCHER, L. and TAPPOLET, C. (2002). 'Fear and the Focus of Attention.' *Consciousness and Emotion*, 3: 105–44.

FORD, C. M. and GIOIA, D. A. (2000). 'Factors Influencing Creativity in the Domain of Managerial Decision-Making.' *Journal of Management*, 26/4: 705–32.

FREDRICKSON, J. W. (1984). 'The Comprehensiveness of Strategic Decision Processes: Extension, Observations, Future Directions.' *Academy of Management Journal*, 27/3: 445–66.

FREDERICKSON, J. W. and IAQUINTO, A. L. (1989). 'Inertia and Creeping Rationality in Decision Processes.' *Academy of Management Journal*, 32: 543–76.

GAZZANIGA, M. S., IVRY, R. B., and MANGUN, G. R. (2002). *Cognitive Neuroscience: The Biology of the Mind*. New York: W. W. Norton and Co.

GIGERENZER, G. (2004). 'Fast and Frugal Heuristics: The Tools of Bounded Rationality,' in D. J. Koehler and N. Harvey (eds.), *Blackwell Handbook of Judgement and Decision-making*. London: Blackwell Publishing, 62–88.

GIGERENZER, G. and TODD, P. M. (1999). 'Fast and Frugal Heuristics: The Adaptive Toolbox,' in G. Gigerenzer, P. M. Todd, and the ABC Research Group (eds.), *Simple Heuristics That Make Us Smart*. New York: Oxford University Press.

GIOIA, D. A. and FORD, C. M. (1996). 'Tacit Knowledge, Self-Communications, and Sense Making in Organizations,' in L. Thayer (ed.), *Organization Communication: Emerging Perspectives*. Norwood, NJ: Ablex, 83–102.

GOLDSTEIN, W. M. (2004). 'Social Judgement Theory: Applying and Extending Brunswik's Probabilistic Functionalism,' in D. J. Koehler and N. Harvey (eds.), *Blackwell Handbook of Judgement and Decision-Making*. London: Blackwell Publishing, 37–61.

HAIDT, J. (2001). 'The Emotional Dog and its Rational Tail: A Social Intuitionist Approach to Moral Judgment.' *Psychological Review*, 108/4: 814–34.

HAMMOND, K. R., HAMM, R. M., GRASSIA, J., and PEARSON, T. (1997). 'Direct Comparison of the Efficacy of Intuitive and Analytical Cognition in Expert Judgement,' in W. M. Goldstein and R. M. Hogarth (eds.), *Research on Judgment and Decision-Making: Currents, Connections and Controversies*. Cambridge: Cambridge University Press.

HINTZMAN, D. L. (1988). 'Judgements of Frequency and Recognition Memory in a Multiple-Trace Memory Model.' *Psychological Review*, 95: 528–51.

HODGKINSON, G. P. and CLARKE, I. (2007). 'Exploring the Cognitive Significance of Organizational Strategizing: A Dual-Process Framework and Research Agenda.' *Human Relations*, 60: 243–55.

—— SPARROW, P. R. (2002). *The Competent Organization: A Psychological Analysis of the Strategic Management Process*. Buckingham, UK: Open University Press.

—— LANGAN-FOX, J., and SADLER-SMITH, E. (2008). 'Intuition: A Fundamental Bridging Construct in the Behavioural Sciences.' *British Journal of Psychology*, 99: 1–27.

HOGARTH, R. M. (2001). *Educating Intuition*. Chicago, IL: Chicago University Press.

HOLLAND, P. C. and GALLAGHER, M. (1999). 'Amygdala Circuitry in Attentional and Representational Processes.' *Trends in Cognitive Science*, 3: 65–73.

JUNG-BEEMAN, M., BOWDEN, E. M., HABERMAN, J. et al. (2004). 'Neural Activity When People Solve Verbal Problems With Insight.' *Public Library of Science Biology*, 2: 97.

KAHNEMAN, D. (2003). 'Maps of Bounded Rationality: Psychology for Behavioural Economics.' *The American Economic Review*, December: 1449–75.

—— SLOVIC, P., and TVERSKY, A. (1982). *Judgement Under Uncertainty: Heuristics and Biases*. New York: Cambridge University Press.

KHATRI, N. and NG, H. A. (2000). 'The Role of Intuition in Strategic Decision Making.' *Human Relations*, 53: 57–86.

KLEIN, G. (1998). *Sources of Power: How People Make Decisions*. Cambridge, MA: MIT Press.

KLEIN, G. (2003). *Intuition at Work*. New York: Bantam Dell.

LANGLEY, A., MINTZBERG, H., PITCHER, P., POSADA, E., and SAINT-MACARY, J. (1995). 'Opening Up Decision-Making: The View from the Black Stool.' *Organization Science*, 6/3: 260–79.

LAUGHLIN, P. (1980). 'Social Combination Processes of Cooperative Problem-Solving Groups on Verbal Intellective Tasks,' in M. Fishbein (ed.), *Progress in Social Psychology*, Vol. 1. Hillsdale, NJ: Lawrence Erlbaum Associates, 127–55.

LE DOUX, J. E. (1996). *The Emotional Brain: The Mysterious Underpinnings of Emotional Life*. New York: Simon and Schuster.

LIEBERMAN, M. D. (2007). 'Social Cognitive Neuroscience: A Review of Core Processes.' *Annual Review of Psychology*, 58: 259–89.

—— JARCHO, J. M., and SATPUTE, A. B. (2004). 'Evidence-Based and Intuition-Based Self-Knowledge: An fMRI Study.' *Journal of Personality and Social Psychology*, 87: 421–35.

LOEWENSTEIN, G. F., WEBER, E. U., HSEE, C. K., and WELCH, N. (2001). 'Risk as Feelings.' *Psychological Bulletin*, 127: 267–86.

LOUIS, M. R. and SUTTON, R. I. (1991). 'Switching Cognitive Gears: From Habits of Mind to Active Thinking.' *Human Relations*, 44: 55–76

MEEHL, P. E. (1954). *Clinical Versus Statistical Prediction: A Theoretical Analysis and Review of the Evidence*. Minneapolis, MN: University of Minnesota Press.

MINTZBERG, H., AHLSTRAND, B., and LAMPEL, J. (1998). *Strategy Safari: A Guided Tour through the Wilds of Strategic Management*. New York: Free Press.

MOLLOY, S. and SCHWENK, C. R. (1995). 'The Effects of Information Technology on Strategic Decision-Making.' *Journal of Management Studies*, 32/3: 283–311.

MOORE, G. E. (1903). *Principia Ethica*. Cambridge: Cambridge University Press.

MURAMATSU, R. and HANOCH, Y. (2005). Emotions as a Mechanism for Boundedly Rational Agents: The Fast and Frugal Way. *Journal of Economic Psychology*, 26: 201–21.

OSBECK, L. M. (1999) 'Conceptual Problems in the Development of a Psychological Notion of " 'Intuition".' *Journal of the Theory of Social Behavior*, 29/3: 229–49.

PAYNE, J. W. and BETTMAN, J. R. (2004). 'The Information-Processing Approach to Decision-Making,' in D. J. Koehler and N. Harvey (eds.), *Blackwell Handbook of Judgement and Decision-making*. London: Blackwell Publishing, 110–32.

—— —— JOHNSON, E. (1993). *The Adaptive Decision Maker*. Cambridge: Cambridge University Press.

POLANYI, M. (1966). *The Tacit Dimension*. London: Routledge and Kegan Paul.

PRIEM, R. L., RASHEED, A. M. A. and KOTULIC, A. G. (1995). 'Rationality in Strategic Decision Processes, Environmental Dynamism and Firm Performance.' *Journal of Management*, 21/5: 913–29.

REBER, A. S. (1993). *Implicit Learning and Tacit Knowledge: An Essay on the Cognitive Unconscious*. New York: Oxford University Press.

SADLER-SMITH, E. (2004). 'Cognitive Style and the Performance of Small and Medium Sized Enterprises.' *Organization Studies*, 25: 155–82.

—— (2008). *Inside Intuition*. Abingdon: Routledge.

—— SHEFY, E. (2004). 'The Intuitive Executive: Understanding and Applying "Gut Feel" in Decision-Making.' *The Academy of Management Executive*, 18/4: 76–92.

SCHOEMAKER, P. J. H. and RUSSO, J. E. (1993). 'A Pyramid of Decision Approaches.' *California Management Review*, Fall: 9–31.

SCHÖN, D. A. (1983). *The Reflective Practitioner*. New York: Basic Books.

SCHOOLER, J. W., OHLSSON, S., and BROOKS, K. (1993). 'Thought Beyond Words: When Language Overshadows Insight.' *Journal of Experimental Psychology: General*. 122/2: 166–83.

SHAFIR, E. and LEBOUEF, A. (2002). 'Rationality.' *Annual Review of Psychology*, 53: 491–517.

SHAPIRO, S. and SPENCE, M. T. (1997). 'Managerial Intuition: A Conceptual and Operational Framework.' *Business Horizons*, 40/1: 63–8.

SHOWERS, J. L. and CHAKRIN, L. (1981). 'Reducing Uncollectible Revenue from Residential Telephone Customers.' *Interfaces*, 11: 21–31.

SIMON, H. A. (1947). *Administrative Behavior*. New York: MacMillan

—— (1982). *The Sciences of The Artificial* (2nd edn.), Cambridge, MA: MIT Press.

—— (1983). *Reason in Human Affairs*. Palo Alto, CA: Stanford University Press.

—— (1987). 'Making Management Decisions: The Role of Intuition and Emotion.' *Academy of Management Executive*, 1: 57–64.

—— (1997). *Administrative Behavior* (4th edn.). New York: Free Press.

SINCLAIR, M. and ASHKANASY, N. M. (2005). 'Intuition: Myth or a Decision-Making Tool?' *Management Learning*, 36/3: 353–70.

SLOVIC, P. (1972). 'Psychological Study of Human Judgment: Implications for Investment Decision-Making.' *Journal of Finance*, XXVII/4: 160–72.

SLOVIC, P., FINUCANE, M., PETERS, E., and MACGREGOR, D. G. (2002). 'The Affect Heuristic,' in T. Gilovich, D. Griffin and D. Kahneman (eds.), *Heuristics and Biases: The Psychology of Intuitive Judgments*. Cambridge: Cambridge University Press, 49–81.

STANOVICH, K. E. and WEST, R. F. (2000). 'Individual Differences in Reasoning: Implications for the Rationality Debate?' *Behavioral and Brain Sciences*, 23/5: 645–65.

SWINK, M. (1995). 'The Influences of User Characteristics on Performance in a Logistics DSS Application.' *Decision Sciences*, 26/4: 503–29.

WAGNER, R. K. (2002). 'Smart People Doing Dumb Things: The Case of Managerial Incompetence,' in R. J. Sternberg (ed.), *Why Smart People Can Be So Stupid*. New Haven, CT: Yale University Press, 42–63.

WILSON, T. D. and SCHOOLER, J. W. (1991). 'Thinking Too Much: Introspection can Reduce the Quality of Preferences and Decisions.' *Journal of Personality and Social Psychology*, 60: 181–92.

YANIV, I. and HOGARTH, R. M. (1993). 'Judgemental Versus Statistical Prediction: Information Asymmetry and Combination Rules.' *Psychological Science*, 4: 58–62.

17

AFFECT AND INFORMATION PROCESSING

KEVIN DANIELS

INTRODUCTION

WHY do some things make us anxious, yet others make us happy? Are we less concerned about risk when in a good mood than in a bad mood? Why do some people feel less confident when they are down, yet others respond to stressful conditions by trying to master their difficulties? These questions concern how our moods and emotions interact with our cognitive processes. There is little dispute that our feelings and thoughts are connected—but the ways in which they are, and how they influence phenomena in work organizations, are far from straightforward.

Definitions of key terms are necessary. The general term "affect" (Parkinson 1995) subsumes both "emotion" (feelings towards an event, object, or person) and "mood" (feelings that are not linked to a specific event, object, or person). Affect has cognitive, expressive, and physiological components (Russell 2003). The focus of this chapter is the cognitive component, because much organizational research on affect has concentrated on this component. Affect also has state and trait aspects. State affect refers to how people feel at a given moment in time, trait affect (or temperament) to dispositions to experience certain kinds of affect (Watson and Clark 1984).

Psychometrically, affective experience can be represented in two dimensional space (Watson and Tellegen 1985). More specific affects cluster at points in this space (Daniels 2000). These two major dimensions are negative and positive affect (Watson and Tellegen 1985). High negative affect relates to the more specific unpleasant affects of anxiety and anger. Its opposite is relaxation. High positive affect relates to more specific pleasant and high activation affects such as enthusiasm. Its opposite relates to the more specific affects of depression and boredom (Watson et al. 1988).

Because of the pervasive nature of affect, organizational research has investigated many theoretical and applied issues. It is not be possible to cover the full range of phenomena investigated, or the full range of theoretical perspectives adopted. Instead, predominantly psychological approaches are the main focus. The topics of this chapter include: how cognitive processes influence affect; how cognitive processes regulate affective experience; how state affect influences cognitive processes; and the role of trait affect. There are organizational applications in each domain. The chapter concludes by highlighting directions for research.

Cognitive Processes' Influence on Affect

Cognitive theories that link judgments to affect are often called appraisal theories, many of which indicate that affect results from an evaluation—or appraisal—that an event, situation, object, or person has or will have an impact on the pursuit of goals (see Power and Dalgleish 1997 for a review). Zajonc (1980) disputed the causal status of appraisals, arguing that affective reactions to events occur too quickly for detailed appraisal of goal progress to occur. To address this, some researchers have argued that appraisals can be made on the basis of slow, deliberative, and detailed cognitive processes, or on the basis of fast, restricted, unconscious cognitive processing (Smith and Kirby 2001). Power and Dalgleish's (1997) SPAARS model is one of the more cognitively detailed accounts of the appraisal process, including both slower and faster forms of appraisal. This model is one of the contributory approaches to a model of affective reactions to work events (Daniels et al. 2004), which contains three major elements that encapsulate how work events are considered to influence initial affective reactions to those events.

Element 1: Categorization

This allows individuals to make inferences, since it allows individuals to use past information from similar situations to predict the consequences of future situations (Smith and Medin 1981). Before an event can influence emotions, it needs to be perceived—consciously or unconsciously—and then categorized as emotionally relevant. Daniels et al. (2004) consider that categorization can occur in two ways, both enabling individuals to use beliefs about similar past events to make inferences about current events. First, an event can be categorized as relevant for current goals. This starts a slow process of goal-related appraisal. Second, an event can be categorized as similar to events that have disrupted goals in the past. Here, categorization is based on a few defining features of an event that are similar to or the same as previously encountered events. This type of process starts the fast process of appraisal.

Element 2: Goal-Related Inferences

Categorization of an event cues the recall of beliefs about that event. For appraisals concerning goals, there are not only beliefs concerning how similar events influence goal progress, but there also needs to be an evaluation of progress towards goals against the desired rate of goal progress (Daniels et al. 2004). Therefore, goal related processing is necessarily slower, because it involves a detailed consideration of current circumstances, informed by beliefs concerning similar kinds of events.

Negative affect is considered to arise from expectancies that an event will reduce the desired rate of goal progress (Carver and Scheier 1990). In contrast, positive affect is thought to arise when events are believed to accelerate progress toward goals at a rate greater than desired (Carver and Scheier 1990). However, the production of low positive affect can arise in two ways: either failure or loss of the desired rate of goal progress or absence of detailed processing about a goal. The specific affect of sadness, related to low positive affect, is thought to result from inferences of a permanent failure to achieve the desired rate of goal progress (Oatley and Johnson-Laird 1987). Boredom, again a specific affect closely related to low positive affect, is thought to be the product of absence of detailed processing about current goals (Daniels et al. 2004).

Element 3: Emotional Associations

When categorization is based on only a few key features of an event, cognitive processing is fast. In this kind of processing, categorization, beyond conscious awareness, cues recall of information concerning previously encountered events that have been learnt to produce specific affects because of their influence on goals. This allows individuals to make inferences concerning current events, without having to process detailed information about goal progress. However, it is considered that the information activated by categorization also activates the phenomenological experience of the specific affect that has been learnt to be associated with similar kinds of event, so causing that affect to be experienced (Power and Dalgleish 1997). Daniels et al. (2004) note that an analogy to this process is classical conditioning.

Cognitive theories of affect in the workplace have received little empirical attention (Cooper et al. 2001; Dewe and Cooper 2007). There has been little investigation of how people categorize work events as a basis for judgments concerning goals and affect. However, evidence does indicate that people can articulate work events that are linked to particular categories of affects or work goals such as performance (Daniels et al. 2002). There are more studies on appraisals of work events and conditions (e.g., Dewe 1989), although these are small in number compared to studies that attempt to link measures of the "objective" work environment to affective and related states. In relation to Daniels et al.'s model, there are three relevant studies, all using experience sampling methods (one in Harris and Daniels 2005; two in Daniels et al. 2006). These studies indicate that beliefs about work stressors' influence on goals and affect may influence affective reactions to work stressors.

Studies also suggest the influence of the social and institutional contexts of organizations in shaping beliefs about stressors and affect at work (e.g., Daniels et al. 2002; Harkness et al. 2005). Understanding the organizational influences on such beliefs may provide a better basis for understanding why some interventions to change objective work conditions appear to have no effect on well-being (Harkness et al. 2005), or provide a basis for prioritizing changes to work conditions to enhance well-being in the workplace (Daniels et al. 2002). The practical importance of examining collective influences on appraisals is underscored by findings that show positive relationships between work performance and work conditions likely to be appraised as challenging, but negative relationships between performance and work conditions likely to be appraised as hindrances (LePine et al. 2005).

COGNITIVE PROCESSES AND THE REGULATION OF AFFECTIVE EXPERIENCE

Daniels et al.'s model of work events and affect also considers the judgments individuals make in order to help them regulate unpleasant affective experience—a process usually referred to as coping and which includes both deliberate and considered decisions to regulate affect, as well as more unconscious and habitual responses (Cramer 2000). Coping consists of cognitive and behavioral elements. The cognitive aspect of coping is the "coping function," or the target of coping. There exist many typologies of coping function (Skinner et al. 2003). Some of the more frequent mentioned functions include: problem focused coping—which is directed at altering things or their consequences; appraisal focused coping—directed at altering the beliefs or inferences that are presumed to cause unpleasant affect; avoidance—directed at suppressing thoughts to regulate affect; and emotion focused coping—directed at changing affect, through for example, cathartic expression of affect.

Coping behaviors are the means through which coping functions come to be (Skinner et al. 2003). For example, eliciting support (behavior) from work colleagues can be used to distract oneself (avoidance), obtain advice (problem focused), ask if one has made the right inferences about consequences (appraisal focused), or validate one's affective reaction by asking how others would respond (emotion focused).

In general, conclusions concerning the effectiveness of coping in work organizations are difficult to draw (Cooper et al. 2001; Dewe and Cooper 2007). It is possible that at least some of the conflicting evidence is because most studies do not link coping functions to coping behaviors explicitly, and because most workplace studies have used measures that require recall of coping activity over several days or weeks. Such retrospective self-report measures of coping are both inaccurate (Todd et al. 2004) and limited in their ability to examine the dynamic processes by which different coping function/behavior combinations may have prolonged, delayed, or decaying effects on affect.

One recent daily diary study examined different coping functions used to deal with daily work demands and brought about by seeking support from co-workers or executing control over work tasks or schedules (Daniels and Harris 2005). Findings indicated that problem focused coping achieved through support was related to better daily affective experience on both the same day as coping and on the following day. In contrast, problem focused coping achieved by executing control was related only to subsequent reports of goal attainment. These results indicate immediate and sustained effectiveness for problem focused coping through support, yet delayed effects of problem focused coping through control. Amongst other results, avoidance through executing control was related to better affective experience on the following morning only, indicating a delayed and rapidly decaying effect. These findings indicate the importance of temporal dynamics, as well as careful consideration of coping functions and behaviors, in relating affective experience to the cognitive regulation of affect.

Understanding the cognitive processes that influence how we come to choose how we cope with aversive work events and situations has received little attention by organizational researchers. In their model, Daniels et al. (2004) consider that judgment concerning coping can again be made on the basis of detailed and deliberative processing, or made by fast processing of a restricted amount of information.

In the former process, it is expected that considerations of what might be effective and capable of being executed influence judgments concerning the most appropriate form of coping. Daniels et al. argue judgments could be based upon recall of past coping successes in situations categorized as being similar to current circumstances, perceptions of the amenability of the environment to executing certain forms of coping (principally in relation to perceptions of support or levels of job control available), the costs of executing certain forms of coping (e.g., in terms of energy expended), and the importance the person accords to resolving the situation. For faster and restricted cognitive processes, Daniels et al. consider that judgments concerning coping are influenced minimally by the environment and its amenability to certain forms of coping, but principally by strongly learnt associations between certain coping functions and the reduction of unpleasant affect.

Considering how individuals regulate affective experience at work has obvious implications for the design of psychologically healthy work conditions. Following from Karasek and Theorell's (1990) job demands–control–support model, Daniels et al. consider the ability for individuals to exert control over working practices or elicit support from colleagues as principal environmental drivers of coping choice and subsequent coping success. However, this goes beyond health considerations. Karasek and Theorell, as well as Wall et al. (2002), consider that the execution of control to solve problems leads individuals incrementally to learn how to improve their work performance. However, detailed links between job design, problem solving, learning, and other cognitive processes still need to be investigated.

Affective Influences on Cognition

It is not surprising that affect influences cognition. There is much evidence to suggest this is the case and many theoretical perspectives attempt to account for affective influences on cognition (e.g., Martin and Clore 2001; Ashkanasy and Ashton-James 2005). This section describes three strands of this research: (1) the "affect as information" hypothesis, and research that qualifies the basic hypothesis of this model; (2) research that examines the influence of affect on the specific cognitive processes of attention and memory; and (3) recent theoretical work on the link between affect and cognitive resource allocation as an explanation for variations in individual work performance (Beal et al. 2005).

The "affect as information" hypothesis starts from the assumption that how one feels *in* a situation might be taken as evidence to integrate into judgments or to compare the favorability of different courses of action (Schwarz 2000; Clore et al. 2001; Peters et al. 2006). This basic hypothesis allows an explanation of "affect congruence," which is where individuals seem to process information in a way that is consistent with their affective state. For example, individuals in a good mood tend to overestimate the likelihood of positive outcomes, whilst individuals with unpleasant affect overestimate the likelihood of negative consequences (Schwarz 2000). In respect of direct judgment, how one feels about a situation, person, or object is used directly as information in coming to a judgment (Clore et al. 2001). For example, people in a good mood at work may decide to help others, simply because they are in a good mood. However, judgments are made often with some input from memory. In respect of recall of information from memory, the affect experienced in a situation may help cue recall information about similar situations where the same kind of affect was experienced (Clore et al. 2001). Here, affect has an indirect effect—the information recalled is about previous similar situations, not situations that evoked similar affects but are otherwise dissimilar.

Another aspect of the "affect as information" hypothesis is that positive affect is associated with more use of heuristic processing relying heavily on existing knowledge, but negative affect with greater use of detailed, deliberative processing of information from the environment. Positive affective is thought to indicate that the environment is benign, allowing us to rely on our usual assumptions and routines of behavior, whereas negative affect is thought to signal that the current state is problematic, encouraging people to resolve their difficulties by close attention to issues in the environment (Schwarz 2000; Clore et al. 2001). In relation to this, the experience of negative affect may lead people to follow decision protocols more closely than if they were experiencing positive affect (Elsbach and Barr 1999).

In general, research evidence does support the "affect as information" hypothesis, but with some qualification. Evidence indicates that the heuristic biasing of positive affect can be overcome where there are various motivational factors (see, e.g., Lassiter et al. 1996; Côté 2005). In additional to these motivational effects, Forgas (Forgas 2001; Forgas and George 2001) also indicates there is no influence of affect for information processing tasks that are so restricted, automatic, and minimally influenced by the environment that more elaborate processing is not required. Further, Forgas indicates affect can influence judgment, so that mood congruency effects occur, only when some degree of "substantive generative" processing is needed—which is fusing information from the environment with pre-existing knowledge to create new knowledge or inferences. Such "substantive generative" processing may be more automatic and truncated. According to Forgas, this is where the "affect as information hypothesis" applies most. Mood congruency can also occur for "substantive generative" processing that is involves more extensive, detailed processing that still requires synthesis of information from the environment and knowledge held in memory.

Research on affective influences on attention and memory has indicated differentiation in how two specific affects influence cognition, specifically anxiety and sadness. These are examples of high negative affect and low positive affect respectively. In both cases, the research perspectives indicate that anxiety and sadness bias information processing toward negative information, but in different ways. Anxiety is thought to bias the allocation of attention toward processing information concerning threats and obstacles in the environment (Dalgleish and Watts 1990). Evidence indicates that such biases are automatic for anxiety, and also anger, another affect characterized as high negative affect (MacCleod 1991; Clore and Gasper 2000). Anxiety is concerned with present threats to goals, and anger with present obstacles to goals (Oatley and Johnson-Laird 1987), which is one explanation for the effects of these affects on attention. In contrast, sadness is concerned with loss or failure of goals (Oatley and Johnson-Laird 1987), and so sadness is thought to orient information processing toward the past and under-standing the causes of loss or failure. This past orientation explains findings that indicate sadness influences recall (Dalgleish and Watts 1990), which occurs because sadness suppresses recall of positive information, so that recall of negative infor-mation is more likely (Wenzlaff and Bates 1998). In both cases, because anxiety and sadness orient the individual to negative information, then there is an explanation why individuals experiencing these kinds of unpleasant affects are more likely to engage in ruminative thinking (Hertel 2004).

As research on cognitive processes indicates, almost any area of organizational life that requires processing of information could be influenced by affect (Forgas and George 2001). Affective experience may influence judgments concerning levels of well-being, job satisfaction, organizational commitment, turnover intentions, and decisions in to engage in organizational citizenship behaviors (Weiss et al. 1999; Thoresen et al. 2003; Lee and Allen 2002). In terms of managerial decision making, affect might influence judgment of risk and whether decision options are considered more or less optimistically (Lerner and Keltner 2001). The "feelings as information" hypothesis may be especially relevant in determining how managers view various decision options, while the influence of anxiety and sadness on attention and recall may be relevant for explaining stability and escalation of poor psychological well-being in some work environments (Daniels et al. 2004) or why senior managers may sometimes pay more attention to threats in the strategic environment rather than opportunities (Daniels 1999).

The heuristic processing associated with high positive affect has at least two organizational implications, one adaptive, the other potentially less so. Although discussing executive job demands, Hambrick et al. (2005) identified two heuristics managers use in strategic decisions (see also Ganster 2005). These are that man-agers can give greater weight to familiar information in coming to strategic decisions or they might imitate strategies of other firms. It might be that positive affect leads managers to adopt either or both of these heuristics, since they are easily accessible heuristics for managers (cf., Ruder and Bless 2003), leading potentially to decisions that are not aligned with the nature of the strategic environment.

The adaptive function of heuristic processing engendered by positive affect is greater levels of creativity. Evidence does indicate associations between positive affect and subsequent creativity in work environments (Amabile et al. 2005). One explanation is that because positive affect indicates no problems in the environment, and therefore no need to engage in detailed information processing, cognitive resources can be directed at elaborating knowledge structures and links between various knowledge structures (Clore et al. 2001). Alternatively, positive affect might promote creativity through a motivational mechanism (Carver 2003). If pleasant affect signals that goal progress is faster than desired, then people may withdraw effort from the current goal and devote effort to other pursuits—including generating solutions to problems that are of no immediate concern.

It may be the case that negative affect can promote creativity in some circumstances. Coping activity directed toward reducing negative affect may engage cognitive processes to the level where extensive elaboration of existing knowledge is not possible. Even so, where resources, such as social support or job control are available (Karasek and Theorell 1990; Wall et al. 2002), then less cognitive effort may be needed to regulate affect and there may be some level of creativity if affect regulation is directed at solving problems by applying and adapting existing knowledge (cf., Erber and Erber 2001). This possibility leads to a consideration that high positive affect might influence both incremental and radical innovations, although the detailed processing associated with negative affect and its regulation may influence incremental innovation only (cf., Karasek and Theorell 1990; Wall et al. 2002).

Beal et al.'s (2005) model of dynamic, within-person variability in work performance includes consideration of how affect regulation impinges upon cognitive capacity, as well as other affective processes. The model indicates that individual variation in task performance is influenced by attentional focus on the task in hand, the level of cognitive resources available for the task, and the resources available to focus attention on the task. In this model, Beal et al. consider that affective influences on performance are stronger on more complex tasks, because more cognitive resources are required for such tasks.

Beal et al. list a number of factors they expect to exert attentional pull away from a work task. Appraisal of non-task related events as causes of unpleasant affect, especially the more deliberative kinds of appraisal and rumination about the events, pull attention away from the work task and toward systematic processing concerning the events. High arousal emotions (both negative and positive affect are "high" arousal emotions, Watson and Tellegen 1985) can divert attention to perceived causes of affect generating events, also potentially drawing information away from the work task. Affect regulation also pulls attention away from the work task. However, because Beal et al.s' model is dynamic, rapidly successful affect regulation, or affect regulation strategies that are well learnt and do not require much cognitive effort, might not interfere with performance over an extended period.

Beal et al. consider that affect regulation also depletes the ability to focus attention on the work task. They consider that attempts to avoid thinking about the affect inducing event and, most especially, attempts to alter the expression or experience of affect might have the most detrimental effects. However, taking breaks to replenish resources might be beneficial for attention regulation, as might affect attributed to the task, for example positive affect attributed to the task or anticipation of future task enjoyment.

AFFECTIVE PERSONALITY

Because affect influences cognition, then the tendency to experience some forms of affect has clear implications for differences between people in judgments concerning work environments (Thoresen et al. 2003). The extent to which trait affect influences judgments and the processes by which it does so are heavily contested among researchers interested in how individuals make judgments concerning their work conditions, but there are implications in other applied areas too.

Findings in this area indicate that measures of trait affect are associated with: individuals' attitudes towards work (Thoresen et al. 2003); perceptions of their work conditions and reports of their health (Fergusson et al. 2006); cognitive failures—lapses of memory, wandering attention and failure to execute actions properly (Wallace and Chen 2005); and managers' perceptions of their organizations' strategic environment (Daniels 1998).

Much organizational research has examined the moderating role of trait affect on work conditions—or job stressors—presumed to cause affective reactions. Many studies have examined interactions between self-reports of job stressors and trait affect, using a range of dependent variables, including attitudes toward work, intentions and behaviors (e.g., Fox et al. 2001; Barsky et al. 2004). Across such studies, the interactions are usually not significant—indicating that trait affect does not alter the influence of the affective impact of work conditions on attitudes towards work or decisions to engage in various behaviors. However, such findings need not be taken to indicate that trait affect influences cognitive processes in a way that is independent of the work environment or state affect.

In respect of the conjoint effects of trait and state affect, Rusting (1998) has indicated that an "independent effects" model is the least likely explanation for a range of cognitive consequences of state and trait affect found in laboratory settings. Although there is evidence from laboratory studies that state and trait affect interact to influence cognitive processes (Rusting 2001; Williams et al. 1996), an explanation based simply on interactions between state and trait affect needs further qualification. As Rusting (1998) noted, as well as interacting with trait affect, state affect could mediate the link between trait affect and cognitive processing, and there is some evidence for this (Hemenover 2001). Moreover, Rusting (2001) has indicated other contingencies need to be taken into account to observe state by trait affect interactions. Outside of laboratory environments, these are motivations (and opportunities) to alter state affect and the extent to which cognitive tasks require the kind of "substantive generative" processing outlined by Forgas (2001). Temporal dynamics seem important to, with the potential for the influence of trait affect on processing to accumulate as minor influences on decisions lead incrementally to a build up of negative inferences, negative mood, and poor judgment (cf., Suls' 2001 description of the "neurotic cascade").

Notwithstanding, these complexities, Williams et al. (1996) have suggested state by trait affect interactions come about because trait affect is associated with more elaborate knowledge structures associated with that affect. For example, people high in trait negative affect are expected to experience negative affect more often, and so develop elaborate knowledge structures containing negatively valenced information. Because of mood congruity effects, when in a state of negative affect, people high in trait negative affect recall these knowledge structures that subsequently direct further information processing towards negative information. This has led Daniels et al. (2004) to propose that inconsistent evidence for interactions between job stressors and trait affect reflects measurement imprecision. Rather than assessing trait affect and assuming links to knowledge structures, they propose researchers assess knowledge structures directly, or at least relevant aspects of them (cf., Daniels et al. 2007).

CONCLUSIONS: FUTURE DIRECTIONS FOR RESEARCH AND RESEARCH METHODS

The complexities of affect–cognition relationships at the individual level are founded on several principles. These principles include reciprocal relationships between affect and cognition; differences in information processing strategies (more deliberative or more restricted); motivations and strategies to regulate affect; the nature of the work environment; and temperamental differences between individuals. The dynamic and ephemeral nature of both affect and cognition add further temporal considerations. Hence, even when considering psychologically focused research on a restricted number of basic affects, it would be simplistic to draw one generalized conclusion about affect and cognition from the diverse research programs that have contributed to our understanding.

Such complexities mean there are inevitably areas where our understanding is not as deep and as full as we may wish. Affect, affective regulation and the cognitive processes that contribute to work performance is one area where major advances in understanding could be achieved rapidly. As well as "on-task" performance (see Beal et al. 2005), close examination of the influence of work design and personal factors on learning and innovation, and the mediating role of affect regulation strategies, would help fill one of the longstanding empirical gaps in our understanding of job design, namely how jobs with seemingly psychological hygienic characteristics contribute to better individual and organizational performance (van der Doef and Maes 1999). Research on the "flow" experience, a state of absorption, positive affect, and motivation, also could indicate how job features might contribute to certain forms of work performance (Bakker 2005).

Of course, affect has a communicative function (Parkinson 1995) and work organizations are social environments. Mood linkage or emotional contagion, whereby people appear to "catch" affective states from others is now well documented in work contexts (Kelly and Barsade 2001). It is not surprising, then, that there is evidence of relationships between the social contexts of organizations, affect and the processes of organizational decision making (Maitlis and Ozcelik 2004; Kopelman et al. 2006). Another fruitful area in which rapid advances could be made is investigation of the interplay between social contexts, affect, and cognition, at all organizational levels. Considering the more complex and overtly social emotions such as jealousy, envy, shame, and embarrassment could also enhance of affect in organizational contexts—although the relatively basic affect of boredom remains conspicuously absent from much organizational research. As noted above, investigation of the social and discursive processes that shape individuals' beliefs about work environment in the context of job redesign may indicate why some job redesign interventions appear to confer benefits, yet others do not (see Briner and Reynolds 1999 for a review).

The evidence reviewed here indicates complex interplays between affect and cognition that unfold over time, yet one in which stable differences in temperament and possibly knowledge structures play a role. Since it is not possible to manipulate stable differences in temperament and knowledge structures in laboratory environments, the clear implication for researchers should adopt real-time, longitudinal methods. Documented inaccuracies in our ability to recall affective states and affect regulation strategies (Parkinson et al. 1995; Todd et al. 2004) further reinforce this conclusion. Where knowledge is lacking, then inductive, longitudinal, ethnographic style methods may be most appropriate for generating knowledge and developing theoretical models. Where there are already strong models to work from, then, structured experience sampling methods, that require individuals to complete short questionnaires once or more times per day over several days, may be the best methods available (Bolger et al. 2003). One significant challenge is to develop methods that can represent knowledge structures but that are also suitable for experience sampling methods (Clarkson and Hodgkinson 2005).

As well as providing high ecological validity, one advantage of experience sampling methods is that they allow simultaneous investigation of differences between individuals (e.g., differences in trait affect), differences within individuals across time (e.g., state affect) and the ability to examine interactions between these two levels of analysis (e.g., state * trait affect; cf., Hofmann and Gavin 1998). Another advantage is that these methods allow investigation of temporal dynamics, including examination of whether changes in affect are concurrent with changes in cognition, and if, over time, any links between affect and cognition accumulate, decay or are delayed.

While there are rich theoretical perspectives to work from, research on affect and cognition in organizational contexts has a limited empirical base—even in those areas traditionally considered more concerned with affect. This limited empirical base also has restricted understanding of many of the more complex affective states, social contexts, and temporal dynamics. What is clear, then, is that organizational investigations of links between affect and cognition are one area of research where there is great promise for developing our understanding of virtually any organizational phenomenon that involves individuals making judgments, taking decisions, or executing plans.

REFERENCES

AMABILE, T. M., BARSADE, S. G., MUELLER, J. S., and STAW, B. M. (2005). 'Affect and Creativity at Work.' *Administrative Science Quarterly*, 50: 367–403.

ASHKANASY, N. M., and ASHTON-JAMES, C. E. (2005). 'Emotion in Organizations: A Neglected Topic in I/O Psychology, But With a Bright Future,' in G. P. Hodgkinson and J. K. Ford (eds.), *International Review of Industrial and Organizational Psychology*, Vol. 20. Chichester, UK: Wiley, 221–68.

BAKKER, A. B. (2005). 'Flow Among Music Teachers and Their Students: The Crossover of Peak Experience.' *Journal of Vocational Behavior*, 66: 26–44.

BARKSY, A., THORESEN, C. J., WARREN, C. R., and KAPLAN, S. A. (2004). 'Modeling Negative Affectivity and Job Stress: A Contingency-Based Approach.' *Journal of Organizational Behavior*, 25: 915–36.

BEAL, D. J., WEISS, H. M., BARROS, E., and MACDERMID, S. M. (2005). 'An Episodic Process Model of Affective Influences on Performance.' *Journal of Applied Psychology*, 90: 1054–68.

BOLGER, N., DAVIS, A., and RAFAELI, E. (2003). 'Diary Methods: Capturing Life as it is Lived.' *Annual Review of Psychology*, 54: 579–616.

BRINER R. B. and REYNOLDS S. (1999). 'The Costs, Benefits, and Limitations of Organizational Level Stress Interventions.' *Journal of Organizational Behavior*, 20: 647–64.

CARVER, C. S. and SCHEIER, M. F. (1990). 'Origins and Functions of Positive and Negative Affect: A Control-Process View.' *Psychological Review*, 97: 19–35.

CARVER, C. S. (2003). 'Pleasure as a Sign You Can Attend to Something Else: Placing Positive Feelings Within a General Model of Affect.' *Cognition and Emotion*, 17: 241–61.

CLARKSON, G. P. and HODGKINSON, G. P. (2005). 'Introducing Cognizer™: A Comprehensive Computer Package for the Elicitation and Analysis of Cause Maps.' *Organizational Research Methods*, 8: 317–41.

CLORE, G. L. and GASPER, K. (2000). 'Feeling is Believing: Some Affective Influences on Belief,' in N. H. FRIJDA, A. S. R. Manstead, and S. Bem (eds.), *Emotions and Beliefs: How Feelings Influence Thoughts*. Paris: Cambridge University Press, 10–44.

—— WYER, R. S., DIENES, B. et al. (2001). 'Affective Feelings as Feedback: Some Cognitive Consequences,' in L. L. Martin and G. L. Clore (eds.), *Theories of Mood and Cognition: A User's Handbook*. Mahwah, NJ: Erlbaum, 27–62.

COOPER, C. L., DEWE, P. J., and O'DRISCOLL, M. P. (2001). *Organizational Stress: A Review and Critique of Theory, Research, and Applications*. Thousand Oaks, CA: Sage.

CÔTÉ, S. (2005). 'Reconciling the Feelings-as-Information and Hedonic Contingency Models of How Mood Influences Systematic Information Processing.' *Journal of Applied Social Psychology*, 35: 1656–79.

CRAMER, P. (2000). 'Defense Mechanisms in Psychology Today: Further Process for Adaptation.' *American Psychologist*, 55: 637–46.

DALGLEISH, T. and WATTS, F. N. (1990). 'Biases of Attention and Memory in Disorders of Anxiety and Depression.' *Clinical Psychology Review*, 10: 589–604.

DANIELS, K. (1998). 'Toward Integrating Emotions Into Strategic Management Research: Trait Affect and the Perception of the Strategic Environment.' *British Journal of Management*, 9: 163–8.

—— (1999). 'Emotion and Strategic Decision Making.' *The Psychologist*, 12: 24–8.

—— (2000). 'Measures of Five Aspects of Affective Well-Being at Work.' *Human Relations*, 53: 275–94.

—— and HARRIS, C. (2005). 'A Daily Diary Study of Coping in the Context of the Job Demands-Control-Support Model.' *Journal of Vocational Behavior*, 66: 219–37.

—— —— BRINER, R. (2002). *Understanding the Risks of Stress: A Cognitive Approach*. Sudbury: HSE Books.

—— —— —— (2004). 'Linking Work Conditions to Unpleasant Affect: Cognition, Categorization and Goals.' *Journal of Occupational and Organizational Psychology*, 77: 343–64.

—— HARTLEY, R., and TRAVERS, C. (2007). 'Beliefs about Stressors Alter Stressors' Impact: Evidence from Two Experience-Sampling Studies.' *Human Relations*, 59: 1261–85.

DEWE, P. (1989). 'Examining the Nature of Work Stress: Individual Evaluations of Stressful Experiences and Coping.' *Human Relations*, 42: 993–1013

—— COOPER, C. (2007). 'Coping Research and Measurement in the Context of Work Related Stress,' in G. P. Hodgkinson and J. K. Ford (eds.), *International Review of Industrial and Organizational Psychology*, Vol. 22. Chichester, UK: Wiley, 141–91.

ELSBACH, K. D., and BARR, P. S. (1999). 'The Effects of Mood on Individual's Use of Structured Decision Protocols.' *Organization Science*, 10: 181–98.

ERBER, R. and ERBER, M. W. (2001). 'Mood and Processing: A View from a Self-Regulation Perspective,' in L. L. Martin and G. L. Clore (eds.), *Theories of Mood and Cognition: A User's Handbook*. Mahwah, NJ: Erlbaum, 63–84.

FERGUSSON, E., DANIELS, K., and JONES, D. (2006). 'The Relative Contributions of Work Conditions and Psychological Differences to Health Measures: A Meta-Analysis with Structural Equations Modelling.' *Journal of Psychosomatic Research*, 60: 45–52.

FORGAS, J. P. (2001). 'The Affect Infusion Model (AIM): An Integrative Theory of Mood Effects on Cognition and Judgments,' in L. L. Martin and G. L. Clore (eds.), *Theories of Mood and Cognition: A User's Handbook*. Mahwah, NJ: Erlbaum, 99–134.

—— GEORGE, J. M. (2001). 'Affective Influences on Judgments and Behavior in Organizations.' *Organizational Behavior and Human Decision Processes*, 86: 3–34.

FOX, S., SPECTOR, P. E., and MILES, D. (2001). 'Counterproductive Work Behavior (CWB) in Response to Stressors and Organizational Justice: Some Mediator and Moderator Tests for Autonomy and Emotions.' *Journal of Vocational Behavior*, 59: 291–309.

GANSTER, D. C. (2005). 'Executive Job Demands: Suggestions from a Stress and Decision-Making Perspective.' *Academy of Management Review*, 30: 492–502.

HAMBRICK, D. C., FINKELSTEIN, S., and MOONEY, A. C. (2005). 'Executive Job Demands: New Insights for Explaining Strategic Decisions and Leader Behaviors.' *Academy of Management Review*, 30: 472–91.

HARKNESS, A. M. B., LONG, B. C., BERMBACH, N. et al. (2005). 'Talking About Stress: Discourse Analysis and Implications for Stress Interventions.' *Work and Stress*, 19: 121–36.

HARRIS, C. and DANIELS, K. (2005). 'Daily Affect and Daily Beliefs about Work Demands.' *Journal of Occupational Health Psychology*, 10: 415–28.

HEMENOVER, S. H. (2001). 'Self-Reported Processing Bias and Naturally Occurring Mood: Mediators Between Personality and Stress Appraisals.' *Personality and Social Psychology Bulletin*, 4: 387–94.

HERTEL, P. (2004). 'Habits of Thought Produce Memory Biases in Anxiety and Depression,' in J. Yiend (ed.), *Cognition, Emotion and Psychopathology*. Cambridge: Cambridge University Press, 109–29.

HOFMANN, D. A. and GAVIN, M. B. (1998). 'Centering Decisions in Hierarchical Linear Models: Implications for Research in Organizations.' *Journal of Management*, 24: 623–41.

KARASEK, R. A. and THEORELL, T. (1990). *Healthy Work*. New York: Basic Books.

KELLY, J. R. and BARSADE, S. G. (2001). 'Mood and Emotions in Small Groups and Work Teams.' *Organizational Behavior and Human Decision Processes*, 86: 99–130.

KOPELMAN, S., ROSETTE, A. S., and THOMPSON, L. (2006). 'The Three Faces of Eve: Strategic Displays of Positive, Negative, and Neutral Emotions in Negotiations.' *Organizational Behavior and Human Decision Processes*, 99: 81–101.

LASSITER, G. D., KOENIG, L. J., and APPLE, K. J. (1996). 'Mood and Behavior Perception: Dysphoria Can Increase and Decrease Effortful Processing of Information.' *Personality and Social Psychology Bulletin*, 22: 794–810.

LEE, K. and ALLEN, N. J. (2002). 'Organizational Citizenship Behavior and Workplace Deviance: The Role of Affect and Cognitions.' *Journal of Applied Psychology*, 87: 131–42.

LEPINE, J. A., PODSAKOFF, N. P., and LEPINE, M. C. (2005). 'A Meta-Analytic Test of the Challenge Stressor-Hindrance Stressor Framework: An Explanation for Inconsistent Relationships Among Stressors and Performance.' *Academy of Management Journal*, 48: 764–75.

LERNER, J. S. and KELTNER, D. (2001). 'Fear, Anger, and Risk.' *Journal of Personality and Social Psychology*, 81: 146–59.

MACCLEOD, C. (1991). 'Clinical Anxiety and the Selective Encoding of Threatening Information.' *International Review of Psychiatry*, 3: 279–92.

MAITLIS, S. and OZCELIK, H. (2004). 'Toxic Decision Processes: A Study of Emotion and Organizational Decision Making.' *Organization Science*, 15: 375–93.

MARTIN, L. L. and CLORE, G. L. (2001). *Theories of Mood and Cognition*. New Jersey: Erlbaum.

OATLEY, K. and JOHNSON-LAIRD, P. (1987). 'Towards a Cognitive Theory of Emotions.' *Cognition and Emotion*, 1: 29–50.

PARKINSON, B. (1995). *Ideas and Realities of Emotion*. London: Routledge.

—— BRINER, R. B., REYNOLDS, S., and TOTTERDELL, P. (1995). 'Time Frames for Mood: Relations Between Momentary and Generalized Ratings of Affect.' *Personality and Social Psychology Bulletin*, 21: 331–9.

POWER, M. and DALGLEISH, T. (1997). *Cognition and Emotion: From Order to Disorder*. Hove, UK: Psychology Press.

RUDER, M. and BLESS, H. (2003). 'Mood and the Reliance on the Ease of Retrieval Heuristic.' *Journal of Personality and Social Psychology*, 85: 20–32.

RUSSELL, J. A. (2003). 'Core Affect and the Psychological Construction of Emotion.' *Psychological Review*, 110: 145–72.

RUSTING, C. L. (1998). 'Personality, Mood, and Cognitive Processing of Emotional Information: Three Conceptual Frameworks.' *Psychological Bulletin*, 124: 165–96.

—— (2001). 'Personality as a Moderator of Affective Influences on Cognition,' in J. P. Forgas (ed.), *Handbook of Affect and Social Cognition*. New Jersey: Erlbaum. 371–91.

SCHWARZ, N. (2000). 'Emotion, Cognition, and Decision Making.' *Cognition and Emotion*, 14, 433–40.

SKINNER, E. A., EDGE, K., ALTMAN, J., and SHERWOOD, H. (2003). 'Searching for the Structure of Coping: A Review and Critique of Category Systems for Classifying Ways of Coping.' *Psychological Bulletin*, 129: 216–69.

SMITH, C. A. and KIRBY, L. D. (2001). 'Affect and Cognitive Appraisal Processes,' in J. P. Forgas (ed.), *Handbook of Affect and Social Cognition*. New Jersey: Erlbaum, 75–92.

SMITH E. E. and MEDIN, D. L. (1981). *Categories and Concepts*. Cambridge, MA: Harvard University Press.

SULS, J. (2001). 'Affect, Stress, and Personality,' in J. P. Forgas (ed.), *Handbook of Affect and Social Cognition*. New Jersey: Erlbaum, 392–409.

THORESEN, C. J., KAPLAN, S. A., BARSKY, A. P., WARREN, C. R., and DE CHERMONT, K. (2003). 'The Affective Underpinnings of Job Perceptions and Attitudes: A Meta-Analytic Review and Integration.' *Psychological Bulletin*, 129: 914–45.

TODD, M., TENNEN, H., CARNEY, M. A., ARMELI, S., and AFFLECK, G. (2004). 'Do We Know How We Cope? Relating Daily Coping Reports to Global and Time-Limited Retrospective Assessments.' *Journal of Personality and Social Psychology*, 86: 310–19.

VAN DER DOEF, M. P. and MAES, S. (1999). 'The Job Demand-Control(-Support) Model and Psychological Well-Being: A Review of 20 Years of Empirical Research.' *Work and Stress*, 13: 87–114.

WALL, T. D., CORBETT, J. M., MARTIN, R., CLEGG, C. W., and JACKSON, P. R. (1990). 'Advanced Manufacturing Technology, Work Design, and Performance: A Change Study.' *Journal of Applied Psychology*, 75: 691–7.

WALLACE, J. C., and CHEN, G. (2005). 'Development and Validation of a Work Specific Measure of Cognitive Failure: Implications for Occupational Safety.' *Journal of Occupational and Organizational Psychology*, 78: 615–32.

WATSON, D. and CLARK, L. A. (1984). 'Negative Affectivity: The Disposition to Experience Aversive Emotional States.' *Psychological Bulletin*, 96: 465–90.

Watson, D. and Tellegen, A. (1985). 'Toward a Consensual Structure of Mood.' *Psychological Bulletin*, 98: 219–35.

—— Clark, L. A., and Carey, G. (1988). 'Positive and Negative Affectivity and their Relation to Anxiety and Depressive Disorders.' *Journal of Abnormal Psychology*, 97: 346–53.

Weiss, H. M., Nicholas, J. P., and Daus, C. S. (1999). 'An Examination of the Joint Effects of Affective Experiences and Job Beliefs on Job Satisfaction and Variations in Affective Experiences Over Time.' *Organizational Behavior and Human Decision Processes*, 78: 1–24.

Wenzlaff, R. M. and Bates, D. E. (1998). 'Unmasking a Cognitive Vulnerability to Depression: How Lapses in Mental Control Reveal Depressive Thinking.' *Journal of Personality and Social Psychology*, 75: 1559–71.

Williams, J. M. G., Watts, F. N., MacLeod, C., and Mathews, A. (1996). *Cognitive Psychology and Emotional Disorders* (2nd edn.). Chichester: Wiley.

Zajonc, R. B. (1980). 'Feeling and Thinking: Preferences Need No Inferences.' *American Psychologist*, 35: 151–75.

18

INDIVIDUAL DIFFERENCES AND DECISION MAKING

EMMA SOANE
NIGEL NICHOLSON

INTRODUCTION

OUR aim in this chapter is to provide an overview and discussion of the sources and effects of individual variation in how people make choices and decisions.

Before we do so let us frame our perspective. Decision making, in this volume and elsewhere, has connotations that are extremely broad, ranging from the reactions of the instant where stimulus meets response through to the major choices that alter the direction of lives, institutions, and business strategies. In the former connotation, people are continually engaged in decision making, much of it unconscious, in ways that shape their everyday experience. The latter life-span view offers a different perspective—that much of the time decision-making processes barely engage active thought, with the stream of decisions operating with a high degree of automaticity via algorithms and heuristics (Bargh and Chartrand 1999). The decisions that change the course of lives are relatively infrequent events and much rarer than actors subjectively assume.

This review encompasses both the micro and the life-span perspective, with the common assumption that individual differences are part of the evolved human design. Individuals reap the benefits of comparative advantage through differentiation, sustaining the survival of the species through complex social organization and their own reproductive fitness by occupying niches within it (Ridley 1999). Behavioural genetics research contains plentiful evidence for the existence of heritable differences in temperament and dispositions that will bear upon how we make decisions at the micro and life-space levels of choice (Ilies et al. 2006).

Scope and Objectives

In this chapter we shall discuss a range of individual difference variables that influence the state and goal orientation of a decision maker, and not the ex post evaluation of the quality of a decision, which is discussed elsewhere in this volume.

The model underlying our review, which we present in the concluding section of this chapter, has five main themes:

1. There are thresholds below which decisions are not consciously be made; rather, automaticity guides behavior.
2. Decisions making occurs within a goal oriented framework that optimises decision outcomes and minimizes decision–situation misfit.
3. A range of individual difference variables influences decision thresholds and goals as well as decision inputs and processes.
4. The interaction between individuals and situations is critical to understanding decision-making behavior. Key inputs include the strength and nature of the situation and individual differences in the strength of traits.
5. Within a life-span perspective, decisions are both a cause and an effect of individual differences and the shape of unfolding life histories.

A Review of Concepts

Our first objective is to summarize the extant literature that bears directly on individual differences and decision making. Since this encompasses a wide range of concepts, we have listed concepts, measures and chief findings in Table 18.1.

The individual difference factors in Table 18.1 operate at a number of levels. At the distal or deep level are deeply internalized states and processes that influence decision

Table 18.1 Summary of Individual Difference Factors and their Influence on Decision Making

Construct	Definition	Influences on decision making
Biographical		
Age	Number of years since birth	With increasing age, there are declines in information processing, but compensatory effects with experience (Salthouse 1984); older adults have more liberal response biases (Huh et al. 2006); there are some changes in personality over the lifespan (McCrae et al. 2005; Roberts et al. 2006).
Gender and sex differences	The blend of biological sex differences and socially constructed and reinforced notions of masculinity and femininity	Gender or sex differences influence: decisions about hiring and firing (Levin et al. 2005); forecasting of own behavior and behavior of others (Song et al. 2004); perceptions of distributive and procedural justice in organizations (Bernerth 2005); stereotyping to increase gender inequality in hiring decisions (Gorman 2005); decisions concerning new technology (Venkatesh 2000); risk-taking (Nicholson et al. 2005); leadership style (Eagly and Johnson 1990); attention to emotion in speech (Schirmer et al. 2005); responsive adaptation to uncertainty (Washburn et al. 2005); and, ethical decision making (Buckley et al. 1998).
Internal processes		
Affect and emotion	The range of short-term feelings and longer-term emotions that people experience	Emotion adds to choice information to aid decision making (Wilson and Arvai 2006); affect influences the role of loss in risk-taking decision behavior (Arkes et al. 1988); affect interacts with risk preferences and influences thoughts about loss (Isen and Geva 1987); affect interacts with task conditions to influence cognitive processes associated with motivation (Erez and Isen 2002); positive affect leads to increased efficiency in decision making (Isen 2001); increases in consumer decision making and in variety seeking (Kahn and Isen 1993).
Attribution	The processes through which people explain their own decisions and actions, and those of others (Martinko 1995)	Learned helplessness shapes choice making (Abramson et al. 1978); attributions influence interpretations of success, and motivation to predict and control environment (Heider 1958).

(Continued)

Table 18.1 (*Continued*)

Construct	Definition	Influences on decision making
Automaticity	Subconscious decision-making processes	Different levels of conscious processing affect decision making (Chartrand 2005); impulsive, goal independent decision making can be automatic (Van Osselaer et al. 2005); habit driven decisions tend to become automatic over time (Kim et al. 2005); conscious and unconscious information processing influence decision efficiency (Dijksterhuis 2004); priming influences decisions differentially depending on whether the focus is on the self or others (Kim and Wyer Jr 2004).
Motivation	Psychological mechanisms that influence the direction, intensity and persistence of actions, and that are distinct from ability or coercive environments (Vroom 1964).	Motivation influences goal choice and striving (Kanfer 1990; Locke and Latham 2002) and allocation of resources (Kanfer and Ackerman 1989).
Personality	The non-physical and non-intellectual qualities that make one person distinct from another (Adler 1996)	Personality type influences ex ante risk tolerance (Filbeck et al. 2005); personality traits influence responses to risk and framing effects (Kowert and Hermann 1997); personality interacts with information framing to influence decision making (Levin et al. 2002).
Risk orientation	The degree to which individuals are willing to accept the potential for loss (risk) in order to achieve a benefit	Individual differences in risk-taking and personality influence willingness to accept risks generally and in specific situations (Soane and Chmiel 2005; (Nicholson et al. 2005).
Self-efficacy	Perceived ability to accomplish a task, generalizable across time	Self-efficacy leads to higher task performance (Bandura 1982; Lee et al. 1997) and influences career choices (Giles 1999); entrepreneurial self-efficacy influences strategic decision making and firm performance (Forbes 2005); self-efficacy links with self-esteem, emotional ability and locus of control, which together influence leadership and strategic decision making (Hiller and Hambrick 2005); self-efficacy can lead to escalating commitment to a losing course of action (Whyte et al. 1997); high self-efficacy can lead to perceptions of risks as opportunities (Krueger and Dickson 1993).
Self-monitoring	The degree to which people monitor and control the self that they project to others in social situations (Snyder 1987)	Self-monitoring influences the ethical decisions of sales persons (Ross and Robertson 2003); and interacts with organizational norms regarding intentions to report

		fraudulent behavior (Uddin and Gillett 2002).
Self-regulation	The cognitive and behavioral adjustments that function to maintain factors such as emotions and performance within acceptable limits (Lord and Levy 1994)	Allocation of attention, sequences of mental operations (Lord and Levy 1994) and self-corrective decision behaviours (Powers 1973) shape decision outcomes.
Traitedness	The degree to which traits are internally consistent	The consistency of individual difference variables is related to consistency of decision making (Baumeister and Tice 1988; Soane and Nicholson 2006).
Attitudes		
Attitudes	A relatively enduring feeling, belief, or behavioural tendency directed towards specific individuals, groups, ideas, philosophies, issues, or objects (Ajzen and Fishbein 1980)	Attitudes towards risk can influence decisions that affect firm performance (Singh 1986).
Values	Core beliefs about acceptable behavior	Values affect the perceptual screening of the decision environment (England 1967), selection, and retention in organizations (Schneider 1987); and responses and adaptations to the environment (Simon 1993).
Ability related		
Ability	Competence in an activity	Cognitive ability influences negotiation style and outcome (Fulmer and Barry 2004); performance on insight and non-insight tasks is related to abilities in task related areas (supporting a dual processing hypothesis) (Gilhooly and Murphy 2005); cognitive ability influences the efficacy of error training (Gully et al. 2002).
Uncertainty	Insufficient or missing information about any aspect of a problem or related choices	Complex, chaotic decision environments are major sources of error in decision making (McKenna and Martin-Smith 2005).
Interactionism	The combined influence of situations and personality and individual level attitudes, behaviors, cognitions, and emotions (Endler and Magnusson 1976)	Interactions between organizational culture, personality, and self-monitoring influence willingness to lie (Ross and Robertson 2000).
Person–job fit	The extent to which there is a match between individual level values, skills, attributes and characteristics, and organizational demands, expectations and rewards	Optimization of performance, person–job fit (Edwards 1991).

making at a subconscious level, such as self-regulation or gender identity. At the proximal or immediate level are psychological attributes, experience, and behavior, for example, competencies or person–job fit. In the discussion that follows, we use this framework to provide taxonomy for some selected aspects of the literature, starting with the internalized processes; then discussing interactions between individual psychology, behavior, and situational characteristics; and concluding with a personological life-span perspective on individual differences and decision making.

Biographical Variables: Age and Gender

A mix of physiological processes control age and gender, including physical, genetic, biochemical, neurological, and social factors. The interaction between age and gender has important effects on decision making. An evolutionary perspective on this theme suggests that innate differences in the fitness enhancing strategies of men and women underlie systematic biases in their dispositions, resulting in gender differentiation in many careers, occupations, and organizational roles (Browne 2006). For example, women often favor and perform better in decisions and roles involving empathy, cooperation, social skills, verbal decisions, multitasking, emotional expression, and nurturing. Men will favor decisions and actions that focus on competition, self-interest, risks, game playing, and serial rather than parallel decision making and task execution (Nicholson 2000a).

Turning to age, few studies have examined decision-making processes over the life span, however a developmental framework comprising five components has been developed that can be applied (Fischhoff 1992).

- Cognitive development enables people to apply greater levels of skill in areas such as focus of attention; use of intellectual resources; drawing on experience to resolve complex issues.
- Greater knowledge can facilitate decision making, however, knowledge might be biased and false. Developmental changes in the capacity for meta-cognition and self-reflection could increase decision performance.
- Skills necessary for making decisions develop with age enabling decision makers to use multiple skills to reach choices (Case 1987; Byrnes 1988).
- There are various changes over the life span that influence decision making. During the adolescent years, hormonal changes exert powerful effects on emotions that influence decision making, with concomitant trends for emotions to become cooler with age (Wallach and Kogan 1961; Botwinick 1966).
- Social development, notably the development of beliefs and values, has an important effect on decision making.

Risk-taking is an area where there has been some investigation of the combined effects of age and gender, with research indicating that the high risk-taking susceptibility of young men is facilitated by their focusing on the benefits rather than the costs of risk-taking (e.g., Martin and Leary 2001). These perceptual biases are subject to individual difference effects as well as to more pervasive cultural influences. For example, one study of race and gender suggested that white men were likely to have a cultural world view that reduced their perceptions of the costs of risks (Finucane et al. 2000).

In sum, the biographical factors of age and gender shape decision content and processes via a range of physiological and psychological processes that can lead to outcomes such as young male risk-taking (e.g., Nicholson et al. 2005) or older female health protective behaviors (Ungemack 1994). These factors can be considered to both shape and interact with the more psychological processes discussed in the following sections.

Internal Self-Regulatory Processes

Internal self-regulatory processes are critical to everyday functioning; reducing dissonance and maintaining cognitions, emotions, and behavior within acceptable boundaries, thus underpinning a coherent self-concept. While individual differences affect subcomponents of the self-regulatory process, some generalities apply. For example, self-regulation influences selective attention such that information needed to make a decision becomes available precisely when required, meaning that goal oriented action directs selective attention (Allport 1989). Selective attention has both conscious and unconscious components (Kuhl 1994a; Neill 1997) components, constituting the threshold below which automaticity influences decision making, and above which conscious decisions will be made.

A significant contribution to the field is Lord and Levy's (1994) paper, which integrates several theoretical areas to understand how information selection functions to guide actions. They draw upon the notion that there is a hierarchy of control systems ranging from abstract concepts to concrete actions (Powers 1973), which enable people to put cognitions into action (Carver and Scheier 1981). This hierarchy influences the activation and inhibition of decision processes and focus on goal attainment. Individual differences in the ability to self-regulate have been characterized as action versus state orientations (Kuhl 1994a, b). Action oriented people are able to suppress cognitions and emotions that might distract them from focusing on the task at hand, while state oriented people are more easily deflected from task focus by emotions and cognitions. Moreover, efficiency in mood self-regulation can improve decision quality (Baumann and Kuhl 2002).

The foundations for self-regulation and related processes are a mix of neurological and psychological functions that relate to govern such consequences as the efficiency of information processing and thresholds for sensory functioning, for example, the trigger for anxiety that might interfere with goal pursuit (Baumann and Kuhl 2002). In the absence of an established agreed model of individual differences in self-regulation, we here define self-regulation as a general adaptive systemic set of interrelated processes that are subject to individual level variation. That is, self-regulation can be dysfunctional and contrary to effective goal attainment for some people some of the time.

Biases and Errors

The pervasive nature of cognitive biases is well documented and discussed in some detail elsewhere in this volume (see Chapter 15 by Zur Shapira). In this section, we will discuss a less well developed literature concerning the individual difference factors that can influence the development and operation of biases and heuristics.

In a review of this topic Stanovich and West (2002) examined theoretical explanations for the observed differences ideal and actual decision making, focusing mainly on two (Stanovich and West 1999): one invokes systematic irrational processes; the other position rejects this idea, and instead implicates computational limits to decision making as the cause of performance errors (Cherniak 1986; Stich 1990; Oaksford and Chater 1998) or from applying the wrong model to solve a problem (Adler 1991; Schwarz 1996).

Other perspectives consider the input of individual differences. Taylor and Armor (1996) propose that biases are states that can be induced, for example, by framing of information, which can itself be subject to individual differences (Carver et al. 1989). There is also growing support for a trait approach to understanding biases. For example, illusion of control has been found to be associated with lower levels of perceived risk and greater risk-taking behavior at the individual level (Houghton et al. 2000). This is associated with traits such as need for control (Burger 1986), neuroticism, and extraversion (Flammer et al. 1995).

Overall, while biases are known to be pervasive and systematic influences on decision making, there are many individual differences that affect both the direction of attention to available information, and decision-making behavior.

Personality

Personality is "that set of non-physical and non-intellectual psychological qualities which make a person distinct from other people" (Adler 1996: 419), and has been found to be relatively robust over the adult life span (Caspi 2000). Research on the relationships between dispositions and decision-making processes can reveal the extent to which particular aspects of decision making are fundamental and enduring versus those that are more situationally induced.

There are two main approaches to the modelling of personality. The type approach is based upon Jungian personality types, as represented by the widely used Myers Briggs Type Indicator inventory (Briggs Myers and McCaulley 1985).

However, recent advances in the psychometric modelling of traits have eclipsed typological approaches. Traits are defined as "internal psychological structures or properties that relate to regularities in behaviour" (Adler 1996: 420) and influence decision making via variations in affect, cognition, and conation (action).

Trait measurement owes much to the pioneering work of Raymond Cattell (Cattell 1950), which spawned numerous general and domain specific inventories. In the past 20 years, researchers have concluded that a five-factor model parsimoniously encompasses all extant trait measures (including the dimensions underlying type approaches) (Digman 1990). The "Big Five" factors are neuroticism, extraversion, openness, agreeableness, and conscientiousness, and the most widely used measurement tool measuring them is the NEO PI-R (Costa and McCrae 1991). The NEO PI-R has been extensively validated cross-culturally (McCrae et al. 2004).

Research mainly focuses on personality as a predictor of behavior, or as a moderator of the effects of other individual differences, influencing decision making through several mechanisms. First, personality directly influences individual goals and preferences. For example, the neuroticism scale is linked with risk avoidance, as we have found in our work on traders in financial markets (Nicholson et al. 2005). Other direct linkages include: extraversion with pro-social choices; openness with venturesome and changeful behavior; agreeableness with high trust relationships and deals; and conscientiousness with control seeking orientations (Costa and McCrae 1991).

Second, personality shapes the perceptual inputs to decision making by directing attention to particular types of information. A notable example is sensation seeking, which relates strongly to risk perception (Zuckerman 1979). Zuckerman's research showed that people with low sensation seeking tendencies attend more closely to information that amplifies risk, thereby reinforcing risk aversion. This is consistent with other research into selective attention and information processing. For example, there is a qualitative difference between a person who has not heard of a hazard, and so cannot act upon it, and a person who has heard of a hazard, and chosen not to act upon it. The former will be open-minded about the hazard but will not actively seek out information (Janis and Mann 1976, 1977). The latter will have a biased commitment to their point of view, selectively attending to information that supports their orientation (Frey 1986).

In sum, personality is important to understanding decision making because it shapes goals that direct decision making, and it shapes the content of decision making via selective attention to salient information and situational influences.

Situation Fit

The fit between individuals and jobs is of particular relevance to organizational decision making. Empirical evidence suggests that, in general, optimal performance is more likely when there is a close association between personal preferences and job demands. Currently there are two dominant, overlapping models that that aid understanding and prediction of career choice, employee suitability, and person–job fit optimization. They are the five-factor model of personality (Digman 1990), discussed above, and Holland's RIASEC (realistic, investigative, artistic, social, enterprising, and conventional) typology (Holland 1985). The model predicts the self-selection of individuals into roles that suit their interests and enable them to express themselves. Research has have found clear connections between the Big Five and the RIASEC types, supporting the proposition that person–job fit and individual career decision making have a dispositional component (Costa et al. 1995; De Fruyt and Mervielde 1999).

Mischel's (1968) critique of the claimed association between personality and behavior helped refocus attention on the interactions between people and situations. His subsequent research (Mischel 1977) drew the important distinction between "strong" and "weak" situations. In strong situations people are influenced more strongly by environmental constraints, reducing the correlation between personality and behavior, whereas in weak situations people are freer to act in accordance with their underlying dispositions. Subsequent work by Mischel has developed the notion of individual personality–behavior links, referred to as 'if...then...personality signatures' (Mischel and Shoda 1995; Kammrath et al. 2005).

The situation fit perspective has two important implications for organizational decision makers. The first concerns the selection of people for specific roles. The work of De Fruyt and Mervielde (1999) suggests that, from an employer's perspective, the five-factor model of personality can complement the frameworks underpinning selection criteria. Specifically, they propose that extraversion and conscientiousness are positively associated with employment status and employability, in other words, these two personality factors operate across situations to aid adaptation to the work environment and goal focus.

The second implication concerns individual level career choices and organizational career counselling within organizations. De Fruyt and Mervielde's work provides some evidence for the superiority of the RIASEC model in these contexts suggesting that person–job fit can be enhanced through the use of matched aptitudes with job categories.

Decisions and Life Histories

Let us now take a step back and considering decision making as a cause and an effect of adult life-span development. Much of the work we have reviewed implies that individual difference related interventions can aid choices and decisions affecting the life course. The logic of the RIASEC and other individual difference measures is that dispositions operate like a gravitational force, largely inborn (McDonald 1991, 1994; Reimann et al. 1997), pulling people towards environments that are congruent with their profile of attributes and dispositions and away from those that are not. In fact, although labor markets have become much more transparent and information flows more freely, job and organization choice remains very much a matter of trial and error. Early theories of career development (Dawis and Lofquist 1984) emphasized this process of assortment by experiential testing, as people take and quit jobs in the search for optimal fit. The process is imperfect of course, and one must allow for the forces of socialization to be also shaping dispositions and behaviors (Chatman 1991). The result of these twin forces of selection and socialization is the sedimentation of like-minded people to particular kinds of jobs and organizations—what has been called the "people make the place" paradigm, or ASA (attraction-selection-attrition) (Schneider 1987; Schneider et al. 1997).

The increased accessibility of information search and self-advertisement via agencies and most recently via the web are creating an increasingly liquid medium for this process to occur (Cappelli and Hamori 2007). This has co-evolutionary implications (Janicki and Krebbs 1998; Nicholson 2000b). Co-evolution here denotes the reciprocal shaping of individual orientations and social contexts: orientations and environments are both cause and consequence of each other. One might conclude that with greater information, awareness, and freedom from compelling social conventions we increasingly are the masters of our own destiny. However, as we pointed out in the introduction, there is another view, which holds that life-span development looks more unpredictable than it really is, especially to the agent (Nicholson et al. 1985).

From an evolutionary perspective, this makes sense. We are "hardwired" to retain a strong sense of agency, internal or external (i.e., ourselves, other agents, gods, etc.) Our persistent belief is that decision making is rational, self-willed, and controlled, held together by self-serving narratives, retrospective sense-making, and hindsight bias (Fischhoff and Beyth 1975; Nicholson 2000a; Nettle 2004). The role of individual differences is thus largely a story of the role of the self deluding itself about its own importance and capacity for self-determination (Leary 2004).

In many cultures and social strata career destinations can be predicted from the time, place, and status of the newborn—decisions affect the course of the journey more than its conclusion, like diversionary tributaries that ultimately rejoin the mainstream. In many societies caste systems dictate the limited set of options the individual may aspire to on the basis on gender and parental status (Kiesing and Kiesing 1971). It remains true today in Western society that life chances and choices are strongly constrained by time, place, and resources available at the time of one's birth (Ellis 1993). One can still find numerous instances of a direct lineage between generations of occupation, craft, or profession, and of the more general phenomenon of parents with wealth channelling their offspring through a predetermined set of elite schooling, military, and blue chip institutions towards a narrow range of elite positions.

From a life-span developmental perspective one might conclude that there has been a historical shift from the normative age graded influences to non-normative, a progression that was also assumed to occur across the individual lifespan (Baltes at al. 1980), in other words, that our lives become freed from timetables the older we get. In the Western twenty-first century, one might perceive this freedom as occurring ever earlier. If this is the case, then it follows that individual differences are assuming increasing importance as determinants of career choice and outcomes.

However, perhaps this just shifts predictability to a more psychological domain. With complete information about a person's psychological profile and their social milieu, choices become predictable, since individuals follow the logic of goal directed search with bounded rationality. An observer can often see this predictability more clearly and dispassionately than does the agent, whose judgment is awash with the fears and wishes that accompany agency. To put it another way, although the individual may agonize over successive decisions, what feels like free choice may in reality be more embroidery of more algorithmic processes (Wegner 1994).

However, what makes biography and history an interesting drama is the fact that reflections, choices, and actions have the capacity to overturn previously predictable lives. This is probably the most uncharted territory of the study of individual differences in life-span decision making. One can only speculate how best to analyze and make sense of such variations, though a self-regulatory framework would seem to fit the bill (Karoly 1993), in other words, how perceptions, goals, and self-concept reconfigure to maintain the functional integrity of personal identity. One might hypothesize via some analogue of catastrophe theory, that the accretion of events, pressures, and emotions trigger a major shift in goals. An individual difference addendum to this explanation might benefit from considering the role of metatraits (Baumeister and Tice 1988). The idea that some people might be less "traited" on personality dimensions, could explain why some people are more changeable than others—in effect the web of interconnections connecting a person's superordinate and subordinate goals is more provisional and fragile.

One conclusion that comes from this review is that the relationship between individual differences looks very different from contrasting levels of analysis, and a challenge for future theory and research is to reconcile them better.

CONCLUSION: UNDERSTANDING INDIVIDUAL LEVEL DECISION MAKING

This chapter has provided an overview of the literature concerning individual difference factors that influence decision making. It is clear that there is potential for complex interactions between individual psychology and situational demands that could lead to numerous decision outcomes, and yet people rarely make decisions either truly randomly or unpredictably. Generally, an overall homeostatic processes of self-identity regulate the interaction between individual choices, goals, and situational forces.

In concluding we would like to propose a self-regulatory model of decision making, based upon theories of individual differences and extrapolating from theories of interactionism and trait activation.

The framework in Figure 18.1 takes into account the impact of individual differences on goal setting, the focusing of attention that shapes decision content and processes, and the decision behavior that follows. Our review and synthesis of the literature shows that numerous psychological characteristics and situational features shape any decision. However, their influence is not random, rather people have systematic and consistent preferences and traits. People choose to be in occupations and situations that suit their tendencies.

The implication is that the full set of influences on individual decision making rarely operates either on most decisions or on most individuals. We use the notion of the self-concept to describe characteristics that are particularly important to a

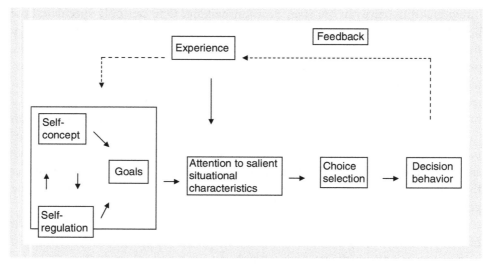

Fig. 18.1 The self–regulatory model of decision making.

given person. These characteristics vary on an individual basis and are regulated by internal processes. Goal processes serve to narrow the field of decision content and focus attention on salient environmental characteristics that are instrumental to goal attainment. Feedback and experience play important roles, too, since they enable learning and the adaptation of goals in the event of environmental changes or failure to reach targets. In sum, we aim to contribute to the understanding of organizational decision making by highlighting the importance of an individually variable set of characteristics that interact with a selectively attended to environment to shape decision behavior.

References

ABRAMSON, L. Y., SELIGMAN, M. E. P. and TEASDALE, J. D. (1978). 'Learned Helplessness in Humans—Critique and Reformulation.' *Journal of Abnormal Psychology,* 87/1: 49–74.

ADLER, N. (1996). 'Personality,' in: N. Nicholson (ed.), *Encyclopedic Dictionary of Organizational Behavior.* Oxford: Blackwell, 419–25.

ALLPORT, A. (1989). 'Visual Attention,' in: M. I. Posner (ed.), *Foundations of Cognitive Science.* Cambridge, MA: MIT Press, 631–82.

ARKES, H. R., HERREN, L. T., and ISEN, A. M. (1988). 'The Role of Potential Loss in the Influence of Affect on Risk-Taking Behavior.' *Organizational Behavior and Human Decision Processes,* 42/2, 181–93.

BALTES, P. B., REESE, H., and LIPSETT, L. (1980). 'Lifespan Developmental Psychology.' *Annual Review of Psychology,* 31: 65–110.

BANDURA, A. (1982). 'Self-Efficacy Theory in Human Agency.' *American,* 37: 122–47.

BARGH, J. A. and CHARTRAND, T. L. (1999). 'The Unbearable Automaticity of Being.' *American Psychologist,* 54: 462–79.

BAUMANN, N. and KUHL, J. (2002). 'Intuition, Affect, and Personality: Unconscious Coherence Judgments and Self-Regulation of Negative Affect.' *Journal of Personality and Social Psychology,* 83/5, 1213–23.

BAUMEISTER, R. F. and TICE, D. M. (1988). 'Metatraits.' *Journal of Personality,* 56/3: 571–98.

BERNERTH, J. B. (2005). 'Perceptions of Justice in Employment Selection Decisions: The Role of Applicant Gender.' *International Journal of Selection and Assessment,* 13/3: 206–12.

BOTWINICK, J. (1966). 'Cautiousness in Advanced Age.' *Journal of Gerontology,* 21: 347–53.

BRIGGS MYERS, I. and McCAULLEY, M. H. (1985). *A Guide to the Development and Use of the Myers-Briggs Type Indicator.* Palo Alto, CA: Consulting Psychologists Press.

BROWNE, K. R. (2006). 'Evolved Sex Differences and Occupational Segregation.' *Journal of Organizational Behavior,* 27/2: 143–62.

BUCKLEY, M. R., WIESE, D. S., and HARVEY, M. (1998). 'An investigation into the Dimensions of Unethical Behavior.' *Journal of Education for Business,* 73/5: 284–90.

BURGER, J. M. (1986). 'Desire for Control and the Illusion of Control—The Effects of Familiarity and Sequence of Outcomes.' *Journal of Research in Personality,* 20/1: 66–76.

BYRNES, J. (1988). 'Formal Operations: A Systematic Reformulation.' *Developmental Review,* 8: 66–87.

Cappelli, P. and Hamori, M. (2007). 'The Institutions of Outside Hiring,' in H. P. Gunz and M. A. Peiperl (eds.), *Handbook of Career Studies*. Thousand Oaks, CA: Sage, 327–49.

Carver, C. S. and Scheier, M. F. (1981). *Attention and Self-Regulation: A Control Theory Approach to Human Behavior*. New York: Springer Verlag.

—— —— Weintraub, J. K. (1989). 'Assessing Coping Strategies—A Theoretically Based Approach.' *Journal of Personality and Social Psychology*, 56/2: 267–83.

Caspi, A. (2000). 'The Child is Father of the Man: Personality Continuities From Childhood to Adulthood.' *Journal of Personality and Social Psychology*, 78/1: 158–72.

Cattell, R. B. (1950). *Personality: A Systematic, Theoretical, and Factual Study*. New York: McGraw Hill.

Chatman, J. A. (1991). 'Matching People and Organizations: Selection and Socialization in Public Accounting Firms.' *Administrative Science Quarterly*, 36: 459–84.

Cherniak, C. (1986). *Minimal Rationality*. Cambridge, MA: MIT Press.

Costa, P. T. and McCrae, R. R. (1991). *Revised NEO Personality Inventory (NEO PI-R) and NEO Five-Factor Inventory (NEO-FFI) Professional Manual*. Odessa, FL: Psychological Assessment Resources.

—— —— Kay, G. G. (1995). 'Persons, Places, and Personality—Career Assessment Using the Revised Neo-Personality Inventory.' *Journal of Career Assessment*, 3/2: 123–39.

Dawis, R. V. and Lofquist, L. H. (1984). *A Psychological Theory of Work Adjustment*. Minneapolis, MN: University of Minnesota Press.

De Fruyt, F. and Mervielde, I. (1999). 'RIASEC Types and Big Five Traits as Predictors of Employment Status and Nature of Employment.' *Personnel Psychology*, 52/3: 701–27.

Digman, J. M. (1990). 'Personality Structure: Emergence of the Five-Factor Model.' *Annual Review of Psychology*, 41/1: 417–40.

Dijksterhuis, A. (2004). 'Think Different: The Merits of Unconscious Thought in Preference Development and Decision Making.' *Journal of Personality and Social Psychology*, 87/5: 586–98.

Eagly, A. H. and Johnson, B. T. (1990). 'Gender and Leadership-Style—A Metaanalysis.' *Psychological Bulletin*, 108/2: 233–56.

Ellis, L. (1993). *Social Stratification and Socioeconomic Inequality. Vol. 1: A Comparative Biosocial Analysis*. New York: Praeger.

England, G. W. (1967). 'Organizational Goals and Expected Behavior of American Managers.' *Academy of Management Journal*, 10: 107–17.

Erez, A. and Isen, A. M. (2002). 'The Influence of Positive Affect on the Components of Expectancy Motivation.' *Journal of Applied Psychology*, 87/6: 1055–67.

Estrada, C. A., Isen, A. M., and Young, M. J. (1997). 'Positive Affect Facilitates Integration of Information and Decreases Anchoring in Reasoning Among Physicians.' *Organizational Behavior and Human Decision Processes*, 72/1: 117–35.

Filbeck, G., Hatfield, P., and Horvath, P. (2005). 'Risk Aversion and Personality Type.' *Journal of Behavioral Finance*, 6/4, 170–80.

Finucane, M. L., Slovic, P., Mertz, C. K., Flynn, J., and Satterfield, T. A. (2000). 'Gender, Race, and Perceived Risk: The "White Male" Effect.' *Health, Risk and Society*, 2/2: 159–72.

Fischer, I. and Budescu, D. V. (2005). 'When Do Those Who Know More Also Know More About How Much They Know? The Development of Confidence and Performance in Categorical Decision Tasks.' *Organizational Behavior and Human Decision Processes*, 98/1: 39–53.

Fischhoff, B. (1992). 'Risk Taking: A Developmental Perspective,' in J. F. Yates (ed.), *Risk Taking Behaviour*. New York: Wiley, 133–62.

—— BEYTH, R. (1975). '"I knew it would happen": Remembered Probabilities of Once-Future Things.' *Organizational Behavior and Human Performance*, 13: 1–16.

FLAMMER, A., ITO, T., LUTHI, R. et al. (1995). 'Coping with Control-Failure in Japanese and Swiss Adolescents.' *Swiss Journal of Psychology*, 54/4: 277–88.

FORBES, D. P. (2005). 'The Effects of Strategic Decision Making on Entrepreneurial Self-Efficacy.' *Entrepreneurship Theory and Practice*, 29/5: 599–626.

FREY, D. (1986). 'Recent Research on Selective Exposure to Information', in L. Berkowitz (ed.), *Advances in Experimental Social Psychology*. New York: Academic Press, 41–79.

FULMER, I. S. and BARRY, B. (2004). 'The Smart Negotiator: Cognitive Ability and Emotional Intelligence in Negotiation.' *International Journal of Conflict Management*, 15/3: 245–72.

GILES, M. and REA, A. (1999). 'Career Self-Efficacy: An Application of the Theory of Planned Behaviour.' *Journal of Occupational and Organizational Psychology*, 72/3: 393–8.

GILHOOLY, K. J. and MURPHY, P. (2005). 'Differentiating Insight from Non-insight Problems.' *Thinking and Reasoning*, 11/3: 279–302.

GLOVER, S. H., BUMPUS, M. A., LOGAN, J. E., and CIESLA, J. R. (1997). 'Re-examining the Influence of Individual Values on Ethical Decision Making.' *Journal of Business Ethics*, 16/12–13: 1319–29.

GORMAN, E. H. (2005). 'Gender Stereotypes, Same-Gender Preferences, and Organizational Variation in the Hiring of Women: Evidence from Law Firms.' *American Sociological Review*, 70/4: 702–28.

GULLY, S. M., PAYNE, S. C., KOLES, K. L. K., and WHITEMAN, J. A. K. (2002). 'The Impact of Error Training and Individual Differences on Training Outcomes: An Attribute-Treatment Interaction Perspective.' *Journal of Applied Psychology*, 87/1: 143–55.

HEIDER, F. (1958). *The Psychology of Interpersonal Relations*. New York: Wiley.

HILLER, N. J. and HAMBRICK, D. C. (2005). 'Conceptualizing Executive Hubris: The Role of (Hyper-)Core Self-Evaluations in Strategic Decision-Making.' *Strategic Management Journal*, 26/4: 297–319.

HOLLAND, J. L. (1985). *Manual for the Vocational Preferences Inventory*. Odessa, FL: Psychological Assessment Resources.

HOUGHTON, S. M., SIMON, M., AQUINO, K., and GOLDBERG, C. B. (2000). 'No Safety in Numbers—Persistence of Biases and their Effects on Team Risk Perception and Team Decision Making.' *Group and Organization Management*, 25/4: 325–53.

HUH, T. J., KRAMER, J. H., GAZZALEY, A., and DELIS, D. C. (2006). 'Response Bias and Aging on a Recognition Memory Task.' *Journal of the International Neuropsychological Society*, 12/1: 1–7.

ILIES, R., ARVEY, R. D. and BOUCHARD, T. J. (2006). 'Darwinism, Behavioural Genetics, and Organizational Behaviour: A Review and Agenda for Future Research.' *Journal of Organizational Behavior*, 27: 121–42.

ISEN, A. M. (2001). 'An Influence of Positive Affect on Decision Making in Complex Situations: Theoretical Issues with Practical Implications.' *Journal of Consumer Psychology*, 11/2: 75–85.

—— GEVA, N. (1987). 'The Influence of Positive Affect on Acceptable Level of Risk—The Person with a Large Canoe has a Large Worry.' *Organizational Behavior and Human Decision Processes*, 39/2: 145–54.

JANICKI, M. and KREBS, D. (1998). 'Evolutionary Approaches to Culture,' in C. Crawford and D. Krebs (eds.), *Handbook of Evolutionary Psychology*. Mahwah, NJ: Lawrence Erlbaum.

JANIS, I. L. and MANN, L. (1976). 'Coping with Decisional Conflict.' *American Scientist*, 64/6: 657–67.

—— —— (1977). 'Emergency Decision-Making—Theoretical-Analysis of Responses to Disaster Warnings.' *Journal of Human Stress*, 3/2: 35–48.

KAHN, B. E. and ISEN, A. M. (1993). 'The Influence of Positive Affect on Variety Seeking Among Safe, Enjoyable Products.' *Journal of Consumer Research*, 20/2: 257–70.

KAMMRATH, L. T., MENDOZA-DENTON, R., and MISCHEL, W. (2005). 'Incorporating *If... Then... Personality Signatures in Person Perception: Beyond the Person–Situation Dichotomy.' *Journal of Personality and Social Psychology*, 88/4: 605–18.

KANFER, R. (1990). *Motivation Theory and Industrial and Organizational Psychology.* Mountain View, CA: CPP Inc.

—— ACKERMAN, P. L. (1989). 'Motivation and Cognitive Abilities: An Integrative/Aptitude–Treatment Interaction Approach'. *Journal of Applied Psychology*, 74/4: 657–90.

KAROLY, P. (1993). 'Mechanisms of Self-Regulation: A Systems View.' *Annual Review of Psychology*, 44: 23–52.

KIESING, R. M., and KIESING, F. M. (1971). *New Perspectives in Cultural Anthropology.* New York: Holt Rinehart and Winston.

KIM, K. and WYER JR., R. S. (2004). 'The Role of Unconscious Processes in Consumer Choice and Decision Making,' in B. E. Kahn and M. F. Luce (eds.), *Advances in Consumer Research*, Vol. 31. Valdosta, GA: Association for Consumer Research, 334.

KIM, S. S., MALHOTRA, N. K., and NARASIMHAN, S. (2005). 'Two Competing Perspectives on Automatic Use: A Theoretical and Empirical Comparison.' *Information Systems Research*, 16/4: 418–32.

KLACZYNSKI, P. A. and DANIEL, D. B. (2005). 'Individual Differences in Conditional Reasoning: A Dual-Process Account.' *Thinking and Reasoning*, 11/4: 305–25.

KOWERT, P. A. and HERMANN, M. G. (1997). 'Who Takes Risks? Daring and Caution in Foreign Policy Making.' *Journal of Conflict Resolution*, 41/5: 611–37.

KRUEGER N. F., Jr., and DICKSON, P. R. (1993). 'Perceived Self-Efficacy and Perceptions of Opportunity and Threat.' *Psychological Reports*, 72/3: 1235–40.

KUHL, J. (1994a). 'Action Versus State Orientation: Psychometric Properties of the Action Control Scale (ACS-90),' in J. Kuhl and J. Beckmann (eds.), *Volition and Personality: Action Versus State Orientation.* Göttingen, Germany: Hogrefe, 47–59.

—— (1994b). 'Motivation and Volition,' in G. d'Ydevalle, P. Bertelson, and P. Eelen (eds.), *Current Advances in Psychological Science: An International Perspective.* Hillsdale, NJ: Erlbaum, 311–40.

LEARY, M. R. (2004). *The Curse of the Self.* New York: Oxford University Press.

LEE, T. W., LOCKE, E. A., and PHAN, S. H. (1997). 'Explaining the Assigned Goal–Incentive Interaction: The Role of Self-Efficacy and Personal Goals.' *Journal of Management*, 23/4: 541–59.

LEVIN, I. P., GAETH, G. J., SCHREIBER, J., and LAURIOLA, M. (2002). 'A New Look at Framing Effects: Distribution of Effect Sizes, Individual Differences, and Independence of Types of Effects.' *Organizational Behavior and Human Decision Processes*, 88/1: 411–29.

LEVIN, I. P., ROUWENHORST, R. M., and TRISKO, H. M. (2005). 'Separating Gender Biases in Screening and Selecting Candidates for Hiring and Firing.' *Social Behavior and Personality*, 33/8: 793–804.

LOCKE, E. A. and LATHAM, G. P. (2002). 'Building a Practically Useful Theory of Goal Setting and Task Motivation—A 35-year Odyssey.' *American Psychologist*, 57/9: 705–17.

LORD, R. G. and LEVY, P. E. (1994). 'Moving from Cognition to Action—A Control-Theory Perspective.' *Applied Psychology—An International Review (Psychologie appliquee—Revue internationale)*, 43/3: 335–98.

MARTIN, K. A. and LEARY, M. R. (2001). 'Self-Presentational Determinants of Health Risk Behavior Among College Freshmen.' *Psychology and Health*, 16/1: 17–27.

McCRAE, R. R., COSTA, P. T., MARTIN, T. A. et al. (2004). 'Consensual Validation of Personality Traits Across Cultures.' *Journal of Research in Personality*, 38/2: 179–201.

—— MARTIN, T. A., and COSTA, P. T. (2005). 'Age Trends and Age Norms for the NEO Personality Inventory-3 in Adolescents and Adults.' *Assessment*, 12/4: 363–73.

MACDONALD, K. (1991). 'A perspective on Darwinian Psychology: The Importance of Domain-General Mechanisms, Plasticity, and Individual Differences.' *Ethology and Socio-biology*, 12: 449–80.

—— (1994). 'Evolution, the Five-factor Model, and Levels of Personality.' *Journal of Personality*, 63: 525–67.

McKENNA, R. J. and MARTIN-SMITH, B. (2005). 'Decision Making as a Simplification Process: New Conceptual Perspectives.' *Management Decision*, 43/6: 821–36.

MISCHEL, W. (1968). *Personality and Assessment*. New York: Wiley.

—— (1977). 'Future of Personality Measurement.' *American Psychologist*, 32/4: 246–54.

—— SHODA, Y. (1995). 'A Cognitive-Affective System Theory of Personality: Reconceptualizing Situations, Dispositions, Dynamics, and Invariance in Personality Structure.' *Psychological Review*, 102/2: 246–68.

NEILL, W. T. (1997). 'Episodic Retrieval in Negative Priming and Repetition Priming.' *Journal of Experimental Psychology—Learning Memory and Cognition*, 23/6: 1291–305.

NETTLE, D. (2004). 'Adaptive Illusions: Optimism, Control and Human Rationality,' in D. Evans and P. Cruse (eds.), *Emotion, Evolution, and Rationality*. Oxford: Oxford University Press, 193–208.

NICHOLSON, N. (2000a). *Managing the Human Animal*. London: Texere.

—— (2000b). 'Motivation-Selection-Connection: An Evolutionary Model of Career Development,' in M. Peiperl, M. Arthur, R. Goffee, and T. Morris (eds.), *Career Frontiers: New Concepts of Working Life*. Oxford: Oxford University Press.

—— WEST, M. A., and CAWSEY, T. F. (1985). 'Future Uncertain: Expected vs. Attained Job Change Among Managers.' *Journal of Occupational Psychology*, 58: 313–20.

—— SOANE, E., FENTON-O'CREEVY, M., and WILLMAN, P. (2005). 'Personality and Domain-Specific Risk Taking.' *Journal of Risk Research*, 8/2: 157–76.

OAKSFORD, M. and CHATER, N. (1998). *Rationality in an Uncertain World*. Hove, UK: Psychology Press.

PARSONS, T. (1978). *Action Theory and the Human Condition*. New York: Free Press.

POWERS, R. (1973). 'Psychology Versus Dissent.' *Journal of Individual Psychology*, 29/1: 96–7.

REIMANN, R., ANGLEITNER, A., and STRELAU, J. (1997). Genetic and Environmental Influences on Personality: A Study of Twins Reared Together Using the Self- and Peer Report NEO-FFI Scales.' *Journal of Personality*, 65: 449–75.

RIDLEY, M. (1999). *Genome: The Autobiography of a Species*. London: Fourth Estate.

ROBERTS, B. W., WALTON, K. E., and VIECHTBAUER, W. (2006). 'Personality Traits Change in Adulthood: Reply to Costa and McCrae (2006).' *Psychological Bulletin*, 132/1: 29–32.

ROSS, W. T., Jr., and ROBERTSON, D. C. (2000). 'Lying: The Impact of Decision Context.' *Business Ethics Quarterly*, 10/2: 409–40.

SCHIRMER, A., KOTZ, S. A., and FRIEDERICI, A. D. (2005). 'On the Role of Attention for the Processing of Emotions in Speech: Sex Differences Revisited.' *Cognitive Brain Research*, 24/3: 442–52.

SCHNEIDER, B. (1987). 'The People Make the Place.' *Personnel Psychology*, 40/3: 437–53.

SCHNEIDER, B., GOLDSTEIN, H. W., and SMITH, D. B. (1995). 'The ASA Framework: An Update.' *Personnel Psychology*, 48: 747–79.

SCHWARZ, N. (1996). *Cognition and Communication: Judgmental Biases, Research Methods, and the Logic of Conversation*. Mahwah, NJ: Lawrence Erlbaum Associates.

SINGH, J. V. (1986). 'Performance, Slack, and Risk-Taking in Organizational Decision-Making.' *Academy of Management Journal*, 29/3: 562–85.

SOANE, E. and CHMIEL, N. (2005). 'Are Risk Preferences Consistent? The Influence of Decision Domain and Personality on Decision Making.' *Personality and Individual Differences*, 38/8: 1781–91.

—— NICHOLSON, N. (2006). 'Traitedness and Intra-Individual Response Consistency on the NEO PI-R: Implications for the Traitedness Construct, and Applications to Personality and Risk Taking.' Working Paper.

SONG, F., CADSBY, C. B., and MORRIS, T. (2004). 'Other-Regarding Behavior and Behavioral Forecasts: Females Versus Males as Individuals and as Group Representatives.' *International Journal of Conflict Management*, 15/4: 340–63.

STANOVICH, K.E. and WEST, R. F. (1999). 'Discrepancies Between Normative and Descriptive Models of Decision Making and the Understanding Acceptance Principle.' *Cognitive Psychology*, 38/3: 349–85.

—— —— (2002). 'Individual Differences in Reasoning: Implications for the Rationality Debate?' in T. Gilovich, D. Griffin, and D. Kahneman (eds.), *Heuristics and Biases: The Psychology of Intuitive Judgment*. New York: Cambridge University Press, 421–40.

TAYLOR, S. E. and ARMOR, D. A. (1996). 'Positive Illusions and Coping with Adversity.' *Journal of Personality*, 64/4: 873–98.

UDDIN, N. and GILLETT, P. R. (2002). 'The Effects of Moral Reasoning and Self-Monitoring on CFO Intentions to Report Fraudulently on Financial Statements.' *Journal of Business Ethics*, 40/1: 15–32.

UNGEMACK, J. A. (1994). 'Patterns of Personal Health Practice: Men and Women in the United States.' *American Journal of Preventative Medicine*, 10/1: 38–44.

VAN OSSELAER, S. M. J., RAMANATHAN, S., CAMPBELL, M. C. et al. (2005). 'Choice Based on Goals.' *Marketing Letters*, 16/3–4: 335–46.

VENKATESH, V., MORRIS, M. G., and ACKERMAN, P. L. (2000). 'A Longitudinal Field Investigation of Gender Differences in Individual Technology Adoption Decision-Making Processes.' *Organizational Behavior and Human Decision Processes*, 83/1: 33–60.

WASHBURN, D. A., SMITH, J. D., and TAGLIALATELA, L. A. (2005). 'Individual Differences in Metacognitive Responsiveness: Cognitive and Personality Correlates.' *Journal of General Psychology*, 132/4: 446–61.

WEGNER, D. M. (1994). 'Ironic Processes of Mental Control.' *Psychological Review*, 101/1: 34–52.

WHYTE, G., SAKS, A. M., and HOOK, S. (1997). 'When Success Breeds Failure: The Role of Self-Efficacy in Escalating Commitment to a Losing Course of Action.' *Journal of Organizational Behavior*, 18/5: 415–32.

WILSON, R. S. and ARVAI, J. L. (2006). 'When Less is More: How Affect Influences Preferences When Comparing Low and High-Risk Options.' *Journal of Risk Research*, 9/2: 165–78.

ZUCKERMAN, M. (1979). *Sensation Seeking: Beyond the Optimal Level of Arousal*. Hillsdale, NJ: Erlbaum.

19

GROUP COMPOSITION AND DECISION MAKING

ELIZABETH GEORGE
PRITHVIRAJ CHATTOPADHYAY

INTRODUCTION

ORGANIZATIONAL researchers have been increasingly exploring the consequences of diversity in organizations. In this chapter we examine one such consequence— the effect of diversity on decision-making processes in organizations. Where management once consisted of mainly white males, organizations are now seeing more women and minorities enter not only the work force but also, gradually, the echelons of senior management. The increase in cross-functional and global teams has also drawn attention to the need for understanding other types of diversity such as functional, national, or cultural diversity (Hambrick et al. 2001). Researchers have also studied other ascriptive characteristics of individuals—such as their age, level and type of education, and tenure—as aspects of diversity in organizations (Tsui and Gutek 1999). Reflecting this trend, there have also been at least five major review articles about diversity in organizations since 1990 (Triandis et al. 1994; Milliken and Martins 1996; Williams and O'Reilly 1998; Jackson et al. 2003; van Knippenberg and Schippers 2007). These reviews reveal that very few researchers have actually focused on the impact of diversity on decision making in groups.

How might the composition of a group affect its decision-making processes? The objective of this chapter is to examine the role of diversity in three key aspects of decision making in groups: (1) access to information; (2) information processing; and (3) building commitment to group decisions. We begin by briefly reviewing the diversity literature. Our review does not attempt to be comprehensive (several such reviews have already been published as noted above), but rather, it attempts to highlight how diversity can influence group decision making. We then discuss how diversity might shape the group's access to information held by its members, the cognitive biases that come in the way of information processing, and finally commitment to the group's decision.

POSITIVE AND NEGATIVE EFFECTS
OF DIVERSITY

In a recent review, van Knippenberg and Schippers (2007) note that the work group diversity literature, though vast, shows rather mixed results: diversity seems to have both positive and negative outcomes for organizations. They speculate that, in part, the reason for these mixed results is the various theoretical frames that inform this line of research—the self-categorization perspective, relational demography, and the information/decision-making perspective. The self-categorization perspective (see Williams and O'Reilly 1998 for a review) usually sees diversity in workgroups as having negative outcomes, since individuals prefer to interact with those who they see as being similar to themselves or whom they can categorize as being part of their in-group (Kramer 1991; Jehn et al. 1999). Relational demography studies exemplify this perspective in finding that individuals whose co-workers include out-group members are less likely to identify with their workgroups, which results in lower levels of innovation and performance (Baugh and Graen 1997; Riordan and Shore 1997; Chatman et al. 1998), lower commitment and higher absenteeism and turnover (Tsui et al. 1992), and lower propensity to display citizenship behaviors (Riordan and Shore 1997; Chattopadhyay 1999). This stream of research leads us to speculate that diversity negatively influences group member interactions such that the group is less effective in sharing information, processing that information, and less committed to the group decision.

The information/decision-making perspective, in contrast, sees a more positive set of outcomes for diverse groups since the group ostensibly has access to greater amounts of information to perform its task. Much of the upper echelon perspective (see Carpenter et al. 2004 for a review) assumes that the diversity of top management teams translates to a greater wealth of knowledge, information, and skills available to that group, which in turn translates to improved firm performance. For instance, Bantel and Jackson's (1989) seminal study reported that a team's heterogeneity correlated positively with organizational innovation, which in turn ostensibly affects the firm's performance. This stream of research leads us to speculate that diverse groups make better decisions because members collectively have more knowledge and information and possess complementary skills. It should be noted that while most of these studies are cross-sectional the arguments they present are causal: group composition precedes the outcomes that are studied and the outcomes are assumed not to have a systematic influence on the attrition of group members belonging to particular demographic categories.

These main effect arguments, that diversity yields positive or negative outcomes in organizations, however, have not always been supported in empirical studies, and van Knippenberg and Schippers (2007) have called for researchers to consider what moderates the relationship between group composition and performance. They have also called for a greater focus on the factors that mediate this relationship. They suggest that researchers search for these moderating and mediating factors with a view to reconciling the self-categorization and informational perspectives on diversity.

Specifically, van Knippenberg and his colleagues have called for research to examine the extent to which categorization processes in groups hinder the elaboration of task-relevant information (van Knippenberg et al. 2004). One stream of empirical work that sheds some light on this topic focuses on the relationship between diversity and conflict (Pelled 1996; Pelled et al. 1999). This body of research associates work group diversity with increased task and emotional conflict. Emotional conflict, on account of categorization processes, has a negative relationship with group performance, whereas task conflict, on account of information elaboration processes, is positively associated with group performance (but see de Dreu and Weingart 2003).

Others have argued that we can understand the positive and negative effects of diversity on performance if we take into account the environmental context (Keck 1997), including the level of uncertainty in the environment (Carpenter and Fredrickson 2001), the level of debate in the team (Simons et al. 1999), the level of task complexity (Pelled et al. 1999), the extent to which the team has a climate that supports shared team objectives (West 2002), or the tenure of the team (Harrison et al. 1998). Some researchers have differentiated between forms of diversity, suggesting that demographic attributes, such as those that are surface (Martin and Milliken 1996; Harrison et al. 1998), relations oriented (Jackson et al. 1995), or fixed (Jackson et al. 1995), are likely to have a negative effect on the group when compared to attributes that are deep, task oriented, or mutable. Many of these studies suggest that the negative effects of categorization can either be mitigated by the pressure to gain information, or will be eroded with time as group members get to know each other and see beyond surface characteristics (Harrison et al. 2002). For instance, Harrison et al. (2002) found that although diversity of surface level characteristics of group members was related negatively to teams' social integration, the longer teams worked together, the less these differences mattered and the more intense was the negative relationship between diversity on deeper level characteristics and team social integration.

These studies do not, however, explicitly consider the link between the categorization and information aspects of diversity and the process through which they might interact with one another. And, as we have noted earlier, decision making has largely been ignored in this context. This chapter proposes an agenda to fill this gap in the literature by examining the relationship between diversity and decision-making processes, with a view to combining explanations from the information and categorization aspects of diversity. Groups are considered to be effective for decision-making tasks because they "(i) can bring many pieces of information together, (ii) they can analyze information critically, and (iii) they can generate commitment in their members" (Leavitt and Bahrami 1988: 173). We consider *how* group composition affects these three aspects of group decision making—access to information in groups, cognitive biases in processing information, and commitment to decisions.

ACCESS TO INFORMATION IN GROUPS

Groups are more effective in decision-making tasks because they ostensibly have more information than individuals do by themselves (Guzzo and Dickson 1996). The information perspective of diversity is also based on this view (Williams and O'Reilly 1998). It argues that diversity is beneficial to groups because group members' diverse backgrounds are a rich informational resource for the group (Williams and O'Reilly 1998). In order for this argument to hold true, that diverse groups have varied informational resources, it is necessary to associate demographic characteristics with unique information. The few researchers who have directly studied this issue question the validity of this assumption, showing that discrete managerial beliefs are sometimes not associated (Chattopadhyay et al. 1999), weakly associated (Marcozy 1997), or associated in a more complex fashion than presented by this view (Beyer et al. 1997), with different functional backgrounds and positions (for reviews see Hodgkinson 2001; Hodgkinson and

Sparrow 2002). Further, groups can benefit from the information held by their members when members are willing to share information with each other. We discuss below the relationship between diversity and information sharing in groups.

Information Sharing

Although we know that each individual might have unique information that others in the group are not aware of, what we do not know is individuals' propensity to share this information in groups. Are individuals likely to share information simply because they have it? To what degree will being similar to others in the group affect a member's willingness to share information with the group?

The categorization-based argument of diversity suggests that when individuals work in groups the social categories to which they belong are salient to them. This affects their interactions with other members of the group, their identification with the group, and their desire to engage in behaviors that are beneficial to the group (Williams and O'Reilly 1998; van Knippenberg and Schippers 2007). Will this categorization preclude them from sharing unique information with others? The similarity attraction paradigm (Byrne 1971) suggests that individuals are less likely to share information with others who are dissimilar to themselves. The relational demography view (Tsui et al. 1992) would suggest that the propensity to share information would also depend on whether the individual derives high status from being a member of that workgroup. Members of low status categories (e.g., women or minorities in organizational contexts) who derive positive self-esteem from belonging to high status, male or white dominated groups, are more likely to identify with such groups (Chattopadhyay et al. 2004), and should therefore be more likely to share information with the group, despite their differences. Moreover, members of low status categories who believe that despite belonging to high status dominated groups their individual status in the organization will remain unchanged are less likely to identify with the high status dominated group, and therefore to share information with the group (Chattopadhyay et al. 2004). Members of high status categories are likely to share information when the group, because of its composition, does not depreciate their status. If, for example, a group is dominated by women, the few male members of the group would be less likely to share information with the others since they would not identify with that group. Thus, the negative effects of categorization are likely to selectively mitigate the positive effects of information diversity.

Diversity researchers have examined the relationship between diversity and firm performance as moderated by the level of debate in the top management team (Simons et al. 1998), as well as the relationship between diversity and communication (Zenger and Lawrence 1989; Bhappu et al. 1997). Bhappu et al. (1997) found that men made more comments than did women in diverse groups, and Zenger and Lawrence (1989) found that the greater the age similarity between members of a project group the more frequently members of the group communicated with each other. While their work suggests that diversity influences information sharing in groups, further research is required to determine the nature of this relationship.

Why do individuals not share information freely in groups? The biased sampling model of group discussion (Stasser and Titus 1985) proposes that the information that is discussed in a group is a function of the information that is available between all the group members prior to the group discussion. If much of the information available to members prior to the meeting favors one point of view then that point of view is likely to get more attention in the subsequent group discussion. One possibility for why this happens is that individuals do not want to destabilize a group by disclosing information that is unknown to some members. Hinsz et al. (1997) argued that group members experience social validation when they discuss information that they have in common with other members of the group, rather than information that they hold by themselves. Thus, the positive feeling that individuals derive from belonging to a group prevents them from sharing information that could potentially help the group make better informed decisions. The implication of the biased sampling model of group discussion (Strasser and Titus 1985) is that groups of demographically diverse individuals are less likely to share information because of group members' perception that the differences in what they share might threaten the cohesiveness of this group. Thus, research based both on social identity theory and on the biased sampling model of group discussion provides complementary reasons why individuals may not share information in groups.

Information Sharing in Heterogeneous Groups

Although much of the research above suggests that individuals are unlikely to share information in diverse groups, additional research has shown that heterogeneous groups do share information. Phillips et al. (2004) found that the kind of group likely to share information was one that could be divided into two equal sized subgroups which had common information within the subgroup but unique information across subgroups. They speculated that there could be two possible explanations for this result. The first, consistent with Strasser and Titus' (1985) work, is that equal sized subgroups increased the possibility that all the information was heard since each piece of information was known to at least two individuals. The second is that since there was no clear minority, the groups focused less on social categorization and more on the task of the group. Thus, when groups are diverse but there is no clear majority subgroup, acting on the basis of category membership is less likely to have a clear outcome. Consequently, the group focuses on the task and the diverse information that is available to it because of the members' heterogeneity. This argument suggests that merely distributing members numerically into equal sized subgroups can affect how the group shares information. The argument does not, however, take into consideration the relative status of the two subgroups (as discussed below).

In summary, these studies suggest that the information perspective on diversity needs to take into account the categorization perspective, which claims that individuals are less likely to share information with others who are different from them, except in very specific circumstances.

Subgroup Size and Salience of Identity

The argument that group members are selective in their sharing of information holds true when individuals' category-based identities are salient. In other words, if members of the group do not notice the gender, age, or race of their fellow members, then they will not react to their fellow members based on attributions that are associated with gender, age, or race. When do individuals notice the demographic characteristics of others? Self-categorization theorists (Turner et al. 1987; Oakes et al. 1994) argue that three factors influence the salience of social categorization and the resultant identity. The first factor, *comparative fit*, refers to the extent to which the categorization provides high within-category similarity and high between-category difference. The second factor, *normative fit*, deals with the extent to which the categorization is consistent with the individual's beliefs, stereotypes, and expectations. Finally, the third factor affecting salience is the *cognitive accessibility* of the categorization, which is the ease with which the categorization comes to mind and can be used in a social context. The greater the extent to which these three factors are present in a categorization situation the more likely it is that the social categories will be salient and hence will be used in deciding whether to share information with group members.

Mullen and his colleagues emphasized the role of group size in making category membership salient (Mullen 1991; Mullen, Anthony et al. 1994; Mullen, Johnson, and Anthony, 1994). Their argument, consistent with Hinsz et al.'s (1997) summary, is that identity is more salient when the individual's identity derives from a category which forms the numerical minority in a group. Mullen explains that the smaller the in-group, relative to the out-group, "the more rare and distinctive the in-group... The underlying assumption for this approach is that the smaller perceptual unit will emerge as the perceptual figure while the larger perceptual unit will recede into a perceptual ground" (1991: 299). This notion of a group (or category) becoming a perceptual figure rather than perceptual ground speaks to the cognitive accessibility of that group or social category. The figure and ground distinction also suggests high comparative fit since the two categories are separate from each other, with some degree of internal homogeneity (at least enough to clearly differentiate between the figure and the ground). Mullen's arguments do not consider normative fit as a key precursor of category salience. Mullen (1991) reported on a series of meta-analyses that provide support for the argument that proportionate group size is predictive of a number of outcomes related to in-group identification such as the tendency to be self-focused or to display in-group bias. The greater the extent to which individuals identify with their in-group, the less likely they are to share information with those in the out-group.

On the basis of Mullen's work, and their own prior research (Chattopadhyay 1999; Chattopadhyay and George 2001) Chattopadhyay et al. (2004) suggest that categorization is least salient in a group dominated by high status individuals and in which lower status members, although a numerical minority, perceive that membership in a group dominated by high status members enhances their own individual status. Under these conditions, members of all categories should identify more with their work group rather than with their demographic categories. In these circumstances, categorization would have less of an impact on decision making and the group would instead focus on the task at hand.

Other Variables that Affect Category Salience

There are a number of studies that have suggested conditions which suppress categorization effects and encourage information sharing in groups. The application of these conditions can capture the benefits of diversity as suggested by the information sharing perspective. Though these studies do not consider the diversity of group membership, they suggest variables that could help in understanding when diverse groups might share information, explicitly shifting the focus from categorization processes to task related, information elaboration processes in the group. Under these conditions, the heterogeneity of a group becomes an information-processing asset since members are encouraged to pool information that is markedly different, rather than share information that is highly similar. We discuss three of these moderators below.

First, norms which promote critical thinking result in a greater sharing of unshared information and better decision quality in groups (Postmes et al. 2001). Second, Galinsky and Kray (2003) showed that the likelihood of discussing unshared information is higher in a group where members have a counter-factual mindset. In their study, Galinsky and Kray these counterfactual mindsets by getting group members to read a story which triggered the consideration of alternate scenarios for causal relationships. Thirdly, framing a problem as having a definite solution caused individuals to share unique information during the group discussion. Stasser and Stewart (1992) argued that because the group knew that the problem had an optimal solution, rather than it being just a matter of opinion, they searched for critical pieces of information rather than aim for consensus. These studies collectively suggest that organizations must manage groups in a way that makes salient their ability to collectively solve the problem at hand rather than the category related differences between group members. Developing norms around sharing information, encouraging individuals to think of alternative causal relationships, or getting groups to focus on an optimal answer could all serve as a useful antidote to group decision fiascos such as groupthink (Janis 1972) and other information-processing-based errors.

INFORMATION-PROCESSING BIASES

One of the reasons for using groups rather than individuals for decision making (Leavitt and Bahrami 1988) is the critical information-processing ability of groups. In this section we consider whether and how group diversity might help or hinder this ability. We examine three factors that might affect the way in which decision-making groups process information: the attention that is paid to information from diverse sources, the levels of cohesiveness of the group, and the influence tactics used by majority and minority factions in the group.

Attending to Information

Information processing in groups is affected by the extent to which individuals are willing to attend to, and be influenced by, information from others in the group. Mullen et al. (1992), working from the perspective of social identity theory, showed individuals tend to believe that the in-group is in agreement with them (false consensus), while the out-group is distinct from them (false uniqueness). This pattern of social projection would lead individuals to pay more attention to the information provided by those in the in-group, and for there to be a greater likelihood for them to agree with those in the in-group.

Similarly, Chattopadhyay et al. (1999) found that one could predict executive beliefs less by the functional background and current functional position of a member of a top management team than the extent to which that individual was similar to others in the team in terms of their functional background. Thus, categorization as a person of a similar functional background was able to explain more of the variance in executive beliefs than was the information held by a person because of their own functional background. Other research has shown that groups are often unable to identify the expertise that exists within their group (Libby et al.

1987), and that controlling for expertise, women are perceived by members of their group to have less expertise than men (Thomas-Hunt and Phillips 2004). These results are difficult to reconcile with the information-processing view of diversity which suggests that group members' actions are based purely on information that is shared in the group rather than being based on the source of the information.

Status characteristics theory (Berger et al. 1966, 1972) helps to explain such results by suggesting that categorization influences individuals to make attributions about abilities in the absence of other information. It proposes that when status characteristics (such as gender, race, or evaluations of competence) are salient in a task context, individuals combine status information to "form beliefs about, and evaluations of, themselves and those with whom they interact" (Cohen and Zhou 1991: 180). If individuals find that their beliefs and evaluations associated with status characteristics are relevant in a particular context, then they use that information to set expectations about performance by themselves and others. These expectations then determine the relative position of members in the group and affect members' abilities to influence each other. Balkwell and Berger (1996) found that one could partly explain influence in gender typed tasks by whether members of groups differed on both gender and task familiarity, and whether these differences were operating in the same direction. Specifically, when the differences operate in the same direction (i.e., evaluations of competence coincide on both trans-situational characteristics such as gender, and task specific characteristics such as time spent speaking about the task), then expectations of the individual's performance are stronger than if the differences are operating in different directions.

These attributions are very specific to a context. Building on Balkwell and Berger's (1996) work, Foschi and Lapointe (2002) examined if gender would be predictive of influence attempts in mixed gender dyads performing a decision task. They found no support for that hypothesis and speculated that their study was conducted in a social system where gender might not have been a relevant indicator of status (their participants were Canadian university students).

Bunderson (2003) tested the idea that group contexts matter in terms of how individuals make expertise attributions. He studied attributions of expertise in self-managed production teams in a technology firm. Bunderson found that gender and race more strongly predicted perceived expertise in centralized, shorter tenure teams, whereas other status cues (linked to the tasks performed by these groups) more strongly predicted perceived expertise in decentralized, longer tenure teams. He argued that in shorter tenure teams, members have less information to make attributions of expertise based on task related characteristics of individuals. In those instances, they fall back on demographic characteristics from which they infer expertise. In teams where power is decentralized, an environment is created where "members are motivated to be careful, effortful, and comprehensive in their assessments of who is more or less expert" (Bunderson 2003: 564). In making attributions of expertise, members are more likely to attend to specific task related status cues rather than status cues that are more categorical. This notion of individuals, when accountable for their decisions, as more likely to engage in deeper information processing has also found empirical support in other studies (e.g., Scholten et al. 2005).

Attention to information and processing of information in a group is also influenced by characteristics of the group, such as the level of cohesiveness in the group. Below we discuss the relationship between diversity, group cohesiveness, and information processing.

Role of Cohesiveness

Janis' (1972) theory of groupthink in its original formulation proposed that group cohesiveness would cause groups to attend more closely to information which supported their positions, and to disregard information which did not. As a result, he argued, groups would suffer from groupthink and would make poorer quality decisions than those groups that did not show the symptoms of groupthink. Mullen et al. (1994) conducted a meta-analysis to test explicitly this putative link between cohesiveness and decision-making quality. They found that cohesiveness impaired decision making when it was operationalized as interpersonal attraction, and enhanced decision making when it was operationalized as task commitment.

The key argument made by researchers investigating the groupthink hypothesis was that individuals are less likely to pay attention to information which differs from that held by well liked colleagues in their group. The similarity–attraction paradigm (Byrne 1971) suggests that we like those who are similar to us. Putting these two argument together we could conclude that the categorization of group members into those who are similar (and liked) and those who are different would affect the cohesiveness of the group and thus hinder the group's ability to process information critically. Relational demographers (e.g., Tsui et al. 1992; Chattopadhyay 1999) suggest one condition under which group cohesiveness might be high despite there being dissimilar members in the group. Specifically, low status individuals (e.g., women in organizations) sometimes identify with groups dominated by high status individuals (e.g., men in organizations). However, the converse is not true: men do not identify with groups dominated by women (e.g., Chattopadhyay et al. 2004). This argument suggests that although, in general, diverse groups will be less cohesive than homogeneous groups, diverse groups that are dominated by high status individuals are more likely to be cohesive, and thus to suffer from groupthink, than diverse groups that are dominated by low status individuals. There are at least two possible explanations for this phenomenon. One is that low status individuals are more likely to identify with the group when they believe that status hierarchies are permeable and that they can get ahead in the organization by working in groups dominated by high status individuals (Haslam 2001). The second explanation is that lower status individuals are politically weaker, and are thus less likely to want to engage in overt conflict in the group (Withey and Cooper 1989; Kabanoff 1991). They thus help retain the cohesiveness of groups through self-censorship.

Group cohesiveness can be built on members' similarity and liking for each other. An alternative conceptualization of group cohesiveness emphasizes the role of shared interests related to the task of the group (Mullen and Copper 1994). When individuals' commitment to the group's task shapes cohesiveness, group members might actually welcome divergent views and information as it will help generate better task related outcomes. In this conceptualization of cohesiveness, diverse groups would be less likely to suffer from groupthink than homogenous groups. However, demographically homogenous groups could also welcome divergent views provided the members of the group share a focus on the task. Thus, with either conceptualization of cohesiveness, diverse groups are likely to suffer less from groupthink than homogenous groups. The one condition under which homogenous groups are also unlikely to experience groupthink is when they focus their cohesiveness on achieving the group's task rather than on the interpersonal relations between group members.

Majority/Minority Influence Processes

A third way in which a group's composition can affect its information processing is the manner in which majority and minority factions in the group attempt to influence group members. Here we are concerned with majority and minority factions that coalesce around shared views on any issue. Moscovici (1980) argued that the numerical majority in a group attempts to influence the others to develop a common view on issues by focusing on social validation and sustenance of the group. He found that the numerical majority's attempts at influencing others in the group results in consensus seeking behaviors by group members. Therefore, when there is any disagreement around majority led influence attempts, the group experiences interpersonal conflict (Moscovici 1985).

The numerical minority, in contrast, attempts to influence the group by focusing on the task. Thus, when the minority attempts to influence the group, any differences that emerge tend to revolve around the task, and result in cognitive conflict rather than interpersonal conflict (Moscovici 1985; Nemeth et al. 1990). We would expect these patterns to be reflected in diverse groups with different influence tactics used by the dominant and minority demographic subgroups within the group.

More recently, Crono and Chen (1998) found that influence of the majority encourages issues related to the focal task to be considered in depth, in contrast to minority influence attempts on related topics. They suggested that both majority and minority focused on the task because the task was central to the identity of the group. We speculate that this was not the case in the research reported by Moscovici (1985) and Nemeth et al. (1990), which found that majority and minority influences were related to different subgroup goals.

The form of influence also correlates with the context within which the group operates (Kruglanski et al. 2006). For instance, Shah et al. (1998) showed that under conditions of time pressure, groups can feel an increased need for closure, and that this need can cause groups to put pressure on members to agree. Kruglanski and Webster (1991) obtained similar findings in respect to groups working in conditions of high ambient noise. The research reviewed above suggests that in groups which pressure members to attain closure, it is the majority members who are likely to exert a greater influence; and when minority members do exert such an influence, they mainly elaborate on the positions developed by the majority members.

The arguments above relate to the numerical distribution of categories in a group. However, this numerical distribution of categories might not correlate completely with the status of the categories. In other words, low status individuals could dominate a group (e.g., a female dominated group in an organization). The question then arises as to whether low status subgroups in the majority position are able to influence high status subgroups that form a numerical minority in the group. Empirical findings by Dovidio and Gaertner (1981, 1983) imply that these low status sub groups will not be able to influence the high status sub groups. In fact, they found high status group members continued to believe in the lack of competence of low status members even when presented evidence to the contrary. Within organizations, Hultin and Szulkin (1999) found that males in the minority retained power even when the proportion of female managers increased. Thus, information processing in diverse groups could be affected by not only the demographic characteristics of group members but also by the cohesiveness of the group and the numerical strength and status of diverse subgroups within a workgroup.

COMMITMENT TO DECISIONS

As noted earlier, the third reason that we consider groups to be effective for decision-making tasks is that they can generate commitment in their members (Leavitt and Bahrami 1988). Management researchers have also been interested in group members' commitment to decisions because this commitment is critical in implementing the decision (Dooley and Frywell 1999). The argument that these and other authors make (e.g., Korsgaard et al. 1995) is that in the absence of commitment to the decision, members who were in any case uncertain about the merits of the decision are unlikely to persist with its implementation in the face of unforeseen obstacles. How does group composition affect group members' commitment to the decisions made by the group?

A willingness by members of the group to exert effort on behalf of the group, and a sense of identification with the group (Guth and Macmillan 1986) could affect an individual's commitment to a decision. As relational demographers argue, identification with a group is affected by the level of diversity in the group and the individual's own position within that diversity (Tsui et al. 1992; Chattopadhyay 1999). Hence, we would expect to find that the extent to which individuals are committed to the decisions of the group would vary with whether they were high or low status members, and on whether the group was dominated by high or low status individuals. Using gender as an example, we would predict that in organizational contexts men in female dominated groups would be less committed to the decisions of their groups than would women in male dominated groups who believe that working in the group enhances their status in the organization. Women who perceive that their gender stands in the way of enhancing their status in the organization, irrespective of what group they belong to, may show as little commitment as men in female dominated groups. These arguments are consistent with our earlier argument that low status individuals (e.g., women) in high status groups (e.g., male dominated groups) are more likely to share information with the group than are high status individuals (e.g., men) in low status groups (e.g., female dominated groups). Diversity thus has the potential of eroding the benefits of using groups in decision making.

Is there any way to mitigate this effect? Kim and Mauborgne (1993) found empirical support for their argument that managers' perceptions of procedural fairness in the strategic decision processes of their organizations causes them, the managers, to cooperate in the implementation of the decisions. Korsgaard et al. (1995) found that group members were committed to a decision when their leader was considerate to them, and that this effect was present only when individuals had little influence on the decisions made by their leaders. Further, they showed that members' perception of there being procedural fairness in their groups at least partially mediated the relationship between commitment to the decision and leader's consideration of group members. These studies suggest that greater inclusion of members in decision-making processes is likely to facilitate commitment to the decision. While the inclusion could be category based (i.e., special efforts are made to elicit the opinions of low status or numerical minority group members), our previous arguments suggest that task-based inclusion would result in greater commitment to the groups' decision.

An alternate way in which one can manage diversity and commitment to groups' decisions is by making sure that category identification does not conflict with group identification. Hornsey and Hogg's (2000) theorizing, and George and

Chattopadhyay's (2005) data suggest that the group as well as the individuals' demographic category can be simultaneous targets for identification when their central defining features coincide, rather than diverge. This work would recommend that groups consider how members belonging to different demographic categories might contribute to the task of the group, rather than only focusing on the task at hand.

CONCLUSION

Our review of the literature leads us to believe that diversity in decision-making groups can be a strength of the group, as the information-processing view of diversity argues. However, salient demography-based categorizations of group members can affect how the group accesses and processes information and the extent to which the members are committed to the group's decisions. Information and categorization processes are tightly interwoven in groups, and diversity research should continue to explore these linkages.

REFERENCES

BALKWELL, J. and BERGER, J. (1996). 'Gender, Status, and Behavior in Task Situations.' *Social Psychology Quarterly*, 59/3: 273–83.

BANTEL, K. and JACKSON, S. (1989). 'Top Management and Innovations in Banking: Does the Composition of the Top Team Make a Difference?' *Strategic Management Journal*, 20: 83–92.

BAUGH, S. G. and GRAEN, G. B. (1997). 'Effects of Team Gender and Racial Composition on Perceptions of Team Performance in Cross-Functional Teams.' *Group and Organization Management*, 22: 366–83.

BERGER, J., COHEN, B., and ZELDITCH, M. (1966). 'Status Characteristics and Expectation States,' in J. Berger, M. Zelditch, and B. Anderson (eds.), *Sociological Theories in Progress*. Boston: Houghton-Mifflin, 29–46.

—— —— —— (1972). 'Status Characteristics and Social Interaction.' *American Sociological Review*, 37: 241–55.

BEYER, J. M., CHATTOPADHYAY, P., GEORGE, E. et al. (1997). 'The Selective Perception of Managers Revisited.' *Academy of Management Journal*, 40: 716–37.

BHAPPU, A., GRIFFITH T., and NORTHCRAFT, G. (1997). 'Media Effects and Communication Bias in Diverse Groups.' *Organizational Behavior and Human Decision Processes*, 70: 199–205.

BYRNE, D. (1971). *The Attraction Paradigm*. New York: Academic Press.

BUNDERSON, J. (2003). 'Recognizing Ultilizing Expertise in Work Groups: A Status Characteristics Perspective.' *Administrative Science Quarterly*, 48: 557–91.

CARPENTER, M. and FREDRICKSON, J. (2001). 'Top Management Teams, Global Strategic Posture, and the Moderating Role of Uncertainty.' *Academy of Management Journal*, 44: 533–46.

—— GELETKANYCZ, M., and SANDERS, G. (2004). 'Upper Echelon Research Revisited: Antecendents, Elements and Consequences of Top Management Team Composition.' *Journal of Management*, 30: 749–78.

CHATMAN, J. A., POLZER, J. T., BARSADE, S. G., and NEALE, M. A. (1998). 'Being Different Yet Feeling Similar: The Influence of Demographic Composition and Organizational Culture on Work Processes and Outcomes.' *Administrative Science Quarterly*, 43: 749–80.

CHATTOPADHYAY, P. (1999). 'Beyond Direct and Symmetrical Effects: The Influence of Demographic Dissimilarity on Organizational Citizenship Behavior.' *Academy of Management Journal*, 42: 273–87.

—— GEORGE, E. (2001). 'Examining the Effects of Work Externalization Through the Lens of Social Identity Theory.' *Journal of Applied Psychology*, 86: 781–8.

—— GLICK, W. H., MILLER, C. C., and HUBER, G. P. (1999). 'Determinants of Executive Beliefs: Comparing Functional Conditioning and Social Influence.' *Strategic Management Journal*, 20: 763–89.

—— TLUCHOWSKA, M., and GEORGE, E. (2004). 'Identifying the In-Group: A Closer Look at the Influence of Demographic Dissimilarity on Employee Social Identity.' *Academy of Management Review*, 29: 180–202.

COHEN, B. and ZHOU, X. (1991). 'Status Processes in Enduring Work Groups.' *American Sociological Review*, 56: 179–88.

CRONE, W. and CHEN, X. (1998). 'The Leniency Contract and Persistence of Majority and Minority Influence.' *Journal of Personality and Social Psychology*, 74: 1437–50.

DE DREU, C. K. W. and WEINGART, L. R. (2003). 'Task versus Relationship Conflict and Team Effectiveness: A Meta-analysis'. *Journal of Applied Psychology*, 88: 741–9.

DOOLEY, R. and FRYXELL, G. (1999). 'Attaining Decision Quality and Commitment from Dissent: The Moderating effects of Loyalty and competence in Strategic Decision-Making Teams.' *Academy of Management Journal*, 42/4: 389–402.

DOVIDIO, J. and GAERTNER, S. (1981). 'The Effects of Race, Status, and Ability on Helping Behavior.' *Social Psychology Quarterly*, 44: 192–203.

—— —— (1983). 'The Effects of Sex, Status, and Ability on Helping Behavior.' *Journal of Applied Social Psychology*, 13: 191–205.

FOSCHI, M. and LaPOINTE, V. (2002). 'On Conditional Hypotheses and Gender as a Status Characteristic.' *Social Psychology Quarterly*, 65/2: 146–62.

GALINSKY, A. and KRAY, L. (2003). 'From Thinking About What Might Have Been to Sharing What We Know: The Effects of Counterfactual Mind-Sets on Information Sharing in Groups.' *Journal of Experimental Social Psychology*, 40: 606–18.

GEORGE, E. and CHATTOPADHYAY, P. (2005). 'One Foot in Each Camp: The Dual Identification of Contract Workers.' *Administrative Science Quarterly*, 50: 68–99.

GUTH, W. and MacMILLAN, I. (1986). 'Strategy Implementation Versus Middle Management Self-interest.' *Strategic Management Journal*, 7/4: 313–27.

GUZZO, R. and DICKSON, M. (1996). 'Teams in Organisations: Recent Research on Performance and Effectiveness.' *Annual Review of Psychology*, 47: 307–38.

HAMBRICK, D., LI, J., XIN, K., and TSUI, A. (2001). 'Compositional Gaps and Downward Spirals in International Joint Venture Management Groups.' *Strategic Management Journal*, 22: 1033–53.

HARRISON, D., PRICE, K., and BELL, M. (1998). 'Beyond Relational Demography: Time and the Effects of Surface and Deep-Level Diversity of Work-Group Cohesion.' *Academy of Management Journal*, 41: 96–107.

—— —— GAVIN, J., and FLOREY, A. (2002). 'Time, Teams and Task Performance: Changing Effects of Surface and Deep Level Diversity on Group Functioning.' *Academy of Management Journal*, 45: 1029–45.

HASLAM, S. A. (2001). *Psychology in Organizations: The Social Identity Approach*. Thousand Oaks, CA: Sage.

HINSZ, V., TINDALE, R., and VOLLRATH, D. (1997). 'The Emerging Conceptualization of Groups as Information Processors.' *Psychological Bulletin*, 121/1: 43–64.

HODGKINSON, G. P. (2001). 'The Psychology of Strategic Management: Diversity and Cognition Revisited,' in C. L. Cooper and I. T. Robertson (eds.), *International Review of Industrial and Organizational Psychology*, Vol. 16. Chichester: Wiley, 65–119.

—— SPARROW, P. R. (2002). *The Competent Organization: A Psychological Analysis of the Strategic Management Process*. Buckingham: Open University Press.

HORNSEY, M. J. and HOGG, M. A. (2000). 'Assimilation and Diversity: An Integrative Model of Subgroup Relations.' *Personality and Social Psychology Review*, 4: 143–56.

HULTIN, M. and SZULKIN, R. (1999). 'Wages and Unequal Access to Organizational Power: An Empirical Test of Gender Discrimination.' *Administrative Science Quarterly*, 44: 453–72.

JACKSON, S., JOSHI, A., and ERHARDT, N. (2003). 'Recent Research on Team and Organizational Diversity: SWOT Analysis and Implications.' *Journal of Management*, 29: 801–30.

JACKSON S. E., MAY K. E., and WHITNEY, K. (1995). 'Understanding the Dynamics of Diversity in Decision-Making Teams,' in R. Guzzo and E. Salas (eds.), *Team Effectiveness and Decision Making in Organizations*. San Francisco: Jossey-Bass, 204–61.

JANIS, I. L. (1972). *Victims of Groupthink: A Psychological Study of Foreign-Policy Decisions and Fiascoes*. Boston: Houghton Mifflin.

JEHN, K., NORTHCRAFT, G., and NEALE, M. (1999). 'Why Differences Make a Difference: A Field Study of Diversity, Conflict and Performance in Work Groups.' *Administrative Science Quarterly*, 44: 741–63.

KABANOFF, B. (1991). 'Equity, Equality, Power, and Conflict.' *Academy of Management Review*, 16: 416–41.

KECK, S. (1997). 'Top Management Team Structure: Differential Effects by Environment Context.' *Organization Science*, 8: 143–56.

KERR, N. and TINDALE, R. (2004). 'Group Performance and Decision Making.' *Annual Review of Psychology*, 55: 623–55.

KIM, W. and MAUBORGNE, R. (1993). 'Procedural Justice, Attitudes and Subsidiary Top Management Compliance.' *Academy of Management Journal*, 36: 502–26.

KORSGAARD, M., SCHWEIGER, and D. SAPIENZA, H. (1995). 'Building Commitment, Attachment, and Trust in Strategic Decision-Making Teams: The Role of Procedural Justice.' *Academy of Management Journal*, 38/1: 60–84.

KRAMER, R. M. (1991). 'Inter-Group Relations and Organizational Dilemmas: The Role of Categorization Processes,' in B. M. Staw and L. L. Cummings (eds.), *Research in Organizational Behavior*. Greenwich, CT: JAI Press, 191–228.

KRUGLANSKI, A. and WEBSTER, D. (1991). 'Group Members Reactions to Opinion Deviates and Conformists at Varying Degrees of Proximity to Decision Deadline and of Environmental Noise.' *Journal of Personality and Social Psychology*, 61: 212–25.

KRUGLANSKI, A. PIERRO, A., MANNETTI, L., and GRADA, E. (2006). 'Groups and Epistemic Providers: Need for Closure and the Unfolding of Group-Centrism.' *Psychological Review*, 113: 84–100.

LEAVITT, H. and BAHRAMI, H. (1988). *Managerial Psychology: Managing Behavior in Organizations.* Chicago: University of Chicago Press.

LIBBY, R., TROTMAN, K., and ZIMMER, I. (1987). 'Member Variation, Recognition of Expertise, and Group Performance.' *Journal of Applied Psychology*, 72: 81–7.

MARKOCZY, L. (1997). 'Measuring Beliefs: Accept No Substitutes.' *Academy of Management Journal*, 40: 1228–42.

MILLIKEN, F. and MARTINS, L. (1996). 'Searching for Common Threads: Understanding the Multiple Effects of Diversity in Organizational Groups.' *Academy of Management Review*, 21: 401–33.

MOSCOVICI, S. (1980). 'Toward a Theory of Conversion Behavior,' in L. Berkowitz (ed.), *Advances in Experimental Social Psychology.* New York: Academic Press, 13: 2209–39.

—— (1985). 'Innovation and Minority Influence,' in S. Moscovici, G. Mugny, and E. van Avermaet (eds.), *Perspectives on Minority Influence.* Cambridge: Cambridge University Press, 9–52.

MULLEN B., and COPPER, C. (1994). 'The Relation Between Group Cohesiveness and Performance: An Integration.' *Psychological Bulletin*, 115: 210–77.

—— DOVIDIO, J., JOHNSON, C., and COPPER, C. (1992). 'In-Group–Out-Group Differences in Social Projection.' *Journal of Experimental Social Psychology*, 28: 422–40.

—— ANTHONY, T., SALAS, E., and DRISKELL, J. (1994). 'Groups Cohesiveness and Quality of Decision Making: An Integration of Tests of the Groupthink Hypothesis.' *Small Group Research*, 25: 189–204.

—— JOHNSON, C., and ANTHONY, T. (1994). 'Relative Group Size and Cognitive Representations of Ingroup and Outgroup: The Phenomenology of Being in a Group.' *Small Group Research*, 25: 250–66.

NEMETH, C., MAYSELESS, O., SHERMAN, J., and BROWN, Y. (1990). 'Exposure to Dissent and Recall of Information.' *Journal of Personality and Social Psychology*, 58: 429–37.

OAKES, P. J., HASLAM, S. A., and TURNER, J. C. (1994). *Stereotyping and Social Reality.* Oxford: Blackwell.

PELLED, L. (1996). 'Demographic Diversity, Conflict and Work Group Outcomes: An Intervening Process Theory.' *Organization Science*, 7: 615–31.

—— EISENHARDT, K., and XIN, K. (1999). 'Exploring the Black Box: An Analysis of Work Group Diversity, Conflict and Performance.' *Administrative Science Quarterly*, 44: 1–28.

POSTEMES, T., SPEARS, R., and CIHANGIR, S. (2001). 'Quality of Decision Making and Group Norms.' *Journal of Personality and Social Psychology*, 80: 918–30.

PHILLIPS, K., MANNIX, E., NEALE, M., and GRUENFELD, D. (2004). 'Diverse Groups and Information Sharing: The Effects of Congruent Ties.' *Journal of Experimental Social Psychology*, 40: 497–510.

RIORDAN, C. and SHORE, L. M. (1997). 'Demographic Diversity and Employee Attitudes: An Empirical Examination of Relational Demography Among Work Units.' *Journal of Applied Psychology*, 82: 342–58.

SCHOLTEN, L., VAN KNIPPENBERG, D., NYSTED, B., and DE DREU, C. (2005). 'Motivated Information Processing and Group Decision Making: Effects of Process Accountability on Information Processing and Decision Quality.' Working Paper, University of Amsterdam.

SHAH, J., KRUGLANSKI, A., and THOMPSON, E. (1998). 'Membership has its (Epistemic) Rewards: Need for Closure Effects on In-Group Bias.' *Journal of Personality and Social Psychology*, 75: 383–93.

SIMONS, T., PELLED, L., and SMITH, K. (1999). 'Making Use of Difference: Diversity, Debate and Decision Comprehensiveness in Top Management Teams.' *Academy of Management Journal*, 42: 662–73.

STASSER, G. and STEWART, D. (1992). 'Discovery of Hidden Profiles by Decision-Making Groups: Solving a Problem Versus Making a Judgement.' *Journal of Personality and Social Psychology*, 63: 426–34.

—— TITUS, W. (1985). 'Pooling of Unshared Information in Group Decision Making: Biased Information Sampling During Discussion.' *Journal of Personality and Social Psychology*, 48: 1467–78.

THOMAS-HUNT, M. and PHILLIPS, K. (2004). 'When What You Know Is Not Enough: Expertise and Gender Dynamics in Task Groups.' *Personality and Social Psychology Bulletin*, 30:1585–98.

TRIANDIS, H., KUROWSKI, L., and GEFLAND, M. (1994). 'Workplace Diversity,' in H. Triandis, M. Dunnette, and I. Hough (eds.), *Handbook of Industrial and Organizational Psychology*. Palo Alto, CA: Consulting Psychologists Press, 769–827.

TSUI, A. and GUTEK, B. (1999). *Demographic Differences in Organizations: Current Research and Future Directions*. Lanham, MD: Lexington Books.

—— EGAN, T., and O'REILLY, C. (1992). 'Being Different: Relational Demography and Organizational Attachment.' *Administrative Science Quarterly*, 37: 549–79.

TURNER, J. C., HOGG, M. A., OAKES, P. J., REICHER, S. D., and WETHERELL, M. S. (1987). *Rediscovering the Social Group: A Self-categorization Theory*. Oxford: Blackwell.

VAN KNIPPENBERG, D. and SCHIPPERS, M. (2007). 'Work Group Diversity.' *Annual Review of Psychology*, 58: 515–41.

—— DE DREU, C., and HOMAN, A. (2004). 'Work Group Diversity and Group Performance: An Integrative Model and Research Agenda.' *Journal of Applied Psychology*, 89: 1008–22.

WEST, M. A. (2002). 'Sparkling Fountains or Stagnant Ponds: An Integrative Model of Creativity and Innovation Implementation in Work Groups.' *Applied Psychology: An International Review*, 51: 355–87.

WILLIAMS, K. and O'REILLY, C. (1998). 'Demography and Diversity in Organizations: A Review of 40 Years of Research.' *Research in Organizational Behavior*, 20: 77–140.

WITHEY, M. and COOPER, W. (1989). 'Predicting Exit, Voice, Loyalty and Neglect.' *Administrative Science Quarterly*, 34: 521–39.

ZENGER, T. and B. LAWRENCE. (1989). 'Organizational Demography: The Differential Effects of Age and Tenure Distribution on Technical Communication.' *Academy of Management Journal*, 32: 353–76.

PART IV

CONSEQUENCES PRODUCED BY DECISIONS

MAKING SENSE OF REAL OPTIONS REASONING: AN ENGINE OF CHOICE THAT BACKFIRES?

MICHAEL L. BARNETT

ROGER L. M. DUNBAR

INTRODUCTION

DECISION makers have long sought ways to effectively yet efficiently generate strategic flexibility within their organizations so that they can quickly adapt to dynamic market conditions (e.g., Ashby 1956). Not surprisingly, decision makers have taken notice of claims that, through real options reasoning, one can design an organization to function as an "engine of choice" (McGrath et al. 2004: 86) that generates unending chains of strategic decision-making opportunities while at the same time limiting the associated costs (Bowman and Hurry 1993). Is real options reasoning actually able to fulfill this promise?

This chapter traces the development of real options reasoning (ROR) and details how problems in assessing the value of real options have made ROR difficult to implement. The chapter then describes how in practice, instead of focusing on explicit valuation, organizations use analogous reasoning to develop, select, and implement options that enable strategic flexibility and so enhance value. An illustrative case demonstrates how financial options can help this process by buffering core operations from changing market environments. The same illustration also shows that ROR fails to simultaneously create future choices while limiting costs. Moreover, where it does generate future choices, it does not prevent decision makers from making poor choices. Thus, the engine of choice that ROR suggests organizations should create may in fact backfire on those decision makers who try to implement it.

The Development of Real Options Reasoning

An option is simply a decision-making opportunity. The finance field formalized an option as a rights contract that transfers market risk; that is, a financial option is the legal right but not the obligation to buy or sell a market asset at a predetermined rate for a prespecified time. By paying an option premium, a buyer buys the rights to any market gains during the option period; by accepting the option premium, a seller agrees to absorb market losses during the same period. A firm may decide, for example, to purchase a financial option to buy a million gallons of oil at US$3 per gallon six months from now. If market prices move above US$3 in the next six months, the firm exercises its option and obtains the million gallons from the option issuer who must absorb the difference between the market price and the US$3 the firm contracted to pay. If prices fall below US$3, the firm buys oil on the open market at less than the contracted amount and abandons its option. From the firm's standpoint, the cost of the option allows the transfer of market risk, after which a firm makes only value enhancing decisions.

Myers (1977) suggested that capital investment projects generate decision-making opportunities similar to financial options. An initial investment that gets a project started, for example, is akin to the premium paid to acquire a financial option. As projects then unfold over time, managers can decide to abandon, defer, expand, or contract them, or they can make new investments in unplanned directions. Each of these possibilities is a decision-making "option." Both "real" and financial options offer these time related decision-making opportunities and so in this sense, they are similar in how they enable strategic flexibility. Real options differ from financial options, however, in how decision makers determine their value. The value of a *real* option directly relates to the value of the associated, ongoing project. This value requires subjective assessment and changes as a project progresses. The value of a *financial* option, in contrast, depends on the market value of a particular asset and on the contractual rights that buyers and sellers agreed to when they transferred the risk associated with this market asset (Myers 1977). Hence, the value of a real option always involves a subjectively determined estimate, while the value of a financial option always reflects a market determined price.

Option traders use the Black-Scholes formula to determine the value of financial options. The formula uses several parameters: a stock price, an exercise price, a time to option expiration, a measure of the volatility underlying the optioned asset's value, and the risk-free interest rate. All of these parameters have current market values, and so the values the formula generates directly reflect market conditions. In fact, the formula establishes a "fair market value" for trading a financial option.

Real option scholars and practitioners have attempted to adapt the Black-Scholes formula to value real options (Brennan and Trigeorgis 2000). To use the Black-Scholes formula to assess real option value, however, one must rely on subjective estimates for the different parameters. An estimate of the project's expected cash flows can substitute for the stock price. Equivalent to the option exercise price, one can estimate the cost of the next project stage. The equivalent of the option expiration date must reflect local circumstances. While competitive pre-emption might suddenly end an option's viability, for example, struggles between optimistic project champions and skeptical upper management might extend its life. To estimate volatility, one should assume that the project's risk profile is similar to the same industry's stocks as they trade on a large financial market. Decision makers must also make adjustments to the risk-free interest rate to account for specific project risk (Fernandez 2002). Bowman and Moskowitz (2001) show that although one could insert such subjective estimates into the Black-Scholes formula, this will necessarily lead to unstable and controversial estimates of what the real option value may be. Ultimately, the approach is practically infeasible because of the unreliability of combining so many subjective estimates.

Consistent with this state of affairs, scholars rarely advise and managers rarely attempt to assign explicit values to real options (Miller and Arikan 2004). Rather, ROR is intended to be primarily a heuristic. Yet even in this regard, ROR research remains vague in terms of what decision-makers should actually do (Adner and Levinthal 2004). Instead of spelling out implementation methods, researchers offer vague analogies. Kogut and Kulatilaka (2001: 756), for example, suggest: "An options approach indicates that firms construct exploratory ridges between peaks to hedge against adverse changes in the landscape." Luehrman (1998: 90) says, "Managing a portfolio of strategic options is like growing a garden of tomatoes in an unpredictable climate." But how should a decision maker decide which exploratory ridges to construct, or which tomatoes to grow?

ROR ignores the value assessment issue and focuses on how time dependent decision making can facilitate organizational flexibility. Kogut (1991), for example, notes how the intention in joint ventures to create time related flexibility is consistent with real options thinking. Finance scholars such as Trigeorgis (1996: ch. 8) and Luehrman (1998) think of "strategic flexibility" and "real options thinking" as essentially synonymous. The common intuition is that, "when the future is highly uncertain, it pays to have a broad range of options open" (Coy 1999: 118).

ROR can be quite specific in its recommendations, however. ROR views the total of an organization's resources as a bundle of real options and argues that decision makers should manage these options over time. It holds that if small investments can initiate new projects and so option costs are low, then decision makers should initiate many projects (McGrath 1997, 1999). Beyond this overarching logic of creating strategic flexibility by initiating many projects, ROR also deals with the need to efficiently abandon significant numbers of these projects. ROR requires decision makers to assess project performance against targets at pre-specified times (Adner and Levinthal 2004). If a project fails to meet a performance target, ROR requires decision makers to abandon the option and avoid further downside loss (McGrath 1999). Disciplined option abandonment is critical to the success of ROR because it ensures that decision makers avoid escalation of commitment to un-promising options (Barwise et al. 1987; Busby and Pitts 1997). Thus, despite the rhetoric of flexibility that ROR emphasizes, a central aim of ROR is to impose discipline that eliminates significant degrees of flexibility—the flexibility to continue investment in unpromising projects. Yet to make this decision, firm decision makers must assess ongoing option value. How to do this is an unresolved issue.

Making Decisions About Options

How do decision makers actually manage options? Levinthal and Rerup (2006) suggest that decision makers learn from earlier situations, and use analogous reasoning to find ways that these insights may apply to new situations. By comparing earlier and current situations, decision makers often find that they can estimate the costs and the benefits of available options sufficiently enough to make decisions; they have enough information to make a decision in favor of one option or another. Decision makers use similar heuristics to assess how available real options match with the requirements of evolving market environments. Of course, situations never replicate exactly and new issues and options inevitably emerge, but for managers to choose between options, it does not seem that they need exact figures—what they do need is contextual appreciation and believable estimates.

As organizations can repeatedly and successfully replicate similar options in new situations, Winter and Szulanski (2001) suggest that managers develop better option management skills even as their organizations develop unique capabilities.

This involves not only analogous reasoning, but also abilities to get agreement on options to choose and options to eliminate (Brunsson 1985). Research on ROR needs to clarify these processes that lead to option generation and a willingness to act out particular options. This would be consistent with the views of Kogut and Kulatilaka (1994:124, emphasis added) who said: "the value of an option stems from the investment in the *capability* to respond profitably to future uncertain events." To date, however, the processes leading to option choice and action are not something that ROR has focused upon.

Trafalgar House Group was faced with increased competition in 1986, for example, and from the range of available options at the time, it resolved to merge with John Brown Engineers and Constructors. In 1995, increased competition from large design construction firms again threatened Trafalgar House Group. Dhillon and Orton (2001) describe an extensive list of strategic options available to the firm in 1995. These included cost leadership strategies, differentiation strategies, strategic alliance strategies, vertical integration strategies, diversification strategies, globalization strategies, and merger and acquisition strategies. Despite these many options, Trafalgar House Group again chose the option of a merger, this time with the Norwegian Group, Kvaerner ASA. While this study reaches no conclusions, it is possible that Trafalgar House's decision makers were using analogous reasoning to link the earlier situation and the option chosen at that time with the later situation and that such a process helped them eliminate other options. It is not clear how in practice, decision making among available options involves or requires a careful or rational evaluation of option costs and benefits (Worren et al. 2002).

The uncertainty that surrounds analogous reasoning may also be something that helps decision makers to explore the potential application of past options, and provides room to assess the merits of new options. Uncertainty may be helpful because it makes it difficult to put a specific value on any real option at a point in time because this value is continuously changing due to managerial efforts to redefine and understand the situation faced. In fact, this characteristic maps reality. To the extent that a new option is similar to what an organization has done before, there is some replication and so insights from the past may be relevant but one cannot be sure. In practice, if the replications are similar enough, decision makers seem able to make rapid decisions. If options involve new things, however, decision makers cannot rely on analogous reasoning. If analogous reasoning is in practice key to making decisions about which options to pursue and which to abandon, one would expect the selection process to slow down drastically and become difficult to implement when there is no previous experience to draw upon.

Garud and Karnoe's (2001: 12) example of innovation in a corporation suggests this may indeed be the case. They describe how at 3M Corporation, Spence Silver created a "glue that did not stick." The company takes pride in making "glues that stick" and so Silver's new compound constituted a very different type of option. Many at 3M were bemused by Silver's new product and didn't recognize it as a new option at all. Silver took ten years to explore ways to combine his glue that did not stick with other 3M resources and create new product options with market appeal. Eventually, it became the basis of Post-It Notes and a huge raft of new but unimagined, commercially successful 3M products. Analogous reasoning could not be used in this context because most people at 3M Corporation had never conceived of glue that did not stick. A trial and error innovation process was necessary to find possibilities but this took years. Had a relevant analogy been available, it would have greatly speeded up the process.

ROR is intolerant of long exploration processes such as this because in many organizations, real options are replications, development processes are based on analogous reasoning, and so many options are non-exclusive and subject to competitive preemption (Pinches 1998). If other firms can imitate a particular option, they can replicate it and compete profits away (Barney 1986). By waiting before committing to such a project, decision makers risk lockout in the face of early mover competitors (Ghemawat and del Sol 1998). Further, low cost activities intended to create real options like research and development, test marketing, or "low cost probes" (Brown and Eisenhardt 1997) may alert others to new opportunities. This may allow competitors to pre-empt or at least shorten periods when an option is a source of competitive advantage (Barwise et al. 1987). Rather than having an ability to respond to emergent events with time dependent options, a firm may find it is left holding "fool's gold" (Garud et al. 1998) as competitors are in position to exploit the opportunity. A viable foothold sometimes requires a quick investment and full commitment (Schilling 1998) rather than time dependent option flexibility.

ROR has not considered how analogous reasoning and organizational consensus making help decision makers sort out which options to pursue and which to abandon. It is likely that such a process allows decision makers to make quick decisions that take many situational subtleties into account while the same process may overlook new information suggesting new options and new directions. Such processes are areas for further research to determine how the time dependent logics that ROR emphasizes may complement the use of analogous reasoning and organizational consensus making. By developing a more complete understanding of these processes and how they may complement one another, decision makers may be able to better manage how organizations generate, select, and implement their options.

USING OPTIONS IN PRACTICE

Guided by their values and expectations and using analogous reasoning, decision makers develop options for current situations. As most organizational situations contain many resources that can be combined in different ways, many options are available. Most decision makers don't recognize most of them, however, and this causes them little concern because they know that if they want to, they can easily draw on vast numbers of unexploited degrees of freedom and develop new options (Bowman and Hurry 1993; Dunbar and Starbuck 2006). They also know that if they apply analogous reasoning and discuss their ideas with others, they will also likely uncover new options. As generating real options is not a problem, decision makers focus on building consensus on the actions to be taken from the options available (Brunsson 1985). They allow values, expectations, and the evolving consensus to guide the process that selects some options and eliminates others.

Although decision makers usually know what ideally they would value, they often have only a vague idea about what options might achieve these outcomes. Discussion often centers not so much on what option to choose but on how to implement it and as a result of talking about it, options get modified in the process of implementation. In this sense, an option constitutes a continuing experiment and decision makers are assessing whether option implementation or a modified option may contribute to organizational value creation. Discussions constitute the ongoing experimental process that creates and modifies and then selects and implements a particular option rather than the alternatives. Continuing discussions explore likely option efficacy.

Over time, distinctions emerge between different types of options. Some options involve critically important tasks in the organization's operating core where the aim is to perform tasks in a predictable and stable manner (Thompson 1967). Options at this level support predictability and efficiency. Decision makers often surround an operating core with support units that protect it, or adapt, evolve, and adjust to developing environments. Options to support an operating core respond to changes in the environment, in the core, in decision makers' beliefs and values, etc. In addition, decision makers may consider new options to rejuvenate an organization with, for example, new products, new services, new facilities, or new capabilities (Burgelman 1983; Dunbar and Starbuck 2006).

OPTIONS SUPPORTING STABILITY IN THE ORGANIZATIONAL OPERATING CORE

After decision makers identify specific tasks and relationships as core operations (Thompson 1967), they train and equip personnel and install rule systems and evaluation criteria to enable repeated and effective task accomplishment. They hone implementation to ensure the operating core is effective and efficient. When an operating core achieves desired efficient performance, decision makers want options that stabilize it. Thompson (1967) said decision makers should stop exploring options to adjust core value generation processes when they generate performance variation, not performance improvement.

As decision makers use options to minimize performance variation in operating cores, if variation occurs, then unanticipated sources of disturbance are often the cause. Changes in implementation of procedures may cause unexpected variation, for example, or changes outside the operating core may cause variation, e.g., variations in input costs or demand levels. Options to introduce additional quality control routines may eliminate implementation variation (Dean and Bowen 1994). Options to increase training and expertise, and to carry out experiments can increase the reliability of technology (Dixit and Pindyck 1994). Variations in input and outputs to the operating core, however, are often beyond decision makers' control. However, in this situation, financial options can help decision makers. Specifically, a financial option can make supplies of critical inputs available at predetermined prices (e.g., oil). In a similar way, a firm may sell options to dispose of its products at predetermined prices. Financial options reduce the impacts of exogenous sources of variation on core operations.

OPTIONS SUPPORTING ORGANIZATIONAL DEVELOPMENT

Decision makers are concerned not only with core operating units but also with options that help organizations evolve, change, and grow. They may be interested in options that introduce new products and services to increase an organization's size and profits, or options to respond to internal and external issues in ways consistent with organization values. They may also consider options that make an organization a better place to live and work.

To stimulate search for new options, decision makers can proceed in two ways. One approach is to rely on the emergence of problems over time. As problems emerge, decision makers then search for options to solve the problem (Cyert and March 1963). Alternatively, if decision makers introduce new evaluation criteria, this may highlight new options for improvement possibilities. Improvement options come from anywhere within an organization, and so decision makers often invite improvement option ideas from all over an organization. As new definitions of value emerge, organizations seek new options to revise current ways of doing things (Usher 1954).

Given an objective organizational problem or a subjective evaluation criterion for defining organizational improvements, decision makers reconfigure available assets to find new organizational options. The problem then is to decide which options to pursue and which to eliminate. Discussions often lead to consensus in support of some options and the elimination of others. Another approach is to predetermine evaluation criteria and have a contest between option possibilities, with the organization committing itself to the competition winners while eliminating the rest. If options are in fact all relatively similar replications, a contest to decide which options to pursue and which to abandon may make sense. To avoid controversy, however, decision makers who mobilize multiple options and use contests for selection must have transparent and fair evaluation processes so that the advocates of unselected options do not reject the organization and its processes.

In some cases, new project options are so different or so unique that a competition or a staged investment process is difficult to conceive. In this situation, errors could be costly and decision makers will want to discuss possibilities widely, bringing in more information and using a variety of assessment criteria. The emphasis is on learning about the option and its implications. A staged investment process with disciplined cutoffs threatens this ongoing learning and analysis cycle (Barnett and Cahill 2007). If a decision maker abandons a unique option without the full participation of those seeking to realize the option, the process generates skepticism and alienation, degrading an organization's capability to create new option value (Barnett 2003).

A continuing process of option development to support an adaptive organization implies that decision makers can revise, change, develop, or abandon options. New options often utilize available resources in new ways. New option possibilities may be most likely to emerge from organizational resources and areas that decision makers always knew were available but which they overlooked and did not particularly value (Bowker and Star 2000). Diverse views, broad participation, and evolving evaluation criteria seem to be the essence of continuing option development and abandonment as the process is currently practiced. This contrasts with the focus of ROR that favors financial criteria and fixed decision points at which time decision makers must either exercise or abandon options (Adner and Levinthal 2004).

OPTIONS IN PLAY: AN EXAMPLE

Suppose that a firm produces the top selling doll, Amiable Amber. Ms Amber has been the best selling doll in the United States since she entered an adoring market some 40 years ago. The firm wants to organize to maximize profitability from continuing sales of Ms Amber. Its decision makers want to protect Ms Amber's production from key uncertainties, such as input price uncertainty and demand uncertainty. Ms Amber's distinctive feature is her amber eyes that are made with a full ounce of authentic high quality amber. The availability of high quality amber varies and, accordingly, so does its cost. Fluctuations in amber availability and price can threaten the ability to produce Ms Amber dolls at a profit.

High volume retailers buy Ms Amber for US$22. The firm can purchase the amber used in Ms Amber dolls for about US$5 per ounce, and so each doll contains about US$10 worth of amber. All other production costs total about US$10, and so it typically costs about US$20 to produce a Ms Amber doll. Amber prices fluctuate from US$4 per ounce to nearly US$9 per ounce, however. As prices for amber exceed US$6 per ounce, it becomes unprofitable to produce Ms Amber. In light of this, the firm could use financial options to maintain a steady supply of amber at a price that allows for profitable production. In particular, the firm could seek option contracts that provide it a guaranteed source of amber at no more than, say, US$5.50 per ounce. If the market price of amber is above US$5.50 per ounce, the firm exercises the option and buys amber for US$5.50. If the market price of amber is below US$5.50, the firm buys it on the open market. The use of financial options enables continued production at a preset level of profitability, despite market price fluctuations, and the door remains open to higher profitability. For example, were amber to drop to US$4 per ounce, the firm would be free to benefit from this drop in price and double its profit margin since the financial option does not require that it purchase amber at US$5.50. Thus, by holding the financial option, the firm has the opportunity to make only those choices that create the most value for it, given changing external market conditions.

In addition to using financial options to protect against input cost uncertainty, the firm could use real options to protect against demand uncertainty. Perhaps due to a saturated US market, the firm may import Ms Amber into Canada. The firm is not certain, however, of the demand for Ms Amber in Canada. If demand is strong, then its current plant will be unable to produce enough dolls and it will need to build additional capacity quickly. Otherwise, rivals could fill the demand that the firm has proven exists. The fastest way to expand is to build a second assembly line adjacent to the current plant. The plot of land next to the plant is available for lease with an associated right to buy it. For the firm, leasing the plot of land is the equivalent of acquiring a real option that gives it the right but not the obligation to build additional production capacity at a maximally convenient location. If the firm discovers that its dolls are not selling, it will not make further investment in plant capacity. When the lease is up, it will not renew it and by so doing, the firm abandons its option. A happy alternative would be that the firm discovers that its dolls are selling well and it wants to produce more. The firm may then exercise the option, buy the land, and build added plant facilities. With increased doll demand, the option to build additional plant capacity has increased in value and it exercises its option. Again, the option allows the firm the opportunity to make only those choices that would increase its value, given changing market conditions.

However, dolls have limited lives, no matter how amiable. Even Barbie innovates as times change. Instead of driving a gas-hogging sports car, perhaps Barbie might sell better if she drove a Prius. The doll firm's chief executive officer (CEO) believes his firm would benefit from offering an evolving portfolio of dolls. He particularly likes the idea of taking real people and offering them for sale in a doll form. The worry is just how well these dolls will sell. Before committing to their production, the CEO would like a better sense of the market for these dolls. He has directed his staff to propose new dolls that the firm could market. Current proposals include marketing a President George W. Bush war-president doll and a Laura W. Bush reading-leader doll. For the purposes of this story, imagine that the White House has agreed to allow the firm to produce and sell dolls that have a likeness of the President and his wife. The doll firm could view the test marketing of these new doll concepts as real options. If the market appears promising, the firm would exercise the option and produce the dolls; if not, it will abandon the new doll concept and so losses would be limited to the cost of the test market program.

Imagine, too, that the firm is very aware of prior experiences where it committed to projects that turned out poorly. The firm has had two dolls that generated legendary but contrasting sales experiences. Beyond Amiable Amber, the firm's best sales success was its beloved Jostle Me Elmer doll that flew off shop shelves for years. The firm's big disappointment was the Ken Lay Ethics Action Figure doll that never took off, even as Enron was one of the world's most admired companies. The losses associated with the full scale launch of the Ken Lay doll eclipsed the profits generated by Jostle Me Elmer. Were it not for the continued success of Ms Amber, the firm would have been bankrupt. Bearing these experiences in mind, the firm wishes to avoid full launches of new product lines until it is sure of adequate market demand. On the other hand, the firm also wants to be able to produce the extra dolls if demand materializes. If the new dolls prove to be a success, the firm will not have enough production capacity.

The value of holding a lease on the land next to the current doll factory increases as uncertainty about the number of dolls the manufacturer will sell increases. If doll sales could vary from ten to ten million units per year, the lease that secures the firm's ability to expand capacity, without obligation, is more valuable than if dolls sales vary from 10,000 to 100,000 units per year. In effect, only the upside matters where option value depends on the exogenous factors that determine doll demand. The downside becomes irrelevant, since additional capacity is not built. The lease allows the firm to "wait and see" what the future holds, delaying any commitment to the large capital project that building new plant facilities will entail.

However, the options of developing new dolls are in many ways replications. The key issue is which doll will have that "X" factor that attracts a market. The firm may be certain there is demand for a doll that exudes ethics but may be uncertain about its ability to produce a doll with the necessary "X" factor. The firm may commission several teams to work independently to make, say, an Ethical Elmer equivalent and so "spread its bets." The firm may fund each team to develop but not produce a doll. This minimizes firm costs until sales efficacy is determined. If the decision maker sets the situation up in this way, the firm holds several "wait and see" options and it can discuss which ones it should proceed with or organize a contest and pick the best.

Decision makers may also seek to influence demand. The doll manufacturer might test market its dolls, for example, to learn about current market demand. The meaning of the time flexibility that the firm's option affords moves from "wait and see" to "act and see." Further exemplifying an act and see stance, decision makers may realize they could add functionalities to the dolls that might appeal to consumers and broaden the potential market. For example, the presidential dolls might say things typical of the president and his wife. This programming could also be flexible, with the dolls saying different things with more appeal in different markets. Yet as the firm has not included such functionality in dolls before, there will be questions as to whether it has the capability to do so.

An additional option is to push established product lines in new directions. Apart from minor changes in the quality of materials, Ms Amber has been the same basic doll since she was first introduced 40 years ago. At the annual toy convention, a Ms Amber fan told the chief executive that she would like to use Ms Amber to learn how to put on makeup properly. With the market evolving toward dolls with greater functionality such as Sewing Sue and Marching Martha, the chief executive took this suggestion seriously. Further, he believes that a doll that helps children to learn critical life skills and respect social models is consistent with the theme he seeks to establish with the President and Mrs Bush dolls. He wonders, though, if it is feasible to make Ms Amber interactive, such that she would display certain facial expressions and voice positive or negative reactions as children apply her makeup correctly or incorrectly.

As always, there are severe cost pressures in this industry and every option to change a doll introduces additional costs. Uncertainty surrounds whether consumers will see the new additions as valuable, whether the firm can make the changes, and whether it can charge sufficiently to recover its costs. This opens many new and interrelated option complexities that ideally the firm will explore and understand. New options also risk disrupting currently well established plant routines.

Without a lot of effort, our doll manufacturer is getting too many good option ideas. Doll demand is certain and it has the technology to produce dolls but should it be meddling with its manufacturing processes? And which new dolls should it bet on? It's difficult to engage in a low cost probe to determine which low cost probe to pick and if you have done so, which option has value and which do you cut off?

ROR is not able to supplant managerial reasoning in decisions to create or destroy organizational value.

Conclusion

Decision makers make choices to generate organizational value from available options. They create options by using the unutilized degrees of freedom surrounding organizational assets. Until they combine organizational assets to form a real option—a specific project in a particular organizational context—the value implicit in combinable organizational assets is unknown. Decision makers know option development requires input from many diverse sources and they repeatedly experiment to find which options are effective. When sources of uncertainty are organizationally endogenous, objective data is not available and so evaluation must be subjective. Decision makers must rely on their experience. Past experience involves the implications of related replications and discussions with knowledgeable colleagues. The decision maker's aim is to develop expectations concerning how long it will take to develop an option and what to expect as a result. Through this process, decision makers initiate and abandon options.

The perspective of decision makers using their experience to develop, choose, and evaluate available options contrasts with the perspective of ROR advocates who assume that options are givens and that option selection involves evaluation routines and the use of time flexibility. For ROR advocates, uncertainty and unpredictability over time require authoritative intervention. They justify their view because some decision makers escalate commitment to costly options that they should abandon. The aim of ROR is to develop a simultaneous solution to the problem of uncertainty and the potential of decision makers to escalate their commitment to expensive options. Their real options solution is claimed to enable an option holder to remain exposed to the upside potential inherent in uncertain and unfolding events but be protected from downside risk. They believe they achieve this aim by waiting for uncertainty to resolve and then at a certain point in time, either exercising the option to gain the upside benefits that have become certain, or abandoning the option as downside losses have also become certain. This reasoning makes it difficult to manage options because the objective data one needs to make decisions about benefits and losses is lacking (Busby and Pitts 1997; Bowman and Moskowitz 2001; Barnett 2003; Adner and Levinthal 2004).

The ROR literature claims the approach is revolutionary because it characterizes an organization as consisting of bundles of options that increase performance uncertainty and variation and contrasts this with the conventional view that decision makers should avoid uncertainty and minimize variance. Specifically, ROR suggests decision makers can embrace uncertainty by pursuing a large number of options and diversifying widely. If a decision maker pursues many options and a few succeed, on balance the decision maker may minimize performance variance (March and Simon 1958; Thompson 1967; Pfeffer and Salancik 1978). On the other hand, this approach makes a relatively simple ongoing problem unnecessarily complicated. Rather than treat all organizational assets as an evolving bundle of options always in play, for example, it seems simpler and more effective to generate options in a one-at-a-time fashion as a way to avoid or embrace uncertainty one step at a time. Moreover, this seems to be how decision makers actually manage options.

ROR is a heuristic that forces a consideration of a bigger field of options but then enforces decisions at time point while ignoring value that it needs to assess but cannot assess. This time-based rigidity destroys the flexibility that is necessary to generate organizational value. The traditional discussion method that decision makers use takes options one at a time and makes a local assessment. This leads to a narrower picture but decision makers face issues of assessing value rather than ignoring them. After examining how decision makers pursue the creation of strategic flexibility in their organizations, and comparing practice against the prescriptions of ROR, it is not clear that ROR improves the decision making process. Rather, it seems that it can make the process worse, at least in comparison with how decision makers usually manage their options.

References

ADNER, R. and LEVINTHAL, D. (2004). 'What is *Not* a Real Option: Considering Boundaries for the Application of Real Options to Business Strategy.' *Academy of Management Review*, 29/1: 74–85.

AMRAM, M. and KULATILAKA, N. (1999). *Real Options: Managing Strategic Investment in an Uncertain World*. Boston, MA: Harvard Business School Press.

BARNETT, M. L. (2003). 'Falling off the Fence? A Realistic Appraisal of a Real Options Approach to Corporate Strategy.' *Journal of Management Inquiry*, 12/2: 185–96.

—— (2005). 'Paying Attention to Real Options.' *R&D Management*, 35/1: 61–72.

—— CAHILL, G. (2007). 'Measure Less, Succeed More: A Zen Approach to Organisational Balance and Effectiveness.' *Philosophy of Management*, 6/1: 91–106.

BARNEY, J. B. (1986). 'Strategic Factor Markets: Expectations, Luck, and Business Strategy.' *Management Science*, 10: 1231–41.

BARWISE, P., MARSH, P. R., and WENSLEY, R. (1987). 'Strategic Investment Decisions.' *Research in Marketing*, 9: 1–57.

BOWKER, G. C. and STAR, S. L. (2000). *Sorting Things Out: Classification and its Consequences*. Cambridge, MA: MIT Press.

BOWMAN, E. H. and HURRY, D. (1993). 'Strategy through the Option Lens: An Integrated View of Resource Investments and the Incremental-Choice Process.' *Academy of Management Review*, 18/4: 760–82.

—— MOSKOWITZ, G. T. (2001). 'Real Options Analysis and Strategic Decision Making.' *Organization Science*, 12/6: 772–7.

BRENNAN, M. J. and TRIGEORGIS, L. (2000). *Project Flexibility, Agency, and Competition: New Developments in the Theory and Application of Real Options*. New York: Oxford University Press.

BROWN, S. L. and EISENHARDT, K. M. (1997). 'The Art of Continuous Change: Linking Complexity Theory and Time-Paced Evolution in Relentlessly Shifting Organizations.' *Administrative Science Quarterly*, 42: 1–34.

BURGLEMAN, R. A. (1983). 'A Process Model of Internal Corporate Venturing in the Diversified Major Firm.' *Administrative Science Quarterly*, 28: 223–44.

BUSBY, J. S. and PITTS, C. G. C. (1997). 'Real Options in Practice: An Exploratory Survey of How Finance Officers Deal with Flexibility in Capital Appraisal.' *Management Accounting Research*, 8: 169–86.

COY, P. (1999). 'Exploiting Uncertainty: The "Real Options" Revolution in Decision-Making.' *Business Week*, June 7: 118–24.

CYERT, R. M. and MARCH, J. G. (1963). *A Behavioral Theory of the Firm*. Englewood Cliffs, NJ: Prentice-Hall.

DEAN, J. W., Jr., and BOWEN, D. E. (1994). 'Management Theory and Total Quality: Improving Research and Practice Through Theory Development.' *Academy of Management Review*, 19/3: 392–418.

DHILLON, G. and ORTON, J. D. (2001). 'Schizoid Incoherence, Microstrategic Options, and the Strategic Management of New Organizational Forms'. *M@n@gement*, 4/4: 229–40.

DIXIT, A. K. and PYNDICK, R. S. (1994). *Investment Under Uncertainty*. Princeton, NJ: Princeton University Press.

DUNBAR, R. L. M. and STARBUCK, W. H. (2006). 'Learning to Design Organizations and Learning from Designing Them.' *Organization Science*, 17/2: 171–8.

FERNANDEZ, P. (2002). 'Valuing Real Options: Frequently Made Errors.' IESE University of Navarra, Research Paper No. 455, January.

GARUD, R., KUMARASWAMY, A., and NAYYAR, P. (1998). 'Real Options or Fool's Gold? Perspective Makes the Difference.' *Academy of Management Review*, 23/2: 212–17.

GARUD, R. and KARNOE, P. (eds.) (2001). *Path Dependence and Creation*. Mahwah, NJ: Erlbaum.

GHEMAWAT, P. and DEL SOL, P. (1998). 'Commitment Versus Flexibility?' *California Management Review*, 40/4: 26–42.

KOGUT, B. (1991). 'Joint Ventures and the Option to Expand and Acquire.' *Management Science*, 37: 19–33.

—— KULATILAKA, N. (2001). 'Capabilities as Real Options.' *Organization Science*, 12: 744–58.

LEVINTHAL, D. and RERUP, C. (2006). 'Crossing an Apparent Chasm: Bridging Mindful and Less-Mindful Perspectives on Organizational Learning.' *Organization Science*, 17/4: 502–13.

LUEHRMAN, T. A. (1998). 'Strategy as a Portfolio of Real Options.' *Harvard Business Review*, 76/5: 89–99.

MARCH, J. G. (1991). 'Exploration and Exploitation in Organizational Learning.' *Organization Science*, 2: 71–87.

MARCH, J. G. and SIMON, H. A. (1958). *Organizations*. New York: Wiley.

McGRATH, R. G. (1997). 'A Real Options Logic for Initiating Technology Positioning Investments.' *Academy of Management Review*, 22: 974–96.

—— (1999). 'Falling Forward: Real Options Reasoning and Entrepreneurial Failure.' *Academy of Management Review*, 24: 13–30.

—— FERRIER, W. J., and MENDELOW, A. (2004). 'Real Options as Engines of Choice and Heterogeneity.' *Academy of Management Review*, 29/1: 86–101.

MYERS, S. C. (1977). 'Determinants of Corporate Borrowing.' *Journal of Financial Economics*, 5: 147–75.

NAYAK P. R. and KETTERINGHAM, J. M. (1986). *Breakthroughs!* New York: Rawson.

PFEFFER, J. and SALANCIK, G. R. (1978). *The External Control of Organizations: A Resource Dependence Perspective*. New York: Harper and Row.

PINCHES, G. E. (1998). 'Real Options: Developments and Applications.' *The Quarterly Review of Economics and Finance*, 38/Special Issue: 533–35.

REUER, J. and TONG, T. (2006). 'Corporate Investments and Growth Options.' *Managerial and Decision Economics*.

SANCHEZ, R. (1993). 'Strategic Flexibility, Firm Organization, and Managerial Work in Dynamic Markets: A Strategic-Options Perspective,' in P. Shrivastava, A. Huff, and J. Dutton (eds.), *Advances in Strategic Management*, Greenwich, CT: JAI Press, 251–91.

SCHILLING, M. A. (1998). 'Technological Lockout: An Integrative Model of the Economic and Strategic Factors Driving Technology Success and Failure.' *Academy of Management Review*, 23/2: 267–84.

SMITH, D. K. and ALEXANDER, R. C. (1988). *Fumbling the Future: How Xerox Invented, then Ignored, the First Personal Computer*. New York: Morrow.

THOMPSON, J. D. (1967). *Organizations in Action*. New York: McGraw-Hill.

TRIGEORGIS, L. (1996). *Real Options: Managerial Flexibility and Strategy in Resource Allocation*. Cambridge, MA: MIT Press.

USHER, A. (1954). *A History of Mechanical Engineering*. Cambridge, MA: Harvard.

WINTER, S. G. and SZULANSKI, G. (2001). 'Replication as Strategy.' *Organization Science* 12/6: 730–43.

WORREN, N. K., MOORE, R., and ELLIOTT, R. (2002). 'When Theories Become Tools: Toward a Framework for Pragmatic Validity.' *Human Relations*, 55: 1227–50.

21

THE SOCIAL CONSTRUCTION OF RATIONALITY IN ORGANIZATIONAL DECISION MAKING

LAURE CABANTOUS

JEAN-PASCAL GOND

MICHAEL JOHNSON-CRAMER

INTRODUCTION

Research on strategic decision making has accomplished an enormous amount since Simon's break from the sterile view of "economic man." (Eisenhardt and Zbaracki 1992: 35)

Yet, homo oeconomicus does exist!... [He] is formatted, framed and equipped with prostheses which help him in his calculations and which are, for the most part, produced by economics. (Callon 1998: 51)

Economists and organization theorists have devoted much attention to understanding organizational decision making. However, since their efforts have often been at cross-purposes, it is unclear how much progress they have made in explaining how organizations make decisions. On one hand, economists have sought to develop a framework for rational decision making. Their quest has a long tradition in the analysis of economic decisions (von Neumann and Morgenstern 1947; Savage 1954; Simon 1976) and has given rise to the subfield of formal decision analysis (e.g., Pratt et al. 1964; Howard 1966; Clemen and Reilly 2001). From this perspective, *homo oeconomicus*, or economic man (Elster 1986), represents a normative ideal and, given the tools of decision analysis, a present possibility. Organization theorists, on the other hand, have consistently rejected the hypotheses of so-called rational choice theory, challenged the explanatory power of the economic model, and deconstructed the myth of economic man (Elster 1989; Eisenhardt and Zbaracki 1992; Langley et al. 1995: 355–6; Laroche 1995; Czarniawska 2003). Their efforts have produced important insights, from the notions of "bounded rationality" (March and Simon 1958) and the "garbage can" model (Cohen et al. 1972) to the "emergent view" of corporate strategy (Mintzberg and Waters 1982). Though fruitful, this organizational perspective all but rules out the possibility that substantive rationality could ever exist in real organizations.

Despite their common interest in decision making, each perspective—the rational and the organizational—has depicted the other in unflattering terms, and in doing so, they have inhibited the emergence of a synthetic understanding of how organizations make decisions. This is a missed opportunity. This chapter attempts to bridge these two perspectives by considering the achievement of rationality in organizational decision making as a process of social construction. Mindful of the contribution of rational decision analysis, we argue (with Callon 1998) that the rational decision maker "does exist" in organizations, not as a natural phenomenon but as a constructed ideal. To lose sight of the central role of rationality—as organization theorists have tended to do—is to ignore the ways in which organizational decision making can produce decisions in line with the premises of rational choice theory. Of course, these decisions do not occur in a social and organizational vacuum. Instead, the rational ideal is the central protagonist in conventions that managers collectively mobilize, commodify as products in a consulting marketplace, and experience through tools designed to produce decisions that accord with this theory. At the heart of this account of rationality is the notion of *performativity* (Latour 1996, 2005; Callon 1998). As economic sociologists have come to see, "economics does not describe an existing external 'economy,' but brings that economy into being: economics performs the economy, creating the phenomena it describes" (MacKenzie and Millo 2003: 108). Likewise, with the support of decision analysts, organizational decision makers can and do *perform* rationality.

This chapter is divided into two parts, each of which helps to elaborate this notion. The first part traces the rise and fall of rationality as a category in organizational decision-making research. The essential story here is one in which the ongoing work of rationalist decision analysts and the growing critique of organization theorists have developed largely in isolation from each other. This occurred not only because their basic premises differed so radically but also because of the sharp distinction drawn between normative and descriptive research on organizational decision making. The second part suggests reconstructing the missing bridge between (rationalist) decision analysis and (organizational) decision-making research and describes how managers enact decision making as a social practice informed by a rational approach to decisions. Finally, the conclusion discusses the implications of this alternative account for both future research and practice.

THE BATTLE OVER HOMO OECONOMICUS

....

The Normative Rationalist Perspective

The starting point for research on how organizations make decisions is the image of *homo oeconomicus*, or "economic man." From this normative perspective, the rational decision maker engages in a process that is, at once, sequential, highly structured, and individual rather than organizational (Elster 1989; Czarniawska 2003). The four stages of this process are straightforward. In the formulative stage, a supposedly goal driven and perfectly rational agent structures the decision problem such that there are several alternatives. In the evaluation stage, the decision maker assesses the impact of each alternative by giving it a subjective value (or utility) and estimates the likelihood of each alternative. In the appraisal stage, the decision maker compares the alternatives and selects the best option through an optimization process, which means choosing the alternative with the higher expected utility. Finally, in the implementation stage, the decision maker carries out the decision through relevant actions (see Keeney 1982: 807–17; Howard 1988: 680). The process rests on subjective judgments about the likelihood of the alternatives (i.e., subjective probabilities) and their desirability (i.e., utility). Decision analysis, which follows from this normative economic model, rests on axiomatic foundations (von Neumann and Morgenstern 1947; Savage 1954; Pratt et al. 1964) and these axioms, in turn, guarantee that the alternative with the higher expected utility is the preferred alternative. Table 21.1 summarizes those axioms in an "informal and intuitive manner" (Keeney 1982: 830–2).[1]

Table 21.1 The Axioms of Decision Analysis

Axioms		Description
1(a).	Generation of alternatives	"At least two alternatives can be specified."
1(b).	Identification of consequences	"Possible consequences of each alternative can be identified."
2.	Quantification of judgment	"The relative likelihoods (i.e., probabilities) of each possible consequence that could result from each alternative can be specified."
3.	Quantification of preference	"The relative desirability (i.e., utility) for all possible consequences of any alternative can be specified."
4(a).	Comparison of alternatives	"If two alternatives would each result in the same two possible consequences, the alternative yielding the higher chance of the preferred consequence is preferred."
4(b).	Transitivity of preferences	"If one alternative is preferred to a second alternative and if the second alternative is preferred to a third alternative, then the first alternative is preferred to the third alternative."
4(c).	Substitution of consequences	"If an alternative is modified by replacing one of its consequences with a set of consequences and associated probabilities (i.e., a lottery) that is indifferent to the consequence being replaced, then the original and the modified alternatives should be indifferent."

Source: Table created from Keeney 1982: 830–2.

This strong form of rationality, also called *substantive* rationality, permeates much of the research on organizational decision making that has followed. Indeed, in much of their work on all manner of economic decisions, economists conceptualize problems such as consumer choice or investment decision along these lines (Mas-Colell et al. 1995). Though individualist in form, the rationalist perspective on organizational decision making assumes that decisions by a group of *homo oeconomici* differ little, if at all (Miller and Wilson 2006: 469), and most economic models assume a representative agent.[2] Since the celebrated Arrow's impossibility theorem (Arrow 1963), economists do indeed know that aggregating individual rational preferences into social decision poses a problem: either the social preference is not rational, as Table 21.1 defines this term, or it is dictatorship. The pursuit of a more naturalistic understanding of how organizations make decisions would ultimately privilege *procedural rationality*, which attempts to make the best possible decision given the circumstances (Simon 1976). Yet, the purpose of the latter would be to approximate the former in organizational settings (Dean and Sharfman 1993).

Paradoxically, substantive rationality remains the structuring reference point in the organizational literature on decision making. Laroche (1995: 65) points out the difficulty organization theorists have in escaping from the rational view on decisions and the very strong attractiveness of "rationality." Integrative models of decision making, even when they try to account for unstructured or non-rational processes tend to reproduce stages of rational decision-making processes (e.g., Simon 1960; Mintzberg et al. 1976), and empirical studies of non-rational processes often acknowledge the presence of some form of "reason" (or rationality) organizing or guiding decisions (Hickson et al. 1986; Miller and Wilson 2006). Arguably, the cognitive perspective in strategy, in some ways, represents yet another revitalization of a rational perspective on organizational decision making (Schwenk 1984; Schneider and Angelmar 1993; Walsh 1995; Hodgkinson et al. 1999; Hodgkinson et al. 2002; Hodgkinson and Sparrow 2002; Wright and Goodwin 2002; Neale et al. 2006). Of course, the cognitive perspective in strategy, rooted in the Carnegie School approach and Simon's (1957) concept of "bounded rationality," belongs to the organizational perspective on decision making (Neale et al. 2006). Yet, it shares many similarities with the decision analysts' perspective; it studies biases and errors in human decision processes (e.g., Kahneman et al. 1982) to deliver prescriptions and "recommendations for improving strategic decision-making" (Schwenk 1988: 53). It can adopt the perspective of the practitioners and seeks to develop decision aiding techniques aiming at "debiasing" top managers (e.g., Hodgkinson et al. 1999; Hodgkinson et al. 2002). In so doing, it constructs, by virtue of an elaborate set of artifacts, a rational decision maker in a way very similar to the one adopted by decision analysts.

The Organizational Perspective

The organizational perspective takes as its departure point the rejection of rational choice principles and their implications for describing decision-making processes. Without question, this departure has proven rich with insights and renewed energy for studying decision making. Each step beyond the strong view of rationality provides a breakthrough contribution to knowledge of how organizations make decisions (Miller and Wilson 2006). The political model of the firm (March 1962; Allison 1971; March and Olsen 1976) challenged the decision maker as a relevant unit of analysis and demonstrated the fact that rationality could be a politically contested term. Decision makers can have good rationales for pursuing their goals, and those rationales can make them act in ways diverging strongly from the economic form of rationality. Finally, the anarchical approach to decision-making processes depicted by the "garbage can model" pushed "bounded rationality" to its logical extent by describing organized anarchies where decisions can occur independently from any form of individual rationality (Cohen et al. 1972; Langley et al. 1995: 261–3). From this new perspective, decisions are political (Pettigrew 1973), unpredictable (Mintzberg and Waters 1985), complex (Langley et al. 1995), and potentially irrational (Brunsson 1982, 1985, 1990). Decision makers are human, subject to powerful external forces, and liable to make mistakes (Langley et al. 1995:

275–7). If the rationalist view of decision making was "sterile" (Dean and Sharfman 1993: 588–90; Eisenhardt and Zbaracki 1992: 35), the organizational perspective has proven fertile. It depicts a landscape peopled by flesh and blood humans experiencing feelings and deploying political strategies.

There is little room in the organizational perspective for the notion of rationality. Because organization theorists systematically emphasize "non-rational" processes, the organization decision-making literature usually provides a relatively naive and simplistic approach of rational decision making. At best, rationality is a simple variable to be included in the overall equation. Those empirical studies that make any mention of rationality tend to treat it as a synonym for "finding the right answer," an elusive goal only rarely achieved by otherwise chaotic processes (Elbanna 2006). Manipulating factors such as perceived competitive threat (Dean and Sharfman 1993), internal context (Papadakis 1998), and conflict (Eisenhardt and Bourgeois 1988) leads the organization toward right answers more consistently. Yet, there is little to be said about the formal analysis undertaken within these firms, except that they may play some symbolic or communicative role in spite of their nominal purpose (Feldman and March 1981; Langley 1989). At worst, however, rationality appears in organization theory as a caricature; little more than an organizing framework (i.e., four sequential stages) from which the real work of theorizing must quickly depart.

The Standoff

Of course, the rise of an organizational perspective on decision making has not hindered the growth of the field of decision analysis. As a result, the two perspectives (rationalist and organizational) have reached an uneasy standoff, in which each has chosen distinctive, if somewhat unsatisfying, strategies for responding to the obvious contradiction. Economists and decision scientists have tended to treat social forces as merely implementation challenges that people can tackle rationally. They have not, it is important to note, assumed that they live in a purely abstract and theoretically world distinct from that described by organization theorists. On the contrary, decision analysts intend to influence organizational life and they insist that they can overcome the non-rational. Howard (1988: 682) wrote, "Decision analysts should realize that not everyone sees the world as they do. They should appreciate the special insights they provide, that can eliminate the "blind-spot" of those who rely mainly on feelings." Consequently, decision analysts have engaged in the creation of tools and practices aiming at implementing that theory, in order to improve organizational decision-making processes. One part of the decision analysis literature focuses on what decision analysts call "applications." Those "applications" are case studies that relate how decision analysts succeeded in performing decision analysis (e.g., Corner and Kirkwood 1991; Keefer et al. 2004).

Meanwhile, organization theorists have responded to the persistence of a rationalist perspective with one of two equally unsatisfying strategies. On the one hand, many have chosen to accommodate the rationalist perspective by labeling it a normative enterprise, without descriptive power in organizational settings or any concrete impact on the organizational world (Eisenhardt and Zbaracki 1992). That early orientation of the organizational literature led to keeping separated a supposedly purely realistic or descriptive perspective on decision making from a purely normative perspective on decision making (e.g., Howard 1966; Brunsson 1990; Laroche 1995). The constitution of two distinct academic fields, the (rational) decision analysis subfield developing a normative theory of decision making and the descriptive organizational decision-making subfield, has essentially ratified that separation. That lasting opposition between those two streams of research, however, is artificial, since normative and descriptive perspectives cannot be so radically distinguished (Putnam 2002). Beyond the epistemologically tenuous underpinnings of this strategy, ignoring the descriptive implications of the normative field leads to a simplistic and incomplete view of what organizations and their managers do when they make decisions.

The second common strategy for organization theorists to cope with the rational–organizational split has been to abandon the concept of a "decision" altogether. Many authors describe the current stagnation in research on decisions by organization theorists. Langley et al. (1995: 260–1) noted that "after more that 30 years of research, the literature of organizational decision-making exhibits its own lethargy" (see also Sfez 1973; Chia 1994; Laroche 1995). This lethargy arises, in no small part, from a fundamental paradox. Because organization theory has progressively deconstructed all forms of rationality within organizational decisions, researchers have enacted a situation which casts doubt on their very categories of analysis, namely "*decisions*," "*decision maker*," and "*decision making*" (Brunsson 1982, 1985; Chia 1994; Laroche 1995). This results not only in a growing gap between decision making as taught and as depicted in research (Czarniawska 2003) but also in a move away from the very idea of decision, which is considered as an artifact. Instead, some theorists seek to elaborate a "theory of action" considering decision as an underlying phenomenon (Starbuck 1983; Laroche 1995). The triumph of the organizational perspective turns out to be a Pyrrhic victory leaving organization theorists to say, as Pyrrhus did, "one more such victory (against the rational choice theory) and we are lost." The destruction of *homo oeconomicus* (a death that decision analysts deny) may also have occasioned the progressive self-destruction of behavioral decision-making research itself.

In sum, the ongoing battle over the state of economic man is currently at a standstill. A new starting point for progress in this area is to re-evaluate the status of rationality in organizational decision making. Rather than considering rationality as an enemy, a myth, or an accident, it is possible to consider rational decisions as a social achievement, produced by a social construction process in which decision makers actually attempt to produce or, more precisely, *perform* rationality. Rationality, then, is not merely a characteristic of decisions but a theory of decision making which many decision makers seek to enact and which resides in their everyday experiences. Only in grasping the complexity of this process can researchers avoid the oversimplification of the behavioralist approach while insisting on the social nature of the process. The next section begins this work.

BRINGING DECISION ANALYSIS BACK IN

The performance of rationality involves three elements that, together, help to constitute the missing link between "decision as a theory" and "decisions as they occur in organizations." Each of them relates to a specific vision of rationality the organizational literature de-emphasizes: rationality as social representations, rationality as commodity, and rationality as tool. These elements help to capture the processes through which decision theory becomes social reality through organizational decision making. Figure 21.1 shows how consultants and decision analysts use rational decision theory to construct rational decisions and to develop markets and products for consumption by decision makers. The performativity perspective suggests mapping the whole chain of translations linking the pure idea (or myth)

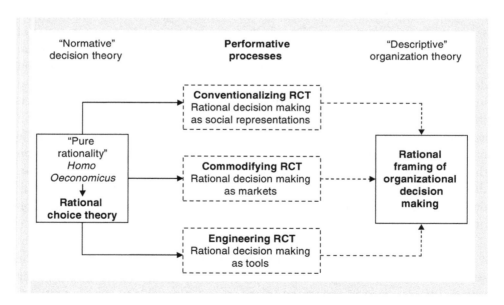

Fig. 21.1 Performing rationality in organizational decision making.

of rationality—expressed in the theory underlying decision analysis—to the practice of decision making within organizations (Callon, 1998; Ferraro, Pfeffer, and Sutton, 2005; Latour, 1996; MacKenzie and Millo, 2003). The embodiment of rationality into organizational decision making is progressive in nature. It passes through three major stages, from: (1) rationality as conventionally conceived in organization theory; to (2) its packaging into a commodity to be sold by consultants on the open market; and (3) its incorporation into products supporting decision making.

Rationality as Convention

Organizational scholars have often considered rationality as a myth influencing decision making mainly through symbolic processes (Meyer and Rowan 1977). Here, it is helpful to grapple with the double meaning of "myth", a term that can connote either a false story or a story meant to make sense of and legitimize a worldview. Rationality is not a myth in the former sense. Yet, in practice, rationality has become more than the formal corpus of knowledge known as rational choice theory; it has become a myth in the latter sense. It is a legitimizing discourse with powerful and tangible effects on organizational decision-making processes. Like any legitimizing discourse, decision theory has its true believers, its heathens and even its heretics (Howard 1992). So defined, the myth of rationality easily transcends its academic origins and becomes a strong social convention in Western cultures and especially businesses (cf., Howard 1980; Feldman and March 1981). Because this discourse has such coherent theoretical roots, it affords managers useful cognitive categories and remains an important part of business language.

Perhaps the most powerful effect of rationality as convention is the way in which it creates strong role categories and organizing principles with which managers naturally identify. Portraying decision making as a form of social representation, Laroche (1995: 68) reminds us that "managers see themselves as conscious decision-makers." They use "decisions" as lenses to make sense of organizational events (Weick 1995) or at least as "useful illusions" to achieve a shared understanding of organizational functioning and therefore help managers to coordinate their actions (Jodelet 1991; Moscovici 1991; Laroche 1995: 70). Moreover, the convention of rationality structures how organizational functioning is taught in business schools. The case method, still prominent in many MBA classrooms, routinely centers on decision points at which students *qua nascent* managers must apply rational tools rather than resting on intuition or impulse (Barnes et al. 1994). All this occurs despite the obvious discrepancy between "taught knowledge" (i.e., the strong form of substantive rationality) and "research knowledge" (i.e., the forbidden knowledge about naturalistic decisions in organizations; see Czarniawska 2003: 353–6). So, too, it privileges the "logic of consequentiality" (i.e., the consideration of consequences) over the "logic of appropriateness" (i.e., the consideration of obligations;

March and Olsen 1989; Czarniawska 2003). In each case, the conventions associated with rationality appear, at least in the minds of students, to be the dominant language of business, despite the more extensive profusion of languages available in actual organizational contexts. It thus becomes appropriate to adopt the logic of consequentiality (Czarniawska 2003). Ultimately, just as Callon (1998: 31) suggests that "the dissemination of students trained in economics is of prime importance" in the performance of the economy as a whole, so too the academic institutionalization of decision analysis and the diffusion of training programs promote the rationality convention in organizational decision making.

Once this convention enters the realm of practice, often via its young initiates (who carry it forth with all of the zeal of the newly converted), rationality plays an important role in coordinating managers' actions within organizations. Rationality becomes an important part of the justificatory regimes—the worlds that managers inhabit (e.g., see the description of the *monde industriel* in Boltanski and Thévenot 1991: 252–62). There, rationality provides the necessary rationales that help managers to defend their positions when controversies occur. But, why should this convention have such power to shape these worlds? In no small part, the power of rationality as convention comes from its repetition. Training programs, executive education, and consulting interventions all play a reinforcing role, ensuring that managers remain cognitively embedded in the conventions of rationality that derive from decision theory. Yet, beyond the simple process of reinforcement, it is also likely that rationality's power as a convention stems from its essentially *performative* nature. Performative conventions travel so readily because they are susceptible to self-validation when diffused; whereas, *a-performative* and *counter-performative* conventions have content that either exercises no influence on its validity, or proves itself empirically invalid by its adoption in social arenas (MacKenzie 2004: 305). It is surely an open question whether the convention of rationality is performative insofar as it possesses proven empirical verisimilitude in organizational life. Yet, in the weaker sense of performativity (attributed to Callon by MacKenzie 2004: 305–6) as being readily translated into social reality for decision makers, rationality as convention lends itself to performance. What remains, then, is a vehicle through which such performances occur. This is the subject of the next subsection.

Rationality as Commodity

To this point, rationality in decision making has been treated primarily in terms of social representations; however, these representations do not fall fully formed from heaven. Rather, their most common manifestation is as "products", rationality as commodified by the consultants and academics seeking to sell solutions to managers primed to expect rationality from their decisions but all too aware of the social constraints preventing its accomplishment in their own organizations.

Rational decision theory has been progressively commodified, to be incorporated into services and tools that are exchanged on consulting markets. Since the 1990s, for example, most consultancies in decision analysis have developed their own decision analysis software, such as PrecisionTree, @RISK, Crystall Ball, and TreePlan (Pearman 1987). This process of packaging and marketing cannot but shape both the context in which it occurs as well as the content of the product itself.

Professional purveyors of decision theory contribute to the framing of organizational decision-making processes by assisting managers in their efforts to make rational decisions. Trigo et al.'s (2004) exploratory study of the influence of consultants on strategic decision-making processes clearly highlights, through an analysis of four cases, the very "rational" approach that those professional decision makers implement. These authors observe a strategic decision-making process perfectly fitting the rational model and attribute it to the presence of consultants (p. 19). Rationality is the essence of what these companies have on offer. Their self-presentations are eloquent in this regard. They "promote innovative and effective management decision-making" (Management Analysis Inc.), "help government, industry, and individuals to understand the implications of complex decision opportunities" (Decision Research) and apply "quantitative management science to help clients improve profitability and performance and gain strategic advantage" (Decision Focus Inc.).

The "supply side" of the market for rationality is made of practitioners, trained in decision analysis courses in famous institutions such as INSEAD, Carnegie-Mellon University, Stanford University, and grouped in associations such as the Decision Analysis Affinity Group. That association, created in the mid-1990s, is

a multi-industry group of decision analysis practitioners who get together once a year to share ideas, successes, and failures. Industries represented include oil and gas, pharmaceutical, utilities, heavy manufacturing, automotive, and chemical—Texaco, Monsanto, Chevron, AT&T, General Motors, Nova Chemicals, TIFOE, Transcanada, ExxonMobil. (www.daag.net)

It includes academics and academic associations promoting the application of decision methods into organizations. Likewise, the International Society on Multiple Criteria Decision Making, which has over 1,400 members, considers its purposes

to develop, test, evaluate and apply methodologies for solving multiple criteria decision making problems, to foster interaction and research in the scientific field of multiple criteria decision making, and to cooperate with other organizations in the study of management from a quantitative perspective. (www.terry.uga.edu/mcdm/)

The academics, practitioners, and managers creating and propagating this marketplace for rationality constitute a powerful field, deploying norms and generating institutional pressures that influence the content of *real* decision-making processes.

These market actors are, indeed, enactors of powerful norms originated by decision theorists themselves. Writing in an editorial for the *Journal of Multi-criteria Decision Analysis,* Simon French, a prominent UK academic, recently insisted that decision analysis is an applied discipline and must not be confined to theory and mathematics. He asked: "Don't we want to provide decision makers with the concepts, tools, analyses and education to help them make better choices? . . . So, let me exhort you to pay more attention to true applications and to report them" (French 1998). In so writing, French merely echoed by Howard's earlier elaboration of the role of decision analysis:

Decision analysis is a profession concerned with helping individuals making decisions. The profession consists of a theoretical paradigm for decision making and a body of practical experiences for using this paradigm to illuminate the decision problem for the decision maker. (Howard 1980: 6)

This exchange between theory and practice is not confined to the academic elite. Previous syntheses of decision analysis applications in a wide range of organizational contexts demonstrate the frequent interactions of academics and practitioners in the production and marketing of rationality (Corner et al. 1991; Keefer et al. 2004). Consequently, rational decision making cannot be conceived as evolving in a "normative bubble" apart from organizations and consultancies. Rather, a more sophisticated treatment of rationality in organizational decision making must include all of these various players. Key academics of the field, such as Keeney (1982) and Howard (1988), have already published retrospective papers synthesizing the steps of decision theory knowledge construction showing how they both concretely performed rational decisions and, in so doing, acted as real "institutional entrepreneurs" of rationality (DiMaggio 1988; Dorado 2005). To date, the effects of this process of commodification on the content of rationality remains largely unexplored, yet it is the very fact of this process, of the translation of rationality into something consumable, that continues the movement from theory into practice. The next section explores this final intervening step by which practicing managers consume these products in the form of decision tools.

Rationality as Tool

Achieving substantive rationality is hard work, and if organization theorists are even half right, it may well be downright unnatural (Callon 1998). Actors such as managers or consultants sometimes find their props not only help to achieve verisimilitude when seen from without, but also inspire them to think differently about their own performance, to "get into character" as it were. So, too, the tools of decision analysis equip managers to pursue rationality with greater confidence in their ability to achieve it. They turn managers into "decision makers". Thus,

Table 21.2 Technical Aspects of Decision Theory: The Engineers' Tools

Examples of decision-making tools	Objectives of the techniques
• Influence diagram	• Structuring the problem
• Decision tree	• Structuring the problem
• Strategy generation table	• Creating alternatives
• Method for eliciting continuous probability distributions	• Assigning subjective probabilities to events (elicitation of probability judgments)
• Certainty equivalent method	• Encoding subjective information about risk attitude and eliciting a utility (or a value) function
• Tornado diagram	• Determining whether the uncertainty in the input variables has a major effect on the uncertainty in the outcome of the model used by the decision makers

decision analysts engage in the development of tools to help managers to decompose decision problems according to the premises of decision theory. Their effect is multilayered, creating the appearance, inspiring the confidence, and ultimately assisting in the substantive performance of rationality. They create material supports that embody decision theory principles and that can be altered, crafted and/or mobilized to perform "rational decisions".

Table 21.2, which presents a selection of those tools, clearly shows that decision analysis is not just about decision trees (Kirkwood 1992). Each step of the decision analysis—problem structure, uncertainty in the outcomes of the alternatives, and decision maker preferences (Keeney 1982; Corner and Corner 1995; Keefer et al. 2004)—is indeed associated with a series of tools and procedures (e.g., Howard and Matheson 1984). And, as "strange as it may seem, many people with what appear to be decision problems have never asked themselves that question [What decision must be made]?" (Howard 1966: 57). The "strategy-generation table" (Howard 1988) was developed to overcome this limitation and make sure that decision makers' problems could be seen as a choice among alternatives (e.g., Arbel and Tong 1982). Similarly, decision analysts have developed tools for structuring decision problems, such as influence diagrams and decision trees (see, for instance, Clemen and Reilly 2001). They have also created tools for assessing the desirability of the various consequences and for eliciting the uncertainty associated with the alternatives (e.g., Keeney and Raiffa 1976; Morgan and Henrion 1990; Clemen and Reilly 2001). These procedures and tools ensure that "real managers" behave as decision makers in ways that conform to the prescriptions of rational decision theory. Specifically, they guarantee that managers have transitive preferences as specified in expected utility theory (see Keeney and McDaniels 1992 for an illustration). After all when preferences are intransitive or cyclical, decision makers are vulnerable to exploitation and may make choices that leave them worse off (cf., the "money pump" phenomenon, Fishburn 1991). These procedures and tools also ensure that decision makers' subjective judgments about uncertainty are made in terms of probability (see Dunning et al. 2001 for an application). Once the subjective judgments about the likelihoods and the desirability of the consequences are elicited, decision makers can then choose the alternative that maximizes their expected utility (von Neumann and Morgenstern 1947; Savage 1954; Pratt et al. 1964).

The rational decision-making tools listed in Table 21.2 contribute to the reconstruction of rational decision making within organizations by putting managers in a context similar to the one described theoretically by the rational choice approach of decision making. They embed theories and form institutional arrangements that frame decision makers' behaviors in such a way that they will adopt the implicit assumptions these theories convey (Ferraro et al. 2005). They help turn the principles of "normative" rational decision making into a social reality directly accessible and potentially useful for decision makers within organizational contexts (Latour 1994, 2005). Their diffusion in organizations can create contexts facilitating the deployment of rational forms of decision making by providing supports and/or by compensating for the rationality deficits of decision makers. Consequently, the tools themselves, which are at the core of the rational decision-making field, become entry points for understanding the making of rational decisions and have to be taken into account in any "thick description" of decision making in organizational contexts. They compensate, often in unexplored ways, for the biases and shortcomings of decision makers' rationality. They contrive to bring the human decision maker into direct contact with, and hence to experience, rationality, often with the effect of creating a kind of "ritual of rationality" for the managers of the firm. Though ritualistic, this experience brings decision makers closer to the theory embedded in the tools in use. These tools thus facilitate the performance of rationality within organizations.

SUMMARY AND CONCLUSION

This chapter suggests bringing "rationality" back in as an object of empirical study in organizational decision making. The skepticism of many organizational analysts regarding the explanatory power of rational choice models of decision making in organizational contexts is not unreasonable. Nevertheless, the glimpses of rationality that do occur are more than mere happenstance. The perspective developed above sketches the processes of social construction underlying the craft of rational decision making. Conventions, markets, and tools serve as key dimensions to capture the performativity of rationality; each could be explored further. As such, this chapter offers many opportunities for future empirical investigation, especially research undertaken in methodologically non-traditional ways. Little is known, for example, about the process by which managers become cognitively embedded within the conventional view of rationality. This may eventually lead researchers to investigate the specific role of business schools where organization theorists are still, ironically, teaching rational choice theory. Likewise, even less is known about the markets for rationality, and some of the main characters and associated props of this play have been kept in the wings: decision analysts, consultants, rational decision-making tools, and, especially, academics. Understanding the social construction of rationality requires that researchers pay greater attention to each of these actors, all of whom are collectively involved in the crafting of rational decisions in organizations.

For practicing managers, this approach should be, at once, comforting and disturbing. The basic premise of this chapter—that the pursuit of rationality might not be the quixotic search for an unattainable ideal, as so often portrayed by organization theorists—should reassure managers that they are not delusional. They might see in the constructivist story of rationality familiar elements, and in so doing, they might see ways in which convention, markets, and tools have either helped or hindered their performance as decision makers. At the same time, though, these same managers might well balk at the complexities of the picture painted herein. If managers could achieve rationality (i.e., some degree of rightness) simply by combining two parts comprehensiveness with one part cognitive conflict and a dash of external threat, how much more preferable would that formulation be to the one presented here? Instead, rationality is an ongoing act, at worst a farce, but, in the best sense, a performance of great depth and sophistication. What remains, however, is for managers and scholars alike to discover the richness of this craft.

ENDNOTES

1 Arguably, the rational *homo oeconomicus* is quite naive from a descriptive perspective. Since three decades almost, behavioral economists have developed psychologically more accurate *homo Oeconomicus* to improve the prescriptive validity of economic models (see Camerer et al. 2003; Camerer et al. 2005). The new "psycho-economic" man is, however, not any more rational in the sense of Table 21.1: to accommodate observed behaviors (e.g., dynamically inconsistent preferences), some normative axioms need to be relaxed (see Laibson 1997 on intertemporal choice for instance). But, it is noteworthy that as a normative figure, the "rational economic man" has not been much challenged yet and Table 21.1 still represents the views of rational theorists.

2 Note that the economic theory of team for instance (Marschak and Radner 1972) extends expected utility theory to several decision makers; it nonetheless considers that no conflict of interest holds and thus assumes that all decision makers have the same utility function and the same beliefs.

REFERENCES

ALLISON, G. T. (1971). *The Essence of Decision: Explaining the Cuban Missile Crisis.* New York: HarperCollins.

ARBEL, A. and TONG, R. M. (1982). 'On the Generation of Alternatives in Decision Analysis Problems.' *The Journal of the Operational Research Society*, 33/4: 377–87.

ARROW, K. J. (1963). *Social Choice and Individual Values* (2nd edn.). New York: Wiley.

BARNES, L., CHRISTENSEN, C., and HANSEN, A. (1994). *Teaching and the Case Method.* Cambridge, MA: Harvard Business School Press.

BOLTANSKI, L. and THÉVENOT, L. (1991). *De la justification: Les économies de la grandeur.* Paris: Gallimard.

BRUNSSON, N. (1982). 'The Irrationality of Action and Action Rationality: Decisions, Ideologies and Organizational Actions.' *Journal of Management Studies*, 19/1: 29–44.

—— (1985). *The Irrational Organization.* Chichester: Wiley.

—— (1990). 'Deciding for Responsibility and Legitimation: Alternative Interpretations of Organizational Decision-Making.' *Accounting, Organizations and Society*, 15/1–2): 47–59.

CALLON, M. (1998). *The Laws of the Markets.* Oxford: Blackwell Publishers.

CAMERER, C., LOEWENSTEIN, G., and RABIN, M. (2003). *Advances in Behavioral Economics.* Princeton, NJ: Princeton University Press.

—— —— PRELEC, D. (2005). 'Neuroeconomics: How Neuroscience Can Inform Economics.' *Journal of Economic Literature*, 43/1: 9–64.

CHIA, R. (1994). 'The Concept of Decision: A Deconstructive Analysis.' *Journal of Management Studies*, 31/6: 781–806.

CLEMEN, R. T. and REILLY, T. (2001). *Making Hard Decisions:* Belmont, CA: Duxbury/Thomson Learning.

COHEN, M. D., MARCH, J. G., and OLSEN, J. (1972). 'A Garbage Can Model of Organizational Choice.' *Administrative Science Quarterly*, 17/1: 1–25.

CORNER, J. L. and CORNER, P. D. (1995). 'Characteristics of Decision in Decision Analysis Practice.' *Journal of the Operational Research Society*, 46/3: 304–14.

—— KIRKWOOD, C. W. (1991). 'Decision Analysis Applications in the Operations Research Literature, 1970–1989.' *Operations Research*, 39/2: 206–19.

CZARNIAWSKA, B. (2003). 'Forbidden Knowledge: Organization Theory in Times of Transition.' *Management Learning*, 34/3: 353–65.

DEAN, J. W. and SHARFMAN, M. P. (1993). 'Procedural Rationality in the Strategic Decision-Making Process.' *Journal of Management Studies*, 30/4: 588–610.

DIMAGGIO, P. J. (1988). 'Interest and Agency in Institutional Theory,' in L. G. Zucker (ed.), *Research on Institutional Patterns and Organizations: Culture and Environment.* Cambridge, MA: Ballinger, 3–22.

DORADO, S. (2005). 'Institutional Entrepreneurship, Partaking and Convening.' *Organization Studies*, 26/3: 385–414.

DUNNING, D. J., LOCKFORT, S., ROSS, Q. E., BECCUE, P. C., and STONEBRAKER, J. S. (2001). 'New York Power Authority Uses Decision Analysis to Schedule Refueling of its Indian Point 3 Nuclear Power Plant.' *Interfaces*, 31/5: 121–35.

EISENHARDT, K. M. and BOURGEOIS, L. J. (1988). 'Politics of Strategic Decision Making in High-Velocity Environments: Towards a Midrange Theory.' *Academy of Management Journal*, 31/4: 737–70.

—— ZBARACKI, M. J. (1992). 'Strategic Decision Making.' *Strategic Management Journal*, 13/8: 17–37.

ELBANNA, S. (2006). 'Strategic Decision-Making: Process Perspectives.' *International Journal of Management Reviews*, 8/1: 1–20.

ELSTER, J. (1986). *Rational Choice*. Oxford: Blackwell.

—— (1989). *Nuts and Bolts for the Social Sciences*. Cambridge: Cambridge University Press.

FELDMAN, M. S. and MARCH, J. G. (1981). 'Information in Organizations as Signal and Symbol.' *Administrative Science Quarterly*, 26/2: 171–86.

FERRARO, F., PFEFFER, J., and SUTTON, R. I. (2005). 'Economic Language and Assumptions: How Theories Can Become Self-Fulfilling.' *Academy of Management Review*, 30/1: 8–24.

FISHBURN, P. C. (1991). 'Nontransitive Preferences in Decision Theory.' *Journal of Risk and Uncertainty*, 4/2: 113–34.

FRENCH, S. (1998). 'Decision Making Not Decision Theory.' *Journal of Multi-Criteria Decision Analysis*, 7/6: 303.

HICKSON, D. J., BUTLER, R. J., CRAY, D., MALLORY, G. R., and WILSON, D. C. (1986). *Top Decisions*. Oxford: Blackwell.

HODGKINSON, G. P. and SPARROW, P. R. (2002). *The Competent Organization: A Psychological Analysis of the Strategic Management Process*. Buckingham, UK: Open University Press.

—— BOWN, N. J., MAULE, A. J., GLAISTER, K. W., and PEARMAN, A. (1999). 'Breaking the Frame: An Analysis of Strategic Cognition and Decision Making Under Uncertainty.' *Strategic Management Journal*, 20/10: 977–85.

—— MAULE, A. J., BOWN, N. J., PEARMAN, A., and GLAISTER, K. W. (2002). 'Further Reflections on the Elimination of Framing Bias in Strategic Decision Making.' *Strategic Management Journal*, 23/11: 1069–76.

HOWARD, R. A. (1966). 'Decision Analysis: Applied Decision Theory.' Proceedings of the Fourth International Conference on Operational Research, 55–71.

—— (1980). 'An Assessment of Decision Analysis.' *Operations Research*, 28/1: 4–27.

—— (1988). 'Decision Analysis: Practice and Promise.' *Management Science*, 34/6: 679–95.

—— (1992). 'Heathens, Heretics, and Cults: The Religious Spectrum of Decision Aiding.' *Interfaces*, 22/6: 15–27.

—— MATHESON, J. E. (1984). *Readings on the Principles and Applications of Decision Analysis*. Menlo Park, CA: Strategic Decisions Group.

JODELET, D. (1991). *Les représentations sociales*. Paris: Presses Universitaires de France.

KAHNEMAN, D., SLOVIC, P., and TVERSKY, A. (1982). *Judgment Under Uncertainty: Heuristics and Biases*. New York: Cambridge University Press.

KEEFER, D. L., KIRKWOOD, C. W., and CORNER, J. L. (2004). 'Perspective on Decision Analysis Applications, 1990–2001.' *Decision Analysis*, 1/1: 4–22.

KEENEY, R. L. (1982). 'Decision Analysis: An Overview.' *Operations Research*, 30/5: 803–38.

KEENEY, R. L. McDANIELS, T. L. (1992). 'Value-Focused Thinking About Strategic Decisions at BC Hydro.' *Interfaces*, 22/6: 94–109.

KEENEY, R. L. and RAIFFA, H. (1976). *Decisions With Multiple Objectives*. New York: Wiley.

KIRKWOOD, C. W. (1992). 'An Overview of Methods for Decision Analysis.' *Interfaces*, 22/6: 28–39.

LAIBSON, D. (1997). 'Golden Eggs and Hyperbolic Discounting.' *Quarterly Journal of Economics*, 112/2: 443–77.

LANGLEY, A. (1989). 'In Search of Rationality: The Purposes Behind the Use of Formal Analysis in Organizations.' *Administrative Science Quarterly*, 34/4: 598–631.

—— MINTZBERG, H., PITCHER, P., POSADA, E., and SAINT-MACARY, J. (1995). 'Opening Up Decision Making: The View from the Black Stool.' *Organization Science*, 6/3: 260–79.

LAROCHE, H. (1995). 'From Decision to Action in Organizations: Decision-Making as a Social Representation.' *Organization Science*, 6/1: 62–75.

LATOUR, B. (1994). 'Une sociologie sans objet ? Remarques sur l'interobjectivité.' *Sociologie du travail*, 4: 587–608.

—— (1996). *Aramis or the Love of Technology* (C. Porter, Trans.) Cambridge, MA: Harvard University Press.

—— (2005). *Re-assembling the Social: An Introduction to Actor-Network Theory*. Oxford: Oxford University Press.

MACKENZIE, D. (2004). 'The Big, Bad Wolf and the Rational Market: Portfolio Insurance, the 1987 Crash and the Performativity of Economics.' *Economy and Society*, 33/3: 303–34.

—— MILLO, Y. (2003). 'Constructing a Market, Performing a Theory: The Historical Sociology of a Financial Derivatives Exchange.' *American Review of Sociology*, 109/1: 107–45.

MARCH, J. G. (1962). 'The Business Firm as a Political Coalition.' *The Journal of Politics*, 24/4: 662–78.

—— OLSEN, J. P. (1976). *Ambiguity and Choice in Organizations*. Bergen: Universitetsforlaget.

—— —— (1989). *Rediscovering Institutions*. New York: Free Press.

—— SIMON, H. A. (1958). *Organizations*. New York: Wiley.

MARSCHAK, J. and RADNER, R. (1972). *Economic Theory of Team*. New Haven, CT: Yale University Press.

MAS-COLELL, A., WHINSTON, M. D., and GREEN, J. R. (1995). *Microeconomic Theory*. Oxford: Oxford University Press.

MEYER, J. W. and ROWAN, B. (1977). 'Institutionalized Organizations: Formal Structure as Myth and Ceremony.' *American Journal of Sociology*, 83/2: 340–63.

MILLER, S. J. and WILSON, D. C. (2006). 'Perspectives on Organizational Decision Making,' in S. R. Clegg, Lawrence T. B., and W. R. Nord (eds.), *The Sage Handbook of Organization Studies*. London: Sage, 468–84.

MINTZBERG, H. and WATERS, J. (1982). 'Tracking Strategy in an Entrepreneurial Firm.' *Academy of Management Journal*, 25/3: 465–99.

—— —— (1985). 'Of Strategies, Deliberate and Emergent.' *Strategic Management Journal*, 6/3: 257–72.

—— RAISINGHANI, D., and THÉORÊT, A. (1976). 'The Structure of "Unstructured" Decision Processes.' *Administrative Science Quarterly*, 21/2: 246–75.

MORGAN, G. and HENRION, M. (1990). *Uncertainty: A Guide to Dealing with Uncertainty in Quantitative Risk and Policy Analysis*. New York: Cambridge University Press.

Moscovici, S. (1991). 'Des représentations collectives aux représentations sociales,' in
  D. Jodelet (ed.), *Les représentations sociales*. Paris: Presses Universitaires de France, 62–86.
Neale, M. A., Tenbrunsal, A. E., Galvin, T., and Bazerman, M. H. (2006). 'A Decision
  Perspective on Organizations: Social Cognition, Behavioural Decision Theory and the
  Psychological Links to Micro- and Macro-Behaviour,' in S. R. Clegg, T. B. Lawrence, and
  W. R. Nord (eds.), *The Sage Handbook of Organization Studies* (2nd edn.). London: Sage,
  485–519.
Papadakis, V. (1998). 'Strategic Investment Decision Processes and Organizational Per-
  formance: An Empirical Investigation.' *British Journal of Management*, 9/2: 115–32.
Pearman, A. (1987). 'The Application of Decision Analysis: A US/UK Comparison.' *The
  Journal of the Operational Research Society*, 38/9: 775–83.
Pettigrew, A. M. (1973). *Politics of Organizational Decision-Making*. London: Tavistock.
Pratt, J. W., Raiffa, H., and Schlaifer, R. O. (1964). 'The Foundations of Decision
  Under Uncertainty: An Elementary Exposition.' *Journal of the American Statistical Asso-
  ciation*, 59/306: 353–75.
Putnam, H. (2002). *The Collapse of the Fact / Value Dichotomy and other Essays*. Cambridge,
  MA: Harvard University Press.
Savage, L. J. (1954). *The Foundations of Statistics*. New York: Wiley.
Schneider, S. C. and Angelmar, R. (1993). 'Cognition in Organizational Analysis: Who's
  Minding the Store?' *Organization Studies*, 14/3: 347–74.
Schwenk, C. R. (1984). 'Cognitive Simplification Processes in Strategic Decision Making.'
  Strategic Management Journal, 5/2: 111–28.
—— (1988). 'The Cognitive Perspective on Strategic Decision Making.' *Journal of Manage-
  ment Studies*, 25/1: 41–55.
Sfez, L. (1973). *Critique de la décision* (3rd edn.). Paris: Presses de la Fondation des Sciences
  Politiques.
Simon, H. A. (1957). *Administrative Behavior* (2nd edn.). New York: Macmillan.
—— (1960). *The New Science of Management Decision*. New York: Harper and Row.
—— (1976). 'From Substantive to Procedural Rationality,' in S. J. Latsis (ed.), *Method and
  Appraisal in Economics*. Cambridge: Cambridge University Press, 129–48.
Starbuck, W. H. (1983). 'Organizations as Action Generators.' *American Sociological
  Review*, 48/1: 91–102.
Trigo, S., Angwin, D., and Wilson, D. C. (2004). 'Strategic Decision Making and
  Management Consultants.' Paper presented at the 21st EGOS colloquium, Bergen,
  July 6–8.
Von Neumann, J. and Morgenstern, O. (1947). *Theory of Games and Economic Behavior*
  (2nd edn.). Princeton, NJ: Princeton University Press.
Walsh, J. P. (1995). 'Managerial and Organizational Cognition: Notes From a Trip Down
  Memory Lane.' *Organization Science*, 6/3: 280–321.
Weick, K. E. (1995). *Sensemaking in Organizations*. London: Sage.
Wright, G. and Goodwin, P. (2002). 'Eliminating a Framing Bias by Using Simple
  Instructions to "Think Harder" and Respondents with Managerial Experience: Com-
  ments on "Breaking the Frame." ' *Strategic Management Journal*, 23/11: 1059–67.

22

WHEN "DECISION OUTCOMES" ARE NOT THE OUTCOMES OF DECISIONS

BÉNÉDICTE VIDAILLET

INTRODUCTION

THE concept of decision making is quite convenient for those who try to understand the origin of organizational outputs. Whether people seek to explain good performances or disasters, they should bear in mind that these outputs are the consequences of certain decisions or of the method of decision making. Quite logically, people consider some organizational outcomes to be decision outcomes, and they suppose that specific decisions produce those decision outcomes.

However obvious these relations may seem, this chapter shows that so-called "decision outcomes" are not necessarily the outcomes of decisions. This demonstration requires: (1) that the chapter identify the implicit assumptions that underlie the hypothesis that decisions determine decision outcomes; and (2) that the chapter confront these assumptions with the empirical reality of organizations' functioning.

COMMON PRESUPPOSITIONS

Though writers have often presented the rational and political models of organizational decision making as being very different or even contradictory (Dean and Sharfman 1993), these models have many things in common and illustrate how researchers in organizational decision making consider "decision outcomes." The implicit reasoning behind those models is the following: (1) different decision-making processes lead to different decisions; (2) different decisions lead to different actions; and (3) different actions lead to different consequences or outcomes. In this reasoning, it is clearly the upstream end of the decision spectrum (how it is made, i.e., the decision-making process) that interests researchers—as several chapters of this book testify—whereas what happens downstream, in other words, between the time the decision is made and the outcomes of the decision, is supposed to be evident. Thus, many authors have failed to explain causal relationships such as different decisions lead to different actions and different actions lead to different outcomes. Many jump from a decision to its consequences, treating an action as the quasi-natural link between a decision and its consequences.

Two essential assumptions influence most studies of organizational decision making. The first assumption is that sequentiality and coherence link the way in which a decision is made initially to the action that implements the decision, then finally to the outcomes of that decision. The second assumption is that this whole process can be isolated from other ongoing processes, thus making it possible to identify the outcomes that a decision produces. This chapter re-examines these two assumptions before presenting other ways of approaching the relations between decisions, actions, and their consequences.

Sequentiality and Coherence Between Process, Decision, Action, and Outcomes

Although researchers have described a variety of decision-making processes in detail, they use the rather simple hypothesis that succeeding phases compose those processes and they try to identify the transitions between those phases. The idea of sequentiality is central to these formulations, not only as the basis for modeling the judgment and choice processes, but also for specifying the links from decisions to actions and in turn from actions to outcomes (cf., Langley et al. 1995). This chapter questions these core assumptions and argues that actions do not necessarily follow decisions in the manner implied by the models that currently dominate the scientific literature; neither does it follow that actions automatically produce outcomes.

When people regard a decision as important, they are actually judging the actions it generates to be important. Thus, they suppose that this decision is turned into action so that it produces decision outcomes (Brunsson 2002). This sequentiality only has merit because there is coherence between the putative phases: not only should action follow a decision and produce certain results, but also these results are supposed to correspond as much as possible to the decision makers' initial intentions. These causality relations are implicit in the dominant theories and models of decision making, but in order to validate them researchers need to identify explicitly the actual, concrete links between processes, choices, actions, and outcomes through empirical investigation. Despite the voluminous data amassed over many years by organizational researchers, these fundamental links have yet to be established. The reason for this gap is not lack of effort, but because the assumptions underpinning researchers' attempts to isolate the connections between processes, choices, actions, and outcomes is found wanting.

The Assumption of Isolability

Identifying the decision outcomes requires that one be able to first isolate the different organizational productions and then attribute them to specific actions, which follow from certain choices that are themselves the products of certain processes. At all levels, there is the assumption that processes, decisions, actions, and outcomes can be clearly disentangled from other processes, decisions, actions, and outcomes. The assumption of isolability has a synchronic dimension (at any time, in the organization, there are processes–decisions–actions–outcomes sequences that are distinct from one another) and a diachronic dimension (these sequences have well defined beginnings and endings).

The methodologies used by researchers clearly rest on this assumption. In general, they isolate, through time and space, either a particular action (for example, the acquisition of a firm) or specific outcomes (say, the performance of the organization or a disaster). Then they assume that some identifiable decision produced this action or those outcomes and identify this decision, while trying to work backwards to the starting point of the process (Langley et al. 1995; Sutcliff and McNamara 2001). Thus, researchers cut up organizational life into "slices" (Laroche 1995) from which they can analyze the cause–effect relationships in connection with a decision more easily.

The assumptions of sequentiality, coherence, and isolability have been, and continue to be, the basis for much of the work on organizational decision making. The "garbage can" model of Cohen et al. (1972) has called into question their validity by describing organizational decision making as a chaotic process; according to this view, streams of problems, solutions, participants, and choice opportunities only coincide by chance. This model replaces sequentiality and coherence by the random assemblage of problems and solutions; it also replaces the division of organizational activity into "slices of decision" by the permanent and intricate interweaving of different activity flows. However, by calling into question simultaneously the validity of all of the core assumptions underpinning the dominant models and theories of organizational decision making, the "garbage can" model does not take into account the existence of a more subtle conception of the potential relations that link decision, action, and decision outcomes.

This chapter shows that so-called "decision outcomes" are not necessarily the outcomes of decisions. It asserts that what people perceive as a "decision outcome" is more an action outcome than a decision outcome. To the extent that this assertion is correct, it calls into question the assumption of sequentiality and coherence in organizational decision making. Furthermore, this chapter backs the claim that so-called "decision outcomes" are more the results of the complex interweaving of organizational issues than the outcomes of specific decisions. To the extent that this second assertion is correct, it calls into question the assumption of isolability.

A COMPLEX RELATIONSHIP BETWEEN DECISION AND ACTION

This section re-examines the coupling between decision and action. According to the hypotheses of sequentiality and consistency, action simply follows and puts into effect a decision and it generates results that are more or less close to what the decision makers expected. However, descriptive studies of organizational decision making have shown that the relationships between decision and action can take diverse forms that do not conform to the dominant formulations in the literature. "Decision outcomes" are the consequences of actions more than of decisions.

Action Precedes Decision: The Retroactive Reconstruction of Decision-Making Processes

The dominant models and theories suppose that action follows decision. However, this sequence can be inverted. Firstly, organizations generate ongoing flows of actions (Starbuck 1983) that do not necessarily originate from decisions. However, organizational actors sometimes present these actions as resulting from decisions: "which are used to describe, understand, interpret, evaluate and explain the actions which the organization has already performed" (Brunsson 2002: 171). Thus, decisions are a possible retroactive explanation of the content of action. A study conducted by Orton (2000) shows that the 1976 re-organization of the US intelligence community was the consequence of many interrelated events generated by the emergent actions of that community. However, its top managers presented this reorganization as the fruit of an intentional decision process to reorganize the community, a decision

> defined here as the presentation of a package of deliberate initiatives that will change formal relationships among organizational components.... Emergent enactments are transformed by organizational members into deliberate decisions... Under the pressures of announcing a decision, organizational members cobble together sensible arguments to support the decision they are announcing. (Orton 2000: 231)

This idea is important in Weick's work (1977); he quotes Garfinkel (1967: 114):

> In place of the view that decisions are made as the occasions require, an alternative formulation needs to be entertained. It consists of the possibility that the person defines retrospectively the decisions that have been made. The outcomes come before the decision... The rules of decision making in daily life... may be much more preoccupied with the problem of assigning outcomes their legitimate history than with the question of deciding before the actual occasion of choice the conditions under which one, among a set of alternative possible courses of action, will be elected.

Decision as a Means of Making Sense and of Coming to an Agreement

In this context, decision making is not an act of choice but an act of retroactive interpretation of certain outcomes. When a group of organizational actors declare that they are "making a decision," it means that they feel a "result" has already been produced and that they must agree on the existence of this "result" and on what led to it. They then engage in a retrospective sensemaking process to agree on where and when a past decision, which might explain a present result, might have been made. Thus, they re-examine history in light of specific outcomes that they retrospectively associate with decisions that can account for them.

Why do organizational actors put so much emphasis on decision making even when what is obviously of import is action? One reason is that this enables them to interrupt the flow of organizational action by organizing it around clusters of decisions. Rather than letting this flow overwhelm them, actors try to establish a semblance of order. Reconstructing events a posteriori around "decisions" makes it possible to punctuate organizational action: making sense of and introducing a degree of sequentiality and duration into the ongoing flow of events and actions is necessary for the latter to appear logical. What is central here is that managers see themselves as decision makers because making "decisions" is a way of being an actor in the organization (Weick 1995). "Organization members explain what they are participating in and what is happening around them in terms of "decisions" (Laroche 1995).

Retrospectively interpreting the action as the result of "decisions" also enables the members of the organization to come to some basic agreement about what is supposed to happen in the organization. "Decisions," seen as plausible stories collectively generated by the members of the organization to account for past and present events, serve to make sense, which is necessary for organizing. That is, "decisions" make organizing possible (Weick 1995).

Decision Making and the Allocation of Responsibility

Isolating decisions helps to identify decision makers clearly. And identifying decision makers makes it possible to assign responsibility (Laroche 1995; Brunsson 2002). To lay responsibility on someone, people need to consider that the person has had a choice, and has voluntarily chosen a course of action.

Responsibility is ascribed to people who are seen (by themselves or by others) to have influenced events by some action (or inaction) freely chosen from among several possible actions and then carried out [that action] ... Decisions produce responsibility. (Brunsson 2002: 181)

Responsibility provides a strong link between actions and decision makers: in this perspective, coming to an agreement about "decisions" implies agreement on the distribution of responsibilities. By clearly attaching some "decision outcomes" to certain people, organizational actors dramatically simplify the answer that they might provide to the question of why things happen. This is particularly evident when they try to explain disasters and to identify potentially responsible—and thus guilty—individuals (Gephart 1993).

Decision makers are aware of this. Thus, they gather information that they might not necessarily use to show that they are "good decision makers" or to be able to justify their decisions should an unexpected event occur (Feldman and March 1981); when making a decision with serious consequences, they might also choose the option that will be the easiest to justify (Tetlock 1983, 1992). For example, when a crisis occurred in France (Vidaillet 2001), the main decision maker decided to implement what he saw as the most justifiable solution to solve this crisis: he chose to evacuate 40,000 people to "protect" them from a "toxic" cloud that turned out to be non-toxic. He said, "I imagined the possible thousands of deaths, the risk of panic. This was a justification for action" (p. 256). He launched the evacuation at the very moment when the firefighters put out the fire that had caused the release of the "toxic" cloud, and when the hospital practitioners found that the cloud was not toxic. Thus, the course of action he had chosen was not the most appropriate, but it was easier to justify an evacuation if it turned out that there was no risk than loss of life if there was no evacuation.

ACTION'S AUTONOMY FROM DECISION

The section above questioned the hypothesis that decisions precede actions. This section concentrates on the generally assumed coherence between decision and action. It examines two types of situations: (1) when a decision problem has different interpretations and therefore cannot determine action; and (2) when action possesses its own dynamic and transforms the initial decision into unexpected outcomes.

Decision, Ambiguity, and Confusion

While the retrospective reconstruction of decisions can create an illusion of order about the past, it is not always order that a decision produces once the decision maker has made it. Indeed, certain decisions can generate surprise (Maitlis 2005), vagueness, confusion, and lack of understanding. Ambiguous decisions are open to interpretation. Thus, they are sources of equivocality defined as "the existence of multiple and conflicting interpretations about an organization situation" (Trevino et al. 1990: 74).

> Once the decision is made, the problem shifts from ignorance to confusion. This counter-intuitive outcome—how can people be confused after a decision—occurs because people temporarily face multiple, conflicting definitions of what their decisions means ... Thus, when the decision means many different conflicting things, the problem is one of too many meanings, not too few, and the problem shifts from one of uncertainty to one of equivocality. (Weick 1993: 30)

This equivocality is particularly well illustrated in Pinfield's study (1986) of a decision-making process that took place in the Canadian government bureaucracy in the 1980s. During an important meeting of the steering committee, members collectively made sense of various issues, but they recorded nothing formally. Within 24 hours following the meeting, a member of the administration who was not part of the committee indicated that the committee had accepted all the arguments his department had provided in favor of changing the existing system. Meanwhile, the manager of another department indicated that the committee had opted for the status quo. These apparently incompatible interpretations of what the committee had decided led to confusion in the action. In the first mentioned department, people did not commit to new projects because they assumed that they would participate to the project decided upon by the committee. After a while, however, as they received no confirmation from the committee that it had made a decision, they got involved in other projects, reinforcing the impression that "no change" was the de facto decision. Thus, the different interpretations of the decision generated confusion about what actions to take, and ended up hindering action.

Post-decisional equivocality and the resulting inconsistencies between decisions, the discussions explaining those decisions and the actions taken are not necessarily a problem; they can be a solution for certain organizations that face many inconsistent demands and standards from their environment (Brunsson 2002). Conversations, decisions, and actions are then separate organizational outputs that do not have to be consistently connected.

Actions Do Not Simply Implement Decisions

Action is not just the dependent child of decision, nor is it the material expression of the latter: the action possesses its own dynamic. It can accelerate decision, exaggerate it, lead the decision maker to feel more committed to his decision than he first was, lead him to pathologically persist in the wrong course of action, or activate deviance amplifying loops. In those cases, "decision outcomes" can be different—sometimes completely different—from the initial intention.

In the case of the re-organization of the US Secret Service studied by Orton (2000), Ford's announcement during a press conference of the decision to redesign the institution led to many questions by the journalists.

There were unintended consequences, unexpected omissions, and unsolved problems in the reorganization decision, and as the press began to identify these, Ford and his staff members had to start improvising the next reorganization decisions. (p. 230)

The very simple action of announcing the redesign decision led to an acceleration of this decision. It obliged the decision makers to imagine the following steps and perhaps to get more involved in the decision than they initially wanted.

More generally, announcing a decision is a crucial point in the process by which action can take its own way. First, it makes the decision concrete—contrary to the case of the Canadian committee that did not clearly announce a decision, which paralyzed action. Second, and more importantly, it can be the moment when specific persons commit themselves in favor of a specific course of action. Not only does it announce *what* the decision is about but it also announces *who* associates her- or himself with the decision. The more public the initial participation is—in a context where the individual appears to have the choice to participate or not—the more she or he might feel bound to her or his decision. The decision maker might consequently get more involved in the action than she or he had intended initially (Weick 1993). These conditions—"high choice" and "high visibility"—are often present in organizations: for example, in meetings, especially when minutes are sent to the participants later. In addition, the binding of decision makers to a course of action is especially likely to occur when advocacy is explicit, high in volition, and repeated (Salancik 1977).

Once decision makers are bound to a course of action, they might have much difficulty to withdraw from a losing project and they might persist even in face of negative feedback. The voluminous body of work on the escalation of commitment concept suggests that the more a decision maker has been invested in the course of action (either psychologically, materially, or both), the more unwilling he or she is to give up, and the more he or she may decide in favor of an even greater commitment of resources to the same course of action. In most cases, decision makers become entrapped in a previous course of action because they do not want to admit—to themselves and to others—that they have allocated prior resources in vain. They try to maintain an appearance of rationality and to prove to others that a costly error was the correct decision over a long-term perspective (Staw and Ross 1978; Brockner 1992). In other cases, they may also be curious about the consequences of persisting in the same course of action, or they may want to learn about the phenomenon ("it's an opportunity to collect additional data" or "the passage of time might allow a better understanding of the situation") (Bowen 1987; Ross and Staw 1993).

It sometimes happens that pathological persistence in action continues, even though the main decision maker wants to stop the project. For example, when the Long Island Lighting Company (LILCO) itself—that had decided and announced the decision to build the Shoreham Nuclear Plant in 1966—agreed to abandon the facility, other external sources of commitment had grown strong enough to hold the organization in its course of action (Ross and Staw 1993). A range of external political parties continued to push for the project. These included public utilities interested in nuclear power, representatives of the nuclear power industry, as well as the federal government, and various citizens' lobbying groups. The focal organization had lost control of the project, which delayed the final decision to abandon Shoreham. Finally, Shoreham's cost, estimated to be US$75 million in 1966, had risen to US$5.5 billion in 1989, when it was abandoned.

In this case, it is clear that the final result was completely different from the initial decision makers' intention. Karl Weick suggested the concepts of "deviance amplification" and "deviation amplifying loops" to explore this idea from a different perspective. In certain systems, small decisions may trigger deviation amplifying loops that *increase* the misalignment between that which was intended and that which actually occurred: for instance, minor changes can change the system from loosely to tightly coupled or increase its complexity (Weick 1990), and end up generating major disasters such as the Bhopal or Challenger accidents (Weick 1988). Small decisions may encourage the occurrence and rapid diffusion of multiple errors by creating a feedback loop which magnifies these minor errors into major problems. In those cases, the decision makers are not aware that their initial decisions may create the preconditions for adverse outcomes (Ramanujam 2003).

A new theoretical framework concerning negative emotions in organizations has recently explored this idea. Certain decisions—such as downsizing, restructuring, organizational change, mergers, or more individual decisions such as the dismissal or promotion of an employee—can give rise to emotions such as anger, frustration, fear, shame, or guilt (Frost 2003). These emotions being "high activation" emotions are all the more likely to permeate the entire organization, spreading to members on whom the decision had no direct impact. For example, a study of three British orchestras examines the role of emotions in six decisions to fire a musician whose performance was no longer satisfactory (Maitlis and Ozcelik 2004). This decision aimed to improve the performance of the orchestra. However, it provoked negative emotional reactions among the other musicians (e.g., fear about their own future, guilt, and indignation). The decision makers sought to minimize these "inappropriate" emotions. This response not only failed to diffuse members' emotions but also incited still further toxicity, in a vicious cycle of emotions and actions. The recursive interplay of organizational members' actions and negative emotions led to the cumulative build-up of toxicity. Whereas the initial decision aimed to improve the performance of the orchestra, some decision outcomes were actually detrimental to the collective work (e.g., demotivation of the musicians, defiance toward the decision makers, and decision making avoidance). The organization was like a resonating chamber in which the effects of certain factors were amplified.

INTERCONNECTEDNESS AND INTERACTIONS BETWEEN DECISIONS

The previous section emphasized that action can have its own dynamic apart from decision, which makes it possible to consider the complexity of the relationships between decisions and decision outcomes. This section shifts the level of analysis and envisages an organization as a system of decision processes that interact. Most studies of organizational decisions focus on specific decisions and decision outcomes. They do not mention potential relations among the many decisions in the organization. This implies that studies assume either there are no relations among decisions or their effects on organizational outcomes are not significant. Although the garbage can model moved the level of analysis from single decisions to streams of problems, random assemblage of problems and solutions led researchers to a loss of interest in the potential relations among decisions This section explores the ways in which the interactions among the myriad of ongoing organizational decision processes can impact variously on decision outcomes.

From Decisions to Sets of Issues

Jane Dutton's works on strategic agenda building have certainly been pioneering in systematically focusing not on specific decisions but on "sets of issues" that mobilize the collective attention of the organization at a given time (Dutton and Duncan 1987; Dutton 1988; Dutton et al. 1989; Dutton et al. 1990). In this "attention-based view of the firm" (March and Olsen 1976), the main research question has been to understand the process through which some issues capture the attention of decision makers, while others do not. Several hypotheses underlie this body of work:

1. The organization does not produce discrete events that researchers could analyze separately because it is, at all times, engaged in a set of decisional processes. It is therefore more useful to examine this set of processes holistically to understand better what the organization produces. For example, organizational change is described not as a discrete event but as what emerges from the organization, that is "a cacophony of complementary and competing change attempts, with managers at all levels joining the fray and pushing for issues of particular importance to themselves" (Dutton et al. 2001: 716).

2. Organizational members' allocation of attention to an issue is a necessary precursor to their making a decision and taking substantive action on this issue. Given that management time and attention are finite (March and Shapira 1982), a major question that has occupied organizational decision researchers is the question as to why certain issues capture the organization's attention and others do not (Kingdon 1990). Research suggests that the more decision makers frame an issue as involving bigger stakes, the more they perceive it as a threat (Dutton and Jackson 1987), as urgent (Dutton and Duncan 1987), uncertain (Milliken 1990), and resolvable (Dutton and Duncan 1987), the more attention they will devote to it. Furthermore, in this perspective, middle managers play a central role in strategic and organizational decision making, through patterns of upward influence (Floyd and Wooldridge 2000): for issues to attract top managements' attention, they have to be "sold" via the persuasive efforts of middle managers and "bought" by top managers (Dutton et al. 2001). Thus, for an issue to be "sold" it must generate a consistent flow of attention from many different people, at different organizational levels.

These studies draw the attention to the whole set of decisions being made at a particular time in an organization. However, placing the concept of attention at the center of analysis emphasizes competition between potential issues. This approach uses the ideas of attention, which is central in the bounded rationality model (Simon 1947), and of competition between "issue sellers," which is in keeping with the political conception of decision making (cf., Eisenhardt and Zbaracki 1992 for a review). In this perspective, researchers have rarely considered the potential relations between issues, and when they did, they considered that bundling an issue with other issues would increase the level of top management's attention (Dutton et al. 1993) and hence the resources invested in the issue (Dutton et al. 1990). They have presented it as an influence strategy to "package" an issue so as to sell it better, which implies that most issues are, in their ordinary state, distinct from one another.

From Sets of Issues to Streams of Issues

Cutting the decisional fabric into separate processes is quite questionable. At individual level, firstly, the decisional context is in itself extremely complex: it forms a whole, made up of elements that interact with each other, mingling in complex relationships (Weick 1995). In this environment, managers are not simply "assigned" prestructured problems. Issues are conceptual entities that do not exist in the real world (Smith 1989). Managers have to construct issues they will be able to cope with. Treating the issues as if they were separate from each other would be tantamount to denying the idea that managers try to construct a decision-making environment that has an overall sense.

Second, at the organizational level, considering issues as being "sold" by some managers and "bought" by others, implies a rather static conception of the organization as being composed of hierarchical layers (middle managers, managers, and top managers) between which these issues circulate. However, many issues flow and intersect with other issues and it is difficult to identify continuity in their evolution. Do they have a rigid outline? Do they have a precise beginning and a precise ending? Many issues persist in some form or other for considerable lengths of time and "do not necessarily die even when key decisions are made" (Langley et al. 1995: 270). Thus, in Pinfield's (1986) study of a decision process in the Canadian government bureaucracy, the issue of the senior executives' management policies persisted for over two years, giving the impression that the decision process had apparently recycled to its original starting point.

Thus this author can only concur with Langley et al.'s suggestion (1995: 270) that "Research in [the area of organizational decision making] would be more productive if conceived in terms of continuing and interacting streams of issues that spin off actions, sometimes through identifiable decisions." The research focus then shifts from the "set of issues" to the "stream of issues" and from the competition between issues to their linkages, in an attempt to understand what organizations produce and how they produce it.

The Need for a Theory of Issue Interconnectedness

No comprehensive theory of issue interconnectedness currently exists. However, there are two essential—though underused—contributions to this point in the field of organizational decision making.

The first contribution is the typology proposed by Langley et al. (1995). They identify three types of linkages between decisions. Sequential linkages are inter-relationships between different decisions concerning the same issue at different times. The same decision situation may recur because prior decisions did not manage to resolve the issue or large decisions may generate a nested series of smaller ones. For instance, Kriger and Barnes (1992) described the relationships between various levels of decision activities associated with the same major issue. Alternatively, a series of minor decisions may accumulate overtime to generate a major one (Braybrooke and Lindblom 1963; Quinn 1980). In Pinfield's (1986) study, actors made numerous minor staffing decisions in any one year. The choice of any action that could produce more than marginal change was unlikely, because of the opposition this would meet. However, over two years, the effect of these multiple interdependent issues was substantial.

Lateral linkages are the links between different issues being considered concurrently. The most relevant way of describing these lateral linkages is to consider that issues bathe within the same organizational context, involving the same people, ideology, structural design, and strategies. Issues are driven by actors who hold similar interpretations of the world. At individual level, for example, Kotter (1982) or Isenberg (1984) emphasize the ability of senior managers to fuse seemingly isolated experiences into an integrated whole. According to Noel (1989) senior managers have "magnificent obsessions" that dictate what issues the leaders concentrate on, the way in which they address these problems and organize their activities as a whole; the influence of a dominant chief executive creates tight linkages between issues. In an 18-month study of six executives, Vidaillet (1997) has shown that those executives formulated issues that were all linked to a central cognitive structure. At the organizational level, deeply rooted shared beliefs may develop, framing what decision makers consider as an issue and linking issues together (Donaldson and Lorsch 1983; Boland et al. 1990). The structural design of organizations may also create linked issues: planning systems of various sorts (budgeting, scheduling, programming), rules, and procedures are powerful mechanisms coupling decision processes.

Finally, some linkages are precursive, cutting across different issues and different times, as a decision taken on one issue can critically affect subsequent decisions on a variety of other issues within the same organization. One decision may set off a series of decisions on a wider range of issues. Alternatively, decision makers may come to see a set of previously unrelated issues as related and thus merge them into a single decision. Furthermore, one decision may evoke new issues or render other issues obsolete (see Langley et al. 1995 for a richer description). Issues can interweave more or less closely, and the organization can be described as a complex issue network "in which almost everything seems to impinge on everything else" (Langley et al. 1995: 275). The idea of the plasticity of issues is central here, with issues

sometimes getting washed up on shore as actions, sometimes sinking and disappearing, and often bumping into each other with the effect of changing another's direction, slowing one down, speeding one up, joining two together. (Langley et al. 1995: 275)

From this perspective, decisions are events that punctuate and modify the network of issues that pervade the entire organization.

Brunsson (2002) made another essential contribution to the study of issue interconnectedness. An organization must produce highly varied outcomes to be able to cope with the diversity and incoherence of the demands it faces. Brunsson gave the example of an organization, in which actors made contradictory decisions. This was possible because action did not necessarily follow those decisions. In Brunsson's view, organizations produce talk, decisions, and actions:

In traditional administrative and decision theories, management talk and decisions point-ing in one direction are assumed to increase the likelihood that corresponding action will be taken. When hypocrisy obtains, there is still a causal relation between talk, decisions and actions, but the causality is the reverse. Talk or decisions pointing in one direction *reduce* the likelihood of the corresponding action actually occurring, while actions in a particular direction reduce the likelihood of any corresponding talk or decisions taking place. Talk and decisions pointing in one direction do not encourage actions in the same direction; rather, they *compensate* for actions in the opposite direction, just as actions in one direction compensate for talk and decisions in a different one. Or, to use the popular concept of "coupling", when hypocrisy obtains, the talk and decisions and actions are not de-coupled or loosely coupled. Rather, they are coupled, albeit in another way than is usually assumed. (Brunsson 2002: xiv)

In an organization crisscrossed by streams of issues, talk, decisions, and actions are different means of capturing those issues. Thus, Brunsson points to one additional mode of linkages. It is what one might call compensatory linkages: that is, issues can cancel each other out, compensate for one another, or system-atically contradict one another. There is no congruence, but there is a relationship, which can be the answer to the problems posed by the inconsistent demands the organization faces.

Finally, shifting the approach from a decisional fabric made of specific decisions to issue interconnectedness questions the very notion of decision outcomes. If outcomes can be identified, it is particularly difficult to map them directly onto specific decisions without resorting to an arbitrary segmentation exercise that bears little correspondence to organizational reality.

CONCLUSION

This chapter has discussed a conception that prevails in organizations and in research on organizational decision making. In this conception, managers as well as researchers consider some organizational outcomes as decision outcomes, and they assume that specific decisions produce those decision outcomes. Though this logic definitely applies in certain situations, it would be simplistic to assume that it describes all that goes on in organizations in terms of decision making. Indeed, the so-called "decision outcomes" are not necessarily the outcomes of decisions.

First, "decision outcomes" are the outcomes of actions at least as much as the outcomes of decisions. Action is not the mere enactment of a decision: it has its own dynamic that strongly affects "decision outcomes." This chapter does not propose that researchers focus all their attention on action rationality—which would imply dropping the concept of decision; rather, researchers should explore the complex and subtle relations that link decision to action and action to decision. How and when does one reinforce the other? How and when do they cancel each other out? How do the rationale of the decision and that of the action combine to produce certain outcomes?

Second, "decision outcomes" can be the product of the interaction of multiple issues that mobilize the organization's attention, rather than the outcomes of specific and identifiable decisions. Here again, by artificially isolating decisions and by examining the causal links, upstream, of those decisions, research on decision processes has omitted to consider an important aspect of organizational reality. Researchers should change their level of analysis and pay attention to the links between different issues, in order to advance understanding of how streams of issues interact and produce organizing.

One reason why researchers so far have traveled only a short way down these two paths is that such work renders irrelevant the attribution of responsibility. Systematically linking what happens in the organization to distinct and identifiable lines of decisions, which are then turned into actions congruent with the initial intention, makes it possible to attribute outcomes to specific individuals. However, what distinguishes organizational decision making from individual decision making is the complex linking of multiple processes and people.

The ideas developed here have practical implications. First, if people in organizations need to construct stories that may plausibly account for specific outcomes, and if locating past "choices" is central in these stories, a fundamental managerial ability is to know how to create collectively these stories. The classical approach of decision making emphasizes the future related to a decision and envisages decision makers as people of vision who create ambitious plans. Conversely, if managerial ability to reinterpret the past is important,

it implies that any decision maker is only as good as his or her memory... Not only does a good decision maker have a good, active memory, that person is especially attentive to choice points that could plausibly be punctuated into an earlier flow of events. (Weick 1995: 185)

In this perspective, the future still matters: the richer the stories the actors agree on, the more useful they will be for construing the meaning of future action.

Second, if "deciding" is an act of interpretation, another quality of the decision maker is to be opportunistic in the best sense of the word. She or he has numerous interpretative opportunities at her or his disposal to make sense of specific outcomes and can use one that creates the most coherent story or one that incorporates more cues.

Third, as decisions are not end points and as action has its own autonomy, managers had better spend more time on action: to adjust it, to correct it, to link it to decision, to stop amplifying loops or, conversely, to use them opportunistically (for example, to undertake radical organizational change).

Finally, managers play a vital role in linking issues together. They can make these relations purposeful: they can link issues together; undo links; transform issues; couple them in an antagonistic way if it has an overall sense (for example, if it enables the organization to cope with contradictory demands). They can also create infrastructures that can help develop "intelligent" linking. This analysis points to a central role for sensemaking processes in organizational decision making. More specifically, it highlights how the activity of connecting and linking different issues is fundamental in those processes, as research on social processes of sensemaking among large groups of diverse organizational stakeholders (Maitlis 2005), or on heedful interrelating (Weick and Roberts 1993) has started to explore. In this perspective, it would be interesting to consider wether particular forms of linking among issues are likely to produce specific organizational outcomes such as innovation, efficiency, radical change, or disasters.

REFERENCES

BOLAND, R. J., GREENBERG, R. H., PARK, S. H., and HAN, I. (1990). 'Mapping the Process of Problem Reformulation: Implications for Understanding Strategic Thought,' in A. S. Huff (ed.), *Mapping Strategic Thought*. New York: John Wiley and Sons, 195–226.

Bowen, M. G. (1987). 'The Escalation Phenomenon Reconsidered: Decision Dilemmas or Decision Errors?' *Academy of Management Review*, 12/1: 52–66.

Braybrooke, D. and Lindblom, C. E. (1963). *A Strategy of Decision*. New York: Free Press.

Brockner, J. (1996). 'The Escalation of Commitment to a Failing Course of Action: Toward Theoretical Progress.' *Academy of Management Review*, 17/1: 39–61.

Brunsson, N. (2002). *The Organization of Hypocrisy: Talk, Decisions and Actions in Organizations* (2nd edn.). Copenhagen: Copenhagen Business School Press.

Cohen, M. D., March, J. G., and Olsen, J. P. (1972). 'A Garbage Can Model of Organizational Choice.' *Administrative Science Quarterly*, 17: 1–25.

Dean Jr., J. W. and Sharfman, M. P. (1993). 'The Relationship Between Procedural Rationality and Political Behavior in Strategic Decision Making.' *Decision Sciences*, 24/6: 1069–83.

Donaldson, G. and Lorsch J. W. (1983). *Decision Making at the Top: The Shaping of Strategic Direction*. New York: Basic Books.

Dutton, J. E. (1988). 'Understanding Strategic Agenda Building and its Implications for Managing Change,' in L. R. Pondy, R. T. Boland, and H. Thomas (eds.), *Managing Ambiguity and Change*. Chichester: Wiley, 127–44.

—— Duncan, R. B. (1987). 'The Creation of Momentum for Change Through the Process of Strategic Issue Diagnosis.' *Strategic Management Journal*, 83: 279–95.

—— Jackson, S. B. (1987). 'Categorizing Strategic Issues: Links to Organizational Action.' *Academy of Management Review*, 12: 76–90.

—— Walton, E. J., and Abrahamson, E. (1989). 'Important Dimensions of Strategic Issues: Separating the Wheat from the Chaff.' *Journal of Management Studies*, 26/4: 379–98.

—— Stumpf, S. A., and Wagner, D. (1990). 'Diagnosing Strategic Issues and Managerial Investment of Revenues,' in P. Shrivastava and R. Lamb (eds.), *Advances in Strategic Management*. Greenwich, CT: JAI Press, 143–67.

—— Ashford, S. J., O'Neill, R. M., and Lawrence, K. A. (2001). 'Moves that Matter: Issue Selling and Organizational Change.' *Academy of Management Journal*, 44/4: 716–36.

Eisenhardt, K. E. and Zbaracki, M. J. (1992). 'Strategic Decision Making.' *Strategic Management Journal*, 13: 17–37.

Feldman, M. S. and March, J. G. (1981). 'Information in Organizations as Signal and Symbol.' *Administrative Science Quarterly*, 26: 171–86.

Floyd, S. W. and Wooldridge, B. (2000). *Building Strategy from the Middle: Reconceptualizing Strategy Process*. Thousand Oaks, CA: Sage.

Frost, P. (2003). *Toxic Emotions at Work*. Boston, MA: Harvard Business School Press.

Garfinkel, H. (1967). *Studies in Ethnomethodology*. Englewood Cliffs, NJ: Prentice-Hall.

Gephart, R. P. (1993). 'The Textual Approach : Risk and Blame in Disaster Sensemaking.' *Academy of Management Journal*, 36: 1465–514.

Isenberg, D. J. (1984). 'How Senior Managers Think.' *Harvard Business Review*, 62/6: 81–90.

Jackson, S. E. and Dutton, J. E. (1988). 'Discerning Threats and Opportunities.' *Administrative Science Quarterly*, 33: 370–87.

Kingdon, J. W. (1990). 'How Do Issues Get on Public Policy Agenda?' Paper presented at the annual meeting of the American Sociological Association, Washington, DC.

Kotter, J. P. (1982). *The General Manager*. New York: Free Press.

Kriger, M. P. and Barnes, L. B. (1992). 'Organizational Decision-Making as Hierarchical Levels of Drama.' *Journal of Management Studies*, 29/4: 439–58.

LANGLEY, A., MINTZBERG, H., PITCHER, P., POSADA, E., and SAINT-MACARY, J. (1995). 'Opening Up Decision Making: The View from the Black Stool.' *Organization Science*, 6/3: 260–79.

LAROCHE, H. (1995). 'From Decision to Action in Organizations.' *Organization Science*, 6/1: 62–75.

MAITLIS, S. (2005). 'The Social Processes of Organizational Sensemaking.' *Academy of Management Journal*, 48/1: 21–49.

—— OZCELIK, H. (2004). 'Toxic Decision Processes: A Study of Emotion and Organizational Decision Making.' *Organization Science*, 15/4: 375–93.

MARCH, J. G. and OLSEN, J. P. (1976). *Ambiguity and Choice in Organizations*. Bergen: Universetet-forlaget.

—— SHAPIRA, Z. (1982). 'Behavioral Decision Theory and Organizational Decision Making,' in G. R. Ungson and D. N. Braunstein (eds.), *Decision Making: An Interdisciplinary Inquiry*. Boston, MA: Kent Publishing Company, 92–115.

MILES, R. H. (1982). *Coffin Nails and Corporate Strategies*. Englewood Cliffs, NJ: Prentice-Hall.

MILLIKEN, F. (1990). 'Perceiving and Interpreting Environmental Change: An Examination of College Administrators' Interpretation of Changing Demographics.' *Academy of Management Journal*, 33: 42–63.

NOËL, A. (1989). 'Strategic Cores and Magnificent Obsessions: Discovering Strategy Formation through Daily Activities of CEOs.' *Strategic Management Journal*, 10: 33–49.

NUTT, P. (2002). 'Making Strategic Choices.' *Journal of Management Studies*. 39/1: 67–96.

PINFIELD, L. (1986). 'A Field Evaluation of Perspectives on Organizational Decision Making.' *Administrative Science Quarterly*, 31: 365–88.

QUINN, J. B. (1980). *Strategies for Change: Logical Incrementalism*. Georgetown: Irwin-Dorsey.

RAMANUJAM, R. (2003). 'The Effects of Discontinuous Change on Latent Errors in Organizations: The Moderating Role of Risk.' *Academy of Management Journal*, 46/5: 608–17.

ROSS, J. and STAW, B. (1993). 'Organizational Escalation and Exit: Lessons from the Shoreham Nuclear Power Plant.' *Academy of Management Journal*, 36/4: 701–32.

SALANCIK, G. R. (1977). 'Commitment and the Control of Organizational Behavior and Belief,' in B. M. Staw and G. R. Salancik (eds.), *New Directions in Organizational Behavior*. Malabor, FL: Kreiger, 1–54.

SIMON, H. A. (1947). *Administrative Behavior: A Study of Decision-Making Processes in Administrative Organization*. New York: Macmillan.

SMITH, G. E. (1989). 'Defining Managerial Problems: A Framework for Prescriptive Theorizing.' *Management Science*, 35/8: 963–81.

STARBUCK, W. H. (1983). 'Organizations as Action Generators.' *American Sociological Review*, 48: 91–102.

STAW, B. and ROSS, J. (1978). 'Commitment to a Policy Decision: A Multitheoretical Perspective.' *Administrative Science Quarterly*, 23: 40–64.

SUTCLIFFE, K. M. and MCNAMARA, G. (2001). 'Controlling Decision-Making Practice in Organizations.' *Organization Science*, 12/4: 484–501.

TETLOCK, P. (1983). 'Accountability and the Complexity of Thought.' *Journal of Personality and Social Psychology*, 45: 74–83.

—— (1992). 'The Impact of Accountability on Judgment and Choice: Toward a Social Contingency Model.' *Advances in Experimental Social Psychology*, 25: 331–76.

TREVINO, L. K., DAFT, R. L., and LENGEL, R. H. (1990). 'Understanding Media Choices: A Symbolic Interactionist Perspective,' in J. Fulk and C. W. Steinfield (eds.), *Organizations and Communication Technology*. Newbury Park, CA: Sage Publications, 71–94.

VIDAILLET, B. (1997). 'La formulation de l'agenda décisionnel des dirigeants: Structure et évolutions dans une perspective cognitive.' Doctoral thesis, University of Paris-Dauphine, Paris.

VIDAILLET, B. (2001). 'Cognitive Processes and Decision Making in a Crisis Situation: A Case Study,' in T. Lant and Z. Shapira (eds.), *Organizational Cognition: Computation and Interpretation*. Mahwah, NJ: Lawrence Erlbaum Associates, 241–63.

WEICK, K. E. (1977). 'Enactment Processes in Organizations,' in B. Shaw and G. Salancik (eds.), *New Directions in Organizational Behavior*. Chicago, IL: St Clair.

—— (1988). 'Enacted Sensemaking in Crisis Situations.' *Journal of Management Studies*, 25/4: 305–17.

—— (1990). 'The Vulnerable System: An Analysis of the Tenerife Air Disaster'. *Journal of Management*, 16/3: 571–93.

—— (1993). 'Sensemaking in Organizations: Small Structures with Large Consequences,' in J. K. Murninghan (ed.), *Social Psychology in Organizations: Advances in Theory and Research*, Englewood Cliffs, NJ: Prentice Hall, 10–37.

—— (1995). *Sensemaking in Organizations*. Thousand Oaks, CA: Sage Publications.

—— ROBERTS, K. H. (1993). 'Collective Mind in Organizations: Heedful Interrelating on Flight Decks.' *Administrative Science Quarterly*, 38: 357–81.

23

WHAT LIES BEHIND ORGANIZATIONAL FAÇADES AND HOW ORGANIZATIONAL FAÇADES LIE: AN UNTOLD STORY OF ORGANIZATIONAL DECISION MAKING

ERIC ABRAHAMSON

PHILIPPE BAUMARD

INTRODUCTION

WHILE stakeholders search for visible signs of or organizational efficiency and effectiveness, organizations, in turn, depend on these stakeholders for resources.

Therefore, organizations display what Nystrom and Starbuck (1984) called "façades"—a symbolic front erected by organizational participants designed to reassure their organization's stakeholders, of the legitimacy of the organization and its management. In the classical formulation, façades act as buffers, allowing managers to gain new resources for their ongoing projects—regardless of their efficiency, effectiveness, and institutional legality (Pfeffer and Salancick 1978).

Why focus on façades in a book about decision making? First, because, investors, managers, leaders, employees, competitors, and regulators all make decisions about organizations based primarily on organizations' façades and less so on what lies behind these façades. In other words, companies hide behind a so-called façade or front stage (Goffman 1974; Nystrom and Starbuck 1984). The façade hides the backstage, which if revealed might make organizational stakeholders decide that problems beset the organization. This would cause stakeholders to withdraw their support—they would disinvest, quit, sue, and generally disparage the unveiled organization (Meyer and Rowan 1977). Second, because as they case study revealed, a lot of organizational decision making involves what façades to erect.

Originally, this chapter was to serve a two-fold purpose. First, it was to investigate what lies behind the façades facing individual decision makers; secondly, to examine the way in which a façade influenced organizational stakeholders. As it turns out, this grounded analysis took us in a very different direction.

What do Façades Look Like?

The orienting framework to this case study, taken from the extant literature on the subject, conceived of façades as unitary—there existed one façade, for one organization (Meyer and Rowan 1977; Pfeffer and Salancick 1978). It also visualized façades as somehow stable and ready made, rather as evolving works in progress. Our orienting framework also assumed that façades served only one function—creating organizational legitimacy in the eyes of stakeholders, in order for the organization to continue receiving stakeholder support. Façades, therefore, we assumed, served to hide the ugly truth from stakeholders, thereby misleading their decisions.

The article's first section describes the case. Then, the second section discusses the conclusions drawn from the case. As will become apparent shortly, this case study undermined many aspects of our orienting framework. The study suggested that façades, far from being unitary, have different facets serving very different roles with respect to stakeholders' decision making. Moreover, the case study revealed that not only entire organizations, but also headquarters, departments, small units, even individuals decide to display façades. Finally, the case study demonstrated that façades do not only serve to legitimize organizations—they serve many other functions. Some of these functions do in fact deceive stakeholders, but this deception, as well as façades other functions, can also benefit stakeholders.

SOGENIOUS LABS CASE STUDY

This chapter investigated a firm caught between contradictory prescriptions forced on it by its main stakeholder; a firm pushed by headquarters to display the ambitious and risky results in a foreign environment; a firm also forced to display a highly positive image for the firm in a completely new market. This European firm, Sogenious Labs (a fictitious name), belonged to a large industrial group. Its specific mandate calls for it to exploit innovation and partnerships in the United States. Thus, it had to supervise ongoing partnerships with US firms, as well as building a small R&D capacity in the emergent West Coast high-tech industry.

In all fairness to the leaders of Sogenious Labs (SL), headquarters gave them little direction. Consequently, over time, SL employees started to capitalize on their own interpersonal networks to respond to various demands from dispersed units belonging to the parent company. Besides, nobody fought to become SL's CEO. Senior managers felt that accepting such a mission would drive them away from the corporate center, and that it would diminish their chances to climb the corporate later to the center's corporate team. Consequently, SL had several CEOs until its parent company decided it should put in place some "strategic consistency." To do so, they selected one of their senior managers who had an honorable record in rejuvenating one of their slow moving business units, and "promoted" him to the strategic reorientation of SL.

Employees of SL had mixed feelings about this entirely new endeavor. On one hand, they welcomed change after so many years of reckless "entrepreneurship." As the former CEOs did not receive much direction from the parent company, management had conducted hiring in the most haphazard fashion, and gaps in income had become clearly visible at SL. This new "strategic reorientation" appeared as an opportunity to reshuffle responsibilities, and more surely, redress salary injustices. On the other hand, the small island that SL represented had become most comfortable. There "no project office" policy placed constraints. Evaluations of work occurred by self-appraisal. A friendly consensus reigned over a multitude of discretionary, and most of the time, totally unknown projects of which peers remained blissfully ignorant.

When the new CEO took office, a breeze of sheer wariness infiltrated SL's cubicles. Many of SL's engineers had defined their efficiency as a combination of attending industry conferences and engaging in "talks" with vendors and local high-tech firms. In fact, they never filed reports of what they had learned at these industry shows. Moreover, the culture assumed that most of these conference "talks" did not lead to any observable industrial development. Surely, something "interesting" to report would materialize when the time had come. However, when the time did come, they had little or nothing to show for it.

From his armchair, the CEO lacked perspective. He could not see that the most valuable assets of his new organization were the outcomes of personal projects that SL employees had undertaken at their own discretion with various levels of success. Nor was he aware that over time, departmentalization had grown to record proportions, and the small SL had almost as many departments as it had employees, people often teaming up in "cross-departmental" projects when new opportunities arose. Two to three employees constituted most of these "departments."

Neither did SL excel in its planning. The parent company always asked that management consume their budget by the end of the fiscal year, and that a particular SL developer budget each new project. SL employees launched most projects that fitted their highly personal tastes. The game became to find a kind manager who would sign onto new and ongoing projects for the annual report. SL employees invested a lot of energy reverse engineering existing solutions to find matching problems, and a potential ownership of the problem in one of the 200 business units of the parent company. Occasionally, a "genuine" demand would fall in the engineers' laps. Most likely, however, ongoing projects already swallowed up their time and budget allocation. This mechanistic budgeting system, in short, militated against any healthy collaboration with the parent's company units. It would instead entangle the small SL "departments" in yearlong "commitments" to self-declared or negotiated projects.

Although the whole picture was quite messy, employees were displaying tremendous creativity in producing outcomes of dubious utility. Various prototypes were piling up on engineers' desks, and surely, the mother company had many opportunities to extract from this total mess valuable innovations. Things did not turn out this way, however.

The parent company itself suffered heavy turmoil after its stock lost more than 40 percent of its value. Because most of the industry faired no better, SL's parent company headquarters did not perceive the stock market collapse, though spectacular, as particularly dramatic. However, analysts' pressure for greater stock values led the CEO of SL's parent to take a drastic decision. "Time to market" became the new religion, and the slow pace of SL's R&D labs became the sin to cure. The firm's reputation was at stake, and consultants from McKinsey and fellow Big Four management consulting firms flocked to examine the situation. A new word appeared recurrently in the headquarters' memos that now rained torrentially onto the small SL: "strategic alignment." The whole plan, the headquarters' document proudly read, would "strategically align the R&D organization with market demands, i.e. the business unit's strategic objectives." This shocked most SL's employees as they spent most of their time trying to convince the so-called "strategic business units" to buy their creative outputs in order to justify their annual budget. To date, the experience has most clearly resembled that of an apostle trying to convince a heretic to join a lost, obscure, and distant faith.

The intervention was doomed from the start. The parent company initiated this so-called "re-orientation" from quite a distance—8,000 miles away, to be precise. Moreover, culturally, as one SL employee put it during an interview, SL basked in a "self-designing chaos" philosophy. As a result, when a doubtful local executive examined carefully the first set of "official" headquarters PowerPoint slides, he confided in the interviewer that: "It's going to be like putting squares into triangular holes, this new plan."

Time pressure exacerbated the sense of local puzzlement. Coming up with a new organization, aligned with something rather distant and mysterious with no additional input appeared to SL employees as complete nonsense. Most engineers relented, however. Nevertheless, one thought impressed itself on them: this was no time for being overcreative. Recycling existing material did not sound like such a bad idea. This involved no malicious intent; as one employee put it: "realigning implies we have to reuse what we've done before, init?"

Unfortunately, SL had lived a lie. What SL had done previously had little to do with the parent company's endeavor. People became aware of the discrepancy soon enough; but, again, they absorbed it. SL could not panic, as the parent company's executives were due shortly for a courtesy visit. This looming deadline blurred the boundaries between future and current achievements. Engineers started to mix old PowerPoint slides with new ones, past, present, and "under progress" with "completed." Some moments of panic struck here and there when young interns pointed out that SL employees showed slides that they had already shown to the same executives, during their previous visit. A parent company's executive receiving a set of slides from SL notice it, and informally got in touch with one of SL's employees to inquire if someone had mishandled the slides. A little fine-tuning fixed the glitch, and managers kept engineers busy on their slides manufacturing for two full weeks.

Some employees noticed that, in its very paradoxical way, this "re-organization" gave them at least the impetus to do their own "write-up" for their "department." The whole exercise also gave opportunities to get rid of fellow workers, reassigning them to the brand new, and "so promising" new domains. The result looked good. SL leaders re-organized into five departments, perfectly "realigned" with the five competitive domains of the parent company. Each subsection contained a detailed plan of grand schemes they would achieve, with the obligatory rational of increased "time to market." When local imagination failed to provide a credible rationale, SL employees called the latest management theories to the rescue. The "re-org" also became an opportunity to lay claim to future hot new topics that would later provide justifications for grabbing or negotiating new demands.

A quick look at the intranet statistics during these two weeks showed that engineers rushed to the corporate web site for tips on the proper jargon to use, and on domains that would make their own write-up attractive. As days passed, the project had less and less to do with SL's reality, but instead of just "putting up with it." Managers started to have real conflicts over the definition of their domains. Upward appeals and inflated past achievements served in management meetings to justify further territorial expansion. Somehow, many of these statements became exaggerated, and after-meeting comments became harsher: "That was pure BS. She's no expert in that field, never accomplished anything in that, and look now, she is manager of the domain."

The fact that everyone had slightly distorted reality never became the subject of debate because of the obvious and keen interest not to report one's neighbor. Indeed, the entire peer review process meant that denouncing one's neighbor would eventually lead to counter-denunciations. Of course, not everyone reacted the same way. A small group of engineers escaped the ongoing mess by quickly re-affirming their affiliation to a single parent unit, and stood aside, laughing as the craziness unfolded.

When SL's parent company executives stepped in, the façade they heard and saw pleased them. The parent company executive congratulated SL's CEO for such a successful "re-org", and they put up the company as an exemplar for all other subsidiaries to imitate. Two weeks later, headquarters invited SL's CEO to share his successful experience and to participate in the global strategic reorientation meeting. All SL perceived this honor as legitimating the work that they had done.

When the manager of the Chinese subsidiary heard of the success story, he immediately took a plane, and flew directly to SL. For people who have suffered from being distant from the heartbeat of the company, the news was truly refreshing. Every actor put on the proper performance; Chinese executives received proper tours of this exceptional re-organization. The Chinese executive left with all necessary documentation, including the hundreds of PowerPoint slides manufactured for the event.

As SL fell back into its old routine, nothing truly changed. People went back to their old projects, leveraging their old connections and fine-tuning reports so that they would fit the new matrix. The beautiful intranet displayed for the occasion had fewer and fewer visitors, and fewer and fewer contributions. At one point, the "chief information officer," who had recently been anointed with this new title, discovered that the last and only two readers of his knowledge management creation were the CEO and himself.

China, was an all together different story. This young and affluent subsidiary adopted the new organization plan and projects swiftly. People in China did not fight the new organization because their personal history was not, as of yet, entangled in the old budget system. There were no problems to invent ongoing solutions for, so a set of fresh and neatly designed problems were very welcome.

When transposed elsewhere, the purportedly exact copy of SL's emergent fallacy turned into a real success. This success reinforced SL's legitimacy and reputation. In fact, all the group subsidiaries dealing with innovation, in short order, adopted SL's organization as the canonic, innovative organization form.

Headquarters' pressure to comply with the new form left the small subsidiary puzzled, and subsidiaries in turn put up façades displaying the requisite form. Meanwhile, at SL certainly did not focus on shareholder wealth, but instead on displaying an image that would exemplify the organization exemplar. Yet, in the end, they did produce overall shareholder value. A façade built out of desperation became a fashionable technique that gave the adequate impression that the firm had successfully managed the analyst driven turnaround. When the new Chinese creation had cloned SL's façade, it had no messes to hide, no previous history to accommodate, no irrational budgeting to circumvent. A façade on one side of the Pacific became a successful design on the other.

DECIDING ON FAÇADES

The SL case offers up many lessons. First, decision makers took decisions based on one main evolving input: SL's slowly *emergent* façade. Indeed, if one thing became clear, SL constantly fixed cracks in the façade, added entirely new walls, and pulled down others. Such "façade labor," the case revealed, became a full time job. Employees did not erect a façade once and hide behind it forever. Rather they constantly engaged in a decision-making process of how to recraft the façade in order to maintain dynamically legitimacy in the face of changing threats to legitimacy.

Second, whereas we assumed initially that façades would have one facet, they turned out to have multiple facets. In particular, we recognized at least three types of facets. Each type of facet also served at least one particular purpose.

More specifically, first, to display façades, managers must make their firms conform to expectation or norms that the run the firm rationally; in other words, they must appear to use management techniques believed to serve as efficient means to important ends (Baumard 1999). Second, conforming to existing norms of rationality does not always suffice. Stakeholders also expect the use of new and improved rational management techniques. Organizational leaders must demonstrate to stakeholders their use of the newest and most improved techniques—so called "state-of-the art techniques" (Abrahamson 1996). Third, organizational decision makers must signal that their organizations follow appropriate legal, financial, and professional norms. Hence, managers have to display the signs of respectability and financial solvency in order to create a reputation that satisfies stakeholders' other social expectation (e.g., a safe product, fair accounting, community support, and so on).

This tripartite description suggests at least three types of different façades: *rational* façades, *progressive* façades, and *reputation* façades guiding organizational stakeholders' decisions.

Rational Façades

Meyer (1977) used the term "rational norms" to denote stakeholder expectations that their firm and its management would run the firm rationally. What constitutes rationality remains vague and ambiguous; therefore, a rational façade projects the impression that a firm uses specific rational techniques that serve important ends for stakeholders.

The Consequences of Rational Façades?

The case revealed that purportedly rational operations did not go as smoothly as expected. The rational façade disguising SL's structured finance operations began to crack and collapse. The trading room was overperforming, while the loan activity was failing to provide the performance required to improve expectation of the larger banks (Baumard 1999: 157–9). Organizations eventually used the rational façade as a shield behind which they could innovate; both substantially, by changing their procedures, and then symbolically to create a new rational façade in order to foster stakeholders' support.

More generally, we propose that rational façades hide messes—complete deviations from expected conception of rational order (Abrahamson 2002). Rational façades, by hiding SL's mess, served a critical role in both SL's survival and its strategic reorientation. Behind SL's rational façade, it could act as a kind of organizational garbage can wherein streams of problem bumped in quasi-randomly into a set of solutions (March and Olsen 1976). As solutions were not always available, and the pressure to solve problems grew, engineers stumbled upon or invented solutions, and then created the problems, or the story, that would to justify these solutions. A total organizational mess resulted, as this practice spread throughout the firm. Managers violated egregiously, but highly productively, every rational rule of rational management decision making.

Rational façades help organizations by allowing them to run in non-orderly or messy fashions. This has two advantages; first, as Starbuck pointed out, organizations can forgo the expensive overhead of adopting institutionalized practices of arguably little utility. Indeed, scholars have never calculated the institutional costs of such institutional conformity—but what if they constituted a sizable component of organizational costs, providing few of the many benefits that they promise?

Second, mess allows for chance interactions between components that would have been otherwise been separated by institutionalized order (Abrahamson 2002). Behind façades, employees can interact in the disorganized fashions that best serve their needs. At SL, many project managers used façades in order to cross boundaries, and work with new business units across the group. Shielded by façades, project managers could change the labels defining their responsibilities, and abandon useless activities to take on ones that are more useful. In other instances, project managers employed façades to escape a narrow and tight coupling to one parent business unit, and to connect with many others. For example, the head of business development decided to include "technology benchmarking" to its responsibilities, allowing his group to interact more effectively with chief technology officers at the parent company, thereby by-passing the local CTO.

When employees face supervisors, they need to sound plausible and to appear consistent. A façade hides the trial and errors inevitable in bringing about change. The Chinese subsidiary, for instance, found in SL's façade the positive image it needed to make its launch appear orderly and mistake-free. Moreover, façades reduce the level of uncertainty that surrounds organizational deeds and actions. A façade projects a confident image of unity in both direction and command. Hence, façades allow for the inspired improvisation necessary to respond to urgent demands caused by unexpected events, while maintaining the appearance of a low level of uncertainty (Crossan et al. 2005: 133).

Freed from guilt, employees who work behind a façade can pursue their own logic of organized or even disorganized logic of action. Façades act as ex ante explanations for whatever could happen to the ongoing actions, guaranteeing achieved consistency, for the façade holds a different temporality from action itself. As Fischhoff puts it (1975), quoting Florovsky: "in retrospect, we seem to perceive the logic of events that unfold themselves in a regular or linear fashion according to a recognizable pattern with an alleged inner necessity. So that we get the impression that it really could not have happened otherwise" (p. 369)

Progressive Façades

The theory of fashion introduces the notion that organizational façades must not only fit norms of rationality, but that they must also mirror norms of progress. Norms of progress mandate not just that managers use efficient means to important ends, but rather that they use the *newest* and *most improved* efficient means equally new and improved ends (Abrahamson 1996). In other words, managers must use the latest management fashions offered up by a management fashion market composed of consulting firms, business book publishing houses, business magazines, business schools, and business professional associations.

If most companies have adopted the six-sigma fashion, for instance, pressure builds to create a six-sigma façade—even if this façades is more symbolic than actual. In another instance, Zbaracki (1998) shows how the language prescribing total quality management (TQM) techniques reaches organizations, leads to some TQM experiments, many of which fail, and few of which succeed. As stakeholders ask for evidence of quality management, managers turn these few successes mutate into a rhetorical façade that fully satisfy stakeholder expectations.

The Consequences of Progressive Façades

In our experience, progressive façade can play at least three roles. First, to put it bluntly, progressive façades can hide the fact that organizations continue doing some of the same old stuff despite pressures to change. On occasion the old stuff gets relabeled—what Kimberly (1981) called putting old wine in new bottles.

Second, progressive façades can make organizations appear as if their management uses the state of the art in management technique. This may explain why so many progressive façades collapse over time, because they serve a symbolic rather than utilitarian purpose (Abrahamson and Fairchild 1999).

Third, and to our surprise, SL's progressive façades played a utilitarian adaptive role for SL. It enabled decisions that headquarters would have otherwise rejected. Progressive façades help in experimenting with fashionable techniques that might otherwise fail. The buffer and the oversight that SL's façade created helped managers to escape micro management, to find more room for experimentation, and to feel less scared by failures, out of box design and daring combinations of improbable business processes. Crafting a progressive façade introduced a narrative guideline in the ongoing mess that, in the end, helped SL achieve congruence with the rest of the firm. It seemed that for the progressive façade to succeed, however, no one had to believe it too much and feel constrained by it too closely.

Internal stakeholders can interpret organizational innovation in two ways—as creative or as deviant. The latter puts innovators at risk. Surprisingly, in this case study, progressive organizational façades—far from bringing innovation into firms—served to incorporate existing organizational innovation.

Innovation also requires freedom (Clark and Fujimoto 1991). Progressive façades create a sanctuary wherein engineers can gain discretion over their projects. For instance, technology for compression video fascinated a young engineer with the mother company in the late 1990s. Unfortunately, he worked in a telecommunication firm. In order to pursue his passion, he built a series of progressive façades that made it appear that compression technologies were the path to progress in telecommunication systems. Well hidden behind these progressive façades, he could achieve his real project—creating one of the first video compression encoders. Facing resistance when the façade collapsed, he obtained a spin-off agreement with a large industrial partner, while sharing in the revenues of the forthcoming patent. Out of the 6,800 patents that the group holds today, this compression encoder patent had generated in some years nearly 40 percent of its licensing revenues.

Façades serve the innovation process, because they allow the construction of an ex post convergence between experiments and their outcomes. As in the Mpeg4 case studies, engineers obtain resources and freedom by projecting a desirable image of a positive and rhetorically convergent outcome for their corporation. When stakeheholders accept the rhetoric, employees can thrive behind the esoterism of the put-up façade and do the real work. Hence, façades provide engineers and managers with degrees of freedom that more scrutiny and micro management would kill from the start. As pointed out by Sobek et al. (1999), this gradual convergence provides the group with the possibility of collective learning based on real-time information, not forcing the choice of early, and potentially misleading, convergence points.

Reputation Façades

Reputation serves to indicate that organizations serve stakeholders in some way that benefits these stakeholders—selling them products that do not hurt them, helping some disadvantaged organizational stakeholder, following acceptable accounting standards, and so on. With the current waves of financial scandals, this type of façade has received the most attention. A reputation façade displays accounting and rhetorical symbols desired by critical stakeholders, for example, most commonly analysts and the press. In that sense, reputation façades participate in the crafting of organizational legitimacy by reinforcing the positive image of an organization (Meyer and Rowan 1977; DiMaggio and Powell 1983).

Reputation façades appear as symbols, stories, and attributes that lead observers to believe that an organization can achieve more than it really can. Enron's CEO, Jeff Skilling, put up a reputation façade depicting a crowded trading room when his firm received a visit from members of the Security Exchange Commission. Employees filled the room mimicking the actions of busy energy traders, while bogus information filled the screens. This chapter considers this trading scenery as a story told, a fairytale, narrated to stakeholders to support ongoing decisions that are better kept discreet from external sight.

The Consequences of Reputational Façades

The case study also revealed and interesting feature of reputational façades. When SL had put up its reputational façade, managers felt obliged to deliver on it, as if caught in a self-inflicted, self-fulfilling prophecy. Employees worked long hours to bring the backstage in line with the front stage—the organizational reality with the organizational façade.

To conform by using façades often means to innovate symbolically. When organizations need to bridge the distance separating current and desired façades, they engage in several forms of more or less radical innovations. In the late 1980s, the Indosuez

Bank was facing such a challenge, as its stockholders had decided that it was time for the historical bank to fly apart from its parent company, and gain all the requisite attributes of an international bank. By the end of 1988, the bank has put together a "development charter" that listed all the pieces of its façade "to put Indosuez on the map as a recognized international bank" (Baumard 1999: 156). These pieces included owning a performing trading room in New York, close to the NYSE, climbing up the scale of loan graduation from AA to more, and displaying the same organization and lines of operations that the major AAA banks operating in New York.

Reputational façades also provide shields for pursuing illegitimate actions. Because façades espouse corporate and societal values, stakeholders do not perceive when organizations have violated these values. Moreover, because façades create causal ambiguity, it becomes harder to hold leaders and managers responsible for such illegitimate actions. Moreover, because stakeholders do not associate reputational façades with particular individual, they create an anonymous shield between organizational operations and the image of these operations broadcasted to the outside. A façade becomes a collective fantasy, a shared dream, where no one remains responsible. At least, the managers of Enron, WorldComm, and Mobil-Com thought so.

Reputational façades also contribute to risk-taking in organizational decision making. Façades raise the level of expectation of investors, stakeholders, and managers as they project positive organizational returns. If stockholders were only to invest based on realistic assessments of firms' current capabilities, most innovations might never take place. Hence, like a collective fantasy, a façade encourages investments and support for innovations that would otherwise have never seen the light of day.

From Organizational to Leader Façades

Up until this point, this article has concerned itself with organizations creating façades. Clearly, however, leaders and managers create façades, not organizations. The create façades for entire subsidiaries, for departments, for subunits. In a way, an organizations constitutes a nested set of façades that mediate the interaction between every differentiated part of the organization.

Note, however, that façades don't stop at the boundaries of organizational subunits. Individuals themselves put up rational, progressive, and reputational façades. This becomes particularly interesting when we consider the façades erected by leaders.

Façades legitimate not only means but ends as well. Leader façades communicate that the strategic ends leaders pursue serve their stakeholders' interests: whether they be investors, employees, suppliers, or consumers. Leader façades, therefore, build CEOs reputations (Adler and Adler 1989; Gamson 1994; Rindova et al. 2006).

To further these reputational leader façades, CEOs use the professional services of communication agencies and public relation agents to shape their image. Jeff Skilling, former CEO of Enron, and Time "manager of the year" before the scandalous bankruptcy of his firm, made extensive use of public relations agencies to burnish his image for stakeholders. "Professional image construction," nowadays has become an academic research subject (Roberts 2005). It leads top managers to

invest a considerable amount of energy into constructing viable professional images by enacting personas that represent desirable qualities (e.g., intelligence, confidence, initiative, trustworthiness, gracefulness, and seriousness about one's work) and that elicit approval and recognition from key constituents. (Roberts 2005: 687)

Accordingly, organizational stakeholders have caught many leaders polishing the façade of their resumes, most lately the Director of FEMA, in the aftermath of the Katrina disaster. Managers seek for themselves and their firm's institutional certifications and symbols of recognition (Rao 1994). As a result, leader façades take the form of fairytales, of organizational myths, and of stories of heroic performances. This storytelling contributes to organizational legitimacy by meeting societal expectations and society's fantasies (Lounsbury and Glynn 2001).

Accounts of organizational founder's personal history frequently dramatize corporate histories as well. The media depicted Howard Hughes as a war hero, a fearless pilot, and a breathtaking engineer. This, though he neither fought in any decisive battle nor flew some of his experimental planes more than a couple hundred yards. Dramatization, hence, makes the façade unquestionable. The larger the fantasy, the more acceptable it becomes, as exceptional performance cannot find any rational and reasonable explanation. Rather than crediting serendipity, luck, or accidents to explain organizational discoveries, the mass media produce stories that explain exceptional performance with exceptional traits. Hence,

using dramatic narratives, journalists are able to selectively distill a complex jumble of otherwise ambiguous and contradictory activities, pronouncements, and impressions into a simplified and relatively coherent portrait. (Ashforth and Humphrey 1997: 53)

thereby reducing the uncertainty associated with the events they report on (Lounsbury and Glynn 2001; Rindova et al. 2006: 57).

CONCLUSION

The orienting frame to this grounded theory case study had us thinking that façades were relatively simple, unitary, organizational mechanisms necessary to make stakeholder decide to contribute organizational resources. Surprisingly, the case study revealed different types of façades serving very different role. Moreover, the case study indicated that façades were not exceptional sins of the few. In a world where reputation moves faster than organizational facts, façades pervade organizations both in scale and in scope.

Our orienting framework also focused on the notion that façades served as a mechanism to hide organizational malfeasance. Observing a façade in the making partially undermined this assumption. We discovered that façades could serve as levers of organizational improvement. Rationality façades, for examples, could help employees ignore institutionalized practices and select more effective and efficient ones. Freed from institutional pressure, inventors of progressive façades gained a degree of liberty in innovation. When progressive façades transmitted fictitious organizational progress, they also transmit potentialities for change that would organizational actors would have otherwise rejected. Finally, reputational façades fostered investment, stakeholder support, and contributed to the growth of firms, when the reality of their business idea constituted merely a sketch on a computer screen.

These last observations left us with a disquieting conclusion. The more façades lie, the more façades have the potential to become realities. Freed from the constraints of institutionalized technique by rational façades; freed to innovate by rational façades; and capable of receiving support behind reputational façades, SL and the subsidiaries could change. Had SL managers crafted less powerful façades, stakeholders would have seen through them, and the reality behind the façades could never have become the reality mirroring the new façade.

Put differently, the less façades lie, the more they lose the potential to become realities. The more the firm remains bound by institutional constraints, the less it can experiment with new techniques, and the less stakeholder support it receives. The more likely, therefore, the possibility that the façades lie becomes a real lie.

Clearly, this line of argumentation has disquieting implications. It not so subtlety suggests that managers should lie with façades so that the truth of these façades has a chance of coming about. However, what of the situation when lies do not result in the truth, requiring more lies and thicker façades, until nothing remains but a crooked E?

References

ABRAHAMSON, E. (1991). 'Managerial Fads and Fashions: The Diffusion and Refection of Innovations.' *Academy of Management Review*, 16/3: 586–602.

—— (1996). 'Management Fashion.' *Academy of Management Review*, 21/1: 254–85.

—— (2002). 'Disorganization Theory and Disorganizational Behavior: Towards an Etiology of Messes,' in B. M. Staw and R. M. Kramer (eds.), *Research in Organizational Behavior*, Vol. 24. New York: Elsevier, 139–80.

ADLER, P. and ADLER, P. (1989). 'The Gloried Self: The Aggrandizement and the Construction of Self.' *Social Psychological Quarterly*, 52: 299–310.

ASHFORTH, B. and HUMPHREY, R. (1997). 'The Ubiquity and Potency of Labeling in Organizations.' *Organization Science*, 8: 43–58.

BAUMARD, P. (1999). *Tacit Knowledge in Organizations*. London: Sage.

CLARK, K. B. and FUJIMOTO, T. (1991). *Product Development Performance: Strategy, Organization and Management in the World Auto Industry*. Boston, MA: Harvard Business School Press.

DIMAGGIO P. J. and POWELL W. W. (1983) 'The Iron Cage Revisited: Institutional, Isomorphism and Collective Rationality in Organizational Fields.' *American Sociological Review*, 48/5: 147–60.

CROSSAN, M., CUNHA, M. P. and VERA, D. (2005). 'Time and Organizational Improvisation.' *Academy of Management Review*, 30/1: 129–45.

FISCHHOFF, B. (1975). 'Hindsight Does Not Equal Foresight: The Effect of Outcome Knowledge on Judgment Under Uncertainty.' *Journal of Experimental Psychology: Human Perception and Performance*, 1: 288–99.

FOMBRUN, C. (1996). *Reputation: Realizing Value from the Corporate Image*. Cambridge, MA: Harvard Business School Press.

GOFFMAN, E. (1974). *Frame Analysis: An Essay on the Organization of Experience*. Boston, MA: Northeastern University Press.

GOLEMAN, D. (1985). *Vital Lies, Simple Truths: The Psychology of Self-Deception*. New York: Simon and Schuster.

GAMSON, J. (1994). *Claims to Fame: Celebrity in Contemporary America*. Berkeley, CA: University of California Press.

GIDDENS, A. (1976). *New Rules of Sociological Method: A Positive Critique of Interpretative Sociologies*. Cambridge, UK: Polity Press.

HEDBERG, B. (1981). 'How Organizations Learn and Unlearn,' in P. Nystrom and W. H. Starbuck (eds.), *Handbook of Organizational Design*. New York: Oxford University Press, 1–27.

HENDRY, J. (2000). 'Strategic Decision Making, Discourse, and Strategy as Social Practice.' *Journal of Management Studies*, 37/7: 955–77.

KUBANY, E. S. and WATSON, S. B. (2003). 'Guilt: Elaboration of a Multidimensional Model.' *The Psychological Record*, 53: 51–90.

LIPPMAN, S. A. and RUMELT, R. (1982). 'Uncertain Imitability: An Analysis of Interfirm Differences in Efficiency Under Competition.' *Bell Journal of Economics*, 13: 418–38.

LOUNSBURY, M. and GLYNN, M. A. (2001). 'Cultural Entrepreneurship: Stories, Legitimacy and the Acquisition of Resources.' *Strategic Management Journal*, 22: 545–64.

MARCH, J. G. and OLSEN, J. P. (eds.) (1976). *Ambiguity and Choice in Organizations*. Bergen: Universitetsforlaget.

MEYER, J. and ROWAN, B. (1977). 'Institutionalized Organizations: Formal Structure as Myth and Ceremony.' *American Journal of Sociology*, 80: 340–63.

MEYER J. W. and SCOTT, W. R. (1983). *Organizational Environments: Ritual and rationality*. Beverly Hills, CA: Sage Publications.

MINTZBERG, H. and WATERS, J. (1990). 'Does Decision Get in the Way?' *Organization Studies*, 11/1: 1–6.

NYSTROM, P. C. and STARBUCK, W. H. (1984). 'Organizational Façades.' *Academy of Management*, Proceedings of the Annual Meeting, Boston, MA: 182–5.

PFEFFER J. and SALANCIK, R. S. (1978). *The External Control of Organizations: A Resource Dependency Perspective*. New York: Harper and Row.

POWELL, T. C., LOVALLO, D., and CARINGAL, C. (2006). 'Causal Ambiguity, Management Perception, and Firm Performance.' *Academy of Management Review*, 31/1: 175–96.

RAO, H. (1994). 'The Social Construction of Reputation: Certification Contests, Legitimation, and the Survival of Organizations in the American Automobile Industry.' *Strategic Management Journal*, 1: 29–44.

RINDOVA, V. P., POLLOCK, T. G., and HAYWARD, M. L. (2006). 'Celebrity Firms: The Social Construction of Market Popularity.' *Academy of Management Review*, 31/1: 50–71.

ROBERTS, L. M. (2005). 'Changing Faces: Professional Image Construction In Diverse Organizational Settings.' *Academy of Management Review*, 30/4: 685–711.

SAPOLSKY, H. M. (1972). *The Polaris System Development*. Cambridge, MA: Harvard University Press.

SILLINCE, J. A. A. (2005). 'A Contingency Theory of Rhetorical Congruence.' *Academy of Management Review*, 30/3: 608–21.

SOBEK, D. K., WARD, A. C., and LIKER, J. K. (1999). 'Toyota's Principles of Set-Based Concurrent Engineering.' *Sloan Management Review*, Winter: 67–83.

SMIRCICH, L. (1983). 'Organizations as Shared Meanings,' in L. R. Pondy, P. J. Frost, G. Morgan, and T. C. Dandridge (eds.), *Organizational Symbolism*. Greenwich, CT: JAI, 56–65.

STAJKOVIC, A. D. and SOMMER, S. M. (2000). 'Self-Efficacy and Causal Attribution: Direct and Reciprocal Links.' *Journal of Applied Social Psychology*, 30: 707–37.

STARBUCK, W. H. (1992). 'Strategizing in the Real World.' *International Journal of Technology Management*, Special Publication on Technological Foundations of Strategic Management, 8/1–2: 77–85.

—— Mezias, J. (2003). 'Studying the Accuracy of Managers' Perceptions: A Research Odyssey.' *British Journal of Management*, 14/1: 3–17.

—— HEDBERG, B., and NYSTROM, P. C. (1976). 'Camping on Seesaws: Prescriptions for a Self-Designing Organization.' *Administrative Science Quarterly*, 21: 41–65.

SUCHMAN, M. A. (1995). 'Managing Legitimacy: Strategic and Institutional Approaches.' *Academy of Management Review*, 20/3: 571–610.

WEICK, K. E. (1993). 'The Collapse of Sensemaking in Organizations: The Mann Gulch Disaster.' *Administrative Science Quarterly*, 38/4: 628–52.

ZBARACKI, M. J. (1998). 'The Rhetoric and Reality of Total Quality Management.' *Administrative Science Quarterly*, 43: 602–36.

PART V

TOWARD MORE EFFECTIVE DECISION MAKING

24

TEACHING DECISION MAKING

GERALD F. SMITH

INTRODUCTION

How should business schools help students—undergraduate and MBA—become effective decision makers? What should they teach in decision-making courses and elsewhere, and how should they teach it? The many business schools that offer courses on decision making or claim that their programs develop decision-making skills assume that these questions have been answered. Several considerations challenge those assumptions:

- Along with critical thinking, problem solving, and creativity, decision making is a form of higher order thought. Resistant to theoretical understanding (Fodor 1983), higher order thinking is also hard to teach (Nickerson et al. 1985; Perkins 1995).
- Like other forms of higher order thought, decision making resists crisp conceptualization. Competing accounts of what decision making involves are legion. Management educators cannot claim to teach decision making if they do not agree on what it is.
- Proponents of decision technologies admit that there is scant evidence of the effectiveness of formal techniques (Edwards 1984). If we do not know the methods work, we cannot assume that teaching them promotes effective decision making.

Management educators base their efforts to teach decision making on two arguments: normative and descriptive. The normative argument holds that there are universal principles of rational choice underlying formal methods managers can learn and apply. Its descriptive counterpart contends that empirical research has identified effective and ineffective decision practices managers can learn to emulate or avoid.

Though each approach has legitimacy, there are serious limitations. Normative rules are often not useful in practice since they pass the problems by, leave key challenges unaddressed. The descriptive strategy has an overabundance of material that could be taught. While there are many plausible accounts of decision making, researchers have not identified a useful, empirically validated "right way" of making choices.

This chapter provides a comprehensive account of the teaching of decision making that highlights the educational implications of alternative views of organizational choice

A THOUGHTLESS DICHOTOMY

In the early 1980s, while pursuing a PhD in decision sciences, I learned that there were two ways of making choices: one could rely on "gut feel" intuitions or employ techniques based on the "rational model" developed by decision scientists. Though some might regard this as a meaningful choice, for graduate students in the decision sciences, it was a "no-brainer": Rational methods were the only way to go. Indeed, intuition seemed something of a "straw man," the disreputable refuge of those who, for want of proper training, had no better way of making choices. Since then, skepticism about rational methods has grown and a more formidable notion of intuition has emerged. As a result, the original dichotomy now contains two viable alternatives. However, they share a limitation that impairs their educational value: neither provides much room in the decision-making process for reflective thought.

THE RATIONAL MODEL

The most highly developed account of decision making goes by many names—the normative model, decision theory, utility theory, and variations thereof. Despite the misleading implication that other ways of making decisions are not rational, the approach is herein termed the "rational model," highlighting its connections to economic theories of choice. Unlike most other perspectives on decision making, the rational model features formal theories and techniques—expected utility theory (von Neumann and Morgenstern 1947), multiattribute utility theory (Keeney and Raiffa 1993), social judgment theory (Brehmer and Joyce 1988), and Bayesian inferential methods (Edwards et al. 1963), among others. It is best known to students and practitioners through decision analysis and decision trees.

The rational model presents a simple conceptualization: decision making is a matter of choosing from among a set of alternatives. Alternatives lead to outcomes that can be evaluated in terms of individual preferences. Contingencies—uncertain events or states of nature—may mediate paths from alternatives to outcomes, so an alternative can lead to various outcomes. Rational decision makers select alternatives that maximize their expected preference satisfaction. They judgmentally evaluate outcomes in terms of preferences and assess probabilities regarding contingencies (Hastie and Dawes 2001). Though doubts have been raised about the model's descriptive validity—people do not always (often?) behave this way (Shafir and LeBoeuf 2002)—proponents insist that it is a normative standard: to be rational, decision makers must follow these rules.

Rational model researchers have translated its principles into practical tools and prescriptions, producing decision technologies (von Winterfeldt and Edwards 1986; Edwards and Fasolo 2001) that have met with some applicational success. Texts on quantitative decision methods teach students how to construct decision trees and influence diagrams, assess subjective probabilities and utilities, compute the value of information, and conduct multiattribute utility analyses (e.g., Clemen and Reilly 2001). Of comparable educational significance are principles that inform the model—for instance, the distinction between beliefs and values, using probabilities to represent uncertainty. Programs that teach decision making to adolescents highlight these principles (Baron and Brown 1991).

There are, however, difficulties with this view of decision making. Since the 1940s, critics, led by Herbert Simon (1955), have argued that the model's account is unrealistic, especially in organizational settings. Descriptive researchers have found persistent behavioral violations of rational norms (Einhorn and Hogarth 1981). Evidence that preferences are constructed on the fly (Payne et al. 1992) threatens the model's claim that people have stable preference structures. The discovery that probability judgments are often biased (Kahneman et al. 1982) refuted the assumption that people reliably generate epistemically valid subjective probabilities. These difficulties contribute to a "rationality critique" challenging the model's claims about rational behavior (Shafir and LeBoeuf 2002).

Doubts also exist about the effectiveness of model-based prescriptions. Decision analytic techniques are choice-centric, providing little support for other stages of the decision-making process. They assume that choices are preference driven, whereas managerial decisions usually involve factors—considerations of fairness or precedent, for instance—that are not matters of preference. Most managerial choices—say, deciding which corporate strategy to adopt—are based on an alternative's effectiveness in achieving organizational goals. Preferences are not informative in such cases; liking a strategy does not indicate that it will work.

Since objective probabilities are rarely available in practical contexts, decision analysts use subjective Bayesian probabilities—someone's "degree of belief"—as measures of uncertainty. This undermines the validity of their conclusions. For computational reasons, analysts assume that only a few contingencies affect the outcome of a choice (Behn and Vaupel 1982). In typical organizational decisions, however, uncertainty is diffuse rather than concentrated, there being numerous circumstances and events, some almost unanticipatable, that could decisively influence outcomes.

Formal methods also assume that relatively few attributes of alternatives determine individual preferences, these attributes being common across alternatives and identifiable in the abstract. In reality, we value complex alternatives for many reasons, some so idiosyncratic they can only be identified when that alternative is directly encountered. As a result of these limitations, formal decision methods are "question-begging": they take one through a procedure that seems impressive because it glosses over the "hard stuff"—defining problems, generating alternatives, identifying relevant values and contingencies, predicting outcomes.

For decades managers trained in decision analytic methods declined to use them (Grayson 1973), provoking decision theorists to lament their irrationality. Increasingly, however, proponents of rational methods are recognizing that, except in special circumstances, decision analytic techniques are not useful. Arguably, the most that the teaching of decision making can take from the rational model are a few principles and its conceptual framework, encapsulated in a decision tree.

INTUITION

Once viewed as a third-rate alternative to rational methods, intuition has experienced a boom in popularity and perceived legitimacy. Mass market books (Klein 2003; Gladwell 2005) tout it as a decision-making resource. Proponents of intuition cite research on expertise and implicit learning which indicates that people often possess knowledge they can apply without conscious thought. But while the "intuition boom" has brought attention to mental capacities that might otherwise be underemployed, problems arise because intuition is difficult to define and detect: what is it and how do we know when someone has it? Different notions of intuition co-exist, few of which can be reliably identified. Since most accounts regard it as a highly personalized capacity, different people can have intuitions about different things.

Intuition has been defined as a capacity for direct knowledge or immediate insight that results from subconscious mental activity (Myers 2002; Miller and Ireland 2005). Intuitive insights occur rapidly, effortlessly, unlike the hard earned results of deliberation. A back of the head mental coin toss can produce quick decisions, but these are not intuitions if pertinent subconscious processing and knowledge is not involved.

Admitting the existence of intuition, the question becomes: how can people have valid intuitions? For many cognitive scientists, the most plausible source of intuition is past experience. Endorsed by Simon (1987), this account conceives intuition as knowledge accumulated unconsciously through experience with numerous cases. Such intuitions are evidence of expertise in a domain and the basis for the fluency of expert performance.

Lieberman (2000) argued that intuition is tacit or unconsciously held knowledge acquired through implicit learning. The latter—our ability to acquire knowledge without being aware we are doing so—has been documented by psychological research. Intuition has also been associated with pattern recognition, perception, and the emotional/affective side of cognition. The common thread in such accounts is non-symbolic processing: intuition reflects knowledge that is not expressed in words or symbols and that people acquire through perceptual and other non-symbolic mental processes (Sadler-Smith and Shefy 2004).

A final perspective regards intuition as instinct, a species-specific genetic endowment. People may be instinctually afraid of snakes, and an innate "language instinct" (Pinker 1994) provides reliable intuitions about natural language grammars. Such intuitions are likely to be consistent across cultures. Formed in the "environment of evolutionary adaptation" (Barkow et al. 1992), instinct-based intuitions would not be useful in many modern decision tasks—for instance, picking stocks.

Each account suggests circumstances in which people are likely to have reliable intuitions—for instance, highly repetitive situations, instances where visual information outweighs symbolic data, and when we have natural instincts. Educationally, however, intuitive decision making has limited potential. The most common prescription—"listen to your inner voice"—encourages people to use intuitions they may not have. Can education help decision makers develop intuitive powers? Klein (2003) encouraged people to strengthen their experience base. Hogarth (2001) proposed seven "guidelines for educating intuition." Many of these prescriptions lack operationality and power: People cannot reliably do what is asked of them, and even if they do, results may not be forthcoming. Will acknowledging emotions and exploring connections, as Hogarth advises, develop intuition? Since intuition building advice necessarily involves reflective thought—one must consciously follow the prescription—it is not clear if the advice builds intuition or simply develops one's capacity for deliberation.

Moreover, educators cannot implement these prescriptions in practical teaching contexts. Managers may not be able to select and/or create their environments—one of Hogarth's guidelines for developing intuition. Students and teachers certainly cannot, since intuitions accrue from experiences that cannot be replicated in classrooms. Most intuitions pertaining to management are industry, company, or position specific, not general enough to justify inclusion in a course of study. Insofar as intuition draws on perceptual processing, pattern recognition, and affective responses, courses that are dominated by textual material cannot address them.

What should management educators teach students about intuition? We can make students aware of the sources of legitimate intuitions—repeated experiences, especially with non-verbal stimuli and basic human instincts. Understanding intuition, students will be less likely to fall for bogus "gut feels." They will learn that intuition, like rational technique, plays a limited role in thoughtful decision processes.

Decision Making as Reflective Thought

The dichotomous, rational model vs. intuition, view of decision making has been reinforced by dual process theories of the human mind (Evans and Over 1996; Sloman 1996; Stanovich 1999; Kahneman 2003). These suggest that people can make decisions using an unconscious, affective, association driven, processing mode (system 1) or through a logical, analytical, rule-based process (system 2) that is consciously controlled. Each processing mode is suited for certain kinds of situations. Mistakes result when people adopt the wrong approach—for instance, relying on system 1 intuitions in situations where system 2 rationality is required.

There is growing support for dual processing theories, but even if the existence of two mental systems was established, it would not justify the aforementioned decision-making dichotomy. On the one hand, theorists have conceived intuition too broadly, to include all decisions not made through formal analysis. Doing so fails to differentiate legitimate intuitions from decisions made by habit, random selection, and other essentially mindless mechanisms. Even more seriously, rationality has been construed too narrowly in terms of deductive logic and utility maximization. This conceptualization overlooks the rich array of reflective thinking practices we use to make choices in our personal and professional lives.

This section develops a broader account of decision-making rationality, one that does justice to our capacity for reflective thought. This capacity forms a middle ground between intuition and formal analysis, as depicted in Figure 24.1. The figure's bell-like curve denotes a distribution of practical decision situations, suggesting that few can be successfully addressed by pure intuition or formal methods. The large majority of choices require that people think intelligently about the situation at hand. Such thinking is not part of the rational model, which instead employs a formal calculative procedure. It is not encouraged by proponents of intuition, who rely on effortless insights. Arguably, however, the capacity for reflective thought is a decision maker's most valuable resource.

This view of decision making has the most useful educational content. Scholars and practitioners have developed a vast, but diffuse, body of knowledge in trying to understand the thinking performed as part of decision making. Figure 24.1 suggests five significant ways in which this perspective reaches beyond the rational model–intuition dichotomy. The remainder of this section develops these themes.

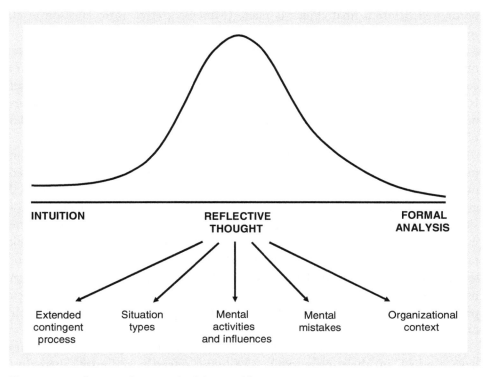

Figure 24.1 Perspectives on decision making.

EXTENDED CONTINGENT PROCESS

Textbook discussions depict the decision-making process as a set of steps or stages. According to these models, decision making consists of tasks or functions performed in order, beginning with problem identification and concluding with post-implementation feedback and control. These are *functional models* of decision making. Similar models have been proposed for problem solving. Some scholars contend that problem solving is part of the larger decision-making process; others view decision making as the back end of the problem-solving process (Smith 1988).

Only a few steps in the decision-making process have been studied in depth. Rational model researchers have focused on predicting outcomes and evaluating alternatives, the choice phase of the process. With rare exceptions—work on decision framing (Kahneman and Tversky 2000), occasional pieces on objective setting and alternative generation (Keller and Ho 1988; Keeney 1992)—decision research is choice-centric. This imbalance extends to texts and the teaching of decision making. Since little research has been done on non-choice activities, text authors have little to say about them. This is unfortunate since organizational decision-making researchers assert that the most consequential developments occur well before a final choice is made (Mintzberg et al. 1976; Hickson et al. 1986; Beach 1997).

Escaping the rational model's myopic view allows one to extend the decision-making process to include other tasks and to develop these into substantive components. Whether it is termed "decision making" or "problem solving," what is being referred to is action oriented thought, the thinking people do in determining how to act. This thinking is an intelligible process guided by heuristic rules of thumb.

Functional models provide a means of analyzing the process. Though decision makers may not perceive themselves as progressing through a series of steps when making choices (Lipshitz and Bar-Ilan 1996), most functions are conceptually well grounded. To initiate the decision-making process, one must recognize that a situation requires attention, thought, and action (problem identification). One must mentally represent or understand the situation (problem definition) to think productively about it. Researchers have paid little attention to these activities (but see Cowan 1986; Jackson and Dutton 1988; and Smith 1989). Yet students can learn useful things about them—for instance, the oft-confused relationship between problems and symptoms, and the danger of defining problems in terms of possible causes.

Some components of functional models are generic thinking tasks that scholars have studied in their own right. Creativity research addresses alternative generation. Diagnosis—determining a problem's causes—has been studied by medical researchers and psychologists interested in causal reasoning. Architects and engineers have developed knowledge of design, featured in Simon's (1977) famous intelligence–design–choice model of decision making. These literatures offer a wealth of material for courses on managerial decision making: concepts, such as different kinds of causes; principles, like the "least commitments" approach to design; heuristics, such as thinking about an abstract version of the problem when generating solution alternatives; and methods, of which there are hundreds for idea generation alone.

This more comprehensive view of the decision-making process highlights its contingency: different tasks or functions are performed in different situations. The process's front- and back-ends are largely immutable: one must always begin by identifying and defining the problem, and end by deciding what to do, implementing the chosen course of action, and using feedback to control the results. Between these endpoints, there is considerable process variability. Consider diagnosis, the task of determining a problem's causes. In some situations—a production line is producing defective outputs—diagnosis is the key mental challenge. In others—hiring a new employee—diagnosis is not required.

Contingency models of decision making are not new. Beach and Mitchell (1978) proposed that the selection of decision strategies, involving the use of formal aids and analytical or non-analytical thinking, depends on characteristics of the problem, the environment, and the decision maker. Payne (1982) discussed research that found decision behavior to be contingent on task and context effects. However, these models posit variability *within* rather than *of* functions. The latter, more radical, contingency implies that standard, one-size-fits-all models of decision making are fundamentally inadequate. Functional models must have the flexibility to make decision processes, defined in terms of functions, contingent on situation or problem types. The next section develops this issue.

Viewing decision making as an extended contingent process has the following educational implications:

- Rather than focusing on evaluation, educators can attend to other parts of the process.
- Tasks that are not always required but which are sometimes critical (e.g., diagnosis) receive attention.
- The inadequacy of standard, one-size-fits-all, functional models is made apparent. Decision makers must tailor their thinking to the situation.
- Scholars can develop knowledge of tasks like problem identification, definition, diagnosis, design, and alternative generation, or borrow it from other disciplines.
- Much of this knowledge—concepts, principles, heuristics, and methods—is teachable.

SITUATION TYPES

Research has shown that situation types play an important role in the decision-making/problem-solving behaviors of experts (Chi et al. 1982). Practitioners use informal, similarity-based, categorization schemes developed through personal experience to make quick "recognition-primed" decisions (Klein 1998). Alternatively, they learn domain specific taxonomies as part of their professional training. Law students distinguish criminal from civil cases. Medical students learn extensive disease taxonomies when developing diagnostic skills (Pople 1982).

Management lags behind other fields in this regard, in part because organizational problems are so diverse (Smith 1995). Presumably, some managers have informal, experience-based, classification schemes specific to their positions. However, scholars have yet to devise a widely accepted taxonomy of managerial problems. Though distinctions among situation types have been made, proposed ways of characterizing managerial problems are not useful. Consider:

- The rational model of decision making differentiates conditions of certainty, risk, and uncertainty. Focused on the predictability of outcomes, this scheme is too narrow.
- Scholars commonly describe problems as being structured or unstructured. Unfortunately, most managerial problems are unstructured and knowing this does not help one solve them.
- Other binary distinctions—strategic vs. operating problems (Brightman 1978) or human vs. technical problems (Cowan 1988)—lack discriminating power and practical utility.
- Researchers (Mintzberg et al. 1976; Nutt 1984) have used "evoking stimuli" to differentiate organizational decision situations into problems, opportunities, and crises. But is a manager's thinking affected by whether a situation is a sales problem, a sales crisis, or an opportunity to increase sales?
- More elaborate problem taxonomies have been proposed (Nadler 1983; Cowan 1990), though none has been widely adopted.

These categorization schemes do not highlight situation characteristics with strong problem-solving implications; knowing you face such-and-such a problem does not tell you how to solve it. As noted earlier, contingency models of decision making presume an ability to differentiate situations in ways that evoke significantly different mental responses. The typologies found in the literature cannot do this. Von Winterfeldt (1980) suggested a more promising direction in a paper that identified facility siting, contingency planning, budget allocation, and regulation as "prototypical decision structures." These categories reflect the underlying nature of the situation. Similarly, practitioners talk about investment, hiring, and make vs. buy decisions. Problems in such categories pose certain challenges, call for certain information, and require certain analyses.

One can differentiate several basic situation types, each having clear problem-solving implications. Though not exhaustive, these types encompass a large portion of the situations encountered by managers.

- *Decision problems.* These are true decision situations that center on a choice. Consumer purchasing decisions are an example. Predicting and evaluating outcomes are key mental challenges. The rational model targets decision problems.
- *Performance problems.* Performance problems are "situations in which an existing system is not performing acceptably" (Smith 1998: 8). A manufacturing process is producing defective outputs; a company is not generating enough revenue because of "sales system" deficiencies. Characteristic of performance problems is the need for diagnosis to determine the causes of the performance shortfall.
- *Design problems.* Design problems require one to create an artifact as the problem's solution. Routinely encountered by architects and engineers, design problems are prominent in organizational life: managers design organizations, business processes, and programs; they are involved in the design of new products and information systems.
- *Negotiation problems.* In these situations, two or more parties are in a state of conflict, disagreement, or possible exchange, and can benefit by reaching an agreement. The topic of considerable research and practical advice (Fisher and Ury 1981; Raiffa 1982), negotiation involves bargaining, coalition formation, and other behavioral dynamics.

Again, this taxonomy is not exhaustive. Many organizational problems cannot be assigned to any of the four categories. Furthermore, some situations have multiple components of different types, so a problem can belong to more than one category.

This categorization scheme possesses the characteristic lacking in other accounts of organizational problems: The types it defines have strong problem-solving implications. Different concepts, heuristics, and techniques pertain to each category. Managers and students can learn these problem types and the knowledge used to address them. Organizing decision-making courses around them would help management education progress along the path followed by medicine and other professional practices.

MENTAL ACTIVITIES

Though decision making can be understood in functional terms, it takes place and can be described at the level of basic mental activities. Intuitive decision making happens so quickly and unconsciously that there is little mental processing to describe. The rational model makes room for conscious thought, but conceives it as purely judgmental. For some time, decision theorists believed this judgmental processing was non-problematic. In the 1970s, "heuristics and biases" research (Kahneman et al. 1982) shattered their complacency, demonstrating that judgmental conclusions can be distorted by people's use of heuristic mental shortcuts. The next section discusses the errors that result. "Heuristics and biases" research is important for present purposes because it aroused interest in the mental side of decision making, suggesting the existence of richer cognitive processes than had been assumed.

Early descriptive research on decision making challenged rational model assumptions (Simon 1955). Subsequent research has shown that problem definition, understanding the situation, is more important than the rational model acknowledges (Isenberg 1984); that decision criteria come to light as alternatives are generated rather than being fully prespecified (Alexander 1979); and that favored alternatives emerge early in a process in which prechoice screening reduces the significance of the final selection phase (Soelberg 1967; Beach 1993; Brownstein 2003). Gigerenzer et al. (1999) identified powerful heuristics like "take the best" that outperform rational methods by exploiting evolved human capacities and environmental structures. Though people often use such heuristics instinctively, they can learn to employ them deliberately on appropriate occasions.

Scholars have proposed other ways, besides judgment, of understanding the thinking performed as part of making decisions. Several perspectives are especially noteworthy:

- *Analogy.* On this account, decisions makers recall past cases that are similar to the current situation (Gilboa and Schmeidler 2001; Gavetti and Rivkin 2005). Courses of action that worked before will be reused or adjusted to fit current needs.
- *Narrative.* This perspective was launched by Pennington and Hastie's (1986) studies of juror decision making, which found that, rather than computing probabilities concerning defendants' guilt, jurors construct stories regarding criminal events and base verdicts on the plausibility of competing narratives. When selecting courses of action, managers might conceive story-like scenarios regarding customer, competitor, and employee responses.
- *Reasoning and Argumentation.* Several scholars have highlighted the role of reasoning in decision making (Shafir et al. 1993; Melone 1994). Unlike judgment, reasoning is an overt verbal way of reaching conclusions. This makes it important in organizational contexts where arguments must persuade executives to authorize courses of action (Garvin and Roberto 2001).

Another source of enrichment is research that has identified psychological influences on decision making. One source of influence—durable mental traits or dispositions—has been conceived in terms of individual "cognitive styles" (Hayes and Allinson 1994). These are habitual ways of thinking—say, being intuitive vs. systematic (McKenney and Keen 1974)—that may reflect innate individual differences. The innateness or durability of individual thinking styles limits the educational potential of this perspective and related research on "decision styles" (Rowe and Mason 1987; Scott and Bruce 1995). Other work on psychological influences has greater educational promise. Argyris (1976, 1991) cited managers' unwillingness to question fundamental value assumptions that frame the decisions they make. He highlighted social dynamics—defensiveness and projecting blame onto others—common in organizational contexts. This research identifies emotional and motivational influences that transform "cool rationality" into "hot cognition" (Nisbett and Ross 1980).

The safest conclusion to be drawn from descriptive studies is that there is no single decision-making (or problem-solving) process. Mental activities vary enormously across individuals and situations/tasks. Decision makers employ a variety of mental resources, not just judgment. Notably, they reason, an overt cognitive process that is amenable to conscious monitoring and control. Finally, decision making is shaped by powerful, non-cognitive influences, including personality, unconscious motives, and emotions.

This enriched view of the mental depths of decision making has significant educational implications. The prominent role of reasoning in the process suggests that business schools teach critical thinking skills. Managers must know how to develop sound arguments supporting intended courses of action and how to recognize weak ones. Research on argumentation in organizations may contribute to this effort (Huff 1990; Sillince 2002). Though it is not easy to "cleanse" decision makers of irrational emotions and motivations, people can develop self-monitoring skills that increase their awareness of such influences, awareness being the first step towards control. Finally, educators can foster "cognitive virtues" like mental flexibility, clarity, depth, soundness, and open-mindedness. These mental habits are responsible for much of the performance difference between good and bad thinkers (Perkins 1995; Ennis 1996).

MENTAL MISTAKES

Although decision scientists have not developed a powerful, general decision-making method, they have compiled an extensive list of mistakes to avoid. Mental errors have been the primary focus of decision research for over 30 years, since Tversky and Kahneman launched the "heuristics and biases" paradigm. As originally conceived, this explanatory scheme—people take mental shortcuts that can lead to mistaken conclusions—was applied almost exclusively to tasks involving predictions and estimations of likelihood. Thus, using the availability heuristic, people overestimate the likelihood of dramatic causes of death (e.g., homicide) because their instances receive more publicity and consequently are easier to recall.

However, studies revealed shortcomings that do not fit under the "heuristics and biases" umbrella and that affect a broader range of mental tasks. The illusion of control (Langer 1975) probably results from culturally derived assumptions about how much influence people have over events. An aversion to waste may dispose people to factor sunk costs into decisions that, logically, they should not affect (Arkes and Blumer 1985). In some cases—neglect of regression effects, for instance—mistakes are made because everyday experience does not reliably teach people the correct way of thinking.

Though decision researchers seem unaware of it, the study of mental errors traces back to classical Greece and Rome. Those cultures identified reasoning mistakes, subsequently called "fallacies of informal logic." If decision making includes reasoning, its instruction should address related errors. Some connect to the "heuristics and biases" paradigm. For instance, use of the representativeness heuristic, an overreliance on similarity, can lead to the fallacy of false analogy. Corporate executives made this mistake when they justified an acquisition by arguing that a company, like a stool, needs at least three legs to be stable (Duhaime and Schwenk 1985). Other reasoning mistakes are cited in works on scientific methodology (Cook and Campbell 1979). Researchers are warned against the fallacy of hasty generalization, basing conclusions on small or biased samples; they learn about erroneous attributions of causality, the fallacy of false cause; and they are taught that hypotheses and other claims should be falsifiable, subject to disproof. The teaching of decision making should address reasoning errors discussed in courses on critical thinking—the genetic fallacy, appeal to tradition, false dilemma, slippery slope, begging the question, and appeal to ignorance, among others (Engel 1976).

Attempts to prevent mistakes through "de-biasing" training have yielded mixed results (Larrick 2004). Instruction in statistical thinking reduces individuals' susceptibility to certain errors—for instance, neglect of regression effects (Fong et al. 1986). Training to reduce hindsight bias and overconfidence has not been successful (Fischhoff 1982). De-biasing's effectiveness may depend on how deeply the relevant error is rooted: mistakes involving unconscious mental processes are difficult to overcome (Arkes 1991). Reasoning errors are susceptible to remediation since reasoning is a consciously controlled mental process. With many errors, the most that can be done is to make people aware of the mistake and the situations in which it usually occurs. Thus, managers can be cautioned not to "escalate commitment" in investment situations when, to save face, they are tempted to "throw good money after bad."

ORGANIZATIONAL CONTEXT

Challenges to the rational model's account of organizational decision making were led by Herbert Simon and his Carnegie School colleagues, who developed decision-centered organization theories that highlight the ways organizations deal with uncertainty (March and Simon 1958; Cyert and March 1963). Lindblom (1959) argued that, not knowing how courses of action will turn out, managers "muddle through" by selecting alternatives that make modest, incremental changes from the status quo. Incomplete information fosters a tentative, trial and error approach to decision making that pursues goals adaptively, what Etzioni (1989) calls "mixed scanning."

Other factors, less prominent in individual choice, shape organizational decision making:

- *Politics.* Organizations are political arenas in which conflicts are resolved, in part, through the exercise of power. Influential parties may choose a preferred course of action whether or not it is best for the organization.
- *History.* The past is a source of precedents that constrain decision makers and of lessons they can learn.
- *Policies and Procedures.* Rather than working through a detailed decision process whenever something must be done, organizations devise policies, procedures, and other devices that specify default courses of action. These are part of the organization's culture, "the way we do things around here" (Schein 1985).

These factors spawn decision processes that deviate wildly from the rational norm. The "garbage can" model of organizational choice postulates a world in which organizational actors have "solutions"—actions they would like to take—and are looking for "problems"—situations that justify the action (Cohen et al. 1972). For some, the notion of "decision" loses meaning when organizations take action without deliberative choice (Langley et al. 1995).

Teams or managers relying on group inputs increasingly make organizational decisions. Since organizational choice is often a group process, participants must understand group dynamics. Managers must be aware of group process dysfunctions, "group-think" (Janis 1982) being the most famous. They should also know how to select the decision making approach—individual, group, or other—to employ in particular circumstances. The Vroom–Jago model (Vroom and Jago 1988) provides useful guidelines.

Managerial decision-making texts and courses should include organizational context issues. Realistic cases make students aware of the effects of power, precedent, and procedures on decision outcomes. Students should understand the pitfalls of group decision making and when to employ individual or group processes.

CONCLUSIONS

This chapter has identified a substantial body of material educators can use to teach decision making. Much of this content consists of concepts, heuristics, and methods pertaining to particular functional parts (e.g., problem definition, diagnosis) of the decision-making process. Another major component is material on mental errors. Educators could incorporate this content into almost any course on decision making, presumably as a substitute for decision analytic techniques. Doing so would transform the teaching of decision making from instruction in impractical quantitative methods into the teaching of action oriented thought, how to think effectively about organizational problems.

In addition to being more relevant to practical needs, moving decision-making instruction away from the rational model has another benefit. While that model, in principle, allows decision makers to maximize any value or objective, it aligns with and tends to support decision practices that maximize profit and easily assessed personal preferences. The rational model is consanguineous with narrow profit maximization messages communicated to students in finance and economics courses, messages that dismiss corporate ethics and social responsibility (Emiliani 2004). The view of decision making presented herein is less vulnerable to this. By highlighting the group and organizational context, and by recognizing the influence of personality, emotions, and unconscious motivations, this account acknowledges that decisions are and should be about more than the maximization of profits or personal preferences. It readily accommodates concerns about ethics, social norms, and social welfare in prechoice deliberations. If educators teach decision making from this perspective, their students will acquire more useful thinking skills and will be better prepared to address the non-economic dimensions of organizational issues.

REFERENCES

ALEXANDER, E. R. (1979). 'The Design of Alternatives in Organizational Contexts: A Pilot Study.' *Administrative Science Quarterly*, 24: 382–404.

ARGYRIS, C. (1976). 'Single-Loop and Double-Loop Models in Research on Decision Making.' *Administrative Science Quarterly*, 21: 363–75.

—— (1991). 'Teaching Smart People How to Learn.' *Harvard Business Review*, May–June: 99–109.

ARKES, H. R. (1991). 'Costs and Benefits of Judgment Errors: Implications for Debiasing.' *Psychological Bulletin*, 110: 486–98.

—— BLUMER, C. (1985). 'The Psychology of Sunk Cost.' *Organizational Behavior and Human Decision Processes*, 35: 124–40.

BARKOW, J. H., COSMIDES, L., and TOOBY, J. (eds.) (1992). *The Adapted Mind: Evolutionary Psychology and the Generation of Culture*. New York: Oxford University Press.

BARON, J. and BROWN, R. V. (eds.) (1991). *Teaching Decision Making to Adolescents*. Hillsdale, NJ: Lawrence Erlbaum Associates.

BEACH, L. R. (1993). 'Broadening the Definition of Decision Making: The Role of Prechoice Screening of Options.' *Psychological Science*, 4: 215–20.

—— (1997). *The Psychology of Decision Making: People in Organizations*. Thousand Oaks, CA: Sage.

—— MITCHELL, T. R. (1978). 'A Contingency Model for the Selection of Decision Strategies.' *Academy of Management Review*, 3: 439–49.

BEHN, R. D. and VAUPEL, J. W. (1982). *Quick Analysis for Busy Decision Makers*. New York: Basic Books.

BREHMER, B. and JOYCE, C. R. B. (eds.) (1988). *Human Judgment: The SJT View*. Amsterdam: North-Holland Elsevier.

BRIGHTMAN, H. J. (1978). 'Differences in Ill-Structured Problem Solving Along the Organizational Hierarchy.' *Decision Sciences*, 9: 1–18.

BROWNSTEIN, A. L. (2003). 'Biased Predecision Processing.' *Psychological Bulletin*, 129: 545–68.

CHI, M. T. H., GLASER, R., and REES, E. (1982). 'Expertise in Problem Solving,' in R. J. Sternberg (ed.), *Advances in the Psychology of Human Intelligence*, Vol. 1. Hillsdale, NJ: Lawrence Erlbaum Associates, 7–75.

CLEMEN, R. T. and REILLY, T. (2001). *Making Hard Decisions with Decision Tools*. Pacific Grove, CA: Duxbury.

COHEN, M. D., MARCH, J. G., and OLSEN, J. P. (1972). 'A Garbage Can Model of Organizational Choice.' *Administrative Science Quarterly*, 17: 1–25.

COOK, T. D. and CAMPBELL, D. T. (1979). *Quasi-Experimentation: Design and Analysis Issues for Field Settings*. Boston, MA: Houghton Mifflin.

COWAN, D. A. (1986). 'Developing a Process Model of Problem Recognition.' *Academy of Management Review*, 11: 763–76.

—— (1988). ''Executives' Knowledge of Organizational Problem Types: Applying a Contingency Perspective.' *Journal of Management*, 14: 513–27.

—— (1990). 'Developing a Classification Structure of Organizational Problems: An Empirical Investigation.' *Academy of Management Journal*, 33: 366–90.

CYERT, R. M. and MARCH, J. G. (1963). *A Behavioral Theory of the Firm*. Englewood Cliffs, NJ: Prentice-Hall.

DUHAIME, I. M. and SCHWENK, C. R. (1985). 'Conjectures on Cognitive Simplification in Acquisition and Divestment Decision Making.' *Academy of Management Review*, 10: 287–95.

EDWARDS, W. (1984). 'Decision Analysis: A Nonpsychological Psychotechnology,' in V. Sarris and A. Parducci (eds.), *Perspectives in Psychological Experimentation*. Hillsdale, NJ: Lawrence Erlbaum Associates, 341–53.

—— FASOLO, B. (2001). 'Decision Technology.' *Annual Review of Psychology*, 52: 581–606.

—— LINDMAN, H., and SAVAGE, L. J. (1963). 'Bayesian Statistical Inference for Psychological Research.' *Psychological Review*, 70: 193–242.

EINHORN, H. J. and HOGARTH, R. M. (1981). 'Behavioral Decision Theory: Processes of Judgment and Choice.' *Annual Review of Psychology*, 32: 53–88.

EMILIANI, M. L. (2004). 'Is Management Education Beneficial to Society?' *Management Decision*, 42: 481–98.

ENGEL, S. M. (1976). *With Good Reason*. New York: St Martin's Press.

ENNIS, R. H. (1996). 'Critical Thinking Dispositions: Their Nature and Assessability.' *Informal Logic*, 18: 165–82.

ETZIONI, A. (1989). 'Humble Decision Making.' *Harvard Business Review*, July–August: 122–6.

EVANS J. St., B. T. and OVER, D. E. (1996). *Rationality and Reasoning*. Hove: Psychology Press.

FISCHHOFF, B. (1982). 'Debiasing,' in D. Kahneman, P. Slovic, and A. Tversky (eds.), *Judgment Under Uncertainty: Heuristics and Biases*. Cambridge: Cambridge University Press, 422–44.

FISHER, R. and URY, W. (1981). *Getting to Yes*. Boston, MA: Houghton Mifflin.

FODOR, J. A. (1983). *The Modularity of Mind*. Cambridge, MA: MIT Press.

FONG, G. T., KRANTZ, D. H., and NISBETT, R. E. (1986). 'The Effects of Statistical Training on Thinking about Everyday Problems.' *Cognitive Psychology*, 18: 253–92.

GARVIN, D. A. and ROBERTO, M. A. (2001). 'What You Don't Know About Making Decisions.' *Harvard Business Review*, Sept: 108–16.

GAVETTI, G. and RIVKIN, J. W. (2005). 'How Strategists Really Think: Tapping the Power of Analogy.' *Harvard Business Review*, April: 54–63.

GIGERENZER, G., TODD, P. M., and the ABC Research Group (1999). *Simple Heuristics that Make Us Smart*. New York: Oxford University Press.

GILBOA, I. and SCHMEIDLER, D. (2001). *A Theory of Case-based Decisions*. Cambridge: Cambridge University Press.

GLADWELL, M. (2005). *Blink: The Power of Thinking without Thinking*. New York: Little, Brown.

GRAYSON, C. J., Jr., (1973). 'Management Science and Business Practice.' *Harvard Business Review*, July–August: 41–8.

HASTIE, R. and DAWES, R. M. (2001). *Rational Choice in an Uncertain World*. Thousand Oaks, CA: Sage.

HAYES, J. and ALLINSON, C. W. (1994). 'Cognitive Style and its Relevance for Management Practice.' *British Journal of Management*, 5: 53–71.

HICKSON, D. J., BUTLER, R. J., CRAY, D., MALLORY, G., and WILSON, D. (1986). *Top Decisions: Strategic Decision-Making in Organizations*. San Francisco, CA: Jossey-Bass.

HOGARTH, R. M. (2001). *Educating Intuition*. Chicago, IL: University of Chicago Press.

HUFF, A. S. (ed.) (1990). *Mapping Strategic Thought*. Chichester: John Wiley.

ISENBERG, D. J. (1984). 'How Senior Managers Think.' *Harvard Business Review*, November–December: 81–90.

JACKSON, S. E. and DUTTON, J. E. (1988). 'Discerning Threats and Opportunities.' *Administrative Science Quarterly*, 33: 370–87.

JANIS, I. L. (1982). *Groupthink: Psychological Studies of Policy Decisions and Fiascoes*. Boston, MA: Houghton Mifflin.

KAHNEMAN, D. (2003). 'A Perspective on Judgment and Choice: Mapping Bounded Rationality.' *American Psychologist*, 58: 697–720.

—— TVERSKY, A. (eds.) (2000). *Choices, Values, and Frames*. Cambridge: Cambridge University Press.

—— SLOVIC, P., and TVERSKY, A. (eds.) (1982). *Judgment Under Uncertainty: Heuristics and Biases*. Cambridge: Cambridge University Press.

KEENEY, R. L. (1992). *Value-Focused Thinking: A Path to Creative Decision-Making*. Cambridge, MA: Harvard University Press.

—— RAIFFA, H. (1993). *Decisions with Multiple Objectives*. Cambridge: Cambridge University Press.

KELLER, L. R. and HO, J. L. (1988). 'Decision Problem Structuring: Generating Options.' *IEEE Transactions on Systems, Man, and Cybernetics*, 18: 715–28.

KLEIN, G. (1998). *Sources of Power: How People make Decisions*. Cambridge, MA: MIT Press.

—— (2003). *The Power of Intuition*. New York: Currency.

LANGER, E. J. (1975). 'The Illusion of Control.' *Journal of Personality and Social Psychology*, 32: 311–28.

LANGLEY, A., MINTZBERG, H., PITCHER, P., POSADA, E., and SAINT-MACARY, J. (1995). 'Opening Up Decision Making: The View from the Black Stool.' *Organization Science*, 6: 260–79.

LARRICK, R. P. (2004). 'Debiasing,' in D. J. Koehler and N. Harvey (eds.), *Blackwell Handbook of Judgment and Decision Making*. Malden, MA: Blackwell, 316–37.

LIEBERMAN, M. D. (2000). 'Intuition: A Social Cognitive Neuroscience Approach.' *Psychological Bulletin*, 126: 109–37.

LINDBLOM, C. E. (1959). 'The Science of "Muddling Through."' *Public Administration Review*, 19, 79–88.

LIPSHITZ, R. and BAR-ILAN, O. (1996). 'How Problems are Solved: Reconsidering the Phase Theorem.' *Organizational Behavior and Human Decision Processes*, 65: 48–60.

MARCH, J. G. and SIMON, H. A. (1958). *Organizations*. New York: John Wiley and Sons.

McKENNEY, J. L. and KEEN, P. G. W. (1974). 'How Managers' Minds Work.' *Harvard Business Review*, May–June: 79–90.

MELONE, N. P. (1994). 'Reasoning in the Executive Suite: The Influence of Role/Experience-Based Expertise on Decision Processes of Corporate Executives.' *Organization Science*, 5: 438–55.

MILLER, C. C. and IRELAND, R. D. (2005). 'Intuition in Strategic Decision Making: Friend or Foe in the Fast-Paced 21st Century.' *Academy of Management Executive*, 19/1: 19–30.

MINTZBERG, H., RAISINGHANI, D., and THEORET, A. (1976). 'The Structure of "Unstructured" Decision Processes.' *Administrative Science Quarterly*, 21: 246–75.

MYERS, D. G. (2002). *Intuition: Its Powers and Perils*. New Haven, CT: Yale University Press.

NADLER, G. (1983). 'Human Purposeful Activities for Classifying Management Problems.' *Omega*, 11: 15–26.

NICKERSON, R. S., PERKINS, D. N., and SMITH, E. E. (1985). *The Teaching of Thinking*. Hillsdale, NJ: Lawrence Erlbaum Associates.

NISBETT, R. and ROSS, L. (1980). *Human Inference: Strategies and Shortcomings of Social Judgment*. Englewood Cliffs, NJ: Prentice-Hall.

NUTT, P. C. (1984). 'Types of Organizational Decision Processes.' *Administrative Science Quarterly*, 29: 414–50.

PAYNE, J. W. (1982). 'Contingent Decision Behavior.' *Psychological Bulletin*, 92: 382–402.

—— BETTMAN, J. R., and JOHNSON, E. J. (1992). 'Behavioral Decision Research: A Constructive Processing Perspective.' *Annual Review of Psychology*, 43: 87–131.

PENNINGTON, N. and HASTIE, R. (1986). 'Evidence Evaluation in Complex Decision Making.' *Journal of Personality and Social Psychology*, 51: 242–58.

PERKINS, D. (1995). *Outsmarting IQ: The Emerging Science of Learnable Intelligence*. New York: Free Press.

PINKER, S. (1994). *The Language Instinct*. New York: W. Morrow and Co.

POPLE, H. E. (1982). 'Heuristic Methods for Imposing Structure on Ill-Structured Problems: The Structuring of Medical Diagnosis,' in P. Szolovits (ed.), *Artificial Intelligence in Medicine*. Boulder, CO: Westview Press, 119–90.

RAIFFA, H. (1982). *The Art and Science of Negotiation*. Cambridge, MA: Harvard University Press.

ROWE, A. J. and MASON, R. O. (1987). *Managing with Style: A Guide to Understanding, Assessing, and Improving Decision Making*. San Francisco, CA: Jossey Bass.

SADLER-SMITH, E. and SHEFY, E. (2004). 'The Intuitive Executive: Understanding and Applying "Gut Feel" in Decision-Making.' *Academy of Management Executive*, 18/4: 76–91.

SCHEIN, E. H. (1985). *Organizational Culture and Leadership*. San Francisco, CA: Jossey Bass.

SCOTT, S. G. and BRUCE, R. A. (1995). 'Decision Making Style: The Development and Assessment of a New Measure.' *Educational and Psychological Measurement*, 55: 818–31.

SHAFIR, E. and LEBOEUF, R. A. (2002). 'Rationality.' *Annual Review of Psychology*, 53: 491–517.

—— SIMONSON, I., and TVERSKY, A. (1993). 'Reason-Based Choice.' *Cognition*, 49: 11–36.

SILLINCE, J. A. A. (2002). 'A Model of the Strength and Appropriateness of Argumentation in Organizational Contexts.' *Journal of Management Studies*, 39: 585–619.

SIMON, H. A. (1955). 'A Behavioral Model of Rational Choice.' *Quarterly Journal of Economics*, 69: 99–118.

—— (1977). *The New Science of Management Decision* (rev. edn.). Englewood Cliffs, NJ: Prentice-Hall.

—— (1987). 'Making Management Decisions: The Role of Intuition and Emotion.' *Academy of Management Executive*, 1/1: 57–64.

SLOMAN, S. A. (1996). 'The Empirical Case for Two Systems of Reasoning.' *Psychological Bulletin*, 119: 3–22.

SMITH, G. F. (1988). 'Towards a Heuristic Theory of Problem Structuring.' *Management Science*, 34: 1489–506.

—— (1989). 'Defining Managerial Problems: A Framework for Prescriptive Theorizing.' *Management Science*, 35: 963–81.

—— (1995). 'Classifying Managerial Problems: An Empirical Study of Definitional Content.' *Journal of Management Studies*, 32: 679–706.

—— (1998). *Quality Problem Solving*. Milwaukee, WI: ASQ Quality Press.

SOELBERG, P. O. (1967). 'Unprogrammed Decision Making.' *Industrial Management Review*, 8/2: 19–29.

STANOVICH, K. E. (1999). *Who is Rational? Studies of Individual Differences in Reasoning*. Mahwah, NJ: Erlbaum.

VON NEUMANN, J. and MORGENSTERN, O. (1947). *Theory of Games and Economic Behavior* (2nd edn.). New York: John Wiley.

VON WINTERFELDT, D. (1980). 'Structuring Decision Problems for Decision Analysis.' *Acta Psychologica*, 45: 71–93.

—— EDWARDS, W. (1986). *Decision Analysis and Behavioral Research*. Cambridge: Cambridge University Press.

VROOM, V. H. and JAGO, A. G. (1988). *The New Leadership*. Englewood Cliffs, NJ: Prentice-Hall.

25

FACILITATING SERIOUS PLAY

MATT STATLER

DAVID OLIVER*

INTRODUCTION

THIS chapter provides a descriptive account of how researchers at the Imagination Lab Foundation (I-Lab) designed, facilitated, and followed up on organizational interventions involving a process called "serious play" (Roos et al. 2004; Jacobs and Statler 2005; Statler 2005; Roos 2006; Oliver and Roos 2007). It additionally describes the outcomes observed in association with these interventions, and closes with a series of reflections on the significance of those outcomes for organizational decision making, especially with regard to the relationship between strategy process and content; the overcoming of psychological defenses; the role of power; and the cultivation of adaptive potential.

To begin, consider the following mini-case descriptions:

- The division management team from a Swiss chemical company completed a six-month strategic planning process and submitted their five-year plan to the firm's senior management. Management critiqued the plan, saying that it lacked ambition and bore too great a resemblance to the previous five-year plan. In response to these criticisms, the five-member divisional team engaged in a two-day workshop, during which they constructed a representation of their organization in its business environment using several thousand LEGO™ pieces.

* Acknowledgement: The facilitation practices described here involved productive contributions from the following Imagination Lab Foundation collaborators: Peter Bürgi, Jennie Gertun-Olsson, Claus Jacobs, Greg Holliday, Wendelin Küpers, Mark Marotto, Johan Roos, Madeleine Roos, and Bart Victor.

As the team built and discussed their multicolored, three-dimensional model, they identified shortcomings in their existing strategy, as well as new opportunities within the landscape. They later integrated these insights into a revised strategy document that received management approval and buy-in.

- An international paint company gathered its 20 country managers to reconcile regional differences and develop a more coherent, shared corporate identity. Over the course of two days, the managers broke into two subgroups, engaged in a facilitated process, and explored their organization's identity verbally and using the medium of LEGO™ bricks. They found the process painfully difficult, and struggled to incorporate all the different perspectives at the table. By the end of the second day, however, they had crafted a single, albeit multifaceted model of their organization's identity, and they jointly resolved to refocus their customer strategy around the elements of the model that they thought differentiated their company from its competitors.

- The strategy committee and the human resources director of a European bank gathered their 47 key reporting officers at a resort to build momentum toward the launch of a major new customer service initiative. A team of action researchers designed and facilitated a two-day process during which six cross-functional subgroups used a variety of toy construction and other materials to construct physical representations of their individual and collective views on banker–customer relations. Each group's model presented strikingly different perspectives, and participants raised questions about the new initiative. If customers should know their banker better, did bankers have to know their customers better too? Are some customers better to know than others? Should the initiative focus on personnel training or the enhancement of technical systems? In view of the variety of interpretations, and in order to respond to the serious questions raised, the bank's strategy committee decided to delay the intended rollout pending further analysis.

These mini-case descriptions illustrate dozens of interventions—involving more than 1,000 managers and scholars—organized by the authors and their colleagues at the I-Lab from 2001 to 2005. Founded by Johan Roos in 2000 to conduct research on play, imagination, and emergence in organizing and strategizing, the I-Lab supported a full-time research staff and engaged with academic and business collaborators. To gather data on these topics, the researchers facilitated interventions focused on strategy, organizational change and development, team dynamics, and leadership.

This chapter describes the facilitation practices that emerged through these collaborations over five years. It begins by outlining several basic assumptions. It then describes in detail the design and facilitation of interventions involving serious play in organizations. It closes with critical reflections on the positive and negative organizational impacts associated with these interventions, as well as the significance of these anecdotal outcomes for future organizational decision making research.

Assumptions

The facilitation processes described below rest on several basic assumptions. At an ontological level, organizations are complex adaptive systems, and decision making is a dynamic process through which transformative change can, and sometime does, emerge. Accordingly, the facilitation of organizational processes by Imagination Lab researchers unfolded experimentally, as a series of open-ended interventions into complex system dynamics.

At an epistemological level, because such dynamic processes involve unique sets of interactions among agents and unfold asymmetrically in time, it is difficult if not impossible to control all relevant variables and arrive at generalizable, predictive knowledge. Accordingly, I-Lab researchers employed action research methods involving various forms of data gathering during multiple cycles of action and reflection, while focusing on an agenda developed in collaboration with organizational sponsors and participants.

Methodologically, this chapter interprets available textual and visual data pertaining to facilitation practices that emerged over a five-year time period. Accordingly, the interpretation constructs a partial narrative of those various events. The narrative begins with a conceptualization of serious play as a process through which people can bring not only cognitions, but also embodied experiences, emotions, and social dynamics to bear on their organizational challenges. The narrative serves as a reference point for critical dialogue among scholars and practitioners about the relevance of different dimensions of human experience to organizational decision making.

Describing Facilitation Practices

Conversing with Practitioners

Serious play interventions typically began with a conversation between an organizational leader (hereafter referred to as the sponsor) and members of the research team. The sponsor typically sought an innovative way to address a particular organizational problem, and the first discussion normally addressed that problem within its organizational context. During this conversation, researchers would provide the sponsor with verbal and written descriptions of the concept of serious play and the facilitation methods that it inspired, often telling stories about previous interventions with similar organizations.[1] In some cases, researchers would propose to conduct a sample pilot process to give a smaller group of senior managers a flavor of the character of the experience, and to help them reflect on how serious play could optimally fit in the context of their ongoing initiatives.

The sponsor would specify potential intervention participants, the time available and desired outcomes of the jointly designed process. When a sponsor expressed interest in very specific content outcomes, the researchers would emphasize the impossibility of predicting what would come of the event or of controlling the content generated by the group. Since the process did not lend itself well to instrumentality, sponsors had to have some degree of comfort with open-endedness in order to proceed. Sponsors had to approach the process as a way of generating a multiplicity of outcomes, and remain willing to consider not only new possible solutions to the problem at hand, but also critical reformulations of it.

The researchers would also explain their own interest in developing scholarly research products based on the data gathered during the intervention. If this conversation with the organizational sponsor ended (as some did, while others did not) with an agreement to proceed with an action research project, then the researchers would gather with colleagues and collaborators to design the process.

Designing the Process

The researchers would begin by determining the most relevant unit of analysis for the intervention. Irrespective of the organization or problem, each process participant would construct that unit of analysis using a three-dimensional medium and tell stories about it. It was therefore crucially important to select something—a project, a change initiative, a strategy—that all participants were already aware of, involved in, and willing to discuss.

Struggling with this choice, the researchers would raise questions about the group's size and composition. What different functional roles and responsibilities did people hold? How long had they been with the organization? Were they accustomed to working with each other? Different facilitation exercises could surface different facets of the unit of analysis. Should the exercises lead participants to engage more with their peers or with people at other levels of the organizational hierarchy? Should they build individually, in pairs, or as a group? Any construction exercise could additionally involve different patterns of storytelling. Should participants tell their stories in plenary, in pairs, or in cross-pollinated subgroups?

Depending on the exercises selected for the process, the researchers additionally had to choose among an array of materials. For most interventions, I-Lab researchers chose LEGO™ bricks because they could be configured in so many different ways, and would require a relatively low level of skill (compared to other materials such as paint or even clay) to generate intricate models.[2] The research team also experimented with other three-dimensional materials, including magnets, sand, paint, musical instruments, and found objects such as fruit and office paraphernalia.

The researchers would also help to differentiate roles and responsibilities for each member of the facilitation team. Who should convene the group? Who should handle the various exercises? Who should pose the challenging questions? Who should take primary responsibility for taking participant observation notes? Who should gather visual data including digital photography and/or video?

While making decisions in response to process design questions such as these, the research team also attempted to formulate new research questions and consider the relevance of the intervention to current topics in organizational research. In this way, developments in strategy, teamwork, and organizational development research could shape or inform the unit of analysis.

Facilitating Serious Play

I-Lab researchers also served as serious play facilitators, often working in collaboration with other professional facilitators. Before participants arrived, all the facilitators would work to set up the room, using tables large and wide enough for the construction materials to scatter across but small enough so that people could easily reach the middle from any side. They would position the tables, and arrange the chairs so that no more than ten people would sit at a single table. Facilitators would also position the materials for easy access by participants, often on side tables.

The sponsor would typically start the event with a few words, and then the facilitators would introduce the process. As the practice developed, facilitators tended to keep their verbal introduction short and focus on several key messages to set the frame. They gave a quick account of the overall objectives of the session. They emphasized the importance of maintaining a safe atmosphere in which people could play around with serious issues without fear of undue recrimination from colleagues. Finally, they sketched out the various process stages so that people would know the pace of the experience without knowing what would happen.

The active process would begin with a warm-up exercise involving a simple construction task and a relatively short amount of time. This exercise would drive people's hands into the materials as quickly as possible, and familiarize them with the various ways that the materials could fit together. Some participants exhibited a greater learned familiarity or natural skill with hands-on activities, so the warm up enabled everyone to develop a certain minimal level of skill in manipulating the materials. It also served the purpose of illustrating the many different ways to accomplish the same task. Following the initial and all subsequent exercises, facilitators would encourage participants to discuss how they felt about what they were doing, and what they saw in the models on the table.

The next exercises typically involved asking participants to take a certain number of pieces and ask them to simply "build anything." Anticipating already the chance to describe what they had built, they reacted with surprise when the facilitators would ask them to tell a story that described the model as one of a list of preselected objects (e.g., your car), people (e.g., the head of state), or processes (e.g., your morning commute). Pedagogically, this exercise emphasized the metaphorical potential (Bürgi et al. 2004) of the three-dimensional medium, and additionally, the creative aspect of the group process of analogical reasoning (Statler, Jacobs and Roos, 2006). People who had attempted to build perfect, literal representations (e.g., of the office, etc.) found that meaning need not remain static or intrinsic to the model, but instead could be attributed to the model creatively by anyone who interpreted it, including the builder, the facilitator, and other participants.

To expand on the analogical and metaphorical potential of the materials while connecting the process more closely with the organization's problem, facilitators would then ask people to build a model that told the story of their job or primary activity. This exercise allowed participants to deepen the metaphors used and further practice using the models as prompts for narrative. It also personalized the dialogue at the table to the extent that people often built their aspirations and frustrations as prominent features of their job, and presented these emotions as part of the three-dimensional model by telling their stories to colleagues.

The facilitators would pose questions to the participants about the significance of particular aspects of these models. The variety of colors and shapes and configurations available in LEGO™ materials could lead to a wide range of possible interpretations, where everything was potentially significant or banal. "Why did you choose red? Why did you make this side so big and the other so small? Has your job always been this way?" Questions such as these could lead nowhere, or they could lead to novel interpretations and elaborate narratives. Facilitators encouraged participants to pose similar questions to each other, while calling attention to different perspectives around the table.

The subsequent exercise usually involved constructing the identity of the pre-selected unit of analysis—the organization, project, or team. Facilitators allocated more time for this exercise, and it usually began with people working individually although at times participants worked in pairs or subgroups of three or four. Sometimes, participants would start building immediately, while others would pause for reflection or appear blocked. In the latter case, facilitators often encouraged people to start simply putting pieces together while thinking about something else, whistling a song, or looking out the window. They discouraged people from excessive, anguished rumination, and encouraged them instead to engage with their work issues in playful manner, using a playful *mode* of intentionality in which they did not seek to control, but instead remained open to emergent change. Following the individual construction of the identity of the unit of analysis, facilitators would encourage participants to share the story of their own construction with other participants.

Participants often exhibited deeply entrenched habits of dealing with their work issues using certain vocabularies, metaphors, rhetorics, and technologies, but this process allowed them to use an entirely different, three-dimensional *medium*. Working with that alternative communication medium, almost all participants could build and describe at least something. In some rare cases, participants rejected the medium outright and ceased to participate or became disruptive. Facilitators generally encouraged such participants to adopt the role of process observer, and occasionally they would re-enter the process at a later moment.[3]

Following these exercises, facilitators would often invite participants to take their various models, and attempt to construct a single, collective model of the content unit of analysis per table. Over time, during different process interventions with different organizations, the facilitators experimented with a series of simple rules to guide this difficult and important transition. They phrase these rules as instructions to participants: "(1) eliminate redundancies; (2) keep everything from your own model that you feel is very important; and (3) ensure that the collective model includes at least one element from each of the individual models."

If the tables were large and there had been no previous collective construction activity, participants could begin by pushing their individual models toward the center of the table. Facilitators would pose questions about commonalities, patterns of similarity, and difference. Non-directive questions—"does anybody see anything in common?"—tended to serve the design purpose best. Sometimes, a moment of silence would ensue, and nobody would move or say anything. If the process stalled, facilitators would sometimes ask someone to step up and take a first shot at building the construction. In all cases, participant groups would eventually begin to construct a collective three-dimensional model of the unit of analysis.

The variety and intensity of dynamics in group play would become especially visible in cases where two or more subgroups worked in parallel, and one group would jump ahead and make decisions about what to keep and what to cast aside, while another subgroup remained locked in stasis, with no clear path forward. In such cases, facilitators encouraged participants to work together using their hands to construct or transform the model, asking for clarification on new changes that were not collectively discussed. Facilitators frequently improvised and adjusted or redesigned these exercises to address emergent phenomena in the group. Once participants were satisfied that the construction was complete, facilitators would invite one or several volunteers to recount the overall story.

Shifting the focus to the world outside the model, subsequent exercises would encourage participants to construct other elements of their organizational landscape, including competitors, partners, funding sources, regulators, clients, and/or customers. Facilitators experimented with different specifications for these models, sometimes asking each individual to build several landscape elements, other times asking that those landscape elements include only decision-making agents, instead of general economic phenomena such as currency fluctuations, changes in inflation, or rising consumer demand. In any case, participants would integrate those elements into the organizational landscape, whether by setting them apart from the collective model, attaching them to each other, or otherwise positioning them in terms of their relative significance. Facilitators also sometimes instructed participants to focus explicitly on the nature of the linkages between the various landscape elements.

With enough time and sufficient mandate from the sponsor to engage participants in a lengthier, potentially more intense set of exercises, facilitators would ask them to reflect on the model they had constructed and imagine possible events that might impact it (regarding scenario planning and serious play, cf., Jacobs and Statler 2006). In some cases, each participant would generate three scenarios, one likely, one possible, and one long shot. In other cases, pairs or groups would identify three different events, at the short-, medium-, and long-term time horizons. Participants would describe which part of the model would be most directly impacted by the scenario, and what the effects might be. In general, facilitators encouraged the participants to articulate scenarios as concretely as possible, avoiding generalities such as "declining sales" in favor of specificities such as "losing the XYZ account because Jones botched the presentation."

As participants played through a series of disruptive scenarios, facilitators would ask them: "what is the right thing to do today in order to mitigate the negative impact of this potential future event?" If participants could answer this question, the facilitators would ask further, "Why is that the right thing to do?" As the group played through several of the scenarios, sometimes someone would write the answers to these questions down on a flip chart. Reflecting on this list of core justifications for strategic action, participants articulated simple principles that they thought could provide guidance in the event that one of these scenarios, or one like them, should arise unexpectedly. In this sense, the serious play process would deal not only with the content of the problem identified in conversation by the sponsor, but additionally with individual and collective notions of how best to respond to unexpected events (Oliver and Roos 2005).

As the process frame ended, facilitators would reserve a significant amount of time for reflective discussion and debrief. On many occasions, the sponsor or some participant took great care to close the frame by drawing close connections between the model and the organization itself, typically in the form of action plans or lists of tasks and next steps. Sometimes facilitators instructed participants to take written notes of the stories they found most compelling. Sometimes participants would take a favorite segment of the model back to work with them as a memory aid. At least one manager closed a session by giving the LEGO™ bricks to his team as a Christmas present for their kids. Some sponsors saved the entire model and displayed it at the office on a conference table. Often participants would snap their own digital pictures of the models and email them around to family and friends. Facilitators would close the session frame by thanking the participants for the opportunity to collaborate with them, packing up the gear and taking the data back to the Imagination Lab, usually engaging in an immediate, preliminary debrief of what they had experienced.

Following Up

When following up after a serious play intervention, facilitators and researchers usually focused on the problem that the sponsor had presented prior to the event. Did the process effectively address the problem? Did other outcomes emerge during the process? What organizational dynamics unfolded during the process?

Researchers began to answer these questions by transcribing the participant observation notes, reviewing the visual data, and engaging with colleagues in reflective dialogue. This dialogue would often focus specifically on key comments made by participants, as well as on what remained unsaid. It would address the overall energy levels and power dynamics within the group, as well as the physical body language and positioning that the facilitators observed in the room. Video cameras positioned in the corner of the room provided a wide-angle overview of the interactive and communicative process of building the models. Digital photos from a variety of angles captured images of group in action, shots of pair and group level interactions, shots of individual people presenting their models and telling stories to the group, and close-up shots of the models themselves.

Typically the researchers would develop a set of first-order analyses and communicate them in an insight memo addressed to the sponsor and all process participants. The insight memo typically included key digital photographs and extensive written interpretations of the data gathered. These interpretations typically included content findings and process findings—dealing at a content level with what was said or unsaid, and at a process level with how these discursive and performative interactions unfolded. In many cases, researchers had a further debriefing conversation with the process owner and key participants, to discuss additional potential courses of action.

Outcomes

The preceding description of facilitating serious play cannot generate generalizable research findings for several reasons. First, the serious play interventions do not provide a uniform control variable, and the research team did not attempt to systematize across various empirical settings the inherently open-ended and malleable character of play (Csikszentmihalyi 1990). Second, since the serious play process occurred in a wide variety of different organizational contexts, under different circumstances, and with different explicit process goals, a potentially wide range of additional factors shaped the practices as well as the outcomes. Third, since the data derives largely from the authors' own personal experiences, it gives rise not to objective measures, but to transparent and self-reflexive interpretations, guided by the methodological notion of participant-objectification (Bourdieu and Wacquant 1992).

Yet, Imagination Lab researchers and facilitators did consistently intervene in organizational systems using a process that introduced a new medium for communication and gave participants the opportunity to approach their organizational problems with a playful attitude, or mode of intentionality. Process participants did consistently rely on haptic, spatial and interpersonal intelligences (Buergi and Roos 2003; Oliver and Roos 2007) in addition to the verbal, logical, and mathematical intelligences (cf., Gardner 1983) more commonly relied upon in organizations. Facilitators consistently called upon participants to relax their desires to command or control situations, and to remain intentionally open to emergent change within the frame of the play process. These activities led to positive as well as negative outcomes.

Positive Outcomes

Almost invariably, participants reported gaining *new insights* into the unit of analysis that the process focused on. Participants would routinely jump up from their chairs and rove around the room to gain different perspectives on the model as others built and described it. For example, once a six-member strategy team saw their organization laid out on the table in three dimensions, they realized that they had previously held at least four different understandings of the term "network," a term that figured prominently in their strategic plan. In another case, participants realized that an important customer service initiative meant vastly different things to different parts of the organization. In another case, a non-profit's senior leadership realized that it had been strategically constrained by the symbolic presence of the group's charismatic, but long deceased, founder. In such cases, the insights led participants to reconsider the problem that had driven them to engage in serious play in the first place.

Participants also consistently reported that the serious play process had led to the development of *different social relationships* with their peers and colleagues. For example, the members of a leadership team of an information technology firm had not previously taken the time, in their hectic work environment, to understand each other's roles and responsibilities. However, once they built and saw each other's jobs as well as each others' models of the organization's identity, they realized how much they actually had in common. They reported that on the basis of that realization, they began to share more information and work more collaboratively with each other. In another case, functional and divisional managers blamed the senior manager in charge of logistics for slow delivery. That individual found himself forgiven by his peers once they saw the complexity of the organization's operations built in three dimensions. In another case, when a managing director used a very detailed model to tell a story about the difficult relationship he had with his own boss, the room fell silent, and other participants expressed a new appreciation for his predicament, with one participant stating that he could now accept the managing director as one of them. This story marked a critical incident in this group's building process, and led to an openness of dialogue that had previously been absent in the group. One participant said: "I've been working with [this colleague] for 14 years and never knew this about him."

Participants also consistently reported experiencing *positive emotions* atypical for normal meetings of those same individuals. Most commonly, participants exhibited the kind of affective dynamics associated with having fun, as manifested by laughter, smiling, excitement, and unbridled enthusiasm to continue. For example, the HR director of one company drew everyone's attention to his good humor by climbing up onto the table to add a component to the emerging construction. Some participants claimed that they had "never had so much fun at a strategy meeting" and others made jokes about how they should not "let their colleagues back at the office know how much fun" they had during the process. Beyond the general climate of light-heartedness, participants also consistently expressed higher levels of emotional commitment and acceptance of the serious issues on the table. In several cases, people reported associating positive emotions with the other participants who had shared the experience, and in at least two cases, participants reported feeling better about the organization as a whole because it provided a place for them to engage in serious play. As a senior academic participant wrote in a comment sheet, the serious play process allowed participants "to know each other in a more genuine way" and start "to commit as people, and not as status, role, power, etc."

Negative Outcomes

On some occasions, participants expressed a degree of confusion about the purpose of the activity and its relationship to the overall purpose of the group or the organization. In a few instances, participants complained that they found the process a distraction or waste of time from the critical matters at hand. Some participants reported that the process was unnecessary to develop the outcomes, and that a traditional verbal discussion would have led to the similar outcomes in a shorter amount of time.

Power dynamics in the group would occasionally intensify and threaten to break the playful frame. Because the process of meaning construction left so much room for interpretation (as opposed, for example, to financial analysis of "the numbers"), it sometimes made it more difficult for people to defend themselves against domineering or abusive colleagues. In addition, beyond clashes of individual personalities, certain power dynamics endemic to specific organizational cultures intensified within the frame of the play process. For example, in organizations with established cultures of hierarchically based evaluation, some participants expressed a fear that their constructions and contributions to the discussion were not sufficient to gain approval.

On several occasions, participants reacted to the process with intensely negative emotions. In one case, a participant became so upset with another group's representation of her organization that her voice began to waver and she began to cry. In another case, a participant became increasingly frustrated with his perceived inability to construct and describe his models. After the third exercise, he began to make loud disruptive comments, and by the fourth exercise, he began to throw materials around the room and at other participants. On another occasion, two members of a subgroup announced that they could not continue with the process because of their intense disagreement with the narrative presented by another participant, and walked away from the table.

Longer-Term Outcomes

Some of the longer-term impacts and outcomes that participants attributed or traced back to the serious play process include:

- A manufacturing organization decided to revise its entire five-year strategic plan.
- A services organization decided to abandon an unrealistic organizational learning initiative.
- A manufacturing firm decided to refocus its strategy development process on key account management.
- A telecommunications firm decided to re-emphasize its historical brand image following a merger process.
- An information technology firm decided that it should focus more attention during its strategy development processes on the expertise in the human resources function.
- The leadership team of a large non-profit organization decided that it should be more aggressive with its organizational change efforts.

- A telecommunications firm decided to design and develop an organization wide management development program based on the serious play process.
- An international non-government organization decided that it could not go forward with the rollout of a management development technique without the firm commitment of its senior leadership.
- The senior management of a large national bank decided that they needed to obtain the buy-in of the front line staff to implement a new customer service initiative effectively.
- A group of university leaders decided to move ahead with a campus wide diversity initiative.
- A rapidly growing company decided that it needed to downplay the influence of its home-country national culture on the organization to pursue its global expansion more effectively.
- A consumer products company decided that it needed to diversify its distribution channels in order to keep pace with changing demographics.
- A manufacturing firm's leadership team decided that they needed to improve the quality and frequency of communication among themselves.

REFLECTIONS

New Process, New Content

Other action research intervention data supports the notion that changes in an organization's strategy process can lead to changes in strategy content (cf., Roos et al. 2004). Reflecting on the facilitation practices described above, the serious play process involved a distinct *mode* of intentionality (i.e., playful openness to emergent change), as well as an alternative *medium* in which to express strategic content (i.e., 3-D materials). Moreover, in view of the outcomes reported in association with these facilitation practices, specific shifts of mode and medium appear to have enabled participants to generate new insights about their organization and the problems faced by it.

Beyond the playful mode and the 3-D medium, another factor may have contributed to the generation of new insights. Unlike standard, discursive decision-making processes in which certain voices dominate and others recede, the serious play process explicitly included content generated by all people present. Of course, not all constructions equally captured the attention of other participants, but each participant did have his or her own constructions out on the table where other participants could see them, comment or ask questions about them, and even incorporate them into their own models. Thus whereas often the qualitative parameters for group decision-making activities are set in advance by a team of analysts or by the senior leadership, serious play process participants all contributed to the exploration and definition of the terms of the debate.

The projective aspect of the serious play process appears as another factor that contributes to the generation of insightful content (Barry 1994). From a rigorous, constructionist analytic perspective, organizational actors always project meaning, whether onto spreadsheets and presentation slides or onto a pile of modeling clay. However, clay (or LEGO™ bricks) may provide more of a blank slate than a spreadsheet, if only because the spreadsheets and the presentation slides remain so embedded in existing habits and patterns of communication. Indeed, inasmuch as strategic thinking in organizations typically involves a set of familiar metaphors, the objects used to construct a physical image schema can range from more familiar, even stereotypical, to unfamiliar, amorphous, and unconstrained (cf., Doyle and Sims 2002). By giving participants the opportunity to project tacit, unconscious meanings on ambiguous, and multidimensional, multicolored objects, the serious play process allowed them to express new thoughts and feelings. Even participants whose voices would typically dominate reported saying things that they had never said before, and the projective aspect of the process helped to make that happen.

Overcoming Defenses? Yes, But...

Privately held, tacit knowledge and affect can additionally lead to biases and conflicts in organizational decision-making processes (cf., Hodgkinson and Wright 2002; Maitlis and Ozcelik 2004). The possibility that processes involving three-dimensional representations of strategic decision content can serve to overcome such psychodynamic defenses motivates research as well as practice focused on cognitive mapping (Huff 1990; Ambrosini and Bowman 2002; Eden and Ackerman 2002; Hodgkinson and Maule 2002; Johnson and Johnson 2002). The serious play process did on many occasions appear to break down individual psychological defenses as well as social antipathies that had previously inhibited decision making in an organizational context. Participants sometimes reported the models they had built represented the organization more accurately and truthfully than any other internal document. On several occasions, after a participant had presented an emotionally sensitive aspect of his job, others would appear more willing to put themselves and their own aspirations on the table.

But while emotion can constrain cognition, the reverse can also be true. Sometimes a preconceived notion (e.g., about a colleague's role in the organization) appeared to preclude the experience and expression of emotions that, from a group dynamics perspective, would have enabled more effective decision making. In the facilitation practices described above, emotional, social, and cognitive dimensions of human experience did not function discreetly from each other, but instead functioned so interdependently as to appear co-constitutive. Thus any attribution of causality with regard to X constraining Y with effect Z should meet with skepticism.

Even if it were analytically possible to differentiate these dimensions of experience and control for variability in any one of them, any organizational system would still include a multiplicity of dynamics at different levels of scale. The same emotional constraint on the same cognition may have positive and/or negative effects on the decision-making process and content depending on the time frame as well as other dynamics within the organizational system. Thus while "think harder" may serve in controlled experiments involving undergraduates and managers to limit the damage that accrues due to framing biases (Hodgkinson et al. 1999; Hodgkinson and Maule 2002; Wright and Goodwin 2002), experienced people in real-life organizational contexts may on occasion respond well to other admonitions including "think less," "feel more," and even "play seriously."

Power and Decision Making

Other researchers have made similar claims—for example, the relevance of power dynamics to decision-making processes has been well established (e.g., Pfeffer and Salancik 1974; Eisenhardt and Bourgeouis 1988). Although such dynamics play out in ways that may often be invisible to external facilitators, the serious play frame and process structure often did serve to de-emphasize the importance of hierarchical power. Each participant had to engage in the same, occasionally embarrassing, process of constructing a model using materials not commonly found in the workplace. Frequently the most effective builders and original storytellers were not necessarily those with the highest hierarchical position in the room. Thus instead of rewarding the ability to generate and comprehend jargon-laden statements about the nature of the organization, this process called for the ability to construct models and tell original stories. The process had the effect of broadening and democratizing the interaction and exchange of opinions about important organizational issues among participants, making them more open and less prone to self-censorship due to concerns associated with power issues.

At the same time, this observation also suggests caution about the potential for misuse of the serious play technique. Since participants frequently made very open and revealing statements about themselves or about what might be considered sensitive issues during the process, facilitators of such processes should remain sensitive to the possibility of abuse by individuals in power, and, if necessary, intervene to mitigate such occurrences. More broadly, decision-making researchers need to acknowledge the extent to which the strategic landscape as well as the parameters of value do not exist in a static or objective form, but instead are creatively enacted by the participants, shaped by narrative convention as well as power dynamics, and subject to transformation and renewal.

Adaptive Potential

People who make decisions in organizations deal as a matter of course with a certain degree of uncertainty and ambiguity (March 1991; Shapira 1997). At a process level, people commonly use decision support techniques designed to reduce that uncertainty, whether through algorithmic modeling or statistical analysis. At a certain point however, the utility of such techniques may be limited, and organizations require other techniques that incorporate an experiential confrontation with unexpected change. In cases of extreme or protracted uncertainty (e.g., due either to the time horizon or to volatility in the environment—cf., Weick and Sutcliffe 2001) organizations simply cannot reduce uncertainty. In such instances, they strive instead to identify and develop sources of resilience (Sheffi 2005) or robustness (Eccles and Nohria 1992; Light 2005) that enable the organization to become more prepared for unexpected events (Statler and Roos 2006, 2007).

In this sense, serious play may increase the adaptive potential of decision-making processes in organizations. Just as scenario planning may require technologies of foolishness in complement to technologies of rationality (Jacobs and Statler 2006), organizational decision-making processes may require a measure of serious play in order to remain resilient and adaptive in the face of uncertainty, ambiguity, and change.

Psychological researchers have argued that the sheer ambiguity of play provides a frame within which humans can express adaptive variations (Sutton-Smith 1997). Organizational researchers have additionally recognized that improvisational play in the workplace can have significant benefits associated with learning, personal fulfillment, and even performance (e.g., Sandelands and Buckner 1989; Starbuck and Webster 1991; Hatch 1999; Ibarra 2004).

By facilitating serious play interventions in an open-ended, experimental fashion, the researchers enabled participants to gain new insights, interact differently with their peers, and feel more satisfied and committed to their organizations. In addition, participants put cognitive, social, and emotional dimensions of their own experience directly to use—both by attempting to solve a particular problem and by cultivating their own capacities to adapt to emergent and unexpected change.

DIRECTIONS FOR FUTURE RESEARCH

This chapter described serious play interventions designed and facilitated by researchers at the I-Lab. This description of facilitation practices can serve as a basis for insights relevant to the organizational decision-making research literature. In particular, the facilitation described here represents an attempt to draw upon more of the emotional, imaginative, context specific, and human elements of decision making (Langley et al. 1995). In this sense, the study follows a stream of research into notions of "intuitive" decision making (Simon 1987), by providing a context within which participants could draw upon their unconscious understandings and impressions. By asking managers to develop shared constructions of their organizations in their environments, the serious play process drew on social, emotional, and embodied aspects of their human experience in addition to rational cognition.

A change in the *process* of decision making enabled the generation of novel decision *content* in these organizations. The process of projecting meaning on multidimensional objects led to the expression of new thoughts and feelings, which were then integrated into a wide variety of decision outcomes. The serious play interventions de-emphasized established power hierarchies by imposing what was for many a radically novel form of expression on all participants. The process encouraged participants to think through scenarios that emerged in the course of the play activity, thus providing a context for testing prior assumptions and possibly modifying existing knowledge structures used in organizational decision processes.

While scenario development has been widely studied (e.g., Schoemaker 1993), much of this research is grounded in assumptions of rational cognition. Future research might continue to explore forms of scenario development that include social, emotional and embodied aspects of human experience in addition to purely rationalist ones. In particular, organizational aesthetics researchers (cf., Guillet de Monthoux 2004; Taylor and Hansen 2005) might address the physical image schemas associated with the notion of cognitive sculpting (Doyle and Sims 2002) and develop an expanded theory of how creative, embodied perception impacts judgments of fit and proportion in organizational decision-making processes.

Additional questions relate to the use of storytelling in decision-making processes. A number of scholars have called for further analysis of the role of narratives in organizational life (cf., Dyer and Wilkins 1991; O'Connor 1997). Storytelling functions as an informal social process that integrates emotional as well as cognitive dimensions of decision making (cf., Oliver and Roos 2005; Oliver and Jacobs 2007). In view of the serious play facilitation practices described above, decision-making research could focus not only on the ways in which decision parameters and optimality criteria are shaped by narratives, but also on the interplay between cognition, emotion, and physical performance as organizational actors construct and interpret models of their organization (cf., Hodgkinson and Wright 2006; Whittington 2006).

ENDNOTES

1 This research on serious play influenced, and was in turn influenced by, the development of a branded process technique called LEGO™ Serious Play TM (LSP). For several years, the authors were licensed LSP facilitators, interacting with a community of practice comprising other licensed and prospective LSP facilitators.

2 Full disclosure: LEGO™ provided sponsorship to the Imagination Lab, a non-profit Swiss foundation making LEGO™ materials readily available for experimental use.

3 The use of three-dimensional objects to construct meaningful models of organizational phenomena has been previously documented and referred to as "cognitive sculpting" (Doyle and Sims 2002). In reference to the typology of different objects used in cognitive sculpting, the various LEGO™ materials served less as distinct metaphors than as a medium with which to create metaphors, thus defying "neat categorization, and, à la Rorschach, support[ing] a variety of different projections" (Doyle and Sims 2002: 75). The serious play process also appears to differ significantly from cognitive sculpting insofar as it (1) involves a series of different structured exercises and facilitation techniques; (2) encourages sensemaking on individual, pair, and group levels; and, as noted above, (3) calls upon participants to adopt a playful mode of intentionality.

REFERENCES

AMBROSINI, V. and BOWMAN, C. (2002). 'Mapping Successful Organizational Routines,' in A. S. Huff and M. Jenkins (eds.), *Mapping Strategic Knowledge*. London: Sage.

BARRY, D. (1994). 'Making the Invisible Visible: Using Analogically-Based Methods to Surface Unconscious Organizational Processes.' *Organization Development Journal*, 12/4: 37–47.

BOURDIEU, P. and WACQUANT, L. (1992). *An Invitation to Reflexive Sociology*. Chicago, IL: University of Chicago Press.

BÜRGI, P. and ROOS, J. (2003). 'Images of Strategy.' *European Management Journal*, 21/1 : 69–78.

—— JACOBS, C., and ROOS, J. (2004). 'From Metaphor to Practice in the Crafting of Strategy.' *Journal of Management Inquiry*, 13/4: 1–17.

CSIKSZENTMIHALYI, M. (1990). *Flow: The Psychology of Optimal Experience*. New York: Harper and Row.

DOYLE, J. R. and SIMS, D. (2002). 'Enabling Strategic Metaphor in Conversation: A Technique of Cognitive Sculpting for Explicating Knowledge,' in A. S. Huff and M. Jenkins (eds.), *Mapping Strategic Knowledge*. London: Sage.

DYER, W. and WILKINS, A. (1991). 'Better Stories, Not Better Constructs, to Generate Better Theory: A Rejoinder to Eisenhardt.' *Academy of Management Review*, 16: 613–19.

ECCLES, R. and NOHRIA, N. (1992). *Beyond the Hype: Rediscovering the Essence of Management*. Boston, MA: Harvard Business School Press.

EDEN, C. and ACKERMAN, F. (2002). 'A Mapping Framework for Strategy Making,' in A. S. Huff and M. Jenkins (eds.), *Mapping Strategic Knowledge*. London: Sage.

EISENHARDT, K. and BOURGEOIS, L. (1988). 'Politics of Strategic Decision Making in High-Velocity Environments: Toward a Mid-Range Theory.' *Academy of Management Journal*, 31: 737–70.

GARDNER, H. (1983). *Frames of Mind*. New York: Basic Books.

GRANOVETTER, M. (1985). 'Economic Action and Social Structure: The Problem of Embeddedness.' *American Journal of Sociology*, 91: 481–510.

Guillet de MONTHOUX, P. (2004). *The Art Firm: Aesthetic Management and Metaphysical Marketing*. Palo Alto, CA: Stanford University Press.

HATCH, M. J. (1999). 'Exploring the Empty Spaces of Organizing: How Improvisational Jazz Helps Redescribe Organizational Structure.' *Organization Studies*, 20/1: 75–100.

HODGKINSON, G. P. and MAULE, A. J. (2002). 'The Individual in the Strategy Process: Insights from behavioural Decision Research and Cognitive Mapping,' in A. S. Huff and M. Jenkins (eds.), *Mapping Strategic Knowledge*. London: Sage.

—— WRIGHT, G. (2002). 'Confronting Strategic Inertia in a Top Management Team: Learning from Failure.' *Organization Studies* 23/6: 949–77.

—— —— (2006). 'Neither Completing the Practice Turn, nor Enriching the Process Tradition: Secondary Misinterpretations of a Case Analysis Reconsidered.' *Organization Studies*, 27/12: 1895–901.

—— BOWN, N. J., MAULE, A. J., GLAISTER, K. W., and PEARMAN, A. D. (1999). 'Breaking the Frame: An Analysis of Strategic Cognition and Decision Making Under Uncertainty.' *Strategic Management Journal*, 20/10: 977–85.

HUFF, A. S. (ed.) (1990). *Mapping Strategic Thought*. Chichester: Wiley.

—— JENKINS, M. (2002). *Mapping Strategic Knowledge*. Thousand Oaks, CA: Sage.

IBARRA, H. (2004). *Working Identity: Unconventional Strategies for Reinventing Your Career*. Cambridge, MA: Harvard Business School Press

JACOBS, C. and STATLER, M. (2005). 'Strategy Creation as Serious Play,' in S. W. Floyd, J. Roos, C. Jacobs, and F. Kellermanns (eds.), *Innovating Strategy Process*. Oxford: Blackwell.

—— —— (2006). 'Toward a Technology of Foolishness—Developing Scenarios Through Serious Play.' *International Studies of Management and Organization*, 36/3: 77–92.

JOHNSON, P. and JOHNSON, G. (2002). 'Facilitating Group Cognitive Mapping of Core Competencies,' in A. S. Huff, and M. Jenkins (eds.), *Mapping Strategic Knowledge*. London: Sage.

LANGLEY, A., MINTZBERG, H., PITCHER, P., POSADA, E., and SAINT-MACARY, J. (1995). 'Opening Up Decision Making: The View from the Black Stool.' *Organization Science*, 6: 260–79.

LIGHT, P. (2005). *The Four Pillars of High Performance*. New York: McGraw-Hill.

MAITLIS, S. and OZCELIK, H. (2004). 'Toxic Decision Processes: A Study of Emotion and Organizational Decision Making.' *Organization Science*, 15: 395.

MARCH, J. (1991). 'How Decisions Happen in Organizations.' *Human-Computer Interaction*, 6: 95–117.

O'CONNOR, E. (1997). 'Telling Decisions: The Role of Narrative in Organizational Decision Making,' in Z. Shapira (ed.), *Organizational Decision Making*. New York: Cambridge University Press, 304–23.

OLIVER, D. and JACOBS, C. (2007). 'Developing Guiding Principles: An Organizational Learning Perspective.' *Journal of Organizational Change Management*, 20: 813–28.

OLIVER, D., and Roos, J. (2005). 'Decision Making in High Velocity Environments: The Importance of Guiding Principles.' *Organization Studies*, 26: 889–913.

—— —— (2007). 'Beyond Text: Constructing Organizational Identity Multimodally.' *British Journal of Management*, 18: 342–58.

PFEFFER, J. and SALANCIK, G. (1974). 'Organizational Decision Making as a Political Process: The Case of the University Budget.' *Administrative Science Quarterly*, 19: 135–51.

Roos, J. (2006). *Thinking from Within: A Hands-On Strategy Practice*. Basingstoke: Palgrave Macmillan.

—— VICTOR, B., and STATLER, M. (2004). 'Playing Seriously with Strategy.' *Long Range Planning*, 37/6: 549–68.

SANDELANDS, L. and BUCKNER G. C. (1989). 'Of Art and Work: Aesthetic Experience and the Psychology of Work Feelings,' in L. L. Cummings and B. M. Staw (eds.), *Research in Organizational Behavior*. Greenwich, CT: JAI Press.

SCHOEMAKER, P. (1993). 'Multiple Scenario Development: Its Conceptual and Behavioral Foundation.' *Strategic Management Journal*, 14: 193–213.

SHAPIRA, Z. (ed.) (1997). *Organizational Decision Making*. New York: Cambridge University Press.

SHEFFI, Y. (2005). *The Resilient Enterprise*. Boston, MA: MIT Press.

SIMON, H. (1987). 'Making Management Decisions: The Role of Intuition and Emotion.' *Academy of Management Executive* 1/1: 57–64.

STARBUCK, W. H. and WEBSTER, J. (1991). 'When is Play Productive?' *Accounting, Management, and Information Technology*, 1: 71–90.

STATLER, M. (2005). 'Practical Wisdom and Serious Play: Reflections on Management Understanding,' in H. Schrat and M. Brellochs (eds.), *Sophisticated Survival Techniques / Strategies in Art and Economy*. Berlin: Kulturverlag Kadmos.

—— JACOBS, C., and Roos, J. (2006). 'Performing Strategy—Analogical Reasoning as Strategic Practice.' Proceedings of the Academy of Management Annual Meeting.

—— Roos, J. (2006). 'Reframing Strategic Preparedness: An Essay on Practical Wisdom.' *International Journal of Management Concepts and Philosophy*, 2/2: 99–117.

—— —— (2007). *Everyday Strategic Preparedness: The Role of Practical Wisdom in Organizations*. Basingstoke, UK: Palgrave Macmillan.

—— —— VICTOR, B. (2006). 'Illustrating the Need for Practical Wisdom.' *International Journal of Management Concepts and Philosophy*, 2/1: 1–30.

SUTTON-SMITH, B. (1997). *The Ambiguity of Play*. Cambridge, MA: Harvard University Press.

WEICK, K. and SUTCLIFFE, K. (2001). *Managing the Unexpected: Assuring High Performance in an Age of Complexity*. San Francisco, CA: Jossey-Bass.

TAYLOR, S. S. and HANSEN, H. (2005). 'Finding Form: Looking at the Field of Organizational Aesthetics'. *Journal of Management Studies*, 42/6: 1211–32.

WRIGHT, G. and GOODWIN, P. (2002). 'Eliminating a Framing Bias by Using Simple Instructions to "Think Harder" and Respondents with Managerial Experience: Comments on Breaking the Frame."' *Strategic Management Journal*, 23: 1059–67.

WHITTINGTON, R. (2006). 'Learning More from Failure: Practice and Process.' *Organization Studies*, 27/12: 1903–6.

26

DO ACTIVITIES OF CONSULTANTS AND MANAGEMENT SCIENTISTS AFFECT DECISION MAKING BY MANAGERS?

ALFRED KIESER

BENJAMIN WELLSTEIN

INTRODUCTION

MANAGERS, consultants, and management researchers are not three of a kind. On the contrary, they are members of different social systems in which they pursue different goals, apply different criteria for success and speak different languages. A basic hypothesis of our analysis is that the differences between these systems hamper communication between them. Our discussion is inspired by Luhmann's theory of social systems (Luhmann 1977, 2005; Seidl 2005a, b; Seidl and Becker 2006). That managers and management researchers have trouble communicating with each other is well-known. That consultants and managers should have similar difficulties may appear astonishing at first sight. Would managers pay consultants if they did not understand them? However, the authenticity of communication between consultants and managers, in the sense that both groups aim for the same goals, is questionable. In any case, consultant talk is different from manager talk and one can question whether understanding between consultants and managers is without complications.

The communication between researchers and managers seems even more problematic. Managers are not familiar with scientific methods. Researchers may be more familiar with formulations of management problems in scientific articles than with the ways in which managers define their problems. When representatives of the two groups meet, they usually find out that they speak of different problems.

In order to assess what kind of knowledge consultants and management researchers can contribute to support managers' decisions, one first has to find out how *managers* make decisions. Hence, this chapter starts by discussing some results on decision making by managers. It then analyzes what kind of knowledge *consultants* produce and how they produce it. The chapter also asks why there has been such an enormous growth in the demand for consulting. This growth seems to indicate that managers appreciate the consultants' contributions to their decision making. Then the chapter argues that the system of science follows its own logic and dynamics and thus necessarily produces a rigor relevance gap: the problems that management researchers analyze are not the problems that managers experience.

How Managers Make Decisions

It is common to frame managerial decisions as responses to problems that the environment poses upon organizations. However, the environment does not present problems by itself. Managers have to decide what to observe in the environment and how to assess what they observe. Thus, in the same industry, managers of comparable organizations often perceive—can decide to perceive—different problems in the environment (Barr et al. 1992). Managers also have to make decisions on how to evaluate the outcomes of previous decisions in order to find out whether decision-making procedures are in need of a redesign.

Seen from this perspective organizations consist of decisions or communication concerning decisions (Luhmann 2000). Every decision within an organization is the product of earlier decisions and gives rise to ensuing decisions (Seidl 2005a). The basic function of a decision is to solve a problem and thereby reduce uncertainty. Once a decision has been made, the uncertainty that originally triggered that specific decision is absorbed: "Uncertainty absorption takes place when inferences are drawn from a body of evidence and the inferences, instead of the evidence itself, are then communicated" (March and Simon 1958: 165). However, the decision may produce new uncertainties that succeeding decisions will have to reduce. In this respect, the organization, on the basis of decision-making processes, is "pulsating between reduction and production of uncertainty" (Seidl 2005a: 43).

From this perspective, each organization is a *closed system*: decisions follow from decisions, not from changes in the environment. Only the members decide what information to include in a decision. People from outside of the organization—management researchers or consultants—can only influence organizational decision makers; they cannot make organizational decisions in lieu of the managers.

As a consequence of their bounded rationality (Simon 1976) managers do not (cannot) attempt to optimize or maximize, they only satisfice, and, over time, adapt their aspiration levels to the success or failure of their decisions, as they assess it (Simon 1979). They show a tendency to start search for better solutions in the neighborhood of the symptoms that indicate that an existing solution is not good enough (Cyert and March 1963). Having defined problems, managers, on an ad-hoc basis, generate alternatives and choose the ones that appear most promising. If managers evaluate the outcomes of decisions as unsatisfactory, they choose another or a new alternative. If, after several rounds, the expected improvements do not realize, managers consider changing the goals that guide the evaluation of the decision. "[T]he manager acts in serial or stepwise fashion, making an incremental change, interpreting the feedback, making another change, and so on" (Mintzberg 1973: 16).

Managers reduce search efforts by following a "logic of appropriateness" (March 1991a: 105, 1994: 58). In decision situations they ask themselves: "What does a person such as I do in a situation such as this?" (March 1991a: 105). In other words, they refer to generalized rules.

Decision-making processes typically encompass a number of interconnected decisions made by individual members or in groups. In organizations one finds streams of choice opportunities in which streams of organizational members, problems, and solutions meet each other (March and Olsen 1976; March 1994). Organizational members try to link problems with solutions but often do not succeed. The absence of relevant problems facilitates the selection of solutions in certain choice opportunities. Relevant problems are sometimes not present because the organizational members who might have an interest in solving them have overlooked this opportunity or because they have wandered with these problems to other choice opportunities that they find more promising.

Managers often do not engage in intensive search for information concerning problems about which they have to decide. They prefer "conditional reasoning [involving] more explicit speculation and figuring out the meaning of facts" (Isenberg 1986: 782). This does not preclude extensive analyses for "big" decisions like acquisitions or investments in new production capacities. The question is, however, what elements of these analyses managers ultimately consider when they, as individuals or in groups, make up their minds for decisions.

In the absence of information, managers rely on intuition (Mintzberg 1973; Shrivastava and Mitroff 1984; Isenberg 1986). "The manager literally wades into the swarm of 'events' that surround him and actively tries to unrandomize them and impose some order" (Weick 1983: 148). This does not mean that managers do not reflect. However, they reflect and think differently than management researchers think that they should.

Conditioned by linear, stage models of problem solving and by scientific thinking as the representative anecdote, observers have suspected that thinking is visible in the form of long reflecting episodes in which managers sit alone, away from the action, trying to make logical inferences from facts. Since observers do not see many episodes that look like this, they conclude that managers do not do much thinking. (Weick 1983: 222)

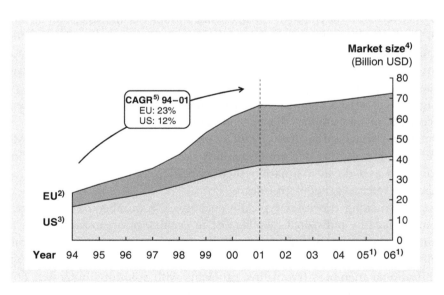

Fig. 26.1 Market development in the EU and US for operations and corporate strategy consulting, 1994–2006.

Notes: (1) Datamonitor forecast; (2) Converted to US$ (EUR=1.24 US$); (3) Figures for 94–99 calculated*; (4) Operations and corporate strategy services (approx. 50% of the total market size for mgmt. consulting); (5) Compound annual growth rate.

Sources: *US Department of Commerce, ITA (2000); FEACO (2003); Datamonitor (2005).

Intuition often flows from *subjective models* (Argyris and Schön 1978; Weick 1983; Shrivastava and Mitroff 1984; Mintzberg 1994). Managers do not regard intuition as inferior. "Intuition...refers to the smooth automatic performance of learned behavior sequences" (Isenberg 1984: 85).

Managers test the appropriateness of their assumptions by assessing their plausibility. The manager's "work pace is unrelenting and his work activities are characterized by brevity, variety, and fragmentation. The job of managing does not develop reflective planners; rather it breeds adaptive information manipulators who prefer a stimulus-response milieu" (Mintzberg 1973: 5).

Intuition encompasses various "solution identification tactics" (Nutt 1993a, b) such as trying out ideas that the manager has taken over from other persons or the literature or revitalizing some schemes that proved helpful in similar situations in the past. Many managerial decisions imply micro politics, including persuading, deceiving, or compensating opponents or winning and nursing allies (Cohen and March 1986). Managers know that those who have a chance to define a problem (including its causes) can influence the search for solutions and the direction that the flow of ensuing decisions takes.

How Management Consultants Produce Knowledge to Assist Managerial Decision Making

Over the last decades, the market for management consulting has undergone impressive growth. This chapter focuses on consulting for operations management (e.g., business process reengineering, cost reduction) and corporate strategy (e.g., strategic planning, M&A). In the 1990s, this kind of advice saw double digit annual growth rates (see Figure 26.1 across). Thus, the consulting sector itself has grown much faster than the sectors most of its clients belong to (Ernst and Kieser 2002). Even though the industry faced something like a crisis in the years following 2000 (Kipping 2002), considering forecasts for 2006 one can conclude that the demand for management consulting has virtually tripled within the last 12 years.

This is even more impressive as, in contrast to the services of public accountants and lawyers, no manager has to obtain consultants' advice. Some companies (e.g., Aldi, General Electric, Procter and Gamble) have decided to do without it (Wooldridge 1997; Brandes 2001)—without suffering obvious disadvantages.

What Kind of Knowledge do Management Consultants Produce?

Consultants predominantly produce and exploit knowledge on *methods*—methods to tackle problems (e.g., Alavi 1997; Werr et al. 1997; Werr 1999; Barlett 2000; Morris 2001; Petersen and Poulfelt 2002). Most methods structure clients' problems to make them accessible to problem solving. To some extent, the kind of knowledge that consultants apply depends on the role that they assume. Basically two role models are relevant (Schein 1978, 1987): the *expert model*, according to which the consultant develops solutions and sells them to the client, and the *process consultation model*, according to which consultants and members of the client organization jointly diagnose the problem and generate a solution. If not noted otherwise, arguments in this chapter apply for both models. From the managers' point of view, consultants are experts in both models though their expertise extends to different problems.

Most consulting methods serve to structure and—in many cases—to simplify decision problems. BCG's share growth portfolio is a good example (O'Shea and Madigan 1997). Despite massive criticism from management research, the portfolio matrix became an overwhelming success (Morrison and Wensley 1991). Consultants who follow the expert model design packaged programs that usually encompass a number of standardized methods besides some other ingredients. Typical are stage processes that contain several elements including the following (e.g., Kubr 2002):

1. *Developing a vision for the change* (e.g., for re-engineering or lean production) that comprises a couple of performance goals and some guiding principles (e.g., process orientation, reduction of interfaces, continuous improvement). Consultants are specialists for communication, including design of slides. They test presentations for impact and, for example, replace slides that do not work. For example, the presentation for the corporate culture concept ("7S-diamond") was tested in different audiences of managers and turned out to be a very powerful symbol (Crainer 1997).

2. *Screening of the "as is" situation.* Here standardized methods for assessing processes, resources, competencies of jobholders, costs, etc., including visualization, evaluation, and presentation, are used.

3. *Developing alternative solutions* based on the evaluation of the "as is" situation. In this phase that requires creativity consultants employ predominantly heuristic methods.

4. *Evaluating and ranking these alternatives.* This step often takes place in a group exercise in which consultants and managers participate in using structured evaluation methods.

5. *Setting up an action plan*, again based on programmed procedures that specify the steps that are necessary to implement the preferred alternative.

The methods for process consultation concentrate on increasing problem-solving skills of groups, including communication (Schein 1987), analytical skills, and learning (Argyris 2000). The assumption behind process consultation is that problem-solving knowledge that members possess is superior to consultants' expertise, it is only necessary sometimes to employ consultants to unlock that knowledge (Argyris 2000). The big consultancies tend to concentrate on methods that rather structure the clients' problems like portfolio analysis or the balanced scorecard than unlock group skills.

The development and application of standardized methods requires *experience* (Werr 1999). Consultants accumulate this kind of experience in all the projects they are involved. It consists of, for example, experience on how to effectively deal with skeptical managers or with conflicts within rival management groups. This also includes tackling with opposing representatives of groups of employees that are disadvantaged by changes recommended by consultants. Expert consultants create the impression that their packaged approaches imply the transfer of "best practices," in other words, solutions that they have been able to isolate in the most successful companies and to incorporate in their redesign packages (Werr 1999; Petersen and Poulfelt 2002; Werr and Linnarsson 2002).

What Kind of Functions Besides Providing Methods and Experience do Consultants Offer their Customers?

Consultants offer their clients more functions—official and unofficial—than those of providing methods and experience, for example:

- *Legitimization.* Consultants convince analysts, shareholders, and an increasingly critical public that the managers of its client organizations use state of the art practices.
- *Providing temporary management capacity.* Consultants help clients to overcome bottlenecks or carry out tasks for which it is not efficient for the client organization to invest in management capacity since these tasks do not have to be performed regularly (e.g., assessing the public image of the organization).
- *Need for an external view.* Consultants act as neutral observers from outside of the organization. "The unattached, unrestricted judgement is what a consultant is supposed to deliver" (Oetinger 2002: 267, all German quotes translated by authors), as one of BCG's top managers coins it. In addition, managers tend to often value external knowledge more highly than internal knowledge (Menon and Pfeffer 2003).
- *Communication and stimulation of acceptance after top management has decided on a change process.* Consultants have well tried presentation techniques and rhetoric at their disposals that enable them to overcome resistance to change.

Unofficial (latent) functions:

- *Providing weapons for politics.* Consultants are instrumental for increasing the power of groups of managers to have their projects accepted and to undermine the projects of rival groups (Littrell and Glen 1982). They sometimes take on the role of scapegoats. In addition, consultants promote the careers of managers who sponsor them.
- *Providing interpretation and reassurance.* Consultants offer "ideas, metaphors, models, and words that impose order on a confusing world, thus reconstructing our appreciation of experience" (March 1991b: 29).

The (demand producing) skill of the consultant consists in sounding out the expectations of the powerful actors and in handling these expectations in such a way that client satisfaction is maximized while the interests of the consultant's company are also taken care of. The satisfied client is likely to prolong and, eventually, renew the cooperation with the consultancy. The individual consultants who are successful in selling following up projects receive special incentives from their consultancy (e.g., Student 2006).

Why is There so Much Demand for Consulting?

The usual explanation for the growth of the consulting market, as shown in Figure 26.1, is that the increase in complexity and dynamics of the environment compels managers to seek consultants' advice (e.g., Hasek 1997; Jackson 1997; Kipping 2002). Another explanation takes into account the managers' *perception of control loss*—a perception that consultants' communication induces (Ernst and Kieser 2002). Thus, consultants are able to influence managers' decisions without being in direct contact with them:

Consultants are agents for *creating a complex environment.* They propagate the installation of experts who are capable of applying sophisticated methods for analyzing and dealing with the environment. However, these methods make the environment look even more complex. Enhanced complexity calls for more experts and techniques that are more powerful. For general top management it gets increasingly difficult to coordinate highly specialized functions that apply sophisticated methods. That means that the perception of control loss increases and, consequently, also the need to seek advice from consultants.

Whereas consultants do not necessarily intend to pursue this development, they do the following: they convince organizations hitherto unaware of their need for consulting that they confront just those problems for which consultants happen to have the solutions. Potential clients who are convinced by this argument perceive control loss: there is knowledge for superior solutions that they do not possess. In this way, consultants increasingly find clients in small and medium-sized companies, the bureaucracies of the public sector, and not for profit organizations such as hospitals, universities, theatres, and churches (Galvin et al. 2004).

Consultants also try to expand the scope of their services by *colonizing new areas of knowledge*. They propose to institutionalize new functional specializations such as real estate management, pricing specialists, business ethics, or sponsoring. Each new specialization is a claim that a company can increase its competitive advantage by establishing new functional departments staffed with professionals. Managers, who become convinced that their organizations lack the expertise that these functional departments provide, experience control loss.

Consultants create *management fashions*. Usually, a fashion contains a number of expressions or principles that are vague like "empowerment," "internal customers," or "process ownership." Vagueness is advantageous since it triggers discussions among those who hear about the fashion and increases their desire to learn more about it. At certain points in time, it appears inevitable to consult experts, and the best experts are the consultants who praise themselves having successfully implemented the respective fashion. The more companies that are reported as having achieved competitive advantages through the implementation of a management concept—and the consultancies are eager to spread success stories—the higher the propensity of non-adopters to get on to the bandwagon until saturation and disillusionment sets in (Loh and Venkatraman 1992; Zbaracki 1998; Strang and Macy 2001). The strategy of increasing demand by creating management fashions has proven highly effective.

By adopting a fashion to bring about change with the help of consultants managers can distinguish themselves from the crowd and, at the same time, belong to a group of managers around the world who are part of this movement (Simmel 1957). Belonging to the group of adopters of a fashion can increases the company's reputation and, thereby, its success (Westphal 1998; Staw and Epstein 2000).

Pressure of constituents for performance improvements is another factor that increases managers' perceptions of control loss. Managers are threatened by shareholder activism (Proffitt and Spicer 2005) and hostile takeovers (Schneper and Guillén 2004). The best response is to seek constant performance improvements. Again, consultants amplify this control loss inducing pressures from the outside by promoting benchmarks that they help to carry out and by propagating shareholder value including all the strategies that are seen as drivers for this concept (downsizing, outsourcing, concentrating on core competencies, etc.) and by assisting hostile takeovers.

Consultants can help to reduce perceived control loss (which they have partly induced):

1. They offer managers approaches like reengineering, total (!) quality management, or target costing that, if applied promise to accommodate the managers' need for control over organizational processes. Thus, a management fashion simultaneously increases and reduces perception of control loss.
2. The sheer presence of experts often appears sufficient to heighten managers' perceptions of controllability.

3. Managers who associate with consultants are often convinced that they profit from their ability to foresee the threats of the future, as this will ensure that they will be prepared.

4. From consultants, managers often learn that the problems they are facing are common and not caused by management failures.

The demand for consulting also profits from the fact that the assessment of the success of consulting is almost impossible: "Clients may be unable to assess experts' advice by acting on it and watching the outcomes: the clients do not know what would have happened if they had acted otherwise" (Starbuck 1992: 731). And there is also the problem of interactivity: consultants and clients always interact in complicated ways so that in case of a failure it is impossible to figure out whose fault it was. Ultimately, the evaluation of a consulting project is always a "social construction"—by managers who have been involved in choosing the consultant and in carrying out the project (Ernst 2002). This inability to assess consulting projects reinforces management's perception of control loss: it seems as if a permanent personal presence of consultants is needed to reduce the perception of control loss what might indicate a certain dependency on consultants.

How Management Consultants Affect Decision Making by Managers

Both, managers of the client organization and consultants are managers trying to achieve "a sense of identity and control over others and the environment" (Sturdy 1997: 392). In doing so, consultants are eager to increase client satisfaction and, thereby, future revenue potentials. Even though consultants stay inside the client firm for a certain time and form teams with members of the client organization, they remain part of the client's environment (Kieser 2002). The relationship between the consultants and their clients can be compared to a situation in which the client's system virtually lies on the consultant's "dissection table" (Nicolai 2000: 240). The consultant's view of the client's systems differs from the self-observation of the client (Luhmann 1992). When consultants communicate observations to their clients, two separate systems are in communication, constituting a social system of its own kind: a "contact system" (Luhmann 1992: 221).

Consultancies try to avoid being drawn into power struggles within the client system (Luhmann 1992). Thus a communication barrier is inherent in the contact system. Consultants prefer to communicate their "true" impressions among themselves and not to the client's managers. If consultants eliminated this communication barrier, the effects and consequences would be hard to control (Luhmann 1992; Nicolai 2000). This and the following observations not only apply to the expert model but also to the process consultation model according to which the consultants "heal" deficient group processes.

As noted, the contact system constitutes an analogy to the relationship between physicians and their patients (Clark 1995; Nicolai 2000). In both models there is an expert to whom the client, or patient, attributes superior knowledge. On the basis of their knowledge, the experts diagnose, conceptualize solutions, and if necessary implement them. However, like the physician, the consultant is supposed to deliver something the client does not (yet) know. Thus, there is an information asymmetry at the very heart of any consultant–client relationship (Arrow 1985; Ernst and Kieser 2002).

This may be an advantageous position for the consultants. Projects often contain a diagnostic phase in which consulting companies gain deep insights into their clients. Hence they are able to "bias" (Armenakis et al. 1990) a problem's definition in two ways. On the one hand, consultants can *define new problems* that have not been revealed by the client's self-observation (Nutt 1993a). On the other hand they can *interpret and reframe problems* so that they fit their solutions and methods (Fincham 1995).

Furthermore the information asymmetry between the client and the consultancy allows management consultants to pursue *impression management*. "The creation, management and regulation of impressions and images is . . . a central feature of consultancy work" (Clark 1995: 91–2). Managers engage consultants "in order to check the sanity of their ideas and plans" (Werr and Linnarsson 2002: 14). Since consultants have a wide experience base they are able to offer "benchmarks" and business acumen to assist managers to select adequate solutions. However, engaging a consultancy with a high reputation (Fincham 1995: 76) reduces the danger that a project in poorly evaluated after its completion.

Expert consultants restructure organizations, implant new information systems and decision-making procedures and thereby *change the conditions* under which managers make decisions. Like traffic lights, these systems deliver decision relevant information for managers; for example, a portfolio analysis suggests a strategy of pushing the sales of "babies" through advertising or of taking "poor dogs" out of the market. Consultants not only propose procedures through which superfluous human resources can be identified but also accompany management in realizing downsizing potential by identifying the employees who are to be laid off, assisting those in finding new jobs, etc. Consultants cannot control how managers react to the new conditions, and therefore they eventually concentrate on the part they can control: managing the impression that one is better off engaging them.

How Management Researchers
Produce Knowledge

Science as a Highly Autonomous System

Science, including management science, is a highly autonomous, even self-referential, social system. It produces knowledge that is difficult to access by individuals outside its borders. Outsiders have to acquire a substantial amount of scientific knowledge before they can take actively part in communication within the system. They need to acquire formal qualifications to become full members. Likewise, for members of the scientific system it is impossible to grasp entirely the problems of business organizations. Communication barriers of this kind are annoying for management researchers since, belonging to an applied science they are supposed to generate knowledge that managers understand and find useful.

Observers of the output from management research diagnose a gap between its scientific rigor and its relevance for practice (Anderson et al. 2001 present empirical evidence that the gap is widening). In 1990, in the inaugural issue of Organization Science, Daft and Lewin (1990: 1) asked: "Is the field of organization studies irrelevant? Organizations have become the dominant institution on the social landscape. Yet the body of knowledge published in academic journals has practically no audience in business or government." The rigor–relevance gap became a reiterating issue in the yearly presidential addresses at Academy of Management meetings. For example, Hambrick (1994: 13) exclaimed:

Each August [at the AoM meeting], we come to talk with each other; during the rest of the year we read each others' papers in our journals and write our own papers so that we may, in turn, have an audience in the following August: an incestuous, closed loop...It is time for us to break out of our closed loop. It is time for us to matter.

Presidents who followed Hambrick, e.g., Huff (2000), Van de Ven (2002), and Rousseau (2006) came back to this issue in their presidential addresses without presenting any evidence that the appeals of their predecessors had improved the situation. In recent years, academic journals have dedicated special issues to the rigor-relevance gap like *Administrative Science Quarterly* (Beyer 1982), *Academy of Management Journal* (Rynes et al. 2001), and *British Journal of Management* (Hodgkinson 2001). An increasing number of articles outside these special issues on this problem have also appeared (LaForce and Novelli 1985; Daft and Lewin 1990; Buckley et al. 1998; Beer 2001; Lallé 2003) as well as books (Campbell et al. 1982; Hakel et al. 1982; Murphy and Saal 1990) or edited books (Noll 1998; Larwood and Gattiker 1999).

There is wide agreement on the diagnosis on the gap's causes: it is not just attributable to differences in language and style between the worlds of science and practice, however differences in logics and communication patterns are. Van de Ven (2002: 180) refers to this cause when he observes that management science is split into two different subsystems—one that "gets absorbed in the applied culture of managers and businesses" and another one whose scientists are "[f]or the most part sealed off from the practitioner's community." Calhoun and Starbuck (2003: 486–7) also point to the self-referential system of science: "People...draw value from the process of doing research whether or not the research produces useful results."

The task of the social system of science, including the subsystem of management science, is to produce theories and results from (predominantly) empirical research. The scientific community alone determines what kind of communication counts as scientific (Stichweh 1994). Only knowledge that results from scientific operations, for example, from scientific experiments, scientific surveys, or other methods acknowledged as scientific, is accepted. Researchers have to prove that their methods qualify as scientific, for example, by pointing out that acknowledged members of the scientific community have included these methods in their books on methods or that their usage is undisputed in the community.

Researchers are supposed to criticize research results from colleagues as well as their own ones (e.g., by pointing to limitations, Merton 1973). This includes identifying results that contradict each other. Critique leads to the advancement of theories and methods and to additional empirical analyses. The growth of knowledge induces spin-offs of disciplines and subdisciplines. In the social sciences, especially in management science, it is easier than in the natural sciences to create new concepts and theories what further increases the number of subdisciplines (Whitley 2000). It is obvious that researchers need not import research problems from outside the scientific system. They have no difficulties to produce an abundance of problems for their research themselves. For outsiders who search for scientific information it is getting increasingly difficult to bushwhack through the jungle of subdisciplines, theories, methods, and contradictory results.

Operations of science always refer to other operations within this system. For example, a scientific publication always refers to other scientific publications—to theoretical concepts and methods it builds on and develops further. "One publishes to get quoted and to increase one's chances for additional publications" (Stichweh 1994: 72). The "incestuous, closed loop" that Hambrick (1994: 13) bemoans is not pathological but a characteristic of "normal science." Communication within the scientific system cannot integrate communication from the outside like, for example, companies' communication on management problems. When, for example, management researchers communicate with managers about problems these managers experience in their practice this communication is similar for them to the one with a rodeo rider. As long as communication that originates from other social systems lacks a theoretical frame, it does not qualify as scientific. The transformation of a problem from practice into a scientific problem, changes its content.

The code of managers' communication refers to the criteria of *profitability* and *efficiency*. In contrast, the code of scientific communication is *true/false*. In other words, it is the basic task of actors in the scientific system to identify deficient theories and research results and to replace them with true theories and results. Scientists test a communication on a result by confronting it with other communication regarding its trueness. For example, reviewers evaluate articles submitted for publication. Researchers are supposed to validate results before using them in their own research. However, the sheer quantity of communication in the scientific system is so immense that it is impossible to "test" carefully all the underlying assumptions. Therefore, reputation often serves as an indicator of truth: communication from reputed members of the scientific community benefits from a leap of faith. The scientific system—and only it—grants scientific reputation in form of titles, positions or citations. In this way, the scientific system stays operatively closed as it does not take into consideration the reputations a scientist has gained in other systems, for example, as a politician, sportsman, or consultant.

The Insurmountable Obstacles of Creating Scientific Knowledge that is Rigorous and Relevant

The problem that members of the scientific system have enormous difficulties to absorb communication from outside into their system has led authors to call for joint research by practitioners and researchers. The underlying assumption is that the dependency in knowledge production helps to overcome communication barriers between the two groups.

Action research was the first approach to advance this concept (Susman and Evered 1978; Eden and Huxham 1996; Reason and Bradbury 2001) in the hope that collaboration "brings rigor and relevance together" (Greenwood and Morten 1998: 238). Following Tranfield and Starkey (1998) proponents of mode 2 research and related alternatives have repeated the call for collaboration (e.g., Gibbons et al. 1994; Hatchuel 2001; Nowotny et al. 2001; Starkey and Madan 2001; MacLean et al. 2002; van Aken 2005). Anderson et al. (2001) argue for "pragmatic science," while Huff and Huff (2001) advocate mode 3. For mode 2 research, it is essential that knowledge production is "guided by specifiable consensus" that "is conditioned by the context of application and evolves with it" (Gibbons et al. 1994: 5). The proponents argue that "to the criterion of intellectual interests and its interaction, further questions are posed, such as 'Will the solution, if found, be competitive in the market?' 'Will it be cost effective?' 'Will it be socially acceptable?' " (Gibbons et al. 1994: 8). In other words, in assessments of scientific knowledge criteria for usefulness have to complement criteria for trueness. However, is it possible to produce scientific knowledge that is equally rigorous and relevant? Ford et al. (2005) assume that a trade-off has to be made when they demand that "[u]niversities should recognize the importance of research that is critical, verifiable, valid, useful, and clear, even if it is not published in the most prestigious journal of the field." Other authors (e.g., Hodgkinson 2006; Van de Ven and Johnson 2006) reject the argument of a possible trade-off between relevance and rigor but fail to outline how to operationalize relevance. At any rate, just as only scientists can legitimately assess scientific rigor, the evaluation of practical relevance has to be left to the system of practice. It is hard to imagine, though, how communication with the code true/false is, at the same time, applying the code relevant/irrelevant (producing practical solutions / not producing practical solutions). It would for example require that practitioners join researchers as reviewers of articles submitted to journals. Moreover, it would require rules for impartially resolving eventual conflicts between the two groups.

Additional questions pose themselves when it comes to the implementation of collaborative teams. To list just a few: who selects the participants? In particular, who selects the subdisciplines for the team of the researchers and the specialized departments for the team of the practitioners? Problems identified in practice seldom correspond to only one or a few scientific disciplines and one or only a few organizational specializations. Which norms govern the overall team's discourse? How are conflicts of interests handled? A conflict that is most likely to emerge is what kind of output the team should seek—knowledge that contributes to the specific problems of the participating organization(s) or general knowledge that can be published in scientific journals? (McSweeny 2000 has formulated questions of this kind in his critique of action research). Perhaps, after a collaborative analysis of a practical problem, managers find researchers inspiring for the search of solutions. They may even find the collaboration with researchers more inspiring than cooperation with consultants. However, it remains to be seen whether the knowledge produced in such discourses qualifies as scientific communication. Perhaps the communication in collaborative teams will prove heuristically valuable for practitioners and researchers when they develop their respective knowledge. Such an outcome one should not regard as of minor value. Why do researchers who propagate collaboration always imply that scientific knowledge should be the outcome—scientific knowledge that is relevant for practitioners? Would not practitioners' knowledge that adds to problem solutions in new ways and scientific knowledge that adds to extant theories in new ways—ways that do better correspond to processes in practice—also constitute positive outcomes of such collaborations?

It is perhaps due to problems of this sort that empirical results from action research or mode 2 research or any other collaborative efforts have only extremely rarely found their way into prestigious journals (concerning action research see Greenwood 2002; Eikeland 2003; Gustavsen 2003). The vast majority of articles originating from these research programs prefer to discuss epistemological problems instead of presenting results from collaborative research.

Why Management Researchers
Do Not Significantly Affect Decision
Making by Managers

Except for collaborative projects that still are extremely rare, management researchers are not able to establish a contact system between themselves and managers. In comparison with consultants, their impact on managers' decisions is therefore low. Some management researchers fluctuate between the roles of researcher and consultant. When acting as consultants they influence managers' decisions in the same ways as consultants do. Their reputation as scientists may increase their authority in this role. In this respect Nicolai (2004) has shown that Michael Porter argues in different styles and tells different stories in his texts that address managers and in those that are directed to the scientific community.

Practitioners do not take much notice of the output of management research. They do not read academic publications. Some journals such as *Harvard Business Review* or *Sloan Management Review* claim to publish popularized versions of the results of management research. However, is it possible to "translate" results of management research for managers so that these are able to understand and apply them properly to their problems? Kelemen and Bansal (2002) compared an article from a scientific journal by Brown and Eisenhardt (1997) with an article by these authors in a management magazine (Eisenhardt and Brown 1998) that, according to the authors, presents the implications of the research results for practice. In the managerial article, the authors develop a concept that is much simpler than that in the scientific journal. They do not discuss their methods but present success factors that did not occur in the scientific article. The analysis in this chapter suggests that such a gap between texts that present research results for the two audiences is unavoidable.

Conclusion

Consultants are in a better position than management researchers to influence managers' decisions. Managers actively seek their advice—and pay for it. Nevertheless, consulting knowledge does not meld in a taken for granted way with knowledge held by managers in a specific company.

Knowledge that management researchers produce is difficult to apply by managers since its logic is different from the logic that characterizes managers' decisions. Some management researchers switch to the role of a consultant and a non-scientific communication style when managers ask them for advice. Whether collaboration between researchers and practitioners will prove as a way to bridge the rigor–relevance gap in production of *scientific* knowledge is difficult to decide. Even though practitioners and researchers will maintain their own way of knowledge production, the two groups may identify procedures by which both profit from collaboration. Such a result would suffice to justify collaboration, though in a less spectacular fashion.

References

ALAVI, M. (1997). *KPMG Peat Marwick U.S.: One Giant Brain.* Case 9-397-108. Boston, MA: Harvard Business School.

ANDERSON, N., HERRIOT, P., and HODGKINSON, G. P. (2001). 'The Practitioner–Researcher Divide in Industrial, Work and Organizational (IWO) Psychology: Where are We and Where do We Go from Here?' *Journal of Occupational and Organizational Psychology,* 74: 391–411.

ARGYRIS, C. and SCHÖN, D. A. (1978). *Organizational Learning: A Theory of Action Perspective.* Reading, MA: Addison-Wesley.

ARGYRIS, C. (2000). *Flawed Advice.* Oxford: Oxford University Press.

ARMENAKIS, A. A., MOSSHOLDER, K. W., and HARRIS, S. G. (1990). 'Diagnostic Bias in Organizational Consultation.' *Omega,* 18: 563–72.

ARROW, K. J. (1985). 'The Economics of Agency,' in J. W. Pratt and R. J. Zeckhauser (eds.), *Principals and Agents: The Structure of Business.* Boston, MA: Harvard University School Press, 37–51.

BARLETT, C. A. (2000). *McKinsey and Company: Managing Knowledge and Learning.* Case 9-396-357. Boston, MA: Harvard Business School.

BARR, P. S., STIMPERT, J. L., and HUFF, A. S. (1992). 'Cognitive Change, Strategic Action, and Organizational Renewal.' *Strategic Management Journal,* 13: 15–36.

BEER, M. (2001). 'Why Management Research Findings are Unimplementable: An Action Science Perspective.' *Reflections,* 2: 58–65.

BEYER, J. M. (1982). 'Introduction.' *Administrative Science Quarterly,* 27/4: 588–90.

BRANDES, D. (2001). *Die ALDI-Erfolgsstory.* Frankfurt: Campus Verlag.

BROWN, S. L. and EISENHARDT, K. M. (1997). 'The Art of Continuous Change: Linking Complexity Theory and Time-Paced Evolution in Relentlessly Shifting Organizations.' *Administrative Science Quarterly,* 42: 1–34.

BUCKLEY, M. R., FERRIS, G. R., BERNADIN, H. J., and HARVEY, J. G. (1998). 'The Disconnect Between the Science and Practice of Management.' *Business Horizons,* 41: 31–8.

CALHOUN, M. and STARBUCK, W. H. (2003). 'Barriers to Creating Knowledge,' in M. Easterby-Smith and M. A. Lyles (eds.), *The Blackwell Handbook of Organizational Learning and Knowledge Management.* Malden, MA: Blackwell. 473–92.

CAMPBELL, J. P., DAFT, R. L., and HULIN, C. L. (1982). *What to Study: Generating and Developing Research Questions.* Beverly Hills, CA: Sage.

CLARK, T. (1995). *Managing Consultants—Consultancy as the Management of Impressions.* Buckingham: Open University Press.

COHEN, M. D. and MARCH, J. G. (1986). *Leadership and Ambiguity* (2nd edn.) Boston, MA: Harvard Business School Press.

CRAINER, S. (1997). *The Tom Peters Phenomenon: Corporate Man to Corporate Skunk.* Oxford: Capstone.

CYERT, R. M. and MARCH, J. G. (1963). *A Behavioral Theory of the Firm.* Englewood Cliffs, NJ: Prentice-Hall.

DAFT, R. and LEWIN, A. (1990). 'Can Organization Studies Begin to Break Out of the Normal Science Straitjacket?' *Organization Science*, 1: 1–9.

DATAMONITOR (2005). *Management and Marketing Consultancy in the United States—Industry Profile.* New York: Datamonitor.

EDEN, C. and HUXHAM, C. (1996). 'Action Research for Management Research.' *British Journal of Management*, 7: 75–86.

EIKELAND, O. (2003). 'Unmet Challenges and Unfulfilled Promises in Action Research.' *Concepts and Transformation*, 8: 265–73.

EISENHARDT, K. M. and BROWN, S. L. (1998). 'Time Pacing: Competing In Markets That Won't Stand Still.' *Harvard Business Review*, 76/2: 59–69.

ERNST, B. (2002). *Die Evaluation von Beratungsleistungen: Prozesse der Wahrnehmung und Bewertung.* Wiesbaden: Deutscher Universitäts-Verlag.

——— KIESER, A. (2002). 'In Search of Explanations for the Consulting Explosion,' in L. Engwall and K. Sahlin-Andersson (eds.), *The Expansion of Management Knowledge: Carriers, Flows, and Sources.* Stanford, CA: Stanford University Press, 47–73.

FEACO (2003). *Survey of the European Management Consultancy Market.* Brussels: FEACO.

FINCHAM, R. (1995). 'Business Process Re-engineering and the Commodification of Management Knowledge.' *Journal of Marketing Management*, 11: 707–20.

FORD, E. W., DUNCAN, J. W., BEDEIAN, A. G. et al. (2005). 'Mitigating Risks, Visible Hands, Inevitable Disasters, and Soft Variables: Management Research that Matters to Managers.' *Academy of Management Executive*, 19/4: 24–38.

GALVIN, T. L., VENTRESCA, M. J., and HUDSON, B. A. (2004). 'Contested Industry Dynamics.' *International Studies of Management and Organization*, 34/4: 56–82.

GIBBONS, M., LIMOGES, H., NOWOTNY, S. et al. (1994). *The New Production of Knowledge: The Dynamics of Science and Research.* London: Sage.

GREENWOOD, D. J. (2002). 'Action Research: Unfilled Promises and Unmet Challenges.' *Concepts and Transformation*, 7: 117–39.

——— MORTEN, L. (1998). 'Action Research, Science, and the Co-optation of Social Research: Studies in Cultures.' *Organizations and Societies*, 4/2: 237–62.

GUSTAVSEN, B. (2003). 'Action Research and the Problem of the Single Case.' *Concepts and Transformation*, 8: 93–9.

HAKEL, M. D., SORCHER, M., BEER, M., and MOSES, J. L. (1982). *Making It Happen: Designing Research with Implementation in Mind.* Beverly Hills, CA: Sage.

HAMBRICK, D. C. (1994). 'What if the Academy Actually Mattered?—1993 Presidential Address.' *Academy of Management Journal*, 19: 11–16.

HASEK, G. (1997). 'The Era of Experts.' *Industry Week*, 246/10: 60–7.

HATCHUEL, A. (2001). 'The Two Pillars of New Management Research.' *British Journal of Management*, 12/Special Issue: S33–S39.

HODGKINSON, G. P. (ed.) (2001). 'Facing the Future: The Nature and Purpose of Management Research Reassessed.' *British Journal of Management*, 12/Special Issue: S1–S80.

—— (2006). 'The Role of JOOP (and Other Scientific Journals) in Bridging the Practitioner–Researcher Divide in Industrial, Work and Organizational (IWO) Psychology.' *Journal of Occupational and Organizational Psychology*, 79/2: 173–8.

HUFF, A. S. (2000). '1999 Presidential Address: Changes in Organizational Knowledge Production.' *Academy of Management Review*, 25: 288–93.

—— HUFF, J. O. (2001). 'Re-Focusing the Business School Agenda.' *British Journal of Management*, 12/Special Issue: 49–54.

ISENBERG, D. (1984). 'How Senior Managers Think.' *Harvard Business Review*, 62/November/December: 81–90.

—— (1986). 'Thinking and Managing: A Verbal Protocol Analysis of Managerial Problem Solving.' *Academy of Management Journal*, 29: 775–88.

JACKSON, T. (1997). 'Survey—Management Consultancy: Growth and Revenues Seem to be Unstoppable.' *Financial Times*, September 19.

KELEMEN, M. and BANSAL, P. (2002). 'The Conventions of Management Research and their Relevance to Management Practice.' *British Journal of Management*, 13/2: 97–108.

KIESER, A. (2002). 'On Communication Barriers between Management Science, Consultancies and Business Companies', in T. A. Clark and R. Fincham (eds.), *Critical Consulting: New Perspectives on the Management Advice Industry*. Oxford: Blackwell, 206–27.

KIPPING, M. (2002). 'Jenseits von Krise und Wachstum.' *Zeitschrift Führung + Organisation*, 71/5: 269–76.

KUBR, M. (2002). *Management Consulting: A Guide to the Profession* (4th edn.). Geneva: International Labour Office.

LaFORCE, J. C. and NOVELLI, R. J. (1985). 'Reconciling Management Research and Practice.' *California Management Review*, 27/3: 74–82.

LALLÉ, B. (2003). 'The Management Science Researcher Between Theory and Practice.' *Organization Studies*, 24: 1097–114.

LARWOOD, L. and GATTIKER, U. E. (1999). *Impact Analysis: How Research Can Enter Application and Make a Difference*. Mahwah, NJ: Lawrence Erlbaum.

LITTRELL, E. K. and GLEN, R. H. (1982). 'Playing the Consulting Game.' *Management Accounting*, 7: 56–60.

LOH, L. and VENKATRAMAN, N. (1992). 'Diffusion of Information Technology Outsourcing: Influence Sources and the Kodak Effect.' *Information Systems Research*, 3: 334–58.

LUHMANN, N. (1977). 'Differentiation of Society.' *Canadian Journal of Sociology*, 2: 29–53.

—— (1992). 'Kommunikationssperren in der Unternehmensberatung,' in N. Luhmann and P. Fuchs (eds.), *Reden und Schweigen* (2nd edn.). Frankfurt: Suhrkamp, 209–27.

—— (2000). *Organisation und Entscheidung*. Opladen: Westdeutscher Verlag.

—— (2005). 'The Concept of Autopoiesis,' in D. Seidl and K. H. Becker (eds.), *Niklas Luhmann and Organization Studies*. Kristianstad: Liber and Copenhagen Business School Press, 54–63.

MacLEAN, D., MacINTOSH, R., and GRANT, S. (2002). 'Mode 2 Management Research.' *British Journal of Management*, 13: 189–201.

MARCH, J. G. (1991a). 'How Decisions Happen in Organizations.' *Human-Computer Interaction*, 6: 95–117.

—— (1991b). 'Organizational Consultants and Organizational Research'. *Journal of Applied Communication Research*, 19: 20–33.

MARCH, J. G. (1994). *A Primer on Decision Making: How Decisions Happen.* New York: The Free Press.

—— OLSEN, J. P. (1976). *Ambiguity and Choice in Organizations.* Bergen: Universietsforlaget.

—— SIMON, H. A. (1958). *Organizations.* New York: Wiley.

McSWEENY, B. (2000). '"Action Research": Mission Impossible? Commentary on "Towards the Increased Use of Action Research in Accounting Information Systems" by C. Richard Baker.' *Accounting Forum,* 24: 379–90.

MENON, T. and PFEFFER, J. (2003). 'Valuing Internal vs. External Knowledge: Explaining the Preference for Outsiders.' *Management Science,* 49/4: 497–513.

MERTON, R. K. (1973). *The Sociology of Science: Theoretical and Empirical Investigations.* Chicago, IL: University of Chicago Press.

MINTZBERG, H. (1973). *The Nature of Managerial Work.* New York: Harper and Row.

—— (1994). *The Rise and Fall of Strategic Planning.* New York: The Free Press.

MORRIS, T. (2001). 'Asserting Property Rights: Knowledge Codification in the Professional Service Firm.' *Human Relations,* 54/7: 819–38.

MORRISON, A. and WENSLEY, R. (1991). 'Boxing Up or Boxed In? A Short History of the Boston Consulting Group Share/Growth Matrix.' *Journal of Marketing Management,* 7: 105–29.

MURPHY, K. R. and SAAL, F. E. (1990). *Psychology in Organizations: Integrating Science and Practice.* Hillsdale, NJ: Erlbaum.

NICOLAI, A. T. (2000). *Die Strategie-Industrie.* Wiesbaden: Gabler.

—— (2004). 'Bridges to the Real "World": Applied Science Fiction or a "Schozophrenic Tour de Force"?' *Journal of Management Studies,* 41: 951–76.

NOLL, R. G. E. (1998). *Challenges to Research Universities.* Washington, DC: Brookings Institution.

NOWOTNY, H., SCOTT, P., and GIBBONS, M. (2001). *Re-thinking Science: Knowledge and the Public in an Age of Uncertainty.* Cambridge: Polity Press.

NUTT, P. C. (1993a). 'The Identification of Solution Ideas during Organizational Decision Making.' *Management Science,* 39/9: 1071–85.

—— (1993b). 'The Formulization Processes and Tactics Used in Organizational Decision Making.' *Organization Science,* 4/2: 226–51.

OETINGER, B. v. (2002). 'Der immer während Wert des Beraters.' *Zeitschrift Führung + Organisation,* 71/5: 226–68.

O'SHEA, J. and MADIGAN, C. (1997). *Dangerous Company: The Consulting Powerhouses and the Businesses they Save and Ruin.* London: Nicholas Brealey.

PETERSEN, N. J. and POULFELT, F. (2002). 'Knowledge Management in Action: A Study of Knowledge Management in Management Consultancies,' in A. F. Buono (ed.), *Developing Knowledge and Value in Management Consulting.* Greenwich, CT: Information Age Publishing, 33–60.

PROFFITT, W. T. and SPICER, A. S. (2005). 'Shaping the Agenda of Shareholder Activism: Institutional Investors and Global Corporate Social Responsibility.' *Academy of Management Proceedings*: H1–H6.

REASON, P. and BRADBURY, H. (2001). 'Inquiry and Participation in Search of a World Worthy of Human Aspiration,' in P. Reason and H. Bradbury (eds.), *Handbook of Action Research: Participative Inquiry and Practice.* London: Sage, 1–14.

ROUSSEAU, D. M. (2006). 'Presidential Address: Is There Such a Thing as "Evidence-Based Management"?' *Academy of Management Review,* 31/2: 256–69.

RYNES, S. L., BARTUNEK, J. M., and DAFT, R. D. (2001). 'Across the Great Divide: Knowledge Creation and Transfer Between Practitioners and Academics.' *Academy of Management Journal*, 44/2: 340–55.

SCHEIN, E. H. (1978). 'The Role of the Consultant: Content Expert or Process Facilitator?' *Personnel and Guidance Journal*, 56: 339–44.

—— (1987). *Process Consultation Volume I: Its Role in Organization Development*. Reading, MA: Addison-Wesley.

SCHNEPER, W. D. and GUILLÉN, M. F. (2004). 'Stakeholder Rights and Corporate Governance: A Cross-National Study of Hostile Takeovers.' *Administrative Science Quarterly*, 49: 263–95.

SEIDL, D. (2005a). *Organisational Identity and Self-transformation: An Autopoietic Perspective*. Aldershot: Ashgate.

—— (2005b). 'The Basic Concepts of Luhmanns Theory of Social Systems,' in D. Seidl and K. H. Becker (eds.), *Niklas Luhmann and Organization Studies*. Kristianstad: Liber and Copenhagen Business School Press, 21–53.

—— BECKER, K. H. (2006). 'Organizations as Distinction Generating and Processing Systems: Niklas Luhmann's Contribution to Organization Studies.' *Organization*, 13/1: 9–36.

SHRIVASTAVA, P. and MITROFF, I. I. (1984). 'Enhancing Organizational Research Utilization: The Role of Decision-Makers Assumptions.' *Academy of Management Review*, 9: 18–26.

SIMMEL, G. (1957). 'Fashion.' *American Journal of Sociology*, 62: 541–58.

SIMON, H. A. (1976). *Administrative Behavior* (3rd edn.). New York: Free Press.

—— (1979). 'Rational Decision Making in Business Organizations.' *The American Economic Review*, 69: 493–513.

STARBUCK, W. H. (1992). 'Learning by Knowledge-Intensive Firms.' *Journal of Management Studies*, 29: 713–40.

STARKEY, K. and MADAN, P. (2001). 'Bridging the Relevance Gap: Aligning Stakeholders in the Future of Management Research.' *British Journal of Management*, 12/Special Issue: S3-S26.

STAW, B. M. and EPSTEIN, L. D. (2000). 'What Bandwagons Bring: Effects of Popular Management Techniques on Corporate Performance, Reputation, and CEO Pay.' *Administrative Science Quarterly*, 45: 523–56.

STICHWEH, R. (1994). *Wissenschaft, Universität, Professionen*. Frankfurt: Suhrkamp.

STRANG, D. and MACY, M. W. (2001). '"In Search of Excellence": Fads, Success Stories, and Adaptive Emulation.' *Journal of Sociology*, 107: 147–82.

STUDENT, D. (2006). 'Powerpoint of No Return.' *Manager Magazine*, 8: 26.

STURDY, A. (1997). 'The Consultancy Process—An Insecure Business.' *Journal of Management Studies*, 34: 389–413.

SUSMAN, G. I. and EVERED, R. D. (1978). 'An Assessment of the Scientific Merits of Action Research.' *Administrative Science Quarterly*, 23: 582–603.

TRANFIELD, D. and STARKEY, K. (1998). 'The Nature, Social Organization and Promotion of Management Research: Towards Policy.' *British Journal of Management*, 9/4: 341–53.

US Department of Commerce, ITA (2000). *US Industry and Trade Outlook*. New York: McGraw-Hill.

VAN AKEN, J. E. (2005). 'Management Research as a Design Science: Articulating the Research Products of Mode 2 Knowledge Production in Management.' *British Journal of Management*, 16/1: 19–36.

VAN DE VEN, A. H. (2002). 'Strategic Directions for the Academy of Management: This Academy is for You.' *Academy of Management Review*, 27: 171–84.

—— JOHNSON, P. E. (2006). 'Knowledge for Theory and Practice.' *Academy of Management Review*, 31/4: 802–21.

WEICK, K. E. (1983). 'Managerial Thought in the Context of Action,' in S. Shrivastva (ed.), *The Executive Mind*. San Francisco: Jossey-Bass, 221–42.

WERR, A. (1999). *The Language of Change—The Roles in the Work of Management Consultants*. Stockholm: School of Economics.

—— LINNARSSON, H. (2002). 'Management Consulting for Client Learing? Clients' Perceptions of Learning in Management Consulting,' in A. F. Buono (ed.), *Developing Knowledge and Value in Management Consulting*. Greenwich, CT: Information Age Publishing, 3–31.

—— STJERNBERG, T., and DOCHERTY, P. (1997). 'The Functions of Methods of Change in the Work of Management Consultants.' *Journal of Organizational Change Management*, 10: 288–307.

WESTPHAL, J. D. (1998). 'The Symbolic Management of Stockholders: Corporate Governance Reforms and Shareholder Reactions.' *Administrative Science Quarterly*, 43: 127–54.

WHITLEY, R. (2000). *The Intellectual and Social Organization of the Sciences*. Oxford: Oxford University Press.

WOOLDRIDGE, A. (1997). 'Management Consultancy: The Advice Business.' *The Economist*, 342/8009: 3–5.

ZBARACKI, M. J. (1998). 'The Rhetoric and Reality of Total Quality Management.' *Administrative Science Quarterly*, 43: 602–36.

27

RISK COMMUNICATION IN ORGANIZATIONS

A. JOHN MAULE

INTRODUCTION

ORGANIZATIONS take decisions about managing risks across different domains of their activity. This includes decisions about chronic risks relating to staff (e.g., threats to well-being), infrastructure (e.g., threats to on-line computing facilities), customers (e.g., negative performance of their financial products) or members of the public over which they have some responsibility (e.g., air pollution around production plants). It can also include decisions about acute risks associated with unexpected events requiring immediate actions (e.g., product contamination or unscheduled release of toxic gas). Structured techniques have been developed to derive quantitative estimates of the risks involved that entail calculating the likelihood of undesired states, the magnitude or impact of these states, and then some weighted combination of the two (e.g., NRC 1983).

Until recently, people managing risk have sought primarily to develop techniques to determine whether they need to act and if so what actions to take. When these actions involve communicating the nature or extent of the risk to others, the assumption has been that the outcomes of formal risk assessments suffice (Fischhoff 1995). Risk managers have paid little attention to whether the recipients of communications accept the assumptions underlying the assessment procedures, how they interpret these assessments, and whether they act in ways the communicator intended. However, several high profile cases have demonstrated the folly of ignoring communication issues in the management of risk (e.g., Barnett and Breakwell 2003; Poortinga et al. 2004).

Given that communication issues are a key factor for effective risk management, it is perhaps surprising that it is only over the last few years that there has been systematic research in this area (Gurabardhi et al. 2004). This rise in interest is due to increasing public concerns about risk issues that have increased pressures on organizations to demonstrate they have effective management strategies in place and to communicate these to all concerned (Tulloch and Lupton 2003). Beck (1992) argued that Western societies are becoming "risk societies" in which "goods" associated with industrialization accompany "bads" associated with pollution and contamination as well as social problems such as unemployment and family break-down. In addition, he suggested that realization that experts often disagree and sometimes make mistakes has led to increased public concerns and a lack of trust in those responsible for managing risk. These changes have put organizations under increased scrutiny, led to demands for them to communicate with the public and other stakeholders, and for the development of regulatory laws and authorities to ensure that they carry out these activities appropriately.

The primary objectives of this chapter are to review theory and research on risk communication and identify gaps and limitations in this body of knowledge; to identify current trends and findings in this area; and to determine whether there are any general principles that organizational decision makers can use to improve their own communications. To achieve theses objectives the chapter contains short reviews of the primary areas of research on how people perceive and act in the face of risk. Following each of these reviews is a brief discussion of the implications of this work for the development of effective communication about risk. The recurrent theme running throughout the chapter is that effective communication depends upon taking account of a range of social factors that are not included in formal risk assessments.

COMMUNICATING PROBABILISTIC INFORMATION

Misperception of Quantitative Risk

Research shows that the public often misinterprets communications based on quantitative assessments (Berry 2004: ch. 3). For example, Gigerenzer et al.

(2005) showed that people often misinterpret risk when expressed as a percentage (e.g., 40 percent likelihood of storm damage). Yamigishi (1997) observed that people are sensitive to the number of people at risk leading them to judge that a threat of death expressed as killing 1,286 people out of every 10,000 is more risky than a threat expressed as killing 24.14 people out of every 100 people (despite the contrary being the case). Fetherstonhaugh et al. (1997) showed that people are more concerned about the proportion than the actual amount of risk reduced (e.g., people valued saving 4,500 lives more when 11,000 were at risk than when 250,000 at risk). McDaniels (1988) showed such biases also occur in legislators, leading to imbalances in expenditure on preventing deaths from different hazards. Fahey et al. (1995) showed that communicating risk reduction in relative rather than absolute terms has a bigger impact (e.g., the benefits of protective clothing are assessed more positively when expressed as a 50 percent reduction in accidents per year as compared with a reduction from 10 to 5 percent per 1,000 employees per year). Fischhoff and MacGregor (1983) reported one from a large number of studies demonstrating the importance of framing effects that indicate that expressing risks in terms of the likely losses rather than the gains can crucially affect risk estimates and behavior (see also Salovey and Williams-Piehota 2004 for a recent review of framing effects in health). These examples demonstrate that simply presenting the output of a formal assessment is unlikely to be an effective way of communicating risk. However, the disparate nature of this body of research and the fact that much of is not theory driven makes it difficult to draw conclusions other than that people often have difficulty understanding statistical information (work on cognitive heuristics and relative frequencies, to be reviewed later, are two exceptions that do provide relevant theoretical accounts). Despite the lack of a unifying theory, researchers have offered several recommendations about how to develop approaches to communication that address these limitations. The next section reviews these approaches.

Procedures for Overcoming Misperceptions of Quantitative Risk

One approach to overcoming misperceptions of statistical risk information has been to use words or phrases rather than numbers. For example, European Union (EU) legislation stipulates using words to communicate the risk of side effects associated with medicines (EC Directive 92/27) with each of five statistical bands associated with particular words (e.g., "very rare" for the lowest band, "very common" for the highest band). However, Berry et al. (2002) showed that people interpret the words differently from that assumed by risk regulators (e.g., whereas regulators defined "very rare" as less than .01 percent, people gave a mean estimate of 4 percent). There are other problems with the use of words.

For example, Lichtenstein and Newman (1969) showed variability in the way people interpret particular words (e.g., "probable" elicited numerical probabilities as low as .01 from some and as high as .99 from others). Moxey and Sanford (1993) showed that people interpret the same probabilistic word differently in different contexts. Jardine and Hrudey (1997) showed that these terms are confusing to lay audiences. Renooij and Witteman (1999) concluded that there are no empirical grounds to prefer numerical or verbal probability expressions but argued that, at least in some situations, clearly interpretable verbal expressions are better because people are more comfortable with them. Weber and Hilton (1990) went further by suggesting that communications should contain appropriate combinations of both words and numbers, though they do not specify precisely how to achieve this. In general, words do not necessarily fare better than numbers as a means of conveying risk. This suggests that communicators need to test out different modes in their own domain and context to determine which, if any, is better.

Second, Gigerenzer and his co-workers (e.g., Gigerenzer and Hoffrage 1995) have challenged the idea that people have a fundamental inability to process statistical risk information, suggesting instead that the difficulties arise because of the way that this information is presented. For example, Gigerenzer and Edwards (2003) argued that communications using single event and conditional probabilities are inherently ambiguous and confusing. They showed that people gave more accurate risk judgments when conveying this information in terms of a frequency format.

A third approach has advocated the use of ladders and scales that display by name and risk level (e.g., risk of dying over a specified period) the target hazard and a number of common hazards all presented in order of magnitude of the risk involved. Proponents of this approach assume that putting the target hazard in the context of known risks aids understanding (Sandman et al. 1994; Paling 1997). However, these techniques have not been without their critics. For example, Lipkus and Hollands (1999) argued that ladders help people locate risk levels in relative, but not absolute terms, thus replicating any biased assessments already present for the reference risks. Calman and Royston (1997) presented a community risk scale involving statistical estimates supplemented by a qualitative scale based on people's understanding of the sizes of different communities (e.g., one in ten or "one adverse event per family"; one in ten million or "one adverse event per country"). A virtue of this scale is that it uses a frequency-based format, as proposed by Gigerenzer. However, to date there is no evidence that it is effective. Related to ladders and scales is the use of comparators, where target risks are explained with reference to a particular "known" risks with a similar statistical profile (Slovic et al. 1990). Again, there is no conclusive evidence that they work (Johnson 2004) and some suggestion that their effectiveness may vary across situations, for example, with and without conflict (Slovic et al. 1990).

Finally, some authors have advocated the use of graphical techniques to aid statistical understanding (Tufte 1999), though evidence on their effectiveness in risk communication is rather mixed (Lipkus and Hollands 1999). For example, simple graphical displays may be effective when dealing with low probabilities (Schirillo and Stone 2005) but this may depend upon the nature of the graphical display and the degree of risk involved (Keller et al. 2006).

The evidence reviewed above shows little agreement about which procedures, if any, remedy the general tendency for people to misinterpret statistical risk information. This lack of agreement is due in part to the diversity of the situations and domains used to test these procedures and to the general lack of theory explaining why people have difficulty interpreting risk information. However, two areas of work have the potential to resolve these problems. As described above, Gigerenzer and his colleagues suggested that people might be naturally adapted to understanding frequency-based statistical information. This provides one useful principle to follow when communicating risk. In addition, there is a body of work showing that people use heuristic forms of thinking to make judgments of risk and uncertainty. The next section outlines this work and explores the extent to which it can provide a basis for understanding and improving risk communication.

Heuristic Forms of Thinking

People rarely think in ways that are comparable to the statistical methods used in formal risk analyses. Instead, they use simpler forms of thinking, referred to as cognitive heuristics, when making risk judgments. These heuristics can induce inaccurate judgments, which, in turn, lead to inappropriate actions (Gilovitch et al. 2002). For example, the representativeness heuristic is a form of thinking where people derive the likelihood of occurrence in terms of resemblance to existing categories of knowledge (Kahneman and Frederick 2002). Individuals using this heuristic evaluate the risk associated with an unfamiliar situation or event by assessing the degree to which it resembles or matches other known risky and safe situations and events. They use the degree of match as a proxy for probability, without taking account of other normatively important principles such as its a priori likelihood of occurring (i.e., base rate). Thus, a new situation may indeed strongly match previously experienced threatening situations but this does not mean that the risks are severe; the base rate or prevalence of such situations also need to influence the overall assessment, but is often overlooked. For this reason, people often misperceive the risks involved, which can lead them to take inappropriate actions.

A second heuristic, availability, uses the ease with which people can imagine an event happening, or with which they can bring an instance of it happening in the past to mind, as the basis for determining its future likelihood (Schwartz and Vaughn 2002). This heuristic has face validity since, all other things being equal, those events brought to mind more readily are likely to have occurred more often in the past and so more likely to occur in the future. However, other factors can influence ease of retrievability and imaginability, such as their impact or personal significance. Consistent with this line of reasoning, Lichtenstein et al. (1978) showed that the risks associated with memorable causes of death are overestimated whereas those from causes of death that are not memorable are underestimated. The author recently analyzed confidential statistics on information security showing that organizations commit too many resources to "high availability" threats to information systems (e.g., hackers) and not enough on "low availability" threats (e.g., underpowered systems that cannot manage peaks in demand). This occurred despite the fact that these organizations kept formal statistics on the primary causes for downtime that showed greater losses associated with these low availability threats.

Recent research has identified a third heuristic, the affect heuristic, where people base their risk assessment on how a situation makes them feel. Slovic and his co-workers have shown a reduction in perceived risk if an event or situation elicits positive affect and an increase in perceived risk if an event or situation elicits negative affect (Finucane et al. 2000). Emotional reactions of this kind are automatic, often precede conscious thought and can be strong motivators of behavior (Damassio 1994). Indeed, stigmatization of a hazard may occur if it automatically elicits strong negative emotions, which, through the application of the affect heuristic, consistently determine risk perception. In addition, perceptions derived in this way are often very resistant to change given they are occurring automatically and outside of conscious thought (Flynn et al. 2001).

Recently, discussions about these and other heuristics have drawn on suggestions that there are two cognitive systems, referred to as system 1 and system 2 (Stanovich and West 2000). System 1 thinking is heuristic, relatively fast, intuitive, associative, and often emotionally charged, whereas system 2 is systematic and deliberate, slower, effortful and more likely to be under conscious control. System 1 thinking allows people to make judgments of risk in situations where there are no formal data available or where the data are available but the person either cannot understand them or not inclined to use them because of the effort required. System 2 thinking monitors the quality of the output of system 1 but may not always detect error, particularly if the problem is difficult or the mechanisms for identifying the correct answer are unknown. The system engaged determines what information is attended to and how it is processed (Chun and Kruglanski 2006).

There are four reasons why work on heuristics is important for risk communicators. First, the system adopted by an individual determines what aspects of a communication they process, how they process it and the impact that it has on their judgments of the risks involved. This highlights the need to evaluate communications under both modes given that people differ in terms of which system of thinking they adopt. Second, the potentially less reliable system 1 thinking may predominate where people are confused by the communication, a situation particularly likely to occur when risk issues are complicated and/or communications focus on scientific issues and statistical risk. Under these circumstances people are likely to use availability or affect, completely ignoring the statistical content of any communication. Third, work on stigmatization suggests that if emotional reactions determine risk judgments then communications based on scientific risk assessments may have limited or no effect on people. Finally, knowledge of heuristics can help in designing communications. For example, Keller et al. (2006) showed that presenting photographs of houses in flood led to higher flood risk judgments. However, their study failed to distinguish whether this was due to availability or affect, highlighting that it is often difficult to determine which heuristic people adopt in particular situations.

This section has demonstrated that people often misperceive statistical risk information, outlined some of the reasons why this is the case and considered the implications of this for developing effective communications. However, much of the work reviewed in this section assumes there is an objective and quantifiable definition of risk and that any differences between this and public perceptions reflect errors and bias in human judgment. The next section reviews work that challenges this assumption and considers the implications it has for effective communication about risk.

DEFINITIONS OF RISK

Qualitative Aspects of Risk Judgments

Slovic and his colleagues demonstrated that people focus on qualitative aspects of risk situations not modeled in formal assessments, and this can lead to important and predictable differences between their evaluations and those derived from formal assessments (Slovic 1992). This research, referred to as the psychometric approach, has identified two aspects, "Dread" and "Unknown." Dread is associated with aspects such as a perceived lack of control, inequitable distribution of the benefits among those at risk, considered a threat to future generation, irreversible effects that increase over time and having catastrophic potential (i.e., a large number of fatalities). Unknown is associated with aspects such as a perception that the threat is unfamiliar, unobservable, and unknown to science. People judge hazards perceived high on these aspects as risky, irrespective of scientific evaluations based on formal assessments. This helps to explain why people voluntarily expose themselves to hazards that formal assessments indicate are relatively high risk (e.g., smoking or fast driving), yet are averse to other "low risk" hazards (e.g., nuclear power). Many more people are killed by the former two, yet they are perceived to be high in controllability, known to science, not a threat to future generations, and so on; the reverse is true for nuclear power.

These qualitative aspects also have a powerful influence on risk regulation. For example, Viscusi et al. (1997) showed that hazards strongly associated with unknown aspects elicited undue risk aversion in regulators leading them to take unnecessarily cautious actions. Slovic (1997) has also outlined situations where these factors have determined the legislative agenda. He showed how this can lead to anomalies in risk mitigation expenditure (e.g., the costs of a year of life saved—in the US—is just US$500 for flu shots—low in dread and unknown—but is US$10 million for radiation controls—high in dread and unknown).

This work has considerable potential for understanding and improving risk communication. First, busy risk managers often prioritize their communications, responding only to those hazards that they perceive as posing the greatest risk to the public. However, prioritizing based on formal assessments may not reflect actual public concerns in situations where relatively low threats are associated with high dread or unknown characteristics (Bennett 1998). Under these circumstances, the public may be highly critical of organizations for what they perceive as their lack of concern about important threats. Second, there is the potential to increase or reduce perceived risk by emphasizing or playing down dread and unknown factors in communications (see Bennett 1998). However, there is to date no research indicating how to do this or whether it affects risk perception in the way predicted. Third, and perhaps most importantly, this work shows that the public takes account of factors that are not included in formal risk assessments. This has led some to argue that public risk perception is irrational so should be excluded from the risk management process altogether (Cohen 1983). From this standpoint, risk is objective and calculable scientifically. The next section reviews work indicating that such a view is untenable and considers the implications of this for risk communication.

Subjectivity in Risk Definitions

Although there are generally agreed objective definitions of risk, Slovic (1997, 1999) has argued that subjectivity pervades all aspects of the risk management processes and that what constitutes risk and how it should be measured are often subject to debate and controversy. For example, Crouch and Wilson (1982) showed how different representations of the same "risk" give very different impressions. Drawing on data from the US coal mining industry between 1950 and 1970 they showed that accidental deaths per million tons of coal mined decreased during this period, but that accidental deaths per 1,000 coalmine employees increased. It is not possible to argue scientifically that one of these measures is "correct" and the other "incorrect", yet each is likely to lead to different conclusions about the risk profile and the communication needed (Slovic 1997). These findings have led to proposals that risk is socially constructed rather than an objective state of nature and that what is taken into account and how is determined by social and political debate rather than scientifically (Funtowitcz and Ravetz 1992). Powell and Leiss (1997) suggested there are two languages of risk: an "expert" language grounded in scientific, specialized, and statistical knowledge and a "public" language grounded in social and intuitive knowledge. Although early research attributed differences between scientific and lay evaluations as being indicative of lay ignorance and/or faulty expert communication, there is now greater acceptance of the need to take account of both with science "on tap not on top" (Stirling 1999).

This work challenges previously held assumptions that in all threat situations there is just one "true," scientifically derived, risk estimate and that conveying this to the public should be the primary goal of risk communication. In addition, it suggests that managers and communicators need to understand and accept non-scientific definitions and consider the implications of these when communicating with the public. The next section outlines and develops one approach that takes these views as a starting point, the Mental Models Approach (Morgan et al. 2002).

The Mental Models Approach (MMA)

The MMA builds on the idea that people internally represent the world in terms of small scale mental models of external reality and the actions they might take (Craik 1943). The approach involves eliciting and comparing expert and lay mental models of a hazard in order to identify misunderstandings and errors in lay understanding and then to construct risk communications that rectify these shortcomings (Morgan et al. 2002). Cassidy and Maule (2006) argued that the MMA has a sound theoretical base, user-centered and that there is evidence that it works (e.g., Cox et al. 2003). However, they outlined three problems with the approach. First, it conceptualizes risk knowledge at the individual level, overlooking social and cultural factors (Breakwell 2001). Second, it takes the "expert" view as fact, yet scientific knowledge is constantly evolving and often contested even among experts themselves, thereby calling into question the possibility of deriving a valid and reliable expert model, particularly in complex, new or poorly understood situations. Third, it is a "deficit" model that places scientific knowledge as primal with lay knowledge flawed and in need of correction, so runs contrary to earlier conclusions that risk is socially constructed. Wynne (1996) showed that, following the Chernobyl disaster, regulatory authorities failed to take account of the individual, social and cultural knowledge held by Cumbrian sheep farmers in the UK and that this considerably reduced the effectiveness of risk communications and advice given by these authorities. In addition, Michael (1996) argued that people use a failure to take account of "non-scientific" risk information as a reason for ignoring expert advice, particularly if they perceive it to be irrelevant, patronizing, or unhelpful for everyday life.

The MMA is distinctive in that it is theoretically driven, provides a clear procedure and is effective (see, for example, Cox et al. 2003), but it may need adapting when the body of scientific knowledge being drawn upon is uncertain or contested (Cassidy and Maule 2006). In these latter situations, it may be necessary to take account of the views of the public and other stakeholders when conceptualizing, managing, and communicating risk. However, this raises theoretical, philosophical, and methodological issues about how to deal with conflicting beliefs about the nature of risk and levels that are acceptable. The next section addresses these issues by reviewing stakeholder involvement in risk management and communication.

Stakeholder Involvement in Managing and Communicating Risk

Although not the first to advocate it, Fischhoff (1995) argued that making the public and other stakeholders partners is critical for effective risk communication. Renn and his colleagues (e.g., Renn 1998) have provided the foundation for the development of a broad range of public involvement techniques, including stakeholder and consensus workshops, citizen's juries, focus groups, and electronic forums (Rowe and Frewer 2005).

These participatory techniques provide ways of exploring and bridging gaps between different conceptions of risk and for resolving dilemmas. They also increase public acceptance of risk related decisions (Charnley and Elliott 2002; Slovic 2003). However, Rowe and Frewer (2005) argued that there are no comparative studies so there is little known about what works in any particular risk context. Perhaps the most important contribution of stakeholder engagement is the positive effect that it has on public trust. Trust in the communicator is critical in determining how the public perceives and acts following a communication (Frewer 2003) and the next section explores theory and research on how and why this is the case.

Trust

People internalize information from trusted sources in ways that are highly likely to influence how they perceive and respond (Petty and Cacioppo 1984), particularly in risk situations (Cvetkovich and Lofstedt 1999). In contrast to this, information from distrusted sources is likely to be disregarded as unreliable or self-serving, may result in attitudes opposite to those intended (Frewer 2003) and seriously reduces the effectiveness of risk communication (Flynn et al. 1998). Trust is fragile in that it is difficult and time consuming to develop and very easily lost (Slovic 1997). Once lost, the outcomes can be disastrous, as evidenced by a recent example in the UK where a government ministry (Ministry of Agriculture Fisheries and Food) was dismantled following loss of public trust in the way this organization managed the BSE crisis (Phillips 2000)

There is general agreement that trust is important and multifaceted, though researchers disagree about the nature of these facets (Johnson 1999). Renn and Levine (1991) identified five facets associated with perceptions that the communicator is competent (has the appropriate expertise), objective (messages free from bias), fair (all points of views are acknowledged), consistent (in terms of behaviors and statements made over time), and is acting in good faith (a perception of goodwill). Frewer (2003) suggested that trust is associated with perceptions of accuracy, knowledge, and concern with public welfare, distrust with perceptions of deliberate distortion of information, bias, and poor past performance. These studies reveal facets that are broadly overlapping and, when taken together, they provide useful insights about the factors that risk communicators should address if they wish to enhance public trust in their organization.

A second group of studies has sought to explain how trust affects perception and action by drawing on the elaboration-likelihood model (Petty and Cacioppo 1986), an approach broadly similar to the dual-process theory discussed earlier in the context of cognitive heuristics. Under system 2 thinking, people undertake in-depth analyses of the contents of communications that are both thoughtful and complex, where external cues such as characteristics of and trust in the communicator are of minor importance. In contrast to this, under system 1 thinking people engage in superficial thought, using external cues such as trust for determining attitudes and behavior, with little or no in-depth analysis of the content of the communication (Frewer et al. 1997). As indicated earlier in the section on cognitive heuristics, people adopt system 1 thinking when they have insufficient understanding of the content of the message and/or the time or inclination to engage in effortful processing. Communicators often have to manage complex physical and biological processes that people do not fully understand, and usually convey the relevant risks in numerical terms. For these reasons, people are likely to rely heavily on peripheral processing and therefore influenced by external cues such as trust (Siegrist et al. 2000).

Developing and sustaining high levels of trust in communicators is important, though there is surprisingly little research on how to achieve it. However, the research literature provides some suggestions that include involving individuals or groups already accorded high levels of trust and through public involvement in the management of risk issues (Frewer 2003). An alternative but untested way of dealing with trust is to encourage system 2 rather then system 1 processing of relevant risk information thereby minimizing the influence that it has on risk perception. This switch in processing modes should occur following a sustained program of activities highlighting the importance of risk issues or by presenting information that people readily understand.

General Conclusions

The foregoing review has complemented earlier reviews (Covello et al. 1986; Bier 2001; Bostrom and Lofstedt 2003) in identifying theoretical, methodological, and practical aspects of risk communication, showing that that these are underpinned by a broad range of individual and social processes. A major problem, at least until recently, has been determining how these different processes interact. However, the last ten years has seen the emergence of the social amplification of risk framework (SARF) that integrates many of the findings in the area, including those reviewed above (Kasperson et al. 2003). The central tenet of SARF is that risk events, such as accidents or incidents, remain neglected until people notice them and communicate them to others. Once communicated, risk information passes through various social agents who generate, receive, interpret, and pass on this information, and in doing so can transform it by increasing or decreasing its "volume". The nature of these transformations depends upon the kinds of individual and social processes reviewed in this chapter, each of which can attenuate (e.g., trust in the communicator) or amplify (e.g., perceived high in dread) the initiating risk information. Thus, "the experience of risk therefore is not only an experience of physical harm but the results of processes by which groups and individuals learn to acquire or create interpretations of risk" (Kasperson et al. 2003: 15). The clear message from SARF and from research reviewed in this chapter is that effective risk communication involves much more than simply communicating the outcomes of formal risk assessments. In addition, it requires knowledge of the broad range of individual and social processes involved.

A second problem is that aspects of risk associated with uncertainty have dominated the research agenda, with comparatively little work on impact, particularly in the context of the values held by the recipients of the communication. French et al. (2004) highlight the importance of taking account of values and consider how these determine the actions that people take. In addition, they present a number of small scale soft modeling techniques to help identify the nature and impact of values on risk communication. A third problem is that research often fails to distinguish between different communication objectives (e.g., to inform or persuade, Covello et al. 1986) and in doing so whether the processes involved and their effectiveness vary accordingly.

In conclusion, risk communication presents an important challenge both for organizations that take decisions regarding the management of hazards and for researchers interested in how people perceive and act in the face of risk. Future research needs to clarify further the range of individual and social processes involved, the interactions between these processes, and the extent to which these differ across different domains of human activity.

REFERENCES

BARNETT, J. and BREAKWELL, G. M. (2003). 'The Social Amplification of Risk and the Hazard Sequence: The October 1995 Oral Contraceptive Pill Scare.' *Health, Risk and Society*, 5: 301–13.

BECK, U. (1992). *Risk Society: Towards a New Modernity*. London: Sage.

BENNETT, P. (1998). *Communicating About Risks to Public Health: Pointers to Good Practice*. Department of Health: HMSO.

BERRY, D. C. (2004). *Risk, Communication and Health Psychology*. Maidenhead: Open University Press.

—— RAYNOR, D. K., KNAPP, P. R., and BERSELLINI, E. (2002). 'Official Warnings on Thromoembolism Risk with Oral Contraceptives Fail to Inform Users Adequately.' *Contraception*, 66: 305–07.

BIER, V. M. (2001). 'On the State of the Art: Risk Communication to the Public.' *Reliability Engineering and System Safety*, 71: 139–50.

BOSTROM A. and LOFSTEDT, R.E. (2003). 'Communicating Risk.' *Risk Analysis*, 23: 241–8.

BREAKWELL, G.M. (2001). 'Mental Models and Social Representations of Hazards: The Significance of Identity Processes.' *Journal of Risk Research*, 4/4: 341–51.

CALMAN, K. C. and ROYSTON, G. H. (1997). 'Risk Language and Dialects.' *British Medical Journal*, 315: 939–42.

CASSIDY, A. and MAULE, A. J. (2006). '*Building Partnership in Risk Communication: Evaluating and Developing the Mental Models Approach*.' Paper presented at RiskComm Conference, Gothenburg, Sweden.

CHARNELY, G. and ELLIOT E. D. (2002). 'Democratization of Risk Analysis,' in D. J. Paustenbach (ed.), *Human and Ecological Risk Assessment: Theory and Practice*. New York: Wiley.

CHUN, W. Y. and KRUGLANSKI, A. W. (2006). 'The Role of Task Demands and Processing Resources in the Use of Base-Rate and Individuating Information.' *Journal of Personality and Social Psychology*, 91, 205–17.

COHEN, B. L. (1983). *Before it's Too Late: A Scientist's Case for Nuclear Energy*. New York: Plenum.

COVELLO, V. T., von WINTERFELDT, D., and SLOVIC, P. (1986). 'Risk Communication: A Review of the Literature.' *Risk Abstracts*, 3: 171–82.

COX, P., NIEWOHNER, J., PIDGEON, N. et al. (2003). 'The Use of Mental Models in Chemical Risk Protection: Developing a Generic Workplace Methodology.' *Risk Analysis*, 23/2: 311–24.

CRAIK, K. (1943). *The Nature of Explanation*. Cambridge: Cambridge University Press.

CROUCH, E. A. C. and WILSON, R. (1982). *Risk/Benefit Analysis*. Cambridge, MA: Ballinger.

CVETKOVICH, G. and LOFSTEDT, R. E. (1999). *Social Trust and the Management of Risk*. London: Earthscan.

DAMASSIO, A. R. (1994). *Descartes' Error: Emotion, Reason and Human Brain*. New York: Avon.

European Commission (1992). European Commission Council Directive 92/27/EEC, OJ No. L113, April 30. 8.

FAHEY, T., GRIFFIN, S., and PETERS, T. J. (1995). 'Evidence Based Purchasing: Understanding Results of Clinical Trials and Systematic Reviews.' *British Medical Journal*, 311: 1056–9.

FETHERSTONHAUGH, D., SLOVIC, P., JOHNSON, S. M., and FRIEDRICH, J. (1997). 'Insensitivity to the Value of a Human Life: A Study of Psychophysical Numbing.' *Journal of Risk and Uncertainty*, 14: 283–300.

FINUCANE, M. L., ALHAKAMI, A., SLOVIC, P., and JOHNSON, S. M. (2000). 'The Affect Heuristic in Judgments of Risks and Benefits.' *Journal of Behavioral Decision Making*, 13: 1–17.

FISCHHOFF, B. (1995). 'Risk Perception and Communication Unplugged: Twenty Years of Process.' *Risk Analysis*, 15: 137–45.

—— MACGREGOR, D. (1983). 'Judged Lethality: How Much People Seem to Know Depends Upon How They are Asked.' *Risk Analysis*, 3: 229–36.

FLYNN, J., SLOVIC, P., and KUNREUTHER, H. (eds.) (2001). *Risk, Media and Stigma: Understanding Public Challenges to Modern Science and Technology*. London: Earthscan.

FRENCH, S., MAULE, A. J., and MYTHEN, G. (2005). 'Soft Modeling in Risk Communication and Management: Examples in Handling Food Risk.' *Journal of the Operational Research Society*, 56: 879–88.

—— —— —— et al. (2003). 'Understanding Stakeholder Concerns in Relation to Communications on Food Safety.' Report to Food Standards Agency, UK.

FREWER, L. J. (2003). 'Trust, Transparency, and Social Context: Implications for Social Amplification of Risk,' in N. Pidgeon, R. E. Kasperson, and P. Slovic (eds.), *The Social Amplification of Risk*. Cambridge: Cambridge University Press.

—— HOWARD, C., HEDDERLEY, D., and SHEPHERD, R. (1997). 'The Use of the Elaboration Likelihood Model in Developing Effective Food Risk Communication.' *Risk Analysis*, 17: 269–81.

FUNTOWICZ, S. O. and RAVETZ, J. R. (1992). 'Three Type of Risk Assessment and the Emergence of Post-Normal Science,' in S. Krimsky and D. Golding (eds.), *Social Theories of Risk*. Westport, CT: Praeger.

GIGERENZER, G. and EDWARDS, A. (2003). 'Simple Tools for Understanding Risks: From Innumeracy to Insight.' *British Medical Journal*, 327: 741–4.

—— HOFFRAGE, U. (1995). 'How to Improve Bayesian Reasoning Without Instructions: Frequency Formats.' *Psychological Review*, 102: 684–704.

—— HERTWIG, R., VAN DEN BROEK, E., FASOLO, B., and KATSIKOPOULOS, K. V. (2005). '"A 30% Chance of Rain Tomorrow": How Does the Public Understand Probabilistic Weather Forecasts.' *Risk Analysis*. 25: 623–9.

GILOVICH, T., GRIFFIN, D., and KAHNEMAN, D. (2002). *Heuristics and Biases: The Psychology of Intuitive Judgment*. Cambridge: Cambridge University Press.

GURABARDHI, Z., GUTTELING, J. M., and KUTTSCHREUTER, M. (2004). 'The Development of Risk Communication.' *Science Communication*, 25/4: 323–49.

JARDINE, C. G. and HRUDEY, S. E. (1997). 'Mixed Messages in Risk Communication.' *Risk Analysis*, 17: 489–98.

JOFFE, H. (2003). 'Risk: From Perception to Social Representation.' *British Journal of Social Psychology*, 42: 55–73.

JOHNSON, B. B. (1999). 'Exploring Dimensionality in the Origins of Hazard-Related Trust.' *Journal of Risk Research*, 2: 325–73.

—— (2004). 'Varying Risk Comparison Elements: Effects on Public Reactions.' *Risk Analysis*, 24: 103–14.

KAHNEMAN, D. and FREDERICK, S. (2002). 'Representativeness Revisited: Attribute Substitution in Intuitive Judgment,' in T. Gilovich, D. Griffin, and D. Kahneman (eds.), *Heuristics and Biases: The Psychology of Intuitive Judgment*. Cambridge: Cambridge University Press.

KASPERSON, J. X., KASEPRSON, R. E., PIDGEON, N., and SLOVIC, P. (2003). 'The Social Amplification of Research: Assessing Fifteen Years of Research and Theory,' in N. Pidgeon, R. E. Kasperson, and P. Slovic (eds.), *The Social Amplification of Risk*. Cambridge: Cambridge University Press.

KELLER, C., SIEGRIST, M., and GUTSCHER, H. (2006). 'The Role of Affect and Availability Heuristics in Risk Communication.' *Risk Analysis*, 26: 631–9.

LICHTENSTEIN, S. and NEWMAN, J. R. (1969). 'Empirical Scaling of Common Verbal Phrases Associated with Numerical Probabilities.' *Psychonomic Science*, 9: 563–4.

—— SLOVIC, P., Fischhoff, B., LAYMAN, M., and COMBS, B. (1978). 'Judged Frequency of Lethal Events.' *Journal of Experimental Psychology: Human Learning and Memory*, 4: 551–78.

LIPKUS, I. M. and HOLLANDS J. G. (1999). 'The Visual Communication of Risk.' *Journal of National Cancer Institute Monograph*, 25: 149–62.

McDANIELS, T. L. (1988). 'Comparing Expressed and Revealed Preferences for Risk Reduction: Different Hazards and Question Frames.' *Risk Analysis*, 8: 593–604.

MICHAEL, M. (1996). 'Ignoring Science: Discourses of Ignorance in the Public Understanding of Science,' in A. Irwin and B. Wynne (eds.), *Misunderstanding Science? The Public Reconstruction of Science and Technology*. Cambridge: Cambridge University Press.

MORGAN, G., FISCHHOFF, G., BOSTROM, A., and ATMAN, C. (2002). *Risk Communication: A Mental Models Approach*. Cambridge: Cambridge University Press.

MOXEY, L. M. and SANFORD, A. J. (1993). *Communicating Quantities: A Psychological Perspective*. Hove: Erlbaum.

NRC (1983). *Risk Assessment in the Federal Government: Managing the Process*. Washington, DC: National Academy Press.

PALING, J. (1997). 'Up to Your Armpits in Alligators: How to Sort Out What Risks are Worth Worrying About.' Gainesville, FL: Risk Communication and Environmental Institute.

PETTY, R. E. and CACIOPPO, J. T. (1984). 'Some Factors and the in the Elaboration Likelihood Model of Persuasion.' *Advances in Consumer Research*, 11: 668–72.

—— —— (1986). *Communication and Persuasion: Central and Peripheral Routes to Attitude Change*. New York: Springer-Verlag.

PHILLIPS, LORD (2000). *The Report of the Enquiry into BSE and variant CJD in the UK*. London: The Stationary Office.

POORTINGA, W., BICKERSTAFF, K., LANGFORD, I., NIEWOHNER, J., and PIDGEON, N. (2004). 'The British 2001 Foot and Mouth crisis: A Comparative Study of Public Risk Perceptions,

Trust and Beliefs About Government Policy in Two Communities.' *Journal of Risk Research*, 7: 73–90.

POWELL, D. and LEISS, W. (1997). *Mad Cows and Mother's Milk: The Perils of Poor Risk Communication*. Montreal: McGill-Queen's University Press.

RENN, O. (1998). 'The Role of Risk Communication and Public Dialogue for Improving Risk Management.' *Risk, Decision and Policy*, 3/1: 5–30.

RENN, O. and LEVINE, D. (1991). 'Credibility and Trust in Risk Communication,' in R. E. Kasperson and P. J. M. Stallen (eds.), *Communicating Risks to the Public*. Dordrecht: Kluwer Academic Publishers, 175–214.

RENOOIJ, S. and WITTEMAN, C. (1999). 'Talking Probabilities: Communicating Probabilistic Information with Words and Numbers.' *International Journal of Approximate Reasoning*, 22/3: 169–94.

ROWE, G. and FREWER, L. J. (2005). 'A Typology of Public Engagement Methods,' *Science Technology and Human Values*, 30/2: 251–90.

SALOVEY, P. and WILLIAMS-PIEHOTA, P. (2004). 'Field Experiments in Social Psychology: Message Framing and the Promotion of Health Protective Behaviors.' *The American Behavioral Scientist*, 47: 488–505.

SANDMAN, P. M., WEINSTEIN, N. D., and MILLER, P. (1994). 'High-Risk or Low—How Location on a Risk Ladder Affects Perceived Risk.' *Risk Analysis*, 14: 35–45.

SCHAPIRA, M., NATTINGER, A., and McHORNEY, C. (2001). 'Frequency or Probability: A Qualitative Study of Risk Communication Formats Used in Health Care.' *Medical Decision Making*, 21: 459–67.

SCHIRILLO, J. A. and STONE, E. R. (2005). 'The Greater Ability of Graphical Versus Numerical Displays to Increase Risk Avoidance Involves a Common Mechanism.' *Risk Analysis*, 25: 555–66.

SCHWARTZ, N. and VAUGHN, L. A. (2002). 'The Availability Heuristic Revisited,' in T. Gilovich, D. Griffin, and D. Kahneman (eds.), *Heuristics and Biases: The Psychology of Intuitive Judgment*. Cambridge: Cambridge University Press.

SIEGRIST, M., CVETKOVICH, G., and ROTH, C. (2000). 'Salient Value Similarity, Social Trust and Risk/Benefit Perception.' *Risk Analysis*, 20: 353–62.

SLOVIC, P. (1992). 'Perception of Risk: Reflections on the Psychometric Paradigm,' in S. Krimsky and D. Golding (eds.), *Social Theories of Risk*. Westport, CT: Praeger.

—— (1997). 'Trust, Emotion, Sex, Politics and Science: Surveying the Risk Assessment Battlefield,' in M. H. Bazerman and D. Messick (eds.), *Environment, Ethics and Behavior*. San Francisco, CA: New Lexington.

—— (1999). 'Trust, Emotion, Sex, Politics, and Science: Surveying the Risk Assessment Battlefield.' *Risk Analysis*, 19: 689–701.

—— (2003). 'Going Beyond the Red Book: The Sociopolitics of Risk.' *Human and Ecological Risk Assessment*, 9: 1181–90.

—— KRAUS, N., and COVELLO, V. T. (1990). 'What Should We Know About Making Risk Comparisons?' *Risk Analysis*, 10: 389–92.

STANOVICH, K. E. and WEST, R. F. (2000). 'Individual Differences in Reasoning: Implications for the Rationality Debate.' *Behavioral and Brain Sciences*, 23: 645–65.

STIRLING, A. (1999). 'Rethinking Risk.' A pilot multi-criteria mapping of a genetically modified crop in agricultural systems in the UK, SPRU, University of Sussex.

TUFTE E. R. (2001). *The Visual Display of Quantitative Information* (2nd edn.). Cheshire, CT: Graphics Press.

TULLOCH, J. and LUPTON, D. (2003). *Risk and Everyday Life.* London: Sage.

VISCUSI, W. K., HAMILTON, J. T., and DOCKINS, P. C. (1997). 'Conservative Versus Mean Risk Assessments: Implications for Superfund Policies.' *Journal of Environmental Economics and Management,* 34: 167–206.

WEBER, E. U. and HILTON, D. J. (1990). 'Contextual Effects in the Interpretations of Probability Words—Perceived Base Rates and Severity of Events.' *Journal of Experimental Psychology: Human Perception and Performance,* 16: 781–9.

WYNNE, B. (1996). 'May the Sheep Safely Graze? A Reflexive View of the Expert–Lay Knowledge Divide,' in S. Lash, B. Szerszinski, and B. Wynne (eds.), *Risk, Environment and Modernity: Towards a New Ecology.* London: Sage.

YAMAGISHI, K. (1997). 'When a 12.86% Mortality is More Dangerous Than 24.14%: Implications for Risk Communication.' *Applied Cognitive Psychology,* 11: 495–506.

28

STRUCTURING THE DECISION PROCESS: AN EVALUATION OF METHODS

GEORGE WRIGHT
PAUL GOODWIN

INTRODUCTION

THIS chapter examines the effectiveness of methods that are designed to provide structure and support to decision making. Those that are primarily aimed at individual decision makers are examined first and then attention is turned to groups. In each case weaknesses of unaided decision making are identified and how successful the application of formal methods is likely to be in mitigating these weaknesses is assessed.

Individual Decision Making

Supporting Decisions Involving Multiple Objectives

To make decisions, humans have evolved simplified mental strategies, or heuristics (Tversky and Kahneman 1974). These heuristics are well adapted to some environments and can be particularly useful where quick decisions need to be made with minimal cognitive effort (e.g., choose a brand of coffee that you recognize rather than an unknown brand) (Gigerenzer et al. 1999).

However, consider the problem of choosing a used car. The car buyer is likely to have a diverse set of objectives. The application of one well-known heuristic, lexicographic ranking (Tversky 1969), would involve the buyer simply comparing the cars on the attribute that is judged to be most important (e.g., price) and selecting the car that performs best on this attribute. If several cars offer the best performance on this attribute (i.e., if there is a tie) then performance on the second most important attribute will be compared and so on. Clearly, the heuristic avoids complexity by making no attempt to consider all of the attributes associated with the cars or to consider trade-offs between them—a car that was rejected because it was relatively expensive may offer other features that would have more than compensated for its greater cost. A more demanding heuristic, elimination by aspects (EBA) (Tversky 1972), *would* consider all of the cars features. Cars would be eliminated from consideration if they failed to meet a minimal requirement on any attribute. For example, any car that had a top speed of below 90 mph would be ruled out, as would any car that did not have electric windows, and so on. However, EBA still fails to consider trade-offs between the attributes. Thus, a car that was rejected because it had a top speed of only 85 mph might have had many other desirable features that would have made it worth purchasing despite its slightly lower top speed. Such heuristics characterize the way in which busy decision makers make choices between alternatives with multiple objectives.

A number of methods have been developed to support decision makers faced with multiple objectives. These methods, which fall within the discipline of decision analysis, include the simple multiattribute rating technique (SMART) (Edwards 1971), the simple multiattribute rating technique exploiting ranks (SMARTER) (Edwards and Barron 1994), the analytic hierarchy process (AHP) (Saaty 1990), and outranking (e.g., Roy 1991). The common idea underlying these methods is that the complexity of the judgments required from the decision maker can be reduced if the problem is decomposed into a set of separate smaller problems—the so-called divide and conquer principle. The decision maker can then apply his or her judgments to each of these (hopefully) simpler problems in turn. The resulting judgments are then recomposed, in accordance with a set of axioms, so that the best course of action can be identified.

For example, in SMART the objectives are decomposed into "subobjectives" that are specific enough for the decision maker to make a relatively straightforward comparison of how well the options perform on that subobjective. Thus the objective of minimizing pollution might be decomposed into subobjectives of minimizing CO_2 emissions, minimizing sulphur emissions, and minimizing noise. Each subobjective is then considered separately and independently, and the options rated according to their performance on that subobjective (usually on a 0 to 100 scale). Weights are then assigned to these subobjectives to reflect their importance in the decision (technically swing weights should be used, see Goodwin and Wright 2004) and the "best" option is identified as the one achieving the highest weighted average score.

It can be seen that SMART enables the decision maker to take into account all of the objectives that are pertinent to the decision (unlike lexicographic ranking). Furthermore, by requiring the assignment of weights, it also ensures that the decision maker evaluates trade-offs between these objectives (unlike EBA).

However, there are several other advantages that emanate from this formal structuring of the decision process. The decision model, at the heart of the technique, automatically documents the rationale for the decision, effectively providing an audit trail that allows the reasons for the decision to be made explicit and, if necessary, defended. Also, methods like SMART are straightforward and transparent so that individuals from a range of specialisms can easily participate in the process and see how their judgments impact on the overall decision. Participation, in turn, can lead to a commitment to the chosen course of action. Decision makers can also use the "common language" of the model to clearly communicate their thinking to other participants (French 1996). Where there are disputes between individual decision makers about the weights to assign to different objectives, sensitivity analysis can often reveal that the same decision should be made regardless of which set of proposed weights is used, thereby avoiding unnecessary debate. Finally, the recommendations of the model may seem counter-intuitive to the decision makers upon whose judgments it is based. However, this challenge to intuition can serve to motivate decision makers to explore their problem more deeply. Indeed Phillips (1984) argues that formal decision models can be at their most valuable when these discrepancies occur because the ensuing exploration yields deeper insights and understanding of the issues. This in turn leads to enhancements of the model until eventually the intuitive view and the model converge, at which point the model is described as being "requisite". (The section on decision conferencing explores this idea further.)

Published examples of the application of SMART include the selection of a wide area network system by a logistics company (Marples and Robertson 1993), systems acquisition decisions by the US military (Buede and Bresnick 1992), the selection of a clinical information system (Graeber 2001), priority setting for research funds by the New Zealand Ministry of Agriculture (Mabin et al. 2001), the design of a

bioreserve network in Canada (Rothley 1999), and fisheries management i
Shetland Islands (Hilden 1997).

The role of these models is not to take the responsibility for decisions from
decision makers or to identify "optimal" courses of action. Instead, they merely
provide support and their purpose is to yield insights and to promote creativity so
that better informed decisions can be made. However, even in this support role
their usefulness is not assured. As Goodwin and Wright (1993) point out, decomposition is unlikely to aid judgment where the decision maker is skeptical about the
technique that is being employed. For example, there may be a reluctance to try to
represent one's preferences, particularly for qualitative attributes, on a numeric
scale (Boyle 2000). Decomposition is also likely to be unsuccessful where the
judgments required by the technique are poorly understood, or are less familiar
and more complex than the holistic judgments that the decision maker may be
used to making. Similar problems are likely to occur when the number of judgments required by the decomposition increases to a level where the decision maker
experiences fatigue or boredom.

There are two further potential limitations associated with the application of
structured models to decisions made by individuals where there are multiple
objectives. The first relates to a criticism by Keeney that traditional decision
analysis methods are "alternative focused" in that they start with a list of alternative
courses of action (Keeney 1992), allowing the decision maker to focus on the
objectives that he or she would like to achieve. Keeney argues that this sequencing
of the process severely restricts the decision maker's perception of opportunities
that may be available. Values are fundamental to decision making and therefore any
support method should commence with the recognition and articulation of these
values—so called "value focused thinking." In this way the decision maker will be
enabled to identify opportunities and create better alternatives. Such an approach
would seem to be particularly appropriate for major strategic decisions where there
may be a need to review and explore the key values and objectives of an organization and to develop innovative ways forward. However, Keeney's approach, perhaps, would be enhanced if it provided more guidance on how fundamental values
might be identified. Exhortations to ask yourself, "What would you like to achieve
in this situation?" and, "If you had no limitations at all, what would your objectives
be?" may not be sufficient to stimulate the creativity required. Wright and
Goodwin (1999a) discuss this issue in more detail.

The second potential limitation of structured modeling approaches is that they
can serve to reinforce the decision maker's existing decision frame (i.e., his or her
current way of defining the decision problem) when "thinking outside the box" is
likely to lead to a superior solution. There is nothing inherent in the application of
decision analysis models that will cause the decision maker to question the frame
and this may lead to considerable effort being wasted on solving the "wrong"
problem. This suggests that, in many circumstances, "softer" techniques, such as

scenario planning or soft systems analysis, should be used to explore the dimensions, nature, and context of the problem first (see, e.g., Rosenhead and Mingers 2001).

Supporting Decisions Involving Risk and Uncertainty

When faced with the complex task of assessing risk, it appears that people again resort to the use of heuristics. While these heuristics can allow risks to be assessed quickly and efficiently in some circumstances their use is also associated with biased judgments.

For example, the availability heuristic (Tversky and Kahneman 1974) is invoked when people assess the probability of an event according to how easily similar events can be recalled or imagined. Thus the probability of a major corporate customer going into receivership may be judged to be higher if the person making the assessment can recall a recent example of the bankruptcy of a similar company. Such assessments will be biased when ease of recall or ease of imagination are not associated with the true risk. Thus rare events, that have been highlighted in the media precisely because they are rare, may be overassessed in terms of their risk, while mundane events that pass largely unnoticed but actually pose greater dangers will have their risks underestimated.

Another heuristic, anchoring and adjustment, is employed when people are required to provide a numerical estimate of a quantity. It involves starting with an initial estimate, the anchor, and adjusting from it to obtain the final estimate. Problems arise when the anchor is a long way from the true value of the quantity because people tend to make insufficient adjustment from it. For example, suppose it is thought that the most likely time that it will take to launch a new product is 35 weeks, but a pessimistic estimate is also required (assume that this will be a launch time that only has a 1 percent chance of being exceeded). It is likely that the 35 weeks will act as an anchor and the pessimistic estimate will be set too close to it. This may lead to insufficient contingency planning for a launch that turns out to be considerably delayed.

Many other biases have been documented when people face uncertainty and risk. In estimating the costs and durations of major projects there is usually a bias towards optimism (indeed several UK government web sites provide optimism bias calculators that are intended to enable the effect of this bias to be removed from estimates). Similarly, when people receive new information that should cause them to substantially revise their original estimates they tend to display conservatism in that they pay too little attention to this information and make insufficient changes to their estimates.

Can managers be helped to produce better assessments of the risk they face? As in the case of multiobjective decision support, decomposition methods seek to improve the accuracy of management judgment by breaking the assessment task down into smaller tasks. Typical tools include probability trees and fault trees. In the former, a tree diagram is used to depict the sequences of events that need to occur for the target event to take place. For example, suppose that it is necessary to assess the risk of an explosion at a chemical plant in the course of a year. Rather than assessing the probability directly the combinations of events that might lead to an explosion are identified (e.g., leakage of a coolant *and* overheating of a processor *and* failure of a reserve cooling system *and* failure of a shutdown mechanism). Probabilities are estimated separately for these precursor events and the rules of probability (e.g., the multiplication rule) are applied to combine the estimates and obtain the desired probability. Fault trees adopt a similar procedure. Note that the decomposition procedure allows the decision maker to focus on each precursor event separately, rather than being forced to consider simultaneously all of the combinations of events that might impact on the target event.

Risk analysis based on simulation, is another decomposition-based approach to assessing risks. Consider the problem of assessing the probability that an investment in a new confectionery product will yield a negative net present value (NPV). The manager making the assessment would first be asked to identify all of the factors that would affect the NPV (e.g., the price of raw materials, manufacturing costs, packaging costs, distribution costs, the extent of competition from rival companies, and sales). For each of these factors a probability distribution would be elicited. A computer risk analysis package would then be used. For example, if it was estimated that there was a 5 percent chance that raw material costs would exceed £5 per tonne then there would only be a 5 percent chance of the simulated combination including raw material costs of over £5. The package would then calculate the NPV that would result from the combination. After repeating this simulation process thousands of times the proportion of combinations resulting in a negative NPV could be obtained. Recent published examples of risk analysis include its use in designing corporate investment, financing, and risk management strategies for financially constrained firms (Casey 2001), decisions relating to the restoration of contaminated land (Oberg and Bergback 2005) and oil and gas estimates for a region of Alaska (Rocha-Legorreta and Lerche 2004).

Decisions involving risk and uncertainty often have another attribute that creates further difficulties for the unaided decision maker: a complex structure. Events may occur in the future that require further decisions to be made or rule out other options. For example, if a decision is made to launch a new product but first year sales are low then a subsequent decision on whether to advertise, relaunch or abandon the product will need to be faced. Decision trees enable this sort of complexity to be represented in a diagrammatic format so that the decision maker can understand the underlying structure of the problem and communicate it to others. Published applications where decision trees have been found to be effective tools include decisions on petroleum exploration (Hess 1993), a decision on automation by the US postal service (Ulvila 1987), forestry management decisions (Cohan et al. 1984), management–union bargaining (Winter 1985), and a decision on an auction bid for the salvage rights of a ship (Bell 1984).

There are limitations associated with these techniques. Many of the potential problems of decomposition that were discussed earlier can reduce the effectiveness of probability and fault trees and risk analysis. For highly complex problems, decision trees can become "bushy messes" and the benefits of clarity that they bring to the decision process can be lost. Decision trees also emphasize the alternative focused approach to decision making criticized by Keeney (Keeney 1992), and they require estimates of probabilities, which may be subject to biases. Indeed, the fundamental structure of decision trees encourages the assumption that outcomes and risks are predicated on the course of action that is being selected. Thus they might reinforce managers' existing views of the world and not alert them to potential changes that could have serious implications for their business. Wright and Goodwin (1999b) discuss this issue in more detail.

SUPPORT FOR GROUPS OF DECISION MAKERS

Do groups of individual decision makers make better decisions than the average of the individuals who make up the groups? This section of the chapter reviews research into the quality of group judgment and then considers the ways that have been proposed and implemented to aid the judgment of groups of individuals.

Unstructured Group Decision Making

One of the major conclusions of research work on descriptions of group decision making is that of shortcomings. Irving Janis (1982) has documented a phenomenon that he has termed "groupthink" within group decision processes. Groupthink is essentially the suppression of ideas that are critical of the "direction" in which a group is moving. It is reflected in a tendency to concur with the position or views that are perceived to be favored by the group. Of course, such forces may produce speedy judgments and commitment to action. However, such cohesive groups may develop rationalizations for the invulnerability of the group's decision and inhibit the expression of critical ideas. These pitfalls of groupthink are likely to result in an incomplete survey of alternative courses of action or choices. Such an incomplete search through the decision space may result in a failure to examine the risks of preferred decisions and a failure to work out contingency plans if the preferred course of action cannot be taken.

Overall, there have been very few laboratory tests of Janis's theory. One main reason is that laboratory researchers have found it difficult to achieve high levels of group cohesiveness, a primary antecedent of groupthink. Another approach to the verification of the theory has been the study of case histories.

One study, by Esser and Lindoerfer (1989) analyzed the decision to launch the space shuttle Challenger on January 29, 1986. The outcome of that flight—the death of all seven crewmembers within minutes of launch—focused attention on the process leading to the decision to launch. In these researchers' content analysis of the verbal transcripts of a presidential commission report on the disaster, statements therein were coded as either positive or negative instances of the observable antecedents and consequences of groupthink. During the 24 hours prior to the launch of the Challenger the ratio of positive to negative items increased significantly. During this time, the Level III NASA management were facing increased difficulties in maintaining their flight schedule, and this was expressed as direct pressure on the dissenters who wanted to delay the flight (the engineers) and "mindguarding". Mindguarding essentially refers to the removal of doubts and uncertainties in communications to others. In this instance, the Level III NASA management said to the engineers that they would report the engineers' concerns to the Level II NASA management, but they did not.

Janis argues that the group-based "victims" of groupthink feel invulnerable in their decision making and so fail to re-appraise initially rejected alternative courses of action and do not search for information that could disconfirm the selected course of action—the so-called confirmation bias. Edmondson et al. (2005) provide a discussion of groupthink as a potential explanation of the second ill-fated shuttle launch—that of Columbia.

Structured Group Processes

Awareness of the factors that can degrade group decision making, combined with the implicit belief that group judgment can potentially enhance decision making, has led to a number of *structured* methods to enhance group decision making by removing or restricting interpersonal interaction and controlling information flow. One such major method has been Delphi. Essentially, Delphi consists of an iterative process for making *quantitative* judgments. The phases of Delphi are:

1. Panelists provide opinions in answer to questions about issues such as the likelihood of future events, when events will occur, what the impact of events will be. These opinions are often given as responses to questionnaires that are completed individually by members of the panel.

2. After tallying the results, individual panelists are provided with *statistical* feedback of the whole panel's opinions (e.g., range or medians), before a

re-polling takes place. At this stage, dissenting opinion is aired so that anonymous discussion (often in written form) may occur.

3. The output of the Delphi technique is a quantified group "consensus," which is usually expressed as the median response of the group of panelists.

After the feedback at phase 2, the Delphi method assumes that the median response of the re-polled individuals is likely to shift nearer to the true value of the outcome to be predicted. Improvement is thought to result from opinion changes in "swingers," who change their less firmly grounded opinions, and the opinion stability of "holdouts," who are assumed to be more accurate than "swingers."

Indeed, Delphi was designed to improve upon the traditional group by adding structure to the process. Results generally suggest that Delphi groups are more accurate than traditional groups. Rowe and Wright (1999, 2001) found that Delphi groups outperformed traditional groups by a score of five studies to one, with two ties, and with one study showing task specific support for both techniques.

The research studies seem to show that collections of individuals make judgments that are more accurate and forecasts in Delphi groups than in unstructured groups, and that Delphi should be used in preference. One point of caution, however, is that the groups used in Delphi studies are usually highly simplified versions of real-world groups, comprising individuals with a high degree of expertise who genuinely care about the result of their meeting and have some knowledge of the strengths and weaknesses of their colleagues (or think they do). On this basis they may be able to selectively accept or reject their opinions. It may be that in a richer environment, the extra information and motivation brought to a task by those in a traditional group may make it of greater value than the limiting Delphi procedure.

Would it be Better to Simply Average the Forecasts of Several Individuals Rather Than Use Delphi?

Averaging of probability forecasts, scores, or weightings is one approach to reconciling differences in group judgments in applications of decision analysis. Another approach is to conduct sensitivity analysis to see if differences between individuals—in terms of probability judgments and value scores/weights—have any impact on the decision recommended by the modeling approach. Sensitivity analysis and averaging are a practical response to situations where individuals differ in their assessments and there is no "gold standard" against which to compare the relative validity of individuals' assessments.

Researchers have compared the *accuracy* of such statistical groups to Delphi groups in two ways: through a straightforward comparison of the two approaches, and through a comparison of the quality of averaged estimates on the first and the final round in a Delphi procedure. The first, pre-interaction, round is equivalent to a statistical group in every way except for the instructions given to individuals: Delphi panelists are led to expect further polling and feedback from others, which may lead panelists to consider the problem more deeply and possibly to make better "statistical group" judgments on that first round than individuals who do not expect to have their estimates used as feedback for others. A first round Delphi may, however, provide a better benchmark for comparison than a separate statistical group, because the panelists in the two "conditions" are the same, thus reducing a potential source of great variance.

Rowe and Wright (2001) reviewed the evidence for the relative values of statistical groups and Delphi groups. Although it should be possible to compare averages over rounds in every study of Delphi accuracy or quality, researchers in a number of evaluative studies have not reported the differences between rounds (e.g., Fischer 1981; Riggs 1983). Nevertheless, in their review of those studies that have examined such differences Rowe and Wright found that results generally support the advantage of Delphi groups over first round or statistical groups by a tally of 12 studies to two. In five studies, the researchers reported significant increases in accuracy over Delphi rounds. Seven more studies produced qualified support for Delphi: in five cases, researchers found Delphi to be better than statistical or first round groups more often than not, or to a degree that did not reach statistical significance. Two further studies, found Delphi to be better under certain conditions but not others. Parenté et al. (1984) found that Delphi accuracy was worse. The overall weight of empirical evidence, however, suggests that Delphi groups should be used instead of statistical groups whenever feasible, because generally they lead to judgments that are more accurate. This could result from the additional interaction during Delphi following the averaging of first round estimates.

Delphi has value in a number of situations. When experts are geographically dispersed and unable to meet in a face to face group, Delphi would seem an appropriate procedure. It enables members of different organizations to address industry wide issues, or experts from different facilities within a single organization to consider a problem without traveling to a single location. Indeed, experts with diverse backgrounds are liable to have different perspectives, terminologies, and frames of reference, which might easily hinder effective communication in a traditional group. The facilitator (or monitor team) can iron out such difficulties before the structured rounds of a Delphi.

Delphi might also be appropriate when disagreements between individuals are likely to be severe or politically unpalatable. Under such circumstances, the quality of judgments and decisions is likely to suffer from motive conflicts, personality clashes, and power games. Refereeing the group process and ensuring anonymity should prove beneficial.

Rowe and Wright (2001) summarize the following principles for using expert opinion in applications of Delphi:

- Use experts with appropriate domain knowledge.
- Use heterogeneous experts.
- Use between five and 20 experts.
- For Delphi feedback, provide the mean or median estimate of the panel plus the rationales from all panelists for their estimates.
- Continue Delphi polling until the responses show stability; generally, three structured rounds are enough.
- Obtain the final forecast by weighting all the experts' estimates equally and aggregating them.

In contrast to Delphi techniques, decision conferencing presents a socially interactive approach to decision making in order to generate a shared *understanding* of a problem and to produce a commitment to action.

Decision Conferencing

Decision conferencing brings together decision analysis, group processes, and information technology over an intensive two- or three-day session attended by people who wish to resolve a complex issue or decision. In this context, a small group of people who have an input to a major decision often sit on the perimeter of a round table and talk through their problem with a decision analyst, who acts to facilitate group interactions and knowledge sharing. In the background, another decision analyst uses interactive decision aiding technology to model individual and group views on such issues as multiattribute option evaluation and resource allocation. However, as can be inferred from the earlier discussion of unaided decision making, the outputs of such modeling seldom agree with unaided holistic judgments. One major responsibility of the decision analyst is to explain the underlying logic of the modeling methods to the decision makers. Only if the decision makers can fully appreciate the methods are they likely to accept model-based choices over their own intuitive judgments. To quote Phillips (1984):

As the results of the modeling become available to the participants, they compare these results to their holistic judgments. It is the inevitable discrepancies that arise, especially early in the modeling process, that drive the dialectic. By exploring these discrepancies, understanding deepens and changes and new perspectives are reflected back as adjustments. Eventually, participants are satisfied with the model and unable to derive any further insights from it ... The model has served its purpose.... (p. 32)

Phillips is concerned not to impose an optimal solution by black box methods:

If exploration of the discrepancy between holistic judgment and model results show the model to be at fault, then the model is not requisite—it is not yet sufficient to solve the problem. The model can only be considered requisite when no new intuitions emerge about the problem ... Requisite models are not produced from people's heads, they are *generated* through the interaction of problem owners. (p. 34)

Participants gain a sense of common purpose and a commitment to action. Sensitivity analysis allows participants to see if individual disagreements make a difference in the final preferred alternative or decision. Decision analytic principles provide a *guide* to action, not a black box prescription for action.

It is intuitively reasonable that discussions about decisions leading to consensus are more likely to be implemented than the output prescriptions of complex black box decision analyses, which involve but a single decision maker who may well have to justify his or her decision to others in the organization. In addition, decisions made by such groups are likely to be "made" to work because of the group commitment.

Are such more or less valid than unaided judgment or prescriptive solutions? For example, does the situational context of decision conferencing produce conditions for groupthink? Phillips (1984) has argued that this is not so, since:

1. Participants are not on home ground. Often decision conferences take place in hotels or an especially designed room on the decision analyst's premises.
2. The small group is carefully composed of people representing *all* perspectives on the issue to be resolved so that adversarial processes operate in the group to check bias and explore alternative framings of the decision problem.
3. The decision analyst who acts to facilitate the conference is a neutral outsider who is sensitive to the unhelpful effects of groupthink and reflects this back to the group.

In a pioneering study, McCartt and Rohrbough (1989) addressed the problem of evaluating the effectiveness of decision conferencing. These investigators argued that attempts to link good decision outcomes to particular types of group decision support are extraordinarily difficult, since virtually all real-world applications of group decision support do not provide enough baselines of comparison (e.g., tests of alternative methods/techniques or alternative decisions) to satisfy laboratory-based experimental researchers.

For example, with group commitment, poor decisions may be "made" to produce good outcomes, otherwise the credibility of the senior executives who attended the decision conference would be in trouble. Good judgment and decision making have been seen as one of the major characteristics of good managers! McCartt and Rohrbough conclude that any assessment of the effectiveness of a group decision process must look at the *process* itself and not subsequent outcomes. In their study, these investigators followed up a cross-section of 14 decision conferences held by Decision Techtronics at the State University of New York at Albany. Using mailed questionnaires, they enquired about the perceived organizational benefits in the form of improved information management, planning, efficiency, and morale. Effective decision conferences were found to be ones where participants perceived real benefit in the support of the decision analysis techniques and in the opportunity for open and extended discussion about the models that had been built. Ineffective decision conferences were characterized by executive teams who convened to discuss a problem but felt little pressure to reach consensus or construct a plan of action.

Scenario Planning

The practice of scenario planning implicitly accepts that managers are *not* able to make valid assessments of the likelihood of unique future events and that "best guesses" of what the future may hold may be wrong. Advocates also argue that it can counter groupthink by allowing minority opinions about the future to have "airtime," relative to majority opinion, although not always successfully (see, e.g., Hodgkinson and Wright 2002).

A scenario is not a forecast of the future. Multiple scenarios are pen-pictures of a range of *plausible* futures. Each individual scenario has an infinitesimal probability of actual occurrence but it is possible to construct the *range* of a set of individual scenarios in such a way as to bound the uncertainties that are seen to be inherent in the future—like the edges on the boundaries surrounding a multidimensional space.

Scenarios focus on key uncertainties *and* certainties about the future and use this information to construct pen-pictures in an information rich way in order to provide vivid descriptions of future worlds. In contrast, subjective probabilities entered into a decision tree provide numerical values that can be used in an expected utility calculation. The judgment process that produced such values is often not justified. When individuals disagree about their subjective probabilities for a critical event within decision analysis, practice is often to take an average, or weighted average. The relationship between the *critical* uncertainties, important predetermined trends (such as demographics, e.g., the proportion of the US population who are in various age bands in, say, ten years' time) and the behavior of actors who have a stake in the particular future (and who will tend to act to preserve and enhance their own interests within that future) are thought through in the *process* of scenario planning such that the resultant pen-pictures are, in fact, seen as plausible to those who have constructed the scenarios.

The outcome of the decision process in scenario planning is *not* the selection of the option with the highest expected value or utility but the selection of the most "robust" decision in the face of an unpredictable future. However, even if the development of a fundamentally robust option is not possible, scenario thinking also provides other benefits. Communication of world views can be easy in an organization via the medium of the scenario "stories". Additionally, rehearsing a future can provide a better understanding of the reasons underlying a situation. Thus, once the early events in a scenario occur, the decision maker will be able to anticipate how the future will unfold. These trigger events will be seen as *information* among the stream of *data* that impacts upon the decision maker.

Table 28.1   The Components of the Three Techniques to Aid Group-Based Decision Making

	Scenario planning	Decision analysis	Delphi
Future orientation:	Scenario planning constructs multiple frames of the future.	Decision analysis is conventionally undertaken within a single general frame of the future.	Delphi is usually focused on forecasting the occurrence of a single event or quantity.
Structure of judgment inputs:	Structuring is achieved by qualitative decomposition into critical uncertainties and trends. An emphasis on understanding causality.	Structuring is achieved by quantitative decomposition into probabilities, payoffs, and decision trees or values and weights.	Structuring is achieved by the controlled exchange of information between anonymous panelists over a number of rounds (iterations).
Information orientation:	Scenario team members exchange existing opinions on issues of concern and systematically provide insight on issues of critical uncertainty.	Fresh information may be sought if the analysis indicates that a decision is sensitive to small changes in judgmental inputs.	Expert panelists exchange their existing estimates. Individual experts can hold, or change, their estimates on the basis of feedback of the estimates of other panelists.
Process orientations:	Dissenting opinions are given "airtime" that is preserved, and combined with the opinions of others, while maintaining divergence.	Divergent opinions are combined by averaging and reduction.	The statistical average of the estimates on the final Delphi round is taken as the group judgment.
Action orientation:	The result is shared understanding within the management team, of causally determined futures that can galvanize managerial action to avoid unfavorable futures or facilitate the occurrence of favorable ones.	The result of the analysis is a single recommended decision for subsequent implementation.	None.

Just as the new purchaser of a particular make of car becomes very sensitive to the number of models of that make on the road and the differences in levels of equipment, etc., the scenario thinker becomes sensitive to a scenario starting to unfold and becoming reality. Such sensitivity can lead to *early* contingency action towards an unfavorable future (see Wright and Goodwin 1999b; Wright et al. 2004). Alternatively, new business opportunities can be quickly grasped as soon as favorable scenarios begin to unfold. Some practitioners see early recognition and reaction to an emerging future as more useful than the creation of robust strategic options (see van der Heijden et al. 2002).

Typical outcomes of the scenario planning process include:

1. Confirmation that the business idea is sound or that new strengths need to be added to create more robustness.
2. Confirmation that lower level business choices are sound or that alternative new options are more robust.
3. Recognition that none of the business options are robust and, therefore, contingency planning against unfavorable futures is necessary.
4. Sensitivity to the "early warning" elements that are precursors of desirable and unfavorable futures.

Often, in practice, scenario workshops invoke an "organizational jolt" to routine, "business as usual," thinking. A major insight can be that continuing with business as usual is a fragile strategy against the constructed futures. Wright et al. (2004), and Cairns et al. (2004, 2006) discuss these issues in more detail.

Comparative views on scenario planning, decision analysis, and Delphi as aids to group decision making are given in Table 28.1.

CONCLUSIONS

This chapter has illustrated the use of heuristics in unaided decision making at both the individual and small group level of analysis. In individual decision making, individuals tend to use simplified mental strategies to make choices between multiattributed alternatives. Such strategies often don't involve trade-offs and so are non-compensatory. By contrast, decision aiding techniques such as SMART, SMARTER, and the AHP aid the decision maker to make trade-offs and so provide support in compensatory decision making. These decision tools have been used in a wide variety of practical business applications. Such compensatory decision aiding techniques are based on the principle of decomposing the decision maker's judgmental task into attribute identification, value scoring, and attribute weighting. The recomposition of these judgments, via the decision modeling, is likely to challenge the decision maker's unaided choice preference. This challenge is the essential value of the decision aiding approach. A similar approach, that of decomposition and recomposition of judgmental estimates, underpins the decision aiding of decisions involving risk and uncertainty. In such decisions, also, heuristics are commonly used by busy decision makers assessing the likelihood of future events. Here, techniques such as fault trees, risk analysis, and decision analysis rebuild decomposed judgmental assessments in ways that will, likely, also challenge unaided, holistic intuition.

With the sphere of group decision making, Delphi can aid convergence of opinion between group members through anonymous interaction. The structuring of group interaction can overcome the process loss inherent in unstructured groups—such as the domination by assertive and talkative individuals. In contrast, decision conferencing and scenario planning interventions allow group members to interact but the interaction is moderated by facilitators who either: (1) implement decision analysis technologies; or (2) implement scenario construction methodologies. As in individual decision making, both decision conferencing and scenario construction, involve the decomposition, and subsequent recomposition, of judgment. As was shown, Delphi, decision analysis and scenario planning can be compared and contrasted in terms of differences in: (1) future orientation; (2) structure of judgmental inputs; (3) information orientation; (4) process orientation; and (5) action orientation.

In summary, there exists a range of methods to aid both individual and group decision making. This chapter has described and contrasted the domains of applicability of a range of well utilized decision aiding technologies. The key, of course, is to match particular methods to particular decision situations.

REFERENCES

BELL, D. E. (1984). 'Bidding for the *S. S. Kuniang*.' *Interfaces*, 14: 17–23.

BOYLE, D. (2000). *The Tyranny of Numbers: Why Counting Can't Make us Happy*. London: Harper Collins.

BUEDE, D. M. and BRESNICK, T. A. (1992). 'Applications of Decision Analysis to the Military Systems Acquisition Process.' *Interfaces*, 22: 110–25.

CAIRNS, G., WRIGHT, G., VAN DER HEIJDEN, K., BURT, G. and BRADFIELD, R. (2004). 'The Application of Scenario Planning to Internally-Generated e-Government Futures.' *Technological Forecasting and Social Change*, 71: 217–38.

—— —— BRADFIELD, R., VAN DER HEIJDEN, K., and BURT, G. (2006). 'Enhancing Foresight Between Multiple Agencies: Issues in the Use of Scenario Thinking to Overcome Fragmentation.' *Futures*, 38: 1011–25.

CASEY, D. (2001). 'Corporate Valuation, Capital Structure and Risk Management: A Stochastic DCF Approach.' *European Journal of Operational Research*, 135: 311–25.

COULTER E. D., SESSIONS J., and WING M. G. (2006). 'Scheduling Forest Road Maintenance Using the Analytic Hierarchy Process and Heuristics.' *Silva Fennica*, 40: 143–60.

EDMONDSON, A. C., ROBERTO, M. A., BOHMER, R. M. J., FERLINS, E. M., and FELDMAN, L. R. (2005). 'The Recovery Window: Organizational Learning Following Ambiguous Threats,' in W. H. Starbuck and M. Farjoun (eds.), *Organization at the Limit: Lessons for the Columbia Disaster*. Malden, MA: Blackwell, 220–45.

EDWARDS, W. (1971). 'Social Utilities.' *Engineering Economist*, Summer Symposium Series: 6.

—— BARRON, H. F. (1994). 'SMARTS and SMARTER: Improved Simple Methods for Multiattribute Utility Measurement.' *Organisational Behavior and Human Decision Processes*, 60: 306–25.

ESSER, J. K. and LINDOERFER, J. (1989). 'Groupthink and the Space Shuttle Challenger Accident: Towards a Quantitative Case Analysis.' *Journal of Behavioral Decision Making*, 2: 167–77.

FRENCH, S. (1996). 'Multiattribute Decision Support in the Event of a Nuclear Accident.' *Journal of Multi-Criteria Decision Analysis*, 5: 39–57.

GIGERENZER, G., TODD, P. M., and the ABC Research Group (1999). *Simple Heuristics that Make Us Smart*. Oxford: Oxford University Press.

GOODWIN, P. and WRIGHT, G. (1993). 'Improving Judgmental Time Series Forecasting: A Review of the Guidance Provided by Research.' *International Journal of Forecasting*, 9: 147–61.

—— —— (2001). 'Enhancing Strategy Evaluation in Scenario Planning: A Role for Decision Analysis.' *Journal of Management Studies*, 38: 1–16.

—— —— (2004). *Decision Analysis for Management Judgment*. Chichester: Wiley.

HODGKINSON, G. P. and WRIGHT, G. (2002). 'Confronting Strategic Inertia in a Top Management Team: Learning from Failure.' *Organization Studies*, 23: 949–77.

GRAEBER, S. (2001). 'How to Select a Clinical Information System.' *Journal of the American Medical Informatics Association*, Supplement S: 219–23.

HESS, S. W. (1993). 'Swinging on the Branch of a Tree: Project Selection Applications.' *Interfaces*, 23: 5–12.

HILDEN, M. (1997). 'Conflicts Between Fisheries and Sea Birds—Management Options Using Decision Analysis.' *Marine Policy*, 21: 143–53.

JANIS, I. R. (1982). *Groupthink* (2nd edn.). Boston, MA: Houghton Mifflin.

KEENEY, R. L. (1992). *Value Focused Thinking*. London: Harvard University Press.

MABIN, V., MENZIES, M., KING, G., and JOYCE, K. (2001). 'Public Sector Priority Setting Using Decision Support Tools.' *Australian Journal of Public Administration*, 60: 44–59.

MARPLES, C. and ROBERTSON, G. (1993). 'Option Review with HIVIEW.' *OR Insight*, 6: 13–18.

McCARTT, A. and ROHRBOUGH, J. (1989). 'Evaluating Group Decision Support System Effectiveness: A Performance Study of Decision Conferencing.' *Decision Support Systems*, 5: 243–53.

OBERG. T. and BERGBACK, B. (2005). 'A Review of Probabilistic Risk Assessment of Contaminated Land.' *Journal of Soils and Sediments*, 5: 213–24.

PARENTÉ, F. J., ANDERSON, J. K., MYERS, P., and O'BRIEN, T. (1984). 'An Examination of Factors Contributing to Delphi Accuracy.' *Journal of Forecasting*, 3: 173–82.

PHILLIPS, L. D. (1984). 'A Theory of Requisite Decision Models.' *Acta Psychologica*, 56: 29–48.

ROCAH-LEGORRETA, F. and LERCHE, I. (2004). 'Oil and Gas Estimates for Arctic National Wildlife Refuge Area 1002, Alaska.' *Energy Exploration and Exploitation*, 22: 161–230.

ROSENHEAD, J. and MINGERS, J. (eds.) (2001). *Rational Analysis for a Problematic World Revisited: Problem Structuring Methods for Complexity, Uncertainty and Conflict*. Chichester: Wiley.

ROTHLEY, K. D. (1999). 'Designing Bioreserve Networks to Satisfy Multiple, Conflicting Demands.' *Ecological Applications*, 9: 741–50.

ROWE, G. and WRIGHT, G. (1999). 'The Delphi Technique as a Forecasting Tool: Issues and Analysis.' *International Journal of Forecasting*, 15: 353–75.

——— ——— (2001). 'Expert Opinions in Forecasting: Role of the Delphi Technique,' in J. S. Armstrong (ed.), *Principles of Forecasting: A Handbook for Researchers and Practitioners*. Norwell, MA: Kluwer Academic Publishers.

ROY, B. (1991). 'The Outranking Approach and the Foundations of Electre Methods.' *Theory and Decision*, 31: 49–73.

SAATY, T. L. (1990). *The Analytic Hierarchy Process*. Pittsburgh, PA: RWS Publications.

STARBUCK, W. H. and FARJOUN, M. (2005). *Organization at the Limits: Lessons for the Columbia Disaster*. Malden, MA: Blackwell.

TVERSKY, A. (1969). 'Intransitivity of Preferences.' *Psychological Review*, 76: 31–48.

——— (1972). 'Elimination by Aspects: A Theory of Choice.' *Psychological Review*, 79: 281–99.

——— KAHNEMAN, D. (1974). 'Judgement under Uncertainty: Heuristics and Biases.' *Science*, 185: 1124–31.

ULVILA, J. W. (1987). 'Postal Automation (Zip 1 4) Technology: A Decision Analysis.' *Interfaces*, 7: 1–12.

VAN DER HEIJDEN, K., BRADFIELD, B., BURT, G., CAIRNS, G., and WRIGHT, G. (2002). *The Sixth Sense: Accelerating Organizational Learning through Scenarios*. Chichester and New York: John Wiley and Sons.

WINTER, F. W. (1985). 'An Application of Computerized Decision Tree Models in Management-union Bargaining.' *Interfaces*, 15: 74–80.

WRIGHT, G. and GOODWIN, P. (1999a). 'Rethinking Value Elicitation for Personal Consequential Decisions.' *Journal of Multicriteria Decision Analysis*, 8: 3–10.

——— ——— (1999b). 'Future-Focussed Thinking: Combining Decision Analysis and Scenario Planning.' *Journal of MultiCriteria Decision Analysis*, 8: 311–21.

——— VAN DER HEIJDEN, K., BRADFIELD, R., BURT, G., and CAIRNS, G. (2004). 'The Psychology of Why Organizations Can Be Slow to Adapt and Change: And What Can Be Done About It.' *Journal of General Management*, 29: 21–36.

29

STRATEGY WORKSHOPS AND "AWAY DAYS" AS RITUAL[*]

NICOLE BOURQUE
GERRY JOHNSON

INTRODUCTION

THERE seems to be an assumption that getting away from the everyday hurly burly of managing and bringing together executives, often to spend a day or two focused on key issues, will aid in the decision-making process and, in turn, in the implementation of the decision. Such events typically involve a one to three day stay at a hotel or conference facility and the use of an external facilitator. For example, according to Hodgkinson et al. (2006), over 60 percent of UK organizations hold such events at least once a year, 73 percent of which take place off-site. These events may lead to heated debate, the surfacing of deep resentments/fears, cathartic resolutions, and/or excitement at the formation of a new intended strategy. Our research suggests, however, that while there may be many benefits in workshops or away days, including the production of decisions on intended strategy, there is a

* We would like to acknowledge the invaluable contribution of Shameen Prashantham and Steve Floyd to the formulation of the theoretical framework we use in this chapter. The financial support of the UK ESRC/EPSRC Advanced Institute of Management (AIM) Research, under grant number RES-331-25-0015, is also gratefully acknowledged.

much lower success rate in converting this to realized strategy when participants return to their everyday place of work.

Common as such events are, there is a lack of research in this field. Management researchers have made few attempts to study strategy events and to build explanations from theories (for exceptions, see Hodgkinson and Wright 2002; Whittington 2006). In particular, the management literature has failed to explain why the social dynamics, the often intense emotional experiences of participants, and the intended strategies formed at these events are not always realized after the event.

This chapter will use ritual theory, developed by anthropologists, in order to shed light on these processes. In particular, this will entail a focus on theories of rites of passage (van Gennep [1909] 1960; Turner 1969) and of ritualization (Bell 1992; Humphrey and Laidlaw 1994). This chapter will describe a "typical" strategy event (see above) and discuss the similarities between this event and a rite of passage. Then, it will use ritual theory to analyze this case study and explain the phenomena that arise during and following the event. Finally, it will suggest areas of future research and offer some advice for managers and facilitators of such events.

A Strategy Away Day

The following case description portrays an actual strategy away day. Of course, this information is generalized to protect the anonymity of the company involved.

The new chief executive of the European division of a multinational corporation convened a three-day weekend workshop that involved the chief executive and two levels of management. The event brought together 20 managers from Germany, France, and the UK. They met at a hotel in an attractive tourist venue in the UK about 40 miles from the UK-based European head office. The managers came from businesses merged together into a single division following a series of acquisitions over the previous decade, so each had a residual culture of its own. The chief executive had two main goals in arranging this away day: (1) to decide the strategic priorities for the division; and (2) to better integrate the operations of the geographically (and culturally) dispersed parts of the business to deliver these.

The chief executive worked with a strategy consultant who facilitated the workshop. They agreed that the goals would be unachievable unless the managers surfaced and discussed some of the hidden agendas that were preventing integration and cooperation. The chief executive, though new to the division, felt he knew what some of the problems were, but was facing difficulties in getting managers to surface problems openly and confront them: "If we can't even admit we have problems, let alone address them, how do we move forward?" The workshop was structured along two lines: (1) a discussion of the required strategy for the organization (which employed a number of standard strategy models and concepts); and (2) the discussion and identification of the different cultures of the organization in order to encourage participants to surface their taken for granted assumptions and ways of behaving.

The first day involved the discussion of strategy. This consisted of competitor analysis and competence analysis. The chief executive was delighted that his managers had little problem in addressing and agreeing upon the required future strategic priorities for the organization in terms of the divisions' products and markets. He regarded the day's activities as a success. However, it was clear to him and to the facilitator that there were underlying tensions. Despite the chief executive's efforts to try to encourage integration that night in the bar, the managers from the different business units clustered in their own groups.

The second day involved the analysis of organizational culture. The participants from the UK, French, and German businesses went to separate breakout groups to discuss the culture of their organization using a framework designed to encourage group discussion (Johnson 1992). They then presented their "cultural analysis" to each other. What emerged were some commonalities—not surprising since they were all in the same industry with the similar technologies—but some differences too. The groups identified the similarities fairly clearly. What they were much less precise about were the differences. The chief executive argued that they would have to clarify these differences before they could deal with the difficulties of integration that they all acknowledged. He pushed to find out what "was really going on." In so doing, it became clear that tensions were rising further. Managers became defensive and uncomfortable. Eventually, one of the French managers cracked: pointing to the German managers he said, "They are the problem. They are raping us!" The German contingent demanded an explanation. It became clear that the UK and French businesses regarded the German operation as being overprotective of what had once been their own superior technology and were using the transfer pricing mechanisms between businesses to inflate their profit performance at the expense of the other businesses in the division. An intense argument ensued, so the CEO called for a break in the proceedings. The German managers then left the hotel and went for a walk; the others went to the bar. Two hours later, the Germans returned to the hotel, spoke with the chief executive and agreed to return to the workshop with the others. Participants then spoke openly, and eventually less emotionally, about problematic issues. Later in the more informal setting of the bar, the managers were able to "sort things out." By the following morning, the participants agreed that the "blood-letting" had been helpful and could lead to more open and honest discussions.

On the final day, the mood of the meeting had changed dramatically from day two. Participants were willing and active in the formation of an agenda for the long- and short-term in order to address both the strategic imperatives and requirements necessary for the development of a more integrated and cooperative organization. Participants identified an action plan and agreed on a timetable for the next six months. These emphasized the need for immediate change in order to encourage greater integration around product and service delivery. There was an air of excitement as individuals volunteered to be responsible for the various action points. Named managers accepted responsibility for overseeing the implementation of each decision. By the end of day three, the participants were enthusiastic about the agenda for change. Moreover, the chief executive proclaimed that the agreed agenda would form the basis of the agenda for the executive team's future monthly meetings. There was general agreement that the event had been a great success.

Three months later, the workshop facilitator was working in another division of the corporation where he met one of the workshop participants. On asking how the agenda had progressed, the participant told the facilitator that not much had happened. The facilitator contacted the European chief executive, who told him that this was indeed the case: the pressures of everyday work had "got in the way of change." The headoffice imposed cost cutting measures on the division. This affected the implementation of the intended strategy.

In summary, this event, conducted at a location away from the everyday workplace, entailed a focus on strategically important issues. Working through a program of strategy analysis and evaluation, the participants identified a number of strategic priorities and explored the prevailing organizational culture. The foregoing steps led to a cathartic episode, followed by efforts to specify action plans. However, the participants subsequently did not implement their plans.

THEORIES OF RITUAL AND RITUALIZATION

There has long been an acknowledgement by management writers that organizations and organizational activities are ritualistic. Some researchers have discussed rituals as key aspects of organizational culture (Trice and Beyer 1984; Deal and Kennedy 1988; Johnson 1992) and culture change (O'Day 1974; Trice and Beyer 1985). Hamel (1996: 70) refers to strategic planning as a "calendar driven ritual." This is echoed by Mintzberg (1994). However, a good deal of this literature does not attempt to explain the meaning and significance of ritual by making reference to anthropological theory.

Anthropologists have indicated that rituals make up a significant part of activity in many societies. Rituals fulfill a range of social functions, including the expression of emotion; the reinforcement of behavior; the support and/or subversion of the status quo; an indication of ethnic, gender, or social status; the initiation of change; and the restoration of harmony (Gluckman 1965; Geertz 1973; Bell 1992; Bowie 2000). Indeed, one reason to study rituals is that they influence the everyday world. Rituals help to shape a group's shared understanding of reality, and in so doing, they legitimize some representations of everyday life and either ignore or actively suppress others (Gluckman 1965; Geertz 1973). Rituals contribute to the development of social order, the preservation of traditions, and the reinforcement of the social status quo (Durkheim [1912] 1954). Some rituals also induce behavior among participants that are socially unacceptable under normal circumstances (e.g., the bride-to-be kissing total strangers during a hen night or a king washing the feet of paupers). In such ways "reversals" of social norms may actually serve to highlight social norms. For example, the astonishing sight of a king washing the feet of the poor ironically emphasizes the importance of the king (Gluckman 1965). However, a challenge to the status quo may possibly arise from the "reversal" of social norms (Turner 1969). Thus, in addition to reinforcing the existing social and cultural environment, rituals also serve as an important means of social change (Kertzer 1988).

Rituals were a subject of anthropological inquiry long before Durkheim's (1912) classic, *The Elementary Form of the Religious Life*. Because of this prolonged inquiry, there is no one agreed definition. However, there is sufficient agreement among the various definitions to distill some common core elements, ones that can usefully inform the analysis of strategy away days. Alexander (1997: 139) defines ritual as "a performance, planned or improvised, that effects a transition from everyday life to an alternative context within which the everyday is transformed." Similarly, Roth (1995: 313), in summarizing Victor Turner (1969), says that "ritual consists of actions that remove individuals and groups from the mundane features of their daily routines, by relocating them outside of the geographical boundaries as well as 'betwixt and between' the social boundaries that define the group." Essentially, the anthropological literature indicates that rituals involve: patterns of formalized behaviour, repetition, separation from everyday life, performance, symbolic communication, the ability to cause transformations, and the capacity for arousing strong emotions.

Recently, anthropologists have shifted their focus from the study of rituals per se, to the study of *ritualization* (Bell 1992; Humphrey and Laidlaw 1996). Ritualization is

a way of acting that is designed and orchestrated to distinguish and privilege what is being done in comparison to other, usually more quotidian, activities... for creating and privileging a qualitative distinction between the "sacred" and the "profane." (Bell 1992: 74)

Certain actions achieve privileged differentiation in a range of ways. Differentiation can entail delineated and structured space with restricted access; special periodicity; restricted codes of communication; distinct and specialized personnel; designated objects, text, and dress; verbal/gestural combinations; special preparations; and/or unique constituencies or audiences (Bell 1992: 204).

In their study of ritualization, Humphrey and Laidlaw (1996) suggest that rather than look at ritual as a particular class of activity, researchers should consider what makes particular actions ritualistic. They point out that a key feature of ritualized action is a disjuncture between action and the direct intent behind that action. For example, under ordinary circumstances, the cutting of hair is not ritualistic, in part because the personal grooming intention (to have shorter hair) represents the purpose behind the behavior. In contrast, in an initiation rite, the liturgy leads to hair cutting rather than the intention of having shorter hair. Because the initiate's behavior is almost entirely scripted and driven by what Humphrey and Laidlaw call "liturgy," such actions are "ritualized."

Liturgy, the script for a ritual, prescribes participants' behavior by restricting communication to particular concepts or a vocabulary that may involve the use of symbols (Durkheim [1912] 1954; Bell 1992). Typically, the most important liturgical element entails "getting it right" (i.e., conforming to liturgical expectations, Humphrey and Laidlaw 1996).

Although anthropologists cannot agree on a definition of ritual/ritualization, there is agreement that rituals: (1) are a performance that is scripted by liturgy and played out within constraints of power relations (Alexander 1977; Turner 1982; Bell 1992; Humphrey and Laidlaw 1996); (2) remove people from the context of everyday life; and (3) have the power to effect social transitions (van Gennep [1909] 1960; Turner 1969).

The literature on rites of passage is especially useful for the analysis of strategy away days. However, before discussing the similarities between rites of passage and away days, it is important to consider what anthropologists have to say about rites of passage. Sociologists and anthropologists regard van Gennep's ([1909] 1960) work on rites of passage as a classic. As a result of comparative analysis, van Gennep ([1909] 1960) determined that all rituals where an individual changes from one status to another (i.e., baptism, initiation, marriage) have a similar structure. Such rituals begin with rites of *separation*. Rites of separation have the social and psychological function of "separating" the person undergoing the ceremony from their old identity or status. This is reflected at a symbolic level by cutting hair, removing clothing, or going away to a place that is very much different from everyday life. The second stage is a *liminal* period, during which the person undergoing the ritual is between statuses. The symbolism that appears during the liminal stage very often depicts images of death and rebirth. Symbols may also reflect a reversal of social norms. The final stage is *re-integration* into society in your new status. Again, symbols are important at this stage, since they emphasize the new status. For example, a priest says, "I now pronounce you man and wife" at the end of a wedding ceremony, or a king who washed feet during the liminal period of his coronation appears before his subjects fully robed and crowned.

Victor Turner (1982: 28) refined van Gennep's theory by focusing on the middle, liminal, part of the process. He noted that during a rite of passage, ritual participants moved from a state of structure during the separation process, to anti-structure during the liminal period, and back to structure during the re-integration process. Turner's (1969, 1982) use of the term "structure" refers to what anthropologists call social structure. This is the matrix of social relation that make up society. Anti-structure does not mean *opposition* to structure. Rather, it describes "the liberation of human capacities of cognition, affect, volition, creativity, etc., from the normative constraints incumbent upon occupying a sequence of social statuses" (Turner 1982: 44). It is "more in contrast than in active opposition to social structure...a way of being detached from social structure—and hence potentially of periodically *evaluating* its performance" (Turner 1982: 51). As indicated above, this may lead to a reversal of social norms, which may reinforce the status quo, but may also serve to signal a rejection of the established social order (rituals of rebellion) (Gluckman 1965).

Turner (1969) further noted that during a state of anti-structure in the liminal period of a rite of passage, ritual participants experienced a sense of communitas. Turner defines this as the "spontaneous, immediate, and concrete relatedness typical of the bonds formed between people in the middle, liminal stage of a rite of passage" (Bowie 2000). Communitas can be "a cathartic experience" (Bell 1992: 172), sometimes associated with descriptors such as "openness" and "potentiality" but also with being a temporary state. Turner (1969) was not the first to study the high emotions that can accompany ritual. Durkheim ([1912] 1954) attempted to explain the high level of emotions displayed at funerals. The key to his analysis was his conception of symbols. He noted that the symbols manipulated during rituals reminded people of important social values. Turner (1969) refined Durkheim ([1912] 1954) by looking at the use of "dominant" symbols. An example of a dominant symbol would be a national flag. A characteristic of dominant symbols is the ability to have a number of different, but linked, meanings in a variety of contexts. Some of these meanings can be quite concrete, symbolizing things that are physically tangible. For example, the red color of the Bolivian flag symbolizes the blood of Bolivians who have died fighting for their country. Other meanings can be quite abstract, such as the American flag standing for "the American" way of life. Since there is a link between dominant symbols and strong social values, their manipulation during a ritual can lead to strong emotions. Moreover, the symbols that people manipulate during rituals can have very different meanings to different groups of participants. For example, as American soldiers tore down the statue of Saddam Hussein in Baghdad, one of the soldiers climbed up and attached an American flag to the statue. The American flag is a powerful symbol across the world, but exactly what it represents can differ if you are an American or Iraqi. Someone on the ground quickly realized this and another soldier quickly replaced the American flag with an Iraqi one.

BACK TO AWAY DAYS

Clearly, strategy workshops or away days share some similarities to rites of passage. *Separation* appears in the tendency to leave the normal operational site to a place that is distinctly outside of the ordinary (Hodgkinson et al. 2006). The separation or removal from everyday life that occurs in strategy away days is symbolized in a variety of ways, such as wearing informal dress or engaging in social activities in addition to business related work. Such activities help move the participants from the structure of everyday life to the anti-structure of the transitional, liminal period. In this case study, the decision of the chief executive officer to hold an away day initiated the separation stage. He also chose the location for the meeting with the express intent of "getting people away somewhere pleasant where they can get to know each other." For many of the participants, there was, of course, substantial geographic separation from their place of work.

The *liminal* period of an event such as a strategy away day starts when participants shift attention away from the everyday routine toward evaluation and planning (Marks et al. 2001). This is an important stage because the activity that occurs during this phase is what distinguishes such episodes from other everyday activities, such as operational decision making. During a strategy episode, liminality may arise from thinking about "big picture" issues and contemplating the long run future of the organization. To enhance the sense of openness, facilitators may use brainstorming, scenario planning, or other techniques from the liturgy of strategy literature and consultancy in an attempt to free participants from ordinary assumptions and inspire creativity.[1] Turner observed that in this state "... people play with the elements of the familiar and de-familiarize them" (Turner 1982: 27).

Such techniques may lead to what Turner (1969) called anti-structure. Unfettered by conventional thinking and the constraints of "structure," participants in a situation of "anti-structure" feel free to critique existing ways of doing things and consider radically new alternatives (Hodgkinson and Wright 2002). Such practices may also help participants reach consensus (Amason 1996; Kellermanns et al. 2005), share goals (Kerr 2004), develop collective vision (Larwood et al. 1995) or otherwise develop the sense of common purpose and emotional closeness that Turner (1969) identified as communitas. There are several ways to symbolize consensus: the most mundane might be the joint production of a flip chart with an agreed diagnosis of a problem, a recommendation, or an action plan. This might, however, be reinforced by emotional bonding around such an output. There may also be an enactment of some dimension of crisis. As Randall Collins observed:

I have often noticed that in a conference of this sort, if it starts out with a conflict during the first day, it will resolve into a high degree of solidarity by the third day when everyone departs; i.e. the originating emotion serves to get the group focused, and later this can be transformed into positive emotions.[2]

In this case study, there is clear evidence of a liminal stage that displays anti-structure and the development of communitas. This occurred as participants worked through a scripted program (i.e., a strategy discussion followed by an exploration of organizational culture). Such scripting corresponds to a "liturgy" that, while in part tailored to the needs of the event, drew heavily on concepts and techniques well rehearsed in similar events by the facilitator. During the first day, the liturgy went to plan. The strategic devices used by the facilitator encouraged participants to "think outside of the box" and together come up with a new strategic priorities for the organization. People ended the day feeling satisfied that the processes in which they were participating had lead to a successful outcome.

On the second day, the facilitator used a different liturgy in order to expose cultural differences and assumption and thereby reveal "hidden tensions." In this, it was spectacularly successful, though the level of emotion was probably unexpected. During this period, the use of space was significant. When tensions reached a head, participants left the physical space of the main workshop room in order to allow "things to cool down." The Germans' decision to go for a walk while everyone else headed to the bar symbolized the split between the Germans and the rest of the participants. The return of the Germans to the bar indicated, at a symbolic level, their willingness to reparticipate in the process. It is interesting that the "cooling off" period and the recognition that differences had to be resolved happened within spaces where activities were not scripted. Returning to the boardroom symbolized the resolution of the cathartic event and also a joint willingness to re-engage in the strategy liturgy.

On day three, the participants released, but did not fully resolve, their tensions. This explains the strong degree of communitas exhibited by all participants. The participants were eager to follow the liturgy and form clear intentions and a detailed action plan. The buzz of excitement that infused the creation of the action plan (particularly when contrasted with the strong divisions that emerged during day two) led everyone to leave the event feeling convinced of the success of the event.

The final stage of a rite of passage is *integration* (van Gennep [1909] 1960; Turner 1969). This is when the individuals undergoing the ritual return to everyday life in their new status—in this case here, supposedly as "converts" to a new integrated way of doing things. Commonly, in a rite of passage, an individual receives a symbol of their new status (for example, a wedding ring). Such symbols serve to remind people of their new status and accompanying rights and obligations. Over time, various societies have developed methods of ensuring that integration takes place during rites of passage. Strategy consultants and organizations have been less successful in this regard. This occurred in this case study. An action plan with designated responsibilities and a promise by the chief executive to prioritize these on the executive team agenda did not have sufficient material or symbolic power. Three months after the event, there was little evidence that the participants made any efforts to realize the action plan. The workshop had not seemed to make any meaningful difference.

CONCLUSION AND CONSIDERATIONS

This chapter began with the observation that there is little research into strategy away days. This is in spite of the fact that away days are very common organizational events, which managers regard as an important forum for strategic decision making. The examination of this one case does not constitute a basis for general findings and recommendations and there is certainly a need for more structured research for this purpose. However, this chapter does clearly indicate support for the contention that away days are ritualistic in nature. As such, it is possible to gain insights and learn lessons into such events from a body of theory that is well developed: ritual theory. It also provides the basis for some tentative recommendations—or, at the least, considerations for managers:

- *Strategy workshops encourage "blue skies" strategic thinking.* If managers who initiate and plan strategy workshops hope to provide a forum in which they question and challenge strategy, their intentions may be well founded. Ritual theory tells us that the removal from everyday life and scripted prompting that appears in such events have three effects and a likely outcome. One effect is "liminality." In this "betwixt and between" state of being, participants address key aspects of their organization culture while being removed from it. Another effect is "anti-structure," which leads participants to question or challenge what they have previously taken for granted. "Communitas" is yet another effect. Participants feel a sense of togetherness and openness to new ideas and ways of being. These effects will create a context positively associated with blue skies thinking.
- *Workshops and away days, as ritualized events, are highly meaningful in and of themselves.* It is misleading to assume that a ritual has a direct function outside itself. Indeed the characteristics of ritual described here indicate that a ritualized

event may be highly significant in and of itself. The more the characteristics are emphasized, for example the geographic or psychological removal, and the novelty and emotional appeal of the liturgy, the greater that significance. It would be wrong to assume, however, that such meaningfulness of and within the event necessarily translates into action or change outside the event.

- It follows *that the ritualization of strategy workshops increases the potential for decisions on intended change within the event but decreases the likelihood that such decisions will lead to realized change*. Decisions within a workshop may not have an impact on everyday organizational life. Indeed the cathartic experience of the workshop may highlight the dangers of too much disruption of the status quo. Victor Turner, the anthropologist, could have been describing this workshop case study when he explained that rituals may "subvert the status quo, the structural form of society" and that ritual participants "can for a brief while have a whale of a time being chaotic ... but they had better stick to the order of things" (1969: 41). In other words, the more energized and questioning the workshop, the more likely it signals the need for change in the order of things: quite a challenge if a workshop is to come up with anything that will result in significant realized change.

- *Different roles for different workshops*. The foregoing suggests that events such as strategy workshops and away days can be valuable, but that the people organizing away days need to carefully assess the role of the event. It is probably wrong to assume that such events can be forums where participants will make major strategic decisions that will be translated into organizational action—at least as single events. Rather, different degrees of ritualization may have different and useful effects. For example, a highly ritualized event (e.g., in terms of degree of removal and liturgy) leading to high levels of questioning and challenge may be used as a way to break down social barriers and facilitate new ways of thinking about and responding to the environment. However, less ritualized workshops may play the different role of grounding decisions. These might be physically less removed from the workplace, with less use of strategy concepts and their associated tools and frameworks and more concerned with day to day implications.

- *Incorporation matters*. If strategy workshops are to be successful other than in and of themselves, if they are to translate into organizational action, then the incorporation stage would seem to be especially important. Interestingly, anthropology and ritual theory has less say about this. This is precisely because anthropologists are interested in rituals as meaningful in themselves. However, there are at least two insights.

   The first is that the shift from intention to realization may benefit from a nested series of strategy workshops that progress from highly ritualized, to moderately ritualized, and then to minimally ritualized.

The second is the reminder that rituals have an emotional character and are often concerned with highly ambiguous conditions. Yet, as with the workshop reported here, attempts at incorporation are purely cognitive (here it was an action list) and do little to help participants cope with the ambiguities they face as they compare the ritual with their more mundane organizational experience. In many cases, there may be a need for *emotional* as well as cognitive continuity between episodes or between an episode and everyday life.

In summary, those involved in the design of strategy episodes should attend to the paradox created by ritualization. All else being equal, episodes that are more removed from the work environment and that rely more on a formal script are more likely to create changes in how a group thinks and feels about strategy. Back at work, however, these ideas and feelings are likely to be more difficult to sustain precisely because participants produced them in a ritualized context. More ritualization, therefore, decreases the potential for the transfer of ideas from the episode to everyday work and puts a heavier burden on the incorporation phase to achieve such transfer. Thus, unless designers are aware of the effects of ritualization and are able to orchestrate an effective incorporation phase, many strategy episodes may be built to fail.

Endnotes

1 We argue, using Humphrey and Laidlaw's (1994) view of ritualization, that the techniques employed by strategy consultants, such as SWOT analysis or scenario planning, are ritualistic. The direct intent behind the participants' actions of filling in squares is not to have a filled in grid, but to stimulate thought and discussion within the group.

2 Email correspondence with Randall Collins, author of *Interaction Ritual Chains* (published in 2004 by Princeton University Press).

References

Alexander, B. C. (1997). 'Ritual and Current Studies of Ritual: Overview,' in S. D. Glazier, (ed.), *Anthropology of Religion: A Handbook*. Westport, CT: Greenwood Press, 139–60.

Amason, A. C. (1996). 'Distinguishing the Effects of Functional and Dysfunctional Conflicts on Strategic Decision Making: Resolving a Paradox for Top Management Teams.' *Academy of Management Journal*, 39: 123–48.

Bell, C. (1992). *Ritual Theory, Ritual Practice*. Oxford: Oxford University Press.

Bowie, F. (2000). *The Anthropology of Religion: An Introduction*. Oxford: Blackwell.

Deal, T. and Kennedy, A. (1988). *Corporate Cultures: The Rites and Rituals of Corporate Life*. Harmondsworth: Penguin.

DURKHEIM, E. ([1912] 1954). *The Elementary Forms of the Religious Life* (J. W. Swain, trans). New York: Free Press.

GEERTZ, C. (1973). *The Interpretation of Cultures*. London: Fontana.

GLUCKMAN, M. (1965). *Politics, Law and Ritual in Tribal Society*. Chicago, IL: Aldine.

HAMEL, G. (1996). 'Strategy as Revolution.' *Harvard Business Review*, 74/4: 69–80.

HODGKINSON, G. P. and WRIGHT, G. (2002). 'Confronting Strategic Inertia in a Top Management Team: Learning from Failure.' *Organization Studies*, 23: 949–77.

—— WHITTINGTON, R., JOHNSON, G., and SCHWARZ, M. (2006). 'The Role of Strategy Workshops in Strategy Development Processes: Formality, Communication, Coordination and Inclusion.' *Long Range Planning*, 39/5: 479–96.

HUMPHREY, C. and LAIDLAW, J. (1994). *The Archetypal Actions of Ritual: A Theory of Ritual Illustrated by the Jain Rite of Worship*. Oxford: Clarendon Press.

JOHNSON, G. (1992). 'Managing Strategic Change—Strategy, Culture and Action.' *Long Range Planning*, 25/1: 28–36.

KELLERMANS, F. W., WALTER, J., LECHNER, C., and FLOYD, S. (2005). 'The Lack of Consensus about Strategic Consensus: Advancing Theory and Research.' *Journal of Management*, 31: 719–37.

KERTZER, D. (1988). *Rituals, Politics and Power*. New Haven, CT: Yale University Press.

KERR, J. L. (2004). 'The Limits of Organizational Democracy.' *Academy of Management Executive*, 18: 81–95.

LARWOOD, L., FALBE, C. M., MIESING, P., and KRIGER, M. P. (1995). 'Structure and Meaning of Organizational Vision.' *Academy of Management Journal*, 38: 740–70.

MARKS, M. A., MATHIEU, J. E. and ZACCARO, S. J. (2001). 'A Temporally Based Framework and Taxonomy of Team Processes.' *Academy of Management Review*, 26/3: 356–76.

MINTZBERG, H. (1994). *The Rise and Fall of Strategic Planning*. London: Prentice Hall.

O'DAY, R. (1974). 'Intimidation Rituals: Reaction to Reform.' *Journal of Applied Behavioural Science*, 10: 373–86.

ROTH, A. (1995). '"Men Wearing Masks": Issues of Description in the Analysis of Ritual.' *Sociological Theory*, 13/3: 301–27.

TRICE, H. M. and BEYER, J. M. (1984). 'Studying Organizational Cultures through Rites and Ceremonials.' *Academy of Management Review*, 9/4: 653–69.

—— —— (1985). 'Using Six Organizational Rites to Change Culture,' in R. H. Kilmanm, Saxtibm, M., Serpa, R. et al. (eds.), *Gaining Control of the Corporate Culture*. London: Jossey Bass.

TURNER, V. (1969). *The Ritual Process: Structure and Anti-Structure*. Chicago, IL: Aldine.

—— (1982). *From Ritual to Theater: The Human Seriousness of Play*. New York: Paj.

VAN GENNEP, A. ([1909] 1960). *The Rites of Passage* (M. B. Vizedom and G. B. Caffee, trans.). Chicago, IL: University of Chicago Press.

WHITTINGTON, R. (2006). 'Completing the Practice Turn in Strategy Research.' *Organization Studies*, 27/5, 613–34.

30

TROUBLING FUTURES: SCENARIOS AND SCENARIO PLANNING FOR ORGANIZATIONAL DECISION MAKING*

MARK P. HEALEY
GERARD P. HODGKINSON

INTRODUCTION

To thrive, organizations must be equipped to anticipate tomorrow's social, economic, political, and technological advances, thereby ensuring that their products and services do not become outmoded. However, since organizational environments are inherently uncertain, decision makers cannot possibly foretell the future.

* The financial support of the UK ESRC/EPSRC Advanced Institute of Management (AIM) Research in the preparation of this chapter, under grant number RES-331-25-0028, is gratefully acknowledged.

Rather, they must attempt to devise strategies of sufficient robustness and flexibility to enable effective responses to shifting contingencies under turbulent
conditions. Many organizational decision makers turn to scenario planning techniques to help them meet this fundamental goal. In a recent UK survey, over a third
of organizations reported using scenario planning in their strategy workshops
(Hodgkinson et al. 2006), reinforcing the results of previous surveys demonstrating
the popularity of scenario-based techniques across Western Europe more generally
(Malaska 1985) and among large US firms (Linneman and Klein 1983).

Porter (1985: 447) describes scenario planning as "a powerful device for taking
account of uncertainty in making strategic choices." Other popular writings tout
scenario planning as a means of developing organizational foresight and facilitating
organizational adaptation by boosting learning (Wack 1985a, b; Hamel and Prahalad
1994; van der Heijden 1996; Fahay and Randall 1998; Ringland 1998; van der Heijden
et al. 2002). Unfortunately, these writings say little about the potential pitfalls of
scenario-based techniques, thus creating the impression that these techniques are a
panacea for strategic decision making under uncertainty. In practice, using scenarios
to inform organizational decisions is a complex matter and can yield mixed psychological effects, some of which might actually impair judgment and decision making.

Drawing on research in the psychological sciences that has largely been overlooked
in the scenario planning literature, this chapter argues that when used unskillfully
scenarios can anchor and confine, rather than stretch and expand, strategic thinking
and that constructing scenarios can itself be a biased activity, one that can induce
new and amplify extant biases rather than remove them. Furthermore, unless
skillfully introduced, scenario techniques can reduce or increase disproportionately
the confidence and uncertainty of decision makers, leading correspondingly to
misplaced optimism and threat rigidity among decision makers. In addition, the
chapter highlights how, in some circumstances, the negative emotional impact of
scenario analysis can override the potentially positive cognitive effects. Guidelines
for using scenarios in organizational decision making are offered throughout.

SCENARIOS AS COGNITIVE DEVICES

In the context of organizational decision making, the term "scenario planning"
refers generically to a group of techniques that use multiple scenarios to depict a
range of contingencies that the organization might plausibly have to face at future
points in time. These scenarios comprise "stories about the future" (Kuhn and
Sniezek 1996: 232), portrayed in "script-like narratives that paint in vivid detail
how the future might unfold in one direction or another" (Russo and Schoemaker
1992: 13). Typically, scenario analysts construct positive, negative, and status quo

futures, depicting strategically important variables (e.g., market demand, product technology) taking divergent forms (e.g., low vs. high demand; technological obsolescence vs. technological continuation). The aim is to stimulate decision makers to engage in deeper critical reflection on the causal processes underlying external events, in turn developing their understanding to inform appropriate strategic responses (Porter 1985; Wack 1985a, b; Schoemaker 1993; van der Heijden 1996).

The roots of scenario usage in organizations lie in forecasting and strategic planning. When used in forecasting applications the ultimate aim is to enable decision makers to assess the viability of strategic alternatives across a range of future scenarios, rather than plan for a single future. In such applications, multiple scenarios replace conventional single point predictions (see, e.g., Schoemaker 1991). Point predictions that take the form of best estimates or single probability distributions assume a solitary basis for action and are notoriously unreliable over the longer term (cf., Hogarth and Makridakis 1981; Pant and Starbuck 1990). Rather than represent uncertainty as deviations from a single best estimate, multiple scenario analysis attempts to place a bound on uncertainty across a range of possible future states (Schoemaker 1991, 1993). When used for strategic planning, the aim is to foster "alertness and responsiveness among decision makers to changing market conditions" (Grant 2003: 506). This entails evaluating how robust current and potential strategies would be under various plausible industry futures depicted in scenarios. Decision makers can evaluate the effectiveness of various strategic alternatives under different scenarios either subjectively or more formally using decision analytic methods (e.g., Goodwin and Wright 2001).

The mainstay of scenario-based techniques is that scenarios act as a "cognitive device" (van der Heijden 1996: 51). Advocates maintain that the process of reflecting on potential events in the operating environment forces decision makers to surface their underlying assumptions about their organization and the dynamics of its operating environment and, in so doing, confront future uncertainties and engage in critical debate regarding strategic responses to environmental change (Schwartz 1991; Fahay and Randall 1998; Ringland 1998). Van der Heijden (1996) claims this process improves the fitness of organizations in two ways. In the short-term, more skillful observation of the business environment is purported to increase organizational adaptability. Over the longer term, the robust strategic alternatives generated by this process equip the organization to withstand major shocks or environmental jolts.

Breaking the Shackles: Scenarios and Cognitive Inertia

A substantial body of theory and research has shown that an overdependence on extant mental representations of the organization and its operating environment is a major cause of organizational inertia (Porac et al. 1989; Barr et al. 1992; Reger and Palmer 1996; Hodgkinson 1997). The mental models[1] developed by decision makers can fail to change adequately and sufficiently quickly to reflect shifts in the wider organizational environment. Techniques that purport to help decision makers adjust their mental models in a timely fashion thus have a potentially important role to play in alleviating such cognitive inertia. Advocates of scenario planning and related techniques have consistently alleged that scenario-based techniques constitute one such means of evincing adaptive cognitive change (Wack 1985a, b; Schoemaker 1993; van der Heijden 1996; Fahay and Randall 1998; Ringland 1998; van der Heijden et al. 2002). For instance, in his famed account of the success of scenario planning in helping Royal Dutch/Shell anticipate the downturn in world oil prices in the 1970s, Wack (1985a: 84) maintained that the aim was "to design scenarios so that managers would question their own model of reality and change it when necessary." De Geus (1988: 71) similarly argued that the real purpose of scenario-based techniques in planning is to "change...the mental models that decision makers carry in their heads." Schoemaker (1993: 200–9) expounded the organizational consequences of these effects, suggesting that scenarios "stretch as well as focus people's thinking...challenge people's mental boundaries" and can be used for "overcoming corporate blind spots and myopic thinking frames." Unfortunately, however, hard empirical evidence to substantiate these fundamental claims concerning the cognitive benefits of scenario-based techniques is both highly equivocal and limited in scale and scope, comprising in the main descriptive case accounts of apparently successful applications of the techniques in action.

The remaining sections of this chapter provide a more thorough analysis of the psychological issues and associated evidence base supporting the use of scenario-based techniques. Five major challenges confront organizational users: (1) managing the effects of scenarios on uncertainty and (over)confidence; (2) the tendency to anchor on single scenarios; (3) the potential of scenarios to exacerbate biases; (4) the plausibility paradox; and (5) the potentially overpowering influence of affective reactions to scenario planning processes and outcomes. The sections that follow consider each of these challenges in turn. First, however, to place these challenges in context it is necessary to consider the rudimentary cognitive effects of scenario thinking.

BASIC EFFECTS OF SCENARIOS ON JUDGMENTS AND DECISIONS

Researchers in the fields of social cognition (e.g., Carroll 1978) and behavioral decision research (e.g., Kahneman and Tversky 1982) construe scenarios as mental simulations of causally related events with the potential to alter expectations and judgments of their likelihood (for a review, see Gregory and Duran 2001). The most reliable finding to emerge from this body of work is that considering a scenario leads people to believe that the events depicted could occur in reality; that is, the perceived likelihood of scenario events increases or is upwardly biased (Carroll 1978; Gregory et al. 1982; Anderson 1983). This effect obtains because considering a scenario makes images of the events depicted come to mind more easily, increasing their availability in memory and hence their influence on judgments (Tversky and Kahneman 1973; Carroll 1978; Kahneman and Tversky 1982). Importantly, however, two factors moderate this effect. Scenarios may not influence judgments when people have strong prior beliefs or preferences about events (Carroll 1978), or when scenarios are difficult to imagine or considered implausible (Anderson 1983; Dougherty et al. 1997). In addition to influencing likelihood judgments, mentally simulating a particular scenario can also incline people to engage in the behaviors simulated (Anderson 1983; Gregory et al. 1982).

Knowledge of the above effects is potentially useful as a basis for persuading key organizational stakeholders to buy into the plausibility of a given scenario unfolding, thereby motivating them to take the necessary action to bring about or avoid certain outcomes (e.g., Hamel and Prahalad 1994; Gregory and Duran 2001). However, heeding scenarios can lead decision makers to overestimate significantly the likelihood of particular events when they focus or anchor on a given scenario. Kahneman and Lovallo (1993) argue that this occurs because considering scenarios leads to the adoption of an "internalized view" when forecasting events relevant to a decision. This occurs when people focus on information that is distinctive to the decision, treat forecasts as independent of prior probabilities for the class of events, and extrapolate current trends in attempting to: "sketch a representative scenario that captures the essential elements of the history of the future" (Kahneman and Lovallo 1993: 25).

Writers on, and practitioners of, organizational scenario planning (e.g., Schoemaker 1993; van der Heijden et al. 2002) frequently warn of the dangers of using single scenarios as a basis for forecasting, which can increase the perceived likelihood or favoring of a focal future state (cf., Gregory and Duran 2001). As noted above, the likelihood of occurrence of any single complex, long-term scenario is too low to provide a reliable basis for planning and decision making, and anticipatory action taken on such a basis may be maladaptive. Since it is undesirable to rely on a single scenario, scenario planners typically advocate considering multiple scenarios to reduce overconfidence in and reliance on favored futures (Porter 1985; Wack 1985b; van der Heijden 1996). However, constructing and analyzing multiple scenarios has mixed effects on uncertainty and confidence that require further illumination.

EFFECTS OF SCENARIOS ON UNCERTAINTY AND CONFIDENCE

Although there is little if any direct evidence that analyzing multiple scenarios can significantly revise mental models, there is some evidence that it can change beliefs about the future. Specifically, researchers have found that considering multiple scenarios can increase uncertainty in predictions. Kuhn and Sniezek (1996) and Schoemaker (1993) both found that analyzing multiple scenarios resulted in widened confidence intervals for forecasts. Schoemaker (1993, experiment 1) had students predict the ranges variables such as product sales or the price of a commodity would obtain in the future. Participants made their predictions before and after constructing several scenarios depicting how future events might influence the focal variables. Comparisons of pre- and post-scenario predictions revealed significantly widened ranges following scenario exposure; that is, considering scenarios stretched participants' beliefs about the future. A second experiment showed that these effects are contingent upon the plausibility of scenarios. Considering scenarios depicting extreme (implausible) events resulted in reduced ranges, making decision makers more certain of their predictions, narrowing rather than stretching thinking.

Other evidence suggests that scenario techniques can reinforce rather than challenge predictions of the future. In an apparent paradox, analyzing multiple scenarios can increase subjective confidence in predictions while simultaneously increasing uncertainty over the states predicted. Kuhn and Sniezek (1996) demonstrated this in an experiment using scenarios to inform forecasts. Measuring uncertainty and confidence separately, the latter on a direct rating scale, they showed that although considering multiple scenarios widened the credible ranges participants predicted (showing increased uncertainty), it also increased participants' subjective confidence in the accuracy of their predictions. Schnaars and Topol (1987) also found that scenario analysis increases confidence in predictions. They provided forecasters with three narrative scenarios depicting optimistic, pessimistic, or middling sales conditions for a new product, and then asked them to predict product sales using point estimates rather than ranges. After considering the scenarios, forecasters showed greater confidence in their own subsequent sales predictions than their counterparts who did not consider scenarios. Schnaars and Topol (1987: 416) found "no evidence that multiple scenarios caused sales forecasters to hedge their bets in light of an uncertain future," because participants tended to "focus on a single, favored scenario rather than the whole set." The process of considering scenarios makes decision makers more assured of their understanding of the causal forces shaping future events, and the uncertainty emphasized by considering multiple scenarios legitimizes subsequent predictions.

In sum, although exposure to multiple scenarios depicting varied states can reinforce perceived uncertainty, it can also make decision makers more confident in the judgments they subsequently make. These mixed effects are potentially problematic for organizational decision makers. Increased uncertainty can be beneficial when it reduces overconfidence in unwarranted prior assumptions (Russo and Schoemaker 1992) and increases information search to benefit judgment accuracy (Lanzetta and Driscoll 1968). In this way, increased uncertainty following multiple scenario analysis might stimulate contingency planning and aid flexibility (cf., Gregory and Duran 2001), when uncertainty is within tolerable limits. Yet, paradoxically, increased confidence in subsequent judgments might constrain actors' thinking about the future. Research has shown that overconfidence biases information search toward sources that confirm favored judgments (Schulz-Hardt et al. 2000) and leads to a neglect of decision aids that improve decision quality (Arkes et al. 1986). Overconfidence in beliefs and prospects after scenario analysis might demotivate and restrict efforts to consider alternative futures and anticipate change, reducing sensitivity and responsiveness to information signaling environmental changes. It is difficult to predict the consequences when scenario analysis increases confidence concomitantly with uncertainty, since research on these joint effects is in short supply. However, three factors are important in addressing the mixed effects of scenario analysis on confidence and uncertainty: (1) differentiating between uncertainty and confidence; (2) generating versus receiving scenarios; and (3) the timing of scenario analysis relative to judgment.

Firstly, some researchers have inferred confidence from predicted ranges (e.g., Russo and Schoemaker 1992; Schoemaker 1993), whereas others have measured subjective confidence directly with self-reported ratings (e.g., Schnaars and Topol 1987; Kuhn and Sniezek 1996), differentiating this from uncertainty as indicated by predictions of ranges. Conceiving uncertainty as a person's beliefs about the variability of possible outcomes and confidence as the belief that a prediction is correct distinguishes the two constructs. Making this distinction, Peterson and Pitz (1988) showed in a series of experiments analyzing sports predictions that confidence and uncertainty have different determinants. They demonstrated that providing decision makers with more information on which to base predictions increased their confidence in predictions, irrespective of the nature of that information. These effects obtained because people believed more information should increase the accuracy of their predictions. In contrast, the effect of increased information availability on uncertainty was contingent upon the nature of the information provided. When the information was equivocal regarding the outcomes of events, decision makers considered a greater number of plausible outcomes than when the information suggested a specific outcome; and the greater the number of different plausible event outcomes decision makers generated, the greater their uncertainty. These findings explain why analyzing multiple competing scenarios can increase uncertainty over predictions but also heighten confidence in the judgments made.

Secondly, there is an important distinction between actively self-constructing and passively considering scenarios. Exemplifying this, whereas studies finding that scenarios increase confidence have presented pre-prepared scenarios to participants (Schnaars and Topol 1987; Kuhn and Sniezek 1996), those finding increased uncertainty and reduced confidence have required participants to generate their own scenarios (Schoemaker 1993; see also Dougherty et al. 1997; Newby-Clark et al. 2000). However, organizational users frequently assume equivalence between the uninvolved consideration and the active self-construction of scenarios. Internal strategy specialists or external futures experts often build scenarios that, once developed, are subsequently rolled out for decision makers to receive passively (e.g., Klein and Linneman 1981; Schwartz 1991; Ringland 1998), with the result that scenarios can fail to stretch thinking (see, e.g., Wack 1985a, b). This assumption of equivalent effects is problematic, because it is the act of mentally simulating different scenarios that forces decision makers to generate and accept the validity of multiple alternatives and reduces their willingness to rely on a single prediction (Koehler 1991, 1994). Research on counterfactual thinking suggests that self-constructing scenarios is likely to encourage decision makers to adopt a mental simulation mindset that enhances these effects by stimulating the liberal generation of options (Galinsky and Moskowitz 2000; Hirt et al. 2004). Groups that adopt such a mindset also tend to share information more effectively and make better use of evidence that disconfirms assumptions, leading in turn to higher quality decisions (Kray and Galinsky 2003; Galinsky and Kray 2004). The use of others' scenarios, in contrast, requires less cognitive effort and does not encourage requisite mental simulation. Hence, this approach is unlikely to reduce decision makers' perseverance with and overconfidence in their own beliefs, and may actually lead to overconfidence in the events depicted (see Koehler 1994). When, therefore, the goal of scenario planning is to stretch thinking, challenge restrictive assumptions, or reduce overconfidence in favored predictions and beliefs, users should encourage decision makers to generate their own scenarios depicting contrasting but equally plausible events and outcomes, and prioritize scenario techniques that stimulate mental simulation.

Thirdly, the impact of scenario analysis depends on its timing relative to judgment. As noted above, the effect of scenario analysis is somewhat recursive. When decision makers use multiple scenarios to increase uncertainty and reduce overconfidence in prevailing prior beliefs, they may actually become overconfident in their subsequent judgments. Hence, decision makers need to be aware of the potential impact of scenarios not only on their extant mental models and prior assumptions, but also on their subsequent cognitions. Several methods are available for reducing overconfidence in judgments and beliefs formed following scenario analysis (for an overview see Russo and Schoemaker 1992). Encouraging more effortful processing and greater scrutiny of new judgments generally reduces overconfidence (Arkes 1991). For this reason, holding decision makers accountable for judgments made subsequent to scenario analysis or having them explain and justify their new beliefs might help reduce overconfidence (Tetlock and Kim 1987). Feedback on the accuracy of judgments also reduces overconfidence in beliefs about the future (Lichtenstein et al. 1982; Mahajan 1992), suggesting a role for using structured feedback to question assumptions formed after scenario analysis.

SCENARIOS CAN ANCHOR AND
RESTRICT THINKING

As noted earlier, effective scenario planning requires unbiased consideration of multiple futures. In practice, however, there are least three reasons why biases toward single scenarios are likely to be evident in judgments and decisions made following scenario analysis, even when multiple scenarios are explicitly considered.

First, not withstanding the dangers highlighted above, decision makers motivated to avoid uncertainty and reduce complexity will often be inclined to anchor on a particular favored scenario, even when considering multiple futures, as illustrated by Wack's (1985a) account of the use of scenario planning in Royal Dutch/Shell to confront the uncertainty surrounding the world petroleum market in the 1970s. Despite having gained an incomplete appreciation of the true complexity facing it, fortunately, in this instance the focal scenario turned out to be sufficiently close to the actual events that subsequently prevailed and the organization was in a position to respond effectively. More generally, however, decision makers who gamble on one particular scenario might not be so fortunate.

Second, decision makers have a tendency to anchor on self-relevant scenarios, i.e., ones depicting futures likely to have a greater impact on the status, goals, resources, and identities of the groups to which they belong. Hence, in general, self-relevant scenarios are likely to attract greater attention, be given greater credence, and weigh heavier on decision makers' judgments and decisions than less self-relevant ones (Gregory et al. 1982; Anderson 1983; Koehler 1991).

Thirdly, recent work on multiple scenario analysis indicates that decision makers tend to anchor their judgments on the first scenario considered. For instance, in a study of new product forecasting Bolton (2003) found that participants who first generated a scenario depicting a successful outcome then generated an opposing failure scenario were significantly more optimistic about the product's future than those who generated scenarios in the opposite order. Moreover, when the researchers attempted to debias participants' judgments by presenting information conflicting with the scenarios generated, participants actually shifted their judgments further in the direction of the first scenario considered; that is, debiasing efforts exacerbated the primacy bias. Bolton theorized that primacy effects occur because the process of generating detailed narrative scenarios entails significant cognitive elaboration, leading in turn to the development of complex causal schemas in memory that act as strong anchors on subsequent judgments. Once developed, these schemas act as conditional frames of reference, leading decision makers to assume the initial scenario is true and thus processing subsequent information in a confirmatory fashion.

In sum, even when analyzing multiple futures decision makers' judgments can be biased toward a single favored scenario as a result of anchoring. Hence, contrary to popular wisdom, scenario analysis can narrow and confine as well as stretch thinking. Removing biases toward particular scenarios is therefore critical to achieving an even-handed consideration of multiple alternatives. There are two main determinants of scenario anchoring effects: motivational and cognitive. Successful debiasing efforts must address both of these factors.

Reducing the pressure to act upon or proactively bring about a particular scenario (rather than anticipate a set of scenarios) is one possible means of reducing the motivation to anchor on a particular scenario. Moreover, encouraging tolerance and acceptance of uncertainty regarding future states and reducing the emphasis on achieving closure by settling on a specific future both have roles to play in alleviating scenario anchoring effects. Reducing the pressure to justify scenarios to others might represent a further means of counteracting the tendency to focus prematurely on a single scenario in an attempt to reduce ambiguity (see Curley et al. 1986). However, since such justification may be required for evaluating the internal consistency of scenarios, or to heighten group dialectical inquiry using scenarios, the latter approach requires users to strike a fine balance between reinforcing anchoring and evaluating scenario consistency.

Although it is tempting to instruct decision makers to consider competing scenarios as a means of removing anchoring effects, this strategy can exacerbate the problem, as highlighted by Bolton's (2003) studies, discussed above. Hence, scenario planners need to adopt alternative strategies to address this problem. As argued above, constructing each scenario with equal cognitive elaboration in the first instance might attenuate the tendency to anchor on initial scenarios. Involving all decision makers in the construction of all scenarios under consideration should hopefully yield similar effects, whereas allotting different individuals or groups to focus on constructing different (single) scenarios, as is often the case in practice (e.g., Schwarz 1991), encourages them to anchor on their own focal scenario. Using decision analytic methods to stimulate equal consideration of multiple scenarios appears particularly amenable to reducing scenario-anchoring effects. Evaluating scenarios systematically using formal evaluation procedures will help structure the attention afforded to multiple scenarios and should mitigate against imbalanced consideration (for a similar approach see Goodwin and Wright 2001).

Given the evident links between cognitive elaboration and anchoring effects, it might be desirable to conduct multiple scenario analysis regularly in short bursts rather than in elaborate but infrequent episodes. The former approach should prevent decision makers from developing and reinforcing detailed scenarios of the sort that encourage the formation of elaborate schemas and thus fuel anchoring bias. Brown and Eisenhardt's (1997) study of strategic decision making in high velocity environments supports this idea. They found that firms making successful decisions used scenarios as fast, undemanding probes into the future. Such "quick and dirty" usage of scenarios contrasts markedly with the lengthy and involved corporate scenario planning exercises typical of those reported in the popular management literature.

THE ROLE OF SCENARIOS IN ATTENUATING AND EXACERBATING BIASES

As noted above, writers often posit scenario techniques as a means of debiasing judgments and overcoming reliance on potentially suboptimal cognitive heuristics. However, the situation is more complex than is sometimes presented. As noted in the previous section, scenarios can act as anchors and thus create new biases within the wider organizational decision-making process. Moreover, scenarios can both attenuate and exacerbate extant biases. The act of generating scenarios is also prone to bias, undermining their effectiveness as decision aids.

Schoemaker (1993) argues that scenarios overcome certain biases by exploiting others. Reducing overconfidence with the help of the conjunction fallacy (Tversky and Kahneman 1983) provides a convenient example. Although the greater the causal complexity of a given scenario, the greater its perceived plausibility, the actual likelihood of occurrence of a scenario actually decreases as progressively greater numbers of causally related events are woven into the accompanying narrative. As scenarios become more causally complex they become credible alternatives to currently held views of the future, reducing overconfidence (Russo and Schoemaker 1992; Schoemaker 1993).

A further claim made by advocates is that scenario analysis can attenuate the availability bias (e.g., Schoemaker 1993). This is the tendency for people to base judgments on information that comes easily to mind and undervalue information that is difficult to imagine or recall (Tversky and Kahneman 1973). Scenario thinking attenuates availability effects through two mechanisms: by increasing the availability of less familiar information and by encouraging the simulation heuristic. In the first instance, constructing scenarios with less familiar content can increase the availability of information that decision makers might otherwise neglect. For example, constructing unfavorable and counterintuitive scenarios may increase the availability of negative and disconfirmatory information respectively, both of which are generally less available in memory than their opposites (Newby-Clark et al. 2000; Jonas et al. 2001). The simulation heuristic overcomes availability effects through a different means. In this case, judgments of the likelihood of an event are based on the ease with which scenarios leading to the event can be mentally constructed or simulated, rather than on the availability of prior beliefs or similar past events (Kahneman and Tversky 1982). Simulating several plausible scenarios makes it apparent that credible alternative futures exist, thus challenging prior beliefs in a single future.

When decision makers consider a plausible scenario for the outcome of an event, the scenario acts as an explanation of the event that they can rely on when predicting how the event will unfold (Hirt and Sherman 1985; Hirt and Markman 1995). However, mentally simulating alternative plausible explanations reduces bias towards an initial explanation (Hirt and Markman 1995). Consider the following. When financial analysts view managers' self-servingly positive plans in the form of narrative scenarios, they are often seduced into making over-optimistic forecasts (e.g., Kadous et al. 2006). However, providing analysts with counter-explanations, outlining why managers' plans might fail, for example, reduces the optimism induced by scenarios and makes forecasts more realistic (Kadous et al. 2006; see also Dougherty et al. 1997). Nevertheless, considering counter-explanations that are implausible or difficult to generate strengthens the bias towards prior beliefs (Hirt and Markman 1995; Dougherty et al. 1997; Kadous et al. 2006). Scenario anchoring effects appear to be less prominent in multiple explanation research than in the forecasting studies reviewed above (Schnaars and Topol 1987; Kuhn and Sniezek 1996; Bolton 2003). This is perhaps because in multiple explanation studies participants do not themselves explicitly generate the kind of detailed narrative scenarios that require significant cognitive effort and encourage the development of elaborate schemas that act as anchors on judgments, which are evidently not so easy to shift.

One factor that can militate against the ability of scenarios to reduce biases is that the very process of constructing scenarios is also susceptible to bias. For example, when making predictions people often construct overly optimistic scenarios that do not adequately account for negative events, falling foul of the so-called positivity bias. This bias can yield inaccurate forecasts that envisage largely positive events and minimize potential problems with particular courses of action (Buehler et al. 1994; Schoemaker 1995). Even when people consider both pessimistic and optimistic futures, negative scenarios are not only considered less plausible, they are given less credence and have less impact on judgments than positive ones (Newby-Clark et al. 2000). Moreover, generating scenarios collectively in groups rather than individually may worsen the bias towards positive or optimistic information. In a series of laboratory and field studies Buehler et al. (2005) showed that because groups typically focus on "planning for success" when making predictions, group discussion makes positive information more available, thus accentuating the optimism bias.

The above effects suggest a role for purposively giving greater emphasis to negative events when constructing scenarios. Developing "worst case" scenarios is an obvious remedy that can reduce bias toward positive information (Buehler et al. 1994). Since the ambiguity of future events accentuates positivity bias, when decomposing future events into their constituent components and consequences, scenario planners should systematically simulate the potential negative consequences of these events rather than accept positive construals at face value.

THE PROBLEM WITH INCREDIBLE FUTURES: THE PLAUSIBILITY PARADOX

To be effective, on one hand, scenarios must challenge and, where necessary transform, actors' mental models and beliefs to inform and stretch strategic thinking. On the other hand, scenarios must be plausible so that decision makers meaningfully accept them. Only then, will scenarios foster involvement in explorative analyses, convince of the need for change and motivate action to anticipate change. However, achieving these twin imperatives can be problematic because they do not sit together comfortably. Specifically, the nature of plausibility creates difficulties, because "a highly plausible scenario is one that fits prior knowledge well" (Connell and Keane 2006: 95). The problem here is that highly plausible scenarios are likely to reaffirm what decision makers already know; hence, they are unlikely to challenge their core assumptions or change their mental models. Yet, when scenarios do not fit with current ways of thinking borne of prior knowledge, decision makers may reject them out of hand.

A further problem with attempting to generate requisitely challenging scenarios is that decision makers may be predisposed to generating undemanding scenarios. Concepts that are central to the way decision makers' mentally represent and comprehend objects and events are cognitively immutable; in other words, they are resistant to change in mental simulation (see Sloman et al. 1998). For this reason, decision makers may be prone to constructing scenarios that are constrained by their extant mental models, tending to construct scenarios consonant with their pre-existing worldviews. Consequently, there is a danger that that self-constructed scenarios constrained by extant mental models may fail to break the beliefs embedded in those models and challenge sufficiently status quo thinking.

One way of helping decision makers avoid the tendency to construct unchallenging scenarios based on extrapolations from extant mental models is to introduce novel outsider perspectives and diverse information sources at the early stages of scenario generation, without losing the benefits of mental simulation that accrue from self-constructing scenarios. This reasoning supports the use of industry experts to inform the scenario construction process, as, for example, by incorporating the counter-intuitive ideas of so-called "remarkable people" (Schwartz 1991; van der Heijden 1996) to first stretch thinking then increase the plausibility of future events that might otherwise be dismissed as outlandish.

Blowing Hot and Cold: Affective Dimensions of Scenario Planning

Practitioners typically design the scenario planning process to emphasize uncertainty, instability and precariousness rather than to underline surety or make accurate predictions (e.g., Porter 1985; Wack 1985a; Schoemaker 1993; van der Heijden 1996; van der Heijden et al. 2002). Although the cognitive consequences of this approach may be beneficial, the emotional or affective effects of uncertainty can present decision makers with considerable difficulties. Specifically, perceived uncertainty over anticipated events, decisions, and their outcomes has been linked with rigidity and slower decision making (Staw et al. 1981; Wally and Baum 1994), escalation of commitment to a failing course of action (Bragger et al. 1998), and increased interpersonal conflict and reduced performance among decision making groups (Argote et al. 1989). Affective mechanisms are largely responsible for these effects. Uncertainty and risk generally increase negative affectivity among decision makers; for example, risky decisions stimulate worry, fear, dread, and anxiety (Loewenstein et al. 2001). When facing decisions where significant negative consequences are possible but the best strategy is uncertain, people become anxious and process information in a narrow and labored manner (Luce et al. 1997). Such findings are highly relevant since these are the circumstances often occupied by organizational decision makers using scenarios to inform their choices.

Scenario planning processes are likely to heighten negative affectivity among decision makers for at least two reasons. Firstly, achieving emotional impact is a stated aim for scenario practitioners. According to van der Heijden and colleagues (2002: 263), the scenarios that have the strongest influence are those that "elicit feelings of fear, hope, security, and threat" since these "create the jolt needed for action." Secondly, even without the explicit aim of provoking emotional reactions, evoking strong feelings is an inherent consequence of articulating and simulating future events through scenarios rich in imagery. As Loewenstein and colleagues (2001: 275) asserted, "one of the most important determinants of emotional reactions to future outcomes is the vividness with which those outcomes are described or mentally represented." In extensive scenario planning exercises decision makers are compelled to heed elaborate scenarios in which futures are articulated through multimedia sources rich in imagery (see example cases from British Telecom: Moyer 1996; and from Royal Dutch/Shell: Kassler 1995). Merely simulating potentially threatening events is enough to create anxiety, for "emotions arise in large part as a reaction to mental images of a decision's outcomes," decision makers being "sensitive to the possibility rather than the probability of negative consequences" (Loewenstein et al. 2001: 276). It is the possibility of a negative event highlighted by a scenario with affective prospects, such as the failure of the current business model in a hostile future, that can "lead to an affective reaction to a salient image, and this feeling (not explicit consideration of the scenario's probability) may guide behavior" (Hsee and Rottenstreich 2004: 28).

The above body of work suggests that the "hot" emotive effects of scenario induced uncertainty (e.g., heightened anxiety and threat rigidity) may overpower its "cold" cognitive effects (e.g., stretched thinking, open-mindedness, desire for more information, decisional flexibility). When rational cognitive reactions conflict with more visceral affective reactions, and when the latter are of sufficient intensity, visceral responses often dominate decision-making behavior, including the assessment of prospects and choice of alternatives (for reviews, see Loewenstein 1996; Loewenstein et al. 2001).

Hodgkinson and Wright (2002) graphically illustrated how emotional reactions to scenario planning processes can overpower their putative cognitive effects. These researchers attempted to use scenario techniques to help a publishing firm confront the implications of market changes so that it might put itself in a position to adapt. The organization faced a highly uncertain future. Industry advances looked set to displace the company's main offering, but it was unclear which business model and technologies would provide the best route(s) to survival. In constructing the scenarios, the management team focused on envisaging quite vividly a threatening future in which technological changes would replace their main offering, to the extent that this triggered defensive avoidance (Janis and Mann 1977) and threat rigidity (Staw et al. 1981) effects. Consequently, they were unable to reach a consensus on an alternative to the current failing strategy. This proved to be anything but an anhedonic process. The scenario intervention "raised the levels of decisional stress and conflict within the organization to unacceptably high levels" (Hodgkinson and Wright 2002: 964). The stress created by attempting to face an uncertain future with a disparate team led the decision makers to adopt a variety of dysfunctional coping strategies, including bolstering commitment to the current failing strategy, procrastinating, and shifting responsibility for maintaining the inert status quo to other stakeholders within the firm.

The implications here, then, are that effective scenario planning requires understanding of the mechanisms and consequences of the emotional processes at work, the ability to identify signs of the impact of negative affect, and techniques for dealing with the potentially overpowering affective consequences of scenario activities. Scenario planners can attempt to reduce anxiety borne of perceived lack of control by systematically incorporating activities to develop plausible contingencies for dealing with specific threatening events highlighted by scenario analysis. Similar strategies have proven effective for dealing with the mental simulation of important personal events (e.g., Pham and Taylor 1999). Emphasizing collective responsibility for responding to difficult situations might also reduce felt isolation for key decision makers, creating reassurance and mitigating avoidance behavior. Furthermore, the emotional effects scenarios have on decision processes highlight the importance of developing a supportive psychological climate to lessen the impact of future focused anxiety on learning. The role of the facilitator in identifying the signs of the dysfunctional coping strategies highlighted above and taking actions to re-engage participants displaying defensive avoidant behavior in connection with the scenario planning process is crucial.

Summary and Conclusions

Applying scenario techniques to inform organizational decisions requires confronting several important but underappreciated difficulties highlighted in this chapter. Understanding and surmounting these problems is critical if these techniques are to produce the decisional benefits sought through the putative cognitive mechanisms.

As we have seen, scenarios exert mixed effects on uncertainty and confidence. They can heighten or reduce overconfidence, contingent upon the nature and timing of scenario analysis relative to judgment, and reinforce as well as stretch staid thinking about the future. There are several ways of maximizing the ability of scenario techniques to evince cognitive change. The decision makers expected to benefit from broadened thinking should themselves generate and analyze scenarios, and planners should strive to make scenarios plausible but challenging. Decision makers should be aware of the effects of scenarios on overconfidence in subsequent judgments. Scenario planners can mitigate these effects by providing decision makers with continuous feedback on predictions and encouraging effortful processing of new judgments formed after multiple scenario analysis.

Unfortunately, unless deployed skillfully, scenario-based techniques can replace old biases with new ones. The use of decision analytic techniques to systematize scenario analysis and structuring the scenario construction process to equalize the elaboration of competing scenarios should help overcome biases toward particular scenarios. Regularly analyzing multiple scenarios in a fast and simple manner, rather than elaborately but infrequently, is another potentially useful means of reducing scenario anchoring effects. As discussed earlier, decision makers' extant mental models can potentially restrict the scenarios produced. To overcome such biases, facilitators of the process should systematically introduce types of information that decision makers may otherwise overlook in scenario generation, particularly negative and disconfirmatory/counterintuitive information regarding future events, with a view to aiding the development of challenging and unbiased scenarios that are more likely to stimulate meaningful cognitive change. The plausibility paradox dictates that such scenarios must be challenging enough to stretch thinking but plausible enough to foster engagement in analyzing, and acting to anticipate, the future.

Arguably, the most significant problem facing would-be users is how best to manage the emotional outcomes that scenario-based techniques can yield, specifically threat rigidity and defensive avoidance. This requires careful handling of the anxiety and decisional stress that can arise when users imagine and simulate future threats with scenarios. Increasing perceived control by focusing attention on the plausibility and attainability of strategies for dealing with specific threats highlighted by scenario analysis can help achieve alleviate such effects, as can the fostering of collective responsibility for dealing with impending problems. Developing a supportive psychological climate is paramount for reducing anxiety, maintaining a future-focus, and alleviating avoidant and dysfunctional behavior.

Scenario-based techniques promise much, but are fraught with many potential difficulties. Although the skillful deployment of these methods cannot guarantee that organizational decision makers will always anticipate the shifting contingencies confronting them in an increasingly uncertain world, ignoring the insights of the work reviewed in this chapter is a sure fire way of making the future more troublesome.

ENDNOTE

[1] A mental model is an internal representation of entities and the relations between them that "mirrors the relevant aspects of the corresponding state of affairs in the world" (Johnson-Laird 1980: 98).

REFERENCES

ANDERSON, C. A. (1983). 'Imagination and Expectation—The Effect of Imagining Behavioral Scripts on Personal Intentions.' *Journal of Personality and Social Psychology*, 45/2: 293–305.

ARGOTE, L., TURNER, M. E., and FICHMAN, M. (1989). 'To Centralize or Not to Centralize: The Effects of Uncertainty and Threat on Group-Structure and Performance.' *Organizational Behavior and Human Decision Processes*, 43/1: 58–74.

ARKES, H. R. (1991). 'Costs and Benefits of Judgment Errors: Implications for Debiasing.' *Psychological Bulletin*, 110/3: 486–98.

—— DAWES, R. M., and CHRISTENSEN, C. (1986). 'Factors Influencing the Use of a Decision Rule in a Probabilistic Task.' *Organizational Behavior and Human Decision Processes*, 37/1: 93–110.

BARR, P. S., STIMPERT, J. L., and HUFF, A. S. (1992). 'Cognitive Change, Strategic Action, and Organizational Renewal.' *Strategic Management Journal*, 13: 15–36.

BOLTON, L. E. (2003). 'Stickier Priors: The Effects of Nonanalytic Versus Analytic Thinking in New Product Forecasting.' *Journal of Marketing Research*, 40/1: 65–79.

BRAGGER, J. D., BRAGGER, D., HANTULA, D. A., and KIRNAN, J. (1998). 'Hysteresis and Uncertainty: The Effect of Uncertainty on Delays to Exit Decisions.' *Organizational Behavior and Human Decision Processes*, 74/3: 229–53.

BROWN, S. L. and EISENHARDT, K. M. (1997). 'The Art of Continuous Change: Linking Complexity Theory and Time-Paced Evolution in Relentlessly Shifting Organizations.' *Administrative Science Quarterly*, 42/1: 1–34.

BUEHLER, R., GRIFFIN, D., and ROSS, M. (1994). 'Exploring the Planning Fallacy: Why People Underestimate their Task Completion Times.' *Journal of Personality and Social Psychology*, 67/3: 366–81.

—— MESSERVEY, D., and GRIFFIN, D. (2005). 'Collaborative Planning and Prediction: Does Group Discussion Affect Optimistic Biases in Time Estimation?' *Organizational Behavior and Human Decision Processes*, 97/1: 47–63.

CARROLL, J. S. (1978). 'Effect of Imagining an Event on Expectations for Event-Interpretation in Terms of Availability Heuristic.' *Journal of Experimental Social Psychology*, 14/1: 88–96.

CONNELL, L. and KEANE, M. T. (2006). 'A Model of Plausibility.' *Cognitive Science*, 30/1: 95–120.

CURLEY, S. P., YATES, J. F., and ABRAMS, R. A. (1986). 'Psychological Sources of Ambiguity Avoidance.' *Organizational Behavior and Human Decision Processes*, 38/2: 230–56.

DE GEUS, A. P. (1988). 'Planning as Learning.' *Harvard Business Review*, 66/2: 70–4.

DOUGHERTY, M. R. P., GETTYS, C. F., and THOMAS, R. P. (1997). 'The Role of Mental Simulation in Judgments of Likelihood.' *Organizational Behavior and Human Decision Processes*, 70/2: 135–48.

FAHAY, L. and RANDALL, R. M. (eds.) (1998). *Learning from the Future: Competitive Foresight Scenarios*. New York: Wiley.

GALINSKY, A. D. and KRAY, L. J. (2004). 'From Thinking About What Might Have Been to Sharing What We Know: The Effects of Counterfactual Mind-Sets on Information Sharing in Groups.' *Journal of Experimental Social Psychology*, 40/5: 606–18.

—— MOSKOWITZ, G. B. (2000). 'Counterfactuals as Behavioral Primes: Priming the Simulation Heuristic and Consideration of Alternatives.' *Journal of Experimental Social Psychology*, 36/4: 384–409.

GOODWIN, P. and WRIGHT, G. (2001). 'Enhancing Strategy Evaluation in Scenario Planning: A Role for Decision Analysis.' *Journal of Management Studies*, 38/1: 1–16.

GRANT, R. M. (2003). 'Strategic Planning in a Turbulent Environment: Evidence from the Oil Majors.' *Strategic Management Journal*, 24: 491–517.

GREGORY, W. L. and DURAN, A. (2001). 'Scenarios and Acceptance of Forecasts,' in J. S. Armstrong (ed.), *Principles of Forecasting: A Handbook for Researchers and Practitioners*. London: Kluwer Academic Publishers, 519–40.

—— CIALDINI, R. B., and CARPENTER, K. M. (1982). 'Self-Relevant Scenarios as Mediators of Likelihood Estimates and Compliance: Does Imagining Make it So?' *Journal of Personality and Social Psychology*, 43: 89–99.

HAMEL, G. and PRAHALAD, C. K. (1994). *Competing for the Future*. Boston, MA: Harvard Business School Press.

HIRT, E. R. and MARKMAN, K. D. (1995). 'Multiple Explanation: A Consider-an-Alternative Strategy for Debiasing Judgments.' *Journal of Personality and Social Psychology*, 69: 1069–86.

—— KARDES, F. R., and MARKMAN, K. D. (2004). 'Activating a Mental Simulation Mind-Set Through Generation of Alternatives: Implications for Debiasing in Related and Unrelated Domains.' *Journal of Experimental Social Psychology*, 40/3: 374–83.

HODGKINSON, G. P. (1997). 'Cognitive Inertia in a Turbulent Market: The Case of UK Residential Estate Agents.' *Journal of Management Studies*, 34: 921–45.

HODGKINSON, G. P. and WRIGHT, G. (2002). 'Confronting Strategic Inertia in a Top Management Team: Learning from Failure.' *Organization Studies*, 23: 949–77.

—— WHITTINGTON, R., JOHNSON, G., and SCHWARZ, M. (2006). 'The Role of Strategy Workshops in Strategy Development Processes: Formality, Communication, Coordination and Inclusion.' *Long Range Planning*, 39: 479–96.

HOGARTH, R. M. and MAKRIDAKIS, S. (1981). 'Forecasting and Planning: An Evaluation.' *Management Science*, 27/2: 115–38.

HSEE, C. K. and ROTTENSTREICH, Y. (2004). 'Music, Pandas, and Muggers: On the Affective Psychology of Value.' *Journal of Experimental Psychology-General*, 133/1: 23–30.

JANIS, I. and MANN, L. (1977). *Decision Making: A Psychological Analysis of Conflict, Choice, and Commitment*. New York: Free Press.

JOHNSON-LAIRD, P. N. (1980). 'Mental Models in Cognitive Science.' *Cognitive Science*, 4: 71–115.

JONAS, E., Schulz-HARDT, S., FREY, D., and THELEN, N. (2001). 'Confirmation Bias in Sequential Information Search After Preliminary Decisions: An Expansion of Dissonance Theoretical Research on Selective Exposure to Information.' *Journal of Personality and Social Psychology*, 80/4: 557–71.

KADOUS, K., KRISCHE, S. D., and SEDOR, L. M. (2006). 'Using Counter-Explanation to Limit Analysts' Forecast Optimism.' *Accounting Review*, 81: 377–97.

KAHNEMAN, D. and LOVALLO, D. (1993). 'Timid Choices and Bold Forecasts: A Cognitive Perspective on Risk-Taking.' *Management Science*, 39: 17–31.

—— TVERSKY, A. (1982). 'The Simulation Heuristic,' in D. Kahneman, P. Slovic, and A. Tversky (eds.), *Judgment under Uncertainty: Heuristics and Biases*. New York: Cambridge University Press, 201–10.

KASSLER, P. (1995). 'Scenarios for World Energy: Barricades or New Frontiers?' *Long Range Planning*, 28: 38–47.

KLEIN, H. E. and LINNEMAN, R. E. (1981). 'The Use of Scenarios in Corporate-Planning: 8 Case-Histories.' *Long Range Planning*, 14: 69–77.

KOEHLER, D. J. (1991). 'Explanation, Imagination, and Confidence in Judgment.' *Psychological Bulletin*, 110: 499–519.

—— (1994). 'Hypothesis Generation and Confidence in Judgment.' *Journal of Experimental Psychology-Learning Memory and Cognition*, 20: 461–9.

KRAY, L. J. and GALINSKY, A. D. (2003). 'The Debiasing Effect of Counterfactual Mind-Sets: Increasing the Search for Disconfirmatory Information in Group Decisions.' *Organizational Behavior and Human Decision Processes*, 91: 69–81.

KUHN, K. M. and SNIEZEK, J. A. (1996). 'Confidence and Uncertainty in Judgmental Forecasting: Differential Effects of Scenario Presentation.' *Journal of Behavioral Decision Making*, 9: 231–47.

LANZETTA, J. T. and DRISCOLL, J. M. (1968). 'Effects of Uncertainty and Importance on Information Search in Decision Making.' *Journal of Personality and Social Psychology*, 10: 479–86.

LICHTENSTEIN, S., FISCHHOFF, B., and PHILIPS, L. D. (1982). 'Calibration of Probabilities: The State of the Art to 1980,' in D. Kahneman, P. Slovic, and A. Tversky (eds.), *Judgement under Uncertainty: Heuristics and Biases*. Cambridge: Cambridge University Press, 306–34.

LINNEMAN, R. E. and KLEIN, H. E. (1983). 'The Use of Multiple Scenarios by United-States Industrial Companies: A Comparison Study, 1977–1981.' *Long Range Planning*, 16: 94–101.

LOEWENSTEIN, G. (1996). 'Out of Control: Visceral Influences on Behavior.' *Organizational Behavior and Human Decision Processes*, 65: 272–92.

—— WEBER, E. U., HSEE, C. K., and WELCH, N. (2001). 'Risk as Feelings.' *Psychological Bulletin*, 127: 267–86.

LUCE, M. F., BETTMAN, J. R., and PAYNE, J. W. (1997). 'Choice Processing in Emotionally Difficult Decisions.' *Journal of Experimental Psychology—Learning Memory and Cognition*, 23: 384–405.

MAHAJAN, J. (1992). 'The Overconfidence Effect in Marketing-Management Predictions.' *Journal of Marketing Research*, 29: 329–42.

MALASKA, P. (1985). 'Multiple Scenario Approach and Strategic Behavior in European Companies.' *Strategic Management Journal*, 6: 339–55.

MOYER, K. (1996). 'Scenario Planning at British Airways—A Case Study.' *Long Range Planning*, 29: 172–81.

NEWBY-CLARK, I. R., ROSS, M., BUEHLER, R., KOEHLER, D. J., and GRIFFIN, D. (2000). 'People Focus on Optimistic Scenarios and Disregard Pessimistic Scenarios While Predicting Task Completion Times.' *Journal of Experimental Psychology-Applied*, 6: 171–82.

PANT, P. N. and STARBUCK, W. H. (1990). 'Innocents in the Forest: Forecasting and Research Methods.' *Journal of Management*, 16: 433–60.

PETERSON, D. K. and PITZ, G. F. (1988). 'Confidence, Uncertainty, and the Use of Information.' *Journal of Experimental Psychology-Learning Memory and Cognition*, 14: 85–92.

PHAM, L. B. and TAYLOR, S. E. (1999). 'From Thought to Action: Effects of Process-Versus Outcome-Based Mental Simulations on Performance.' *Personality and Social Psychology Bulletin*, 25: 250–60.

PORAC, J. F., THOMAS, H., and BADEN-FULLER, C. (1989). 'Competitive Groups as Cognitive Communities—The Case of Scottish Knitwear Manufacturers.' *Journal of Management Studies*, 26: 397–416.

PORTER, M. E. (1985). *Competitive Advantage—Creating and Sustaining Superior Performance*. New York: Free Press.

REGER, R. K. and PALMER, T. B. (1996). 'Managerial Categorization of Competitors: Using Old Maps to Navigate New Environments.' *Organization Science*, 7: 22–39.

RINGLAND, G. (1998). *Scenario Planning: Managing for the Future*. Chichester: Wiley.

RUSSO, J. E. and SCHOEMAKER, P. J. H. (1992). 'Managing Overconfidence.' *Sloan Management Review*, 33/2: 7–17.

SCHNAARS, S. P. and TOPOL, M. T. (1987). 'The Use of Multiple Scenarios in Sales Forecasting—An Empirical-Test.' *International Journal of Forecasting*, 3: 405–19.

SCHOEMAKER, P. J. H. (1991). 'When and How to Use Scenario Planning—A Heuristic Approach with Illustration.' *Journal of Forecasting*, 10: 549–64.

—— (1993). 'Multiple Scenario Development—Its Conceptual and Behavioral Foundation.' *Strategic Management Journal*, 14: 193–213.

—— (1995). 'Scenario Planning—A Tool for Strategic Thinking.' *Sloan Management Review*, 36: 25–40.

SCHULZ-HARDT, S., FREY, D., LUTHGENS, C., and MOSCOVICI, S. (2000). 'Biased Information Search in Group Decision Making.' *Journal of Personality and Social Psychology*, 78: 655–69.

SCHWARTZ, P. (1991). *The Art of the Long View*. New York: Currency Doubleday.

SLOMAN, S. A., LOVE, B. C., and AHN, W. K. (1998). 'Feature Centrality and Conceptual Coherence.' *Cognitive Science*, 22: 189–228.

STAW, B. M., SANDELANDS, L. E., and DUTTON, J. E. (1981). 'Threat-Rigidity Effects in Organizational Behavior: A Multi-Level Analysis.' *Administrative Science Quarterly*, 26: 501–24.

TETLOCK, P. E. and KIM, J. I. (1987). 'Accountability and Judgment Processes in a Personality Prediction Task.' *Journal of Personality and Social Psychology*, 52: 700–9.

TVERSKY, A. and KAHNEMAN, D. (1973). 'Availability—Heuristic for Judging Frequency and Probability.' *Cognitive Psychology*, 5: 207–32.

—— —— (1983). 'Extensional Versus Intuitive Reasoning: The Conjunction Fallacy in Probability Judgment.' *Psychological Review*, 90: 293–315.

VAN DER HEIJDEN, K. (1996). *Scenarios—The Art of Strategic Conversation*. Chichester: John Wiley.

—— Bradfield, R., BURT, G., CAIRNS, G., and WRIGHT, G. (2002). *The Sixth Sense: Accelerating Organizational Learning with Scenarios*. New York: John Wiley.

WACK, P. (1985a). 'Scenarios: Uncharted Waters Ahead.' *Harvard Business Review*, 63/5: 72–89.

—— (1985b). 'Scenarios: Shooting the Rapids.' *Harvard Business Review*, 63/6: 139–50.

WALLY, S. and BAUM, J. R. (1994). 'Personal and Structural Determinants of the Pace of Strategic Decision-Making.' *Academy of Management Journal*, 37: 932–56.

SUBJECT INDEX

Personal Name Index: Includes All Referenced Authors